RESOURCE AND ENVIRONMENTAL ECONOMICS

Modern Issues and Applications

(Second Edition)

RESOURCE AND ENVIRONMENTAL ECONOMICS

Modern Issues and Applications

(Second Edition)

Clement A Tisdell

The University of Queensland, Australia

World Scientific

NEW JERSEY • LONDON • SINGAPORE • BEIJING • SHANGHAI • HONG KONG • TAIPEI • CHENNAI • TOKYO

Published by

World Scientific Publishing Co. Pte. Ltd.
5 Toh Tuck Link, Singapore 596224
USA office: 27 Warren Street, Suite 401-402, Hackensack, NJ 07601
UK office: 57 Shelton Street, Covent Garden, London WC2H 9HE

Library of Congress Cataloging-in-Publication Data
Names: Tisdell, C. A. (Clement Allan), author.
Title: Resource and environmental economics : modern issues and applications / Clement A. Tisdell.
Description: Second edition. | New Jersey : World Scientific, [2021] | Includes bibliographical references and index.
Identifiers: LCCN 2020056884 | ISBN 9789811230035 (hardcover) | ISBN 9789811230936 (ebook) | ISBN 9789811230943 (ebook other)
Subjects: LCSH: Natural resources. | Environmental economics.
Classification: LCC HC85 .T57 2021 | DDC 333.7--dc23
LC record available at https://lccn.loc.gov/2020056884

British Library Cataloguing-in-Publication Data
A catalogue record for this book is available from the British Library.

For any available supplementary material, please visit
https://www.worldscientific.com/worldscibooks/10.1142/12093#t=suppl

Desk Editor: Lum Pui Yee

Typeset by Stallion Press
Email: enquiries@stallionpress.com

Endorsements

Professor Tisdell's expository skills are unmatched. This volume conveys complex material with great clarity, using case examples with unusual effectiveness. Furthermore, it is more inclusive than many books on these topics in its extensive international coverage. This is a most useful contribution.

Jane V Hall
Co-Director, Institute of Economic and Environmental Studies
California State University

This textbook provides an excellent introduction, which is easily accessible and readable and benefits greatly from the author's life-long career as an environmental and resource economist.

Eric Neumayer
Professor of Environment and Development and
Head of the Department of Geography and Environment
London School of Economics, UK

Preface

I was very pleased when I received a request from Lum Pui Yee, on behalf of World Scientific, to prepare the manuscript for a second edition of *Resource and Environmental Economics: Modern Issues and Applications*. This was not only because the first edition was sufficiently well received to justify a second edition but because it provided me with the opportunity to update material in this book and enabled me to introduce new relevant material and ideas in this edition. Furthermore, it was possible for me to correct a few errors that were overlooked when the earlier edition was prepared. As a result, this edition is longer than the earlier edition and is a thoroughly revised version of it. For example, two new chapters have been added (namely Chapter 11, "Problems involving the availability of natural resource stocks and flows" and Chapter 12 "More on mineral resources: their economic significance, sustainability and environmental issues") and Chapter 13, "Energy use, global warming and air pollution" has been significantly updated and extended. Several other chapters also have added sections. In order to make the e-book version of this volume more readable and attractive, color has been used in presentation of the figures for this version.

In covering the topics in this book, I have concentrated on the critical presentation of ideas and have presented alternative points of view. I have also endeavored to be constructive. It is very important for scientific and scholarly work (in my view) to be subjected to Socratic questioning which is a systematic method of critical thinking. This approach is important to facilitate the development of new ideas, to test and qualify existing theories, hypotheses and findings; and to develop intellectual skills to respond effectively to changing situations. Furthermore, I consider it to be inappropriate to present ideas as if they exist in a historical vacuum. Therefore, I have tried to provide, wherever possible, information about the historical development of ideas and have placed natural resource and environmental issues and problems in their historical contexts wherever I could.

As pointed out in the Preface to the first edition of this book, the prime stimulus to write that edition was from a series of guest lectures which I gave to postgraduate students at Humboldt University in Berlin and at the University of Ghent in Belgium. My thanks once again go to those who helped the first edition to come to fruition. I would now like to thank Douglas Hunt for his useful feedback on some material that has been added to this new edition and once again, I am grateful to the School of Economics at The University of Queensland for the use of its excellent facilities. As well, I appreciate the help of Evelyn Smart who (relying on my handwritten drafts) prepared the manuscript for this edition in a form suitable for the publisher, and who also provided some basic research assistance needed to update the first edition. Preparing the second edition has involved many hours of work. Much of this work was completed at home, particularly after COVID-19 became prevalent. I thank my wife, Mariel, for taking an interest in this project and for allowing me to remain incommunicative for longer than most people would consider to be reasonable while I was writing up the text for this edition.

Clement Tisdell

Contents

PART I
GENERAL ISSUES

Chapter 1

The Nature and Significance of Resource and Environmental Economics

1.1. Introduction

Global concerns and social conflicts about the use of natural resources have intensified in recent times, as is evidenced in many countries by frequent public demonstrations, such as the "Save the Planet" demonstrations. As is shown in this book, the use of natural resources and the occurrence of environmental change raise a diversity of issues which significantly affect the well-being of people. These issues range geographically from local and regional ones to global ones. We have now reached a stage in the evolution of global economic growth and development where our need to consider the economics of natural resource uses and environmental change is more important than ever for the maintenance of our well-being and for sustaining that of future generations. The types of environmental economic issues requiring attention are extensive. For example, apart from those involving climate change, they even include the control of pandemics, such as the COVID-19 pandemic, because these have economic and environmental or ecological dimensions.

Economic thought about matters involving the economics of natural resource use and environmental change have evolved over a long period of time and the amount and the value of attention given to these matters by economists have varied with the passage of time. Therefore, in this chapter, after giving attention to how the subjects of economics, natural resource economics, environmental economics and ecological economics are inter-related, a brief historical account is provided of the development of economic thought which addresses the significance of natural resource use and environmental conditions for human welfare.

In this book, the term "resource economics" refers principally to natural resource economics. Originally, economists referred to all natural resources as land and vestiges of this earlier usage are retained in the title of a leading academic journal entitled *Land Economics*, which focuses on the economics of the utilization of natural resources. The concept of land adopted by classical economists included not only natural terrestrial resources but also marine and other aquatic resources as well as those below the Earth's surface, such as minerals.

Originally, economists considered land (natural resources), labor and capital to be the main factors of production and believed their availability to be the prime determinants of national wealth and economic welfare. While this conception of classical economists might have been reasonably appropriate in Europe in the 18th and 19th centuries, it became less relevant as economic growth and changes in the nature of economic activity occurred. As outlined below, this led economists to revise their views about the main resources contributing to economic welfare and to extend their views about what resources are significant for economic welfare.

This chapter commences with a discussion of the relationships between natural resource economics, environmental economics and ecological economics and then outlines changing views about the basic economic problem (the presence of economic scarcity). It then outlines *general* factors that add to or ameliorate this problem and indicates how the views of economists about this subject have altered with the passage of time. The penultimate section of this chapter highlights major modern issues (covered in this book) that can be assessed by applying methods developed in natural resource economics or in closely related environmental and ecological economics. The final section contains general observations about the nature of models used in resource and environmental economics.

1.2. How are the Subjects of Economics, Natural Resource Economics, Environmental Economics and Ecological Economics Related to One Another?

1.2.1. *The subject matter of economics*

Economics has been defined as the science of the administration or management of scarce resources. Its focus is mainly on the social mechanisms used for this purpose and their consequences for the satisfaction of human wants. The satisfaction of human wants is seen as depending primarily on the quantity (and quality) of goods and services available to individuals. Consequently, even though economics is concerned with important factors that influence human well-being, it does not study *all* such factors. For example, it does not take into account the value to individuals of different possible types of social relationships, which may affect their sense of belonging and personal satisfaction. Such aspects are taken into account in sociology, social psychology and similar areas of study.

Economic scarcity exists because collectively individuals want more commodities that can be produced with the resources available to them. Consequently, organizational changes that increase economic efficiency and thereby make it possible to supply a greater quantity of wanted commodities (relative to resources used) are desired by most societies. An important objective of economics is to suggest ways in which the social management (administration) of resources can be improved to reduce the scarcity of available commodities. For example, to what extent do market mechanisms help to minimize scarcity? In what respects do such mechanisms have shortcomings and what can be done (if anything) to remedy these shortcomings? What effect do different political systems have for the efficient administration of scarce resources?

However, the problem of making efficient use of available resources is not easily solved. One complication is that the use of resources now affects their availability in the future. In some circumstances, this may add to future scarcity but in other cases, it can reduce future scarcity.

For example, if a fixed stock of water is available for use over two periods, using more of it in the first period will reduce its availability in the next. How should the available quantity of water be allocated between the periods in order to obtain the greatest economic value from its uses? On the other hand, greater use of resources in a current period need not spell greater scarcity in the future. For example, if resource use is increased in the current period to support research and development efforts and if this results in scientific advances that reduce the quantity of resources needed (or alters the type or resources required) to produce commodities in the future, this can reduce future resource scarcity. Economics is concerned not only with current scarcity but also with features of economic scarcity likely to emerge in the future, such as the nature of economic scarcity that is likely to occur with the advent of global warming. The connection between current resource use and future economic scarcity is one of the subjects studied in economics.

1.2.2. *The nature and coverage of natural resource economics, environmental economics and ecological economics*

The subjects of natural resource economics, environmental economics and ecological economics overlap substantially in their coverage but all are concerned with the analysis of the basic economics of managing resource use so as to reduce economic scarcity. These subjects (all subsets of economics) have evolved and have, to some extent, altered their content as the economic problems facing society have changed. It is useful to consider the nature of their evolution.

Natural resource economics (previously known as land economics) emerged as a focus of interest in the early development of economics. Sometimes the French physiocrats (writing about the mid-1700s) are credited with being the pioneers of natural resource economics (see Cleveland, 2010). Possibly, Quesnay (1694–1774) is the most widely known physiocrat. He tended to stress agriculture and the quality of land as the foundation for the circulation of economic wealth and developed the "Tableau economique" (see, for example, Roll, 1945, pp. 130–138; Quesnay and Cartelier, 1991). However, the European mercantilists who wrote at an earlier time also placed emphasis on natural resources as a source of wealth, particularly the importance of mines. Furthermore, Kautilya writing in (what is now India) about 300 BC gave considerable attention to the importance of natural resources as an influence on national wealth (Shamasastry, 1961; Tisdell, 2006). Therefore, the interest of political scientists and economists in natural resources as influences on economic wealth is one of very long standing. Nevertheless, during the late 18th century and in the 19th century, interest in natural resource economics accelerated as a result of enquiries about whether there are limits to economic growth and if so, what determines these limits. In other words, what are the main factors that determine long-term economic possibilities and the likely extent of economic scarcity in the future?

Two main constraints on economic growth were identified:

(1) the diminishing marginal productivity of land suitable for agriculture; and
(2) the need to engage in more marginal mining operations as minerals in the most productive mines are exhausted or become more difficult to recover.

Given the constraints on economic growth posed by what Malthus (1798) called the "niggardliness of nature", it was thought likely that an increase in income levels would be unsustainable should there be a significant rise in population levels. This led Malthus to suggest policies to restrain population growth. However, the debate did not end there. An important issue became the extent to which scientific and technological progress could stave off this specter of increasing resource scarcity. Ricardo (1817) recognized that scientific and technological progress could be counteracting force to the effects of diminishing resource productivity or economic scarcity. However, Engels (1959), writing in 1844, was most dismissive of the possibility that limited available natural resources of diverse productive quality would place a limit on economic growth — he optimistically declared that nothing was impossible to science. The debate about the ability of the development of science and technology to offset increasing scarcity of natural resources continues today. It is unresolved because the future development of scientific and technological knowledge is highly uncertain.

In due course, more detailed analysis of the economic exploitation of natural resources emerged. Analysis was extended in relation to the economics of mining, the economics of utilizing natural forests, and wild fish stocks and the role of natural resource use in agriculture. The main focus was on primary production and the production of industries depending heavily on the use of natural resources. At the same time, it was recognized that the production of these industries did not depend only on the natural resources available to them. Other factors of production such as man-made capital, labor, human capital and ingenuity were also important contributors to production. While some attention was given to environmental externalities in later developments of natural resource economics, these were usually limited to negative externalities confined to the primary-industries studies, for instance, the negative economic impacts of open-access to fisheries.

The development of environmental economics resulted in a broadening of economic analysis involving natural resources. It made it clear that the quality of these resources could decline due to pollution and environmental deterioration caused by human activity. Pigou (1932) pointed out how such environmental externalities could add to economic scarcity and reduce economic welfare. The examples that he used were not confined to primary industries but included air pollution caused by manufacturing industries and the risk of fire caused by sparks from steam locomotives. His analysis was based on neoclassical economic analysis and emphasized marginal or small changes in economic activity. The larger picture was ignored because of his focus on microeconomic analysis. His work, however, became a starting point for the development of environmental economics, which relied heavily on the application of neoclassical economic techniques. Ecological economics began developing from the late 1960s onwards. It was more eclectic in its use of analytical methods, favored a holistic approach stressing interdependence between economic activity, the natural world and social systems. For example, Boulding (1966) used the spaceship analogy to emphasize the type of situation facing humankind on Earth — those living on a spaceship only have limited resources (many of which are used up during their mission) and they must be careful not to pollute the capsule in which they exist. Boulding's analogy highlighted resource depletion on Earth and pollution as potential limits to economic growth. These theories were further developed by Georgescu-Roegen (1971) and Daly (1973) and other economists. Focus shifted to the sustainability of economic growth and the factors that do (or could) limit this growth. Natural resource depletion and adverse changes in the quality of natural resources (due to human activity such as the emission of air and water pollutants) were identified by ecological economists as major constraints on the sustainability of economic growth. Misallocation of resources (such as may occur when there is open-access to natural resources) also continued to interest ecological economists. In line with their eclectic approach, ecological economists did not reject completely the type of microeconomic analysis used in environmental economics but emphasized its limits.

As a result of these developments, a synthesis of economic thought has emerged that draws on the development of natural resource economics, environmental economics and ecological economics. Such a synthesis was already apparent in some texts that appear in the 1980s, such as Pearce *et al.* (1989). Resource and environmental economics as outlined in this book incorporates material that has been developed by economists who have primarily concentrated on the advancement of ecological economics, as well as more traditional materials covered in natural resource economics and environmental economics. Figure 1.1 provides a rough sketch of the historical development of natural resource economics, environmental economics and ecological economics. It indicates that a synthesis of these approaches seems to be emerging. This book is based upon this eclectic synthesis.

For clarification purposes, it is worthwhile considering a definition of ecological economics. It studies the economics of the interdependence between living things (especially humans) and the nature of their environments, including changes in the characteristics of these environments. These environments consist of living and abiotic components. The coverage of environmental economics is in fact, similar to that of ecological economics, but traditionally, the type of economic analysis used by the latter has relied heavily on neoclassical economics.

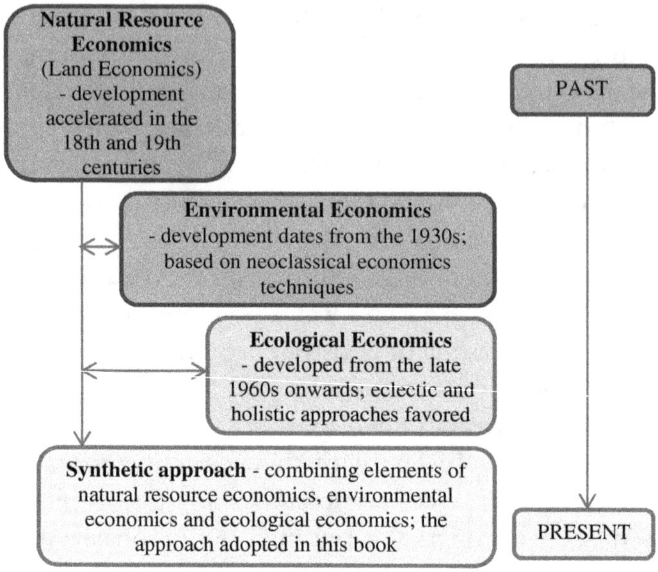

Fig. 1.1. A sketch indicating the pattern of historical development of natural resource economics, environmental economics and ecological economics and the emergence of a synthesis of these subjects.

Therefore, possibly more appropriately, this book could have been given the alternative title of *Resource and Ecological Economics.*

1.3. Further Observations on the Development of Economic Thought About the Significance of Natural Resources and Environmental Conditions

1.3.1. *Changing emphasis on the relevance of natural resources for economic growth and scarcity*

As mentioned above, classical economists in the 18th and 19th centuries emphasized the importance of the supply and quality of natural resources as constraints on economic growth and as major determinants of economic supplies. The main constraint to economic growth and production was, in their view, the operation of the laws of diminishing marginal returns and declining marginal productivity.

In their view, the main reasons why these laws apply to economies are that most natural resources (for example, land for agriculture) are in fixed supply and are of uneven quality in terms of their productive potential. However, it was conceded that some natural resources (for example, minerals) are depletable and not reusable, and that as superior grades of these resources are depleted, inferior stocks of these are exploited. Nevertheless, the finiteness of the availability of such resources did not obtain emphasis. Diminishing marginal returns from increased economic activity was seen as arising

(1) from the intensified exploitation of natural resources already utilized; and
(2) the extension of economic activity to involve the use of previously unused natural resources of lower productivity that those already utilized.

Although classical economists emphasized the role of natural resource availability as limiting growth, they did not stress exhaustion of natural resources as a serious barrier to economic growth and they paid no attention to the possibility that environmental pollution would inhibit economic growth. Because these did seem to be serious problems at the time, the economic implications of biodiversity loss and global warming received no attention.

Economists, during most of the 20th century, retreated from the view that the availability and quality of natural resources posed a significant impediment to economic growth. In fact, the expansion of manufacturing industry led to the view that increasing returns to expanded economic activity rather than decreasing returns might be more characteristic of expanding economies (Young, 1928). Emphasis now shifted to the availability of man-made physical capital (the produced means of further production) as being the most significant determinant of economic growth. Economic models were developed that no longer took natural resources into account as a determinant of economic growth. These models include the Harrod–Domar growth model (Harrod, 1948; Domar, 1946) and the models of Solow (1956) and Swan (1956). Solow (1957) later extended his model to include exogenous technological progress as an important influence on economic growth.

Further extensions to these types of growth models were, for example, made by Romer (1986). Studies by Denison (1962) found that economic growth in many countries depended not only on the supply of physical capital but also on human capital (for instance, the level and quality of the education of their populations) as well as technological progress.

Nevertheless, beginning around the early 1970s, a small group of economists (for example, Boulding, 1966; Mishan, 1967; Georgescu-Roegen, 1971; Daly, 1973, 1999, 2007) plus some noneconomists (for example, Meadows *et al.*, 1972, 2005; Ehrlich *et al.*, 1973, 1977) began to emphasize the possibility that depletion of natural resources and the pollution and degradation of natural environments could become serious impediments to sustained economic growth. Thus, a significant group of economists (and some influential noneconomists) have reasserted the importance of natural resources (assets) for economic processes. Pearce (1988), in particular, stressed the vital economic role of the availability of natural capital (resource stocks) as a complement to man-made capital. The views of these scholars are given particular attention in Chapter 7 of this book but these concerns are also reflected in other chapters such as Chapters 10–13.

1.3.2. *Changing emphasis on the significance of material versus nonmaterial goods for economic welfare*

On the whole, classical scholars only ascribed economic value to material commodities and tended to dismiss nonmaterial commodities as a source of economic value. In line with this view, labor producing physical goods was described as productive labor whereas that supplying services was designated unproductive labor. Thus, labor helping to supply grain was considered productive but that supplying tourist services fell into the unproductive category of labor.

This may have been a reflection of the fact that classical economists wrote at a time when per capita incomes were low and possibly in those times, increased supplies of basic necessities were valued most by society. This implied that in the hierarchy of wants or needs (Anon, 2020; Maslow, 1987), goods (for example, food) to satisfy *basic* physiological needs were valued most highly, and services and nonmaterial goods were regarded as unessential luxuries. However, even the poor appear to have a demand for nonmaterial goods. This accords with the theory of Max-Neef (1992) that a *strict* hierarchy of wants does not exist. It cannot be taken for granted that the poor place no economic value on intangible commodities. Depending on their cultures and religions, even the poor in some developing countries value the conservation of living things (see Bandara and Tisdell, 2003).

During the early 20th century, there was growing emphasis by economists on subjective valuation of economic commodities as a basis for economic theories of rational choice. Cardinal scaling of consumer preferences based on the measurement of utility was replaced by the mere ordering of preferences (ordinal utility). This has been described as the ordinal revolution (Little, 1957). Probably as a result of this and because of rising incomes, the concept (accepted by the community) of what had economic value began to widen. It soon became accepted that any item (tangible or intangible) could have economic value provided some individuals are willing to pay for its supply. The desired commodity could be of a material or a nonmaterial nature as pointed out by Robbins (1937).

This changed outlook provided an opening for new developments in natural resource economics and in environmental economics. For example, the way was now open for assessing the value of natural resources (such as national parks) for outdoor recreation and methods developed for valuing wild species taking into account such intangible attributes as their existence value, option value and bequest value (see Chapters 6 and 10). It was shown that species and environments possessing little material economic value could have considerable economic value in view of the value placed on their intangible attributes. In general, the evolution of economic thought has widened the scope of economic enquiry and enriched it. This evolution has also influenced the development of resource and environmental economics (and closely related studies in ecological economics). Further evolution of these subjects can be expected in the future.

1.4. Notes on the Coverage in This Book of Modern Issues in Resource and Environmental Economics

This book is divided into two parts. Part I focuses on general issues and economic principles relevant to resource and environmental economics, and Part II applies these general principles to specific topics of current concern. These specific topics include the development of agriculture and its impacts on environments and resource availability, water management, biodiversity conservation, global warming and air pollution, recycling and solid waste management, and environmental health. Several important general issues are covered in Part I. For example, Chapter 2 outlines varied theoretical perspectives that can be used to analyze issues involving environmental and resource economics. The coverage of this book is intended to emphasize the following points:

(1) No single economic approach is suitable for solving all problems in resource and environmental economics. The most appropriate method can change with the purpose of the analysis and the availability of data.
(2) Often it is useful to examine issues in resource and environmental economics from several different perspectives.
(3) Economic thought offers a variety of approaches to economic analysis, and resource and environmental economics can be strengthened by drawing on all of these different types of analyses.
(4) The body of economic thought is not static but has evolved and continues to do so. This evolution is partly a response to the need for new and improved analyses to address novel and emerging issues, such as global resource and environmental issues that have become apparent in modern times. These include global warming and biodiversity loss. Nevertheless, many economic scarcity problems have been studied for a long time and are of enduring concern, as will also be clear from the coverage in Part I of this book.
(5) In addressing the complexities of contemporary environmental and natural resource challenges, it is beneficial for economics to

draw on the knowledge, value systems and analytical methods of other disciplines such as ecology, psychology and sociology. Furthermore, the solution to most environmental and natural resource problems requires account to be taken of knowledge provided by natural scientists. Consequently, economists need to interact with scholars in other disciplines and take account of their knowledge to solve economic problems and advance economic theory.

In addition, this book provides a detailed account of why social systems (principally economic and political systems) may fail to use natural resources and the environment in ways that minimize economic scarcity. It gives particular attention to how market systems may fail in that regard and considers the extent to which laws and property rights can be used to rectify these failures. Government policies for regulating natural resource use and pollution emissions are given particular attention in light of the fact that markets and the bestowal of private property rights can fail to minimize economic scarcity. However, there are also limits to the extent to which governments can rectify this situation and this is kept in mind in the text.

Economic valuation of commodities plays a central role in procedures for determining how well natural resources (including environments) are used to minimize economic scarcity. Consequently, Chapter 6 gives considerable attention to economics methods for valuing environmental spillovers and natural resources.

Environmental and economic sustainability have become major issues and there are fears that scarcity reduction now may result in unwanted economic and environmental impoverishment in the future. Chapter 7 of this book provides a realistic analysis of the issues involved.

1.5. Concluding Comments

While neoclassical economic theory is not rejected in this book as a means of appreciating some important issues in environmental and resource economics, it is nevertheless considered to be a special case, which needs to be supplemented or complemented in many cases by other economic theories and perspectives. Therefore, in order to provide a better understanding of several important modern issues involving the use of natural resources and environments, the coverage in this book also draws on perspectives provided by new institutional economics and behavioral economics, for example. A useful test of the value of any theory is whether it improves our perception or understanding of observed phenomena. This is the basic test, which has shaped the presentation of materials in this book.

1.6. Keywords

Cardinal utility; classical economics; decreasing economic returns to scale; diminishing marginal productivity; ecological economics; economics; economic scarcity; economic value of intangibles; environmental economics; factors of production; future economic scarcity; hierarchy of wants; increasing economic returns to scale; land; limits to economic growth; material goods; natural resource economics; non-productive labor; ordinal utility; productive labor.

1.7. Questions for Review and Discussion

1. What factors of production were considered by classical economists to be the main determinants of economic production? What factor of production was regarded by classical economists as being the main constraint on economic growth?
2. What is the basic economic problem and how does it influence the nature of economic studies? How do the subjects of natural resource economics and environmental economics relate to the basic economic problem?
3. Compare and contrast the subjects of natural resource economics, environmental economics and ecological economics and outline and discuss their historical evolution.
4. The theories that classical economists developed to predict limits to economic growth (and therefore, limited prospects for reducing economic scarcity) differed in important respects to modern theories (such as those developed by ecological economists), which also predict limits to economic growth. Explain.

5. Several economic growth theories developed since the 1930s fail to include natural resource availability and environmental conditions as influences on economic growth. Do you consider this to be a shortcoming? Why?
6. Why do you think that classical economists only considered material goods to be of economic value? Do you agree with the views of classical economists that labor employed in the production of material goods in production but that employed in the supply of services is unproductive? Why do you think that economists extended their views about the type of things that possess economic values? How did their altered perception influence the development of resource and environmental economics?
7. Do you think it is useful to conceptualize human wants as being hierarchical? In such a system of hierarchy, higher-order wants are only satisfied once lower-order ones are satisfied to an "adequate" extent. Does this mean that the poor are only interested in satisfying basic physical wants? What implications could this have for environmental conservation?
8. Do you think it is important to realize that economic thought about resource and environmental economics has evolved and altered with the passage of time? Why do you think this? To what extent do you believe that the theories involving resource and environmental economics are responses to major economic issues of their times?
9. Why is it beneficial to realize that there are a variety of theories and economic perspectives that can throw light on issues involving resource and environmental economics? Outline the type of benefits that could be obtained by making use of different theories dealing with the same economic phenomenon.

Readings* and References

Anon (2020). *Maslow's hierarchy of models,* Wikipedia, https://en.wikipedia.org/wiki/Maslow%27s_hierarchy_of_needs [Accessed 3 August 2020].

*The highlighted items can constitute suitable readings for students. Some are also references. This identification procedure applies to all subsequent chapters.

Bandara, R. and C.A. Tisdell (2003). Use and non-use values of wild Asian elephants, *Sri Lankan Economic Journal*, 4, 3–30.

Boulding, K.E. (1966). The economics of the coming spaceship Earth. In H. Jarrett (Ed.) *Environmental Quality in a Growing Economy*, 3–14. Johns Hopkins University Press, Baltimore, MD, USA.

Cleveland, C.J. (2010). Biophysical Economics. *Encyclopedia of Earth*. In R. Costanza (Ed.) Environmental Information Coalition, National Council for Science and the Environment, Washington DC. https://editors.eol.org/eoearth/wiki/Biophysical_economics.

Costanza, R., H.E. Daly and J.A. Bartholomew (1991). Goals agenda and policy recommendations for ecological economics. In R. Costanza (Ed.) *Ecological Economics: The Science and Management of Sustainability*, 1–20. Columbia University Press, New York and Chichester, West Sussex.

Daly, H.E. (1973). *Toward a Steady-State Economy*, Freeman, San Francisco, USA.

Daly, H.E. (1999). *Ecological Economics and the Ecology of Economics: Essays in Criticism*, Edward Elgar, Cheltenham, UK and Northampton, MA, USA.

Daly, H.E. (2007). *Ecological Economics and Sustainable Development: Essays in Criticism*, Edward Elgar, Cheltenham, UK and Northampton, MA, USA.

Denison, E.F. (1962). *The Sources of Economic Growth and the Alternatives Before Us*, Committee for Economic Development, New York.

Domar, E.D. (1946). Capital expansion, rate of growth, and employment, *Econometrica*, 14, 137–147. doi: 10.2307/1905364.

Ehrlich, P.R., A.H. Ehrlich and J.P. Holdren (1973). *Human Ecology, Problems and Solutions*, W.H. Freeman, San Francisco.

Ehrlich, P.R., A.H. Ehrlich and J.P. Holdren (1977). *Ecoscience, Population, Resources Environment*, W.H. Freeman, San Francisco.

Engels, F. (1959). Outlines of a critique of political economy In K. Marx (Ed.) *Economic and Philosophic Manuscripts of 1844*, Foreign Languages Publishing House, Moscow.

Georgescu-Roegen, N. (1971). *The Entropy Law and the Economic Process*, Harvard University Press, Cambridge, MA.

Harrod, R.F. (1948). *Towards a Dynamic Economics*, Macmillan, London.

Little, I.M.D. (1957). *A Critique of Welfare Economics*, 2nd edn. Oxford University Press, Oxford.

Malthus, T.R. (1798). *An Essay on the Principle of Population as it Effects the Future Improvement of Mankind*, J. Johnson, London. Reprint 1976, Norton, New York.

Maslow, A.H. (1987). *Motivation and Personality*, 3rd edn. Harper and Row, New York.

Max-Neef, M. (1992). Development and human needs. In P. Ekins and M. Max-Neef (Eds.), *Real-Life Economics: Understanding Wealth Creation*, Routledge, London, New York.

Meadows, D.H., D.L. Meadows, J. Ronders and W. Behrens (1972). *The Limits of Growth: A Report for the Club of Rome's Project on the Predicament of Mankind*, Universe Books, New York.

Meadows, D.H., J. Randers and D.L. Meadows (2005). *The Limits to Growth: The 30 Year Update*, Earthscan, London.

Mishan, E.J. (1967). *The Costs of Economic Growth*, Staples, London.

Pearce, D., A. Markandya and E.B. Barbier (1989). *Blueprint for a Green Economy*, Earthscan Publications, London.

Pearce, D.W. (1988). Economics, equity and sustainable development, *Futures*, 20, 598–605. doi: https://doi.org/10.1016/0016-3287(88)90002-X.

Perman, R., Y. Ma, M. Common, D. Maddison and J. McGilvray (2011). *Natural Resource and Environmental Economics*, 4th edn. Pearson, Harlow, Essex UK. [Chapter 1].

Pigou, A. (1932). *The Economics of Welfare*, 4th edn. Macmillan, London.

Quesnay, F. and J. Cartelier (1991). *Physiocratie: droit naturel, tableau économique et autres textes*, Flammarion, Paris.

Ricardo, D. (1817). *The Principles of Political Economic and Taxation*, Dent, London. Reprint, 1955.

Robbins, L. (1937). *An Essay on the Nature and Significance of the Economic Science*, Macmillan, London.

Roll, E. (1945). *The History of Economic Thought*, 2nd edn. Faber and Faber, London.

Romer, P.M. (1986). Increasing returns and long-run growth, *Journal of Political Economy*, 94, 1002–1037. doi: 10.1086/261420.

Shamasastry, R. (1961). *Kautilya's Arthasastra*, R. Shamasastry [trans.], Mysore Printing and Publishing House, Mysore, India.

Solow, R.M. (1956). A contribution to the theory of economic growth, *Quarterly Journal of Economics*, 70, 65–74. doi: https://doi.org/10.2307/1884513.

Solow, R.M. (1957). Technical change and the aggregate production function, *The Review of Economics and Statistics*, 39, 312–320. doi: 10.2307/1926047.

Swan, T.W. (1956). Economic growth and capital accumulation, *Economic Record*, 32, 334–361. doi: https://doi.org/10.1111/j.1475-4932.1956.tb00434.x.

Tisdell, C.A. (1990). *Natural Resources, Growth and Development*, Praeger, New York, Westport CT and London. [Chapters 1, 3 and 4].

Tisdell, C.A. (2005). *Economics of Environmental Conservation*, 2nd edn. Edward Elgar, Cheltenham, UK and Northampton, MA, USA. [Chapter 1].

Tisdell, C.A. (2006). Arthasastra as a basis for economic science? In R.K. Sen and R.L. Basu (Eds.), *Economics in the Arthasastra*, 36–49. Deep & Deep, New Delhi.

Young, A.A. (1928). Increasing returns and economic progress, *The Economic Journal*, 38, 527–542.

Chapter 2

Different Types of Approaches to Environmental and Resource Economics

2.1. Introduction

There are many different approaches to economics and, therefore, to resource and environmental economics. The subject matter of natural resource economics and environmental economics overlaps almost completely, but not entirely (Tisdell, 1999a, Chapter 2; Harrison and Tisdell, 1994). Consequently, it is convenient to combine the discussion of these subjects. The purpose of this chapter is to outline the range of different approaches to economics and to indicate their implications for the nature of resource and environmental economics. In subsequent chapters, analysis and policy proposals will be considered from multiple perspectives reflecting these different approaches.

The approaches or perspectives to economics outlined here should be regarded as a *selection* designed to highlight important differences. There are many variations in perspectives and not all of these can be covered in a single chapter. Furthermore, analytical approaches sometimes overlap. In addition, the question arises of whether different economic perspectives or paradigms result in theories and techniques that are mutually exclusive. In my view, different paradigms are useful for different purposes and it is often illuminating to consider an issue in resource and environmental economics from several different perspectives. Nevertheless, for understanding the nature of a particular environmental or resource issue, some approaches are likely to be superior to others. Approaches to economics which will be outlined are:

1. neoclassical economics;
2. new institutional economics;
3. behavioral or psychological economics;
4. old or orthodox (conventional) institutional economics; and
5. evolutionary economics including co-evolution.

Some attention will also be given to views associated with the Austrian School of Economics and its relationship to the perspectives listed above and to game theory. Figure 2.1 provides a representation

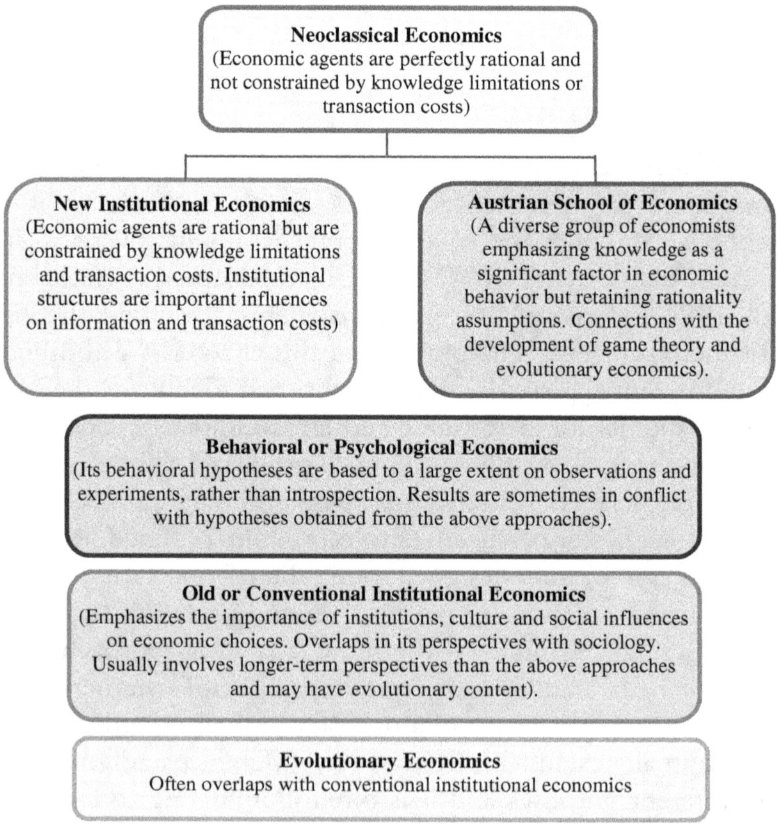

Fig. 2.1. Different approaches to economic analysis with some of their features indicated.

of most of the economic perspectives to be considered and indicates some features of each.

The main purpose of this chapter is to illustrate how these different approaches to economics result in resource and environmental issues being examined in different ways. For this purpose, very basic models are used here and more advanced models are introduced in later chapters.

2.2. Neoclassical Economics and Environmental and Resource Economics

The early development of resource and environmental economics was embedded in neoclassical economics. The neoclassical perspective relies on the following assumptions:

1. Economic agents have perfect knowledge.
2. They maximize their own gains in economic transactions. Thus, consumers are assumed to maximize their utility and businesses their profit. The theory adopts the concept of rational economic man; a human being unconstrained by knowledge or information limitations in making rational choices.
3. The focus of analysis is on equilibria, with comparisons of equilibria (comparative statics) being of central importance.
4. The transaction costs involved in exchange, economic administration, and in policy-making and implementation are largely ignored.
5. Costs of decision-making by individuals and limits to such decision-making (bounded rationality) are ignored.
6. The preferences (values) of individuals are taken as given and social influences on these are not studied.

This means that there is little attention to disequilibria, to dynamic processes involving change, and to knowledge constraints. Nevertheless, it can be argued that neoclassical economics provides a useful, if incomplete, *first* overview of how market systems work and how they in some respects, fail to minimize economic scarcity. Neoclassical economic models provide a starting point for identifying market failures (due to factors such as environmental spillovers), for examining the economic consequences of these failures and for proposing policies that may "correct" these. Neoclassical economics can, for example, be used to show that even perfectly competitive market systems will fail to minimize economic scarcity if environmental spillovers occur. This can be illustrated by a very simple model developed by A. Pigou.

The British economist, Arthur Pigou (1932), built the foundations of environmental economics on neoclassical economics. He proposed that economic activities resulting in negative environmental externalities should be taxed and those generating positive environmental externalities should be subsidized. He recommended a tax on the output of industries that generate negative externalities and a subsidy on those that generate positive externalities.

An *economic externality or spillover* occurs when an economic agent as a consequence of her/his activity, provides a benefit to others without being paid for it, or when an activity results in a disbenefit to others without the originator of the activity being charged for it. In the former case, there is a favorable externality and in the latter case an unfavorable externality. In the former situation, the economic agent receives less than the economic benefit created by her/his activity whereas the opposite occurs in the latter case. Because neoclassical economic theory assumes that individuals act in their own self-interest, the activity is likely to be under supplied in the former case and to be over supplied in the latter case from a social point of view.

The type of model that Pigou (1932) used to examine this economic problem and to suggest policies that could be used to remedy it can be illustrated by Fig. 2.2. There the line marked DD represents the industry demand curve for a product X, for instance steel. It indicates the extra value which buyers of steel place on its extra production. The industry's supply curve is shown by the line marked SS and represents the extra (marginal) private costs of producing steel. In a competitive market, the industry will come into equilibrium at point E_1 with X_2 of steel being produced per period of time and being sold at a price per unit of P_1.

The production of this industry, however results in negative environmental externalities. The steel industry can, for example, emit particulate matter (dust and soot), and gases that result in acid rains. These emissions may damage buildings, crops, and cause ill health in some

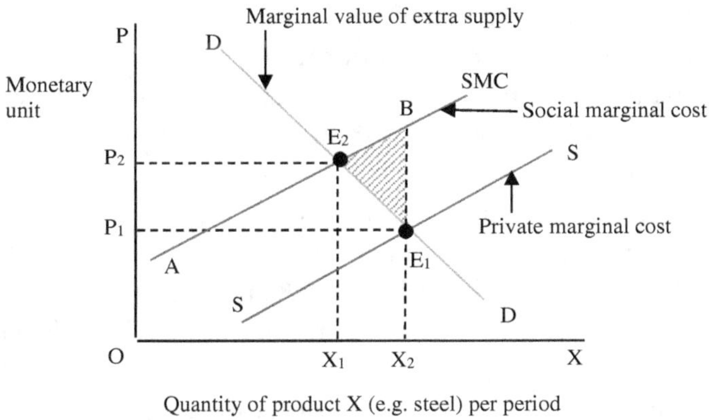

Fig. 2.2. Pigou's approach for analyzing and regulating environmental externalities is based on neoclassical economics.

localities. The line *AB* identified by SMC in Fig. 2.2 is assumed to be the social marginal cost of producing steel when the costs of these spillovers are taken into account. The difference between the lines *SS* and *AB* represents the marginal externality costs of steel production. Hence, if the steel market is perfectly competitive, its market equilibrium at E_1 will not be socially ideal.

In the absence of externalities, the private and social marginal costs of production of steel will coincide and production of X_2 of steel (corresponding to equilibrium point at point E_1) will be socially ideal in the sense that the extra value placed on steel production by buyers will just equal its extra social cost of its production. The presence of an externality, however, destroys this relationship. In the case illustrated, the free market results in the social marginal cost of production of steel corresponding to point *B* being in excess of the private marginal cost of production corresponding to E_1. Given existing production methods, the socially optimal amount of steel to produce per period of time is X_1 (not X_2) because at this level of output the extra value placed on steel by buyers is just equal to the extra social marginal cost of producing it. The area of the hatched triangle E_2E_1Brepresents the loss in the net economic value of production (sometimes called the deadweight social loss) that occurs if externality costs are not taken into account in this case.

Pigou's suggested solution was that the government should impose a tax or charge on the production of the commodity generating a negative externality to bring private marginal costs into line with social marginal costs. This procedure is sometimes described as one of internalizing the negative externality. In the case shown in Fig. 2.2, this would involve the imposition of a tax on each unit of steel produced of BE_1. After the imposition of this tax, private marginal costs of supplying steel would coincide with line AB and the market would come into equilibrium at E_2. As a result, the social deadweight economic loss would be eliminated.

Note that Pigou's analysis relies on comparative statics, assumes perfect knowledge and self-interested rational economic agents. Processes of change and any institutional difficulties in imposing this environmental tax are not considered. No account is taken of agency costs involved in implementing policy and policy-makers are assumed to have perfect knowledge of the relevant supply and demand functions and to know the level of externality costs. Agency costs refer to the costs which would be incurred by a government in monitoring the quantity of output produced by businesses and ensuring that businesses pay the amount of environmental taxation for which they are liable.

Ignoring agency costs, it is usually more efficient to tax directly a pollution emission that gives rise to a negative externality than to tax the quantity of output of the product associated with the externality (see Chapter 5). Taxing emissions of a pollutant will encourage suppliers to reduce their emissions in relation to whatever level of output they produce. This will not happen if their level of output is taxed.

For example, suppose that emissions from coal-fired power stations of gases and particulate matter are of concern. Pigou's approach would be to attempt to control the unfavorable externalities involved by taxing the amount of electricity produced by the power stations in the expectation that this would reduce their level of output and thus, indirectly reduce their levels of emission of pollutants. An alternative method would be to impose taxes or charges on the offending emissions themselves. In contrast with the Pigovian approach, this will encourage these power stations to use coal that generates less emission of gases contributing to acid rains, such as low sulfur coal, and to adopt techniques, such as scrubbers, that reduce emissions of particulate matter.

Despite the apparent economic superiority of the imposition of pollution charges on emissions of pollutants rather than the quantity of output of products generating pollutants, agency costs do have to be taken into account. When they are taken into account, regulating output will *sometimes* be more economic than controlling emission levels as a means of managing environmental externalities.

As discussed in Chapter 5, standard economic models of controlling emissions of pollutants are also based on the assumptions of neoclassical economics outlined above. They assume a world in which, for example, economic agents are rational, well-informed and self-seeking. Neoclassical economists in addition assume a perfectly informed government motivated only by the desire to reduce economic scarcity. Furthermore, institutional constraints (such as difficulties associated with public bureaucracies) are not considered to be constraints on environmental policy.

Nevertheless, neoclassical economic models show that even under relatively ideal conditions, competitive market systems can fail to minimize economic scarcity, if environmental externalities occur. They also indicate that it is economically possible for government intervention to correct for these market failures, a matter discussed in more detail in the next chapter. Nevertheless, government intervention in practice is not costless, governments are not perfectly informed and as the economics of politics and of bureaucracies indicates, governments are not always motivated by the desire to minimize economic scarcity. New institutional economics has focused on such issues.

2.3. New Institutional Economics

The impact of new institutional economics on environmental and resource economics has yet to be fully realized. Dominant scholars in new institutional economics retain the assumption of rational economic man but envisage economic agents and policy-makers as having to cope with transaction costs in economic exchange, the costs of decision making and the cost of administrating institutions. These factors are all neglected in neoclassical economics.

Williamson (1985) has been one of the main advocates of new institutional economics but he has not given much attention to its consequences for environmental and resource economics. However, other contributors to new institutional economics such as North (1990), North and Thomas (1973), Demsetz (1967) and Coase (1960) have given attention to its consequences for environmental and resource economics.

Douglas North and H. Demsetz argue that property rights depend on economic considerations. As the costs of exclusion from private property fall and as the economic benefits to be had from private property rights rise, it becomes more economic to establish private property rights and enforce these rights. In general, North believes that societies evolve towards extension of private property rights, and towards market economies. In his view, those societies are likely to be more efficient economically and growth-oriented than earlier ones, most of which were organized to a large extent by custom or command.

Robert Coase is often regarded as a pioneer of new institutional economics in view of his article on the nature of the firm (Coase, 1937). Writing on environmental issues, he also put forward the view that many environmental problems arise because property rights in the environment are not clearly defined. The Coase theorem (Coase, 1960), for example, is that in the absence of transaction costs, bargaining can result in an optimal resolution of environmental problems provided either polluters have the right to pollute or the victims of pollution have a legal right to a pollution-free environment. Coase argues that either of the distribution of rights leads as a result of bargaining to a socially optimal position if transaction costs are absent.

However, transaction costs make a major difference. For example, if there are many victims of pollution, none may take action to enforce their property rights. The benefit to each may be small, so none may act to control pollutors. Consequently, only if a class action is allowed, might an “optimal” solution be possible.

Furthermore, major differences in income distribution occur depending on whether the right to pollute is given to polluters or to their victims. If the rights are given to polluters, victims will need to transfer income to polluters to achieve social optimality. If the rights are given to the victims, the polluters will have to transfer income to victims to achieve social optimality, that is Paretian optimality in this case, a situation in which it is impossible to make anyone better-off without making somebody worse-off (see Section 3.2.1).

Given that Coase (1937) put so much emphasis on the importance of transaction costs for the existence and operation of business firms, it is surprising that he did not put greater emphasis on their significance when proposing the conferment of clearly specified private property rights as a way to overcome economic problems arising from environmental spillovers. Possibly, he did not want to detract from the extension of private property rights as a solution to environmental problems. This issue will be discussed in Chapter 3.

The question could also be considered of whether property rights should always be exclusive. Shared rights might be socially acceptable on occasions. For example, in Nordic countries, a right exists to trespass on private lands. In many European countries, communal rights exist to use beaches and rivers for some purposes.

Baumol and Quandt (1964) are not often associated with the new institutional economics. However, they put forward a theory of optimally imperfect decisions. This fits well into the new institutional framework. They argue that it is only optimal to refine decisions (collect information and analyze it and decide) up to the point where the extra cost of decision-making equals its extra expected benefit. This can be applied to the formulation of policies for environmental management. Baumol and Quandt show that approximations or rules of thumb may be optimal given decision-making costs (Tisdell, 1996, Chapter 1).

Because uncertainty and information inadequacies are prevalent in the consideration of environmental issues, the theory of optimally imperfect decisions has applications to the making of environmental policy as is illustrated later in this book.

Mancur Olson, author of *The Economics of Collective Action*, (1965) can also be regarded as a new institutional economist. He examines the economic incentives for collective action and the likely distribution of gains from such action.

Although Williamson (1985) has not contributed much to environmental economics, he does examine the efficiency of hierarchies and emphasizes the principal–agent problem. The principal–agent problem can occur when the principal has limited knowledge and control of the actions of his/her agent. This provides the agent with scope to undertake behavior that may not be in the best interest of the principal or which is at odds with the objectives of the principal. For example, members of large conservation organizations (its principals) may have limited control over the behavior of its executives because it is costly to monitor their behavior and members are reliant on its executives for much of their information about the organization. This type of problem is not new. It was raised by Berle and Means (1932) and discussed by Penrose (1964) in relation to the performance of public companies. Writers such as Niskanen (1971) and Downs (1957) raised it in relation to public administration. Public servants (agents of the government) may follow their own agenda up to a point. They may not, for instance, implement policies, including environmental policies, in a cost-effective manner. Costs of implementing policy may be inflated so that the size of the public administration is larger than it otherwise would be.

The writings of some economists and social scientists are not easily categorized by the classification of economic thought adopted here because their views straddle more than one category. This is true for example, of the works of Simon (1957). Although he was a mentor of Williamson, Simon rejects the concept of rational economic man in favor of satisficing and administrative man (Simon, 1961). His emphasis on the cost of decision-making and constraints on decision-making overlaps with that of the new institutionalists. On the other hand, his rejection of optimization as a realistic theory of human behavior distinguishes him from the new institutionalists and his models of behavior are more akin to those advocated in behavioral or psychological economics. His views and their implications will, therefore, be discussed below when behavioral and psychological approaches are considered.

The main difference between the new institutional approach to economics and the neoclassical one is the emphasis of the former on the importance of information or knowledge constraints, many of which cannot be removed. Therefore, environmental behaviors and environmental policies must be assessed in this context. Nevertheless, subject to these constraints, optimizing, rational, and self-interested behavior are assumed. The strong rationality assumptions of neoclassical economics are retained but knowledge and decision-making costs are taken into account. As in neoclassical economics, the analysis used in new institutional economics is based on comparative statics.

In relation to the Pigovian model (Fig. 2.2) one might expect that a new institutional economics perspective would emphasize the agency costs involved in implementing policies to control pollution as an important consideration in deciding if control is in the public interest. This contrasts with the neoclassical approach which gives little or no attention to agency costs. Furthermore, the neoclassical approach assumes that the economic relationships shown in Fig. 2.2 are known by the regulatory authority. In practice, they are not usually well known. Therefore, it would be consistent with the approach of new institutional economics to take into account the costs of estimating these and the administrative costs generally of devising environmental policies. Decision costs are a part of optimizing problems in the new institutional economics. More attention than in neoclassical economics is also given to how different institutional structures affect the efficiency of achieving economic goals, particularly when information constraints are taken into account. This, however, is not peculiar to new institutional economics but is also a feature of parts of Austrian economics.

Table 2.1 summarizes stock features that help to differentiate the neoclassical approach to economic analysis from that of the new institutional economics. These differences have implications for the way in which environmental policy is devised and for how economic agents are assumed to act.

Table 2.1. Comparison of some "stock" attributes of neoclassical and new institutional economic models.

Attribute	Feature of neoclassical economics	Feature of new institutional economics
Perfect knowledge	Yes	No
Decision-making costs	No	Yes
Agency costs	No	Yes
Institutional structure emphasized	Limited	Yes
Comparative statics emphasized	Yes	Yes
Optimizing behavior	Yes	Yes
Objectives of economic agents given (exogenous)	Yes	Yes

2.4. Behavioral and Psychological Economics

In its assumptions and approach, new institutional economics is much closer to neoclassical economics than is behavioral or psychological economics. Theories based on behavioral economics do not as a rule suppose that individuals always optimize and are as rational as assumed in the previously mentioned theories. Furthermore, its behavioral assumptions are less likely to be based on introspection and more likely to be grounded on experimentation and empirical evidence. Behavioral assumptions of these theories are usually derived from psychology. There is acceptance of the fact that not all human behavior is likely to be rational and that such behavior is limited by uncertainty and the costs involved in decision-making. By contrast, new institutional economists normally suppose that individuals act in a rational optimizing manner subject to the presence of uncertainty and the need to take account of the costs of decision-making. In addition, behavioral economists often take into account dynamic processes involved in choices whereas this is less common in new institutional economics (which along with neoclassical economics) relies heavily on comparative statics.

Behavioral or psychological economics is still developing and does not yet constitute a completely settled body of thought. Its nature and its applicability to environmental and resource economics can, however, be illustrated by considering some of the prominent contributors to this field.

Simon (1955) was an early contributor to the development of psychological economics and indirectly through his influence on Williamson (1985) contributed to the development of new institutional economics. Simon argued that due to uncertainty and the cost of decision-making individuals strive for satisfactory outcomes rather than optimal ones in their behavior. He termed this "satisficing" behavior to distinguish it from optimizing behavior. Once an individual's effort results in his/her aspiration levels being achieved, the individual is satisfied and does not engage in further effort or search to achieve an optimal outcome. If aspiration levels are not being achieved in the time-frame set by individuals, they are either lowered or effort is increased. Therefore, one needs to study the dynamic process of the formation of aspiration levels and their adjustment in relation to effort. It is possible that different individuals may have different subjective estimates of the effort required to reach their aspiration levels, and this would result in different estimation of effort to reach the same goal.

Herbert Simon did not apply his satisficing concept to environmental economics. However, there are possible parallels between his approach and the adoption of safe minimum environmental standards, for example, the setting of targets not to permit levels of water or air pollution to rise above specified levels. This approach may be influenced by the presence of uncertainty and the costs and difficulty of specifying optimal standards. However, in the case of such standards, social and political factors come into play and influence how stringent the standards are. This is not a subject studied by Simon but is worthy of investigation. Simon's satisficing approach introduces thresholds into models of decision-making; a feature absent in neoclassical theory. In some cases, it is difficult to decide whether these thresholds reflect the nature of decision-making or are a consequence of biophysical phenomena. For example, it is sometimes argued that a core of natural/environmental resources needs to be conserved if economic sustainability is to be achieved. To what extent this core is determined by attitudes to risk-taking or by biophysical factors is unclear. It is also possible for a satisficing approach to decisions about natural resource use to be combined with optimization. For example, one might wish to maximize the aggregate income of future generations subject to the condition that the income level of no future generation falls below some acceptable or satisfactory level (Tisdell, 1999b).

A further feature of Simon's approach is his view that the concept of optimizing economic man be replaced by that of administrative man when studying the behavior of organizations. Administrative man searches for satisfactory solutions rather than optimal ones and takes into account the cost of decision-making (Simon, 1961). In doing so, the administrator may use rules-of-thumb and cryptic procedures.

The question has arisen of whether economic actors who behave in the way described by Simon may in fact by optimizing. George Stigler (1961) showed that search models in which the aim is to maximize expected gain taking into account the costs of search and the expected benefits of further search can generate similar behavior to that described by Simon. The models Stigler has in mind involve optimal stopping rules. Baumol and Quandt (1964) have also shown that in some cases rules-of-thumb maximize expected gains when the costs of decision-making are taken into account. There is, therefore, argument about whether the type of behavior described by Simon is in fact optimizing behavior or whether it is best modeled as if it is optimizing behavior. There are similar implications for environmental policy no matter which of these views is adopted. Both involve bounds on rationality.

First, they imply that the behavior of economic agents may not exactly coincide with that predicted by neoclassical economic theory. Secondly, decisions involved in policy-making should not be regarded as costless. Costs and uncertainty are involved in formulating and administering environmental policy. Sometimes these costs are so high that they make public intervention to regulate natural resource use socially undesirable, even though it would be desirable in their absence. Furthermore, in deciding on environmental regulation, the application of rules-of-thumb or approximations may give satisfactory results or even ones that are nearly optimal. However, not all such procedures are equally satisfactory and they need to be assessed individually.

Kahneman and Tversky (2000) have presented empirical evidence of what has been called the endowment or status quo effect. A useful summary of this anomaly is available in Kahneman *et al.* (1991). It has been found that in many cases, the maximum amount that individuals are willing to pay to obtain a commodity is less than the minimum amount they must be paid to forgo the same commodity. This is inconsistent with the implications of neoclassical economic theory. As discussed in the next chapter, it creates a complication for Coase's theorem. It implies that the willingness to pay to retain an environmental good by those who possess it exceeds the amount they are willing to pay to restore it if it is lost.

Why does the endowment effect exist? To some extent, an income effect may help to explain the result. But the lack of reversibility might also be a psychological response to a feeling of being dispossessed if one "owns" a commodity and it is taken away. A premium may be sought to compensate for the feeling of dispossession.

In some cases, it may also be that possession of a commodity alters tastes or values and this could give rise to ratchet-like (limited reversibility) effect. This aspect does not however, seem to be explored by Kahneman and associates, probably because their experiments are of a short-term nature. Nevertheless, changes in tastes or values or their formation as a result of experience or information provision to individuals do fall within the ambit of psychological economics. Tisdell (2007) and Tisdell *et al.* (2008) have, for example, explored ways in which information and experience alter the demand for conservation of wildlife species. These species can be regarded as public or quasi-public environmental resources.

The question of the extent to which values and demand for environmental goods are dependent on previous experiences, knowledge and preconceptions (path dependence) is also a subject of psychological studies. In practice, tastes and values evolve over time but this is not a focus in neoclassical and in new institutional economics. Furthermore, social influences on individuals' demands and values are not considered in neoclassical and new institutional economics. But they are an interest in social psychology, sociology, and conventional institutional economics.

Etzioni (1988) argues that the behavior of individuals is influenced by social values and considerations. In his view, most individuals do not act solely in their own selfish interest. Most, in his view, temper their pursuit of personal self-interest by taking into account social (moral and similar) values. This suggests that the behavior of individuals can be altered by propagating appropriate social values (for example, in schools) about how individuals or groups should act in relation to their environment and by making individuals aware of environmental concerns. While such an approach may not be entirely effective, it may nevertheless have some effect on the behavior of individuals. Furthermore, once social values are established which provide individuals with a moral obligation to be careful of the environment, social reprobation become more likely for those who flout their moral responsibilities. Tisdell (2003a, Chapter 9) also points out that the behavior of individuals is influenced by the social roles they occupy and society's expectation of persons occupying these roles. Neither neoclassical economics nor new institutional economics give particular attention to social influences on human values and behavior. However, this aspect is usually a central interest in conventional institutional economics and can be a feature of psychological economics (via social psychology) as the discussion of Etzioni's view indicates.

2.5. Conventional (Old) Institutional Economics

The terms "old", "conventional", "orthodox" in institutional economics are used to distinguish this line of thought from new institutional economics. This terminology is rather unfortunate because "old" often carries a negative connotation and "new" a positive one. But there is nothing old-fashioned, conventional or orthodox about classical institutionalism even though it developed before the term "new institutionalism" was coined.

Conventional institutional economics has much in common with sociology. It recognizes that social institutions and values change or evolve with the passage of time and followers of this approach usually adopt a long-term perspective. It is much broader in its scope of its enquiry than the other approaches to economics outlined above. It examines how social and cultural settings influence economic behavior and activity and the role of institutional structures and the legal system in this. On the other hand, it also recognizes that the pattern of economic activities helps to shape the institutions, social values and cultural patterns of communities. As pointed out by Myrdal (1958) circular causation is present. Furthermore, path dependence is likely to be present because pre-existing institutional features, cultural structures and social values limit possibilities for the future development of communities; that is they create a degree of "lock-in" to the past.

In short, conventional institutionalism stresses that economic activity is embedded in a social system involving institutions and social values and that these are of major significance for the way in which economies operate or perform. In turn, this has important consequences for the impact of economic systems on the state of the environment and on the use of natural resources.

In America, Veblen (1934) and Commons (1974, 1951) were early advocates of this approach. Bromley (1991) is a more recent advocate of the approach. Conventional institutionalists argue that to understand influences on resource use one has to study legal systems, cultural factors and the historical backgrounds of societies. Orthodox institutionalists maintain that what is valued by individuals is to a large extent culturally conditioned. This then raises the question of how social values are formed and change. Myrdal (1958) says that social values are capable of altering quickly whereas some others, institutionalists, believe that social values only change slowly. Possibly, such values are normally slow to change but in particular circumstances (such as a political and social crises), could alter rapidly.

Consider the following as an example of changing social values. In most Western countries the attitudes of humans to nature have changed with the passage of time (Passmore, 1974). Whereas cruelty to animals was widely practiced in early times, for example, by the Romans and in Elizabethan England (for instance, bull- and bear-baiting), now cruelty to animals is regarded as a serious offence by society. The view that other species have a right to exist independently of their utility to human beings has also gained ground.

Orthodox institutionalists are skeptical of neoclassical welfare economics and tend to reject individual preferences (utility) as a basis for social choice because it is argued that these preferences are to a large extent socially determined. For example, the willingness to pay of individuals to conserve a particular object may be to a large extent a consequence of their culture and institutions. Thus, the merit of what individuals want may depend on the merit of the institutional and cultural context in which they are embedded. Therefore, this limitation should be kept in mind when using neoclassical economic techniques to make recommendations about the conservation and use of natural resources based on estimates of the demands (preferences) of individuals for these. An example is the application of contingent valuation techniques, but this reservation applies to most methods discussed in Chapters 6 and 7.

Conventional institutional economists vary in the amount of attention they give to issues involving natural resource and environmental economics. Whether or not Malthus (1798) should be regarded as an institutional economist is unclear. He argued that there is a natural tendency for the level of human population to rise rapidly with the available means of subsistence so that any increase in per capita income is likely to be short-lived. His suggested remedy was social in nature — encourage late marriages and sexual abstinence.

Both Karl Marx and Friedrich Engels rejected Malthus' population theory arguing that improvements in science and technology can ensure that levels of economic production can expand at a faster rate than the rate of population increase (Marx, 1988). Although both Marx and Engels were classical institutionalists and believed that institutions mirrored the prevailing economic system (for example, they argued that the institutions that evolved under Capitalism reflected its needs and underpinned it), they were nevertheless, technological optimists (Marx and Engels, 1969–1970). They had great faith in the ability of the increasing use of capital to increase productivity but believed that under the capitalist system, workers would be exploited and deprived of the benefit of this increased productivity. The distribution of income was unjust. They did not expect the system to improve the lot of workers and thought that it would only be changed by a revolt of the workers culminating in the establishment of communism. It is interesting that the former centrally planned economies of the Soviet Union and (prior to its economic reforms) the People's Republic of China put great faith in the ability of science and technology and in huge levels of investment in physical capital to promote the economic growth of their economies. Their approach to resource use and economic development was top–down and technocratic (Tisdell, 1993a). This approach resulted in serious pollution and natural resource problems, some of which are still evident today, for example, problems with the diversion of streams and rivers flowing into the Aral Sea to irrigate cotton, and the melt down of the nuclear power station at Chernobyl. Furthermore, Mao Zedong adopted a policy which encouraged population growth.

The idea that technocratic-economic power structures can have major influences on resource use has also been applied to Capitalist economies by Galbraith (1957, 1967). He argues that a small group of business leaders and technocrats in Capitalist economies have a disproportionate impact on the way resources are used, on what technologies are developed and used, and on the pattern of public expenditure and the support of governments for the private sector. Furthermore, large corporations significantly influence what consumers want, encourage increasing expenditure by consumers, and may resist measures to conserve natural resources and the environment. Similar views have been expressed by socialist writers such as Marcuse (1991). These features can create problems for sustainable development, for example, because they accelerate natural resource depletion, and add to pollution problems. Furthermore, changes in public policy, including environmental policy, are likely to be easier to achieve if this dominant social group can be convinced of their desirability.

As capitalist systems have developed their economic institutions have altered and have evolved. The joint stock company (usually with many shareholders) has emerged as an important business entity, and many of these corporations are multinational in their operations. Furthermore, impersonal market systems have expanded in their scope. As discussed by Tisdell (1991, Chapter 1), these institutional changes could weaken individual's feelings of social and moral responsibility for their economic and environmental behavior. Individuals are increasingly divorced from the locality in which their enterprises engage in economic activity. This makes them less subject to local concerns and social pressures. Furthermore, it has been claimed that growing economic globalization decreases economic dependence on local areas and consequently, there is reduced care for ensuring sustainability of economic production. This is because people alter from being ecosphere-oriented to being biosphere-oriented (Dasmann, 1984). There is also strong evidence to support the view that growing economic globalization has led to considerable biodiversity loss, particularly in relation to domestic livestock (Tisdell, 2003b) and cultivated crops. While growing economic globalization is not bound to have adverse environmental consequences, legitimate concerns exist about some of its possible environmental consequences, such as its impact on the level of greenhouse gas emissions (Tisdell, 2001). There are also major institutional restraints to altering the current global economic system so as to moderate its adverse environmental effects, for example, by reducing consumption levels or moderating economic growth (Tisdell, 1999a, Chapter 6).

Veblen (1934) did not consider environmental issues but his observations about social influences on economic demands and lifestyles are relevant to a consideration of such matters because the pattern of economic demands and lifestyles impacts on natural resource use and the state of the environment. In some cases, social effects encourage environmentally damaging economic activities and in other cases, environmentally friendly activities, for instance compare motor car racing with bicycling as leisure activities. If the buying of "green" products has a positive social demonstration effect (for example, within the social group to which buyers belong), this will encourage the buying of such products. Individuals who engage in ecotourism and greenhouse neutral activities apart from purchasing their own moral satisfaction ("warm glow effect"), may achieve extra standing with their friends and contacts with similar attitudes. The social dimensions of both values and beliefs can be important influences on human behavior and alter with the passage of time and economic change.

Some institutionalists, such as Commons (1974), stress the importance of legal systems and changes in these as influences on economic and social behavior. Legal systems, the laws and their interpretation alter as societies evolve and change, and in so doing cause variations in permitted behaviors. For example, the laws relating to legal liability in relation to environmental damages and product liability (and their interpretations) have altered in recent centuries. In general, these laws have changed so as to increase the legal liability of those who perform acts that may cause damage to others (Tisdell, 1993b, Chapter 5). Legal transaction costs and uncertainties, as well as the allocation of rights influence the way in which the legal system works and whether it is favorable to the conservation of natural resources or not. The party or parties charged with the burden of proof in the event of disputed economic or environmental changes can also be material for outcomes, for instance, whether the burden of proof is placed on developers or conservationists (Tisdell, 2002, Chapter 3). With changes in values and technologies, legal systems alter but very often with lags and imperfectly.

2.6. The Austrian School of Economics

The Austrian School of Economics is diverse but is frequently portrayed by the work of F.A. Hayek (Colonna *et al.*, 1994). Such a portrayal gives a narrower impression of the School than is justified. Virtually all members of the Austrian School of Economics believe that a study of knowledge (lack of knowledge, costs of knowledge acquisition and use, creation of new knowledge involving inventions and innovations) is essential to the understanding of the functioning of economic systems.

Hayek argued that centralized economic systems are likely to be less efficient than decentralized market systems because the latter can use the knowledge available in society more effectively than the former (Hayek, 1948; Machlup, 1976). This means that there is some overlap in the interests of the Austrian School and that of the new institutional economists, for example, in the efficiency of different institutional structures where knowledge limitations and transaction costs are taken into account. In addition, given Schumpeter's theses (Schumpeter, 1942), one would expect capitalist market systems to show greater innovation and technical progress than centralized ones. Hayek emphasizes processes and change rather than equilibria. He is critical of the use of comparative statics widely employed in neoclassical economics and in new institutional economics.

Followers of Hayek usually regard externalities as unimportant phenomena. This may be because of their strong support for liberalism and individualism (see for example, Hayek, 1982). In general, they oppose state intervention in society and are prepared to forgo economic benefits, if necessary, to secure liberalism. On the other hand, it is accepted that society needs rules to reduce uncertainty.

Joseph Schumpeter is also a member of the Austrian School. His emphasis in *Capitalism, Socialism and Democracy* is on innovations as a source of economic change and progress (Schumpeter, 1942). He sees bureaucracies as bodies that stifle economic change. He argues that the strength of capitalism is in its power to support technical progress and innovation. In the end, however, he believes that very large corporations will develop in capitalist societies and that they will be bureaucratic and will slow economic progress. There are important institutional components in Schumpeter's work. Nevertheless, Schumpeter does not address environmental problems but basically accepts the thesis that economic growth is good. He also has an evolutionary component to his theory, as indicated above. There is no hint in Schumpeter's work that continuing economic growth could eventually become unsustainable because of natural resource-scarcity or environmental pollution.

2.7. Game Theory and Some of Its Applications to Environmental Conflict

Despite the fact that many followers of Hayek reject mathematical economics and the use of equilibrium concepts, the development of game theory and its application to economics and the social sciences is associated with the Austrian School. The development and application of game theory owes much to two scholars of Austrian origin, John von Neumann, a mathematician, and Oskar Morgenstern, an economist. They published the *Theory of Games and Economic Behavior* in 1944. The basic theory relies on rationality and equilibrium concepts to provide solutions. However, aspects of knowledge are an important component of it. It is concerned with how to behave given that the choice of others in a game may not be perfectly known in advance. The basic theory is built on strong rationality assumptions. Herbert Simon claims that its knowledge assumptions are even more demanding than those assumed in neoclassical economics (Simon, 1957).

Players are assumed to know all the possible strategies in a game and the associated payoffs and to act to maximize their own gain given that other players are doing likewise. This is unlikely to be so in practice. However, the theory makes us aware of the limits of rationality and provides some useful insights into issues involving social conflict about the use of the environment. It supports the idea that social rules may be necessary in some cases to reduce uncertainty and ensure socially optimal results.

2.7.1. *A prisoners' dilemma problem*

The prisoners' dilemma problem is widely used to show that in relation to environmental behavior, the pursuit of individual self-interest can lead to a socially suboptimal outcome. Consider a two-person game in which each player has only two strategies, s_1 not to pollute and s_2 to pollute. The players might be two nations, and the strategies might be to restrict greenhouse gas emissions or not to do so.

The hypothetical payoffs to Player 1 and Player 2, respectively, from their alternative combinations of strategies are shown in the matrix in Table 2.2. If each player acts in its self-interest, both will pollute and each will receive a payoff of 2. However, both will be better-off if neither pollutes because then both will receive a payoff of 3.

Table 2.2. A matrix used to illustrate the application of the prisoners' dilemma game to social conflict involving use of the environment.

		Strategies of Player 2 ⟶	
Strategies of Player 1		s_1	s_2
↓	s_1	(3, 3)	(1, 4)
	s_2	(4, 1)	(2, 2)

The problem is how to ensure that the socially ideal outcome is achieved. Social obligation or morality could play a part and trust can be important. In some cases, a third party (such as the state) could enforce agreements to achieve social optimality. For example, parties that adopt s_2 rather than s_1 might be fined 2 units. However, third party enforcement is not always an option. This is frequently the case in international agreements involving the environment which are often described as protocols or accords.

The above dilemma is illustrated by a one-shot game. It can be regarded as the so-called normal form of a game rather than its extensive form. However, repetitive games of the above type have been considered. It has been argued that a tactic of adopting tit-for-tat is most effective to ensure compliance. But tit-for-tat may only work in the small group case. Furthermore, if there are a finite number of repetitions, then on the last repetition both parties have an incentive to adopt anti-social strategies. The use of the religious notion of an all-knowing God and subsequent judgment after death with assignment to Heaven or Hell according to past actions could be regarded as a social mechanism to deal with situations in which the following of selfish interests causes social damage. Those who engage in anti-social behavior on the last repetition of a game might be assigned to Hell.

2.7.2. *A game involving a battle of the sexes — further application*

Two types of games can be distinguished here: (1) those which involve no conflict but require coordinated actions by the players to ensure a socially optimal outcome, and (2) those that do involve conflict between the players but which require coordination of strategies to avoid socially inferior outcomes. The original battle-of-the-sexes problem involved a stereotype of a female and a male. Both would be happier if they went together to the same entertainment. The man wants to go to the wrestling and the woman wishes to be at the opera. So there is a conflict that corresponds to case (2).

Consider the first case. It may apply to a decision of farmers about whether to grow genetically modified (GM) crops in a region. For simplicity, consider a case involving just two farmers having two

Table 2.3. A matrix illustrating an environmental coordination problem. A decision about whether or not to grow GM crops in a region.

		Farmer 2's Strategies	
		s_1	s_2
Farmer 1's Strategies	s_1	(3, 3)	(1, 1)
	s_2	(1, 1)	(3, 3)

Table 2.4. A matrix illustrating social conflict and the need for coordination of strategies in addressing an environmental issue.

		Farmer 2's Strategies	
		s_1	s_2
Farmer 1's Strategies	s_1	(2, 3)	(1, 1)
	s_2	(1, 1)	(3, 2)

alternative strategies: s_1 not to grow GM crops and s_2 to grow GM crops. The corresponding payoffs may have the structure shown in the matrix in Table 2.3. Farmers will be best off in the region if either none of them grow GM crops or if all grow GM crops. There is no conflict; merely a co-ordination problem.

On the other hand, Table 2.4 illustrates a case in which there is both the presence of social conflict and the need for coordination of strategies for addressing this environmental issue. The same strategies as before are available to the farmers but the pattern of their payoffs differs from that in Table 2.3. Farmer 1 would prefer GM crops only to be grown in the region whereas Farmer 2 would prefer no GM crops to be grown in the region. For both, however, a regional mixture is the worst outcome. How to address such social problems is one of the concerns of game theory.

2.7.3. *Games against nature and environmental outcomes*

Game theory has also been applied to the making of policy decisions about natural resource use when the outcomes depend on uncertain events or states of nature. In these games, the inanimate opponent, nature, is treated as being a rational player aiming to maximize its own gains (or to minimize its own losses) from the game. While such an assumption is unrealistic, the game-theory framework structures the choice problem in a simple way that allows the implications of varied rules for decision-making under uncertainty to be easily appreciated.

Adoption of the maximin gain rule (minimax loss rule) in games against nature (or in relation to fictitious opponents that are not deliberately reacting to the possible strategic choices of the policy-maker) implies a very conservative attitude by the policy-maker to the bearing of risk or uncertainty or alternatively a very pessimistic view about which state of nature will prevail. The policy-maker assumes that no matter what strategy he/she adopts, nature will adopt a countervailing strategy that minimizes the gains of the policy-maker. Therefore, the policy maker should maximize his/her gain given this countervailing strategy. However, use of the minimax gain rule does not necessarily result in an increased incentive to conserve natural resources.

This can be illustrated by the case shown in the matrix displayed as Table 2.5. There it is supposed that a policy-maker has two choices: to conserve a species, strategy α_1, or eliminate it, α_2. Two alternative states of nature are considered to be possible, namely that the value of payoffs of the alternative strategies of the policy-maker turn out to be as currently assessed (s_1) (namely 2 or 3) and the possibility (s_2) that the value or payoff from concerning the species is much higher (100) than now with the payoff from eliminating it (3) being unchanged.

Table 2.5. An illustration of a game against nature in which the policy maker has two alternative strategies, to engage in development that eliminates a species (α_2) or to forgo that development and retain the species (α_1). Nature has two alternative strategies s_1 and s_2. The solution shown assumes that the policy-maker adopts a maximin gain approach.

		Possible states of nature				
		s_1	s_2	Min		
Strategies of policy-maker	α_1	2	100	2		
	α_2	3	3	3*	←	Maximin Gain

Hypothetical payoffs to the policy-maker are shown in Table 2.5. If the policy-maker adopts strategy α_1 his/her minimum payoff is 2 and if α_2 is adopted it is 3. Therefore, the policy-makers' minimax gain strategy is to adopt α_2, that is the strategy of eliminating the species. In effect, this implies that a "bird in the hand is preferred to one in the bush".

An example of the above case is where a slow growing species of naturally occurring forest is replaced by a plantation forest involving monoculture but growing at a faster rate and giving a return higher than the native forest. But as a result of the elimination of the native forest, a species is extirpated that could be very valuable in the future if retained.

On the other hand, a different attitude to decision-making under uncertainty can result in the strategy, α_1, that of conserving species, being adopted. For example, if the opportunity costs (the possible benefits forgone in this case) of the alternative strategies of the policy-maker are taken into account and the minimax strategy is applied to these, α_1 is the optimal choice. Opportunity cost is called regret in this decision theory context. The regret matrix derived from Table 2.5 is shown in Table 2.6. The maximum possible regret of the policy-maker is 1 if α_1 is adopted and is 97 if α_2 is adopted. Therefore, given this decision-making rule, α_1 (retaining the natural forest) is optimal because it minimizes the maximum possible regret of the policy-maker.

Ciriacy-Wantrup (1968) and Bishop (1978) suggested that because the costs of conserving most species is small and the possible gains from conserving a species could be very high, it is rational to err in favor of

Table 2.6. A regret matrix (opportunity cost matrix) derived from Table 2.5. The minimax regret strategy is α_1, that is to forgo development and conserve the species at risk of extinction.

		Possible states of nature				
		s_1	s_2	Min		
Strategies of policy-maker	α_1	1	0	1*	←	Minimax regret
	α_2	0	97	97		

a policy that conserves biodiversity, for example, by maintaining minimum viable populations of species. This is consistent with a matrix having the structure shown in Table 2.6 if α_1 is interpreted as maintaining the minimum viable population of a species and α_2 involves not maintaining this population, and if the minimax regret criterion is adopted. Depending on the structure of the payoffs, other criteria for decision-making under uncertainty can also support this point of view. For instance, given the irreversibility of extinction of species and the possibility that one may learn in the future that a species has extra economic value to that currently known, the expected gain criterion can also favor conservation of biodiversity (see Krutilla, 1967; Tisdell, 1996, Chapter 5). Learning possibilities usually favor strategies which keep options open.

There are games also against nature where uncertainty favors a policy of conservation of resources if the maximin gain approach is adopted, even though it did not do so in the case illustrated by Table 2.5. For example, situations can arise in which the elimination of a natural resource could threaten the functioning of a whole ecosystem and reduce the value of its services greatly. In such a case and adopting similar interpretations to those above, a payoff matrix of the type shown in Table 2.7 might apply. For the state of nature s_1, the relevant ecosystem still continues to provide satisfactory services but if the state of nature s_2, prevails, then the relevant ecosystem collapses or degenerates considerably. In these circumstances, the payoff of the policy-maker may fall drastically as a result of eliminating the natural

Table 2.7. A game against nature in which removing a natural resource could result in an adverse payoff for the decision-maker. In this game, the maximin gain strategy favors conservation of the natural resource.

		Nature's strategies			
		s_1	s_2	Min	
Decision-maker's strategies	α_1	2	2	2*	← Maximin Gain
	α_2	3	0	0	

resource in the process of development. The minimax gain strategy is not to eliminate the natural resource to make way for development but to adopt strategy α_1 (the conservation of the resource) rather than α_2 its elimination.

An implication of the above discussion is that a precautionary approach to decision-making about resource use does not necessarily favor the conservation of natural resources. The results vary with the structure of payoffs and even with the same structure of payoffs, different risk-averse criteria can give unlike results. For example, in the situation illustrated by Table 2.4, the maximin gain and minimax regret criteria give conflicting recommendations about whether biodiversity conservation is optimal. However, when these criteria are applied to the situation illustrated by Table 2.6, they give the same recommendation, namely that the natural resource should be conserved. The minimax regret matrix corresponding to the matrix shown in Table 2.7 is shown in Table 2.8.

Of course, many other criteria for decision-making under uncertainty exist, and several other lines of enquiry are also possible. For example, what determines beliefs about what is possible and what influences the choice of decision-making criteria? How do beliefs and attitudes to the bearing of uncertainty vary with changing institutions and external factors (aspects of conventional institutionalism)? How in reality do individuals choose under conditions of uncertainty? The latter is a particular interest of psychological or behavioral economists. They have found that individuals are not as rational as has been traditionally assumed.

Table 2.8. The regret (opportunity cost) matrix corresponding to Table 2.7. The minimax regret rule favors conservation of the natural resource in this case.

		Nature's strategies				
		s_1	s_2	Max		
Decision-makers strategies	α_1	1	0	1*	←	Minimax regret
	α_2	0	2	2		

2.8. Evolution, Coevolution and Limits to Economic Growth Imposed by Natural Resource and Environmental Constraints

It is not intended to review in depth the above-mentioned concepts in relation to a resource and environmental economics but merely to indicate their basic relevance.

2.8.1. *Evolutionary economics and the environment*

There are a variety of approaches to evolutionary economics but most evolutionary economists have not given much attention to resource and environmental issues. Marx's theory of successive stages in the economic development of economics (Marx, 1999), also subscribed to by Engels (Marx and Engels, 1969–1970), is evolutionary in nature but Marx's writings did not specifically relate economic development to changes in the state of the environment and the availability of natural resources, although Marx was well aware of the horrible levels of pollution associated with early industrialization in Britain. Once again, Schumpeter's theory of economic development includes evolutionary elements but he does not draw any conclusion from these about the natural environment (Schumpeter, 1942).

Possibly, the theories of North (1990) can be regarded as having an evolutionary focus and from this environmental implications are drawn. For example, North argues that with economic development, the extent to which natural resources become private property increases and market mechanisms become more widely used as mechanisms for resource use and allocation. This in turn tends to increase the efficiency of natural resource use and stimulate further economic growth. It can have positive consequences for the conservation of natural resources that produce private goods. However, as is clear from the views of neo-Malthusian (for example, Daly, 1980; Daly and Farley, 2004), the increasing occurrence of private property rights combined with greater use of the price mechanisms does not eliminate significant environmental problems nor ensure the sustainability of economic growth.

2.8.2. *Coevolution of economic practices, social systems and environmental conditions*

Norgaard (1994) has put forward the view that coevolution occurs in economic practices, in the nature of social systems (institutions) and in environmental conditions. In earlier historical times, this type of coevolution tended to occur at a fairly localized level. This may have resulted in relatively stable economic, social and environmental conditions, that is relatively sustainable paths of economic activity and development.

With the integration of local communities into more global relationships, coevolutionary patterns can be threatened. With the introduction of guns and other technologies to some tribal hunting societies as a result of European contact, the economic patterns of many such communities were disrupted and their economic activities became unsustainable because many species were hunted to extinction. Stable coevolutionary patterns no longer prevailed.

Tisdell (2003a, Chapter 19) has pointed out that the increasing concentration of agricultural research development in the hands of large corporations and big organizations is likely to circumvent the process of coevolution in agricultural communities. It could result in the introduction of riskier technologies than otherwise (for example, the use of genetically modified organisms) and significantly disrupt the social fabric of rural communities. It may result in rapid and large discrete jumps in agricultural practices rather than gradual changes which might occur when the evolution of agricultural practices is grounded in local communities. In many cases, the technology developed by large organizations is also decoupled from local environmental conditions, and this could add to sustainability risks (Tisdell, 2003b). A coevolutionary perspective is illustrated in Fig. 2.3.

2.8.3. *Limits to economic growth*

Traditionally economic growth has been seen as an effective way to reduce economic scarcity. However, not all economists are convinced that ever continuing economic growth is sustainable.

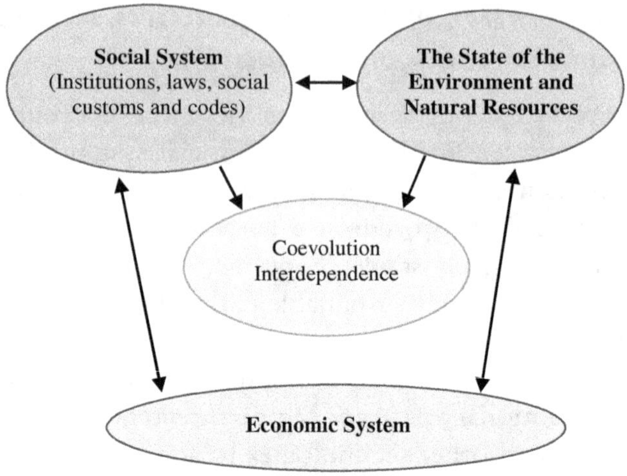

Fig. 2.3. Patterns of coevolution of the state of the environment, social systems and economic systems have been typical of most communities in the past but modern economic systems seem to involve less gradual change and to be more weakly embedded in coevolutionary patterns.

Beginning in the second half of the 20th century, an increasing number of economists expressed the view that continuing global economic growth could become unsustainable. These economists, often called neo-Malthusians, argue that global economic growth can be jeopardized by increasing depletion of natural resources and by burgeoning levels of pollution. While some neo-Malthusians foresee the possibility that continuing global economic growth will result in an economic catastrophe or disaster, others see it as activating negative resource and environmental forces that create a growing drag on economic growth. Thus, the sustainability of continuing economic growth is a major issue and the possibility is flagged that continuing economic growth rather than reducing economic scarcity in the long-term, will add to it for future generations. The opportunity cost of rapid economic growth now could be a reduction in the economic welfare of future generations according to this dynamic perspective.

Although the theories of the neo-Malthusians are not all identical and differ in emphasis, contributors to this stream of economic thought include Boulding (1966), Mishan (1967), Pearce (1988),

Pearce *et al.* (1989), Pearce and Barbier (2000), Georgescu-Roegen (1974), Daly (1980), and Daly and Farley (2004). Neo-Malthusians also include several natural scientists and engineers such as Ehrlich and Ehrlich (1990) and Meadows *et al.* (2005).

Opponents of the neo-Malthusian perspective usually rely on one or more of the following counterarguments:

1. natural resources are more abundant than realized;
2. there is considerable scope for substituting natural resources in production, for example, nuclear energy for fossil fuels;
3. continuing technological progress will continue with several new production possibilities being developed (these are grounds for technological and scientific opportunism);
4. the population problem is not a problem because rising per capita income will lead to a reduction in family sizes naturally;
5. pollution emissions (for various reasons) will decline with continuing economic growth; and
6. human beings can be expected to cooperate to arrest environmental and economic disaster if it is imminent.

It is not intended at this point to debate the merits or otherwise of the outlook of the neo-Malthusians compared to those of the economic growth-optimists. However, it can be noted that the pro-growth argument becomes vulnerable if technological progress is not maintained, if the extent of resource substitutability proves to be limited and if economic growth activates irreversible (or nearly irreversible) environmental changes (such as those associated with the greenhouse gas effect) which shrink the global natural resource-base.

2.9. Concluding Comments

From the above review, it can be seen that approaches to economic analysis are very diverse. This is because different theories usually have different primary purposes. Economic theories are simplified approximations to reality and their simplifications, to some extent, reflect the bounded rationality of human beings. Depending on the resource and environmental economic issue to be addressed and the depth of the analysis required, it is often useful to consider the matter from several economic perspectives. For example, the economics of regulating pollution emissions might be initially assessed from a neoclassical perspective and if greater depth is required, from the perspective of new institutional economics or psychological economics. Therefore, methodological pluralism needs to be considered as a means for formulating public policies. Nevertheless, the adoption of this view does not imply that all available theories are relevant to the problem at hand, nor that all are equally reliable or illuminating. Judgment is still needed.

The choice of appropriate theories also depends on the time-frame being considered and on how wide and encompassing the analysis is supposed to be. Often the dynamics and nature of the processes involved in economic and environmental change are important. When this is so, neoclassical and new institutional models (based as comparative statics) are likely to be of limited value for policy purposes. Furthermore, some economic models ignore the "big" picture because they proceed on the basis that biophysical systems are independent of economic systems. This is unrealistic when considering many long-term environmental and resource issues.

2.10. Keywords

Agency costs; Austrian School of Economics; battle of the sexes; behavioral economics; Coase theorem; coevolution; conventional institutional economics; endowment effect; environmental externalities; evolutionary economics; favorable externalities; maximin gain; minimax regret; neoclassical economics; neo-Malthusians; New Institutional Economics; optimally imperfect decision; principal-agent problem; prisoners' dilemma problem; psychological economics; satisficing; unfavorable externalities

2.11. Questions for Review and Discussion

1. Because different approaches to economics exist, issues involving natural resources and environmental economics can be analyzed

in diverse ways or from diverse perspectives. Explain and list five or so major streams of economic thought and in doing so state their basic assumptions.

2. Outline the main assumptions underlying neoclassical economics. To what extent are these assumptions likely to be satisfied in practice?
3. Arthur Pigou relied on neoclassical economics to specify public policies for regulating environmental externalities. Illustrate his approach, specify why it relies on neoclassical economics and indicate its limitations.
4. Compare and contrast the approach to economic analysis employed in new institutional economics with that employed in neoclassical economics. In what ways might the approach of new institutional economics to regulating environmental spillovers (the case illustrated in Fig. 2.2) differ from that of neoclassical economics?
5. What is behavioral or psychological economics? Why might its implications for resource and environmental policy differ from those of new institutional economics and neoclassical economics? How does it differ from these two approaches in its view of human behavior?
6. To what extent (in your view) are social and moral influences important determinants of human behavior? If they are influences, what consequences does this have for environmental policy?
7. How does conventional institutional economics differ in its perspectives from new institutional economics? What elements do these perspectives have in common? What types of implications does conventional institutionalism have for environmental economics?
8. Some conventional institutionalists see individual preferences and values as being to a large extent, products of the society in which individuals are embedded. They, therefore, believe that only limited reliance should be placed on individual preference as a guide to social (including environmental) choice. Discuss.
9. The Austrian School of Economics is diverse but has some common threads. Explain. Because of Hayek's support for liberty and

individualism (including private property rights), Austrian economics has not given much attention to the regulation of environmental spillovers. Do you think that this is because it is wary of state intervention? Why is it wary of such intervention?

10. Why is game theory consistent with the tradition of the Austrian School of Economics? Do you think it is a useful approach to the consideration of social issues involving the use of natural resources and the environment? Why?
11. The prisoners' dilemma game and the battle-of-the-sexes game have resource and environmental applications. Illustrate. In doing this, try to think of examples additional to those given in the text.
12. Some natural resource and environmental problems can be modeled as games against nature. To what extent is this a justifiable approach?
13. What is the maximin gain and the minimax regret rule? Does their application always favor the conservation of natural resources? Illustrate.
14. What conditions are likely to make it socially optimal to conserve a species if its future value is uncertain?
15. Conventional institutional economics often encompasses evolutionary perspectives but it has paid little attention to evolving natural resource and environmental issues. While there are evolutionary patterns of resource ownership in the theories of North, these do not come to grips with the problems raised by neo-Malthusians. Discuss.
16. Explain the concept of coevolution of economic, social and biophysical systems. To what extent have modern economic systems disrupted traditional modes of agricultural coevolution? Are there social and sustainability dangers as a result of this disruption? What are they?
17. Neo-Malthusians have listed several factors that may interfere with the sustainability of economic growth and pro-growth protagonists have specified a series of counterarguments. Outline the claims of each group. Which view do you favor and why?

Readings and References

Baumol, W.J. and R.E. Quandt (1964). Rules of thumb and optimally imperfect decisions, *American Economic Review*, 54, 23–46. doi: https://www.jstor.org/stable/1810896.

Berle, A. and G. Means (1932). *The Modern Corporation and Private Property*, Harcourt Brace, New York.

Bishop, R.C. (1978). Endangered species, irreversibility and uncertainty: The economics of a safe minimum standard, *American Journal of Agricultural Economics*, 60, 10–18. doi: 10.2307/1242715.

Boulding, K.E. (1966). The economics of the coming spaceship Earth. In H Jarrett (Ed.) *Environmental Quality in a Growing Economy*, 3–14. Johns Hopkins University Press, Baltimore, MD, USA.

Bromley, D. (1991). *Environment and Economy: Property Rights and Public Policy*, Basil Blackwell, Oxford.

Ciriacy-Wantrup, S.V. (1968). *Resource Conservation: Economics and Policies*, 3rd edn. Division of Agricultural Science, University of California, Berkely, CA.

Coase, R.H. (1937). The nature of the firm, *Economica, New Series*, 4, 386–405. doi: https://doi.org/10.1111/j.1468-0335.1937.tb00002.x.

Coase, R.H. (1960). The problem of social cost, *Journal of Law and Economics*, 1–44. doi: https://doi.org/10.1057/9780230523210_6.

Colonna, M., H. Hagemann and O.F. Hamouda (1994). *The Economics of F.A. Hayek: Capitalism, Socialism and Knowledge*, Vol. 2 Edward Elgar, Aldershot, UK, Brookfield, VT, USA.

Commons, J.R. (1951). *The Economics of Collective Action*, Macmillan, New York.

Commons, J.R. (1974). *Legal Foundations of Capitalism*, Routledge, (Originally published in 1924 by Macmillan, New York).

Daly, H. E. (1980). *Economics, Ecology, Ethics*, Freeman, San Francisco,.

Daly, H.E. and J. Farley (2004). *Ecological Economics: Principles and Applications*, Island Press, Washington, DC.

Dasmann, R. (1984). *Environmental Conservation*, Wiley, New York.

Demsetz, H. (1967). Toward a theory of property rights, *The American Economic Review*, 57, 347–359. doi: https://www.jstor.org/stable/1821637.

Downs, A. (1957). *An Economic Theory of Democracy*, Harper and Row, New York.

Ehrlich, P.R. and A.H. Ehrlich (1990). *The Population Explosion*, Simon and Schuster, New York.

Etzioni, A. (1988). *The Moral Dimension: Towards a New Economics*, The Free Press, New York.

Galbraith, J.K. (1957). *American Capitalism*, Hamish Hamilton, London.

Galbraith, J.K. (1967). *The New Industrial State*, Hamish Hamilton, London.

Georgescu-Roegen, N. (1974). *The Entropy Law and The Economic Process*, Harvard University Press, Cambridge, MA, USA.

Gowdy, J. and J. Erickson (2005). Ecological economics at a crossroads, *Ecological Economics*, 53, 17–20. doi: https://doi.org/10.1016/j.ecolecon.2005.01.010.

Harrison, S.R. and C.A. Tisdell (1994). Resource economics and the environment, *Review of Marketing and Agricultural Economics*, 62, 399–413.

Hayek, F.A., von (1948). *Individualism and Economic Order*, Chicago University Press, Chicago, IL.

Hayek, F.A., von (1982). *Law, Legislation and Liberty: A New Statement of the Liberal Principles of Justice and Political Economy*, Routledge and Kegan Paul, London.

Kahneman, D. and A. Tversky (2000). *Choices, Values and Frame*, Cambridge University Press, Cambridge UK.

Kahneman, D., J.L. Knetsch and R.H. Thaler (1991). The endowment effect, loss aversion and status quo bias, *Journal of Economic Perspectives*, 5, 193–206. doi: 10.1257/jep.5.1.193.

Krutilla, J.V. (1967). Conservation Reconsidered, *The American Economic Review*, 57, 777–786. doi: https://www.jstor.org/stable/1815368.

Machlup, F. (1976). Hayek's contribution to economics. In F. Machlup (Ed.) *Essays on Hayek*, 13–60. New York University Press, New York [Advanced].

Malthus, T.R. (1798). *An Essay on the Principle of Population as it Effects the Future Improvement of Mankind*, J. Johnson, London. Reprint 1976, Norton, New York.

Marcuse, H. (1991). *One-Dimensional Man: Studies in the Ideaology of Advanced Industrial Society*, Beacon Press, Boston, MA, USA.

Marx, K. (1988). *Economic and Philosophic Manuscripts of 1844*, Promethus Books, Buffalo, NY, USA.

Marx, K. (1999). *Capital*, abridged edn. Oxford University Press, Oxford.

Marx, K. and F. Engels (1969–1970). *Karl Marx and Frederick Engels: Selected Works*, Progress Published, Moscow.

Meadows, D. H., J. Randers and D.L. Meadows (2005). *The Limits to Growth: The 30 Year Update*, Earthscan, London.

Mishan, E.J. (1967). *The Costs of Economic Growth*, Staples, London.

Myrdal, G. (1958). *Value in Social Theory: A Selection of Essays on Methodology*, Harper, New York. Edited by P. Streeten.

Niskanen, W.A. (1971). *Bureacracy and Representative Government*, Aldine, Chicago.

Norgaard, R.B. (1994). *Development Betrayed*, Routledge, London.

North, D.C. (1990). *Institutions, Institutional Change and Economic Performance*, Cambridge University Press, New York.

North, D.C. and R.P. Thomas (1973). *The Rise of the Western World: A New Economic History*, Cambridge University Press, London.

Olson, M. (1965). *The Logic of Collective Action*, Harvard University Press, Cambridge, MA.

Passmore, J.A. (1974). *Man's Responsibility for Nature: Ecological Problems and Western Traditions*, Duckworth, London.

Pearce, D. (1988). Economics, equity and sustainable development, *Futures*, 20, 598–605. doi: https://doi.org/10.1016/0016-3287(88)90002-X.

Pearce, D., A. Markandya and E.B. Barbier (1989). *Blueprint for a Green Economy*, Earthscan Publications, London.

Pearce, D.W. and E.B. Barbier (2000). *Blueprint for a Sustainable Economy*, Earthscan, London.

Penrose, E. (1964). *The Theory of the Growth of the Firm*, Macmillan, London.

Pigou, A. (1932). *The Economics of Welfare*, 4th edn. Macmillan, London.

Schumpeter, J.A. (1942). *Capitalism, Socialism and Democracy*, 2nd edn. Harper Brothers, New York.

Simon, H. (1955). A behavioral model of rational choice, *The Quarterly Journal of Economics*, 5, 99–118. doi: 10.2307/1884852.

Simon, H. (1957). *Models of Man*, John Wiley, New York.

Simon, H. (1961). *Administrative Behavior*, The Macmillan Company, New York.

Stigler, G.J. (1961). The economics of information, *Journal of Political Economy*, 69, 213–225. doi: 10.1086/258464.

Tisdell, C.A. (1991). *Natural Resources, Growth and Development*, Praeger, New York.

Tisdell, C.A. (1993a). *Economic Development in the Context of China: Policy Issues and Analysis*, Macmillan, Basingstoke and London.

Tisdell, C.A. (1993b). *Environmental Economics: Policies for Environmental Management and Sustainable Development*, Edward Elgar, Aldershot, UK and Brookfield, VT, USA.

Tisdell, C.A. (1996). *Bounded Rationality and Economic Evolution: A Contribution to Decision Making, Economics and Management*, Edward Elgar, Cheltenham, UK and Brookfield, VT, USA.

Tisdell, C.A. (1999a). *Biodiversity, Conservation and Sustainable Development: Principles and Practices with Asian Examples*, Edward Elgar, Cheltenham, UK and Northampton, MA, USA.

Tisdell, CA (1999b). Conditions for sustainable development: weak or strong. In A.K. Dragun and C.A. Tisdell (Eds.), *Sustainable Agriculture and Environment*, 23–36. Edward Elgar, Cheltenham, UK and Northampton, MA, USA.

Tisdell, C.A. (2001). Globalisation and sustainability: environmental Kuznets curve and the WTO, *Ecological Economics*, 39, 185–196. doi: 10.1016/S0921-8009(01)00234-8. .

Tisdell, C.A. (2002). *The Economics of Conserving Wildlife and Natural Areas*, Edward Elgar, Cheltenham, UK and Northampton, MA, USA. [Chapter 8].

Tisdell, C.A. (2003a). *Ecological and Environmental Economics: Selected Issues and Policy Responses*, Edward Elgar, Cheltenham, UK and Northampton, MA, USA.

Tisdell, C.A. (2003b). Socio-economic causes of loss of animal diversity: analysis and assessment, *Ecological Economics*, 45, 365–376. doi: https://doi.org/10.1016/S0921-8009(03)00091-0.

Tisdell, C.A. (2005). *Economics of Environmental Conservation*, 2nd edn. Edward Elgar, Cheltenham, UK and Northampton, MA, USA. [Chapter 1].

Tisdell, C.A. (2007). Knowledge and the valuation of public goods and experential commodities: information provision and acquisition, *Global Business and Economics Review*, 9, 170–182. doi: https://dx.doi.org/10.1504/GBER.2007.013699.

Tisdell, C.A. and K. Hartley (2008). *Microeconomic Policy: A New Perspective*, Edward Elgar, Cheltenham, UK and Northampton, MA, USA. [Chapter 3].

Tisdell, C.A., C. Wilson and H. Swarna Nantha (2008). Contingent valuation as a dynamic process, *Journal of Socio-Economics*, 37, 1443–1458. doi: 10.1016/j.socec.2007.04.005.

Veblen, T. (1934). *The Theory of the Leisure Class: An Economic Study in the Evolution of Institutions*, The Macmillan Company, New York.
von Neumann, J. and O. Morgenstern (1944). *Theory of Games and Economic Behavior*, Princeton University Press, Princeton, NJ.
Williamson, O.E. (1985). *The Economic Institutions of Capitalism*, Free Press, New York.

Chapter 3

Economic Failures in Using Natural Resources and the Environment

3.1. Introduction

Economics focuses on factors that limit the satisfaction of human wants and explores organizational methods that will enable human wants to be more fully satisfied. The need for economics arises because available resources are limited relative to their ability to satisfy human desires. In its widest sense, economics is the science of the administration or management of scarce resources.

Traditionally economic resources are classified as consisting of natural resources, capital (the produced means for further production) and labor (the human resource). Natural resources include items such as wild fish, natural stands of forests, soil, water, minerals, fresh air and most genetic material. If the use of natural resources is not well organized in society, this will result in greater economic scarcity than needs to exist. An important concern in this book is to identify inadequate organizational features that result in economic scarcity being greater than it need be and to explore managerial mechanisms that will reduce this scarcity. Its concentration is on natural resource use and the use and conservation of natural environments. Much of the analysis of the latter can also be applied to human-modified environments and to built environments such as the Forbidden City in Beijing and St Peters (the Vatican) in Rome.

Not all objects or things that are wanted by individuals are included in the core of economic studies. Organizational structures are valued by economists solely in terms of their impact on the availability of commodities. They are assessed only on their ability to reduce scarcity; that is by how well they meet this end. However, individuals are usually not indifferent to the mechanisms used for social choices. They may, for example, desire inclusion in the choosing process itself (even if it is not fully efficient as a mechanism for reducing scarcity) or may have a desire for a system that ensures a high degree of personal liberty, or one that provides a sense of community or promotes belonging to a social group, such as a family.

Nevertheless, some economists believe that particular economic systems which, in their view, minimize economic scarcity also support a desirable social system. For example, Hayek (1982) argues that free market systems combined with private property regimes are comparatively efficient in reducing scarcity and at the same time, support individual liberty, a desirable attribute of social systems according to Hayek. Libertarians are reluctant to accept an economic system or social choice mechanisms that reduce economic scarcity if this is at the expense of personal liberty. Socialists are more inclined to accept a reduction in personal liberty if this is considered to be in the collective interest. The main point, however, is that individuals are not indifferent about the actual mechanisms used to make social choices about resource use.

Another difficult social issue is whether the desires of everyone for commodities (relative to their incomes) should count equally in social decision-making and whether all desires are equally worthy of being fulfilled. Libertarians generally start from the position that all should count equally. Exceptions are possible but have to be considered on a case-by-case basis. For example, the preferences of lunatics and children do not usually count equally with those of sane adults. In relation to environmental issues, there is also the question of whether the preferences of the ill-informed should count equally with those of the better-informed. Although a remedy to this problem could be to provide the ill-informed with more knowledge, they may not want to or may not be able to take advantage of it, and the knowledge provided may itself be incomplete or even biased. As the new institutionalists point out, knowledge-acquisition and dissemination is not a costless process. Other biases can also arise when information is transmitted (Tisdell, 2007).

Neoclassical economics assumes that economic agents are all well informed. Therefore, it does not emphasize economic choice problems that arise from lack of knowledge. Knowledge limitations are likely to be more serious in relation to the demand for public goods (or public bads) than for private goods (Tisdell, 2007). An attribute of public goods is that their supply is available to all without payment whereas private goods are only available to those who purchase these or possess them. Thus, pollution-free air in open spaces would be a public good (polluted air is a public bad) whereas bread is a private good.

In this chapter, the neoclassical approach to identifying economic failures and measuring the resulting economic losses will be reviewed. Such failures can occur as a result of market, political, legal and administrative limitations, and these are outlined. General possible policy responses to economic failures are then discussed and information problems that occur in formulating policies for use of natural resources and the environment are explored. Specific policy options for regulating the use of natural resource and the environment are outlined and assessed in Chapters 4 and 5.

3.2. Identifying Economic Failures and Measuring Economic Loss

3.2.1. *Pareto optimality*

An economic failure occurs when economic scarcity is greater than it need be. Neoclassical economists argued that economic failure is present in an economic system if it is possible by better management of available resources to make any individual better-off without making another worse-off. Therefore, a necessary condition for minimizing scarcity in society is that it be impossible to make anyone better-off without making someone else worse-off. *Pareto optimality* is said to exist when this condition is satisfied. In this context, each individual is assumed to be the best judge of his/her self-interest.

It has been shown that Pareto optimality can be achieved in principle under conditions of perfect competition if externalities are absent, if there are no public goods and if economies of scale are unimportant. This is, however, only a theoretical possibility because the knowledge requirements needed for perfect competition cannot be satisfied in practice. This is mainly because most economic systems are changing constantly and often in uncertain ways. Nevertheless, the economic conditions that need to be satisfied to achieve Pareto optimality do provide an initial guide to procedures for minimizing scarcity.

These conditions are outlined in Tisdell and Hartley (2008, Chapter 2). They imply the following:

(1) production be efficiently organized so that in relation to the quantity of resources employed, it is impossible to increase the supply of any wanted commodity without reducing that of another;
(2) that available commodities be efficiently exchanged so as to reflect fully the differences in preferences of individuals for the commodities;
(3) that the composition of the supply of commodities accords with what consumers want; and
(4) that resources be utilized and conserved taking into account their anticipated future scarcity compared with their current scarcity.

In brief, there should be economic efficiency in production and exchange, the composition of commodities which sellers supply ought to accord with what buyers want, and resource use should take appropriate account of user costs.

For well-behaved mathematical specifications of the functions involved, the mathematical conditions for minimizing scarcity can be specified (see Ng, 1979, Chapters 2 and 3). Detailed empirical specification of the relevant functions would, however, be very challenging: (probably impossible) given the degree of knowledge required. Furthermore, the way in which future generations' wishes should be taken into account is unclear.

3.2.2. *Taking account of future economic scarcity*

An important issue in the use of natural resources and the environment is that their current use be balanced appropriately against the demands to use these resources in the future, that is that condition (4) mentioned above be satisfied. The profligate use of a natural resource now may add undesirably to its future scarcity. The benefits to be obtained from current use of a resource should be compared with the future benefits forgone (if any) of its future use. The latter is described as *user costs.*

This issue is illustrated in Fig. 3.1. Assume a non-renewable natural resource (for example, oil) available in a fixed quantity, x^*. Its fixed available stocks can be allocated between present uses or future uses. Line *ABC* represents the marginal economic benefit from present use of the resource and *DBE* indicates the marginal benefit from its future use that is the marginal user cost incurred as a result of current use of the resource. Given these relationships it is optimal to utilize x_1 of the resource now and conserve $x^* - x_1$ of it for future use. Should, however, marginal user costs be lower than that shown by line *DBE,*

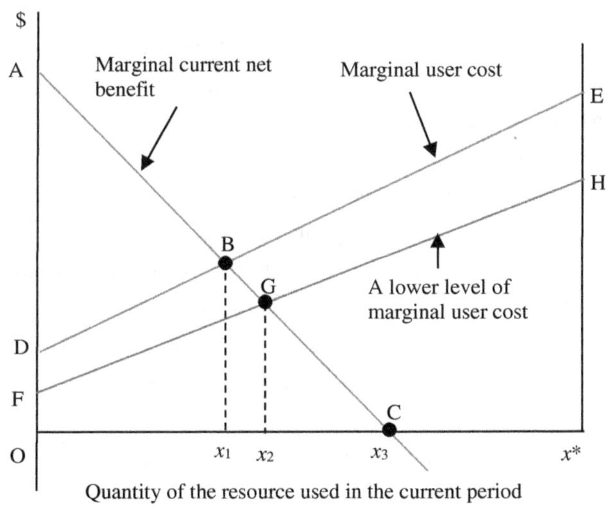

Fig. 3.1. As illustrated, the marginal current net benefit of using a natural resource needs to be balanced against future marginal benefits forgone (marginal user cost) of this utilization.

say *FGH*, less conservation of the natural resource will be optimal. In this case, it will be optimal to use x_2 of the resource now and conserve $x^* - x_2$ for future use. One reason why a lower level of marginal user costs may apply could be the anticipated discovery of competitive substitutes for the natural resource or expected discovery of previously unknown deposits or stocks of the natural resource.

When combined with private property rights, market systems are responsive to user cost. If a natural resource is likely to be scarcer in the future than now, its expected future prices will exceed its current price. Therefore, other things held constant, resource-holders have an economic incentive to conserve more of the resource for future use, the higher is the expected future price of the resource. For example, Fig. 3.1 can be reinterpreted. Let line *ABC* represent the marginal net profit which the resource-holder can earn by using the stock of its resource now. Let line *DBE* indicate the future (discounted) net profit which the resource-holder can earn by deferring use of the resource to the future. Given this interpretation, the resource-holder maximizes its benefit by using x_1 of the resource now and conserving $x^* - x_1$ for future use.

If the price of the resource is expected to be lower in the future than in the case just considered or if a higher discount is applied to future profit, this will move the marginal user cost curve downwards, for instance to *FGH*. This will increase the current use of the resource and reduce the amount of it conserved.

The discount rate applied by a resource-holder may be equal to the rate of interest plus an addition for risk or uncertainty. The greater the degree of uncertainty about the future economic return from the resource, other things held constant, the more rapidly the resource is likely to be depleted. Insecurity of future property rights can for example, accelerate the rate of depletion of natural resources. Furthermore, as discussed in the next chapter, when there is open-access to the use of natural resources, no account is taken of user costs. In such cases, there is no private property in the resource or collective control of the use of the resource and this results in profligate use of the resource. In the case illustrated in Fig. 3.1, x_3 of the resource will be used now, if there is open-access to it, rather than x_2 or x_3 of it. In some cases, the resource may be completely exhausted now or become so depleted (if it is a renewable resource, such as a fish species) that it is driven to extinction. The fact that the resource is likely to be in great demand in the future has no positive impact on the outcome in this case.

3.2.3. *Potential Paretian improvement criterion*

The *Paretian improvement criterion* implies that any economic change that makes at least one individual better-off and none worse-off (in terms of their own preferences) is a social improvement. This is equivalent to a "win–win" situation. Unfortunately, such possibilities are uncommon but can occur. Sometimes, for example, the planting of hedges for windbreaks or to reduce soil erosion on farms can have a positive impact on farm income and profit. As well, it may generate favorable externalities, such as improved air visibility and air quality if wind-blown dust is a problem (as in parts of northeast China) or reduce the extent of flooding.

If losers are fully compensated for any economic change that would otherwise affect them adversely, this extends the scope for mutually beneficial economic change. Thus, if the building of a river dam (such as the Three Gorges Dam) is contemplated, there will be losers (such as those who have their lands and dwellings flooded) and gainers, such as those who will have more regular supplies of irrigation water or more abundant supplies of electricity. If the gainers fully compensate the losers, then after this, gainers *may* still be better-off than before the building of the dam, and therefore, a Paretian improvement can occur. Nevertheless, significant transaction costs can sometimes be involved in fully compensating the losers from an economic change. Kaldor (1939) and Hicks (1939) suggested that if the gainers from an economic change *could* potentially compensate the losers and be better-off than before the change, the change is socially desirable. This is known as the *potential Paretian improvement criterion* or the *Kaldor–Hicks criterion*. Unlike the Paretian improvement test, the potential Paretian improvement criterion does not require actual compensation to be paid to losers. The Kaldor–Hicks test tends to favor economic change or development whereas the Paretian improvement criterion favors the status quo as far as the distribution of income and resources are concerned. Hicks (1939) suggested that use of the potential Paretian improvement criterion might be justified because when many economic changes are being made, the economic losses and benefits of individuals from the various changes will tend to average out so that on the whole, all will be better-off as a result of the adoption of this criterion.

While this might be true in the very long-run, application of the criterion could lead to injustices in some cases if compensation is not paid. For instance, those who are deprived of their land or fixed assets by the building of a dam experience major economic losses. In the absence of compensation, they may be net losers in their life-time because faster economic development may not compensate them fully for these losses, and Hicks' averaging rule would not apply to them. To take account of such problems, Little (1949, 1957, Chapter 6) suggested that an economic improvement satisfying the potential Paretian improvement test be only accepted without further questioning if it does not worsen the distribution of income. If the distribution of income is worsened, a judgement is required about whether the net economic gain from the change more than compensates for the deterioration in the distribution of income.

The potential Paretian improvement criterion is widely adopted as the basis for social cost–benefit analysis, including assessments of the use of natural resources and the environment. It is important to keep this in mind because one may want to take into account income distribution effects and questions of social justice before opting for an economic change that results in a *potential* Paretian improvement.

3.3. Markets and Economic Failure

3.3.1. *Economic failure generally*

Economists conclude that there is economic failure in the use of resources when it is theoretically possible by re-organizing the use of the resources employed to bring about a potential Paretian improvement. While markets have considerable ability to minimize economic scarcity, they are not perfect administrative mechanisms for doing this. Market failure can occur for a variety of reasons. These include the presence of externalities (such as environmental spillovers), some consequences of uncertainty, the presence of monopolies, the existence of commodities (such as pure public goods) that are unable to be marketed or which are only partially marketable (mixed goods), and open-access to resources the products of which are private goods and which are therefore, capable of being marketed. The reason for such failures will be outlined below. Nevertheless, it should also be borne in mind that alternative organizational mechanisms, such as political and administrative ones, are subject to economic failure and some of their failures will be outlined subsequently. Few, if any, mechanisms for social organization are free of the possibility of economic failure and therefore, social choice often involves deciding on the organization that is the best of the imperfect ones available. Furthermore, the political acceptability of the allocative mechanism being considered will also need to be taken into account.

Consider now the particular factors that may lead to market failure. Specific policies for addressing such failures will be discussed in Chapters 4 and 5.

3.3.2. *Externalities, particularly environmental spillovers*

As illustrated in the previous chapter using the analysis of Pigou (1932), externalities can be a source of market failure. Environmental externalities or spillovers from economic activities can be very diverse, and may be favorable or unfavorable. For example, bee-keepers often create favorable externalities for farms near their hives because the bees help pollinate many crops. Some types of agriculture create attractive or scenic landscapes. Forestry in some areas may also have positive externalities by improving micro-climates, by reducing the degree of flooding and fluctuation of water in streams and by sequestering carbon. Nevertheless, modern economic activities can also give rise to adverse environmental spillovers. These include spillovers associated with air, water and soil pollution, noise pollution, crowding and congestion, solid waste disposal, exclusion of light and air by large buildings, deterioration in landscapes and views, and the presence of offensive smells. Virtually all industries are capable of generating adverse externalities. Such externalities add to dissatisfaction of individuals about their environment and may be the source of ill-health. They may impose avoidance costs on potential victims of the externalities and distort the pattern of economic production by favoring the growth of industries generating unfavorable externalities and disadvantaging those that do not.

If an environmental externality exists, a potential Paretian improvement is usually theoretically possible. Nevertheless, it should be noted that there are circumstances in which environmental externalities can be Paretian irrelevant (Tisdell, 1970, 2005, Section 3.2; Walsh and Tisdell, 1973). Despite this, economic scarcity is not normally minimized from a Kaldor–Hicks point of view when environmental spillovers occur. This can be illustrated by giving further consideration to the Pigovian case depicted in Fig. 2.2 and by introducing another model in which the quantity emitted of a pollutant is the focus rather than the supply of a product associated with the externality.

Figure 3.2 illustrates the same type of situation as shown in Fig. 2.2, except for minor changes in labeling. Line *CD* represents the market

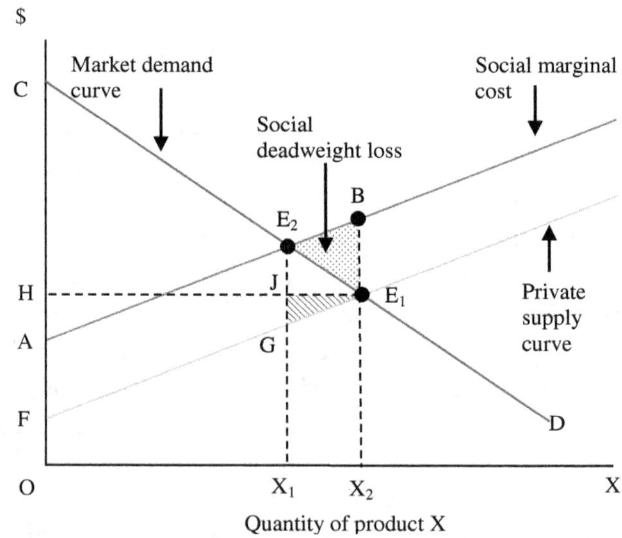

Fig. 3.2. When an adverse externality of the type illustrated occurs, a potential Paretian improvement is possible by moderating the externality.

demand curve for product X, and line FE_1 is the market supply curve for the product and reflects the private marginal costs incurred by suppliers in supplying the product. Line AB represents the social marginal cost of supplying the product and the difference between it and line FE_1 measures the marginal external costs or marginal spillover costs associated with the supply of product X. Market equilibrium occurs at E_1 and X_2 of the commodity is supplied. But as pointed out in Chapter 2, this is not ideal because when X_2 of the product is supplied, the social marginal cost of its supply (corresponding to point B) exceeds its marginal value to consumers (corresponding to E_1), and a deadweight social loss equal to the dotted area of triangle E_2E_1B occurs. By reducing the supply of X from X_2 to X_1, a potential Paretian improvement is possible. Because a potential Paretian improvement is possible, there is a market failure.

In order to show more precisely that a potential Paretian improvement is possible where negative externalities of this type occur, it is useful to introduce the concepts of consumers' surplus and producers' surplus. *Consumers' surplus* (if Alfred Marshall's definition is adopted) is the difference between what consumers actually pay for a quantity of a product and the maximum amount they would be prepared to pay for this amount of the product. *Producers' surplus* is the difference between the income producers actually earn from supplying a quantity of a product and the minimum income they would require to supply it. In Fig. 3.2, consumers' surplus when the market is in equilibrium at E_1 is equal to the area of triangle HE_1C and producers' surplus is equal to the area of triangle FE_1H. The victims of the unfavorable externality generated by the production of X have total additional externality costs imposed on them of an amount equal to the area of trapezium GE_1BE_2 when output is expanded from X_1 to X_2. However, the extra benefit to those trading in X is equal only to the area of triangle GE_1E_2. Consequently, those injured by the externality could pay the equivalent of the amount of the area of triangle GE_1E_2 to traders in X (the amount equal to the hatched area of triangle GE_1J to suppliers of X, and the amount equal to the area of triangle JE_1E_2 to buyers of X) to reduce the supplies of X from X_2 to X_1 thereby fully compensating the traders for this action. They could then reap a gain equivalent to the dotted

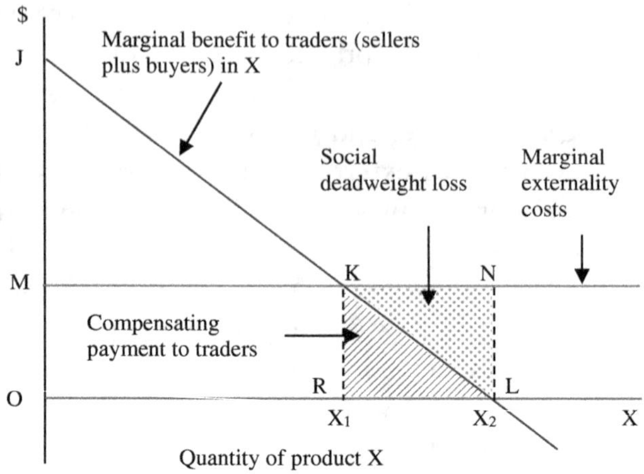

Fig. 3.3. An alternative illustration of the potential economic gains that may be obtained by moderating an adverse externality.

area of triangle E_2E_1B for themselves. This is why the area of the latter triangle is said to indicate the social deadweight loss.

This matter can also be illustrated in a somewhat different manner. In Fig. 3.3, let line *JL* represent the marginal benefits to buyers and sellers combined of being able to trade in commodity *X* when its price is OH. It is the marginal change in consumers' plus producers' surplus given the situation illustrated in Fig. 3.2. Line *MN* represents the marginal externality costs imposed on those adversely affected by the spillover from the production of *X*. In a perfectly competitive market, X_2 of *X* will be produced. At this level of output, the marginal benefits to traders in supplying *X* are zero but the marginal externality costs imposed on those who suffer from associated pollution (or similar spillovers) is *LN*. A potential Paretian improvement is possible by reducing supplies of the product from X_2 to X_1. The payment of an amount equivalent to the hatched area of triangle *KRL* to traders by victims of the adverse externality would compensate traders for their economic loss and the victims of the externality would have a net gain equivalent to the dotted area of triangle *KLN*, the social deadweight loss that would otherwise occur.

Note that such a solution has little to do with justice. It in effect accepts that polluters have the right to pollute and it does not compensate the victims of the pollution or of the externality for the adverse spillover they endure. If those adversely affected by the externality have a right to an environment free of it, then those who want to supply the product would have to compensate the victims for any adverse spillover produced. This would involve paying marginal compensation to victims equal to *OM* on each unit of *X* produced. This would once again result in X_1 of *X* being marketed but now an amount equal to the area of rectangle *ORKM* would be transferred to those adversely affected by the externality. Compared to a situation where *X* is not produced at all, there would be a potential Paretian improvement because those wanting to trade in *X* would have an economic gain and those who are adversely affected by the externality are fully compensated for its presence. However, the income distributional consequences are entirely different in this case compared to the previous one.

A more economical way of controlling emissions of pollutants that give rise to adverse externalities is often to regulate the level of these emissions rather than the quantity supplied of products which are associated with these emissions. A simple diagram (not unlike the previous one) can be used to illustrate this approach and to indicate the relevance of the potential Paretian improvement criterion.

In Fig. 3.4, let line *ABC* indicate the marginal benefit to polluters of being able to emit a pollutant, *X*, and let line *OBD* represent the marginal externality cost imposed on those who suffer as a result of the emission. Unless the level of emission of the pollutant corresponds to that for which the marginal benefit to those polluting equals the marginal externality cost of the emissions, a potential Paretian improvement is possible. For example, if the emission of the pollutant per period is X_2 (which it will be if there is no regulation of the externality), those adversely affected by it can gain a benefit equal to the area of quadrilateral *FCDB* if the level of its emissions is reduced to X_1. At the same time, polluters have an economic loss equal to the hatched area of triangle *FCB* if this reduction occurs. Consequently, the victims of the pollution after compensating polluters for this loss would have a net

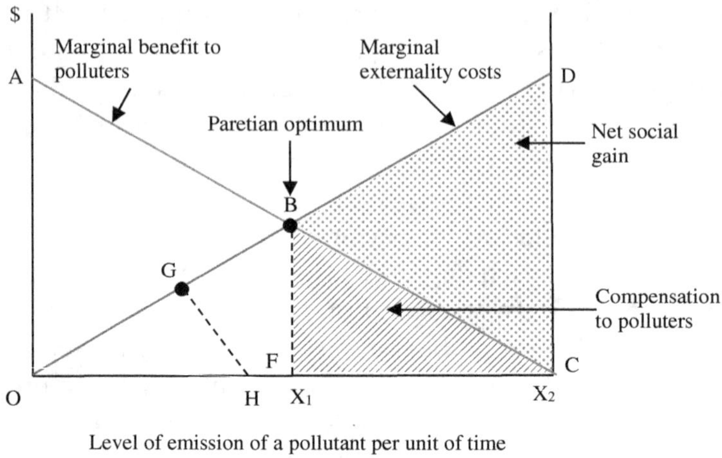

Fig. 3.4. If the emission of a pollutant is unregulated, as in the above case, X_2 of it will be emitted. This does not minimize scarcity because a potential Paretian improvement is possible.

economic gain equivalent to the dotted area of triangle *BCD*. Thus, a potential Paretian improvement can be achieved.

Similarly, if there are no emissions of the pollutant, those who want to emit it could gain an amount equal to the area of the quadrilateral *OFBA* by being able to emit X_1 units of it per period of time. After paying those adversely affected by the emissions an amount equal to the area of triangle *OFB* to compensate them for damages, the net benefit to polluters would be equal to the area of triangle *OBA*. Once more, a potential Paretian gain is possible. Observe that point *B* (corresponding to a level of emissions of X_1) represents a Paretian optimum.

Note that not all externalities are Pareto relevant (Tisdell, 2005, pp. 58–60; 1993, Chapters 3 and 4). For example, if in Fig. 3.4 marginal external costs rise until point *G* is reached and then drop rapidly (along say line *GH*) so they reach zero for $X \leq X_1$, they would be Pareto irrelevant if emissions reach X_2. On the other hand, if emissions are at zero both victims of pollution and polluters can gain by agreeing to a level of pollution of X_2. The total gain for polluters will be equivalent to the area of triangle *OCA* and after paying an amount equal to the area of triangle *OHG* to "victims", polluters will have a net gain. Whether or not compensation should be paid is primarily a matter of justice rather than efficiency in cases such as this.

3.3.3. *Uncertainty and market failure*

Economic agents live in an uncertain world and this is one of the reasons why markets and other forms of economic organization do not operate perfectly. In such cases, scope usually exists in theory for a potential Paretian improvement. However, achieving such an improvement in practice can be much more problematic. In fact, some economists argue that markets are very efficient in using available information and that it is difficult or impossible to improve on their performance in this regard. This could, however, be too pessimistic or optimistic, depending on one's viewpoint. In any case, scope often does exist in market systems to reduce uncertainty and thereby, bring about a Paretian improvement. For example, market failures occur in the production of knowledge and provision of information, including that relating to the state of the environment and general features of the availability of natural resources. These failures occur because of externalities in the supply of information. Once such information is supplied, access to it may be virtually free or only be partly paid for. This may lead to governments subsidizing the provision of such information, for example, via research in universities.

Institutional factors can also add to the uncertainty of market operations. If property rights are uncertain (such as the length of land tenure and its conditions, as has been experienced by Indian farmers in Fiji (Prasad and Tisdell, 2006, Chapter 5), or if the period of entitlement to mine or to harvest natural resources is uncertain, this is likely to have a negative effect on resource conservation and accelerate resource depletion or extraction. An example of this was given in Section 3.2.2 (using Fig. 3.1) where it was argued that such factors reduce marginal user cost, that is they reduce the future economic profits forgone by exploiting a natural resource now.

Increased uncertainty about future economic prospects has a similar effect on business decisions to an increase in the discount rate (see Section 3.2.2). More certain and longer periods of tenure are likely to favor resource conservation whereas great uncertainty and shorter periods of tenure tend to accelerate resource depletion.

Again, lack of clarity about legal liability for environmental damages (as for instance specified in the law of torts, that is law dealing with wrongs, other than criminal wrongs, including environmental negligences) can be a source of uncertainty and can potentially add to costs because of the transaction costs that may be incurred in legal proceedings. In general, clearer specification of the law and cost-effective legal procedures are an economic advantage. Poor institutional structures can add to economic scarcity.

When environmental outcomes are not perfectly correlated, the risk faced by the individual is greater than that on average of the group to which the individual belongs. Scope, therefore exists for insurance as a way to mediate these risks. Insurance markets and other market mechanisms (such as the presence of futures markets) help to reduce economic risks. Whether they are so efficient that there is no scope for a potential Paretian improvement is unclear.

There may be some environmental hazards for which monetary compensation is often believed to be an inadequate substitute, for example, those potentially resulting in death or permanent personal incapacity. See Chapter 15 for further discussion of this aspect and Tisdell (1993, Chapter 5) for an analysis of environmental risk-taking and the law. Political action may be taken to try to prevent economic developments that entail risks of death or permanent injury. In some cases, for example, local communities strongly oppose the setting up of nuclear power stations in their neighborhoods because of the perceived environmental risks involved. That a potential Paretian improvement is possible for the whole community in such cases does not cut much ice with locals.

There is also the further problem that when individuals in communities are exposed collectively to an environmental risk, different individuals in the community will have different perceptions of the risk involved as well as different attitudes to the bearing of the risks. Social conflict can, therefore, arise about whether the community should be subjected to the risk. Ways to resolve the conflict and do so equitably, may not be easily found. The fact that a community can obtain a potential Paretian improvement from an economic change is not sufficient for resolving social conflict.

3.3.4. *Public goods, mixed goods, and quasi-public goods*

Not all commodities are marketable even when they are demanded. When the use or provision of a commodity cannot be made dependent on a payment to the owner of the commodity, then *exclusion* is said to be impossible. In such cases, a commodity cannot be marketed.

Another attribute of economic interest is whether use of a commodity involves *rivalry* in its use. Consumption or use of some commodities involves complete rivalry. For example, food or wine consumed by one person is not available to another. On the other hand, any number of people can share the same idea without reducing its availability to others, or all can enjoy the continuing existence of a wildlife species, such as the giant panda, without diminishing the ability of others to enjoy its continuing existence.

Using these attributes, four particular types of economic commodities can be identified. These are:

(1) Pure private goods — these involve the possibility of complete exclusion and involve complete rivalry.
(2) Pure public goods — these involve the impossibility of exclusion once they are supplied and the complete absence of rivalry.
(3) Open-access commodities, such as fish in international waters — these involve complete rivalry but there is no exclusion in accessing these.
(4) Commodities for which there is no rivalry but for which exclusion is possible. These include pay-television programs. They are sometimes called quasi-private goods.

These categories correspond to points C, A, D, and B, respectively, of the set of possibilities represented in the diagram shown in Fig. 3.5. While commodities involving partial rivalry and partial exclusion are possible, the diagram in Fig. 3.5 does not identify all relevant economic classifications of commodities. For example, mixed goods

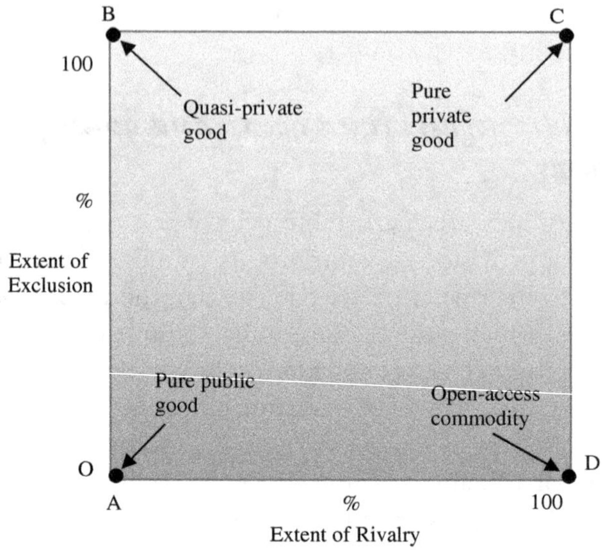

Fig. 3.5. A simplified approach to classifying economic commodities.

are not well identified nor are quasi-public goods, as will be evident from the discussion below of those. Let us now consider how lack of exclusion as well as lack of rivalry can give rise to market failure.

A *pure public* good involves the absence both of exclusion and rivalry in the use of the commodity. This may be confined to individuals in a particular locality or extend over a wider region. For example, works to reduce flooding in a river basin will produce a pure public good for those in the basin or local area. On the other hand, efforts to reduce greenhouse gases (for example, by planting trees to sequester carbon) can produce a global pure public good by reducing the predicted negative effects associated with the accumulation of greenhouse gases in the atmosphere. Also the continuing existence of some wildlife species (such as elephant species and species of whales) may at least in part have the attributes of a pure public good.

Because of the impossibility of exclusion, suppliers of pure public goods cannot market these. Consequently, in a free market system these goods will either not be supplied or will be supplied in smaller quantities than are necessary to achieve a Paretian optimum. Unless they are supplied collectively (by government action or by community cooperation), economic scarcity is greater than it need be and scope for a potential Paretian improvement exists. This can be illustrated by a simple example.

Take the case of a possible flood mitigation project and assume (for simplicity) that two landowners are equally affected by floods in a river valley and that they are the only ones affected. A dam can be built on the river to mitigate flooding, and the extent of the mitigation depends on the height of the dam wall. Again, for simplicity, assume that there are no adverse economic consequences from impoundment of the water. Usually, of course, there will be and these would have to be offset against any economic benefits otherwise received. Each of the landholders may have a demand for flood mitigation as indicated by line *AB* in Fig. 3.6. This may reflect the marginal increase in income expected by each from greater flood mitigation. It represents the marginal evaluation that each landholder places on the supply of the public good. Their combined marginal evaluation (or demand for flood mitigation) is represented by line *DB* which is twice the height of *AB* given the presence of non-rivalry in economic benefits. If the

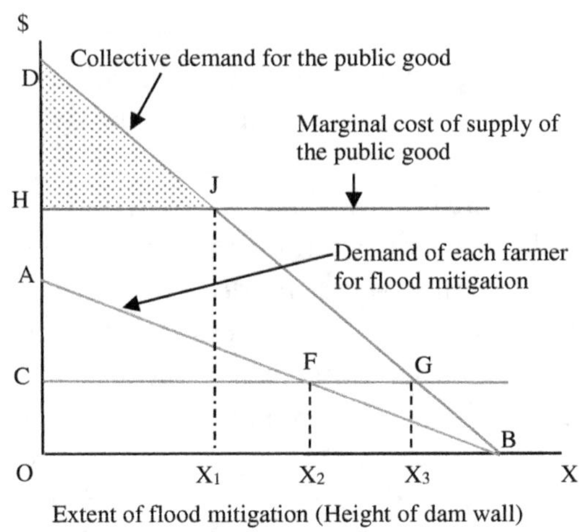

Fig. 3.6. Markets can fail to supply pure public goods even when their supply reduces economic scarcity. This is illustrated by a flood mitigation example.

marginal cost of extra flood mitigation is shown by line *HJ*, neither landholder has any individual economic incentive to supply flood mitigation because the marginal evaluation of each is less than the marginal cost of flood mitigation. However, flood mitigation to the extent X_1 can bring about a Paretian improvement.

This optimal level (X_1) of flood mitigation implies that the sum of the marginal evaluation of landholders for extra flood mitigation equals the marginal cost of its provision. The total net benefit of the landholders from flood mitigation in this case is equal to the dotted area of triangle *DHJ*. If both contribute equally to the cost of the flood mitigation (and if average cost and marginal cost are identical in this case) each has a net economic gain equal to half of the area of the triangle *DHJ*. If the cost of supplying the public good is low (say corresponds to line *CG* in this case), then one of the beneficiaries may supply the good but will do so on a smaller scale than is collectively optimal. In the case illustrated, X_2 of the good might be supplied by one landholder and the other may free-ride. All, however, could obtain a Paretian improvement by increasing the supply of the public good to X_3. The main point is that in the case of pure public goods, markets are incapable of minimizing economic scarcity.

Some goods (*mixed goods*) have more than one set of economic attributes in terms of Fig. 3.5. Whales are an example. For those who wish to eat whale meat, whales are a rivalrous commodity. For those who do not want to eat such meat but enjoy the existence of whales, the existence of whales is a pure public good. Such goods are mixed economic goods. Where commodities are mixed goods, the marketed component is likely to dominate their use and conservation. Hence, a socially optimal economic outcome does not normally eventuate in the absence of mechanisms to counteract market dominance.

This can be illustrated by a case involving the logging of a private forest. Suppose that line *ABC* in Fig. 3.7 represents the marginal cost of logging a private forest and let *OP* be the price of logs. Logs are private goods. However, a collateral effect of logging can be loss of pure public goods (such as reduced biodiversity, greater levels of greenhouse gases in the atmosphere, greater risk of floods — a localized public bad, and so on). The difference between lines *ABC* and *ADE*

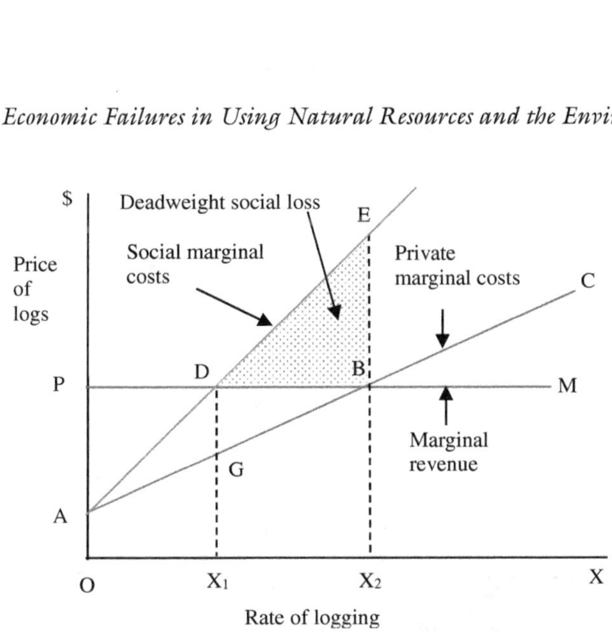

Fig. 3.7. A mixed good case. In the case illustrated market operations do not minimize economic scarcity.

indicates the marginal loss in value of public goods occasioned by the logging. This loss is equivalent to that caused by an adverse economic externality. The private owner will not take this factor into account and will maximize his/her profit by logging at the rate of X_2 per period. This, however, is not ideal from a Paretian point of view. A potential Paretian improvement is possible by reducing the rate of logging from X_2 to X_1 per period of time. Those damaged by a loss of public goods as a result of logging can compensate the forest owner and still be better-off than before the change. After paying a sum equivalent to the area of triangle *DGB* to the forest owner to reduce his/her rate of logging from X_2 to X_1, those who suffer public "bads" as a result of the logging have a net economic gain equivalent to the dotted area of triangle *DBE.*

Sometimes mixed goods are valued using the concept of *total economic value* (see Chapter 6). In such cases, total economic value is divided into use value and non-use value (see for example, Table 11.1 or Tisdell, 2005, Section 5.2). Components of non-use value usually have the attributes of pure public goods whereas use value components can have the characteristics of private goods and may also possess an externality attribute. *Quasi-public goods* are those for which there is

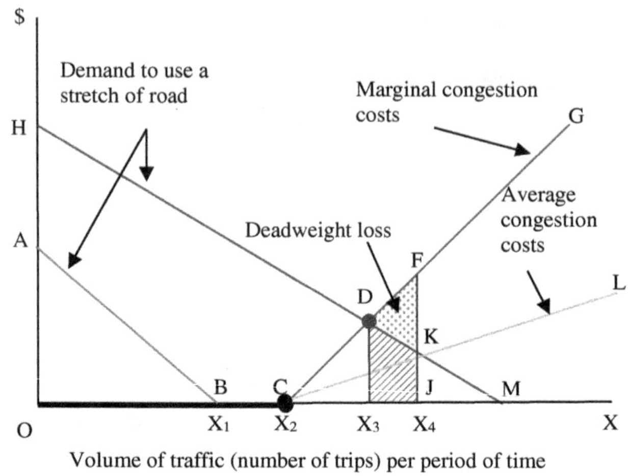

Fig. 3.8. An illustration of the economics of using a quasi-public good, in this case a stretch of road.

non-rivalry in their use up to some particular level of utilization but rivalry develops once some threshold of use is exceeded. [In some cases, they are also quasi-private goods — see Section 3.3.5.] An example is traffic congestion on a particular stretch of road. This can be illustrated by Fig. 3.8. In this figure, the relationship *OBCG* represents the marginal congestion cost of using the road. *OCKL* indicates the average congestion costs per trip of using the road. It is zero until the volume of traffic is X_2 or more. Should the demand to use the road in the absence of congestion be as indicated by *AB*, the equilibrium volume of traffic per period of time is X_1. There are no congestion costs. Should, however, the demand curve to use the road rise to *HM*, an amount of traffic of X_4 will use the road if there is no charge to use the road. At X_4, the average congestion cost per trip is just equal to the value placed on the last trip. However, the marginal cost of the marginal trip is *FJ* and exceeds its marginal value, *KJ*. There is in fact an economic deadweight loss equal to the area of the dotted triangle in Fig. 3.8 due to congestion. Consequently, a potential Paretian gain is possible by reducing the volume of traffic from X_4 to X_3. Those experiencing marginal congestion costs indicated by the segment *DF* of the marginal cost curve could pay those with a low demand to travel an amount equal to the hatched area in Fig. 3.8 not to travel on the stretch of road and would then be better-off by an amount equivalent to the dotted area of triangle *DKF*. Therefore, a potential Paretian improvement is possible.

3.3.5. *Open-access commodities*

In Fig. 3.5, the open-access case corresponds to point *D* and is associated with no exclusion and complete rivalry in use of a commodity. But the aspect of no exclusion in this case needs a slight qualification. There is no exclusion from the commodity *until* it comes into the possession of someone. Once it comes into the possession of someone, it usually becomes their private property and exclusion occurs. Thus, in cases where wild fish are subject to open-access, *once* fish are captured by some individual, they become their exclusive property. The same applies to the gathering of forest resources where there is open-access to these. While in some cases, open-access to natural resources is or has been open to all, in many cases it is restricted to local villagers or communities.

In earlier times, much of the resources in the world's oceans were open-access resources but there has been a global trend towards eliminating or restricting access to natural resources. For example, the United Nations International Convention on the Law of the Sea (UNICLOS) considerably extended the area of the sea over which sovereign nations have exclusive rights to marine resources. Thus, the area of open-access to marine resources is now much diminished compared to the past. While this may have reduced economic misuse of marine resources, it has not solved all economic problems associated with their use. Continuing problems include the difficulties that some nations face in restricting access to these resources and transboundary problems, that is management problems that arise when nations share natural resources, such as stock of migratory fish (see for example, Tisdell, 2003, Chapters 1 and 22).

Economic failures that arise as a result of open-access to resources are discussed in the next chapter and there is some discussion of transboundary problems there and later in this book.

The case represented by point *B* in Fig. 3.5 involves a commodity for which complete exclusion is possible but for which there is no rivalry in its use. This has been called a *quasi-private commodity*. The supply of electronic signals (for instance wireless transmissions for use in information technology) often have this quality. Due to the existence of the patent system, new inventions if patented, also have these characteristics. When these characteristics of a commodity occur, owners of the commodity frequently gain a monopoly or near monopoly in supplying their product. This can lead to a deadweight economic loss because the monopolist may restrict supply of the commodity to users in order to increase its profit. However, the consequences of imperfect market competition for natural resource conservation are complex as the next section indicates.

3.3.6. *Monopolies*

Monopolies can be a source of market failure. If monopolists operate in the manner predicted by neoclassical economic theory, they create an "artificial" scarcity to increase their profit (see Tisdell and Hartley, 2008, Chapters 2 and 8). A potential Paretian improvement is possible in such a case. If the source of the monopoly is a natural resource, they may market it at a slower rate than is socially optimal. On the other hand, several economists believe that monopolies, oligopolies and big business generally are very growth-oriented (Schumpeter, 1947). It has been argued that large businesses are always trying to expand the demand for their products and are active in undertaking research and development to find new uses for their resources (Marris, 1964). This may accelerate natural resource use rather than limit it. Therefore, the net effect of big business on economic scarcity is difficult to access.

3.4. Political and Administrative Mechanisms and Economic Failures

Although markets may fail to minimize economic scarcity for the reasons outlined above, political and administrative mechanisms affecting the allocation of resources and their use can do likewise. In some circumstances, replacing market mechanisms by political and administrative mechanisms will add to economic scarcity, and the converse is also true. Judgment is required about what is the most suitable mechanism or combination of mechanisms to address particular resource and environmental issues.

Reasons why political and administrative mechanisms may fail to establish a Paretian optimum can vary. They vary, for example, with the type of political mechanisms being used for decision-making and with the type of administrative structures that exist. It is only possible here to illustrate a few possibilities.

3.4.1. *Failure of majority voting to bring about a Paretian optimum*

While majority voting is a democratic way to decide whether an economic change or development should be allowed, it may not result in a Paretian optimal outcome. This can be illustrated by the case shown in Fig. 3.9.

Suppose that a fixed area of land is covered in natural vegetation but its development for a housing estate is being considered. Constituents (voters) in the relevant region are divided about whether the land should be retained in its natural state or developed for housing. In Fig. 3.9, line *DBF* may represent the marginal willingness to pay of those who favor conversion of the land for housing and line *ABC* may represent the marginal willingness to pay of those who oppose this land conversion. Given this representation, point *B* corresponds to a Paretian optimum. This involves X_1 of the land being retained in a natural state and the use of $100 - X_1$ of it for housing. Suppose that constituents are asked to vote on whether the land should be used for housing or kept in a natural state. Then if conservationists are in the majority and if majority voting determines the social choice, no development will be allowed. On the other hand, if developers are in the majority, the entire land area will be used for housing.

Either of the extremes mentioned leaves scope for a Paretian improvement. For example, if conservationists were paid an amount

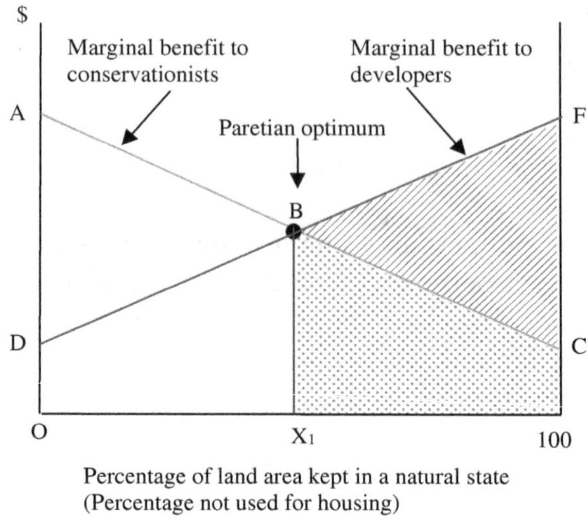

Fig. 3.9. As illustrated, majority voting can fail to minimize economic scarcity if the potential Paretian improvement criterion is used.

equivalent to the dotted area in Fig. 3.9 to allow $100 - X_1$ of the land to be used for housing, this would compensate them for the natural area lost and developers would have a net gain equivalent to the hatched area of triangle *BCF*. Similarly, a Paretian improvement is possible if all the land is initially planned to be used for housing. Furthermore, if developers know that conservationists are in the majority, they might get a majority by proposing development of $100 - X_1$ of the land if they include a package which provides sufficient compensation to conservationists, such as the provision of some environmental feature or service that conservationists would value at least as much as the dotted area in Fig. 3.9. So even when referenda based on majority voting are used to make social decisions, the options presented to voters may already incorporate a compromise and in some cases, could even result in a Paretian optimum.

3.4.2. *Special interest pressure groups*

In many countries, special interest groups can be a source of economic failure. Often they are able to obtain economic benefits for themselves at the expense of the remainder of the community, and the gain to them is usually less than the economic loss to the remainder of the community. This outcome is partly explained by transaction cost theory. When a few can gain considerably (a special interest group) from government policies in their favor, and the costs of this favoritism are spread thinly over a large number of individuals so that the loss of each is small, the cost may be little noticed by this group and none of those disadvantaged are likely to find it economically worthwhile to lobby against the proposals of the special interest group. For example, suppose a country with a population of 200 million and that a special interest group of 10 persons can benefit from a change in government policy that benefits each by $10 million but damages each resident by $1. The former group has a strong economic incentive to lobby in favor of the proposal (they will have large individual gains) but the latter group is unlikely to organize to oppose it because the cost of any individual starting the ball rolling in that respect is likely to be far in excess of $1. Nevertheless, there is a net social economic loss of $100 million as a result if the new policy is adopted.

Apart from political lobbying (which may involve donations to the party in political power by special interest groups in return for political favors), electoral boundaries and structures can favor some special interest groups. For example, in some countries, rural residents have a greater number of representatives in government than urban residents in proportion to their population. This can bias economic policy in favor of particular economic interest groups, for example, farmers. It may, for instance, result in subsidies for agricultural production. While these subsidies add to the income of farmers, they usually result in a net social economic loss. If the production of the subsidized commodity gives rise to negative environmental externalities, the loss will be greater than otherwise. This can be illustrated by applying Pigou's analysis (see Fig. 3.2).

In Fig. 3.10, let the line *AB* represent the market demand for agricultural supplies and let the line *CF* represent the market supply curve of agricultural products (which in turn, reflects the private marginal cost of their supply). Suppose that agricultural production gives rise to negative environmental externalities (due to the clearing of trees

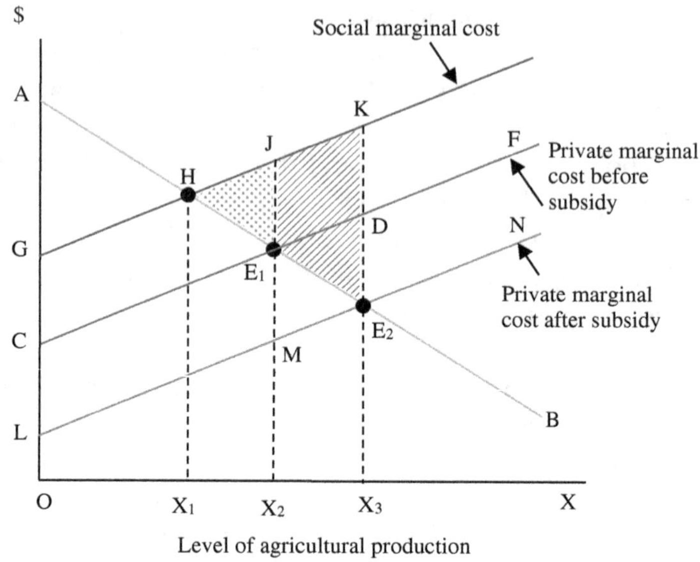

Fig. 3.10. An example of how a government subsidy designed to support special economic interests can add to overall economic scarcity and to environmental deterioration.

and so on) so that the social marginal cost of agricultural production is as indicated by line *GK*. In the absence of government intervention, the market comes into equilibrium at E_1 and, as previously explained, there is a deadweight social loss equivalent to the dotted area of triangle HE_1J. Now imagine that for political reasons, agriculturalists are able to obtain a subsidy of *CL* on each unit of agricultural production. The equilibrium of this market then shifts to E_2. The deadweight social loss is thereby increased from an amount equivalent to the area of triangle HE_1J to an amount equal to the area of triangle HE_2K.

The above means that government intervention has added to overall economic scarcity. The net increase in the social deadweight loss as a result of the subsidy is equal to the hatched area of quadrilateral E_1E_2KJ. This loss can be divided into two components. The area of trapezium JE_1DK represents the economic impact of increased negative environmental spillovers and the area of triangle E_1E_2D is a further loss due to the misallocation of resources.

3.4.3. *Prevalence of myopic and reactive rather than pro-active behavior by governments*

It has been suggested that many governments are myopic in their decision-making. This may partly be because of the limited periods of office of most governments and the felt need of incumbents to impress the electorate with their perceived achievements in order to gain support in the next round of elections. This can lead to distortions in resource use.

Many governments also appear to be reactive rather than pro-active in much of their policy-making. Even though a resource or environmental problem is foreseen, government action to moderate or to prevent the problem emerging may not occur until after the problem emerges or even becomes serious, and the demands of the electorate for action are strongly evident. By taking action, then the government appears to be responding to the will of the electorate. On the other hand, earlier action, in many cases would result in less economic loss, even if the government does not appear to voters to be so responsive as when action is taken once the problem has emerged. This reactive behavior can result in irreversible adverse consequences for natural resource conservation. This can arise because the delay leads to irreversible biophysical consequences or to a socio-economic trap which leaves no scope for effective policy choices by the government. For example, delayed action limiting greenhouse gas emissions could result in irreversible and unwanted biophysical changes. Another example is when government delays in addressing or preparing for increased traffic volume result in increased costs for improved traffic systems later. This seems to be a common phenomenon.

3.4.4. *Failures in public administration*

As the size of government grows, governments usually become more dependent on public administrators for policy advice and for implementing government policies. Although public administrators are the agents of the government, bounded rationality of elected politicians limits their ability to monitor the actions of public servants and to access information directly. This usually provides public administrators with some degree of freedom in their behavior. In other words, principal–agent problems arise. Public administrators may prepare information supplied to politicians in a way that favors their own interests and politicians may not be able to monitor how well public servants carry out their duties because of the costs involved in supervision. Problems involving asymmetry of information arise. Niskanen (1971) and Downs (1967) have claimed that to a large extent, public administrators may be guided by their own self-interest. They may aim for managerial perks, excessive staffing and growth of their individual bureaucracies. This they may achieve by various strategies including the inflation of the demand for their services and by cooperating with pressure groups that may be advantaged by the expansion of particular public bureaucracies. In the case of public regulation of resource and environmental use, these factors encourage excessive administration costs of regulation, inefficient research and data collection, and attempts to capture a large share of the total economic benefits of regulation. All of these factors add to economic scarcity.

The situation is made more problematic because the supply of public administration is subject to limited market competition and contestability. A high degree of imperfect competition prevails in the supply of public services.

In some jurisdictions, corruption of public servants can be a problem. This can occur in complicity with politicians but also may occur secretly. Illegal logging sometimes involves bribery. Hence, state forests are harvested at a faster rate than otherwise as a result of this bribery and public royalties from logging are lost. Cases of this nature have been reported in the past for Indonesia, the Solomon Islands and other developing countries. In some instances, politicians in developing countries appear to have been given financial inducements (bribes) to allow open-cut mining which has had adverse externalities. Such corruption adds to collective economic scarcity.

Apart from self-seeking behavior by public administrators, public administrators can vary in their competency or capabilities. Thus, apart from opportunism by public servants, the potential incompetence of public administrators can sometimes add to economic scarcity and to environmental deterioration.

3.5. Conclusions

The above discussion demonstrates that both market systems and government/public administration of natural resources and the environment can fail to minimize economic scarcity, depending on the circumstances. Both forms of management of resources can fail to achieve a Paretian optimum. However, this does not mean that these managerial systems are complete economic failures but rather that in particular circumstances, scope exists for improving their economic performance, at least in theory. However, because of knowledge limitations and existing institutional constraints, it may be impossible to institute economic reforms that enable a Paretian optimum to be obtained. Or expressed differently, there may be no practical way of achieving 100% economic efficiency in reaching this target or benchmark of economic performance. Given these constraints, at a particular point of time and in a particular economy, potentially realizable performance as a proportion of this target may only be 80%, for instance. If existing economic performance of this economy is 60%, then workable scope exists to increase its economic performance by 20%. A 40% addition to economic performance cannot be achieved in practice. The practical scope for raising the economic performance of economies can be expected to vary with countries and with the stage of their socioeconomic evolution.

A further consequence of this discussion is that in large relatively complex economies, mixed economic systems (systems involving a combination of the use of markets and non-market mechanisms, such as political and administrative ones) are likely to deliver the best achievable level of economic performance. Nevertheless, getting the balance "right" between the use of market systems and non-market systems for the economically efficient use of resources is a difficult choice. Furthermore, even if the balance between different institutional arrangements is "right", scope can still exist to improve the operation of institutions. It should also be borne in mind that what is believed to be an appropriate institutional balance ought not ultimately be judged solely on how well the balance minimizes economic scarcity. It also requires account to be taken of human aspirations for justice and for the achievement of social goals, such as individual liberty and in many cases, the need to belong to a meaningful social group.

Chapter 4 will examine the sanctioning by governments of private rights in natural (and other) resources as a means to reduce economic scarcity within a market system, that is, to avoid market failures that may otherwise occur. The importance of legal rights will also be considered in this context. A subsequent chapter (Chapter 5) examines specific regulations that governments may introduce to avoid or reduce the economic cost of market failures in the use of natural resources and the environment. Apart from considering the likely impacts of these policies on economic scarcity, questions of social justice will also be discussed.

3.6. Keywords

Administrative and political failure; consumers' surplus; economic failure; environmental spillovers; externalities; Kaldor-Hicks criterion; market failure; mixed goods; nonuse value; open-access commodities; Paretian irrelevant externality; Pareto's criterion; Pareto optimality; Pareto relevant externality; potential Paretian improvement; private marginal costs; producers' surplus; pure private goods; pure public goods; quasi-private goods; quasi-public goods; social marginal costs; special interest groups; total economic value; user costs; use value.

3.7. Questions for Review and Discussion

1. In considering the optimal use of natural resources and the environment, the basic economic problem cannot be ignored. Explain this problem.
2. Minimizing economic scarcity is not the only desired goal of societies. Explain and discuss.
3. What is economic failure? How do economists traditionally determine whether it exists?

4. To some extent, market systems take account of future scarcity. Explain and discuss in relation to the use of a non-renewable natural resource, such as crude oil.
5. Explain the potential Paretian improvement criterion. Outline the pros and cons of using this criterion to determine whether a proposed economic change, such as the building of a dam, should proceed.
6. While markets are subject to economic failures so too are many other social mechanisms for administering natural resources. Discuss.
7. Illustrate and explain how the existence of a negative environmental spillover associated with market operations can provide scope for a potential Paretian improvement. Show this both for Pigou's approach and for a model that is focused on the emission of a pollutant as the source of the offending spillover.
8. Outline some of the types of uncertainty that can exist about use of natural resources and the environment and which may add to economic scarcity.
9. Private goods can be supplied by markets but not pure public goods. Why? Give examples of environmental commodities that can be considered to be pure public goods.
10. Explain why pure public goods are usually undersupplied or not supplied even when their supply would reduce economic scarcity. Illustrate and give natural resource or environmental examples.
11. What is a mixed economic good? Give some examples. Explain why market failure can occur in such cases.
12. What is a quasi-public good? Give some examples. Explain how economic failure can arise in such cases.
13. What is an open-access commodity? Give some examples.
14. The impacts of monopolies and of imperfect competition on natural resource use and the state of the environment may be different to that suggested by neoclassical economic theory. Discuss.
15. Explain how majority voting may fail to minimize economic scarcity. Illustrate by considering an example in which loss of natural resources is at stake, such as a natural forest.

16. Explain how the political activities of special economic interest groups can add to economic scarcity. Illustrate this by an example in which subsidies obtained by special interest groups add to an adverse environmental externality.
17. Explain how reactive government behavior in addressing natural resource problems could add to economic scarcity or make it more difficult to reduce economic scarcity.
18. Principal–agent problems can be a source of economic shortcomings in public administration and may inflate the costs of regulating use of natural resources and the environment. Explain.
19. In some cases, bribery and incompetence reduce the potential economic benefits from regulation by the public administration of natural resource use. Discuss and give examples.
20. Neither free markets nor political mechanisms (in association with public administration) provide ideal mechanisms for regulating the use of natural resources and the environment. Why? If this is so, what types of organizational mechanisms should be used, in your view, to administer the use of these scarce resources.
21. In practice, no economy is likely to be able to reach a Paretian optimum and consequently, minimize economic scarcity relative to its available resources. Furthermore, the ability of countries to approach this target will vary with their particular circumstances, for example, their existing institutions and customs. This is particularly evident in relation to the use of natural resources and the environment. Discuss.
22. Should minimizing economic scarcity (for example, by trying to achieve a Paretian optimum) be the prime or sole goal of society? What other social goals could be important? Can methods designed to minimize economic scarcity conflict with these other goals? Explain and illustrate.
23. A mining development is proposed for a remote region in a developing country where it will have a major impact on the local community. The development will result in a *potential* Paretian improvement for the country. Should it be allowed? In discussing the matter, take into account its possible impact on the distribution

of income, for example, whether it will provide an economic benefit to the country and to the affected local community. Does the potential Paretian improvement criterion imply that both the relevant nation and local community will gain? Would you also want to examine its possible social and environmental consequences closely before supporting the development? Why?

Readings and References

Callan, S.J. and J.M. Thomas (2000). *Environmental Economics and Management*, 2nd edn. Dryden Press, Fort Worth, TX. [Chapters 2 and 3, Level: Basic to Intermediate].

Downs, A. (1967). *Inside Bureaucracy*, Little Brown, Boston, MA, USA.

Hayek, F.A. von (1982). *Law, Legislation and Liberty: A New Statement of the Liberal Principles of Justice and Political Economy*, Routledge and Kegan Paul, London.

Hicks, J.R. (1939). The foundations of welfare economics, *The Economic Journal*, 49, 696–712. doi: 10.2307/2225023.

Ison, S., S. Peake and S. Wall (2002). *Environmental Issues and Policies*, Pearson Education, Harlow, Essex, UK. [Chapter 3, Level: Basic].

Kaldor, N. (1939). Welfare propositions of economics and interpersonal comparisons of utility, *The Economic Journal*, 49, 549–552. doi: 10.2307/2224835.

Kolstad, C.D. (2000). *Environmental Economics*, Oxford University Press, New York. [Chapters 4 and 5, Level: Intermediate to Advanced].

Little, I.M.D. (1949). The foundations of welfare economics, *Oxford Economic Papers*, 1, 227–246. doi: https://www.jstor.org/stable/2661708.

Little, I.M.D. (1957). *A Critique of Welfare Economics*, 2nd Edn edn. Oxford University Press, Oxford.

Marris, R. (1964). *The Economic Theory of Managerial Capitalism*, Macmillan, London.

Ng, Y.-K. (1979). *Welfare Economics: Introduction and Development of Basic Concepts*, Macmillan, London.

Niskanen, W.A. (1971). *Bureacracy and Representative Government*, Aldine, Chicago.

Perman, R., Y. Ma, M. Common, D. Maddison and J. McGilvray (2011). *Natural Resource and Environmental Economics*, 4th edn. Pearson, Harlow, Essex UK. [Chapter 3 and 4, Level: Advanced].

Pigou, A. (1932). *The Economics of Welfare*, 4th edn. Macmillan, London.

Prasad, B. and C.A. Tisdell (2006). *Institutions, Economic Performances and Sustainable Development: A Case Study of the Fiji Islands*, Nova Science Publishers, New York.

Schumpeter, J. (1947). *Capitalism, Socialism and Democracy*, 2nd edn. Harper Brothers, New York.

Tietenberg, T. and L. Lewis (2018). *Environmental and Natural Resource Economics*, 11th edn. Routledge, New York and Abingdon, Oxon, UK. [Chapter 2, Level: Basic].

Tisdell, C.A. (1970). On the theory of externalities, *The Economic Record*, 46, 14–25.

Tisdell, C.A. (1993). *Environmental Economics: Policies for Environmental Management and Sustainable Development*, Edward Elgar, Aldershot, UK and Brookfield, VT, USA.

Tisdell, C.A. (2003). *Economics and Ecology in Agriculture and Marine Production*, Edward Elgar, Cheltenham, UK and Northampton, MA, USA.

Tisdell, C.A. (2005). *Economics of Environmental Conservation*, 2nd edn. Edward Elgar, Cheltenham, UK and Northampton, MA, USA. [Chapters 1 and 3. Level: Basic].

Tisdell, C.A. (2007). Knowledge and the valuation of public goods and experential commodities: Information provision and acquisition, *Global Business and Economics Review*, 9, 170–182. doi: https://dx.doi.org/10.1504/GBER.2007.013699.

Tisdell, C.A. and K. Hartley (2008). *Microeconomic Policy: A New Perspective*, Edward Elgar, Cheltenham, UK and Northampton, MA, USA. [Chapters 2 and 16, Level: Basic to Intermediate].

Walsh, C. and C. Tisdell (1973). Non-marginal externalities: As relevant and as not, *The Economic Record*, 49, 447–455. doi: 10.1111/j.1475-4932.1973.tb02282.x.

Chapter 4

Property Rights, Laws, Markets, and Resource Use

4.1. Introduction: General Views about Property Rights, Justice and Economic Efficiency

The purpose of this chapter is to outline the nature of property rights in resources and to show the consequences of such rights (or the lack of such rights) for wealth creation or for a reduction in economic scarcity. While some public policy responses to the issues that are raised are outlined, the next chapter (Chapter 5) focuses mainly on possible policy responses to market failures that occur because of incomplete property rights in resources.

The previous chapter outlined ways in which markets and political mechanisms can fail to minimize scarcity relative to human wants. Some economists believe that if private property rights were universal and if there were no impediments to markets operating freely and competitively, there would be no market failures. For them, an ideal economic system is one in which all economic resources (commodities) are private property and exchanges occur in free and competitive markets. Such a system is seen as being economically ideal for three reasons:

(1) It is seen as ensuring economic efficiency because it is able to minimize scarcity relative to wants so that Pareto's criterion is satisfied (see Chapter 3).
(2) It is believed to provide strong economic incentives to owners of private property to profit from their property. This stimulates economic growth as well as economic efficiency.
(3) According to the Austrian School of Economics (for example, Hayek, 1948, 1994) this system shows outstanding performance in minimizing the amount of (costly) information required to adjust the economy to changing circumstances (see Chapter 2). The market or price mechanism involves processes of self-organization that only require individual economic actors or agents to have limited knowledge of economic variables and prices. The market system is seen as an effective system for managing or organizing an economy efficiently because it minimizes the amount of information needed to do this.

Apart from these considerations, some economists such as Hayek (1994), favor the widespread presence of private property and competitive markets on ideological grounds. This combination is seen as providing a strong basis for personal freedom and liberty.

Richard Posner argues that policies and laws facilitating wealth maximization in society are justified ethically (Posner, 1981, Chapters 2 and 3; 1985). His wealth maximization principle implies support for the potential Paretian improvement criterion (also known as the Kaldor–Hicks principle) which was discussed in Chapter 3. In some cases (but not all) private property combined with competitive markets is wealth-maximizing and therefore, from Posner's perspective, would be ethically justified as a form of economic organization. Furthermore, Posner claims that in such a system, those who are able to add more to the wealth of society than others will accumulate a greater amount of property, thereby obtaining control of a growing amount of resources for the further generation of wealth. The evolutionary selection of such individuals is a powerful force (in his view) for wealth maximization in societies. In his view, the wealth inequality that emerges is justified because it accelerates wealth creation for society.

Posner also accepts the view that economic exchange based on consent is beneficial to both parties involved in the exchange and is wealth-enhancing, if no third party problems exist, for example, if there are no adverse externalities. However, Posner recognizes that the institution of private property is not always economic because the transaction costs involved in the creation and maintenance of private property can exceed the economic benefits obtained. Furthermore, he recognizes that this situation can alter with the stage of development of a society (Posner, 1981, Chapter 7). Consequently, Posner argues that private property combined with competitive markets is not always a recipe for maximizing economic wealth. He is therefore, prepared to accept community intervention in an economy if it can be shown to be wealth-maximizing. Thus, he is less opposed to such intervention than those who strongly support personal individualism or liberty.

Posner is supportive of the view that private wealth (private property) accumulated by free and competitive exchange is an indicator of an individual's social worth. Those who accumulate greater wealth benefit society more than those who accumulate less wealth because given his theory, they are more effective wealth-maximizers. In addition, the former individuals are likely to have benefited others to a greater extent than the latter bearing in mind that exchange benefits both the buyer and the seller. In these circumstances, a wealthier individual could be regarded as being more virtuous than a less wealthy one.

This position has parallels with the Protestant ethic. This ethic extolled hard work, savings and investment, honesty and capital accumulation as indicators of the social and moral worth of the individual. Weber (1930) believed this ethic was an important driving force behind the Industrial Revolution and fostered the development of capitalism. Posner (1985, p. 94) agrees that his wealth maximization norm involves capitalist ethics.

Even if one is inclined to accept Posner's view, it should be noted that not all wealth and private property have been obtained by free and competitive exchange. Illegality, deception and chance can play a major role in the accumulation of personal wealth. In addition, the fortune of individuals depends to a large extent on their initial endowments of resources. These include their inherited abilities and their inherited property rights. Furthermore, when individuals are young, they are dependent on others (such as their parents) for support to develop their abilities, for example, to support their education. This is not normally an exchange relationship. The degree of support for dependents varies amongst other things, with the wealth of carers and their concern for their dependents. All these factors ultimately impact on the wealth of individuals and their ability to add to the wealth of society.

Sen (1981) has stressed the importance of endowments and social entitlements in determining the economic opportunities available to individuals. Posner (1985, pp. 200–201) agrees that the nature of initial endowments can create difficulties for his ethical principle of wealth maximization which "holds that a transaction or other change in the use or ownership of resources is good if it increases the wealth of society" (Posner, 1987, p. 15). He therefore, suggests that ways should be found of ensuring that resources are redistributed as rapidly as possible in society in favor of those who can use these resources to make the greatest contribution to increasing the wealth of society.

Posner's concept of justice is inconsistent with that of Rawls (1971). Rawls in his *Theory of Justice* (Rawls, 1971) emphasizes the significance of chance in determining the initial endowments of individuals and consequently, their economic opportunities. He argues that income should be equally distributed between individuals except in cases where inequality is to the advantage of all.

Rawls' theory of justice has been used by some scholars to support the ideal of sustainable development (see Chapter 7). Attaining this ideal requires present generations to conserve sufficient natural resources for (or more generally, bequest a package of resources to) future generations to enable the level of income of future generations (or more generally their well-being) to be not less than that of current generations. In some circumstances, the existence of private property combined with competitive markets is wealth-maximizing and there is some ethical support for personal wealth accumulated in this capitalist institutional system. However, a fully-fledged system of private property rights in all resources cannot be economically established because of the transaction costs and other difficulties involved in enforcing these rights. In practice, property rights are often incomplete and markets are missing. Furthermore, private property rights are not wholly secure because the state (or a local community) may regulate or change these rights and acquire private property compulsorily in certain circumstances, for example, when this is seen as necessary to increase social welfare or collective wealth. For instance, the state may acquire private land compulsory for the construction of new roads. While this may sometimes be justified on the basis of Posner's wealth-maximization principle, care is needed in such intervention. If the prospect of state acquisition of private property generates insecurity of property rights, it is liable to result in a misallocation of resources and create a disincentive to wealth-creation by the owners of resources.

In order to gain a deeper appreciation of the role of property rights in resource allocation, in the generation of wealth, and in the operation of economic systems, let us in turn consider:

(1) the concept of private property rights and other forms of property rights;
(2) private property rights and the efficient operation of market systems;
(3) transaction costs and limits to the economics of creating private property;
(4) common property, open-access resources and the operation of economic systems; and
(5) the taking of property rights by the state from individuals and from other legal entities.

4.2. Private Property Rights and Other Forms of Property Rights

Property rights provide a set of legal entitlements to individuals or other legal entities to use and transfer resources. These rights can vary widely in their nature and they affect how well economies operate. At one extreme, private property rights could be complete and all pervasive. This, however, is just a theoretical possibility. At the other extreme, there may be no property rights in resources. Numerous possibilities exist between these extremes, and most actual cases fall in this intermediate area.

A complete and strong set of private property rights in resources exist if the following entitlements (and obligations) apply:

(1) *Exclusive use rights.* The owner of the resources has the exclusive right to use these resources or to decide how they are to be used. The owner has the exclusive rights to the economic benefits generated by possession of the resources but at his or her discretion, may transfer these benefits to others by exchange or gift. The owner also has the obligation to compensate other owners of resources for any costs imposed upon them by his/her use or possession of the resources.
(2) *Transferability.* Private ownership of the resource exists in principle in perpetuity but the owner may transfer by exchange, gift or bequest all or part of his or her property rights in the resource to others.

In this extreme case, all private property rights are assumed to be assured and to be costless to protect. Transaction costs are absent. The owner of private property is sure that his/her property will not be seized or encroached upon, for example, by the state.

The above is clearly an extreme theoretical possibility. In practice most private property rights are not as absolute as this. The state, for example, reserves the right to compulsorily acquire private property in particular circumstances, for example, to widen or to improve roads. It may also vary the obligations placed on property owners and limit their use rights. This is discussed later in this chapter. As private property rights become increasingly restricted by governments or other entities, these restrictions limit the power of resource-owners to determine the use of their resources and can reduce economic efficiency and incentives for economic growth. This is not to say that state or communal intervention with private resource use can never be justified. Sometimes, such intervention can increase economic efficiency, ensure economic sustainability and bring about a more desirable distribution of resources and economic opportunities. Nevertheless, insecurity of (private) property rights is a threat to wealth creation. It reduces private incentives to conserve and husband resources for future use.

Common property is another form of property recognized in the relevant literature. It covers a diverse set of possibilities. This category includes resources (such as the commons used for grazing livestock) which are shared by individuals but the use of which is governed by communal rules. Those allowed to use the common resource may also be restricted, for example, to residents of a nearby village.

Common property is usually distinguished from open-access property. In the case of an open-access resource, there are no collective rules governing the nature of its use by individuals or economic entities. However, access to an open-access resource may be limited to a particular group of potential users. For example, villagers living near the resource, residents of a particular tribe, caste or clan, or residents of a particular country. Open-access may only be periodic in some cases, for example, harvesting of some marine animals is restricted to a particular season or period of the year. These observations underline the point that property rights form a continuum of possibilities.

While the presence of common property is not usually associated with modern economies, it is much more prevalent than has often been realized. For example, many local and national facilities are used in common such as roads, parks and waterways and rules have been devised by governing bodies for their shared use.

Again, a large amount of resources in modern economies involve shared ownership through legal entities, such as partnerships and companies (private and public). In the case of companies, the property rights of shareholders are limited by regulations: a shareholder of a public company only has limited legal rights, for instance, in determining how the resources of the shareholder's company are to be used.

Apart from regulating the use of resources, governing bodies may also regulate their transfer. They may decide how, to whom, and on what conditions resources can be transferred. Such regulations will have impacts on economic efficiency, on conservation, on the distribution of income and wealth and on economic growth. Once again, the rules governing transfer of property and resources can vary greatly from society to society and may change with the passage of time.

In practice, the spectrum of property rights involves a multitude of different cases. Two main categories can be identified from the above discussion: (1) situations in which property or resources are shared and (2) cases in which the holder of a resource does not share their use. It is possible for use rights and for transfer rights to be regulated in each of these cases.

4.3. Private Property Rights and the Efficient Operation of Market Systems

In Chapter 3, it was shown how perfectly competitive markets could result (under particular conditions) in economic efficiency when this is judged by applying Pareto's criterion. The neoclassical economic theory supporting this view assumes that all economic commodities involved are private goods. These goods involve rivalry in their use and the possibility of costless exclusion (by their owners) of others from their use. In addition, economic entities are assumed to be well-informed about the relevant economic choices available to them and to maximize the net benefits from their choices. In such a system, consumers are assumed to maximize their utility and businesses their profits. Note that this optimizing or rational behavior can occur even if economic agents have incomplete knowledge (Tisdell, 1996, Chapters 2 and 3). All that economic actors need for this rationality is limited knowledge about their own choice possibilities. Furthermore, as pointed out by Hayek (1948, 1994), individual economic actors need only to have very limited knowledge of the operation of an economy outside their own immediate sphere of control of resources for a competitive system to organize itself in a relatively efficient way.

The institution of private property harnesses the self-interest of resource-owners to make the capitalist market system work efficiently, or at least relatively so. When such a system is in equilibrium, it results in a Paretian ideal allocation of resources and cost efficiency in production given the available set of techniques and the assumptions of neoclassical economic theory.

Figure 4.1 provides a simple illustration of this point. There, the market demand per unit of time for a product *X* is shown by the line marked *DD* and its market supply is indicated by the line marked *SS*. The product might, for example, be wheat. The equilibrium in this

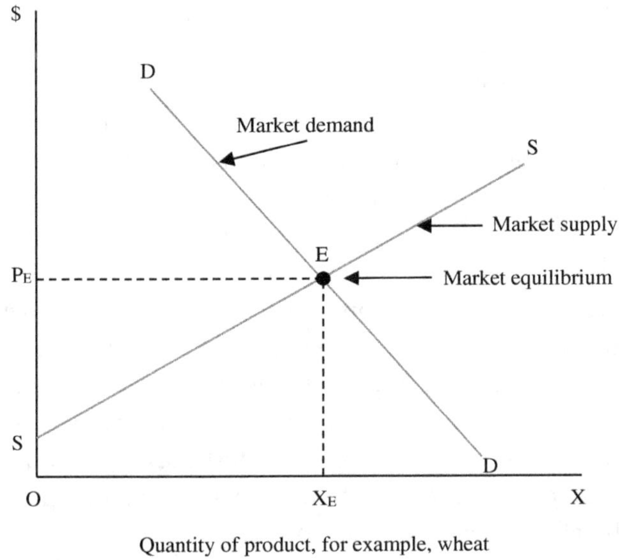

Fig. 4.1. A simple model often used to illustrate the efficiency of perfect market competition in satisfying human wants when such a system is based on private property rights.

market occurs at point *E* and results in a quantity of X_E of the product being traded per unit of time at a price per unit of P_E.

The supply curve, *SS* in Fig. 4.1 reflects the extra or marginal cost involved in supplying quantities of *X*. It reflects the benefits that suppliers of *X* have to forgo to supply *X* rather than other products. It is an indication of the marginal opportunity cost of supplying *X* rather than other products. Line *DD* represents the extra or marginal value that buyers, for example, consumers, place on extra supplies of *X* in comparison to their demands for other products. At point *E*, the extra value placed on the availability of *X* by buyers is just equal to the extra cost of its supply. This is a Paretian efficient outcome.

However, economic systems are always in a process of change and rarely if ever, reach equilibrium. Neoclassical economists, such as Marshall (1920), recognized this. The question then arises of how well do competitive market systems perform given that economic systems are continually changing? Do these markets move in the appropriate directions and do they do so quickly enough? This requires a study of the dynamics of the operation of markets. In many cases, markets do move in the appropriate direction (are stable) but may not operate perfectly. Nevertheless, no alternative preferred system may be available that displays superior dynamic performance. Furthermore, economic systems can be identified that are likely to perform less well in a dynamic situation (as well as in a static one) such as (in particular circumstances) systems involving open-access to resources.

The economic incentives provided by the private ownership of resources generate strong forces within a market system for the efficient allocation of resources if private goods are involved and economic externalities are absent. Furthermore, when combined with private rights in intellectual property for a limited period of time (as in the case of patents for inventions), the market system stimulates economic growth. The above tendencies are present even when the market system is not perfect and private property rights are significant but not absolute. In such circumstances, it can be claimed that workable competition exists (Clark, 1940).

4.4. The Economics of Creating Private Property

Even though an economic system based on the ownership of private property may have economic efficiency and growth advantages compared to alternative systems, it needs to be borne in mind that the creation and enforcement of private property rights is not costless. The lower are the costs of creating rights in private property and enforcing these, and the larger the economic benefits to those holding these rights, the greater is the economic incentive to create and enforce private property rights.

Technological changes which make exclusion more economic provide an impetus to the creation of private property. Wire fencing for example, reduced the costs of enclosing grazing land in Australia and the United States and accelerated the privatization of land in these countries following European settlement. Registration by the state of land titles further facilitated exclusion by making legal enforcement of land rights more certain. The demand for private ownership of land also increased as the profits to be earned from the land rose. Lands which were unprofitable to cultivate or use commercially were not sought by prospective farmers and graziers. Much of this land remained state land and some was subsequently incorporated into national parks and reserves.

The legal system plays an important role in supporting private property rights. The lower are the costs and more certain are the prospects of obtaining legal redress from parties that violate private property or steal it, the more secure is exclusion. Furthermore, the lower are the legal costs involved in transferring private property, the greater are the economic advantages to its owner. In addition, social customs can play an important role in ensuring that the entitlement of owners of private property is secure. If there is a social ethic of respecting the property of others, this will lower the potential cost of protecting private property and ensuring exclusion of those who do not own this property. The economic performance of market systems depends to a large extent on social customs, such as the prevailing degrees of respect for property rights and for business contracts as well as the extent to which individuals are willing to meet their personal economic obligations. Without such customs, the transaction costs involved in economic activity would be very high and economic welfare would be lower than it need be.

As mentioned in Section 4.2, the owner of private property has the exclusive right to decide how it is to be used. However, in many cases in modern economies, the owner appoints an agent to manage his or her property and that property may be owned jointly with others, either directly or indirectly. Transaction costs may prevent the property-owners (the principals) from being able to monitor all the relevant actions of their agents. Consequently, an agent may, to some extent, use the owner's property to his/her advantage and may not exactly pursue the wishes of the principals. This is described as the principal-agent problem in the literature. If the property is jointly owned, its owners may not always operate as a team. Thus, rather than having a common objective, they may have conflicting objectives.

An important development in modern economies is the evolution of public companies. Those who own the shares in a public company (the principals) only have limited control over the way in which the managers of a company use its resources. There is a separation of ownership and management. If shareholders have the common aim of wanting to maximize the returns on their shares, will managers in fact aim to do this? To what extent do company managers aim to maximize the long-run profits (the capitalized value) of their company? Views differ about this (Tisdell and Hartley, 2008, Chapter 7). Marris (1964), for example, argues that as a result of financial competition (for example, the possibility of the take-over of a company by another institution) managers have a strong incentive to maximize the profit of their company or nearly so.

Note that a company is a legal entity and is also able to obtain private property rights. In essence, a public company involves a complex system of property rights and limitations. This property rights situation is much more complicated than that imagined by neoclassical economists who seem to have had in mind the case of single owner of a business who also managed it.

A single proprietor cum manager of a business is likely to live in the community where the business is conducted. In such circumstances, a resident–owner may feel socially more accountable to his/her local community for any adverse externalities created by his/her economic activity compared to a public company. This is because in the latter case, responsibilities for resource use are shared and most public companies do not have a strong association with any local community (see Tisdell, 1990, Chapter 2).

4.5. Common Property

Common property is a property shared by several individuals and social rules govern its use. In the literature, common property is most frequently discussed in relation to local communities, particularly those of earlier times and communities in non-market economies. Nevertheless, much property in modern economies is in fact common property, as was pointed out in the previous section. Resources owned by public companies provide a prominent example of common property in modern economies.

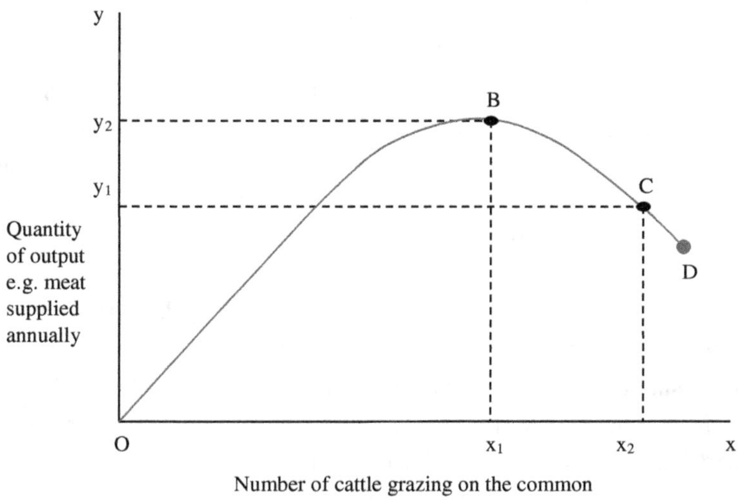

Fig. 4.2. Communal rules can help to raise the productivity of common property as this example illustrates.

In the past and in some places today, local communities devise rules for sharing the use of natural resources. For example, in the case of shared grazing land, the number of livestock that each household is allowed to graze may be limited by the local community. This can reduce the risks of overgrazing or overexploitation of the common resource. This is illustrated in Fig. 4.2. There curve *OBCD* represents total annual production (for example, of beef) obtained from grazing cattle on the village common as a function of the number of head of cattle allowed to graze. Annual beef production is at a maximum when x_1 head of cattle graze on the village common. In the absence of rules to limit the number of head of cattle grazing on the village common, open-access may result in x_2 head of cattle being allowed to graze on the village common. Consequently, the annual output from the cattle herd is y_1 rather than its maximum value, y_2. This is suboptimal if the villagers want to maximize their beef output from the village common. Communal rules which restrict the number of cattle grazing on the village common to x_1 will be collectively beneficial.

A variety of other communal rules may be adopted to increase the productivity of common property and contribute to its sustainability.

For example, harvesting of some shared natural resources may be restricted or banned seasonally, for instance the harvesting of wild animals during their breeding season may be banned. Despite this, there is no guarantee that communal rules for natural resource use will be socially optimal for sustaining levels of economic production and adding to economic wealth. Forms of governance and the type of rules adopted can vary greatly from community to community. Furthermore, the appropriateness of existing communal rules can alter with changing circumstances, such as increasing densities of human population and new technologies. Consider the case of shifting agriculture or slash-and-burn agriculture in Mizoram, India.

The Mizos in the state of Mizoram in Northeast India practiced slash-and-burn agriculture and some still do. In this agricultural system, the local community cultivates a patch of their land and once its fertility declines move on, clear and cultivate a new patch of forested land. The process is repeated and eventually the community returns to the original patch of land which in the meantime has become forested and has had its fertility restored. The village moves as a whole and families are allocated rights to land on each move by the drawing of lots. However, families have no permanent rights to that land. When the village returns to that site at a later time, each family may be allocated a different lot of land.

At low population densities, such an agricultural system is relatively sustainable. However, as the population of a community increases, the plots allocated to families may become smaller, agricultural production per family may decline and the period of time for which an area is fallowed may also decrease. In the latter case, restoration of soil fertility levels by fallowing is reduced and this also causes agricultural productivity to decline. The rate of soil erosion may also rise. In such circumstances, more settled agriculture involving permanent land rights and appropriate crops and cultivation techniques might be more productive and sustainable. While the Indian Government and the Government of Mizoram are encouraging a change from shifting to settled communal agricultural in Mizoram, the transition is not without its economic problems such as difficulties which local people have in predicting prices for agricultural produce (Tisdell, 1999, Chapter 15).

4.6. Open-Access Resources

4.6.1. *The nature of open-access resources*

In the most general case, open-access resources are resources available for use by all without any restriction on their utilization. While no individual property rights exist in the resource itself, any harvest from it normally becomes the private property of those who harvest or capture it. Very often, however, open-access to a resource is not available to all but only to a particular group. The particular group may consist of villagers living near the resource or those identified in some other way, such as those who purchase a license to exploit the resource. These are cases of "restricted" open-access. Many of the economic problems associated with an open-access resource tend to be less acute when the population able to access the resource is limited.

Resources may alter their ownership and management status with the passage of time. Resources may, for example, alter from being communal property (the use of which is closely governed by communal rules) to open-access property and vice-versa, or rights may alter from either of these situations to become private property. For example, forests in the Himalayan region of Nepal were once communal property and their use was regulated by local communities. Subsequently, these forests were put under the nominal control of the Forestry Department of Nepal headquartered in Katmandu. This department could not maintain effective control over distant forests. The result was that villagers obtained *de facto* open-access to the forests which became over exploited. Or to give another example, communal grazing lands in most of Europe eventually became private land as economic circumstances altered.

Let us consider economic shortcomings of complete open-access to resources bearing in mind that despite such shortcomings, open-access may still be the most economic way of using resources in some areas because communal control of the resources is too costly, or effective private property rights cannot be established economically (see Section 4.4).

4.6.2. *Inefficiency of open-access resource use — resource misallocation*

In a society where other resources are mostly private property and their use is determined by the market mechanism, too many resources are likely to be employed in exploiting an open-access resource. Too many resources are allocated to the exploitation of the open-access resource in the sense that it would be *possible* in principle to bring about a Paretian gain by allocating fewer resources to the exploitation of the shared resource and employing more of these elsewhere in the economy. The nature of their economic argument can be illustrated by means of Fig. 4.3.

In Fig. 4.3, it is assumed that one open-access resource (which might, for example, be a fishery, wildlife, a forest) is being exploited by

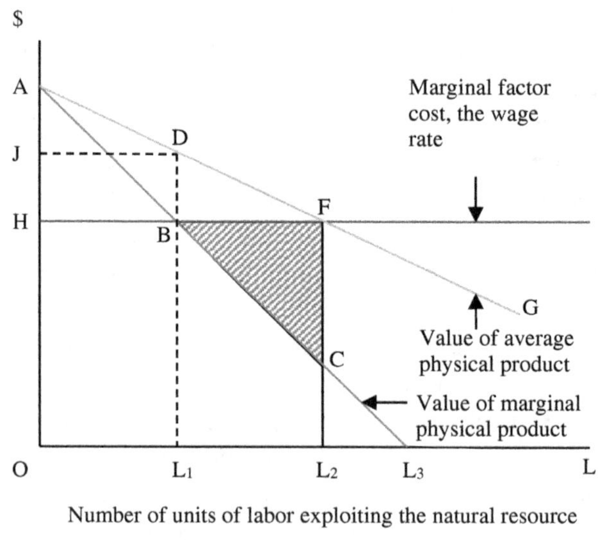

Fig. 4.3. An illustration that in a market economy, an excessive amount of mobile resources is used to exploit open-access resources.

a single variable resource, for example, labor. Each unit of labor may have a fixed quantity of capital which it employs in its harvesting of the open-access resource. Assume that the variable resource is labor and let L represent the quantity of labor used in harvesting the resource. Furthermore, suppose that the economy is a competitive market economy and that the supply of product harvested is insufficient to affect its market price. Consequently, the price of the product is a constant, p. In Fig. 4.3, line ABC represents the value of the *marginal* product of labor which is equal to the price of the product harvested times the marginal physical product of the labor involved in the harvest. Line ADF represents the value of the *average* product of labor. Line ABF indicates the marginal (factor) cost of labor and represents the wage rate that laborers can obtain if employed elsewhere in the economy. It is a measure of the marginal opportunity cost of employing labor to harvest the natural resource. This is because labor is assumed to be perfectly mobile in a perfect market economy and to be fully employed.

A growing amount of labor will be attracted to exploit the open-access resource as long as the value of its average product in doing this exceeds the going wage rate in the economy. Therefore, equilibrium in exploiting the open-access natural resource will be achieved when L_2 units of labor are employed in its exploitation. When this occurs, the value of the average product received by each unit of labor is just equal to the prevailing wage rate in the economy. This allocation is not, however, efficient from the point of view of economics. It does not minimize economic scarcity given the resources employed in this economy.

Economic scarcity will be minimized when L_1 of labor is used to exploit the natural resource. This is because at this level of employment of labor the value placed on the extra production of product obtained from the employment of the last unit of labor exploiting the natural resource just equals the value of the extra contribution to production which it could make if employed elsewhere in the economy. If open-access occurs and L_2 of labor is employed in exploiting the open-access resource, the total loss in value of production for the economy as a whole is equivalent to the area of the hatched triangle

BFC in Fig. 4.3. The excessive amount of labor used in exploiting the open-access resource is equal to $L_2 - L_1$.

Note that it is not always the case that labor is perfectly mobile or fully employed. This assumption may not hold in all regions in developing and transitional economies, for example. This case is discussed below. Observe also that if the employment of labor in exploiting the natural resource is reduced from L_2 to L_1, this will eventually raise the average product of labor employed in exploiting the natural resources from *OH* to *OJ*. However, this adjustment will not be instantaneous because some time is required for natural ecosystems to adjust to reduced harvesting pressure.

4.6.3. *Failure to achieve adequate conservation of natural resources when there is open-access*

When open-access to natural resources occurs, users of these resources have no incentive to take into account the user costs of exploiting them, that is the future benefits that might be obtained by conserving these resources. This is because an individual who conserves an open-access resource in order to maintain or increase its future productivity has to share that gain with all other users of it and indeed, may obtain no benefit at all. Consequently, as discussed in Section 3.3.2 and as illustrated by Fig. 3.1, only current benefits from resource use are taken into account by resource users. If marginal user costs are positive, this behavior will not be economically optimal from a social point of view. On the other hand, if the number of persons exploiting the resource is low relative to its abundance (as could have been the case in some early subsistence communities), the user cost associated with open-access to the natural resource can be negligible. The economic cost of this failure would then be low. But as societies grow and develop and the rate of exploitation of an open-access natural resource increases, the user costs associated with exploitation of the resource are likely to grow in magnitude. One, therefore, expects this type of economic failure to be a more serious problem in modern economies than in “primitive” societies in which population densities and capital accumulation are low, and technologies are little developed.

4.6.4. *Perverse responses to market signals and biodiversity loss as a result of open-access*

Under normal market conditions, a rise in the demand for a product increases its supply. However, when open-access to a resource occurs, rising demand for the product derived from the open-access resource can reduce its supply. In the case of a renewable biological resource, such as fish, open-access can result in its population and biomass being reduced to such an extent that as demand for the product obtained from it rises, its supply falls and at sufficiently high levels of demand, the population of a harvested species may be so greatly reduced that the survival of the species is endangered. This can be illustrated by Fig. 4.4.

In Fig. 4.4, the curve SE_1E_2S represents the supply of a product, for example, fish, obtained from an open-access resource. This supply curve is backward bending. As attempts are made to increase the supply from the open-access resource, this eventually reduces the stock or population of the biological resource and consequently the biomass of the resource available for harvest. For example, when the demand for

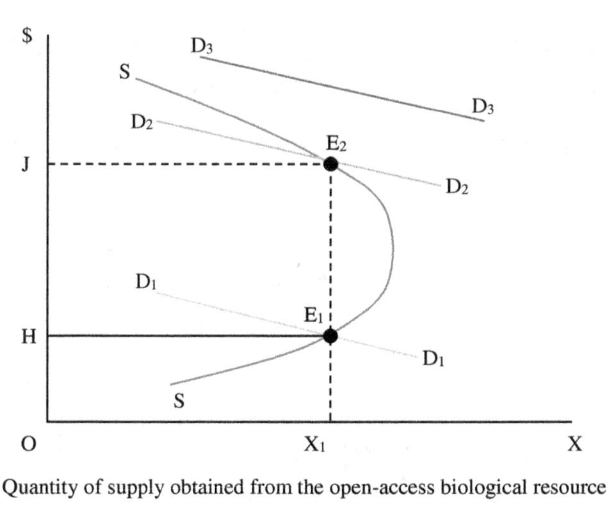

Fig. 4.4. In the case of an open-access biological resource, increasing demand for its product may eventually reduce its supply and therefore the continuing existence of the resource. This perverse response is illustrated by use of this diagram.

the produce from the renewable open-access resource is D_1D_1, market equilibrium (given the situation illustrated in Fig. 4.4) is established at E_1 and X_1 of the product is supplied. If market demand rises to D_2D_2 a new market equilibrium is established at E_2. In this particular case, there is no increase in supply because the extra harvesting effort reduces the biomass of the resource. The same level of supply is achieved before and after the increased harvesting effort but at a high per-unit cost of supply, namely a cost per unit of OJ rather than OH.

If the demand curve in Fig. 4.4 shifts upward so that it is above D_2D_2 but still cuts the supply curve SE_1E_2S, the equilibrium supply of the harvested product actually falls. It can also happen in such a case that the population level of the species harvested falls to such a low level that it is unable to sustain its population. Hence, the species becomes extinct. Furthermore, extinction of the species is bound to occur if the demand curve is above the supply curve, for instance is the one shown by D_3D_3 in Fig. 4.4. In such cases, supply of the product eventually ceases altogether even if demand for it is high and sustained. This would not be so if the resource were private property because the user costs would be taken into account.

4.6.5. *Another perspective on the over exploitation of natural resources when open-access occurs*

When there is open-access to a natural resource, it may be over exploited in at least two senses:

(1) greater effort may be put into harvesting the resource that maximizes economic benefit or yield and
(2) the harvesting effort may be so great that a yield lower than the biological yield is obtained.

Figure 4.5 can be used to illustrate these points.

In Fig. 4.5, the curve *OABD* represents the yield (supply), x, available on a sustainable basis from a renewable biological resource as a function of the amount of effort, L, expended in harvesting it. For example, it might be the sustainable quantity of the harvest of wild fish. As effort in harvesting a renewable biological resource (or species)

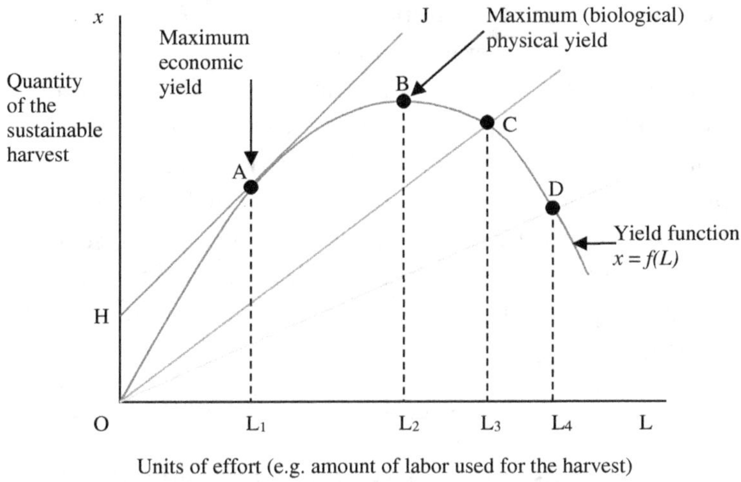

Fig. 4.5. This figure is used to illustrate the point that when there is open-access to a biological resource, it is unlikely to be utilized in a way which maximizes its economic yield. Furthermore, depending on the circumstances, the amount of effort expended in harvesting the resource may exceed (or be less than) that which maximizes the biological (physical) yield of the resource.

increases, its population tends to fall. At first, this effort is associated with an increase in the total sustainable yield of the species but yield levels fall at high levels of exploitation. Curve *OABD* can also be regarded as a sustainable production function. At high levels of effort, the population level of the harvested species declines, a slower rate of growth of the population of the species eventuates and the lower density of its population contribute to a decline in this production function.

The maximum economic yield from a renewable biological resource and the most economical amount of effort to expend in exploiting it is normally less than that which maximizes the maximum physical yield from the resource. The divergence can be expected to increase in size, other things held constant, the higher is the marginal opportunity cost of employing mobile resources to harvest the open-access resource. Only when the marginal opportunity cost of the mobile resources employed in harvesting the natural resource is zero will the maximum economic yield and the maximum physical yield of harvesting coincide.

In order to illustrate this suppose a perfect market economy and a local community that is supplying the harvest from a natural biological resource to the market. Suppose that the supply of the harvest from the local community is insufficient to influence the price of the product. Let the market price of the harvested product be represented by p and let w represent the opportunity cost (income available elsewhere) to the local community employing its resource (labor) to harvest the natural resource. Then if the local community wants to maximize its economic benefit from harvesting the natural resource, it should maximize its net profit function,

$$\pi = px - wL \tag{4.1}$$

(where L represents its units of harvesting effort and π is its net profit) subject to its yield from utilizing the natural resource (its production function)

$$x = f(L). \tag{4.2}$$

The necessary condition for this to be at a maximum is that

$$p\frac{df}{dl} = w \tag{4.3}$$

which implies that the value of the marginal product of L (which also equals its marginal revenue product in this case) be equal to its marginal opportunity cost, that is the level of income which a marginal unit of L can earn if employed elsewhere in the economy. For simplicity, this is assumed to be constant. This result accords with the case illustrated in Fig. 4.3, where L_1 of labor satisfies the necessary condition for maximizing economic benefit from harvesting the relevant natural resource. Rearranging Eq. 4.3 (dividing each side by p), the necessary condition for maximum economic benefit can be re-expressed as

$$\frac{df}{dL} = \frac{w}{p} \tag{4.4}$$

This implies that the marginal productivity of labor in harvesting the natural resource should be equal to the real wage rate which it could earn if employed elsewhere in the economy, that is the real opportunity cost of the labor employed in harvesting the natural resource.

The economic optimum can be illustrated using Fig. 4.5. The profit or benefit which the local community obtains for exploiting the natural resource is equivalent to

$$\pi = px - wL, \tag{4.5}$$

which can be represented by a series of parallel lines in Fig. 4.5. Each of these lines shows combinations of L and x which result in the same level of economic benefit or profit and can be described as isoprofit lines. For example, the isoprofit line corresponding to a profit of π° would be

$$\pi^{\circ} = p - wL. \tag{4.6}$$

Rearranging this equation, it can be expressed as

$$x = \frac{\pi^{\circ}}{p} + \frac{w}{p}L. \tag{4.7}$$

Thus, it has a positive slope of $\frac{w}{p}$ and its intercept is $\frac{\pi^{\circ}}{p}$. Therefore, it has a steeper slope the greater is the opportunity cost of labor. Higher isoprofit lines correspond to a higher level of profit. If economic profit is to be maximized, the local community should expand its amount of effort in harvesting its natural resources until it reaches its highest attainable isoprofit line. However, this attainability is constrained by the yield or production function governing the harvest.

In the particular situation illustrated by Fig. 4.5, line *HJ* is the community's highest attainable isoprofit line. This is tangential to its yield or production function at point A. At this point, the slope of the isoprofit line, $\frac{w}{p}$, is equal to the slope of the yield function, $\frac{dx}{dl}$ and thus the necessary condition for the maximization of profit, specified in Eq. (4.4) is satisfied. Note that *HJ* is one of a series of parallel isoprofit lines, the remainder of which are not shown on Fig. 4.5.

Given this analysis, several consequences can be noted. First, the lower is the opportunity cost of labor (or effort expended) in harvesting the natural resource, the smaller is the slope of the isoprofit lines. This makes it economic to expend a larger amount of effort in exploiting the natural resource. Conversely, other things remaining constant, the greater is the marginal opportunity cost of labor or effort, the smaller is the optimal amount of economic effort for harvesting the natural resource. Thus, if an economy develops and the comparative earnings available to labor elsewhere in the economy rise, this will reduce the most economic amount of effort to expend in exploiting the natural resource, other things remaining constant. Only if the opportunity cost of labor (or effort) employed in exploiting the natural resource is zero will the maximum economic yield coincide with the maximum biological yield. In such a case, the isoprofit lines are all horizontal and the highest attainable one in Fig. 4.5 would be one tangential to the yield function at point B.

Should there be open-access to the natural resource under consideration, the equilibrium quantity of labor employed in harvesting the natural resource will be one which equates the value of its average product to the wage rate assuming perfect mobility of labor (see the discussion relating to Fig. 4.3) this implies in mathematical terms that

$$w = \frac{pf(L)}{L} \tag{4.8}$$

or rearranging, that

$$\frac{w}{p} = \frac{f(L)}{L} \tag{4.9}$$

For example, in Fig. 4.5 let line *OD* represent the total output (x) required to provide each unit of labor employed in harvesting the natural resource with the same level of average income as its available income elsewhere in the economy. This line has a slope of $\frac{w}{p}$. In this case, when L_4 of labor is employed in harvesting the natural resource, the average product available to labor is just equal to that available elsewhere in the economy. *D* is the equilibrium level of employment in harvesting the natural resource given open-access. Should L be less than L_4, then the average product of labor would be higher in harvesting the natural resource than elsewhere in the economy and this would encourage more labor to be used in harvesting the resources. Conversely, if more than L_4 of L is employed in harvesting the natural resource, its average product would be lower than elsewhere in the economy. Hence, there would be a reduction in the amount of labor allocated to harvesting the natural resource. This demonstrates that point *D* corresponds to the equilibrium in this open-access case.

Observe that in this case open-access results in the natural resources being over exploited from two points of view: (1) the amount of harvesting effort results in the yield being less than the maximum biological yield; and (2) effort is greater than that which maximizes economic yield. Note that as $\frac{w}{p}$ increases (as the level of real income available elsewhere in the economy rises), effort expended in exploiting the natural resource falls, other things remaining constant, and the extent of over exploitation is reduced. For example, if the opportunity income line rises from *OD* to *OC*, the quantity of labor employed in exploiting the natural resource falls from L_4 to L_3. Thus, if as a result of economic development, incomes to be earned elsewhere in the economy rise significantly, this may reduce effort put into harvesting open-access natural resources. This, however, depends on the assumption that other things remain constant. If, for instance, new technologies reduce the cost of the harvesting of the open-access resource (see for example, Tisdell, 2005, Chapter 6) or if the demand for its harvest rises, over exploitation of the natural resource could actually increase as economic development proceeds.

Observe that open-access to a biological natural resource does not always result in the amount of effort allocated to harvesting it being greater than that which maximizes its biological yield. For example, if the average level of income is sufficiently high elsewhere in the economy, a line (or ray) similar to *OC* may be so steep that it intersects the yield function between points *A*and *B* in Fig. 4.5. Consequently, effort given to harvesting the open-access resource will be less than that maximizing biological yield.

4.6.6. *Limitations in applying this model in less developed countries*

The above theory of the use of open-access resources assumes a competitive market system in which variable factors of production are completely mobile and fully employed. If the mobility of factors of production, such as labor, is limited, this restricts the applicability of this theory. In some developing regions, labor may find it difficult or impossible to find employment other than by relying on the harvesting of a local open-access resource, the harvest of which might be used primarily for subsistence purposes.

In such circumstances, the supply of effort involved in harvesting a local open-access resource can be expected to depend on the level of population of the local region or community involved. To model this situation, it is necessary to take account of the dynamics of human population growth in the focal region. For example, there may be a tendency for the population in the region to increase provided that the income per capita of residents is above a minimum "satisfactory" level. In some cases, this might be a subsistence level and the population growth theory of Malthus (1798) could apply. Malthus predicted that human population would tend to increase if its income per capita exceeded subsistence level.

In relation to Fig. 4.5, the "satisfactory" subsistence level of per capita income might correspond to the slope of line *OD*. In these circumstances, suppose that the amount of labor used in harvesting an open-access resource in a region is proportional to the region's population. Assume that initially, the amount of labor harvesting the open-access resource is L_1. This results in a level of per capita income higher than the subsistence level: the slope of line passing through points *O* and *A* is greater than the slope of *OD*. Population in the region therefore, increases. As it does so, per capita income falls. Population in the region will continue to increase until L_4 of labor is involved in harvesting the open-access resource and income per head is reduced to subsistence level.

Note that given the situation illustrated in Fig. 4.5, the level of equilibrium effort, L_4, exceeds that which maximizes biological yield. Production could be increased in the long-term by reducing effort from L_4 to L_2. However, this result is not easy to achieve because it takes time for the stock of a harvested biological resource to adjust to the reduced harvesting pressure. Consequently, if initially the local community is in equilibrium at *D*, reduced harvesting effort is likely to depress the per capita income of the community below subsistence level. Such a policy may, therefore, not be practical. To reach point *B*, policies to reduce effort have to be implemented before point *D* is reached. Otherwise the community becomes trapped at point *D*. (see Tisdell, 2007). Furthermore, if effort is reduced to or limited to L_2 and Malthus' theory holds, the level of population in the local region could *still* rise until income falls to subsistence level. The output corresponding to *B* makes a larger level of subsistence population possible than the output corresponding to *D* if output is equally shared amongst members of the population. In that case, even situation *B* might not be socially all that advantageous compared to situation *D* because eventually population growth fritters away its advantages in raising per capita income. If, however, human population growth can be limited or the acceptable level of per capita income in the local community increases as output rises, increased per capita income will not be dissipated by population growth.

The above discussion makes it clear that the type of model used to analyze the consequences of open-access to biological resources in market economies with considerable mobility of labor are not always appropriate for analysis in less developed regions where mobility of labor can be limited. This has important policy consequences.

4.6.7. *Other economic failures associated with open-access resources*

Additional economic failures (some of which were mentioned previously) can occur when there is open-access to biological resources. There is no economic incentive for individuals to undertake investment which may increase the future productivity of the resource because any benefit will have to be shared with everyone else having access to the resource. Secondly, there is no incentive for individuals to avoid incidental damage when harvesting these resources even when this reduces the future productivity of the biological resources. Thirdly, when there is open-access to a biological resource, technological changes which increases the harvest rate in relation to effort can accelerate the over exploitation of the resources and may lead to it being extinguished

(Tisdell, 2005, Chapter 6). In Fig. 4.5, for example, suppose that L_1 units of labor are harvesting the biological resources. Suppose the technological change increases the catch rate so that the amount of effort with the new technique is equivalent to an increase in the amount of labor employed with the previous technique. If this is equivalent to an increase in the amount of labor by $L_2 - L_1$ or less; the total catch rate rises. However, if the equivalent increase in labor is greater than $L_2 - L_2$, total output starts to fall — the greater the increase in the catch rate, the more likely is the catch per unit of labor likely to fall in the long-run. For example, if the productivity increase is equivalent to an increase in the quantity of labor by $L_4 - L_1$, catch or harvest per unit of labor actually falls as a result of technological change. This would not occur if the resource was private property.

4.7. The Taking of Property Rights and Natural Resource Interests

The extent to which private property rights contribute to the achievement of economic efficiency in resource allocation and fosters wealth creation depends on the security of these rights. The more likely these rights are to be taken away by the state or by others without compensation or adequate recompense, the more likely will this result in the inefficient use of resources and deficiencies in their conservation. For example, if there is a risk that private property will be restricted in its use in the future or taken away from its owner, this lowers the expected benefit from conserving it for future use unless adequate compensation is assured. Nevertheless, in some special cases, generous state compensation for the taking of private property rights can result in behavior by property owners that is not Paretian optimal (see for example, Pitchford and Snyder, 2003).

In most countries, the state has the right to seize a person's private property but usually must pay compensation for such seizure and the seizure normally must be in the public interest. This is described as the exercise of *eminent domain* in the United States, compulsory purchase in the United Kingdom, New Zealand and the Republic of Ireland, compulsory acquisition in Australia and expropriation in South Africa and Canada (Anon, n.d.). Procedures for such acquisition, the determination of what is to be paid by way of compensation, and decisions about what constitutes the public interest vary by jurisdictions. It might be argued that just compensation for the taking of private property should be the payment of its market value. However, in many cases the owner may value the property at greater than its market value and suffer economic inconvenience and extra transaction costs by the expropriation of his/her property. This is recognized in Canadian legislation governing such matters (Anon, n.d.).

Sometimes, however, property rights are taken by the state but the title to the property is not transferred to the state. For example, restrictions may be imposed on the way in which private property can be used or on the parties to whom it can be transferred. Environmental regulations usually restrict the way that private property can be utilized and thus, take away some pre-existing rights of owners. For example, the introduction of state restrictions on the clearing of trees or other vegetation on privately owned land in Australia reduces the pre-existing rights of landholders in the use of their land. Such restrictions are usually seen as being in the public interest, and owners of the property involved are often not compensated for the loss of these rights. On other occasions, resource-owners may be partially compensated for a change in their property rights due to environmental regulations by issuing them with tradable pollution permits or resource-use rights; a process described as "godfathering". This is discussed in the next chapter.

If the taking of private property rights by the state is frequent, not very predictable and does not provide just compensation to property owners, it weakens the economic incentive of private persons to accumulate wealth. Consequently, it adds to economic scarcity and is ethically undesirable given Posner's point of view (Posner, 1981, 1985).

Rental of natural resources, such as land, can also have a negative effect on their use and conservation, particularly if the period of rental is short and uncertainty exists about whether a lease will be renewed and on what terms. Uncertainty about renewal of leases by Indian Fijian farmers of land owned by Indigenous Fijians has, for instance, led to reduced investment in leased agricultural land and has contributed to its degradation (Prasad and Tisdell, 2006).

Whether or not compensation should be paid for the taking of natural resource results is a complex matter. It has, however, become an increasingly important issue with the establishment of additional protected areas by the state, the introduction of new environmental regulations, and the resumption by the state of land for public use. These actions appropriate natural resources or restrict private property rights. Some of the principles and practices involved in the taking of natural resources, interests are discussed in Tisdell and Harrison (1999) and Seidl *et al.* (2002).

4.8. Concluding Comments

Private property rights underpin the operation of modern capitalist market economies. They have important implications for the efficiency of resource allocation and economic growth. Nevertheless, even in these economies, private property rights are restricted to a considerable extent by the state and shared property rights are more prevalent than is usually recognized. In practice, it is very difficult to satisfy fully the conditions or attributes associated with private property.

Although in some circumstances, the presence of private property promotes economic efficiency and growth, the creation and maintenance of private property rights is not costless and its creation is not economic in all circumstances. In practice, there is no single form of property rights that is economically ideal in all circumstances. This is why a mixture of systems of property rights exists in most societies. Although the absence of property rights, as illustrated in the case of open-access resources, can have several adverse economic consequences, sometimes no better system of resource use is attainable. Furthermore, at low levels of economic development, including low levels of utilization of open-access resources, no pronounced economic failures may occur from lack of property rights. However, as economic growth gathers pace, economic failures associated with the use of open-access resources and adverse externalities are liable to become more serious and are likely to require state or communal regulation. Such regulation is the focus of the next chapter.

4.9. Keywords

Common property; eminent domain; inefficiency of open-access resource use; open-access resources; principal-agent problem; private property; Protestant ethic; Posner's theory of justice; Rawls's theory of justice; resource endowments; the taking of natural resource rights; the taking of private property rights; wealth maximization.

4.10. Questions for Review and Discussion

1. Posner argues "that a transaction or other change in the use or ownership of resources is good if it increases the wealth of society". Do you agree that society should be organized in a way that maximizes the creation of wealth?
2. Taking into account Posner's principle of wealth maximization, does it follow that wealthier individuals are more virtuous than poorer individuals? Consider the arguments for and against this view taking into account the matter of initial endowments of resources available to individuals as discussed, for example, by A.K. Sen and John Rawls.
3. Outline the conditions that are required for a complete and strong set of private property rights. Why does this set constitute an extreme possibility?
4. Why is the presence of a system of private property in society believed to contribute to the efficient operation of markets and to stimulate economic growth, that is wealth maximization in Posner's terms? Also consider the view that such a system does not result in perfect economic performance.
5. "The creation and improvement of private property rights in resources is not costless". Discuss and consider the economics of creating private property. Why are social attitudes and the way

in which the legal system operates significantly influences on the economics of the creation of private property?

6. In modern societies, the exercise of private property rights is limited by principal–agent problems. Explain paying particular attention to the evolution of public companies. Could the evolution of such companies have adverse environmental consequences? Explain.
7. What is common property? Does it exist in modern economies? Give examples.
8. Explain how communal rules for the use of common property, such as communal grazing land, can be used to maintain its productivity.
9. Communal rules for the use of natural resources are often slow to adapt to changing circumstances, and do not always ensure economic sustainability. Discuss and give examples.
10. What is an open-access resource? Give some examples. Outline in basic terms the types of economic failures that can occur in market economies when there is open-access to biological resources.
11. Explain why in a market economy too many mobile resources will be allocated to harvesting an open-access biological resource. Use a diagram to illustrate this.
12. When there is open-access to a resource, the future benefits forgone from its current use (that is user costs) are ignored. Explain why and outline some of the possible consequences of this.
13. When there is open-access to a resource, the market system can operate in a perverse way. The stock of the resource can be depleted even though the future value of conserving it is extremely high. The system is not favorable to economic sustainability and to the conservation of biodiversity. Explain.
14. The economic theory of the utilization of open-access resources developed for economies in which labor and similar resources are mobile is not applicable to all less developed regions. Discuss and elaborate on this view.
15. When there is open-access to a biological resource, technological change that increases this harvest rate in relation to effort may add to economic scarcity. Explain.

16. In all countries, the state is able to take away private property rights. To what extent can the taking of such rights be justified on economic grounds? Do you think that the taking of such rights should be used sparingly? Why?
17. It is becoming more common for governments to take away a portion of pre-existing private property rights (often for environmental reasons) rather than compulsorily acquiring or expropriating real property. Give examples. To what extent should property owners be compensated for this? What economic arguments may be used to support such restrictions on the use of private property?
18. Sometimes when governments take away access to natural resources which are not private property or restrict such access, they pay compensation to the parties adversely affected or provide adjustment assistance. Give an example. Why might this action be taken?
19. It has been shown that open-access to natural resources can create economic problems. Nevertheless, there are circumstances in which open-access constitutes the most economic available way of utilizing resources. Even in modern economics, there is much common property and property to which there is relatively open-access. Discuss.

Readings and References

Anon (n.d.). *Eminent domain*, Wikipedia, https://en.wikipedia.org/wiki/Eminent_domain [accessed 27 May 2020].

Clark, J.M. (1940). Towards a concept of workable competition, *American Economic Review*, 30, 241–256. doi: https://www.jstor.org/stable/1807048.

Hayek, F.A. von (1948). *Individualism and Economic Order*, Chicago University Press, Chicago, IL.

Hayek, F.A. von (1982). *Law, Legislation and Liberty: A New Statement of the Liberal Principles of Justice and Political Economy*, Routledge and Kegan Paul, London.

Hayek, F.A. von (1994). *The Road to Serfdom*, 50th Anniversary edn. University of Chicago Press, Chicago.

Malthus, T.R. (1798). *An Essay on the Principle of Population as it Effects the Future Improvement of Mankind*, J. Johnson, London. Reprint 1976, Norton, New York.

Marris, R. (1964). *The Economic Theory of Managerial Capitalism*, Macmillan, London.

Marshall, A. (1920). *Principles of Economics*, 8th edn. Macmillan, London. (1st edn. 1871).

Pitchford, R. and C.M. Snyder (2003). Coming to the nuisance: An economic analysis from an incomplete contracts perspective, *Journal of Law, Economics, & Organization*, 19, 491–516. doi: 10.1093/jleo/ewg018.

Posner, R.A. (1981). *The Economics of Justice*, Harvard University Press, Cambridge, MA, and London, UK.

Posner, R.A. (1985). Wealth maximization revisited, *Notre Dame Journal of Law, Ethics and Public Policy*, 2, 85–105. Reprinted in R. A. Posner and F. Parisi (2000). *The Economic Structure of the Law*. Edward Elgar, Cheltenham, UK and Northampton, MA, USA.

Posner, R.A. (1987). The justice of economics, *Economica delle Scelte Pubbliche*, 15–25.

Prasad, B. and C.A. Tisdell (2006). *Institutions, Economic Performances and Sustainable Development: A Case Study of the Fiji Islands*, Nova Science Publishers, New York.

Rawls, J.R. (1971). *A Theory of Justice*, Harvard University Press, Cambridge, MA, USA.

Seidl, I., C.A. Tisdell and S. Harrison (2002). Environmental regulation of land use and public compensation: Principles, and Swiss and Australian examples, *Environment and Planning C: Government and Policy* 20, 699–716. doi: https://doi.org/10.1068%2Fc01103s.

Sen, A.K. (1981). *Poverty and Famines: An Essay on Entitlement and Deprivation*, Clarendon Press, Oxford.

Tietenberg, T. and L. Lewis (2018). *Environmental and Natural Resource Economics*, 11th edn. Routledge, New York and Abingdon, Oxon, UK.

Tisdell, C.A. (1990). *Natural Resources, Growth and Development*, Praeger, New York, Westport CT and London.

Tisdell, C.A. (1996). *Bounded Rationality and Economic Evolution*, Edward Elgar, Cheltenham, UK and Brookfield, VT, USA.

Tisdell, C.A. (1999). *Biodiversity, Conservation and Sustainable Development*, Edward Elgar, Cheltenham, UK and Northampton, MA, USA.

Tisdell, C.A. (2002). *The Economics of Conserving Wildlife and Natural Areas*, Edward Elgar, Cheltenham, UK and Northampton, MA, USA. [Chapter 8].

Tisdell, C.A. (2005). *Economics of Environmental Conservation*, 2nd edn. Edward Elgar, Cheltenham, UK and Northampton, MA, USA. [Chapters 3 and 6].

Tisdell, C.A. (2007). Poverty, political failure and the use of open-access resources in developing countries. In C.A. Tisdell (Ed.) *Poverty, Poverty Alleviation and Social Disadvantage*, 193–202. Serials Publication, New Delhi.

Tisdell, C.A. and S. Harrison (1999). Compensation for taking of natural resource interests: Principles and practices in recent Queensland cases, *Australian Journal of Environmental Management*, 6, 99–108.

Tisdell, C.A. and K. Hartley (2008). *Microeconomic Policy: A New Perspective*, Edward Elgar, Cheltenham, UK and Northampton, MA, USA.

Weber, M. (1930). *The Protestant Ethic and the Spirit of Capitalism*, T. Parsons [trans.], George Allen and Unwin, London.

Chapter 5

Regulating Natural Resource Use and Pollution Emissions

5.1. Introduction

As was demonstrated in the previous chapter, free market systems are unlikely to minimize economic scarcity when any of the following circumstances arise:

(1) there is open-access to natural resources;
(2) environmental spillovers (externalities) are generated by economic activity;
(3) environmental actions result in the supply of a public good or a bad; or
(4) mixed goods are the subject of economic activity.

In such circumstances, governments may be able to reduce economic scarcity by intervening in the operation of the economic system. The purpose of this chapter is to outline and assess methods that may be used by governments to control natural resource use, including the emission of wastes into natural environments or into environments external to economic entities. The assessments made focus primarily on the likely effectiveness of different methods of government interventions in reducing economic scarcity bearing in mind that scarcity reduction is the central focus of the science of economics.

Major types of regulations governing pollution emissions will be discussed in turn. These are taxes or charges on pollution emissions or resource use, tradable permits, subsidies related to resource use, property rights, zoning and administrative rules governing pollution and resource use. The applicability of similar regulations to the management of open-access resources is then considered.

Most economic activities result in pollution emissions or the production of wastes that require disposal. These wastes can take a variety of forms. For example, they may consist of gases, liquids or solids or be in other forms, such as radiation. In the past, such wastes were often discharged into or disposed of in environments to which there was open-access such as air bodies, water bodies (streams, lakes and the sea) and "wastelands" (such as unoccupied wetlands) with little control. While this still occurs in some geographical areas for some wastes, government regulations now control the disposal of many wastes and the extent of this regulation has increased in recent decades. With further economic development globally, the extent of government regulation of the use of environments external to individual economic entities can be expected to increase. For example, concerns about global warming are likely to result in greater government regulation of greenhouse gas emissions worldwide.

There are many different measures that governments can adopt to regulate the disposal of pollutants and wastes. These vary in their economic consequences, efficiency and practicality as well as their political acceptability. No single method of regulation of environmental externalities or spillovers is ideal for all situations. The "best" method of control varies with the circumstances, and requires account to be taken of enforcement and monitoring costs, the geographical spread of the pollutants created by the disposal of wastes plus other factors such as the longevity of the pollutants. Individual cases involving the disposal of wastes can be very complex. The coverage of the alternative methods of environmental regulation given in this chapter is based on simplified models and therefore, should be regarded as introductory.

5.2. Taxes or Charges on Pollution Emissions and on Waste Disposal

5.2.1. *A simple model*

The possibility of controlling pollution by means of taxes on the output of products the production of which causes the emission of pollutants and the alternative of imposing taxes or charges directly on the emissions themselves was raised in Chapter 3. Other things remaining equal, such as monitoring and enforcement costs, it was concluded that it is usually more efficient to impose taxes or charges on the emissions themselves rather than to regulate these indirectly by imposing taxes on the production of a product that generates such emissions. Let us consider more carefully the use of taxes or charges to control pollution emissions or the disposal of wastes. Figure 5.1 provides a useful basis for the discussion. In this figure, line *ABD* shows the marginal economic benefit that producers (or those involved in an economic activity) can obtain from being able to use the external environment as means to get rid of pollutants or wastes. Alternatively, if reductions in emissions commencing at point *D* are considered, it indicates that the additional cost producers will incur if they are forced to curtail their emissions. The line *OBC* indicates the marginal economic costs imposed on those who suffer as a result of the pollution emissions or wastes disposed of externally. At point *B* in Fig. 5.1, the private marginal benefits from being able to pollute just equals the marginal external cost of the pollution generated. Thus, the emission of x_1 units of waste per period of time is socially optimal from an economic point of view. At this level of emissions, the *net* social marginal cost of emissions is zero. In the absence of any mechanism to regulate emissions, polluters will ignore the external costs of their activities and emit x_2 units of waste per period of time. This is a socially excessive amount and results in a social deadweight economic loss equivalent to the dotted area of triangle *BDC*. The area of this triangle represents the amount by which the costs imposed on the victims of the pollution exceeds the economic benefits obtained by those generating the pollution.

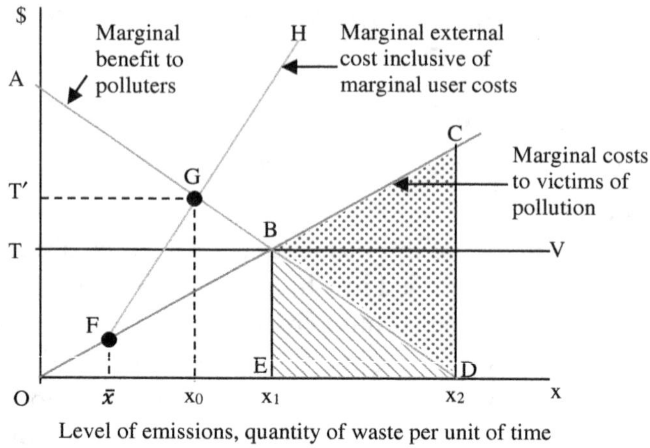

Fig. 5.1. A simple illustration of the use of taxes or charges on pollution emissions or waste disposal as an environmental control.

Note that from the point of view of maximizing aggregate economic wealth, it is not optimal to ban all pollution emissions in the case illustrated. In the case shown, banning emissions would result in an aggregate economic loss of an amount equivalent to the area of triangle *OBA* compared with the level of emission of x_1. Nevertheless, there could be some substances that are so dangerous that their external costs exceed their private benefits for any level of emissions. In such cases, banning their emissions or disposal to shared environments would maximize aggregate economic benefit. The appropriate policy depends on the nature and degree of external damages caused by the pollutants or wastes.

For the type of situation illustrated in Fig. 5.1, the socially "optimal" level of pollution emissions can in principle be achieved by imposing a tax or charge of OT on each unit of the waste or pollutant emitted. As a result, the marginal cost to polluters of emitting the pollutant after the imposition of the emissions tax is as shown by the line TV. Consequently, at point *B*, the marginal benefits that polluters obtain from being able to pollute (*ABD*) just equal their marginal cost of polluting (TV) and profit maximization motivates polluters to emit x_1 of the pollutant per period of time.

This is, however, a highly simplified model even though it is widely used in discussing this topic. Let us consider ways in which the model may have to be varied to accord more closely with reality.

5.2.2. *Limitations of the simple model and their policy consequences*

The simple model shown in Fig. 5.1 has several limitations, which not only affect the economic efficiency of taxes or charges as regulators of environmental use but also limit the efficiency of using other instruments for environmental regulation.

5.2.2.1. *Lack of attention to dynamics and user costs*

Firstly, it should be noted that the model shown in Fig. 5.1 is a static single-period one. In a dynamic context, it may be interpreted as a repetitive model. However, each sequence in the repetition is not linked to the past but is independent of the past. Consequently, it is only the emissions of the current period that influence external costs. This may be because these emissions are absorbed or neutralized by external environments during each period before the next begins. In some cases, however, stocks of pollutants accumulate, particularly when they exceed thresholds beyond which they can no longer be neutralized by external environments, as has happened with the emission of greenhouse gases. This might be allowed for in principle by adding a component to represent marginal external user costs to line *OBC* in Fig. 5.1. For example, if $\bar{x}$ is the level of emissions at which future environmental costs start to be incurred, the external marginal cost of emissions might then be as shown by the kinked relationship *OFGH*. The level of emissions x_0 rather than x_1 would then be socially optimal given that aggregate economic benefits are to be maximized. The higher are the future environmental costs from the pollution emissions, the lower ought to be their allowed level. In the case illustrated in Fig. 5.1, a higher tax rate than *OT*, namely *OT*′, is optimal when account is taken of the marginal user costs generated by the emissions. On the other hand, if user costs do not "kick-in" until the level of emissions exceeds x_1 per period; the "optimal" economic solution is unaltered.

With growing demand to use natural or external environments as sinks for waste disposal, the line *ABD* may shift upward and reach the region where marginal user costs become of serious concern. This appears to have happened for the emission of greenhouse gases, particularly carbon dioxide. If there are low levels of global emissions of greenhouse gases, user costs associated with these emissions may be zero or small.

5.2.2.2. *External environmental impacts modeled as a global or localized pure public bad*

The model illustrated by Fig. 5.1 assumes that the pollution or waste emissions enter a common pool from which no potential victims of the pollution are able to be excluded and that the biophysical external impacts are the same no matter from which geographical location the emissions enter the pool. This may be approximately true for some environmental impacts either globally or locally. For example, carbon dioxide emissions are usually seen as a global economic bad. Or to give another example, the emissions of liquid wastes into lakes, like Lake Biwa in Japan, which disperse evenly throughout the lake, might be modeled as a localized public bad.

In such cases, it has been argued that uniform taxes or charges on each unit of the emissions are economically efficient because they minimize the aggregate cost of limiting allowed emissions (Tisdell, 1993, Chapter 4). This is because each polluter equates its marginal benefit of polluting (or its marginal cost of reducing its emissions) to the *same* tax rate or emission charge. This coincidentally results in the marginal cost of reducing pollution emissions being made equal for all. A necessary mathematical condition for minimizing the aggregate cost of reducing pollution emissions is that the marginal cost of reducing pollution emissions be equal for all polluters. This is often portrayed as a positive feature of the use of an economic price mechanism for controlling pollution emissions. Such price mechanisms include uniform taxes or charges on emissions, as do some systems of tradable pollution permits or resource-use rights to be discussed later in this chapter. However, this favorable characteristic depends on the *common pool assumption* for the disposal of emissions being satisfied, or nearly satisfied. In practice, many situations can occur in which this assumption is not satisfied and this complicates environmental regulation.

Cases arise, for example, where the external effects of pollution emissions depend on the location of their source relative to the possible victims of the pollution. For example, the noise pollution from an airport or road will depend upon where it is located relative to the residents who are likely to be adversely affected by it. Or, if a pollutant is emitted into an air stream or flowing water, its external impacts can vary with the geographical location where it is emitted. For example, if prevailing air flows carry air pollutants from the west to the east, as in California, location of activities creating air pollution in the west may have greater external environmental costs than those located further to the east. To reflect this, charges for pollution emissions should vary with their location. Other things being equal, economic efficiency in this case would require charges for pollution emissions to be higher in the west than in the east. Or again, consider the release of pollutants into a river. Their release upstream may cause more external damage than their release farther downstream and pollution charges would need to vary accordingly. Biophysical, social and geographical factors all need to be taken into account in assessing environmental phenomena and the regulation of human-induced environmental change. The complexities involved are often not highlighted in simple economic models of economic regulation. As will be discussed later, such complexities frequently result in the geographical zoning or separation of different types of economic activities.

5.2.2.3. *Income distribution consequences of environmental regulation are not assessed*

Environmental policy proposals by economists are to a considerable extent based on the "new welfare economics" (Little, 1957). The most commonly used principle in that regard is the potential Paretian improvement (or Kaldor–Hicks) criteria, which regards an (environmental) change as desirable if the gainers *could* compensate the losers for their loss and be better-off than before the change. Actual compensation need not be paid. Therefore, some economic entities are in practice likely to be worse-off after the change than before it. The distribution of income alters, and it may alter in a socially undesirable way.

This raises the question of whether compensation should be paid to losers and if so, how much? If compensation is paid, should it be sufficient to ensure an *actual* Paretian improvement, that is, a situation in which no one is worse-off after the change than before and some are better-off? An actual Paretian improvement may be pursued because it is believed that pre-existing resource-use rights (either *de jure* or *de facto*) should be respected or because of political realities. For instance, a political backlash may be feared if existing resource rights are not respected. However, the transaction costs involved in paying compensation also need to be considered. If these are high, they may annul the aggregate economic gains otherwise available from the proposed change.

This discussion can be related to the situation depicted in Fig. 5.1 assuming for simplicity that user costs are zero. If polluters are already emitting x_2 of pollutants per period of time, a potential Paretian improvement is possible by reducing the level of these emissions to x_1 per period of time. The victims of pollution could, in principle, pay polluters an amount equivalent to the hatched area of triangle *EDB* to reduce their emissions from x_2 to x_1 and be better-off by an amount equal to the dotted area of triangle *BCD*. Thus, there is a potential Paretian improvement: victims of pollution gain and polluters are fully compensated for the alteration of their behavior if the transfer of income is made. Nevertheless, such a transfer may never occur voluntarily given the nature of the transaction costs involved and free-riding by victims, particularly if the number of victims is large.

In the case illustrated in Fig. 5.1 what are the income distribution effects of a government imposing a tax of OT per unit on each unit of emission of the pollutant? Firstly, it can be noticed that the victims of the pollution are better-off by an amount equivalent to the area of quadrilateral *EDCB*. On the other hand, if no compensation is paid to polluters, polluters are worse-off by an amount equivalent to the area of the quadrilateral *ODBT*. *This is on the assumption* that the full incidence of the pollution tax or charge falls on polluters. In most cases, this is unlikely because (depending on the slopes of the market demand and supply curves) if polluters are suppliers of commodities, some of the cost of the pollution tax will be passed on to buyers by an increase in the price of the commodities supplied by polluters. If supply and demand curves are normally sloped then a portion of these pollution emission charges (or the extra control costs of polluters) will be passed on to buyers, as is explained in Section 5.8.

Note that the final welfare effects of a tax of OT on each unit of emissions would depend on what the government does with its tax receipts. Furthermore, observe that if it is considered just that potential victims of pollution should have the right to a pollution-free environment, the tax solution does not compensate them for enduring emissions of x_1 per unit of time. To compensate them for this, the government would need to transfer an amount equal to the area of triangle *OEB* to those affected by the pollution. On the other hand, if polluters are assumed to have the right to pollute, they are penalized rather than rewarded for reducing the level of their pollution emissions.

5.2.2.4. *Uncertainty about the costs and benefits of environmental regulation and about how external economic effects should be evaluated*

The above discussion of the situation illustrated by Fig. 5.1 assumes that the marginal cost and benefit curves used in the analysis are known perfectly. This is unlikely to be so in practice. Both the marginal benefits to polluters of being able to pollute and the marginal external costs imposed on those who suffer from the pollution can be uncertain. Therefore, environmental regulation often is undertaken under conditions involving uncertainty. However, the presence of uncertainty does not necessarily mean that no rational decision can be made about the control of pollution.

Take, for example, the case illustrated in Fig. 5.2. In this case, it is assumed that regulators are uncertain about the marginal benefits

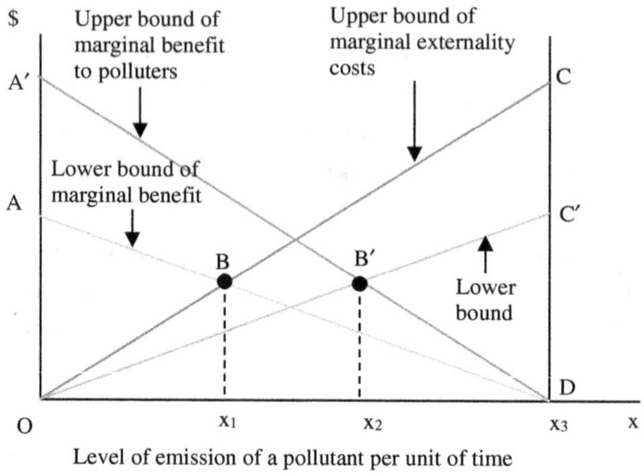

Fig. 5.2. An illustration that uncertainty complicates environmental regulation but does not rule out the possibility of rational intervention to control emissions.

to polluters of being able to pollute and are also uncertain about the marginal external cost imposed by emissions on victims of the pollution. Nevertheless, regulators are confident that the marginal benefits to polluters are at a minimum as indicated by line *ABD* and at a maximum as shown by line $A'B'D$. The maximum possible marginal external costs to those adversely affected by pollution are estimated to be as shown by line *OBC* and at a minimum, these possible marginal costs are believed to be as indicated by line $OB'C'$. In these circumstances, it is certain that a level of pollution emissions of $x < x_1$ or of $x > x_2$ *cannot* be socially optimal because a potential Paretian improvement in the former case can be achieved by increasing the level of emission to x_1 and in the latter case by decreasing the level of emission to x_2. Either policy would be better than non-intervention if the Kaldor–Hicks criterion is adopted. Account would, however, need to be taken of rules for optimal choice under uncertainty to select a value for x in the range $x_1 < x < x_2$.

A further possible complication is that the positions of the marginal cost and benefit curves for the control of pollution can shift depending upon whether their estimates are based on willingness to pay or willingness to accept compensation. Usually the monetary sum based on willingness to pay is less than that based on willingness to accept compensation and the differences can be substantial (Pearce and Markandya, 1989, p. 39; Gregory, 1986; Knetsch and Sinden, 1984). For example, if victims of pollution have to pay to have a reduction in pollution emissions, the estimate of their external marginal costs might be as shown by line $OB'C'$. If, on the other hand, victims have to be paid to allow pollution emissions, their external marginal costs might be indicated by line OBC. Similar reasoning can be applied to polluters. In each case, regulators should decide what is the appropriate basis on which to make the estimates. If, however, regulators are unable to decide this, it may still be rational to regulate emissions to some extent, as in the uncertainty case discussed above.

5.2.2.5. *Government regulators may not always try to adopt efficient economic pricing of pollution emissions via taxes or charges and therefore, transaction costs of regulation could be high*

It cannot be assumed that governments will always want to adopt environmental policies that satisfy criteria used in welfare economics, such as the Kaldor–Hicks criterion. Neither can it be assumed that government agencies responsible for environmental controls will regulate in a way that minimizes their costs of intervention. For example, taxes or charges on pollution emission may be politically determined by taking into account the political reactions of those being regulated as well as those subject to the pollution. In some cases, another consideration of an environmental agency may be raising sufficient revenue to cover its costs of administering environmental regulations. A regulatory agency is liable to act in its own self-interest rather than the general interest. The main concern of agency members may be to secure the future of the agency and, up to a point, expand its operation. Consequently, administrative checks and balances (as well as a free press) can be necessary to increase the public accountability of such agencies.

When the costs of monitoring pollution emissions and enforcing regulations are taken into account, as well as possible economic inefficiencies of agencies administering environmental regulations, these costs can in some cases exceed the aggregate net benefits otherwise obtained from regulating pollution emissions or managing an environmental change. The transaction costs involved in regulation may be so high that sometimes, environmental regulation results in a net economic disadvantage to society.

5.2.2.6. *A system of taxes or charges on adverse environmental externalities encourages research and innovations designed to reduce negative environmental spillovers*

When polluters must pay for their emissions of pollutants or disposal of wastes, they have an economic incentive to adopt techniques that reduce their wastes. This also provides a market for those who develop new patentable technologies that can reduce waste emissions. The development and use of environmentally friendly techniques is encouraged. This is not true of all methods of environmental regulation. For example, administrative rules, which merely set the maximum amount of pollution that a polluter may emit, are likely to provide less economic incentive for the development of pollution reduction technology. However, there could still be some economic incentive to adopt pollution reduction technologies if the administrative rules restrict the level of profitable production by the polluter. Furthermore, mere zoning of polluting activities without any other restrictions or charges for pollution emissions can be expected to have little positive impact on technological change designed to reduce negative environmental spillovers.

5.2.2.7. *Government taxes or charges on pollution emissions may be inflexible*

It is sometimes contended that government taxes or charges on pollution emissions or waste disposal may be "sticky". This, however, depends on the nature of the political or administrative mechanisms used to change these. This has led some writers to contend that systems of tradable permits are superior because charges for pollution emissions alter automatically in these systems due to the operation of market forces. In practice, however, a number of the advantages and problems associated with government-determined pollution taxes or charges also apply to tradable permit systems for waste disposal and resource use. Let us consider such systems.

5.3. Tradable Permit Systems for Pollution Emissions and Waste Disposal

Some writers contend that tradable permit systems for regulating pollution emissions and waste disposal are, as a rule, superior to alternative forms of control such as government taxes on pollution emissions. Despite this, most of the problems mentioned in the previous section in relation to government taxes or charges also occur for systems of tradable permits. These include the possible neglect of user costs, the issue of whether or not the pollution emissions result in a global or a local bad or a more complex set of geographical environmental spillovers, the need to consider the income distribution consequences of such schemes, and uncertainties about environmental costs and benefits. There are also government transaction costs involved in administering tradable permit schemes but they may be lower than in the case of pollution emission taxes or administered charges. These systems also have positive effects on technological progress designed to reduce pollution emissions because they involve the pricing of emissions. Because a market system is involved, if a tradable permit system is adopted, the price tends to be flexible. However, this does not necessarily mean that the price is optimal from a Kaldor–Hicks point of view.

Many different types of tradable permit systems are possible and regulators need to choose between the competing models. In order to introduce the tradable permit method, consider a simple model first by referring to the situation illustrated in Fig. 5.1, assuming that *OBC* is the marginal cost to victims of pollution emissions and *ABD* is the marginal benefit to polluters of being able to pollute. If the government issues permits giving a total aggregate right to emissions of x_1 for the current period, the total supply of rights will be a vertical line located at x_1. Line *ABD* is the demand for these rights and therefore, their market price will be *OT* per unit of the pollutant emitted. If the rights are auctioned, the government would collect revenue equivalent to the area of *OTBE*. Thus, there would for this single-period case be virtually no difference between the economic impact of this system and an ideal tax system. On the other hand, if pollution rights are made available to existing polluters free of charge and issued in proportion to their pre-existing levels of pollution emissions, there would be no income transfer to the government. Furthermore, the benefits forgone by polluters as a result of these measures would only amount to a quantity equivalent to the area of triangle *EBD* rather than an amount equivalent to the area of trapezium *ODBT*. Politically, polluters will prefer such a scheme to the auctioning of pollution rights or to taxes on pollution emissions because it leaves polluters with more income than otherwise. However, tradable permit schemes involve public administration costs because emissions need to be monitored for compliance and penalties may have to be imposed for non-compliance. Furthermore, a record of rights needs to be maintained and their transfer needs to be recorded. Consequently, if polluters are to pay for the public administration of the scheme, the public agency responsible for the administration of the scheme will need to impose a levy on permit-holders in order to fund the administration of the scheme.

Usually tradable pollution rights are issued for longer than one period. They may, for example, be issued in perpetuity. The latter possibility does not, however, allow for flexibility in public policy even though it gives permit-holders a solid long-term property right. If rights are in perpetuity and circumstances alter so that a reduction in emissions becomes desirable, then an option available to the government is to buy back permits by bidding for them. This, however, can be costly to the government. If, on the other hand, the situation changes and a higher level of emissions becomes acceptable, additional permits might be issued by the government. It would then have to decide how these are to be issued, for example, whether existing permit-holders would have priority and what terms and conditions will apply.

Some of the issues that arise when pollution rights are issued in perpetuity are illustrated in Fig. 5.3. Initially, the marginal benefits to polluters of being able to emit a pollutant are as shown by line *ABD*

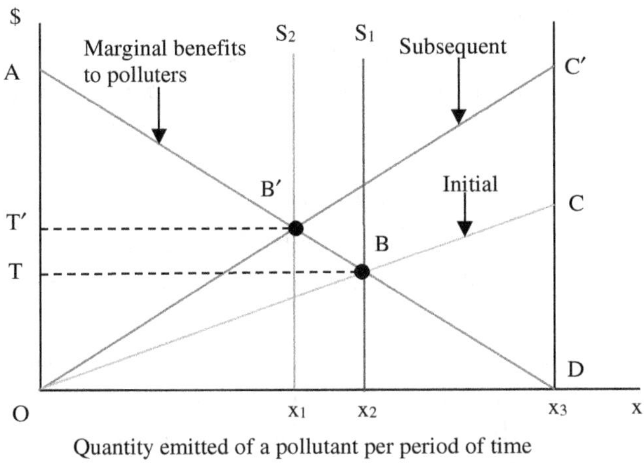

Fig. 5.3. Changing economic and environmental conditions create challenges for the public management of tradable pollution rights schemes, as is illustrated.

and the external costs are as shown by line *OBC*. A tradable emissions scheme is introduced, which gives aggregate rights to emit x_2 of the relevant pollutant in perpetuity. Assuming a competitive market, this results in a price per unit of permitted emissions of *OT* and an "ideal" economic outcome prevails. However, suppose that subsequently the marginal external costs of pollution rise from *OBC* to $OB'C'$. The pre-existing policy solution is no longer ideal. Permission to emit pollutants should be reduced from x_2 to x_1. The government could, therefore, buy back from permit-holders permits giving holders an entitlement to emit $x_2 - x_1$ of the pollutant. Another possibility is that marginal external costs decline (fall below *OBC*) and an upward adjustment by the government of the total allowable level of emission would then be optimal. Or again, variations in the marginal benefit to polluters of polluting may cause line *ABD* to shift and consequently the optimal economic level of pollution emissions. However, the government may be tardy in making variations in the number of permits issued. Hence, there may be some administrative inflexibility in this scheme similar to that for taxes on pollution or administrative charges.

Many other durations for pollution rights are possible between those granted in perpetuity for emissions of a definite quantity of pollutants or just for one period. It is possible that the rights might decline regularly with the passage of time, for example, by 10% per year, or the rights might only be for a specified *proportion* of the total allowable level of emissions. The latter gives the government scope to vary the specified proportion of the total allowable level of emissions but ensures permit-holders of a fixed share of these emissions. It provides a compromise by allowing flexibility in government policy and at the same time ensuring a reasonable degree of security of property rights to permit-holders.

An argument often put in favor of tradable pollution permits is that they promote economic efficiency because those who can profit most from owning the permits will buy them. On the other hand, if the market for pollution permits is not competitive, these permits may create a barrier to entry to an industry. This occurs if existing permit-holders refuse to make permits available to potential entrants.

It has also been argued that if markets for pollution permits are competitive, then price will be the same everywhere. If the common pool assumption applies, this promotes economic efficiency by ensuring that the marginal cost of reducing pollution emissions is the same for all polluters. However, as pointed out above in relation to uniform taxes on pollution emissions, this is only a valid argument if the emissions are a pure public bad. When this is not so, zoning of regions in which trading of permits is allowed may be required and permits then need to be region specific. This may result in "thin" markets in which there are few competitors and can add to administrative costs.

It is clear that the assessment of tradable permit systems is more complex than is often realized. Table 5.1 summarizes factors that need to be considered in designing tradable pollution permit schemes. The economic value of tradable permit systems will vary with how they are designed.

The issues raised by Table 5.1 can be quite complex and political barriers to their resolution are likely to vary with particular cases. The proposal for global greenhouse gas emission permits and their trading highlights the complexities that can arise. For example, there is conflict between countries about how emission rights should be allocated. Allocations based on pre-existing national levels of emissions

Table 5.1. A list of factors that need to be considered in designing a system of tradable pollution rights.

Factor	Comments
How the permits are to be issued	The permits may, for example, be issued by auction or tender, or by allocation free of charge to existing polluters in proportion to their pre-existing levels of emissions (a process known as grandfathering). They can also be issued to existing polluters at a price below what their market price would be
Transferability of rights	Are there to be restrictions on transferability of permits and what restrictions will apply? For example, will transfers be limited to particular geographical zones?
The nature of the entitlement	For example, will the permit enable the holder to emit a fixed quantity of a pollutant or a fixed proportion of the total allowable level of pollution emissions?
Duration of rights	For example, will the rights be granted in perpetuity or for a limited period of time?
How will the public administration of the scheme be funded?	How are the costs of evaluating pollution emissions, monitoring these, and enforcing entitlements to be financed? Will a levy be imposed on those with pollution permits (for example, an annual registration fee) and how will it be determined?

are unacceptable to China and India, and many developed countries might not be prepared to accept initial national allocations based on an equal per capita allocation for all individuals. The latter would, for example, give a much greater share of emission rights to China and India than to the United States. There have also been debates about the extent to which international trading of these rights should be allowed. Some individuals have expressed concern that some less developed countries may sell their emission rights (because of poverty or corrupt leaders) to higher income countries and be disadvantaged in the long run. Therefore, they favor some restrictions on international trade in these rights. A further complication can arise in the regulation of pollution emissions: the emissions may not consist of a single pollutant but of a mixture or cocktail of pollutants. This is not a serious problem if the polluting components are in relatively fixed proportions but it can create difficulties if substitution can occur. For example, if one polluting component is priced and the other components are not, this may result in substitution of pollutants that can be freely emitted for the pollutant subject to a charge. If charges for the emission of a mixture of pollutants are based on an index of its components, this can create challenges for estimating the appropriate index. The index would need to take into account the environmental costs and benefits of the different components. This is an issue in the case of greenhouse gases, for example (see Chapter 13).

5.4. Subsidies for Pollution Reduction

Subsidies for reducing pollution emissions or for engaging in environmentally friendly behavior are likely to be popular with their recipients. However, they do entail a tax burden if financed from general public revenue and they signal that the recipients have a right to engage in environmentally unfriendly behavior. In Fig. 5.1, for example, if a subsidy of *OT* is paid on each unit by which emissions or wastes are reduced, polluters will reduce their emissions from x_2 to x_1. A total subsidy payment of *EDVB* will be paid and polluters will have a net increase in income equal to the area of triangle *BDV*. Victims of the pollution will also benefit by an amount equal to the area of quadrilateral *EDCB*. There will, however, be a burden on taxpayers, the negative effects of which cannot be evaluated in terms of Fig. 5.1.

In some cases, subsidies for improved environmental behavior may be favored by government over charges on negative environmental behavior because of income distribution (or political) considerations. For example, the reformed Common Agricultural Policy of the European Union enables farmers to obtain subsidies for engaging in more environmentally friendly behaviors than they might otherwise adopt (Tisdell and Hartley, 2008, pp. 70–80).

5.5. The Policy of Clearly Defining Property Rights Combined with Bargaining or the Legal Settlement of an Environmental Dispute

As discussed in Section 2.3, Coase (1960) argued that much progress could be made in the efficient control of environmental spillovers, by ensuring that the legal rights of entities to use (or not make use of) external environments are clearly specified. Limits to this approach have already been noted. For example, the transaction costs involved in bargaining and enforcing rights can be so high for injured parties or others with environmental rights that they preclude a bargained solution. The problem can be chronic when public bads occur and a large group of entities have a right to be free of such bads. No individual may be willing to initiate action to reduce the public bad because all victims benefit and many victims may not contribute to the cost of the action. A free-rider problem exists.

This is overcome to some extent when there is a possibility of *class actions*. In such a case, a lawyer or other representative may engage in legal or bargaining action on the condition that if gains are made a part of the benefit will be retained by the lawyer or the negotiating party. Those who wish to be part of the class action must agree to this in advance. In some cases, they may also be requested to pay a small sum in advance to facilitate the class action but in other cases, payment may only be required if there is a "win". If a *tort* (a non-criminal legal wrong) is involved those causing the damage may be required to pay a financial sum to injured parties, a portion of which may be retained by their lawyers. For further discussion of the law and the control of environmental spillovers (particularly when the spillovers are uncertain or probable) see, for example, Tisdell (1993, Chapter 5).

5.6. Administrative Rules or Fiat as Environmental Control Measures

Economists normally argue that when pollution emissions above particular levels are prohibited, this is likely to be inefficient as control measures. For example, a method that sets the same maximum level of pollution emissions for each firm or plant in order to regulate aggregate emissions fails to take account of differences in the marginal benefits that firms obtain from polluting or the differences in the levels of marginal cost which they would experience as a result of reducing their pollution emissions. This policy measure is, therefore, unlikely to maximize the social economic benefits obtained from a given aggregate level of emissions or to minimize the cost of reducing aggregate emissions to a particular aggregate level.

This contrasts with systems, which involve a uniform pollution emission charge, tax or price on each unit of a pollutant emitted. If a global environmental bad is involved, these systems can result in Paretian optimality. If localized public bads are involved in different geographical areas, then uniformity in *each* geographical area in these variables will be ideal but the appropriate price for emissions is likely to differ between regions.

Nevertheless, it would not be correct to maintain that fiat or "non-economic" rules have no place in environmental regulations. Some techniques may be so environmentally dangerous that their use should be prohibited. Furthermore, geographical zoning of facilities on the basis of their environmental impacts can be useful as an administrative mechanism for environmental regulation. Zoning may be used in conjunction with other methods, such as charges on emissions.

5.7. Zoning of Polluting Activities Having External Environmental Consequences

5.7.1. *Introduction*

Zoning of economic activities appears to be relatively common, particularly in urban areas. One reason for this zoning may be to regulate the impacts of adverse environmental externalities from economic activities or in some cases, to take advantage of external economic synergies that can be obtained by concentrating particular types of economic activities in different zones. In practice, the reasons for and the nature of geographical zoning of economic activities can vary widely. Furthermore, this subject appears to be under researched in comparison to its importance. The aim here is to bring attention to a few of the factors that may need to be taken into account in making decisions about zoning of activities that have external environmental consequences.

5.7.2. *Zoning of incompatible activities*

Some activities are incompatible with one another because of their external effects. For example, smoking in areas occupied by non-smokers adversely affects the welfare of non-smokers. The emission of noise or toxic substances from some activities and their presence within short distances can be incompatible with residential dwelling in the area involved. Or, hunting and passive recreation in the same natural areas may be incompatible. Such negative externalities may be regulated by the geographical separation of the activities involved.

Two types of situations are worth identifying, namely those in which all interested parties gain by the separation of their activities, and so separation involves no conflict, and those in which some parties gain and some lose as a result of this policy. In the latter case, there is conflict. It is worthwhile illustrating these cases by an example in order to highlight relevant issues.

For simplicity, assume that there are two groups of relevant parties, I and II, who engage in different activities. These activities may be intermingled or be carried out in separate locations and gains, payoffs or benefits to each of the two parties depend on whether the activities are intermingled or separated.

A case in which there is a Paretian gain from separation of the activities is illustrated in Table 5.2. There the numbers in column 1 indicate the benefits to party I of the alternative policies and in column 2 that for party II. Both gain by separation of activities in this case and there is no conflict.

The second case does involve conflict and is more difficult to resolve politically. In this case, there is an increase in aggregate benefit as a result of separation of the activities but one party loses and the other gains. This case is illustrated in Table 5.3, which has the same interpretation as Table 5.2. In this case, party II loses as a result of separation of economic activities but party I gains. The figures indicate that aggregate benefit rises from 5 units to 7 units and that party I could

Table 5.2. A case in which separation of activities with adverse environmental consequences results in a Paretian improvement.

Policy	Benefit to I	Benefit to II
Intermingling of activities	2	2
Separation of activities	4	4

Table 5.3. A case in which there is social conflict about separation of activities with adverse environmental externalities but for which separation results in a potential Paretian improvement.

Policy	Benefit to I	Benefit to II
Intermingling of activities	2	3
Separation of activities	5	2

compensate party II for its loss as a result of separation of activities and be better-off than before the change. Therefore, a potential Paretian improvement can be realized by having separated activities rather than intermingled ones.

The case in Table 5.2 might (for example) correspond to the separation of body surfers from surfboard riders as happens at most Australian beaches, and the second corresponds to some situations involving smokers and non-smokers. There is little political difficulty in deciding on the optimal policy in the first case (because all gain as a result of separation) but the situation is more complicated in the second case. This is because some gain and some lose in the latter case if compensation is not paid. Furthermore, in the second case, attention has to be given to whether gainers can *really* compensate losers and be better-off than before the social change. This is important if the Paretian improvement criterion is being applied. How accurately can the benefits to the parties be measured and are the numbers representing benefits (such as those in Table 5.3) adequate for determining transferability of benefits from one party to another? Because interpersonal comparisons of benefits are involved, more sophisticated approaches than that adopted above are likely to be required. In the above case, complete transferability of benefits is assumed, that is, units of benefit can be transferred from one party to another and each unit has the same value for each partner. This assumption will often not be satisfied in practice.

In addition, the case illustrated by Table 5.3 highlights the need for strong value judgments in making the policy choice involved. For example, should smokers have the right to a smoke-free environment or should smokers have the right to smoke where they want to? If one opts for the former position, there would be no real need for compensating smokers for policies, which restrict the location of their smoking activities in order to provide smoke-free environments for non-smokers.

5.7.3. *Cases where external pollution damage depends only on the distance between emitters and potential receptors*

Very often the amount of economic damage caused to receptors of pollution emissions depends on their distance from the source of the emission. Planners may take this into account in spatially separating pollution emitters from those who are likely to be adversely affected by the emissions. A simple case can be illustrated by Fig. 5.4. In this figure, x represents the distance between the source at which pollutants are emitted and those who are likely to be adversely affected by them. For instance, the source of pollution may be a set of factories and the potential victims of the pollution might be nearby residents. Curve ABC is assumed to measure the environmental damage suffered by receptors as a function of their distance (x) from the source of emissions. It indicates that if receptors are located more than a distance of x_2 from the source of emissions, they suffer no damage.

Thus, given the situation illustrated by Fig. 5.4, if polluters are placed in a zone at a distance of at least x_2 from potential receptors of these emissions (for example, residents) who could be in a second zone, there would be no externality costs from the polluters. However,

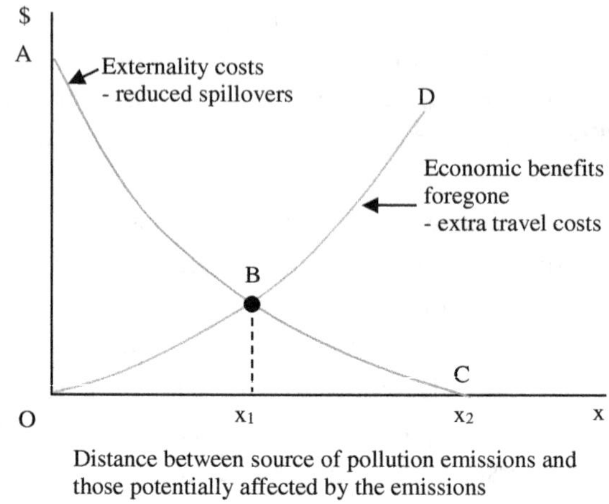

Fig. 5.4. A diagram to illustrate zoning of economic activity based on the distance between polluters and potential victims.

this may not be the most economic strategy because economic benefits foregone may rise as the distance between say the polluting factories and residents increase. For instance, if residents work in the factories, their transport costs to go to work can be expected to rise the greater is the distance of their dwellings from the factories. This cost could be indicated in Fig. 5.4 by line *OBD*. When this is taken into account, the optimal distance between the zone for the source of pollution (for instance, factories) and the zone for reception of it (for instance, dwellings) is x_1.

Note that the nature of the curves in Fig. 5.4 is likely to vary depending on the geography of the areas involved and with the technologies adopted by polluters. High smoke stacks, for instance, may cause the level of air-borne emissions to be higher at some distance from the pollution source than near it.

5.7.4. *Should polluting activities be concentrated by location or dispersed?*

In considering the zoning of activities, authorities may have to consider the extent to which polluting activities ought to be concentrated in particular locations or the extent to which they should be widely dispersed.

A further consideration may be the *mixture* of polluting activities that ought to be allowed in a particular area taking into account possible interactions between emitted substances. These are all complicated issues. The latter situation may result in separate zones for different types of polluting activities.

If the marginal externality costs of pollution emissions from a fixed location tend to decline with the volume of emissions, this will usually favor the concentrated location of the polluting activities concerned. On the other hand, if the marginal externality costs of emissions from a fixed location tend to rise with the level of emissions, this will tend to favor greater dispersion of polluting activities, other things held constant. In both cases, the above are the implications if the aim is to minimize total externality costs.

5.7.5. *Geographical influences*

The particular geography of a region influences the optimal zoning of polluting activities and pollution emission charges associated with zones, as has already been indicated in Section 5.2. Geographical influences can include the direction of winds and air currents as far as wind-borne pollutants are concerned. In the case of water-borne pollutants, the nature of water flows and currents can be important. Many bio-physical factors can be relevant for environmental policy-making such as precipitation and temperatures as well as the nature and location of human settlements. In practice, there may be few situations in which the assumption is fully satisfied that pollutants enter a common pool (discussed in Section 5.2).

5.8. The Economic Incidence of Environmental Regulations

5.8.1. *Introduction*

Growing social concern in the 20th century about increasing pollution levels gave rise to the slogan that "the polluter should pay" for pollution emissions. While this slogan may have political appeal, it ignores the fact that in a market exchange system, polluters supplying commodities usually pass on (by increased prices) at least some of the extra costs they incur as a result of environmental regulation of their activities. This means that (to some extent) buyers rather than suppliers of commodities pay for the cost of environmental regulation. It could be argued, nevertheless, that buyers should pay because it is their demand (consumer sovereignty) that determines the supply of commodities. Therefore, buyers are indirectly responsible for environmental damage if they demand commodities the supply of which causes environmental degradation.

Economists are well aware of the fact that those on whom taxes, levies and other costs are imposed by public policy may not bear the full burden of these impacts but to some extent, may shift this economic burden to others if exchange is involved. In most cases, the *incidence* of the cost of an environmental regulation does not fall fully on the party or parties on which it is imposed. The final incidences of such regulations are usually of political concern.

One of the economic reasons why environmental regulations may be imposed on suppliers rather than buyers is that this results in lower transaction costs in enforcing the regulations than intervening directly to alter the nature of buyers' purchases. There may also be a "mirage effect" because buyers (who are usually more numerous than sellers) may believe that sellers pay the cost of the regulation and may be unaware that there is some economic incidence of the environmental regulations on them as buyers. It is worthwhile elaborating on this matter.

5.8.2. *Implications of the Pigovian approach to environmental policy*

If the Pigovian approach is followed of controlling the negative environmental externalities from an industry by taxing the value of its output, then it is clear that normally a part of the incidence of this tax falls on suppliers and a portion falls on buyers. This is because the imposition of the environmental tax results in a rise in the market price of the product if demand and supply curves have normal slopes (that is, have negative and positive slopes, respectively) and if pure competition prevails in the industry. The extent of the increase in the equilibrium price of the product arising from its environmental regulation will depend on the relative slopes of the industry supply and demand curves (see Tisdell and Hartley, 2008, Section 5.5). Only in the case where the industry demand curve is perfectly elastic (is a horizontal demand line) will the incidence of the environmental control costs fall completely on suppliers. However, if the industry demand curve is perfectly inelastic (is a vertical line), the extra cost imposed on suppliers by the pollution fee will be passed on completely to buyers if the industry supply curve after regulation moves up by a constant throughout its range. However, if the slope of the supply curve changes, this may not happen.

The normal case can be illustrated by Fig. 5.5. In this figure, line *AD* represents the industry demand curve for product *X* and line *DF* represents its supply curve in the absence of environmental regulation. Initially, the industry is in equilibrium at point *C* supplying X_2 of the

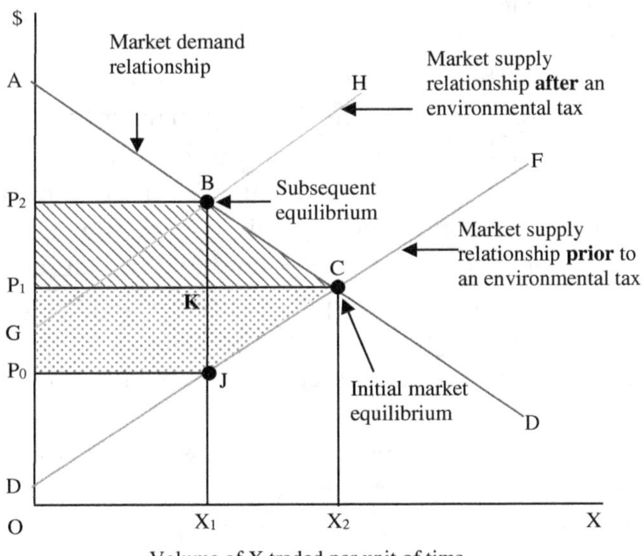

Fig. 5.5. An illustration of how a tax on supplies of producers generating pollution may to some extent be passed on to buyers. The illustration is for a Pigovian-type tax on supply.

product and selling it at a price of P_1 per unit. Now imagine that in order to allow for the presence of negative externalities, a tax of BJ is imposed on each unit of output of product X. Suppliers now find that their private cost of supply increases by this much and therefore, the industry supply curve after the imposition of the tax shifts up to GH. The equilibrium of the industry now alters from C to B, its volume of supply per unit of time falls from X_2 to X_1 and the equilibrium price of the product rises from P_1 to P_2. Buyers pay $P_2 - P_1$ more for the product than formerly and sellers receive $P_1 - P_0$ less for their product after they pay the production tax imposed for environmental reasons. The former amount represents the incidence of the tax on buyers and the latter sum represents its incidence on sellers.

In the case illustrated in Fig. 5.5, consumers of product X have a loss in consumers' surplus equal to the hatched area of quadrilateral P_1CBP_2 and producers have a loss in surplus of an amount equal to the difference between the area of triangle DCP_1 and that of triangle DJP_0 — this is equal to the dotted area shown. Note that Pigou assumed there to be no environmental benefits to buyers and suppliers of X from regulating the environmental impacts of the industry. The environmental effects of the spillovers are assumed by him to be *completely external* to all those trading in the industry. This may not always be realistic. Observe that in the Pigovian case that if the demand curve in Fig. 5.5 is a vertical line passing through B, the full incidence of a Pigovian tax would fall on buyers. In this case, the initial equilibrium of the industry would correspond to point J and the subsequent equilibrium to point B. Thus, the imposition of the Pigovian tax would cause the market price of product X to rise from P_0 to P_1 and the tax of BJ per unit of output levied on suppliers would be fully recovered from buyers.

Although suppliers suffer no economic loss in the case just stated and are just as well off after the imposition of the tax on supply as before, the result depends on the tax being a uniform one on each unit of supply. If the tax rate falls with the volume of output, full tax recovery from buyers does not occur. If the tax rate increases with the volume of output, suppliers recover more than their extra tax payments from buyers. These results are illustrated by Fig. 5.6.

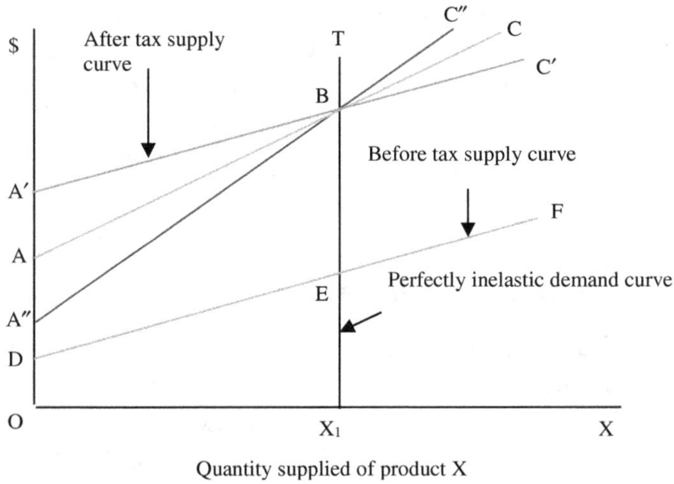

Fig. 5.6. The burden (or incidence) of an environmental tax can be sensitive variations in its marginal rate of the tax as is illustrated by this case.

In this figure, *TV* represents the perfectly inelastic demand curve for product *X* and *DEF* is the market supply curve for *X*. In the absence of government intervention, the equilibrium of the market occurs at *E*. If producers of *X* are required to pay a uniform tax on each unit of production equivalent to *EB*, their marginal costs of production will increase by this amount and the industry supply curve will shift upward from *DF* to *AC*. The market equilibrium alters from *E* to *B* and the price of the product rises by an amount equivalent to the per unit tax on each unit of production. Suppliers fully recover their taxation payments from buyers. Should, however, the tax rate increase with the volume of production of *X* (for example, as is the case where the after-tax supply curve is $A''C''$ as illustrated in Fig. 5.6), suppliers will recover from buyers an amount in excess of their tax payments. This is because the change in the equilibrium market price will correspond to the marginal tax (*EB* in the case shown) and the tax rate will be lower than this for units of production below that corresponding to the market equilibrium supply, X_1. Similarly, if the tax rate declines with the value of production of the product (illustrated by an after-tax supply line in Fig. 5.6 of $A'C'$), suppliers will be unable to recover from buyers the total cost of their tax payments. This is because the infra-marginal tax rate paid by suppliers is higher than the marginal rate and the equilibrium price only rises by an amount equivalent to the marginal tax rate. This underlines the need for care in economic analysis.

5.8.3. *Cases where environmental regulation benefits all market participants*

As mentioned above, Pigou supposed that the benefits of the environmental regulation of an industry would be entirely external to it. However, this is not always the case. For example, regulations that limit the use of dangerous chemicals in agricultural food production may benefit food consumers and increase their demand for purchased food. The control of pesticides drifting from one farm to another may benefit all the farmers involved and increase their productivity thereby lowering their supply curve. In the latter case, there are reciprocal benefits to suppliers as a result of environmental regulations. In both these cases, it is *possible* for both buyers and suppliers of the product to be better-off after environmental regulation than before it, even though this would not be so in every case.

Examples of situations in which all traders in a product benefit from environmental controls on its supply are illustrated by Figs. 5.7 and 5.8. In the case shown in Fig. 5.7, the market demand for a product X is indicated by the line D_1D_1 and in the absence of environmental regulation, its supply is shown by the line S_1S_1. Suppose that reciprocal negative externalities exist between suppliers. After the regulation of these externalities, the industry's supply curve might shift to S_2S_2. As a result, the industry's market equilibrium shifts from E_1 to E_0, the price of the product falls from P_2 to P_1 and supply expands to X_1 to X_2. Both consumers' and producers' surplus increase in the case illustrated. This result is assured provided the industry supply curve after regulation has the same slope as before or is steeper in slope than before (compare Duncan and Tisdell, 1971).

Figure 5.8 illustrates a different case. In this case although environmental regulation in an industry adds to suppliers' cost of production,

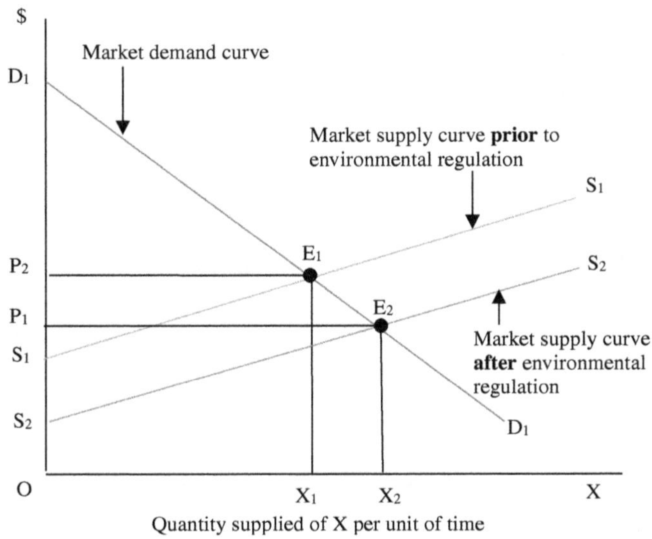

Fig. 5.7. The regulation of reciprocal negative situations between suppliers in an industry can potentially benefit both all suppliers in the industry and purchasers of its product.

it also expands the demand of consumers for product X. Demand may expand because buyers believe, for example, that after environmental regulation the product is safer to consume or they may obtain satisfaction from knowing that they are supporting environmentally more friendly supply behavior. In the case illustrated, the industry supply curve is initially as indicated by the line marked $S_1 S_1$ and the initial demand curve is $D_1 D_1$. After environmental regulation, there is a shift up in the supply curve from $S_1 S_1$ to $S_2 S_2$ and substantial upward shift in the demand curve from $D_1 D_1$ to $D_2 D_2$. Market equilibrium changes from E_1 to E_2 and both the equilibrium price and quantity traded of the product rise. Visual inspection of Fig. 5.8 reveals that both producers' and consumers' surplus rise in this particular case. Thus, while in some cases the economic benefits of environmental regulation may be entirely external to an industry, this is by no means always the case. There are, in fact, several cases where all stakeholders in an industry benefit from its environmental regulation. Pigou's analysis requires modification to allow for this.

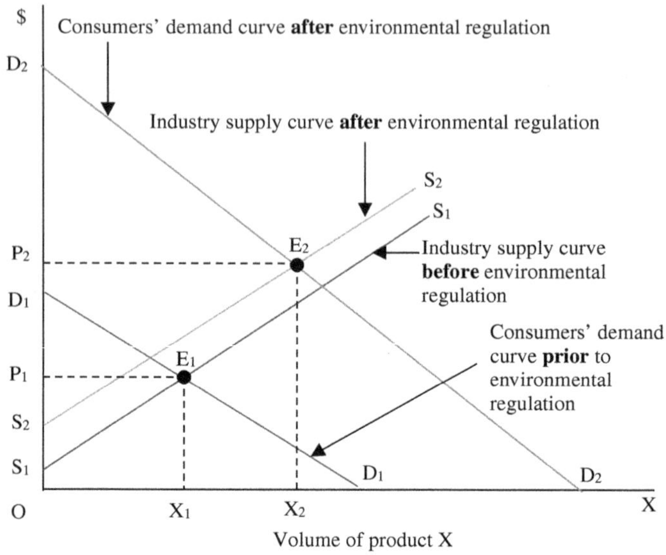

Fig. 5.8. In the case illustrated although environmental regulation adds to the cost of supplies of a product, it increases demand for the product by so much that both suppliers and buyers of the product make an economic gain.

5.9. Regulating the Use of Open-Access Resources

5.9.1. *Introduction*

As demonstrated in Section 4.6 of the previous chapter, allowing open-access of individuals to natural resources can add to economic scarcity. It was also shown that communal control of access to and use of shared resources is capable of reducing the amount of scarcity that would occur if there happens to be open-access to these resources. Writers, however, differ on how effective communal rules for the use of shared resources are likely to be as a scarcity-reduction mechanism. For example, Ostrom (1990) is optimistic about their effectiveness in reducing scarcity whereas Tisdell (2005, Sections 4.6 and 6.4) brings attention to cases where they have proven to be ineffective, particularly in situations of rapid social and ecological change. Communal rules can be regarded as an administrative approach to the management of resource use.

Along with administrative regulations on resource use, all the different types of policy instruments discussed and applied above to the regulation of pollution emissions can also be applied to the management of the use of shared natural resources. The purpose of this section is to demonstrate their applicability. Note that it will be initially assumed that the natural resources involved yield a pure private good, an example of which could be a type of fish, such as cod or tuna. Subsequently, attention will be given to the mixed good case, of which whales, various types of wildlife and some ecosystems provide examples.

5.9.2. *Taxes and charges as a means to govern the use of shared natural resources*

Just as taxes and charges can be used to regulate pollution emissions, they can also in principle be used to regulate natural resource use so as to limit economic scarcity. This will in the first instance be demonstrated by reference to Fig. 4.3 and then an industry-based exposition will be introduced (which is Pigovian in character) because it is easier to follow and allows for some analytical extensions.

In the case illustrated in Fig. 4.3 and as previously explained, open-access to the natural resource involved results in an excessive amount of labor (L_2) being employed in the exploitation of the resource and a potential Paretian improvement is possible by reducing this to L_1. This change could be achieved by imposing a tax or charge of an amount JH on each unit of labor (effort) allocated to the exploitation of the resource (see Fig. 4.3).

At the initial equilibrium level of exploitation of the resource corresponding to point F, labor would earn less than OH per unit after payment of the tax. Initially, this would reduce its earnings per unit to $OH-HJ$ and labor would exit the exploitation of this resource because if line HF represents the opportunity which labor has to earn income elsewhere in the economy, some labor will move elsewhere to earn this level of income. The input, labor, will exit the exploitation of the resource until the quantity engaged in utilizing the resource declines to L_1. At this level of utilization of the resource, each unit of labor earns $OJ-HJ$ equals OH, the level of income that each unit of labor would earn if employed elsewhere in the economy. At the same time, the aggregate value of economic output rises by an amount represented by the hatched triangle in Fig. 4.3. This reflects the fact that in this case the value of the marginal product of labor in utilizing the open-access resource is less than its marginal value, *OB*, in contributing to output elsewhere in the economy. The amount equal to the area of *JHBD* is transferred to the government as tax revenue. After deduction of administrative costs, the remaining net amount could be transferred to the community.

As pointed out in Chapter 4, this analysis has several limitations. It is based on comparative statics and therefore, assumes that adjustment to policy implementation is instantaneous and perfect. Perfect mobility of labor is supposed within the economy as well as full employment of labor. However, especially in developing countries, adjustments may be slow, labor may be relatively immobile and if incomes of those involved in extracting this open-access resource are low, there may be little scope for policy adjustment because adjustment lags may initially depress the income of those extracting the open-access resource below subsistence level (Tisdell, 2007). The latter situation would be socially unacceptable. This problem is not limited to policies relying on taxes or charges on access to resource use. It would also occur if administrative or communal means were used to reduce the amount of labor extracting the open-access resource rapidly from L_2 to L_1.

The model discussed using Fig. 4.3 assumed that labor was used in exploiting the open-access resource in fixed proportions with other factors of production. If other factors are substitutable for labor in production, policies that restrict the use of labor in exploiting the natural resource may be offset to some extent by increasing the use of substitute factors of production. Or, to give another example, if the number of boats involved in fishing is restricted and also their size, this may be partially compensated for by installing more powerful motors in fishing boats.

Sometimes policies to control the exploitation of natural resources regulate the allowable output from them rather than the quantity of inputs used into their exploitation. This policy approach can be illustrated by Fig. 5.9 and has parallels with the Pigovian approach to the regulation of externalities. In Fig. 5.9, line *AD* represents the market demand for a product *X*, which, in the absence of government regulation, is obtained by open-access to a natural resource. Line *BCS*

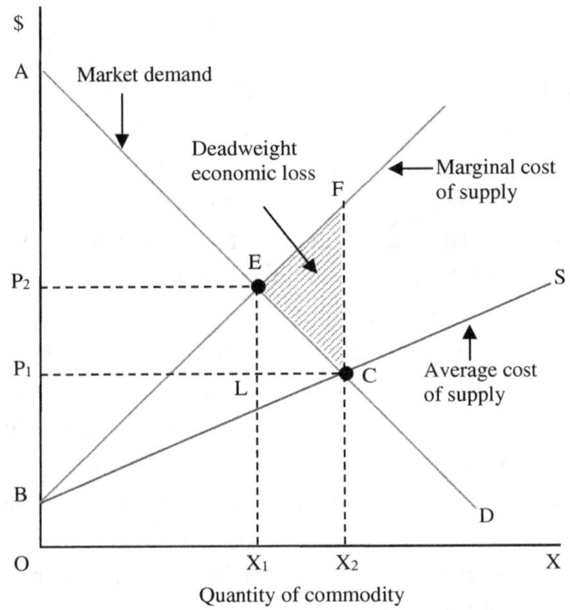

Fig. 5.9. Diagram used to illustrate a type of market failure which occurs when there is open-access to a natural resource and to identify policies to rectify this failure.

indicates the average cost to the industry of supplying the commodity and line *BEF* shows its marginal cost of supplying the commodity. If there is open-access to the resource from which the product is obtained, the industry will come into equilibrium at point *C*. At this point, the average cost of supplying the product just equals its price or the average revenue obtained by the industry. However, there is a deadweight economic loss equal to the hatched area of triangle *ECF* because the marginal cost of supply of *X* in excess of X_1 exceeds the extra value of its supply. Changing the amount of *X* supplied to that corresponding to point *E* results in greater economic efficiency because at *E* the marginal cost of extra supply of *X* equals its extra value and there is no deadweight economic loss.

One possible way to rectify the market failure illustrated by Fig. 5.9 is for the government to impose a tax or charge of $P_1 - P_2$ on each unit of product *X*. The after-tax average cost curve of suppliers will then be one parallel to line *BCS* and will pass though point *E*. In the new industry equilibrium at point E, there will be no deadweight loss and the government will obtain revenue equal to the area of rectangle P_1LEP_2. The final economic welfare effects will be influenced by the administrative costs of the scheme and how any surplus government revenue from the scheme is used. Suppliers who remain in the industry after this intervention will just be able to cover their costs (inclusive of normal profit) as was the situation prior to the intervention. Thus, they will see no advantage to themselves from this type of scheme, and one would expect them to oppose it politically. Furthermore, the dynamics of adjustment complicates the intervention.

For example, if the industry is initially in equilibrium at point C, the imposition of the tax may initially cause some social hardship if movement of firms out of the industry is slow, if it results in sunk costs for those forced to exit the industry, or in the case of a biological open-access resource, if the adjustment of its biomass is slow in relation to reduced harvesting effort. This underlines the point that one needs to be careful in applying comparative statics in determining economic policy.

The type of limitations outlined in Section 5.2.2 in relation to taxes on pollution emissions can also apply to this case. For example, industry demand and supply curves may vary and be uncertain. Thus, the optimal tax rate may be uncertain up to a point and may need to be altered with changing circumstances, and this entails the sort of problems already mentioned in Section 5.2.2.

5.9.3. *The use of tradable permits*

Systems of tradable permits to use open-access resources can relate to inputs or outputs. For example, in relation to Fig. 4.3 licenses could be issued to those laborers allowed to utilize a natural resource but they could be tradable. If they are tradable, they will tend to be purchased by those who can make the greatest economic gain by utilizing the natural resource, that is, those who are most efficient in its utilization. For example, in relation to Fig. 4.3, L_1 units of labor may be issued with permits to use the resource. If these permits are issued free of charge to holders, permit-holders will after adjustment have an increased level of income because there is no income transfer to the government unlike the case where government taxes are imposed on the utilization of the resource. Alternatively, permits may be issued to users of the resource to produce a given quantity of supply from it. This amounts to a quota on output.

In Fig. 5.9, for example, permits may be issued to supply X_1 of commodity X. If the permits are made available free of charge, those who are allocated permits may have an increase in their income after the system adjusts to reduced harvesting effort. If the permits are tradable, they will tend to be purchased by those who can get the highest return from utilizing the resource, that is the most efficient users of the resource. This is a positive economic consequence of transferable (tradable) permits for resource use compared with permits that cannot be traded. Nevertheless, tradable permit systems are not free of limitations.

They are subject to similar limitations to those outlined in relation to pollution emissions and can vary considerably in their conditions (see Section 5.3). Furthermore, public decisions have to be made about changing the aggregate allowable quota as economic and environmental conditions alter. Thus, this regulatory system is *not* a completely automatic one, even though some writers give the impression that it is. In relation to fishing, quotas on the quantity of catch of a particular species (whether transferable or not) can result in low value specimens of the species being discarded by fishers when caught in order to fill the quotas by retaining higher-valued specimens. Many of the discarded specimens may die after being caught and discarded. This is an unwanted side-effect of this regulation.

5.9.4. *Subsidies to refrain from resource use*

Another method that may be used to avoid over exploitation of open-access resources is for the government to pay subsidies for reduced use of the resources. All users of the resource could (depending on how this subsidy is distributed) have increased income as a result of such a policy. However, the subsidy has to be financed by some members of society and places a tax and income burden on them. Nevertheless, subsidies are sometimes paid in higher income countries to owners of fishing boats to exit the fishing industry and to no longer use their boats for fishing. This policy is intended to reduce over capacity in the fishing industry.

5.9.5. *The creation of private property rights*

In some cases, open-access resources may be converted to private property as a way to overcome market failures that are associated with open-access to resources. However, as pointed out in Chapter 4, the benefit from doing this depends on how economical it is to institute and enforce a system of private property rights for the resource involved. As previously noted, the economics of exclusion from property varies with changing market conditions and technologies. The creation of private property is not always the most economical way to regulate the use of open-access resources, even though it may become more economical as economic development proceeds.

5.9.6. *Administrative or communal rules*

To some extent, any form of government regulation of resource use involves administrative rules. However, the degree of economic prescription of economic activity by the government (or community) can vary. For example, the creation of private property regimes combined with markets would involve least government prescription, tradable permit systems would entail somewhat more prescription of economic activity, systems of government taxes or charges for resource use involve even more control, and non-tradable individual quotas on resource use would entail additional government prescription of economic activity. There is a danger that as the degree of regulation of economic activity by government increases that public control will become less efficient from an economics point of view. Particularly if the regulator is a remote central government, it may lack knowledge about local resources and economic activities and have difficulty in enforcing its regulations. Nevertheless, in some cases administrative rules can be the most economical policy option available, for example, banning the use of particular techniques for the exploitation of resources, for instance, dynamiting to cause fish kills in coastal waters. In some circumstances, rules devised by local communities for the use of shared resources may be efficient or socially defensible (Ostrom, 1990) but this is not always so (Tisdell, 2005, Section 4.6).

5.9.7. *Zoning and shared natural resources*

Zoning is a management device that is often applied to the regulation of shared natural resource use. For example, uses of natural resources that would involve conflict between different types of users if conducted in the same proximity are often separated by zoning. In the Great Barrier Reef Marine Park, zoning is used, for example, to separate commercial fishing from non-consumptive tourism and to set aside pure conservation areas that can only be used for scientific research. Furthermore, national parks involve a form of zoning of land use because within their boundaries many types of commercial economic activities are banned but are allowed outside these parks.

Zoning may also be adopted to vary the regulations governing the use of natural resources in different geographical areas. This is likely to be necessary when natural resources do not form a common pool, as is frequent. For example, fishing grounds can be disjoint or almost so and differ in their stocks and productivity. If tradable permit systems are used for resource management, then catch quotas may have to be determined separately for each of the fishing grounds and trading in permits may only be allowed for the fishing grounds to which they are assigned. As a result, prices for permits are likely to differ between fishing grounds.

Also some natural resources such as some marine species of fish are migratory. This complicates the management of their capture, especially if the migratory fish (such as tuna) pass through the marine waters of several countries (see for example, Tisdell, 2003b, Chapters 1 and 22). In the absence of collective agreement between these nations, such species may be overharvested in the areas they initially pass though in the sense that a lower rate of harvesting in the initial areas would enable a greater net value of the catch to be obtained. An increase in the total net value of the harvest might be achieved by taking fish later in their migratory path when they have grown to a larger size. Zoning may be used to regulate the quantity of the catch in different segments of the migratory path of the species. In the absence of collective agreement, those harvesting the species early in their migratory path do not take account of the benefits lost by harvesters involved later in the migratory path of the species.

5.10. Regulating the Use of Shared Natural Resources Supplying Mixed Goods

Frequently, natural resources are capable of providing mixed goods and this leads to conflict about their uses. In the above analysis, it was assumed that natural resources supplied a single private good. They may, however, supply different mixtures of goods. For simplicity, assume that the supply of a private good, X, obtained from a natural resource reduces the supply of a pure public good. For example, the capture of whales for whale meat supplies a private good but impacts negatively on those who want to conserve whale stocks for non-consumptive purposes. Or, in some cases, the mining of minerals (a private good) may conflict with the conservation of heritage sites (such as the preservation of rock carvings by Australian Aborigines) or detract from the quality of valued landscapes. The use of land for agriculture can have similar consequences although agricultural use does not involve open-access as a rule.

Figure 5.9 can be modified (as is done in Fig. 5.10) to take account of the economic interests of those who are adversely affected by the exploitation of an open-access resource, which is undertaken to supply a private good, X. As before, line *BCS* is the average cost of supplying the private good, X, and line *BEF* is the industry's marginal cost of doing this. Line *AD* represents the demand for the private good. If only the worth of the open-access resource for producing the private good is taken into account, ideally the resource should be used to supply X_1 of the private good per period of time, not X_2, as would happen under open-access to the resource. However, this does not take account of the possibility that third parties (parties other than the suppliers and consumers of X) may register an economic loss as a

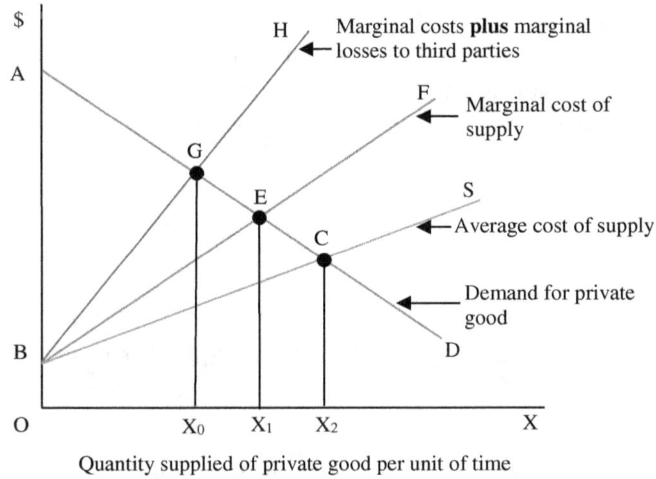

Fig. 5.10. An illustration that policies to manage open-access resources need to be modified to allow for mixed goods.

result of the supply of the private good, as in the case of whales. Let the difference between line *BH* and *BF* indicate the marginal loss of third parties as a result of the supply of X. Taking this into account the socially optimal supply of X from an economic point of view is likely to be lowered. In the case shown, it would be reduced to X_0 and regulations on the allowable supply of X would need to be varied accordingly. In the case of whales, for example, negative feelings endangered by the killing of whales and by a reduction in their stocks as well as the value of their stocks for non-consumptive tourism (whale watching) would need to be taken into account in managing this natural resource.

5.11. Concluding Comments

In this chapter, a variety of methods for regulating pollution emissions and for managing the use of natural resources have been outlined and assessed. Similar management methods can be applied in both cases, and have similar shortcomings and advantages in their applications. There is no universally best or perfect method for managing environmental and natural resources. The best choice of available methods for managing these resources will vary with specific circumstances and will require account to be taken of the knowledge available to policy-makers, the transaction costs involved in administering policy, as well as the volatility and variability of the fundamental biophysical and social relationships associated with the use of these resources.

5.12. Keywords

Administrative and communal rules to regulate the use of shared resources; agency costs; auctioning of permits for pollution emission; charges on the use of shared natural resources; class actions; common pool; economic incidence of the costs of pollution control; emission charges; emission taxes; geographical dispersion of polluting activities; geography and pollution control; global public bad; grandfathering; local public bad; marginal externality costs; mixed goods; natural resources supplying mixed goods; open-access resources; private property as an alternative to open-access; property rights, legal action and pollution control; reciprocal externalities; rules or orders as means for pollution control; subsidies to reduce pollution emissions; subsidies to reduce the use of shared resources; taxes on the use of shared natural resources; the "polluter-should-pay" principle; torts; tradable permits for pollution emission; tradable permits for the use of shared resources; user costs of pollution emissions; zoning and the management of shared natural resources; zoning of polluting activities; zoning of pollution regulations.

5.13. Questions for Review and Discussion

1. Illustrate by means of a diagram how taxes or charges on pollution emissions could in principle be used to ensure that the marginal external cost from such emissions is made equal to the marginal benefit of polluters from pollution emission. Explain how or why such intervention in the market system might be desirable.

2. The socially optimal amount of emission of a pollutant from an economic point of view is often positive but sometimes it is zero. Explain and discuss.
3. Simple economic analysis of pollution emissions often fail to take into account the external *user* costs generated by the emissions. Explain. What implications would the presence of marginal user costs have for the regulation of pollution emissions?
4. The biophysical consequences of pollution emissions can vary by the location of the emissions and this limits the applicability of policies imposing uniform charges on pollution emissions irrespective of their location. Emissions may not form a common pool. Discuss and explain.
5. The income distribution consequences of environmental regulation are frequently ignored in economic analysis but this gives an incomplete picture of the welfare and political consequences of regulatory policies. Explain and outline the consequences for income distribution of a tax on pollution emissions using the model depicted by Fig. 5.1. Do you agree that the final welfare effects of an environmental tax depend on what the government does with the tax revenue it collects from the tax?
6. Governments have imperfect knowledge about the costs and benefits of environmental regulation, for example, about the costs and benefits of regulating pollution emissions. Consequently, it is possible that any regulatory policy will not be socially optimal in retrospect. This, however, does not imply that no policy intervention is optimal. Explain and illustrate.
7. Depending on whether the victims of pollution are required to pay to avoid it or need to be paid to allow it, the optimal cost–benefit solution to pollution emissions differs. Discuss and explain.
8. Government regulators may not always be motivated to adopt schemes that efficiently price pollution emissions and may not minimize their own operational costs. Discuss.
9. Explain why environmental regulations that impose taxes, charges or prices on pollution emissions encourage researchers to develop methods that will reduce pollution emissions.

10. Systems of tradable permits can be used to control pollution emissions. They are often claimed to be more flexible in allowing for changing environmental and economic circumstances than pollution taxes. This is, however, partly illusory. Discuss.
11. Tradable permit systems can have quite different income distribution consequences to pollution taxes, but this depends on how the rights to pollution permits are allocated. Explain.
12. There are many factors that have to be taken into account in designing a system of tradable pollution rights. The consequences of such systems will vary considerably depending on the choices made about the design of the system. Elucidate.
13. Many of the policy limitations noted for pollution taxes also occur for tradable permit systems. Give examples.
14. Why might it be necessary to assign tradable pollution permits by areas or zones? Can tradable pollution permits reduce economic competition within product markets and create barriers to entry of new firms to an industry?
15. In implementing tradable pollution emission schemes, governments face the difficult task of balancing the property rights of permit-holders against their flexibility to alter the direction of the scheme (for example, the total allowable level of emissions) as conditions change. Discuss and consider ways in which these permit schemes can incorporate a compromise between ensuring rights to permit-holders and flexibility of governments to alter the level of emissions.
16. Why are subsidies for pollution reduction likely to be popular with their recipients? What types of economic costs can they impose on non-recipients?
17. It is sometimes claimed that the clear definition of property rights in the environment combined with the scope for aggrieved parties to bargain about environmental changes or to obtain a legal settlement of environmental disputes is an efficient method for environmental management. Discuss. Why *might* the possibility of class actions lead to the increased efficiency of this approach?

18. The use of rules or of fiat to achieve environmental control is often criticized by economists as being relatively inefficient. Do you agree with this point of view?
19. Zoning including *complete or partial* separation of economic activities can sometimes result in an increase in economic welfare when environmental spillovers are taken into account. Explain and discuss.
20. Should polluting activities be concentrated in a particular geographical area or dispersed? Outline the factors that should be taken into account in deciding this matter.
21. The specific geographical features of areas need to be taken into account in designing pollution control policies. Explain why and discuss and illustrate by giving examples.
22. Those economic agents who initially bear the costs of pollution control often pass on the burden of these costs by altering the price of products they supply to the market. Illustrate by considering a tax on the output of a product the production of which creates pollution. In such cases, is it fair for buyers of a product to have to pay a higher price for it?
23. While in most cases regulations on the pollution emissions of suppliers of commodities adds to their costs (with some of these costs being passed on to buyers), sometimes they may reduce producers' costs and raise the demand for commodities supplied by an industry. Explain and discuss.
24. To some extent (but not completely) market failures that occur in the use of open-access or shared natural resources can be overcome by imposing taxes on inputs exploiting these resources or by levying taxes on the output obtained from these resources. Elucidate. In doing so, consider the limitations of these methods of controlling resource use.
25. Tradable permit systems can be a useful means to overcome market failures involved in the use of open-access or shared natural resources. Indicate why they might be useful. Do they eliminate all market failures?

26. Tradable permit schemes for resource use have similar limitations to those for control of pollution emissions using taxes. Discuss. Furthermore, their impacts on the distribution of income vary considerably depending on how those schemes are structured. Explain.
27. Should subsidies ever be paid to individuals or economic agents to refrain from using shared natural resources? What factors would you want to take into account in deciding this matter?
28. It is too simplistic to contend that the most efficient way of managing communal or open-access resources is to convert them to private property. Why is this view too simplistic?
29. Do you believe that there is a place for the use of administrative and communal rules in management of shared resources? What limits do you see to their role?
30. Zoning has an important role to play in the management of shared natural resources. What types of roles does it have in such management? Give examples.
31. When open-access to the use of natural resources alters the availability of mixed goods this requires alterations in government (or communal) policies regulating their use. Use a diagram to explain this. Give examples of such goods and discuss the difficulties involved in resolving social conflict between those who want to use such resources for consumptive purposes and those who want to conserve them for non-consumptive purposes.

Readings and References

Coase, R.H. (1960). The problem of social cost, *Journal of Law and Economics*, 1–44. doi: https://doi.org/10.1057/9780230523210_6.

Duncan, R. and C. Tisdell (1971). Research and technical progress: The returns to producers*, *Economic Record*, 47, 124–129. doi: 10.1111/j.1475-4932.1971.tb00752.x.

Gregory, R. (1986). Interpreting measures of economic loss: Evidence from contingent valuation and experimental studies, *Journal of Environmental Economics and Management*, 13, 325–337. doi: https://doi.org/10.1016/0095-0696(86)90003-3.

Ison, S., S. Peake and S. Wall (2002). *Environmental Issues and Policies*, Pearson Education, Harlow, Essex, UK. [Chapter 4].

Kahn, J.R. (2005). *The Economic Approach to Environmental and Natural Resources*, 3rd edn. South-Western, Mason, Ohio, USA. [Chapter 3].

Knetsch, J.L. and J.A. Sinden (1984). Willingness to pay and compensation demanded: Empirical evidence of an unexpected disparity in measures of value, *Quarterly Journal of Economics*, 99, 507–521. doi: 10.2307/1885962.

Little, I.M.D. (1957). *A Critique of Welfare Economics*, 2nd edn. Oxford University Press, Oxford.

Ostrom, E. (1990). *Governing the Commons: The Evolution of Institutions for Collective Action*, Cambridge University Press, Cambridge, UK and New York.

Pearce, D. and A. Markandya (1989). *Environmental Policy Benefits: Monetary Valuation*, Organization for Economic Co-operation and Development, Paris.

Perman, R., Y. Ma, M. Common, D. Maddison and J. McGilvray (2011). *Natural Resource and Environmental Economics*, 4th edn. Pearson, Harlow, Essex UK. [Chapters 5 and 6, Relatively advanced].

Tietenberg, T. and L. Lewis (2018). *Environmental and Natural Resource Economics*, 11th edn. Routledge, New York and Abingdon, Oxon, UK. [Chapters 12 and 14].

Tisdell, C.A. (1993). *Environmental Economics: Policies for Environmental Management and Sustainable Development*, Edward Elgar, Aldershot, UK and Brookfield, VT, USA. [Chapters 4 and 5].

Tisdell, C.A. (2003a). *Ecological and Environmental Economics: Selected Issues and Policy Responses*, Edward Elgar, Cheltenham, UK and Northampton, MA, USA. [Chapters 16–18].

Tisdell, C.A. (2003b). *Economics and Ecology in Agriculture and Marine Production*, Edward Elgar, Cheltenham, UK and Northampton, MA, USA.

Tisdell, C.A. (2005). *Economics of Environmental Conservation*, 2nd edn. Edward Elgar, Cheltenham, UK and Northampton, MA, USA. [Chapter 6].

Tisdell, C.A. (2007). Poverty, political failure and the use of open-access resources in developing countries. In C.A. Tisdell (Ed.) *Poverty, Poverty Alleviation and Social Disadvantage*, 193–202. Serials Publication, New Delhi.

Tisdell, C.A. and K. Hartley (2008). *Microeconomic Policy: A New Perspective*, Edward Elgar, Cheltenham, UK and Northampton, MA, USA.

Chapter 6

Economic Valuation of Environmental Spillovers and Natural Resources

6.1. Introduction

There are growing concerns about actual and prospective environmental developments, as well as about the declining availability of natural resources. These have stimulated interest in economic methods for evaluating environmental spillovers (externalities) and for determining the desirability of conserving natural resources. The method most frequently used by economists to address such matters is *social cost–benefit analysis*. Economists often endeavor to express the social costs and benefits of alternative economic options in monetary terms in order to determine those possibilities that will increase social net benefit and if possible find the one that maximizes social net benefit. Monetary sums provide the common metric for this analysis. At this level of generality, social cost–benefit analysis seems appealing because of its apparent simplicity. However, such analysis is more complex and controversial than it appears to be at first sight. There are several reasons for this.

First, ethical, moral or normative assumptions have to be made in order to derive measures of social benefits and costs. This is unavoidable. For example, it must be decided whether the preferences of all individuals should count or which subset of individuals should count in estimating social costs and benefits. A further important issue is how their valuations should be combined to obtain aggregate measures of the costs and benefits of the alternative uses of resources. Given that the valuations of individuals are to count, then it is necessary to determine how best they can be measured and to consider how accurate these estimates are likely to be. This aspect also raises the question of whether all valuations can be expressed accurately and meaningfully in monetary terms. Such issues have been discussed in depth by both economists and philosophers.

The main purpose of economic valuation is to identify socially desirable improvements in the allocation of resources. However, apart from the application of economic evaluation techniques to the improved social management of the use of the environment and natural resources, economic valuation techniques are sometimes applied in legal cases to determine damages and compensation to be paid to injured parties, for instance, in tort law. They have, for example, been applied to assess compensation for damages caused by environmental disasters and the loss of environmental amenities resulting from the "wrongful" action of offending parties. This approach was, for instance, adopted in assessing the legal liability of the owners of the *Exxon Valdez* (an oil tanker, which ran aground in Alaska) causing considerable environmental damage (Carson *et al.*, 2003).

The purpose of this chapter is to highlight the basic ideas underlying social cost–benefit analysis, consider some of the limitations of the analysis, such as those involving measurement issues and philosophical questions, and to outline procedures that can be followed in applying social cost–benefit analysis to the evaluation of environmental spillovers and natural resource use. Subsequently, the valuation of spillovers that have an impact on marketed commodities is discussed and the methods for valuing of changes in environments or natural resources that involve non-marketed economic impacts are considered.

6.2. The Basic Ideas Behind Social Cost–Benefit Analysis

6.2.1. *A simple illustration*

Most of the economic analysis undertaken in this book so far has involved simple forms of social cost–benefit analysis based on using

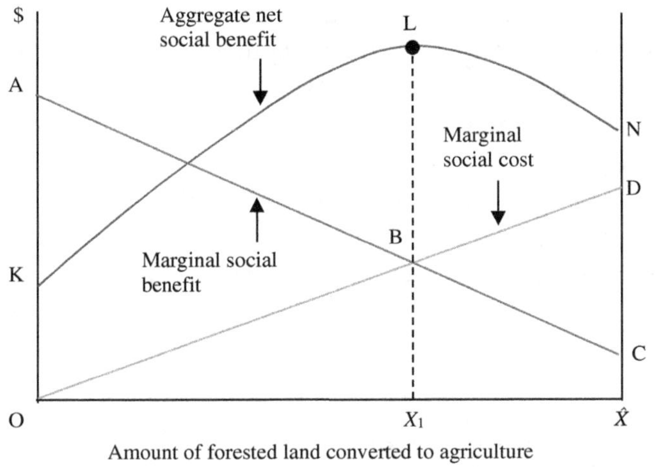

Fig. 6.1. An illustration of a simple social cost–benefit problem involving natural resource use. Note that the aggregate net benefit curve and the marginal curves are drawn to different scales.

either the Paretian improvement criterion or the potential Paretian improvement criterion. The main idea behind this analysis can be illustrated in Fig. 6.1. Suppose that a natural resource has two alternative uses. It may be used for development purposes or conserved. While its use will bring economic benefits, there will also be an opportunity cost in terms of benefits forgone from the loss of the conserved resource. These benefits and costs need to be weighed up. To make this example concrete, suppose that the natural resource is an area of tropical forest. It may be left in its natural state or converted to farmland. It may be logged, cleared and converted to agricultural land growing oil palm. The total area of available forested land is assumed to be $\hat{X}$. Let X represent the amount of this land converted to the growing of oil palm, then $\hat{X} - X$ represents that remaining as tropical forest. In Fig. 6.1, line *ABC* represents the marginal social net benefit in dollars of the land converted to agriculture and line *OBD* represents the *decline* in net social benefit that results from the reduction in the forested area. The former might consist of the change in aggregate net profit obtained from the use of the land for agriculture. Lost marginal benefits as a result of deforestation could consist of the marginal loss from a reduction in environmental services provided by the forest. These services might consist of carbon sequestration, preservation of natural biodiversity, less siltation offsite and more regular water flows. Agricultural use of the land lowers these benefits. This is an opportunity cost of agricultural development.

In the case illustrated in Fig. 6.1, aggregate net social benefit from the use of the available area of tropical land (shown by curve KLN) is maximized when X_1 of this land is converted to agricultural use and $\hat{X} - X_1$ of it is conserved as tropical forest. This corresponds to a situation in which the marginal social benefits from forest conversion to agriculture just equal the marginal social loss from deforestation.

6.2.2. *Some complications*

The simple case shown in Fig. 6.1 glosses over many challenges that can arise in obtaining accurate estimates of the relationships shown. Actual estimates of the relationship may, for example, be subject to considerable error due to uncertainty. Only a limited amount of resources may be available for estimating the relationships involved and this will affect the accuracy of the estimates. Even with a large expenditure on this estimation, it may still be impossible to eliminate all uncertainty. However, as pointed out previously, even imperfect estimates can be a guide to rational decision-making (see Section 5.2.2.4).

Usually, economists suppose changes in the aggregate net social benefits resulting from small variations in resource use to alter by marginal (small) amounts. The aggregate net social benefit function is assumed to be continuous and differentiable everywhere. However, some environmental or resource-use situations occur in which a small change in resource use results in a major (non-marginal) variation in aggregate social net benefits. Such situations are modeled in mathematics by catastrophe theory (Anon, 2020; Zeeman, 1976).

An example can be illustrated in Fig. 6.2, assuming the same land-use problem as outlined above. The relationship $ABCD$ now represents the *most probable* level of aggregate social net benefit as agricultural land use replaces the tropical forest. It indicates that aggregate net social benefits are likely to fall dramatically if more than X_1 of the available land is converted to agriculture. This implies that X_1 is the

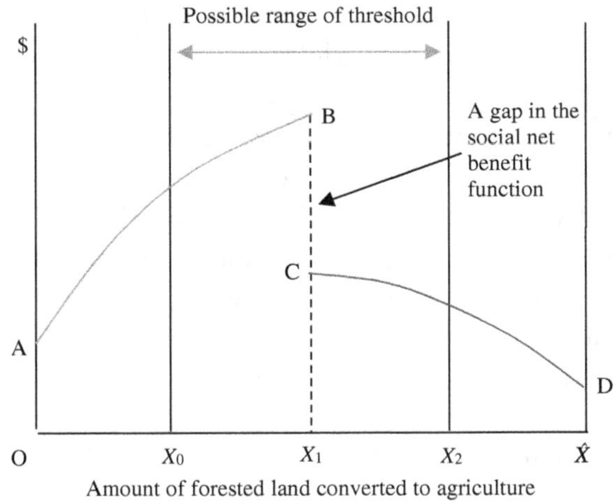

Fig. 6.2. An illustration that the presence of uncertain thresholds complicates social cost–benefit analysis. The broken relationship consisting of curves *AB* and *CD* represents the most probable level of social net benefits from conversion of forested land to agriculture. It is assumed in this example that the gap in this function could be at X_0 or X_2 or anywhere in between.

most probable threshold. However, suppose that it is known that the actual threshold (which corresponds to the maximum of the net social benefit function) is definitely at X_0 or at X_2 or somewhere in between. Assume further that forest conversion is irreversible. Then if society is highly risk-averse, no more than X_0 of the forested land should be converted to agriculture. Given this relationship, it would nonetheless always be irrational from an economics point of view to convert less than X_0 of the available land to agriculture or to do this for more than X_2 of the land area.

6.3. Normative and Philosophical Matters as well as a Measurement Issue

6.3.1. *Ethical and normative assumptions underlying economic valuation*

Ethical and normative assumptions cannot be avoided in the process of social valuation and assessment. Therefore, the extent to which valuations and evaluations of resource-use possibilities are socially acceptable will depend on how widely their ethical and normative bases are accepted.

Economists have endeavored to base their valuations and evaluations on welfare principles, which they believe are likely to be widely accepted. However, not everyone finds these principles to be acceptable and many may only accept them subject to qualification. Most economists believe that economic valuations of the supply of commodities should be based on individuals' desires for these commodities. The most frequently used measure of the strength of this desire for a commodity is the maximum monetary amount that individuals (in aggregate) are *willing to* pay for its supply. However, in some cases (particularly those involving environmental goods) the minimum amount of money, which individuals would *accept as compensation* for the loss of a good rather than the maximum amount they would be willing to pay for its retention, is used as a measure of its economic value. The question then arises of the extent to which willingness of individuals to pay (or accept compensation) should be used as an indicator of value and subsequently, decide policy choices for using resources. Using these measures assumes that individuals are well informed about what is desirable for them or if they are not well informed, and that nevertheless their wishes should be respected. However, the latter point of view may be difficult to accept if the supply of public goods is at stake. This is because catering for the wishes of the ill-informed could lead to a supply of public goods that disappoints them as well as those who are knowledgeable.

There are also many issues that should not be decided by willingness to pay. For example, suppose that a person has been found guilty of a crime and that hanging or life imprisonment is the alternative possible sentences. It would not be morally acceptable to decide this by whether those who are in favor of hanging are willing to pay more for this than those who are opposed to it. Therefore, economic valuation is only relevant to limited types of social choices.

There are values that transcend economic values and as suggested by Kant (1781), these values are likely to transcend what individuals want. However, transcendental values may not be self-evident. In addition, there can be a problem when different individuals hold different transcendental values in resolving social conflict. Furthermore, it seems likely that accepted transcendental values vary from culture to culture and may alter with the passage of time.

Economic values (traditionally) are entirely anthropocentric because they depend only on what humans want. Consequently, other species will only be willingly conserved if this is desired by human beings, that is, if humans place a positive monetary value on their continuing existence. Despite this, it has become more widely accepted in Western countries that humankind has a responsibility to conserve nature and biodiversity independently of individual human wishes (Passmore, 1974). It has also become more widely accepted that humans should not ill-treat animals and that they have some duties of care towards animals (Passmore, 1974).

Given the above observations, economic valuation can only be a partial measure of what is valuable. It may, for example, be a useful guide for valuing necessities and other goods with which individuals are quite familiar but it is liable to falter when commodities need to be valued of which individuals have limited knowledge or which involve intangible considerations.

6.3.2. *A measurement issue*

Economists usually assume that individuals are knowledgeable and engage in rational optimizing behavior. They regard a Paretian improvement as desirable and most social cost–benefit analysis is based on the view that a *potential* Paretian improvement is desirable. Therefore, economists often search for changes in resource use that can bring about an actual Paretian improvement or a potential Paretian improvement. This requires economists to try to elicit the economic values, which individuals place on alternative forms of resource use. For example, the economic value of an environmental amenity may be based on how much individuals are willing to pay in aggregate for its retention if it already exists. Or, alternatively, its economic value might be estimated on the basis of how much, in aggregate, individuals would have to be paid to compensate them for the loss of the amenity.

Which of these bases is chosen will depend upon views about what is just. If it is believed that those who desire the amenity have a right to it, the latter basis of valuation is appropriate. Otherwise, the former has merit.

A problem is that depending on the basis used, estimated economic values differ and often do so substantially. Empirical evidence supports the proposition that willingness to pay for a valued resource is normally less than willingness to accept compensation for its loss (Kahneman *et al.*, 1991; Kahneman and Tversky, 2000; Knetsch and Sinden, 1984). This does not mean (as was pointed out in Section 5.2.2.4) that no rational economic decision can be made (see also Tisdell, 1996, Chapter 2). For example, it may turn out that both measures indicate that an environmental resource should be conserved or both measures may signal that there is no economic demand in aggregate to conserve it. If, however, the measures give different indications, the situation is more difficult. One must choose between the alternatives by making additional value judgments.

6.4. Steps in Applying Social Cost–Benefit Analysis to the Valuation of Environmental Spillovers and to the Valuation of Natural Resources

6.4.1. *Identifying and measuring impacts*

One of the first steps in valuing environmental spillovers and in evaluating natural resources is to identify their attributes that need to be taken into account. In evaluating environmental spillovers from an existing economic activity, or an existing natural resource, or from a projected new economic project, consideration needs to be given initially to

(1) its relevant external biological and physical impacts;
(2) its relevant consequences for social relationships; and
(3) economic variables that are likely to be altered by these.

Identification of relevant impacts of the above type can be quite challenging, especially if new projects are involved. Usually, identification of relevant impacts requires cooperation by experts from different fields or disciplines. Measurement of the impacts is likely to be even more difficult and can be costly. If the project or activity is a new one in a particular location, estimates of its biophysical and social impacts can be expected to be uncertain. Scientists may, for example, be relatively sure of some external impacts but less certain of others. It may be possible, therefore, to order the likely different types of impacts by the degree of confidence that one ought to have in them. Because biophysical impacts contribute to the economic analysis of spillovers, they affect the reliability of economic valuations. Both biophysical and economic impacts can be uncertain.

While it is important to note the likely social and sociological consequences of changes in economic activity or new projects, economic methods possibly only have limited ability to evaluate these. If considerable change occurs in social structures and cultures, economic analysis is unable to provide a clear guide to the value of the changed social situations. This is so even if the changes are associated with a considerable increase in economic wealth. The final valuation of alternative social structures and cultures as such is beyond the bounds of economics. Nevertheless, economists as individuals should have views about these alternatives.

6.4.2. *Identifying the economic nature of the components of environmental spillovers and of natural resources*

In order to value the components of environmental spillovers, it is useful to identify the economic nature of the commodities affected by these spillovers. In some cases, the main consequences of the environmental externalities might be primarily or exclusively on the external supply of marketed commodities, such as a spillover that causes a loss in agricultural production. Or the external loss might be mostly of the supply of a (localized) public good. Often the external economic impacts of a change consist in part of a variation in the availability of private goods as well as the supply of public goods. This means that the external economic consequences are mixed in terms of the nature of the economic goods affected. In some cases, the environmental spillovers involve a variation also in the availability of quasi-public or quasi-private goods (see Chapter 3). The appropriate method for valuing an economic spillover can be expected to vary with the economic type or types of commodities affected by the environmental spillover.

When the supply of marketed commodities is affected by a spillover, it is often possible to base the valuation of the economic consequences of the spillover on market considerations. For example, if an economic activity results in an external loss in agricultural production and if the variation in the farmers' supply is insufficient to influence the market price of their produce, the net loss in their income resulting from the economic activity can be used as a measure of the social economic loss arising from this effect. On the other hand, if the economic activity results (or is predicted to result in) the loss of a public good, such as a wild species that only has existence and bequest value, no markets exist for it. It is, therefore, necessary to use non-market methods of valuation to provide monetary estimates of the economic loss involved. These include methods such as stated preference or stated value methods introduced later in this chapter.

Similarly, if the use of a natural resource is not priced, or only partially priced, relevant methods of economic valuation will depend on its economic nature of the goods and services supplied by the natural resource. For example, if a national park or a protected area is taken as an example and entry to it is free, values will have to be assigned to its on-site recreational use (which basically involves a quasi-private good) and to its off-site impacts. Its off-site consequences could involve conserving nature, which is valued because of its non-use qualities (such as its existence value) and because of the spillover environmental services it provides, such as ensuring high quality and regular water supplies for urban areas downstream of the protected area.

Identification of the type of economic commodities the supply of which is affected by environmental spillovers or by the availability of a natural resource is an important step in the economic valuation process. Note that there are several available types of systems for classifying economic goods. One system is along the lines discussed in Chapter 3 and illustrated in Fig. 3.5. Another is that which subdivides total economic value into sub-components breaking it down first into use value and non-use value categories, and then subsequently further subdividing these into additional categories (see Table 11.1 in this book and Tisdell, 2005, pp. 110–113). Nevertheless, in the end one has to consider the type of classification indicated by Fig. 3.5 in order to select relevant valuation techniques.

6.4.3. *Confidence in estimates of economic value and sensitivity of returns*

Even when one has selected an appropriate technique for estimating economic values, there is bound to be some degree of uncertainty about the accuracy of the estimates obtained. This is usually because only a limited amount of information can be collected given the cost involved and because of constraints on the available time for obtaining estimates. There may also be situations in which the information that can be collected is unreliable. For example, stated values or preferences may be unreliable if respondents engage in strategic bias in their stating values or respondents may have insufficient knowledge to value accurately options presented to them. When valuation of net economic benefits requires future market prices and costs to be taken into account, estimates of these may also be subject to error due to uncertainty about the future.

One way in which such uncertainty is sometimes allowed for is not just to provide a point or a single estimate of net benefits but a range of estimates that vary with different possible values of the key independent variables. This is usually called *sensitivity analysis*. Sometimes, subjective probabilities are placed on these possible alternatives. In such cases, statistical risk analysis can be applied. However, if there is considerable uncertainty about the relevant probabilities, the value of this analysis is sometimes questioned.

Estimates of social economic benefit from an economic change or that from an existing activity usually consist of several components. For example, social benefits may comprise of private benefits plus external benefits. One might be relatively confident about the values of private benefits but less so about the external benefits or costs and their components. In principle, one might be able to identify the extent to which one has confidence in the different components comprising the estimate of social net benefits. This can be very helpful in facilitating rational choice under conditions of uncertainty.

By the way of illustration, one might be certain that the internal *private* rate of return from a new project is 15%. At the same time, it is known that it will have adverse spillovers and that this will reduce the internal rate of return from this project when it is evaluated from a social point of view. The exact amount by which this will happen may be uncertain. However, it may be certain that the reduction will be in the range of 3–6%. Thus one could be confident that the social internal rate of return from the project would be in the range of 9–12%. Despite this uncertainty, policy-makers may conclude that it is a socially worthwhile project if say the prevailing rate of return is 5%. On the other hand, if after allowing for externalities, the social internal rate of return is only 1–4%, the project may be rejected from a social point of view. Should, however, the internal social rate of return from the project be in the range of 3–8%, it is uncertain whether the project will be socially wealth-creating given a rate of interest of 5%. Policy-makers will have to take into account the risks they are willing to take in this case.

6.5. Allowing for the Time Dimension in the Process of Valuation

A difficult issue in economic valuation is how best to value economic benefits obtained in different periods of time. Usually, the same benefit obtained in a future period of time is considered to be worth less than that economic benefit received now. For example, one dollar available 10 years from now is normally considered to be worth less (or of lesser value) than one dollar available now. There are several possible reasons why this is believed to be so. For example, having the one dollar available now rather than in 10 years time gives the holder more options about what to do with it. It adds to its option value. Secondly, if a positive return can be earnt on a dollar now, it can accumulate to much more than one dollar in 10 years' time. Thirdly, there might be some uncertainty about whether the dollar will actually become available in

10 years' time. This will result in a reduction in the perceived value of an offer of this sum in 10 years' time. Fourthly, if price inflation occurs the real value of a dollar 10 years hence is less than it is now worth.

The upshot of the above considerations is that future economic benefits are normally discounted or reduced compared with present benefits and they are more heavily discounted the further into the future is their availability. Often a rate of interest is used in the process of this discounting.

In Section 6.4.3, the notion of the internal rate of return was mentioned. This is the rate of discount or the rate of interest which when applied to the stream of benefits and costs from a project or economic activity results in the sum of discounted benefits just being equal to the sum of discounted costs, that is, result in its net present value being equal to zero. If the going relevant rate of interest or the social rate of discount of net benefits is less than the internal rate of return, then it is implied that the project or activity confers a net economic benefit after making allowance for the time dimension. However, the question of what is an appropriate rate of social discount is a controversial matter because discounting of future benefits from resource use has welfare implications for future generations, and it raises several philosophical issues, which are considered in the next chapter. That chapter deals with sustainability.

The remainder of the discussion in this chapter is based on the use of single-period models and therefore, side-steps problems raised by the dimension of time. This makes the exposition less complex than it otherwise could be. However, these models can be extended so that they take account of costs and benefits for multiple time periods even though their extension can be complex. Nevertheless, they are useful as starting points for considering the valuation of environmental spillovers and natural resources.

6.6. Cases in which Market-Based Valuation of Environmental Spillovers and Natural Resource Use is Possible

Sometimes the impact of environmental spillovers depends solely on the supply of marketed commodities, or virtually so. Furthermore, there may be occasions where all the economic values associated with the use of a natural resource are marketed. In such cases, market values can usually be the basis for economic valuation. Let us consider first cases where market prices are not affected by spillovers from an economic activity and then discuss cases where they are.

6.6.1. *Simple market-based valuations*

Suppose that the economic activity of a particular industry or the completion of a project in a particular location has an adverse external impact on the productivity of supplies of a product X as a result of an environmental spillover. For example, water pollution from factories upstream may adversely affect the quality of water downstream. This may stunt agricultural crops grown by using the water from the stream for irrigation. Or, if the water is used on fish farms, it may add to the costs of its purification or increase the mortality and morbidity of cultured fish.

Let us suppose that the suppliers subject to the adverse externality have no influence on market prices and that the markets in which they trade are competitive. Then the social economic loss that results from the environmental spillover will be equal to the loss in the economic surplus experienced by those suppliers of X who are adversely affected by the environmental externality. This is illustrated in Fig. 6.3 for a single-period case. In this figure, line ACS_1 represents the supply curve of suppliers of X (who are potentially subject to the externality) if the externality is absent. It is their marginal cost of production. Once, however, they experience the adverse environmental externality, their marginal cost of producing X shifts upward and their supply curve becomes DES_2. Assuming that the suppliers affected by the externality have no influence on the price of X (which is assumed to be OP), these suppliers would find it profitable to supply X_2 of product X in the absence of the externality, but only X_1 after its occurrence. Their economic surplus falls from an amount equal to the area of triangle ACP to an amount equal to the area of triangle DEP. The social economic loss arising from the activity causing the externality is equivalent to the area of quadrilateral $ACED$ in Fig. 6.3. In order to determine the net

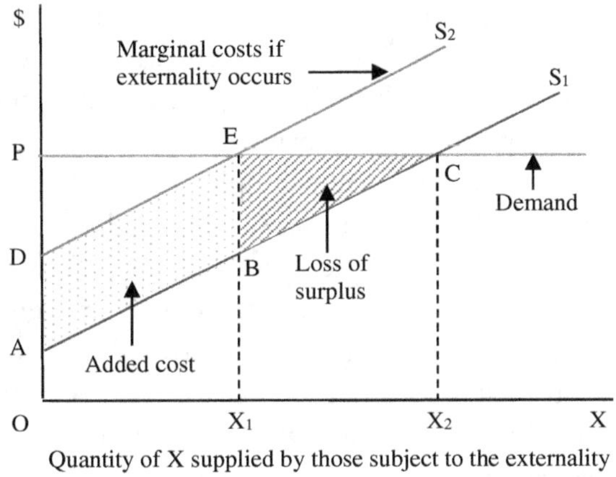

Fig. 6.3. A market-based case in which it is relatively easy to estimate the social economic loss caused by an adverse environmental externality. In the case illustrated, the adverse externality causes marginal costs of those supplying X (who are impacted by it) to rise from AS_1 to DS_2. Because these producers are unable to influence the price of X (which remains constant at P), their marginal revenue function is as shown by the horizontal line *PC* and the social economic loss arising from the adverse externality is equivalent to the area of quadrilateral *ACED*.

social benefit from an activity or project that causes this adverse externality, the loss represented by the area of *ACED* should be deducted from the private economic benefit obtained from the activity or project that causes the adverse externality.

Note that the social economic loss occasioned by the externality can be divided into two components:

(1) the increase in costs experienced by those suppliers of X adversely affected by the externality (shown by the dotted area in Fig. 6.3) and
(2) the loss in their economic surplus as a result of scaling back their production after the occurrence of the externality (shown in Fig. 6.3 by the hatched triangle).

Observe that the area of triangle *BCE* can be small in relation to the area of trapezium *ABED*. When this is so, the increase in costs after the occurrence of the externality will almost account for the entire social economic loss occasioned by the externality.

In some cases, an environmental externality can impact not only on the cost of supplying a commodity adversely affected by it but also on the quality of this product. The affected product may, therefore, have to be sold at a lower price than otherwise or possibly it cannot be sold at all because of health risks, for example, aquacultured fish subject to the externality may be contaminated. In the latter case, given the situation illustrated in Fig. 6.3, the social economic loss occasioned by the spillover would be equivalent to the area of triangle *ACP*. If the affected commodity still remains saleable after the occurrence of the externality but must be sold at a lower price than previously, this can also be allowed for in the analysis. Quality reductions in commodities as a result of adverse environmental spillovers result in social economic losses.

6.6.2. *A more complicated case involving a change in the market price of a product adversely affected by an environmental externality*

The external environmental effects of some spillovers may be sufficient to alter the price of a product that is affected by them. Such a case is illustrated in Fig. 6.4. Suppose that the supply of a product X is adversely affected by an externality. In the absence of the externality, the supply curve for product X is as shown by the line ACS_1 in Fig. 6.4 but after the externality occurs it is DES_2. The shift upwards in the supply curve indicates the increase in marginal costs imposed on industry X by the externality. In the absence of the externality, the equilibrium quantity of X marketed is X_2 which sells at a price per unit of P_1. After the externality occurs, the equilibrium quantity of X supplied falls to X_1 and its prices rises to P_2. There is a reduction in the consumers' surplus from product X as a result of its rise in price. Producers' surplus obtained by the suppliers of X also decreases. The former decreases by an amount equal to the difference between the area of triangle P_1CF and that of triangle P_2EF and the latter falls by the difference between the area of triangle ACP_1 and triangle DEP_2. The total decline in the net economic value of X as a result of the externality is equal to the sum of these differences.

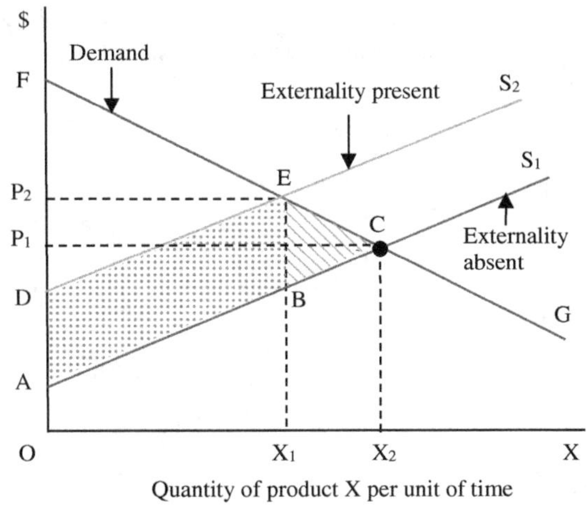

Fig. 6.4. A case in which an adverse externality increases the cost of production of a product X and forces up its price. In the case illustrated, the loss in consumers' surplus plus the loss in producers' surplus from X is equivalent to the area of the quadrilateral *ACED*.

The total loss in surplus obtained by consumers and producers from product X as a result of the externality is in fact equal to the area of quadrilateral *ACED* in Fig. 6.4. This follows because in the absence of the externality consumers' plus producers' surplus from X equals the area of triangle *ACF* and after the externality, it equals the area of triangle *DEF*. The difference between the area of those two triangles is the area of quadrilateral *ACED*. The area of *ACED* consists of the total rise in the cost of producing X_1 (the dotted trapezium) plus the economic losses stemming from the reduction in supply of X from X_2 to X_1 (shown by the hatched triangle).

This decomposition of the change in economic benefits or welfare from a negative environmental spillover can be of considerable practical value because it is often not difficult to estimate the extra production costs associated with such a spillover, and the stemming losses may be relatively small, or able to be approximated without undue difficulty. Less information is required to make such estimates than is needed to estimate consumers' plus producers' surplus *prior* to the environmental spillover and to do this for the predicted situation after the

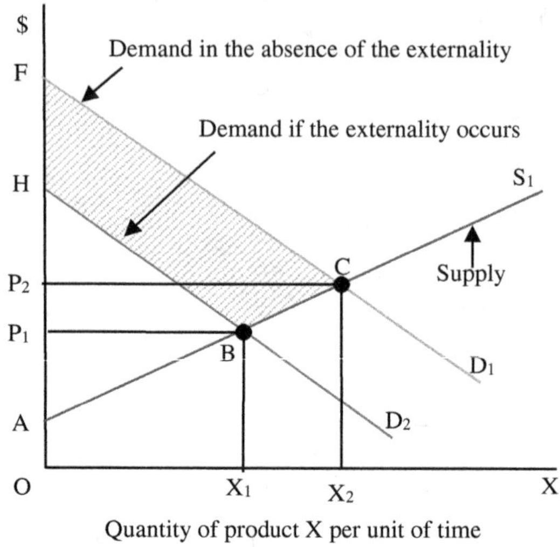

Fig. 6.5. An unfavorable externality may adversely affect the quality of a product. In the case illustrated, this results in the demand curve for product X falling from FD_1 to HD_2 and consequently, the market equilibrium of X alters from C to B. The total loss in consumers' plus producers' surplus from X is shown by the hatched quadrilateral in this figure.

occurrence of the externality. Furthermore, the estimates of changes in economic benefits are likely to be more accurate when the decomposition approach is applied rather than the latter surplus-type approach.

Consider another case in which there is a negative environmental externality. However, assume that this does not alter the marginal cost of producing X but instead reduces the quality of X and consequently, lowers the demand of consumers for it. In Fig. 6.5, the private marginal cost of supplying X is shown by line AS_1. In the absence of an adverse externality, the demand for product X is as indicated by line FD_1. Suppose that the adverse externality just mentioned lowers the demand for the product so that the demand for it drops to HD_2. In the case illustrated, market equilibrium for X alters from C to B. There is a decline in the total economic surplus of consumers plus that of producers equivalent to the area of quadrilateral *HBCF*. It can be readily seen that both the surplus of consumers of X declines (it falls from an amount equal to the area of P_2CF to that of the area of triangle P_1BH)

and producers' surplus falls also. It declines from an amount equal to the area of triangle ACP_2 to that of the area of triangle ABP_1.

In some cases, the quality of a product may decline as a result of an adverse externality and its marginal cost of its production may also rise as a result of the adverse externality. The above analysis is easily extended to cover this case. Similarly, if a favorable externality is generated, this can be analyzed by applying similar analysis.

It should also be noted that environmental spillovers from economic activities at one location can impact on the availability of public goods and unpriced or incompletely priced commodities at other locations. For example, activity at one location may impact on air quality at another location or cause acid rains elsewhere, all of which are likely to reduce environmental quality in the areas affected. The economic evaluation of such spillovers requires the use of techniques of the type outlined in Section 6.7 and in the following sections of this chapter.

6.6.3. *Valuing marketed natural resources that do not generate significant environmental spillovers*

Sometimes the use and management of natural resources do not result in significant externalities but this could be rare. It is conceivable that low impact logging of natural forests in some areas has few environmental spillovers and so might some types of mining in particular areas. In any case, private benefits from the use of a natural resource must be taken into account as part of social cost–benefit analysis.

Economists usually suppose that the private economic value of a natural resource, the product of which is marketed, is equal to its maximum capitalized or net present value. It is assumed that owners (and potential buyers) of such a resource would want to maximize its capitalized value because this accords with the motive of maximizing profit. The capitalized value of a resource from a private point of view is equal to the sum of the stream of future (maximum) profits that can be earned from it discounted back to the present. This value depends on the discount rate applied. The discount rate usually increases with the rate of interest. However, valuation using this method is not as straightforward as it may appear to be at first sight. This is because of the presence of imperfect information or uncertainty and the occurrence of bounded rationality.

There is likely to be some uncertainty about future prices of the products obtained from the natural resource and the private costs of utilizing it. This uncertainty may reflect uncertainties about the availability of substitutes for the resource and new technologies. Sometimes also, the physical or biological properties of a resource may be imperfectly known, for example, the extent of an ore body and its mineral content, or the level of harvest that can be sustained by a forest may be uncertain. Uncertainty is likely to result in different economic entities having different estimates of the private economic value of a natural resource.

Such uncertainties tend to reduce the anticipated capitalized private value of the natural resources and accelerate the rate of their private use. Consequently, production from these resources is tilted in favor of the present period (and those periods not far away) at the expense of supplies in later periods. Production from the resource is liable to be sustained for a shorter period of time than otherwise. This (plus other considerations) has led economists such as Daly (1980a) to warn that natural resources are likely to be utilized at a faster rate than is socially desirable.

Other considerations (discussed in the next chapter) mentioned by neo-Malthusian economists include adverse environmental externalities (such as pollution) generated by a high level of throughput (use) of natural resources in economic production and the possible deprivation of future generations of economic opportunities due to reduced availability of natural resources. Daly (1980b, pp. 337–344) recommends that governments impose depletion quotas on the amount of minerals used annually and that these be auctioned. These depletion quotas can be made tradable. It is not intended to go into the merits and drawbacks of such a policy here but these will be discussed in the next chapter. There is additional discussion of the possible future scarcity of minerals in Chapters 11 and 12. At this point, it is sufficient to note that given current economic systems, there are sometimes concerns that natural resources are being used at a socially excessive rate.

Despite the difficulties created by uncertainties of the type mentioned, social economic evaluation of natural resource use requires account to be taken of private benefits from their use because private benefits are part of the determination of social benefits from economic projects or from economic activities. To allow for uncertainty, benefits may be estimated for a range of possible events or the sensitivity of net benefits to variations in important non-controlled variables may be considered (see Section 6.5).

6.7. Introduction to Methods of Valuing Non-marketed Commodities

Several different methods are available to determine the economic values of non-marketable commodities. Some of these methods (such as contingent valuation) can also be used to value marketed commodities. It is common for environmental commodities (such as air quality, scenic landscapes or seascapes) as well as access to national parks, protected areas and outdoor recreational sites not to be priced, or if access to the latter is priced, the price may only be a nominal one. In order to determine the demand for such commodities and subsequently their economic value, indirect economic methods are used to estimate the demand for these commodities. Usually these methods are classified into two sets: (1) revealed preference methods and (2) stated preference methods.

The revealed preference methods to be outlined in this chapter are as follows: (1) the travel cost method and (2) the hedonic pricing method. The stated preference methods that will be considered are

(1) contingent valuation (of which there are a range of variants) and
(2) choice modeling.

Revealed preference methods infer the demand for a focal commodity (such as an environmental good) from empirical evidence about the demand for a *highly complementary* commodity, which is priced. For example, the demand to travel to recreational sites is highly complementary to the demand to use these sites. This relationship is utilized in applying the travel cost method as a means of determining the recreational value of outdoor sites. Similarly, the demand to live in a location with a good environment is likely to be reflected in variations in land prices according to the quality of the environment in the locality of the land. Hedonic pricing methods use such complementarity as a means for estimating the demand for environmental commodities and consequently, their economic value.

Stated preference methods rely on statements by individuals about their willingness to pay for alternative economic options (including the availability of environmental goods) or to accept monetary compensation for their loss. Contingent valuation approaches adopt relatively direct ways of eliciting these values from individuals whereas choice modeling techniques adopt a more indirect approach. The latter methods rely on the economic evaluation of attributes or characteristics of commodities that determine the final demand for these.

Although economic valuation methods have been divided into two sets (revealed preference and stated preference methods), it is possible to have methods that combine elements of both sets. Furthermore, the methods for valuation outlined in this chapter are those that are most frequently used — additional methods exist. Figure 6.6 provides a summary of the methods that will be considered here.

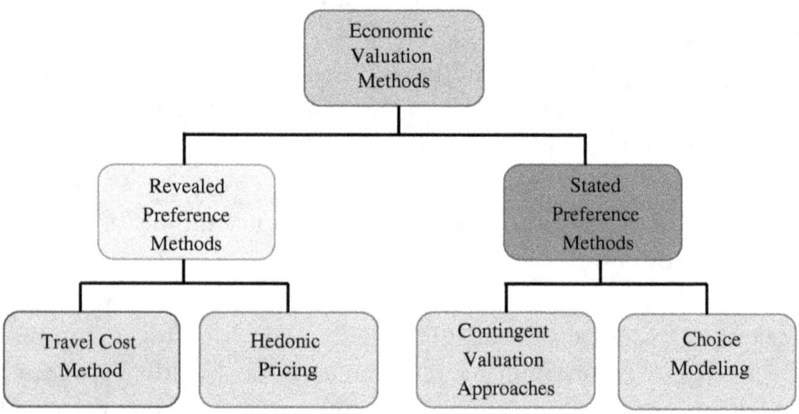

Fig. 6.6. A classification of types of economic valuation methods for non-marketed goods discussed in this chapter.

6.8. The Travel Cost Method of Economic Valuation

6.8.1. *Background about this method*

The travel cost method is a revealed preference method of economic valuation, which infers the demand for the recreational use of an outdoor site from the demand to travel to it. The demand to travel to the focal outdoor site is assumed to depend on the cost of a trip to it. From the demand to travel to a site, the willingness of visitors to pay to visit the site can be obtained.

This can be used to determine the visitors' economic surplus from visiting the site, that is, the difference between the maximum amount visitors would be prepared to spend on visits to the site and the amount they actually spend. Their economic surplus from visits to the site is used as an economic measure of its value for recreational purposes. In recent times, the method has been frequently used to provide one measure of an economic value of national parks and protected areas, namely their value for recreational use. This economic value (although it can be important) is normally only part of the total economic value of such natural resources. It can also be applied to the economic assessment of outdoor human-modified environments that are used for recreational purposes. For example, it was once widely used to help raise the estimated benefit–cost ratios of the building of dams — estimates of the economic benefits from the recreational use of such dams were added to their other total economic benefits.

As mentioned above, the travel cost method relies heavily on the assumption that there is strong complementarity between the willingness of visitors to incur travel costs to visit an outdoor site for recreational purposes and the recreational demand for that site. The cost of visiting a site usually increases with the distance that visitors need to travel to reach the site. Therefore, other things remaining equal, one would normally expect the relative frequency of visits from populations further away from a recreational site to be less than for those populations located closer to the site. This, for example, is likely to be so for outdoor areas used for skiing. Therefore, when the relative frequency of visits from population areas to the outdoor recreational site is related to the cost of travel from these areas, one would expect this relative frequency to decline with the cost of travel. The function that relates the relative frequency of on-site visits from population areas to the cost of traveling to the site is called the *trip generation function* and is an important component of the travel cost method of valuation.

The trip generation function for a particular site is estimated from empirical data. This usually involves interviewing visitors (normally a sample of these) at the site to determine where they began their journey and to obtain an indication of their cost of traveling to the site. Additional questions may also be asked, for example, whether traveling to this site was the sole purpose of their journey. This information may be used in conjunction with data about the size of the population in the areas or zones from which visitors are sourced to estimate the trip generation function for the site being assessed. Let us consider the procedure involved in more detail.

6.8.2. *Procedures for applying the travel cost method of valuation*

In practice, application of the travel cost method involves a series of approximations. A common procedure is to divide the areas from which visitors to a site are drawn into a series of zones. Zones are determined by ensuring that travel costs from any particular zone to the site being assessed are approximately equal. The wider are the defined zones using this *zonal method*, the larger will be the divergence of travel costs within a zone, for example, the less representative will be the median or average cost of travel from the zone to the site be of the travel costs incurred by visitors to the site from the zone. Furthermore, travel costs are unlikely to be uniform for the same aerial distance from a recreational site, and the geography of transport routes has to be taken into account in determining zones.

Let us suppose that once the costs of travel are taken into account that the area from which visitors to a recreational site, *S*, are drawn can be divided into three zones (I, II and III) on the basis of the cost of travel from each of the zones. An example is shown in Fig. 6.7. If the

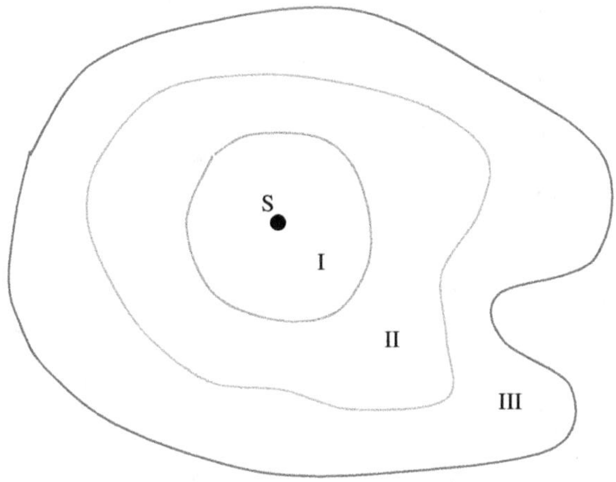

Fig. 6.7. A pattern of travel cost zones for visits to a recreational site, *S*. The borders of each of the zones (I, II and III) correspond to equal levels of cost of those traveling to *S* from a zone.

travel costs of visiting *X* is proportional to the aerial distance from *S* of the residences of visitors, each of the zones would be bounded by concentric circles centered on *S*. However, this is unlikely to be so in practice given the geographically variable nature of connecting roads and transport routes. In Fig. 6.7, the isotravel cost boundaries, which border each of the zones, are shown by "irregular" shapes to reflect the fact that travel costs are unlikely to be proportional to the aerial distance from the start of a trip to a site.

Once the travel cost zones are determined, the next step is to estimate the *trip generation function*. This requires the number of visits to the site from each of the zones (per year) to be divided by the size of the population of each of the zones. This gives the relative frequency of visits by residents of each of the zones from which visitors are sourced. When the relative frequency of visits to the recreational site are related to the (average) cost of travel from each of the zones, this specifies the trip generation function.

To take a simple case, suppose that the average cost of travel to *S* from zones I, II, and III are \$10, \$20, and \$30, respectively, and that the corresponding relative frequency of visits from each of the

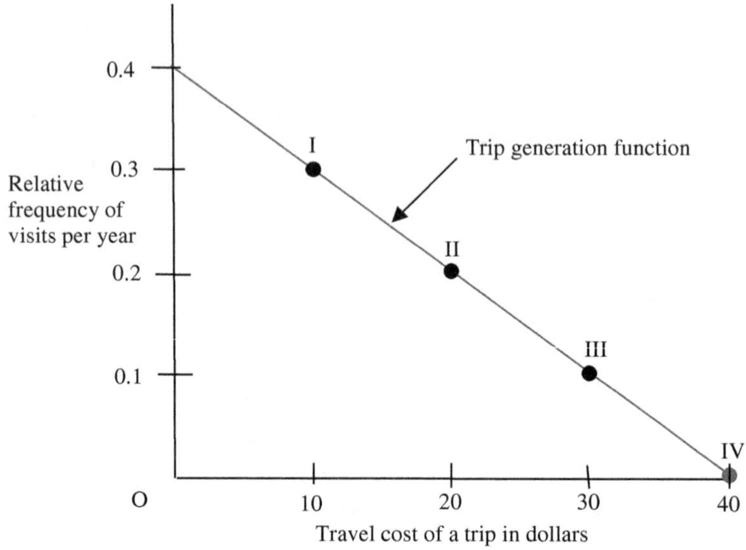

Fig. 6.8. A trip generation function. This shows that the relative frequency of visits to a recreational site declines as the cost of traveling to a site rises.

zones is 0.3, 0.2, and 0.1. Also suppose that the average cost of travel from a zone IV (not shown in Fig. 6.7 but it is the next outside zone after III) is $40 and that there are no visitors from zone IV. Then the travel cost generation function is indicated by the points I, II, III, and IV in Fig. 6.8 and corresponds approximately to a line, which pass through these points. Using the trip generation relationship, the visitors' surplus from visiting the recreational site can be estimated. Or, alternatively, the demand per visit to the site can be constructed and the visitors' surplus inferred from that (Tisdell, 2005, Section 7.4).

In order to estimate the visitors' surplus from visiting the focal recreational site, it is usually assumed that the demand of residents in each of the residential zones for visits is similar and only varies with the cost of traveling to the recreational site. For example, if in the case illustrated in Fig. 6.8, the cost of a visit was to increase by $10 for everyone, there would be no visitors from zone III and the relative frequency of visits from zones II and I to the recreational site would fall to 0.1 and 0.2, respectively.

Taking into account the number of visits from each of the residential zones, the visitors' surplus from the recreational site can be estimated. If it is assumed that \$40 is the critical travel cost at which visits to the recreational site cease, then the maximum price per visit that visitors from each of the zones would be prepared to pay would be just under \$40. Since those from zone I only outlay \$10 on travel cost, their surplus per visit approaches \$30. Similarly, that for visitors from zone II approaches \$20 and from zone III, \$10. The total surplus can, therefore, be found by multiplying the surplus per trip from each zone by the number of trips from that zone and summing these. If there is no entry fee to the recreational site, this sum is an approximation to the economic value of the site for recreational purposes.

However, recreational value is usually only a part of the total economic value of an outdoor area. For example, although most protected areas are used for recreational purposes, they also provide ecosystem services (such as maintaining clean waterflows and acting as carbon sinks) and these are not valued when only the recreational value of a site is estimated. Many of the economic values generated by such areas are obtained off-site. However, it should be remembered that there can also be negative external effects from protected areas. They can, for example, contain "pests" that cause damage to nearby farms or they may increase the risks of wild fires that threaten nearby properties and human lives.

6.8.3. *Some limitations of the travel cost method*

As already noted, the travel cost method only provides a partial estimate of the total economic value of most natural sites and human modified outdoor areas. Furthermore, questions have arisen about how travel costs should be computed. For example, should the amount of time involved in traveling to the site be regarded as a cost and if so, how should this cost be determined? In addition, the travel cost method assumes that the *sole* purpose of a journey is to reach the site to be evaluated to engage in recreational pursuits at this site. Sometimes, however, journeys involve multiple attractions and the value of the journey cannot be attributed to a single site. The method also supposes that the site is relatively small. If the recreational site is very large (as, for example, is the Great Barrier Reef Marine Park), this will not be so and travel costs will vary considerably depending on which part or parts of it are visited. Again, the visitors' surplus derived from this method is usually only for a past period of time. For many problems, the demand for using a recreational area needs to be projected into the future to take account of the future stream of economic benefits from it. This may be possible but it involves predictions and most likely some uncertainties. Additional limitations of this approach are discussed in Tisdell and Wilson (2012). See its index.

Despite these difficulties, the travel cost method can be useful in making economic decisions about land use. For example, suppose that a natural area has two alternative uses: it can either be kept as a natural area and used for recreation or "developed" for beef production. In the former case, if entry is free, it may generate a visitors' surplus of $15 million per year whereas if it is used for beef production, the net profit of pastoralists might be $10 million per year. If that is so, the land area would have a greater economic value if it were left in a natural state and used for recreation rather than developed for beef production.

6.9. Hedonic Pricing as a Valuation Method

The hedonic pricing method of valuation is also a revealed preference method and depends upon strong complementarity between marketed commodities and unmarketed environmental attributes. For example, the price of residential land usually depends on the quality of the environment made available to its holder. Other things equal, the price of residential land will tend to be higher in areas with more scenic views, those with less noise from traffic and if it is located in areas with better air quality, near parks and so on. Similarly, the rental price of apartments and other accommodation can be expected to vary with environmental factors. The following example provides an indication of how this method can be applied.

Suppose that in a residential area the main environmental factor that influences the price of land is the level of noise experienced on this land. From empirical evidence on land sales, suppose that the price of land as a function of the level of noise experienced can be determined. One would expect it to fall with increased noise levels; other things remaining constant. The reduction in the price of land is an indicator of its reduced economic value due to the noise-factor. Or the increase in the price of land as a result of reducing noise is an indicator of the economic value of noise-reduction. This information can be used as a basis for determining the economically optimal level of noise reduction in a city area. It suggests that the marginal cost of reducing noise in an area be pursued up to the point where it equals the marginal increase in land values that result from this.

This case can be made more concrete by reference to Fig. 6.9. In this figure, line *OAB* indicates the increase in land value in a particular area as a result of a reduction of noise levels in this area and line *CAD* shows the marginal cost of adopting measures to reduce noise levels in this area. Noise levels are measured by variable x. The socially optimal level of noise reduction is x_1, which corresponds to the point at which marginal increase in the market value of land in the area equals the marginal cost of lowering noise levels in the area.

Application of the hedonic pricing method is not, however, always as straightforward as in the above example. Usually multiple factors,

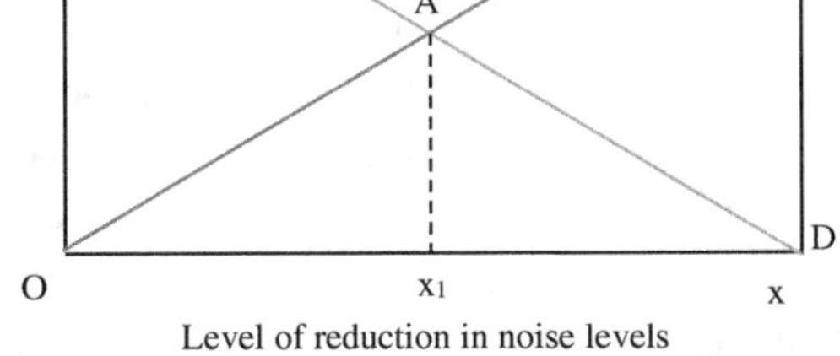

Fig. 6.9. An application of the hedonic pricing method to the determination of the socially optimal reduction of noise levels in an area. In this case, x_1 is the optimal level of noise reduction.

including several environmental factors, influence the price of a commodity, (such as housing) in the area where it is located. Disentangling the separate influences of the factors involved can be quite difficult.

Furthermore, there may be no marketed commodity that is strongly complementary with the environmental factor that needs to be evaluated. In such cases, one may turn to stated preference methods, such as contingent valuation approaches or choice modeling, to provide economic estimates of values associated with environmental phenomena.

6.10. Contingent Valuation — A Stated Preference Approach

6.10.1. *The basics of contingent valuation*

The contingent valuation method of valuing commodities relies on the use of questionnaires designed to elicit from those surveyed the maximum amount they would be willing to pay for the supply of a commodity, or if it already exists, a similar willingness to pay for its retention. Less frequently, but alternatively, it is used to elicit from individuals the maximum amount they would have to be paid to forgo the availability of a commodity. This method can be applied in principle to the valuation of public goods (such as many environmental goods) as well as other types of commodities, such as private goods.

Generally, because of cost and time considerations, a survey for contingent valuation is limited to a sample of the population to be assessed. It is important that the sample be selected so that it is representative of this population. This is to ensure that reliable inferences can be drawn from it about the economic values held by the relevant population. Also consideration has to be given to the size of the sample. While increasing the size of the sample can be expected to increase the accuracy of predictions drawn from it about the population, the increased size of the sample adds to survey costs. Increased sample size needs to be compared with the extra benefits from a larger sized sample to determine the ideal size of the sample from an economics point of view. The ideal sample size is that for which the marginal cost of increased size equals the extra expected benefit from greater accuracy of the predictions that can be drawn from the sample. Sometimes, however, the researcher has little flexibility because the available sum of money that can be spent on a survey is fixed. In such circumstances, the best the researcher can do is to design the survey so as to maximize its expected net benefits given the available budget for the survey.

The way in which the questionnaire is to be administered has to be considered. For example, will direct interviews be undertaken, will mail surveys be used, telephone surveys or internet surveys? These will all vary in their costs and response rates and probably in the accuracy of replies received. The amount of content in the questionnaire will also have to be considered. The longer the questionnaire and the more complicated the questions asked respondents, the lower is likely to be the response rate. Furthermore, response rates and the accuracy of responses may decline once questionnaires become very long because respondents can become fatigued or may resent the amount of time required to complete a long questionnaire.

It is often necessary to describe to those being surveyed the commodity they are supposed to value. This should be done in an objective and as accurate a manner as is possible. If faulty or value-laden information is provided to respondents, this will influence their responses and may result in inappropriate valuations. Questionnaire design and the nature of implementation of the survey are all important. It is advisable to conduct a pilot survey to detect and adjust for any problems with the proposed questionnaire and its administration before undertaking the complete survey.

6.10.2. *Variations in procedures for estimating contingent values — single bids, multiple bids, bounded bids*

Contingent economic values can be elicited from respondents in a variety of ways. Respondents may be asked directly the maximum amount they would be willing to pay for a commodity, or the maximum amount they would need to be paid to forgo the commodity. This is described as a *single bid* approach. *Multiple bids* may also be employed. These rely on trial-and-error search to determine maximum willingness to pay by respondents or to find the minimum amount they need to be paid to forgo a commodity. Let us concentrate on willingness to pay for the supply of a commodity such as an environmental good. Similar procedures can be adopted for willingness to accept compensation for foregoing a commodity, such as an available environmental good.

Respondents may initially be asked if they would be prepared to pay for or contribute to the cost of supplying the commodity to be valued. As discussed later, their willingness to pay is likely to depend on procedures to be used to ensure supply of the good being assessed. Of those who are willing to pay, it is necessary to determine their maximum willingness to pay. From a pilot survey, it may, for example, be known that all likely bids will involve a proposed one-off contribution of \$60 or less. Questions may then focus on sums in this range to determine the maximum amount each respondent would be willing to pay for the supply of the environmental good being assessed (see, for example, Carson *et al.*, 2003). Thus, the bidding values are bounded. As a result of interviewing respondents, their willingness to pay for an environmental good might be found to have the distribution represented by the first two columns in Table 6.1. This indicates that 90% of respondents would be willing to pay \$10 or more for the environmental good, that 80% would be willing to pay \$20 or more and so

Table 6.1. An example to illustrate one way of calculating the contingent value of an environmental good.

(1) Amount in dollars (x) to be paid by the respondent	(2) % of respondents WTP x or more	(3) Mid-point of relevant interval (\$)	(4) Relative frequency of maximum WTP (%)	(5) (3) times (4), where % is a proportion (\$)
0	100			
10	90	5	10	0.5
20	80	15	10	1.5
30	50	25	30	7.5
40	30	35	20	7.0
50	10	45	20	9.0
60	0	55	10	5.5
	Average willingness to pay			\$31.00

on. As would be expected, the percentage of respondents willing to pay declines as the requested level of payment increases. It may also be found that 10% of those sampled are not willing to contribute \$10 or more to financing the supply of the environmental good. This implies that 10% would be prepared to contribute less than \$10, 10% would be willing to contribute \$10 or more but less than \$20. If we assume that the willingness of respondents to pay is equally distributed over the relevant intervals based on column one, the average willingness to pay in each class interval is approximately as is indicated in column three of Table 6.1. The relative frequency of willingness to pay the sums involved are shown in column 4. Therefore, each group is willing to contribute on average per person the sums listed in column 5 towards the supply of the environmental good. Thus, if the distribution of the average willingness to pay per person is representative of the total population, the total willingness to pay of the population for the supply of the environmental good is equal to this average value (\$31) *times* the size of the total population. This is the contingent value of the environmental good.

Note that the above procedure is an approximation because the percentage of respondents willing to pay a requested sum does not usually vary linearly with that sum. An alternative procedure is to fit a relevant mathematical function to the observations and use this to estimate average or median willingness to pay (Carson *et al.*, 2003). Using statistical techniques, factors that may influence the willingness to pay of respondents can be analyzed. For example, it might be found that those with higher incomes or higher levels of education are probably willing to pay more than those with lower levels of income or with lower levels of education for the supply of the environmental good being considered.

6.10.3. *Issues raised by procedures used to estimate contingent values*

The procedures for contingent valuation and its benefits and shortcomings have been assessed in depth by a panel of experts consisting of Arrow *et al.* (1993) and their views have been influential in providing support for this approach. Limitations of techniques for estimating contingent economic values include the possibilities of instrument bias, hypothetical bias, strategic responses, whole-and-part interactions, stating-point bias, uncertainty on the part of the researcher and respondents about the commodity being evaluated, "yeah" saying, attempts to gain moral standing in responding as well as psychological influences that arise from the bounded rationality of individuals. Consider each of these factors in turn.

Instrument bias arises when the method of requiring payment for the commodity being valued is not considered to be credible by the respondents. If, for example, contributions for the supply of a commodity are voluntary and do not appear to be binding, respondents may not give serious bids. Plausible payment vehicles can vary with the issue being considered. In the case of the Alaskan oil spill from the ship *Exxon Valdez*, respondents were, for example, asked whether they would vote for a measure that would increase taxes by specific amounts, the receipts from which were to be used to stop such a disaster occurring again (Carson *et al.*, 2003). Payment of the tax or levy would be compulsory. This is a *referendum method* of determining willingness to pay.

Hypothetical bias occurs when respondents have difficulties in imagining alternative environmental possibilities presented to them for valuation. They may, for instance, have no or only limited experience with the alternatives presented.

Strategic bias occurs when respondents bias their answers to the questionnaire in the hope that this will increase the probability of policies being adopted that are favored by them. Conservationists, for example, may inflate their stated willingness to pay for the conservation of an endangered wildlife species in the hope that this will result in greater public funding for conservation of this species. Or, some respondents may understate their willingness to pay for a commodity in the hope that they will be charged less for its supply than otherwise. Nevertheless, empirical evidence suggests that this is not usually a major problem, particularly when the number of respondents is large.

Whole-and-part distortions occur when respondents instead of valuing a particular environmental good as requested, such as the environmental quality of a particular lake, are influenced in their valuation by the quality of all lakes or a large set of these. This tends to inflate the stated values given by respondents.

It has been observed in multiple bidding valuation that the stated values found by trial-and-error procedures are influenced by the starting values first offered to respondents. This has been called *starting-point bias*. It may not, however, be very serious and it can be allowed for to some extent by varying the starting points of respondents; for instance, randomizing them.

Sometimes respondents reply to interviewers by giving them the answers they think interviewers would like to hear. This has been called *yeah saying*. The extent to which it occurs may vary depending on the social groups interviewed and their culture. Attempts to gain *moral standing* are also related to this aspect. In such cases, the respondent desires to impress the interviewer with her/his moral stance.

Uncertainty can be a major problem in the evaluation particularly of public goods (Tisdell, 2007). In the case of environmental goods both the researcher and the respondents may have imperfect knowledge about the alternatives likely to be available. Furthermore, in many cases, natural scientists may disagree about the likely alternative environments that can be expected to emerge and when. For example, natural scientists disagree about the rapidity with which global warming will result in sea-level rises.

Psychological influences involving the bounded rationality of human beings can have important consequences for stated valuation. Stated values appear to be heavily (disproportionately) influenced by the recent experiences of respondents and by recent information that has come to their attention. The process of seeking values from respondents may focus their attention on the object to be valued to the relative neglect of other objects. This can result in initial over valuation or under valuation of the object being valued, depending on whether it is considered by the respondent to be desirable or not (Tisdell *et al.*, 2008). This makes it difficult to determine the "true" value placed on an object by a respondent because their perceived valuation of the object is influenced by variations in their awareness of the object as time passes. This is a drop-off or decay effect (Tisdell, 2014, Chapter 6).

A further difficulty (but this may not be peculiar to stated preference methods) is that the willingness to pay for the supply of commodity is likely to differ from willingness to accept compensation for its loss. It is normally higher in the latter case (see Section 6.3.2). This seems to be partially for psychological reasons. Value judgments are therefore needed to decide which of these alternative bases of valuation should be adopted.

6.11. Choice Modeling — Stated Preferences Based on Attributes or Characteristics of Commodities

Choice modeling concentrates on valuing the attributes or characteristics which influence the final demand for commodities. In this regard, it differs from contingent valuation, which endeavors to evaluate directly the demand for commodities themselves.

Choice modeling, when applied to valuation of environmental resources, requires respondents to state their preferences about the relevant attributes of the resources to be valued rather than about the resources themselves. The latter are indirectly valued by using this information. While choice modeling is mainly based on stated preferences, it may also make use of revealed information, such as travel costs.

Choice modeling can be regarded as an application of the characteristics theory of demand which was developed by Lancaster (1966a, 1966b). A problem in its application is not to overload respondents with an excessive number of choices about attributes but to nevertheless include all relevant choices. Stages in choice modeling involves the following:

(1) selecting a relevant set of attributes for evaluation;
(2) assigning measures to these attributes (the measures can be cardinal or ordinal);
(3) choosing an experimental design (that is, a method to determine which combinations of attributes could be presented to respondents);

(4) deciding on the choice sets to be presented to respondents for their preference ordering;
(5) completing a survey to determine these preferences; and
(6) constructing preference relationships (in some cases, functions which may be stochastic in nature) on the basis of the survey data.

Further details are available, for example, in Hanley *et al.* (2001, p. 437).

Different methods of specifying preference relationships exist. These have been classified as

(1) choice experiments;
(2) contingent ranking;
(3) contingent rating; and
(4) paired comparisons.

Economists usually prefer the choice experimental method because it is more consistent with the predictions of standard microeconomic theory than the other methods (Hanley *et al.*, 2001, p. 440). However, as discussed later, this method is not entirely consistent with standard economic theory.

A major problem in undertaking choice modeling is to make the empirical evaluation tractable but at the same time to avoid discarding relevant choice sets that should be evaluated. Judgment by the researcher is unavoidable. The bounded rationality of respondents and their time constraints must be taken into account.

When the choice experimental method is adopted, the level of an individual's utility as a function of the attributes being taken into account is usually assumed to be linear; utility is supposed to be a linear function of the value of each attribute plus a stochastic element. While the linearity assumption helps to make the problem tractable, the standard economic theory of demand suggests that utility as a function of quantity of any particular attribute, other things constant, is likely to be nonlinear. For instance, it may be common for marginal utility at first to rise as the quantity of a particular attribute is raised while everything else is held constant and subsequently to decline for higher quantities of the attribute. The linear approximation may, however, not result in significant inaccuracies if the variations being considered in the attribute are small, or if marginal utility changes fairly slowly with the attribute being varied. The slower the rate of change of utility as a function of the "size" of the attribute, the greater is the practical scope for making use of the linear approximation.

Selecting acceptable measures of the attributes to be included in choice modeling can be quite challenging because in some cases attributes are difficult to quantify objectively. Furthermore, it is even possible that the particular attributes may not be known or may not be well known by respondents, or respondents may lack experience with them and consequently cannot easily evaluate them. In addition, there may be interactive effects between attributes, which affect utility. These are not captured if the utility function is assumed to be linear.

Hanley *et al.* (2001) provide an example based on rock climbing in Scotland to illustrate alternative approaches to choice modeling. They point out that if it is intended to value attributes in monetary terms, it is necessary to include among the attributes being evaluated one that includes a price or a monetary cost. They take account of the following attributes:

(1) the length of the climb;
(2) the time needed to approach the climb once in the vicinity of the site;
(3) the quality of the climb as measured by a star rating system used in guidebooks in Scotland;
(4) whether the climbing site is considered to be crowded or not crowded;
(5) the scenic quality of the area measured on a four-point scale; and
(6) the travel distance from home.

The travel distance from home was converted into estimated travel costs that would be incurred by respondents. This was done in order to include a monetary attribute in the set of pertinent attributes.

Assuming a linear utility function, Hanley and co-authors found that climbers would be prepared to pay extra 12 pence for each additional meter length of the climb. The demand for uncrowded sites was relatively high because they discovered that respondents were willing to pay an extra £19.23 to climb at a "not crowded" site compared with a "crowded" one. They also estimated average consumer's surplus per trip. However, they do not seem to use an objective measure of what is considered "crowded" and "not crowded". It is also probably unlikely that climbers would be willing to pay 12 pence per meter for very long extensions of their climb.

Choice experiments may overcome some of the limitations associated with contingent valuation (Hanley *et al.*, 2001). For example, the fact that only attributes are evaluated in choice modeling may lower the likelihood of hypothetical bias and even of strategic bias. Sensitivity to scope may be reduced also. Values obtained from choice experiments can be easier to transfer from one environmental situation to another than those obtained from contingent valuation. This is consistent with Lancaster's view that his theory can be applied to assessing the demand for new technologies, based on the evaluations of attributes contained in these technologies when they are combined in products. Nevertheless, one needs to be sure when transferring valuation results from one set of environmental conditions to another set that the conditions are fundamentally similar in both situations.

6.12. Other Evaluation and Valuation Methods

6.12.1. *Multi-attribute choice models*

Choice modeling is a form of multi-attribute valuation. While in the case of choice experiments the goal of the researchers is usually to express values of attributes in monetary terms, this is not possible with all forms of multi-attribute analysis or may not always be considered to be desirable. Sometimes only the attributes that are relevant for evaluation purposes are empirically determined and policy-makers are left to assign their own weights to these in deciding what is desirable. Or, again predetermined weights may be assigned to each of the attributes so that a valuation index is obtained. These weights can reflect the values that policy-makers place on the individual attributes. Indices of this type imply particular types of preference functions. For example, if the index is a linear function of the values of the attributes being taken into account, they imply straight-line indifference curves and constant rates of substitution between values of the attributes. Such a relationship may only, however, be relevant over a limited range.

Preference functions involving multiple attributes can be *lexicographic*. This implies that one set of objectives is only to be pursued subject to another set (or other sets) of objectives being satisfied. For example, the choice of nuclear technology to minimize per unit cost of production of electricity might be subject to the constraint that the probability of a nuclear accident of a particular kind should not exceed a specified level of probability.

6.12.2. *Citizens' juries*

One of the limitations of economic methods for social evaluation of alternative forms of resource use is their failure to take into account the political acceptability of policies designed to bring about a more economic use of resources. Sometimes policies that would increase economic efficiency (result in a potential Paretian improvement) cannot be adopted because they are not politically acceptable (Tisdell, 2009). Citizens' juries help in some cases to address these problems. They are *focus groups*, and can serve a variety of functions. If members of such juries are representative of the community where resource changes are proposed, they may, as a result of their discussions, be able to identify what policies are likely to be acceptable to the community and could act as advocates for these in their community. They may also identify issues and aspects of a resource problem that have been overlooked by researchers in their initial analysis. However, the value of such groups varies with the extent to which they are representative of their community and with how knowledgeable they are about relevant local conditions.

To a large extent, social or institutional structures determine the costs of implementing policies and their social acceptability as does the cultural background of the societies involved. Sometimes, it is possible to alter institutional structures so that the transaction cost of implementing policies is reduced, and the prospects of particular policies becoming socially acceptable are increased. Nevertheless, scope for institutional engineering and the evolution of institutions is limited by past conditions: it is to some extent dependent on previous institutional structures.

6.12.3. *Cost-effectiveness analysis*

It is sometimes difficult to place a monetary value on particular commodities and the choice of the quantity of their supply may be made independently of such valuation. For example, it may be decided that a particular level of health services should be provided but that these ought to be supplied at minimum costs. Or, to give another example, it may be decided that a minimum viable population of a particular wildlife species should be conserved (in the wild) but this should be done at minimum cost. In the latter case, the problem becomes one of selecting the land area containing suitable habitat, which can be conserved at minimum opportunity cost. For instance, if agriculture is the only alternative land use for the habitat containing the wildlife species, a suitable tract of land, which minimizes the loss in returns from its agricultural uses, would need to be found.

While cost-effectiveness analysis is straightforward in many cases, it can become quite complicated. This can occur, for instance, because opportunity costs consists not only of economic benefits forgone from private goods but also in lost economic benefits from reduced availability of public goods or mixed goods. From a social welfare point of view, it is necessary to take into account *social* opportunity when evaluating alternative economic activities, and in many cases, those will differ from private opportunity costs. For example, suppose that two alternative forms of agricultural land use (I and II) are being considered. Use I gives the higher private returns but has slightly negative environmental externalities whereas II yields slightly lower private returns but provides significant positive environmental externalities. Therefore, the adoption of land use II is likely to give the greatest social returns.

6.12.4. *Cost of replacement of a natural resource as a valuation technique*

Some environmentalists claim that the value of a natural environmental resource might be measured by the cost of replacing it by a man-made alternative. However, if willingness to pay for the survival of an ecosystem or an attribute provided by a natural resource is less than the cost of its replacement, this method will over value the service provided by the natural resource (Tisdell, 2015, Chapter 16). This is not to say that cost of replacement should not be taken into account in social economic evaluation. For example, the New York City water authority is required by law to supply water to New York that meets minimum quality standards. The authority found that it would be more costly to treat water to achieve this quality than paying landholders in its water catchment area to revegetate their properties. This revegetation improved the quality of run-off water and meant that the water treatment costs of the authority were lower than they otherwise would have been.

6.13. Concluding Comments

A wide range of features of economic valuation and evaluation have been covered in this chapter. It began by outlining the basic ideas underlying social cost–benefit analysis and then examined some of the complications that can arise in applying this analysis. It raised normative and philosophical considerations and measurement problems that occur in economic valuation. The steps involved in applying social cost–benefit analysis to the valuation of environmental spillovers and the economic valuation of natural resources were then specified. The question of how to allow for the dimension of time in undertaking economic valuation was discussed.

Subsequently, methods for valuing environmental spillovers (externalities) and natural resource use where market relationships can be the basis of economic valuation were outlined. Attention then turned to commodities that are not marketed but which are of economic value. Several methods for valuing these (some of which were classified as revealed preference methods and others as stated preference methods) were outlined. The main methods considered were the travel cost method, hedonic pricing, contingent valuation, and choice modeling. Finally, some miscellaneous methods of valuation were introduced and discussed. These were multi-attribute analyses, citizens' juries, cost-effectiveness analysis and the cost of replacement of a natural resource. It can be seen that the process of economic valuation and evaluation can be very challenging. While some economic problems involving the conservation and use of natural resources lend themselves to straightforward valuation and evaluation, others require the application of complicated procedures and are subject to significant error. However, economic valuation techniques can help to reduce the margin of error in valuation. In natural resource problems, errors in evaluation will depend not only on the adequacy of the economic assessments involved but on the veracity of the biophysical relationship assumed to be relevant to the analysis.

6.14. Keywords

Aggregate net social benefit; anthropocentrism; bounded bids and contingent valuation; catastrophe theory; characteristics theory of demand; citizens' juries; choice experiments in choice modeling; choice modeling; contingent valuation; contingent valuation by multiple bids; contingent valuation by a single bid; cost-effectiveness analysis; cost of replacement as a valuation technique; discounting of economic values to allow for time; economic valuation of natural resources; environmental spillovers; hedonic pricing; hypothetical bias in contingent valuation; instrument bias in contingent valuation; market-based valuation; multi-attribute choice models; non-market-based valuation; revealed preference methods of valuation; sensitivity analysis; starting-point bias in contingent valuation; stated preference methods of valuation; strategic bias in contingent valuation; travel cost zones; trip generation function; whole-and-part distortions in contingent valuation.

6.15. Questions for Review and Discussion

1. Explain the basics of social cost–benefit analysis. What economic welfare assumptions are usually adopted in this analysis? Use a diagram to illustrate the solution to a simple economic problem requiring social net benefit to be maximized.

2. Outline and discuss the main limitations of social cost–benefit analysis.
3. Ethical and normative assumptions cannot be avoided in the process of social economic valuation and assessment. Explain and discuss.
4. Outline the main steps involved in applying social cost–benefit analysis to the valuation of environmental spillovers. Why is it important to undertake economic valuation of environmental spillovers and of natural resources?
5. Why is it important in social cost–benefit analysis to consider the degree of confidence that one can have in the estimates of relevant economic values? Why should the sensitivity of social net benefits to variations in important variables be taken into account?
6. A dollar that is only available in the future is worth less than a dollar that is available now. Why might this be so?
7. When environmental spillovers only affect the availability (supply) of marketed goods, the economic evaluation of these spillovers is relatively straightforward. Explain and illustrate assuming that the price of a product affected by the externality does not vary as a result of the spillover.
8. Sometimes an environmental externality may cause the price of a product affected by it to alter. Explain why this could happen and illustrate. If the externality is an adverse one, how can its social economic cost be estimated? Use diagrams to illustrate this.
9. How would you go about valuing natural resources that can be fully marketed and which do not generate any externalities? Do you agree with Herman Daly's view that natural resources (such as oil) are likely to be used up at a faster rate than is socially desirable? Explain your answer.
10. Commodities that are valued but not priced by market competition create challenges for economic valuation and the application of social cost–benefit analysis. This includes both the valuation of spillovers (externalities) and natural resources. Why is the situation challenging? Broadly classify methods that have been used to estimate economic values in those circumstances. In doing so,

distinguish between revealed preference methods and stated preference methods.

11. What is the travel cost method of economic valuation? Explain its basic rationale. Why does it only partially measure the social economic value of some recreational sites?
12. Outline the procedures followed in estimating the recreational value of a site when the travel cost method is used. What are the main limitations of this method?
13. Explain the basic rationale that underpins the hedonic pricing method of economic valuation. Illustrate the method by a simple example. What are its main limitations?
14. What is contingent valuation? Why does this method normally involve sampling and what economic considerations should be taken into account in deciding on the size of the sample and its nature? When using this method, what type of factors need to be taken into account in deciding how to administer a questionnaire in order to elicit stated values from respondents?
15. A variety of procedures (for example, single bids; multiple bids) can be used to elicit contingent values from respondents. Explain and consider the advantages and drawbacks of alternative procedures.
16. Outline and discuss the types of biases that can occur in eliciting contingent values from respondents.
17. How does choice modeling differ basically from contingent valuation? Outline the main steps involved in choice modeling and the difficulties that may arise in completing each of these steps.
18. Choice modeling using choice experiments has been claimed to be a better method of economic valuation than contingent valuation. Why? Do you agree with this claim? Explain why and consider some of the limitations of choice experiments.
19. What are citizens' juries? Outline their benefits and drawbacks as mechanisms for social decision-making.
20. What is cost-effectiveness analysis? When is it likely to be useful? Discuss the view that although cost-effective analysis reduces the required extent of economic valuation, it does not entirely eliminate the need for economic valuation.

Readings and References

Anon (2020). *Catastrophe theory*, Wikipedia, https://en.wikipedia.org/wiki/Catastrophe_theory [Accessed 10 June 2020].

Arrow, K.J., R.M. Solow, P.K. Portney, E.E. Leamer, R. Radner and H. Schumand (1993). *Report of the NOAA Panel on Contingent Valuation to the General Council of the US Oceanic and Atmospheric Administration.* Resources for the Future, Washington, D.C.

Carson, R.T., R.C. Mitchell, M. Hanemann, R.J. Kopp, S. Presser and P.A. Ruud (2003). Contingent valuation and lost passive use: Damages from the Exxon Valdez oil spill, *Environmental and Resource Economics*, 25, 257–286. doi: 10.1023/A:1024486702104.

Daly, H.E. (1980a). Introduction to the steady-state economy. In HE Daly (Ed.) *Economics, Ecology and Ethics: Essays Toward a Steady-State Economy*, 1–31. Freeman and Company, San Fransisco.

Daly, H.E. (1980b). The steady-state economy: Toward a political economy of biophysical and moral growth. In H.E. Daly (Ed.) *Economics, Ecology, Ethics: Essays Toward a Steady-State Economy*, 324–356. W.H. Freeman & Co, San Francisco.

Hanley, N., S. Mourato and R.E. Wright (2001). Choice modelling approaches: A superior alternative for environmental valuatioin?, *Journal of Economic Surveys*, 15, 435–462. doi: 10.1111/1467-6419.00145.

Kahneman, D. and A. Tversky (2000). *Choices, Values and Frame*, Cambridge University Press, Cambridge UK.

Kahneman, D., J.L. Knetsch and R.H. Thaler (1991). The endowment effect, loss aversion and status quo bias, *Journal of Economic Perspectives*, 5, 193–206. doi: 10.1257/jep.5.1.193.

Kant, E. (1781). *Critique of Pure Reason*, N. Kemp Smith [trans.], Macmillan, London.

Knetsch, J.L. and J.A. Sinden (1984). Willingness to pay and compensation demanded: Empirical evidence of an unexpected disparity in measures of value, *Quarterly Journal of Economics*, 99, 507–521. doi: 10.2307/1885962.

Lancaster, K. (1966a). A new approach to consumer theory, *Journal of Political Economy*, 74, 132–157. doi: https://www.jstor.org/stable/1828835.

Lancaster, K. (1966b). Change and innovation in the technology of consumption, *The American Economic Review*, 56, 14–23.

Passmore, J.A. (1974). *Man's Responsibility for Nature: Ecological Problems and Western Traditions*, Duckworth, London.

Pearce, D. (1998). Cost-benefit analysis and environmental policy, *Oxford Review of Economic Policy*, 14, 84–100.

Perman, R., Y. Ma, M. Common, D. Maddison and J. McGilvray (2011). *Natural Resource and Environmental Economics*, 4th edn. Pearson, Harlow, Essex UK. [Chapters 11 and 12, Relatively advanced].

Tietenberg, T. and L. Lewis (2018). *Environmental and Natural Resource Economics*, 11th edn. Routledge, New York and Abingdon, Oxon, UK. [Chapters 2 and 3].

Tisdell, C.A. (1996). *Bounded Rationality and Economic Evolution*, Edward Elgar, Cheltenham, UK and Brookfield, VT, USA.

Tisdell, C.A. (2005). *Economics of Environmental Conservation*, 2nd edn. Edward Elgar, Cheltenham, UK and Northampton, MA, USA. [Chapter 7].

Tisdell, C.A. (2007). Knowledge and the valuation of public goods and experential commodities: Information provision and acquisition, *Global Business and Economics Review*, 9, 170–182. doi: https://dx.doi.org/10.1504/GBER.2007.013699.

Tisdell, C.A. (2009). Complex policy choices regarding agricultural externalities: Efficiency, equity and acceptability In V. Beckmann and M. Padmanabhan (Eds.), *Institutions and Sustainability. Political Economy of Agriculture and the Environment — Essays in Honour of Konrad Hagedorn*, 83–106. Springer.

Tisdell, C.A. (2014). *Human Values and Biodiversity Conservation: The Survival of Wild Species*, Edward Elgar Cheltenham, UK and Northampton, MA, USA.

Tisdell, C.A. (2015). *Sustaining Biodiversity and Ecosystem Functions: Economic Issues*, Edward Elgar, Cheltenham, UK and Northampton, MA, USA.

Tisdell, C.A. (2017). *Economics and Environmental Change: The Challenges We Face*, Edward Elgar Publishing, Cheltenham, UK, and Northampton, MA, USA. [Chapter 4].

Tisdell, C.A. and C. Wilson (2012). *Nature-based Tourism and Conservation: New Economic Insights and Case Studies*, Edward Elgar Publishing, Cheltenham, UK and Northampton, MA, USA.

Tisdell, C.A., C. Wilson and H. Swarna Nantha (2008). Contingent valuation as a dynamic process, *Journal of Socio-Economics*, 37, 1443–1458. doi: 10.1016/j.socec.2007.04.005.

Zeeman, E.C. (1976). Catastrophe theory, *Scientific American*, 234, 373–388. doi: 10.1038/scientificamerican0476-65.

Chapter 7

Sustainability as an Environmental and Economic Issue

7.1. Introduction

Reductions in the actual and predicted quantities of available natural resources and the declining quality of many (such as water and air) have led to growing doubt about whether economic growth can be sustained at past levels and by the same methods as those adopted previously. The view has gathered ground that changes in the nature of economic activity are needed to avoid unwanted reductions in economic growth in the future as well as the loss of desired natural environments and living resources. There is no doubt that the type of economic growth achieved since the Industrial Revolution is unsustainable in the long term because of, amongst other things, its high dependence on non-renewable fossil fuels. Significant limits on economic growth and economic activity are already becoming apparent. This is underlined, for example, by current economic and social concerns about the onset of global warming. Rising levels of greenhouse gases in the atmosphere (the cause of global warming) are attributable mainly to the level and nature of economic activity (see Chapter 13). Both the availability of living and inanimate natural resources are being altered by human economic activity in ways that will make it more difficult to sustain future economic growth and human well-being.

This chapter shows why environmental and economic sustainability is now an important issue and then outlines a general classification of natural resources and demonstrates the importance of this classification for analyzing the sustainability of natural resource use. The way in which economies are organized or managed has important implications for the sustainability of the use of natural resources, the preservation of natural environments, the conservation of living organisms and ultimately, the sustainability of economic activities. Deficiencies are likely to occur in the sustainable management of economies when adverse externalities occur, commodities have attributes associated with public goods (or bads), when there is open-access to resources, and when there is "excessive" discounting of future economic benefits from alternative economic choices. As already pointed out (for example, in Chapters 3 and 4), these factors can result in greater economic scarcity than need be and they can reduce economic and environmental sustainability. Their significance in relation to environmental and economic sustainability is stressed in this chapter. Such factors have important influences on the occurrence of environmental and economic sustainability at the local and micro-level as well as at the macro- or aggregate-level. The last portion of this chapter examines macroeconomic aspects of sustainable development.

Before commencing detailed discussion of environmental and economic sustainability, it is important to realize that the word "sustainability" has no practical implications until it is related to an object. It is necessary to know *what* has or can have the attribute of sustainability. A further consideration is whether the sustainability of that object is desirable. Depending on the object involved, its sustainability may be desirable or undesirable. For example, it is generally considered to be undesirable to sustain poverty, but desirable to provide individuals with a fulfilling life free of substantial economic hardship. Therefore, in making economic and other choices, it is important to know what one wants to sustain and what one does not wish to sustain. Furthermore, even if it is possible to sustain an object for an unlimited period of time, one may not want to do this. This means that the time for which something should be sustained ought to be considered, for example, the aim may be to maintain the existence of the human race for as long as is possible, as suggested by Daly (1980) and discussed by Tisdell (1988, 1992). A realistic aim is to adopt actions which avoid unwanted lack of sustainability of desired objects taking into account what is achievable. There are concerns at present that current benefits from economic activity are being obtained at excessive cost because they are reducing future attainable benefits to a greater extent than is desired. In other words, there are concerns that the user costs arising from the operations of current economic systems are too high.

7.2. Why has Environmental and Economic Sustainability Become an Important Issue?

7.2.1. *Human dependence on natural resources*

Humans depend for their continuing existence on the use of natural resources. Therefore, their availability and quality is of crucial significance for humans. Although humans can modify and transform natural resources to increase the availability of commodities, their continuing existence is *essential* for the supply of commodities consumed by humans. However, the supply of commodities and economic welfare do not depend solely on the availability of natural resources. Other factors of production such as labor, know-how, man-made capital and managerial skills also play an important role in helping to supply commodities. Nevertheless, their presence would be to no avail in the absence of natural resources.

Once the pivotal role of natural resources for human existence and economic welfare is recognized, social concerns about a reduction in the availability of these resources is warranted, particularly when these reductions are irreversible, or can only be reversed with considerable difficulty, slowly or at considerable cost. Many natural resources are nonrenewable and their use inevitably reduces their future available stock. This happens, for example, with the combustion of non-renewable fuels such as oil and coal. On the other hand, many biological resources are renewable, but can be extinguished by over harvesting or by planned or incidental destruction as a result of economic activity. Consequently, their demise becomes irreversible and this often results in permanent biodiversity loss. Other natural resources which circulate, such as water, may be reduced in quality because of economic activity and altered in their geographical distribution, thereby generating unwelcome economic losses.

7.2.2. *Historical impacts of humans on natural environments and resources as a reason for concern*

Observable human impacts on the availability and quality of natural resources and natural environments are by no means new. For example, there is strong evidence that some early hunting and gathering societies harvested some vulnerable wild animal species to extinction, for example moas (flightless bird species) in New Zealand were harvested to extinction by Maoris after their settlement of New Zealand. Landscapes were altered by regular burning of natural vegetation by Australian Aborigines. After an area of land was burnt a flush of green grass followed which enticed wild animal species to the burnt area where they could be hunted for food. Swidden or slash-and-burn agriculture (forms of shifting agriculture) also altered landscapes. The development of settled agriculture had an even larger environmental impact because forests and natural vegetation were permanently removed to enable this type of agriculture to succeed. For example, much of Europe was deforested to make way for agricultural development.

Following the Industrial Revolution, the impacts of humans on natural resources *accelerated*. In particular, dependence grew on non-renewable fossil fuels to provide energy for economic production. This resulted in considerable pollution of natural environments and subsequently, rising concentrations of greenhouse gases in the atmosphere. Global reduction of natural vegetation continued globally and levels of use of natural resources in production magnified. Consequently, apart from local and regional environmental problems, several global environmental issues have emerged, such as a massive loss of biodiversity (see Chapter 9) and the occurrence of global warming (see Chapter 13). Furthermore, the economic consequences of reduction in the stocks of some nonrenewable resources, such as mineral oil, have become apparent. John Gowdy (personal communication,

March 21, 2009) has stressed that the period we are in now is quite incredible and unprecedented as far as humankind's impacts on natural resources and the environment are concerned.

Modern economic activity has two very important consequences: (1) it results in the production of wastes which can be a source of pollution; and (2) it results in the irreversible depletion of some natural resources. In some circumstances, wastes from economic production generate cumulative levels of pollution because natural environments are unable to "absorb" or neutralize the levels of pollution generated. The use of some types of natural resources, such as the combustion of fossil fuels, results in the inevitable depletion of their global stock. In other cases, the loss of a natural resource depends on the level of its economic exploitation or the extent to which it is destroyed by human activity. For example, a wild species (such as a fish species) may continue to survive provided that its habitat is not destroyed by human activities and provided it is not hunted or harvested so heavily that it is driven to extinction. Both pollution (or more generally environmental changes caused by economic activity) and reductions in the availability of natural resources can result in lack of economic sustainability. The long-term consequences can be growing impoverishment and falling standards of living. High and growing levels of total global economic production are generating burgeoning levels of natural resource use. Consequently, the economic dangers from a decline in natural resource availability and from environmental change have become more evident than in earlier times. This is probably the main reason why environmental and economic sustainability has become a major social and political issue in recent times.

7.2.3. *Interdependence between economic systems and natural resource systems*

Traditionally, most economists have examined the operation of economic systems independently of the functioning of natural systems. While this reductionist approach is appropriate for some situations, it is wanting in many cases. For example, it is inappropriate for considering the long-term consequences of economic growth, particularly if the level of economic production is already high. Again, where particular types of economic activity have significant impacts on the availability of natural resources and environments, or vice versa, this reductionist approach to economic analysis is likely to be defective. In general, the operation of economic systems and the state of biophysical (natural resource) systems are interdependent and the importance of this interdependence has increased with global economic growth.

Figure 7.1 illustrates and emphasizes the interdependence between economic systems and natural resource systems. Economic systems draw on biophysical systems, and ultimately are dependent on natural resource endowments for their continuing operation. In this process, some natural resources may be depleted or reduced in availability. Economic activity transforms natural resources to provide commodities to help satisfy the human wants. As a result, wastes are created which are added to the biophysical system and environmental changes occur.

The type of interdependence illustrated in Fig. 7.1 was emphasized by Kenneth Boulding (1966) by likening human existence on Earth to being in a spaceship. Daly (1980) has argued that while many

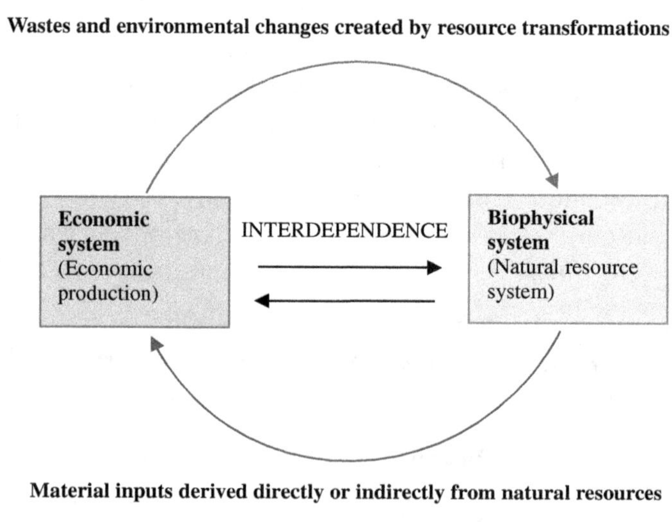

Fig. 7.1. An illustration of interdependence between the state of biophysical systems and the operation of economic systems. Economic systems use natural resources, create wastes, and alter environments and the state of natural resource systems.

economists have been aware that natural resources play a central role in the operation of economic systems, they have tended to neglect the significance of wastes and pollutants generated by economic activity as influences on economic sustainability, that is the upper relationship shown in Fig. 7.1.

Economists, such as David Ricardo (1817), were aware that the utilization of nonrenewable minerals could eventually limit economic growth, but believed that this tendency could be offset by technological progress, and to some extent, discoveries of new mineral deposits. The classical economic view, for example expounded by David Ricardo (1817), was that superior deposits of minerals and other resources would be utilized initially and as these became exhausted, more marginal deposits (of low economic value) would be utilized. Georgescu-Roegen (1971) provided new insights into this process and the impact of economic activity on natural resource availability.

Georgescu-Roegen likened the consequences of economic activity to entropy in physics. Humans draw on rich and geographically concentrated resources and utilize these as inputs into economic activity. This process and human consumption results in the dispersion of these resources, thereby reducing their future availability. While some resources may be recycled, the process of recycling leads to further diffusion of natural resources. Eventually, diffusion of the resources involved becomes complete or virtually so. The Earth has an endowment of rich concentrated nonrenewable resources which are being dispersed by economic activity. Our physical system is closed except for the energy received from the sun. Plants, and some other living organisms, use solar energy to grow and in the process help to offset this diffusion of material resources. Nevertheless, the general tendency is for economic activity to accelerate the dispersion of nonrenewable resources and consequently, to add to the difficulty of sustaining economic production in the long run.

The rate of utilization of natural resources in relation to economic production can be reduced as a result of innovations which lower material inputs per unit of economic output. This can come about as a result of technological and scientific progress, and can also be a consequence of improvements in the organization and management of resource use.

But this resource-saving can be offset, or more than counteracted, by an expansion in the level of economic production. For example, if the amount of input of materials per unit of economic output is reduced by 10% and the volume of economic production rises by 20%, total throughput of materials (derived ultimately from natural resources) increases. The general pattern of global economic growth has been marked by falling input–output ratios and rising levels of throughput of material resources. This has resulted in a continual rise in the rate of utilization of natural resources by the global economy.

Similarly, the level of wastes and pollution emissions generated by an economic system can be related to the efficiency with which materials are used to produce economic output and to the total volume of materials used. Greater efficiency in transforming materials into economic output reduces the amount of wastes and pollutants generated per unit of output. But the volume of wastes and pollutants generated per unit of time will continue to rise if the volume of economic production escalates proportionately more than the relative reduction in wastes and pollutants per unit of economic output. For example, while there is evidence that greenhouse gas emissions per unit of economic production tend to fall eventually with economic growth, the total volume of these emissions may continue to rise. Furthermore, some of these gases, such as CO_2, can accumulate in the atmosphere once their rate of emission exceeds the absorption capacity of the natural environment. Consequently, even when total emissions of these pollutants per unit of time falls, the cumulative level of pollutants in the natural environment can continue to rise.

7.2.4. *Environmental Kuznets curves*

It has been contended that the trajectory of the intensity of pollution emissions of many important pollutants when related to economic output tends to follow an inverted-U pathway. This appears to be so for CO_2 emissions, for example. This inverted-U relationship has been described as giving rise to an *environmental Kuznets curve*.

The curve marked *ABC* in Fig. 7.2 provides an illustration of an environmental Kuznets curve. It represents the level of emissions of

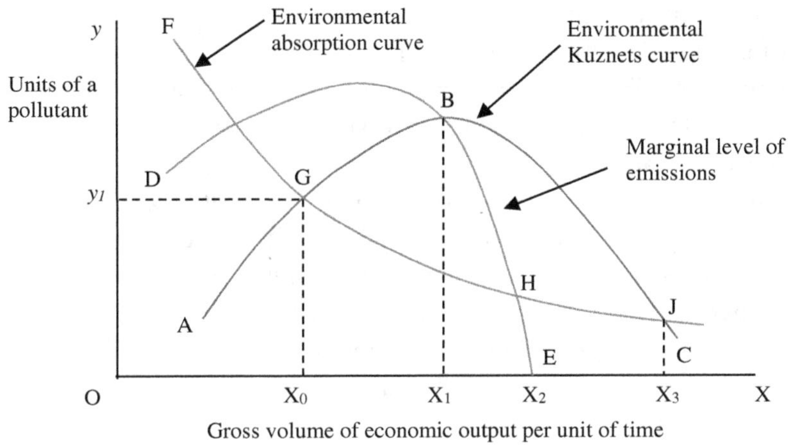

Fig. 7.2. Curve *ABC* in this figure has an inverted U-shape and represents a typical environmental Kuznets curve.

a pollutant as a ratio of the volume of economic output. It is the average rate of emission of the pollutant per period of time relative to the volume of economic production. This implies that pollution intensity relative to the level of economic production is at a maximum when production per unit of time reaches the level X_1. With further expansion in the level of economic production, pollution intensity then declines per unit of time.

The nature of the environmental Kuznets curve (namely, its inverted U-shape) led many to the optimistic view that with sufficient economic growth, levels of pollution would eventually fall. Thus, it seemed possible that economic growth could eventually solve pollution problems. However, this view is too optimistic. Firstly, the inverted U-shape may not apply empirically to the emission of all pollutants. Secondly, the maximum of an environmental Kuznets curve does not correspond to the maximum quantity of emission of a pollutant. This occurs for a higher volume of economic output. In Fig. 7.2, the curve *DBE* is the marginal level of emission of the pollutant corresponding to the environmental Kuznets curve shown. Hence, the total level of emission of the pollutant continues to rise with increasing output after the environmental Kuznets curve reaches a maximum. It does so until the total volume of output per period of time is X_2. At this level of output, the rate of change (marginal value) of the quantity emitted of the pollutant becomes zero. Only after this level of output does the level of emission of the pollutant start to decline. However, even in this case a further complication can arise.

The ability of the natural environment to neutralize ("absorb") a pollutant may be limited and the pollutant may accumulate with the passage of time in the "natural" environment when this limited capacity is exceeded, as for example, has happened with CO_2 emissions. In such cases, even when that level of emissions of the pollutant per period of time declines, the pollutant may still continue to accumulate in the natural environment.

This can be illustrated by reference to Fig. 7.2. Suppose that the natural environment has the ability to neutralize a constant maximum amount of a pollutant per unit of time. In the case shown, assume that this amount is equivalent to y_1 times X_0. The rectangular hyperbole identified by *FGHJ* represents the neutralizing capacity of the natural environment in one time period. For volumes of production between X_0 and X_3, the quantity emitted per period of the pollutant exceeds the capacity of the natural environment to neutralize it. Even after total emissions per unit of time decline, the stock of pollutant continues to accumulate in the natural environment. In the case shown, a decline in the stock of the pollutant in the natural environment would only start to occur once economic output exceeded X_3. There is, however, a *possibility* that an economic output of greater than X_3 will never be achieved because the accumulation of the pollutant in the natural environment erodes the natural resource base for economic production. For example, accumulation of greenhouse gases reduces the global potential for economic production (Tisdell, 2001).

Note that shifts can occur in environmental Kuznets curves for several reasons. For example, technological progress may reduce the amount of pollutant emitted per unit of economic production. Or, a change in the organization of the economy may reduce the amount of material resources used per unit of economic production (see Tisdell, 2001).

7.2.5. *Export of polluting economic activities*

One of the reasons why higher income countries may have been able to reduce their pollution intensities in recent times is by "sending" very polluting industries offshore to developing countries, such as China and India. Growing environmental restrictions usually add to the private costs of locating environmentally unfriendly businesses in higher income countries. This may cause the owners of such businesses to relocate in lower income countries with fewer such restrictions. In addition, production from "dirty" industries already located in developing countries becomes internationally more competitive when restrictions are placed on these industries in more developed nations. Consequently, the location of polluting economic activities tends to gravitate to developing countries. This, however, does not solve global pollution problems.

For example, *one* of the reasons why China and India may have increased their contribution to total greenhouse gas emissions by so much in recent times is that the location of polluting economic activities has gravitated towards these countries from higher income countries. Reduced pollution intensities in higher income countries have been achieved, to some extent, by "exporting" pollution problems to a group of developing countries. This appears to have provided both sets of countries with short-run economic benefits. However, there are long-term costs for both groups of nations. Such export is not a remedy for pollution problems in the case of global environmental bads. No country is shielded from the impacts of these bads, for example greenhouse gas production. Consequently, in such cases, the long-term benefit to higher income countries of offshore production of commodities having adverse environmental effects is illusory.

Apart from the above-mentioned exports of polluting industries, it can also be noted that individual nations via international trade and investment frequently add to environmental degradation in other countries. Examples include the clearing of rainforest in the Amazon Basin to provide soya beans and corn for exports designed mainly to feed livestock, and the loss of forests in Borneo to make way for the expansion of oil palm production. Palm oil is a major export of

Indonesia and Malaysia. Exports of tropical timbers further add to these environmental losses which in turn result in worrying levels of biodiversity loss (see Chapter 10) and exacerbate global warming (see Chapter 13).

7.3. Types of Material Resources, Particularly Natural Resources, and Their Implications for Economic Sustainability

7.3.1. *A classification of material resources*

The classification of resources into mutually exclusive sets is not easy. One possible approach is to divide material resources into biological and non-biological resources and then to further subdivide these categories.

Biological resources may be divided into those that are natural and those which are human-modified. Natural biological resources consist, for example, of wildlife species, natural vegetation and ecosystems. Human-modified living resources consist of, amongst other things different varieties of crops, various breeds of domesticated animals, genetically modified organisms, agricultural ecosystems, systems for silviculture and for aquaculture and so on. These are all developed from natural resources. Biological resources have the property that they are reproducible (can be regenerated) and under suitable conditions, are relatively sustainable.

Non-biological material resources do not have the ability to regenerate. They may be divided into three groups:

(1) those natural resources that are replenished but do not regenerate, such as water,
(2) those natural resources that are not renewable and which are depleted by their use, such as oil and coal used for combustion, and
(3) physical man-made capital, such as buildings and manufacturing machinery.

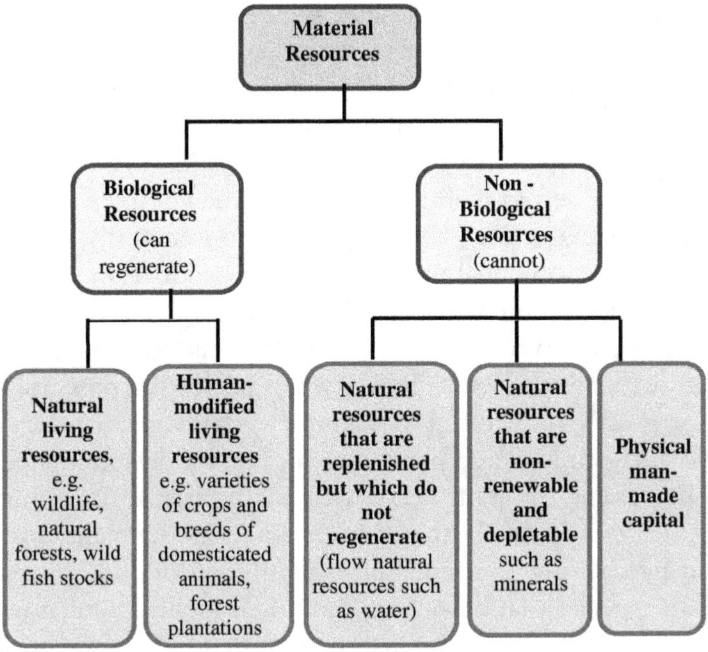

Fig. 7.3. A classification of material resources which includes natural resources as well as natural resources that have been modified or altered by humans.

Physical man-made capital wears out with the passage of time and the materials contained in it eventually become dispersed into the environment. This capital can only be replaced by human effort using additional materials. The chart shown in Fig. 7.3 provides an overview of this classification of material resources.

Economic production utilizing the different types of resources listed in Fig. 7.3 has varied consequences for economic sustainability. Let us consider these consequences in turn for each type of resource.

7.3.2. *Biological resources and economic sustainability*

Humans are dependent on the consumption of food derived from biological resources for their continuing existence. Therefore, sustaining the availability of biological resources has special significance for human beings. Problems can occur because biological resources can be used for economic ends in ways that threaten economic sustainability.

For example, as shown in Chapter 4, living natural resources may be over exploited (for instance, if there is open-access to these) and this can result in falling levels of economic production. In extreme cases, stocks of the harvested living resource may be completely wiped out resulting in the extinction of wild species. Consequently, the resource is no longer able to contribute to economic production at all and the loss is irreversible. A further possibility is that high harvesting rates can cause the population of a harvested species to flip to a low equilibrium level from which it does not recover when harvesting pressure is eliminated, or greatly reduced. For example, populations of the Atlantic cod have not yet recovered from over harvesting despite the cessation of their harvesting for many years. One theory is that the reduction in their populations enabled other fish species to fill the niches previously occupied by cod and the remaining population of cod are unable to displace the species that have "invaded" their niches. Similar possibilities also exist in relation to habitat changes that reduce the population of a species.

Natural living resources are often eliminated by adverse spillovers from human activity which damage the habitat of wild species or reduce their food availability. Humans compete with many other living species for the use of natural resources. This results in some species being branded as pests and being destroyed by humans. Due to such factors, there is considerable human-induced loss of natural biodiversity. There are fears that this loss of biodiversity could result in lack of economic sustainability in the long term (see Chapter 10).

Human-modified living organisms (utilized for example in agriculture) constitute a valuable stock of resources and make possible substantial increases in economic production. However, they sometimes generate adverse externalities which can result in a reduction in the overall level of economic production, or they can have adverse consequences for the conservation of biodiversity in the wild, and in many cases, the level of their productivity can only be sustained by employing nonrenewable natural resources for their culture. All of these factors can pose a challenge for economic sustainability.

In addition, economic growth and development is sometimes associated with the loss of genetic diversity of cultivated crops and domesticated animals. With economic growth and the spread of the market system, many varieties of cultivated plants have been lost as well as breeds of animals (Tisdell, 2003). While some new varieties and breeds have been developed, it is by no means clear that the remaining genetic stock is ideal for ensuring economic sustainability. Production of some crops (such as wheat production) has come to depend on a narrow genetic base. Failure in this base due to disease or other factors can seriously affect the yields of these crops.

Again, humans have developed biological methods of disease and pest control. For example, antibiotics have been developed to treat many diseases. The more widely these are used, the greater the likelihood that the bacteria which they are targeted to kill become resistant to them. There are many situations where their cumulative use reduces their efficiency and consequently, the economic benefits obtained from their use. The user costs associated with such controls need to be taken into account (see, for example, Tisdell, 1993, Chapter 12).

7.3.3. *Replenishable nonbiological natural resources and those not subject to significant depletion*

While many nonbiological resources are neither renewable nor replenishable and are subject to depletion once used for economic production, others are not. Some are replenishable but not regenerative. Some are flow resources and still others are virtually inexhaustible. For example, sunlight, although limited in availability, is a flow resource which becomes available to the Earth each day. This externally supplied resource is essential for supporting most forms of life. For example, it allows photosynthesis to occur in plants, and plants are essential for sustaining the food chain of animals. Furthermore, it has major consequences for physical systems such as for air movements and water currents. It is an essential component in the recirculation of water, which is hydrological cycles. Living organisms either directly or indirectly depend to a large extent on this source of energy to concentrate materials from the environment. It offsets to some extent processes (human and natural) resulting in the diffusion of materials. However, even this solar resource is subject to disturbance by human economic activity. For example, the amount of solar energy reaching and retained by the Earth's atmosphere and surface is affected by the amount of greenhouse gases, such as CO_2, in the atmosphere.

Water constitutes a recirculating resource. However, the amount, quality and the pattern of its availability at different geographical locations can be influenced by environmental changes brought about as a result of economic activity. Its availability at different locations is often less than the demand for the use of this resource.

Natural gravitational forces also provide usable resources and their availability appears to be unaffected by their use. Hydro-electricity generation, for instance, depends on the gravitational pull of the Earth. Tides depend on the gravitational pull of the Moon in relation to the Earth and are energy sources which are not depleted by human use. Nevertheless, attempts by humans to use such sources of energy have environmental consequences, for example, the building of dams for the prime purpose of hydro-electricity generation. The classification of geo-thermal energy is more difficult. Some of this energy is dissipated naturally as the Earth cools whether or not it is put to human use. Techniques are developing to tap this energy source by sinking shafts to access this heat underground and this would accelerate dissipation of this source of energy. It is a nonrenewable source and not a flow or recirculating resource.

7.3.4. *Non-renewable non-biological resources which are depletable, for example, minerals*

Many natural non-biological resources consist of finite stocks and the use of these resources leads at once, or eventually, to their dispersion. As a result, they are reduced in their availability. While some can be recycled, dispersion also occurs as a result of recycling. The act of recycling does not completely offset the forces that make for dispersion of the materials involved. As a result of this dissipation process, it can become increasingly difficult to sustain economic production which is based on the use of non-biological stocks of natural resources

(Georgescu-Roegen, 1971). However, the increasing economic costs of using these resources may be staved off by improvements in their efficient use due to advances in scientific, technological and administrative knowledge and its application. Furthermore, the location of the stocks and quality of these resources are imperfectly known. New discoveries add to the known stock of these resources and extend the extent to which they can continue to support the level of economic production. Nevertheless, the scope for discovering previously unknown high-value deposits of these resources may eventually decline with the passage of time as search techniques improve and as the search encompasses a greater area of the Earth. It has, for example, been claimed that all major oil deposits have now been discovered and that future finds will mostly consist of smaller and more marginal deposits (Roberts, 2008). In addition, there are concerns that improved technology for oil extraction will hasten petroleum exhaustion (Gowdy and Juliá, 2007). Even in the case of coal (which appears to be relatively abundant) some pessimistic predictions have emerged — for example, it has been predicted that coal production might peak around 2020 and then decline due to depletion of deposits (Kerr, 2009).

However, in 2020 scarcity of oil and coal had not become a problem and they are unlikely to become scarce in the foreseeable future. Although there has already been a decline in global coal production, this is not due to depletion of coal deposits but rather a decline in demand for coal due to the substitution of other sources of energy for it (see Chapter 13). Furthermore, the future demand for oil is likely to decline due to the increased substitution of electricity for it in its end-uses, e.g. to power vehicles.

It is difficult to predict accurately the long-term availability of stocks of nonrenewable natural resources, such as minerals. This is mainly because the extent and quality of stocks is not fully known — some deposits remain undiscovered and the extent and quality of discovered deposits is usually not fully proven because in many cases, they remain hidden underground and costs are involved in proving deposits. However, it is not only the extent of deposits that determine their long-term availability. Features such as variations in demand to use them also play a role. These variations can be influenced by such factors such as technological change (for example, technological change that reduces the dependence of automobiles on oil for fuel and moderates demand for oil) and by the use of substitute natural resources and processes (for example, the replacement of coal-based power plants by nuclear energy plants and energy sourced from solar and wind power). These changes are discussed in Chapter 13. All of these factors play a role in influencing the long-term availability of stocks of natural resources.

Despite these difficulties, estimates of the length of life of mineral deposits are frequently made. These methods are given further consideration in Subsection 11.9.3 and Section 12.3. The simplest measure merely involves dividing the stock of known deposits (which it is currently economic to mine) by current annual production from these deposits, that is their rate of mining. This reserve–production ratio represents the number of years of life of the known deposits if the current situation does not alter. While this figure can have some value in signaling the extent of resource scarcity, its value should not be over rated. This is because the current situation can be expected to alter and the extent of known economic reserves depends on economic factors, as does the search for and discovery of new reserves. Other things held constant, the higher the price of the nonrenewable natural resource (for example, a mineral) the larger is the extent of the economically recoverable known deposits and the greater is the effort to discover and prove new reserves.

This is illustrated in Fig. 7.4 by the hypothetical example of world reserves of economically recoverable copper ore from known deposits. The curve *ABCD* represents this relationship. Thus, if the current price of copper per kg is P_1, the level of economically recoverable copper from known global deposits is X_1. If, however, the price of copper should rise to P_2 per kg, the level of economically recoverable reserves rises from X_1 to X_2, other things remaining constant. The length of life of economically recoverable deposits can, therefore, increase.

Furthermore, high prices can be expected to stimulate the search for additional deposits and this can be expected to add to known economically recoverable resources. Nevertheless, this does not necessarily avert increasing resource scarcity.

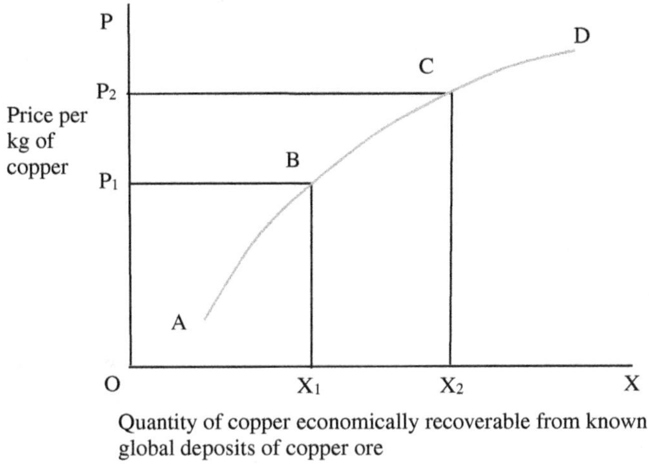

Fig. 7.4. As the price of a mineral increase, other things held constant, the level of economically recoverable known resources increases. This is illustrated here for the hypothetical case of copper. Apart from a rise in the price of a mineral leading to an increase in the level of economically recoverable known resources, it is likely to stimulate the search for new deposits.

The impact on overall economic scarcity of growing shortages of particular natural resources is usually moderated by the use of substitutable natural resources, even though, as a rule, perfect substitutability does not occur. For example, in the illustration given in Fig. 7.5, if the current relative dependence on fossil fuels as a source of energy remains unaltered, the real price of energy may follow a path like that shown by curve *ABC*. However, the rising price of fossil fuels may trigger the use of alternative sources of energy. For example, when the real price of energy from conventional sources reaches P_1, there may be a major shift in the sources from which energy is obtained. For example, nuclear energy and renewable energy may become important sources of energy. Therefore, instead of energy prices following the path *ABC* which would result if fossil fuels continued to be the principal energy source, after t_1 the path may follow *BEG*. However, at t_2, additional sources of energy may become available and economic to use. Therefore, instead of energy prices continuing along *FG*, they follow *FH*. It is even possible that new technologies drawing on new

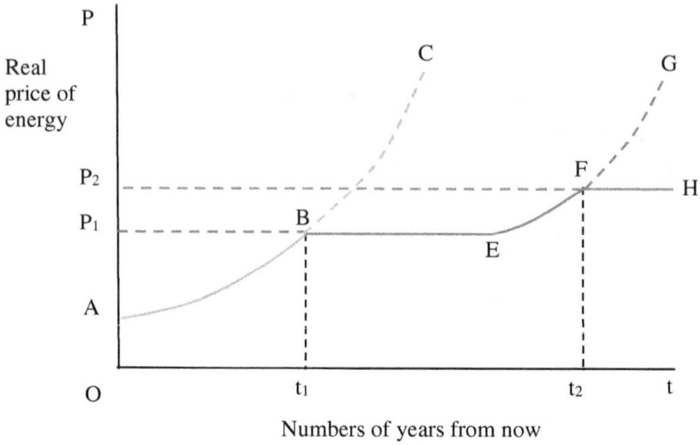

Fig. 7.5. Substitution of new sources of energy is likely to moderate increases in real energy prices as resources conventionally used for energy production are depleted. Consequently, in the case illustrated real energy prices may follow the path *ABEFH* rather than *ABC*, the projection if only the mix of present energy sources is used.

energy sources (such as solar and wind power) could after a time result in a fall in real energy prices. This is, however, not certain to happen.

7.3.5. *Physical man-made capital and human capital*

Accumulation of physical man-made capital has been seen by most economists as an important way to obtain economic growth and reduce economic scarcity. However, as economic growth has proceeded, the level of human capital rather than physical capital has increased in importance as a source of economic growth. Human capital involves investment in human beings to increase their knowledge and skills and their health. Both forms of capital use natural resources either directly or indirectly and neither form of capital lasts forever. Physical capital depreciates and wears out with the passage of time and individual human beings eventually decline in their capacities and die. However, humans can pass on their knowledge to succeeding generations. This process involves some investment. Knowledge can accumulate and be utilized in the future if its accumulation is supported by suitable types and levels of investment.

To some extent, all these forms of capital accumulation use natural resources but the use of such resources is more apparent in the case of man-made physical capital. Basically, capital accumulation increases economic productivity. However, if this accumulation depletes natural resources that are (or can become) nonrenewable, increased economic productivity resulting from capital accumulation may be unable to be sustained in the long run. This is because natural resources are productive assets and unless an adequate supply of these is maintained, higher levels of economic production can become unsustainable. In fact, natural resources are not only productive resources but also they are essential for sustaining economic production. This will be discussed further in this chapter when the concept of sustainable development is considered.

7.4. Microeconomic Phenomena Resulting in a Lack of Economic Sustainability

A number of microeconomic failures which result in lack of economic sustainability have already been identified in this text (see Chapters 2–4). These include the presence of negative externalities from economic activity and public bads (such as those created by the global accumulation of greenhouse gases). These can result in less conservation of natural resources than desired and can cause an unwanted reduction in living standards. Furthermore, in economic systems, failure to conserve public goods can occur because private economic incentives to conserve or provide such goods are lacking. This is because they are characterized by non-rivalry and lack of exclusion. Nevertheless, the conservation of these goods can be important for sustaining economic welfare. For example, biological diversity can be regarded as an important resource that contributes to the level of economic production and helps meet other human wants, for example the demand to enjoy the existence of a diversity of other living things. Some species of living things have attributes that at least partially make them public goods — they are mixed goods and their conservation is subject to market failure.

It was also pointed out (Chapters 3 and 4) that resources to which there is open-access are subject to market failure and their use can result in unwanted lack of economic sustainability. Natural resources (for example, wild fish stocks) to which there is open-access are likely to be unsustainably exploited. Those exploiting these resources take no account of their economic activities on the economic future or on others. No account is taken of user costs. Because no account is taken of user costs, this is likely to result in the natural resource being exploited at a faster rate than is desirable and production based on the use of the resource can fall, or even cease altogether, as a result of collectively unwanted depletion of resources. Nevertheless, it should also be recognized that even if market failure is absent, market systems will not necessarily conserve all natural resources.

As shown by Clark (1976), it is sometimes economic to deplete or extinguish a natural resource. He gives the example of a living species which only has use value and which yields a net rate of return below the going rate of interest. An example would be a slow growing species of tree. Assume that trees of this species are the property of landholders. Suppose that the net internal rate of return from sustainably using these trees is 2%, but that the going rate of interest is 5%. It would be economic for the landholders to harvest all these trees (if the cost of realizing their stock is low) and invest the capital obtained at the going rate of interest if they wish to maximize their economic gains. Alternatively, it may be that another species of tree gives an internal rate of return of 6% when it replaces the slow growing species. In that case, it will be economic for landowners to replace the slow growing species by the faster growing one if the cost of switching is low. As a result, the slow growing species will disappear. Thus, even when the economic system shows no market failures, its operation can result in a reduction in biodiversity. While this choice seems optimal from a purely economic perspective, it is in conflict with the view that human beings have a moral obligation to conserve biodiversity.

Again, it is not always economic to conserve all nonrenewable natural resources. For example, if as a result of technological progress, a cheaper substitute for a mineral will become available in the future, then it pays to accelerate the rate of depletion of this mineral now and before significant substitution occurs. One would expect this to occur in a fully operational market system. This is because the owners of the resources would take into account the future economic benefit they forgo by utilizing the resource now. Significant future substitution is likely to result in falling prices for the resource in the future. Therefore, there would be lower profit if the resource is conserved for future use. Nevertheless, concerns have been expressed that private businesses may discount future benefits too heavily and therefore, utilize a resource at a faster rate than considered to be socially desirable. They may do this because of uncertainty about the future. In the economic system, there may be an "excessive" preference for present gains over future gains. This reflects a *time-preference* for gains in the present or in the near future rather than in the more distant future. This tends to be reinforced by the formation of human economic expectations. As pointed out by Keynes (1936, p. 155), these expectations are heavily influenced by current events and little influenced by more distant considerations. As suggested by Keynes (1936, p. 155), institutional change associated with the development of public companies and the stock exchange seems to have reinforced this tendency. There is also some evidence that many governments take a short-run rather than a long-run perspective in their decision-making about resource use. Consequently, current economic systems may result in economic decisions that result in less sustainability of natural resources use than is socially desirable.

7.5. Sustainable Development

All of the types of market failures mentioned in the previous section can be compatible with initial economic growth and development which in the end proves to be unsustainable. The question, however, has arisen of whether economic growth could prove to be unsustainable even in the absence of market failures. Authors such as Herman Daly (1980) have argued that this is a possibility. In Daly's view, very high levels of economic production may prove to be unsustainable in the long-run because they result in the reduced availability of natural resources and environmental deterioration. Eventually, increasing natural resource scarcity and deteriorating environments will limit economic growth and may result, in due course, in falling standards of living. In order to avert this possibility, Daly believes that it is desirable to aim for a steady state economy. He envisages that this would involve zero population growth and maintaining levels of consumption at moderate levels. He argues that this will enable satisfactory levels of living to be sustained for longer than would be possible by following a strategy for high rates of economic growth. High economic growth rates are unlikely to be sustainable in perpetuity because they rely on the conversion of natural resources into man-made capital and consumer goods and hasten the dispersion of natural resources as foretold by Georgescu-Roegen (1971). Furthermore, they can be a source of environmental deterioration and this involves some destruction of natural resource systems.

This raises the question of the extent to which it is economically justifiable to convert natural resources into man-made capital and use them for the production of economic goods. Clearly in the absence of any such conversion, that human welfare would be much lower than it is today. The conversion process has enabled humans to use new materials to satisfy their wants, exercise greater control over nature and substantially raise their standard of living. However, we cannot conclude that unrestricted natural resource conversion will continue to yield such desirable results in the future.

To some extent, the issue can be illustrated in Fig. 7.6. This figure indicates that there is an inverted-U relationship, *ABCD*, between an indicator of human welfare and the extent of conversion of natural resources to human use, for example, their incorporation into man-made capital and consumer goods. In the absence of any conversion, human welfare remains at low levels, but rises at first with the extent of conversion and then eventually declines as high levels of conversion occur. The question then arises of where economies are located today along such a curve. If they are at a position such as *B*, further conversion is compatible with rising levels of human welfare but if they are at *C* or nearly so, further conversion can be expected to reduce human welfare. Those who believe that the current situation corresponds to a point such as *B* will be optimistic about the economic consequences of further natural resource transformation whereas those who consider

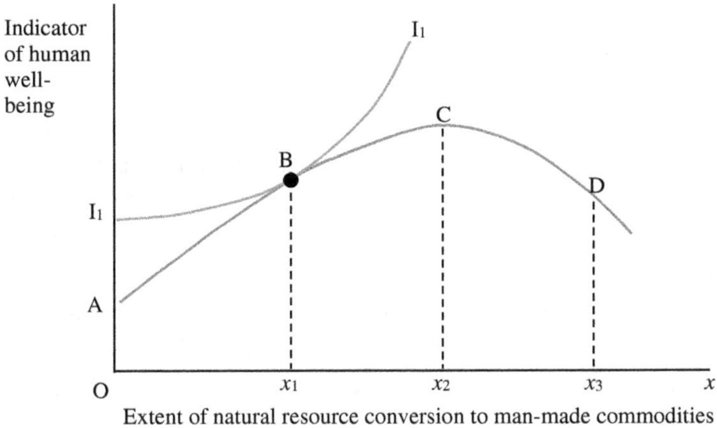

Fig. 7.6. Curve *ABCD* represents a possible relationship between natural resource conversion and an indicator of human well-being.

the situation to be at or near *C* will be pessimistic about the consequence of increased natural resource conversion.

In Fig. 7.6, the extent of natural resource conversion corresponding to x_2 maximizes human well-being. However, not everyone might accept the desirability of this much conversion of natural resources. For example, those who believe that humans have a moral responsibility to conserve biological diversity may not see point *C* as ideal. This is because increased transformation of natural resources can be expected to reduce the extent of biological diversity. For this group, the ideal would be a lower level of conversion. This group may, for example, try to balance human well-being against their feeling that they have a moral responsibility to conserve biodiversity. Their preference would be represented in Fig. 7.6 by a series of upward sloping indifference curves, the highest attainable of which might be like that shown by the curve $I_1 I_1$. Given the preference trade-off of this group, the optimal amount of natural resource conversion would be x_1. They would be opposed to further natural resource conversion because it results in unacceptable increased loss of biodiversity relative to the gain in human well-being.

Note that Fig. 7.6 is illustrative rather than definitive. Furthermore, it is also possible that curve *ABCD* could shift as a result of change in knowledge. However, it can be concluded from Fig. 7.6 that those who believe that strong restrictions should be placed on natural resource use suppose the world has reached a position approaching point *C* whereas those who favor *no* such limitation on natural resource use believe that the extent of natural resource conversion is well below x_2 or are optimistic about the resource conversion curve *ABCD* moving upward, for example, as a result of technological progress. The former believe that human well-being will not be sustained unless natural resource conversion is strongly curtailed, whereas the latter do not, for the time being, consider that additional resource conversion to be a threat to the maintenance of human well-being. The former individuals are said to favor *strong* constraints on resource conversion to ensure sustainable development whereas the latter favor *weak* constraints (or even no constraints) on this conversion. See, for example, Pearce (1993, Chapter 2) and Tisdell (1999).

7.6. Intergenerational Fairness and Sustainable Development

7.6.1. *Rawls' principle of justice and intergenerational equity*

As outlined in Section 4.1 of this book, Rawls (1971) suggested that a just society should aim to ensure that the distribution of income is equal unless inequality is beneficial to all. According to Tietenberg and Lewis (2018, p. 112), this principle requires that resource-use by each generation be such that it does not reduce the well-being of future generations below that enjoyed by each preceding generation. This implies that an ideal development path representing the well-being of all future generations never declines throughout its length.

However, this is a mistaken application of Rawls' principle. This is because a development path could be available which does not have the property just mentioned which is nevertheless, beneficial to all future generations. This is illustrated in Fig. 7.7.

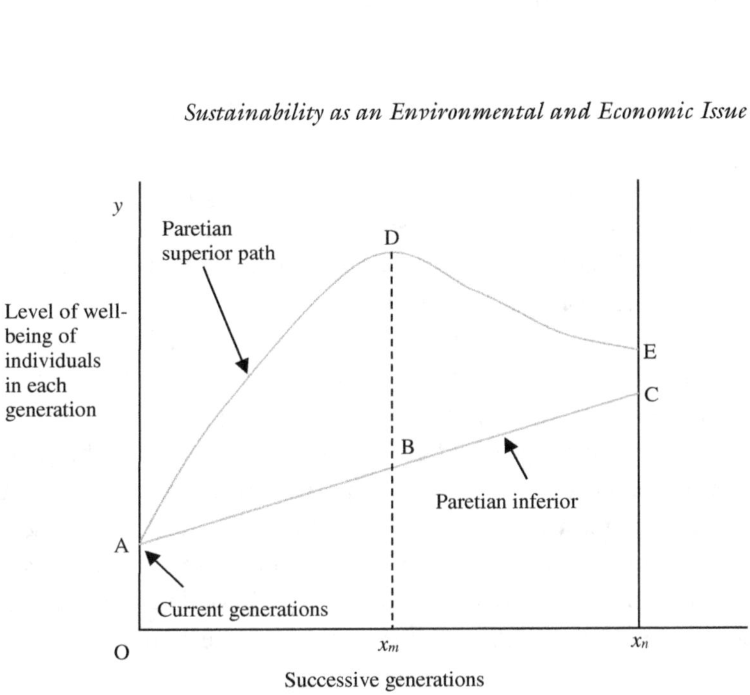

Fig. 7.7. An illustration that Rawls' principle of fairness does not require the well-being of each successive generation to be no less than its predecessor.

In Fig. 7.7, the X-axis indicates the successive generations and the Y-axis indicates the well-being of individuals in each of these generations. The final generation is assumed to be x_n. Two alternative development paths are supposed to be available. The path ABC satisfies the interpretation of Tietenberg and Lewis of Rawls' principle but path ADE does not. This is because if path ADE is followed each succeeding generation born after generation x_m has a lower level of well-being than its predecessor. However, given the correct interpretation of Rawls' principle, path ADE is the socially preferred path because it ensures greater well-being for all future generations than does path ABC. It is Paretian superior to path ABC. In this case, greater intergenerational inequality is beneficial to all.

7.6.2. *An alternative to Rawls' equity principle*

It is by no means clear that all those who are going to be born in the future would (if they were all able to confer before birth) agree to adopt Rawls' distributional objective. Given that none of them know when they are going to be born, they might (for example) opt for a development path that gives each of them the highest level of expected well-being subject to each being assured of a minimum acceptable level of well-being. Basically, those yet to be born are involved (given Rawls' scenario) in decision-making under conditions of uncertainty. This alternative objective of maximizing the expected well-being of individuals subject to assuring them of a minimum level of well-being is a safety-first approach to decision-making under uncertainty. The expected value just mentioned above would be based on the probability of being born into each of the future generations and this would be multiplied by a measure of the well-being of each corresponding generation. Then these values would be summed to give the expected value of well-being of this approach as discussed in Tisdell (2015, Chapter 4).

The application of Rawls' principle to intergenerational equity assumes that the unborn are unwilling to take any risks. This, in my view, is unlikely to be so. Note that criteria for a fair distribution of resources between generations do not indicate how this distribution is to be achieved. The extent to which the use of natural resources is compatible with maintaining the welfare of future generations requires a separate investigation. As pointed out in Section 7.5, views differ about the extent to which natural resources (including environmental resources) should be conserved to benefit future generations.

7.7. The Hartwick Rule, Strong and Weak Conditions for Sustainable Development

Hartwick (1977) developed a particular model to show that the utilization of exhaustible resources (e.g. minerals) could be compatible with future generations having a no lower level of consumption than the present generations. In his model, this is achievable if the rent earned from utilizing exhaustible resources (such as minerals) is invested in the accumulation of man-made capital. However, among other things, this requires that man-made capital is a perfect substitute for natural capital. As has been pointed out by Tietenberg and Lewis (2018, Chapter 5) and others, this assumption is unrealistic. Depreciation and entropy of man-made capital reduces its capacity to perfectly substitute for natural capital. Furthermore, market failures in the conservation of environmental capital result to a significant extent in its socially excessive depletion. This depletion partly occurs because of the accumulation of man-made capital. Consequently, the well-being of future generations can be reduced by substituting man-made capital for natural capital in a world in which there are substantial market failures.

Those economists who believe that sustainable economic development can be achieved by accumulating man-made capital with little regard to the depletion of natural capital, are said to adopt weak conditions for sustainable development. Those who emphasize that sustainable economic development requires this process of accumulation to be restricted by policies to conserve natural capital are said to propose strong conditions for sustainable development. A spectrum of views (from very weak to very strong requirements) exist about how much natural capital (and of what type) ought to be conserved in order to achieve sustainable economic development (Tisdell, 2017, Chapter 3, see especially Fig. 3.3).

Most economic models only take account of the well-being of humans, including most models of sustainable economic development. They are very anthropocentric in their valuations of economic development. These values are, however, not shared by everyone. An increasing number of individuals believe that humankind has a moral responsibility to conserve nature as an end in itself and that humans should be prepared to forgo some material welfare to achieve this. Nevertheless, they differ in their views, about how much economic sacrifice human beings should be prepared to make to achieve this objective.

7.8. The Willingness and the Necessity of Current Generations to Make Economic Sacrifices to Benefit Future Generations

7.8.1. *The willingness to make sacrifices to benefit future generations*

More empirical evidence is needed about the willingness of individuals to make economic sacrifices to benefit future generations. Their willingness to do this sacrifice depends in part on the degree of their concern for the economic welfare of future generations. Pearce (1998) has suggested that individuals are unlikely to show much concern for the welfare of those who will live beyond the life-span of their children and grandchildren. Consequently, the coefficient of concern for the welfare of future generations of most people tapers off sharply after a limited period of time. Furthermore, most people display an unequal amount of concern for the welfare of others. For example, most appear to show the greatest concern for the welfare of their immediate family members. They are likely to be less empathetic to the welfare of other people, for instance those with whom they have little social connection. These factors influence the willingness of current generations to make sacrifices to help others, including those who will live in the future, and they distort the nature of economic bequests left by each generation for future generations. Aspects of these issues are discussed in Tisdell (2017, Chapter 3).

Even if there is a strong desire to maintain the welfare of future generations, the nature of collective decision-making can result in failure to achieve the objective. For example, as pointed out in Section 7.9, social embedding may constitute a significant barrier to social changes needed to ensure this sustainability.

7.8.2. *Is economic sacrificing by current generations needed to sustain the well-being of future generations?*

Not all scholars are convinced that those alive today need to make substantial economic sacrifices to ensure that the well-being of future generations is sustained. Some for instance, are quite optimistic about the role which advances in science and technology can play in sustaining the well-being of future generations. They believe that advances in science and technology will be able to compensate (or more than do so) for natural resource depletion and adverse changes in the environment arising from the economic actions of current generations. In addition, some believe that a point will soon be reached where the natural rate of global population growth falls significantly resulting in a reduced demand for natural resources. Given this point of view, business as usual would not be a disaster for future generations, especially if it results in a larger stock of knowledge of value to future generations and if the occurrence of higher levels of income and other changes (such as increased urbanization) associated with economic growth, lower the global fertility rate. However, those who argue that strong constraints on natural resource use are needed to ensure sustainable development do not support this point of view. They consider it to be overly optimistic.

It should also be noted that some environmental policies are capable of improving the welfare of both current and future generations. Many forms of environmental pollution, degradation and resource depletion have lasting consequences and adversely affect the welfare of both present and future generations. Better management of these problems can benefit not only present but future generations. This book identifies many of these problems and considers how they can be addressed. However, social embedding may prove to be an important obstacle to the adoption of these policies.

7.9. Socioeconomic Embedding as an Obstacle to Achieving Sustainable Development

Our modern market economy is geared to the pursuit of self-interest and this is an obstacle to the adoption of behaviors and policies for promoting sustainable development. Most individuals are unwilling to make major economic sacrifices for the benefit of others, especially if the benefits are spread thinly over an extremely large number of persons; as happens to be so in the case of policies to limit climate change. Climate change provides an example of failure to pursue desirable collective goals as a result of the tyranny of a large number of beneficiaries. As the number of choosers (players in the theory of games) in situations involving a prisoners' dilemma type of structure (see Table 13.9 and surrounding discussion) increases, the possibility of achieving a collective optimum as a result of required actions by each of the choosers (players) decreases. As this number becomes very large, the likelihood of optimal collective action approaches or reaches zero. Olson (1965) has described this as the tyranny of large numbers. A negative outcome is more likely when it is difficult to observe the behaviors of others.

In this case, those who act with social responsibility have little chance of morally condemning those who do not. Situations of this type are more likely when the number of choosers is very large.

Furthermore, many individuals appear to have decreasing concern for the welfare of individuals the further away in the future is their possible existence (Pearce, 1998, p. 71), the more anonymous they are, and the less clearly they are socially linked to the individual, e.g. by family ties (Tisdell, 2015, pp. 68–69). These factors can all impact negatively on the possibility of collective action to achieve sustainable economic development. Their importance still requires more empirical investigation.

The question of the strength of socioeconomic embedding is also important. Gowdy and Krall (2015) argue that today socioeconomic embedding is extremely strong and that contemporary societies therefore, exhibit ultrasociability. Hence, societies are unable to alter their economic development trajectory because all are so strongly embedded in the whole current economic system. A consequence of this is that current societies are unlikely to take effective action to achieve sustainable development unless win-win economic opportunities arise, for example, unless new technologies become available which are both more profitable to adopt and environmentally friendly than existing ones, such as low-cost green technologies for supplying electricity. The adoption of these technologies is discussed in Chapter 13 of this book.

Although socioeconomic embedding occurs in modern societies for several different reasons, it seems to be less absolute than hypothesized by Gowdy and Krall (2015) even if it is strong. The fact that some governments, for example, have subsidized the development and use of solar and wind power as a source of electricity generation (in order to promote sustainable development) indicates that there is some flexibility in social decision-making in the current socio-economic system. Nevertheless, social embedding is a constraint on social choice and restricts adoption of the effective actions to achieve sustainable development.

The type of market failures which were outlined in Chapters 3 and 4 can also contribute to failures to achieve sustainable economic development. However, even if they were eliminated or reduced in significance, the strong desire for continuing substantial economic growth could still overtax our natural environment and create growing scarcity of our natural resources thereby threatening economic sustainability.

7.10. Concluding Comments

The reasons why environmental and economic sustainability have become important subjects in recent times was explained in this chapter. This is partly because economic activity reduces the availability of many natural resources and results in unwanted environmental degradation, such as pollution of air and water resources. The operation of economic systems and the functioning of natural resource systems were shown to be interdependent. The sustainability of natural resource systems was demonstrated to have important implications for the sustainability of economic systems and the operation of economic systems were observed to affect the sustainability of natural resource systems because they extract resources from such systems and dispose of wastes or pollutants into these systems.

Problems of pollution generation and environmental degradation were discussed by reference to the environmental Kuznets curve. It was argued that this curve presents too optimistic a picture of the relationship between economic growth and the occurrence of pollution. It fails, for example, to take account of the fact that some pollutants accumulate, for example, greenhouse gas concentrations, in the biosphere. On its own, economic growth cannot be relied on as a means to mitigate environmental degradation.

Types of material resources, including natural resources, were shown to be quite varied in their attributes. Their different attributes have significant implications for their availability in the long term and consequently, for economic sustainability. Some natural resources, such as living resources, are regenerative but if over exploited or otherwise destroyed or if their habitat is seriously damaged, become nonrenewable. Some natural resources, such as minerals, are depleted by use and are nonrenewable. Others are replenishable but are in limited supply, such as fresh water and sunlight. The available amount of stocks of many types of natural resources are difficult to determine, and their proven reserves depend to some extent on the economic value or price of the resources. Usually, proven resources are less than actual reserves. Consequently, natural resource scarcity can seem to be greater than it really is, particularly once the possibility of substituting the use of other natural resources for those increasing in scarcity is taken into account. Nevertheless, this should not be construed to imply that the possibility of increased natural resource scarcity is not an important economic issue.

Several types of microeconomic market failures were identified as possible contributors to lack of economic sustainability. However, it was also pointed out that when market failure is absent, market systems do not ensure the conservation of all natural resources. In some cases, it is economic to deplete some nonrenewable resources and to extinguish some regenerative resources, such as tree species. This implies that a market system free of market failures may result in loss of biological diversity, a result that is unlikely to be welcomed by those who believe that human beings have a moral responsibility to conserve biodiversity. The possibility that economic systems are too myopic in their operations due to uncertainty and the way in which economic expectations are formed favors policies which increase current economic benefits and reduce resource conservation. Therefore, current economic systems give less consideration to the needs of future generations than might be considered socially desirable.

An important issue in the debate about how sustainable development is to be achieved and about how unwelcome reductions in human welfare are to be avoided is whether this requires restrictions on the rate at which natural resources are being used to produce man-made commodities. Unregulated conversion of natural resources may lead to an undesirable reduction in human well-being in the future. However, it is uncertain how close economic systems are to reaching the critical point where continuing natural resource depletion would reduce future well-being. Furthermore, the scarcity of different types of natural resources varies, and, therefore, the stage can be expected to vary at which their continuing conversion to man-made commodities is likely to reduce economic welfare.

While some economists (such as Engels, 1959, p. 204) have dismissed natural resource constraints as impediments to continuing economic growth on the basis that scientific and technological advance will overcome any emerging limitations, this is a very optimistic point of view. Even if it is true, it should be kept in mind that scientific and technological advances do not occur automatically. Furthermore, natural science does not have a "quick fix" to reverse many of the environmental changes that have emerged or are in the process of occurring, such as climate change, as the result of the type of economic growth which has occurred globally since the Industrial Revolution.

7.11. Keywords

A steady state economy; biological natural resources; diffusion or dispersion of resources; entropy; environmental Kuznets curve; expected economic life of mineral reserves; export of polluting activities; interdependence of economic systems and natural resource systems; lack of environmental sustainability in the absence of market failures; market failures and a lack of economic sustainability; natural resources; natural resource conversion; natural resource substitution; non-biological natural resources; nonrenewable non-biological resources subject to depletion; replenishable non-biological resources; reserve-production ratios of nonrenewable natural resources; strong conditions for sustainable development; sustainability; sustainable development; weak conditions for sustainable development.

7.12. Questions for Review and Discussion

1. The word "sustainability" is without import unless it is related to an object. Explain. Is it always desirable to seek the sustainability of an object?
2. Why has environmental and economic sustainability become an important issue in modern times?

3. Economic systems and natural resource systems are interdependent in their operations. Explain why this is so. Use a diagram to illustrate your answer.
4. According to the theory of Georgescu-Roegen (1971), economic activity utilizes concentrations of natural resources and this use ultimately leads to their dispersion. What long-term consequences might this have for natural resource availability and economic growth? Is there any natural resource process that counteracts this dispersion effect to some extent?
5. Increased economic efficiency does not in itself necessarily result in reduced quantities of natural resources being used for economic production nor a fall in the total levels of wastes and pollutants generated by economic production. Why?
6. What is an environmental Kuznets curve? Illustrate the relationship which is usually assumed for this curve and outline its implications for the levels of pollution emissions.
7. Explain why the environmental Kuznets curve could give too favorable an impression of the reduction in pollution levels that can be achieved by economic growth. In doing so, take into account the possibility that pollutants may accumulate in the biosphere.
8. Higher income countries may send polluting industries offshore to less developed countries. What could cause this to happen? Is it always an effective way for higher income countries to avoid the consequences of increasing environmental pollution? Explain.
9. Natural resources can be divided into three main groups. What are these groups?
10. Explain generally the relationship between the use of each of the three main groups of natural resources and the occurrence of economic sustainability.
11. The conservation of biological resources is vital for continuing human existence. Discuss.
12. What role do replenishable non-biological natural resources play in satisfying human wants? Give examples. Why ought these resources be used carefully in most cases?

13. Current levels of economic production are heavily dependent on the use of nonrenewable, non-biological resources which are depletable. Explain. What sort of challenges does this pose for attaining economic sustainability?
14. It is difficult to determine the stocks or reserves of many non-renewable natural resources. Why? To what extent do reserve–production ratios for minerals depend on economic factors? To what extent are they a limited guide to the length of time for which a mineral will be economically available?
15. Natural resource substitutions can be a powerful force for moderating the economic impact of increasing scarcity of natural resources that are currently major contributors to economic production and human well-being. Explain and discuss.
16. Microeconomic phenomena, such as market failures, can result in lack of economic sustainability. List market failures that can have this consequence and explain the processes by which they can generate unwanted lack of economic sustainability.
17. Even if there are no market failures, market systems may fail to conserve biodiversity and some natural environments. Why?
18. It has been claimed that those involved in resource decisions in market systems have a strong preference for economic gain now, or in the near future, rather than in the more distant future. Why might this be so? Why might it lead to less conservation of natural resources than is considered socially desirable?
19. Explain how the use of natural resources to produce man-made commodities now, and in the near future, could result in human welfare being reduced in the long term. Do you think that greater restrictions should be placed now on natural resource conversion than in previous times? Why?
20. Many economists see the accumulation of man-made capital as an effective means to reduce economic scarcity. However, could such accumulation increase economic scarcity in the long run? Explain your answer. Do you think there are any economic forces that tend to counteract this potential increase in future economic scarcity?

21. What is Rawls' principle of justice? Do you think it provides a sound basis for determining intergenerational fairness? Explain your answer. Do you think it possible that the unborn could adopt a different principle for determining their proposed path of economic development? Why?
22. Is it possible for greater intergenerational equality to be preferred to less generational inequality? Explain why this could happen.
23. A spectrum of views exists about the extent to which present generations would need to conserve natural resources and environments to benefit future generations. Outline the nature of these different views. Which of these views do you favor? Why?
24. In order to devise appropriate policies for sustainable economic development we need to have more empirical knowledge how concerned current generations are for the welfare of members of future generations, that is the nature and characteristics of their coefficients of concern. Discuss.
25. It is possible for some environmental and resource policies to be beneficial to both current and future generations. Discuss. Give examples.
26. Do you think that socioeconomic embedding significantly limits our prospects of achieving sustainable development? Why?
27. Explain why the pursuit of self-interest can make it difficult to achieve sustainable development. In your answer, consider the prisoners' dilemma problem and the issue of the tyranny of large numbers.

Readings and References

Boulding, K.E. (1966). The economics of the coming spaceship Earth. In H Jarrett (Ed.) *Environmental Quality in a Growing Economy*, 3–14. Johns Hopkins University Press, Baltimore, MD, USA.

Clark, C.W. (1976). *Mathematical Bioeconomics: The Optimal Management of Renewable Resources*, John Wiley, New York.

Daly, H.E. (1980). *Economics, Ecology, Ethics: Essays Toward a Steady-State Economy*, W.H. Freeman & Co, San Francisco.

Engels, F. (1959). Outlines of a critique of political economy In K. Marx (Ed.) *Economic and Philosophic Manuscripts of 1844*, Foreign Languages Publishing House, Moscow.

Georgescu-Roegen, N. (1971). *The Entropy Law and the Economic Process*, Harvard University Press, Cambridge, MA.

Gowdy, J. and R. Juliá (2007). Technology and petroleum exhaustion: Evidence from two mega-oilfields, *Energy*, 32, 1448–1454. doi: https://doi.org/10.1016/j.energy.2006.10.019.

Gowdy, J. and L. Krall (2015). The economic origins of ultrasociality, *Behavioral and Brain Sciences*, 39, e92. doi: https://doi.org/10.1017/S0140525X1500059X.

Hartwick, J.M. (1977). Intergenerational equity and the investing of rents from exhaustible resources, *The American Economic Review*, 67, 972–974. doi: https://www.jstor.org/stable/pdf/1828079.pdf.

Ison, S., S. Peake and S. Wall (2002). *Environmental Issues and Policies*, Pearson Education, Harlow, Essex, UK. [Chapter 5].

Kahn, J.R. (2005). *The Economic Approach to Environmental and Natural Resources*, South-Western, Mason, Ohio. [Chapter 6].

Kerr, R.A. (2009). How much coal remains?, *Science*, 323, 1420. doi: 10.1126/science.323.5920.1420.

Keynes, J.M. (1936). *The General Theory of Employment, Interest and Money*, Macmillan and St Martin's Press, London, UK and New York.

Olson, M. (1965). *The Logic of Collective Action*, Harvard University Press, Cambridge, MA.

Pearce, D.W. (1988). Economics, equity and sustainable development, *Futures*, 20, 598–605. doi: https://doi.org/10.1016/0016-3287(88)90002-X.

Pearce, D.W. (1993). *Blueprint 3: Measuring Sustainable Development*, Earthscan Publications, London.

Pearce, D.W. (1998). *Economics and Environment: Essays on Ecological Economics and Sustainable Development*, Edward Elgar, Cheltenham, UK and Northampton, MA, USA.

Perman, R., Y. Ma, M. Common, D. Maddison and J. McGilvray (2011). *Natural Resource and Environmental Economics*, 4th edn. Pearson, Harlow, Essex UK. [Chapter 2].

Rawls, J.R. (1971). *A Theory of Justice*, Harvard University Press, Cambridge, MA, USA.

Ricardo, D. (1817). *The Principles of Political Economic and Taxation*, Dent, London. Reprint, 1955.

Roberts, P. (2008). World oil demand is surging as supplies approach their limits, *National Geographic*, 218, 86–91.

Tietenberg, T. and L. Lewis (2018). *Environmental and Natural Resource Economics*, 11th edn. Routledge, New York and Abingdon, Oxon, UK. [Chapter 5].

Tisdell, C.A. (1988). Sustainable development: Differing perspectives of ecologists and economists, and relevance to LDCs, *World Development*, 16, 373–384. doi: 10.1016/0305-750X(88)90004-6.

Tisdell, C.A. (1992). The nature of sustainability and of sustainable development, *Middle East Business and Economic Review*, 4, 21–25. Reprinted as Chapter 9 in C.A. Tisdell (1993), *Environmental Economics, Policies for Environmental Management and Sustainable Development*, Edward Elgar, Aldershot, UK and Brookfield, VT, USA.

Tisdell, C.A. (1993). *Environmental Economics: Policies for Environmental Management and Sustainable Development*, Edward Elgar, Aldershot, UK and Brookfield, VT, USA. [Chapters 9 and 10].

Tisdell, C.A. (1999). Conditions for sustainable development: Weak or strong. In A.K. Dragun and C.A. Tisdell (Eds.), *Sustainable Agriculture and Environment*, 23–36. Edward Elgar, Cheltenham, UK and Northampton, MA, USA.

Tisdell, C.A. (2001). Globalisation and sustainability: Environmental Kuznets curve and the WTO, *Ecological Economics*, 39, 185–196. doi: 10.1016/S0921-8009(01)00234-8.

Tisdell, C.A. (2003). Socioeconomic causes of loss of animal genetic diversity: Analysis and assessment, *Ecological Economics*, 45, 365–376. doi: 10.1016/S0921-8009(03)00091-0.

Tisdell, C.A. (2005). *Economics of Environmental Conservation*, 2nd edn. Edward Elgar, Cheltenham, UK and Northampton, MA, USA. [Chapter 11].

Tisdell, C.A. (2015). *Sustaining Biodiversity and Ecosystem Functions: Economic Issues*, Edward Elgar, Cheltenham, UK and Northampton, MA, USA.

Tisdell, C.A. (2017). *Economics and Environmental Change: The Challenges We Face*, Edward Elgar Publishing Cheltenham, UK and Northampton, MA, USA. [Chapters 3 and 7].

PART II

MORE SPECIFIC TOPICS

Chapter 8

Agriculture, Agricultural Policies and the Environment

8.1. Introduction

Although this chapter focuses on agriculture, its environmental impacts, its use of natural resources and the consequences of its development for the sustainability of agricultural production, many of the issues discussed here are also relevant to the development of aquaculture and silviculture. All depend to a large extent (but not exclusively) on the use of natural resources for their productivity and transform terrestrial or aquatic areas.

The nature of agricultural production varies in its intensity. Intensive agriculture results in high yields per hectare whereas extensive agriculture results in lower yields and requires greater land use for the same amount of production. However, both forms utilize natural resources to a high degree. For example, intensive agriculture, as a rule, makes use of artificial fertilizers and chemicals ultimately derived from natural-resource stocks. Considerable use of capital equipment and works are also characteristic of modern agriculture. Once again, this man-made capital is ultimately supplied by utilizing natural resources, many kinds of which are nonrenewable. Energy for operating agricultural machinery and equipment is supplied mainly, and increasingly, by the combustion of nonrenewable fossil fuels.

Table 8.1. Agricultural area as a percentage of land area for the world and for selected regions in 2016.

Region	Percentage
World	37.4
UK	71.7
India	60.45
Australia	48.2
Germany	47.7
USA	44.4
EU	42.8

Source: Derived from https://data.worldbank.org/indicator/AG.LND.AGRI.ZS [Accessed 17 June, 2020].

Agriculture has pervasive and environmental impacts (see, for example, Kiers *et al.*, 2008; FAO, 2007). Agriculture has changed the natural environment of a large portion of the globe. It is the main form of land use. Table 8.1 provides some data specifying the area of land used for agriculture as a percentage of total land areas. For the world as a whole, this amounted to about 37% of its total land area in 2016. This percentage varies considerably between countries.

It is for example, quite high for the UK and India but very low for Sweden (7.4% and only 2.7% for Norway) since much of their land area is unsuited to agriculture.

Of course, as a percentage of land which is no longer in a natural (or near natural) state, the proportion occupied by agriculture is much higher than is shown in Table 8.1. The extent to which natural ecosystems are transformed by nature depend on its intensity and type. The statistics in Table 8.1 include land use for both intensive and extensive forms of agriculture. The latter includes land use for the grazing of livestock. Both intensive and extensive agriculture result in the transformation of terrestrial environments, but more so in the former case than in the latter one. Furthermore, in most countries, agriculture is the major user of freshwater.

According to World Bank data, 70% of global withdrawals of freshwater in 2014 were used for agriculture. In South Asia, this figure was extremely high, namely 91.2%. In the USA, according to the United States Department of Agriculture, agriculture accounted for 80% of water use. The amount of water used by agriculture often has significant effects on the state of natural freshwater environments. For example, it can result in much reduced waterflows in streams and rivers, especially during drought. This is a threat to populations of species dependent on these waterbodies and can result in higher concentrations of pollutants in these bodies. However, the amount of water used by other industries and for domestic purposes also adds to environmental problems of this type.

As the global population continues to increase and more people exist with higher incomes, the demand to use freshwater will increase. This will add to growing social conflict about access to freshwater. Furthermore, protecting the quality of this water will become more important. More attention will need to be paid to water management. Some of the issues involved in this management are considered in Chapter 9.

As outlined in this chapter, agricultural development has a major ecological and environmental footprint. Nevertheless, agricultural development (together with other biologically based food-supplying industries) is needed to provide enough food for the world's growing level of human population. This chapter begins by discussing the general impacts of agriculture on the environment and the use of natural resources, then considers market failures as influences on the occurrence of agriculture's environmental impacts and its use of natural resources before examining economic factors that affect agricultural sustainability. Subsequently, the implications of agricultural policies for the state of the environment and for the availability of natural resources are outlined.

8.2. General Impacts of Agricultural Development on the Environment and on the Availability of Natural Resources

8.2.1. *Broad environmental concerns*

The development of agriculture has a heavy ecological and environmental footprint because the productivity of agriculture depends on the transformation of natural environments. It generally requires the clearing of land of natural vegetation, thereby altering landscapes, and the greater is its intensity, the more it modifies the natural environments and regulates the environment in which agriculture takes place. This often results in considerable environmental costs and can raise concerns about the sustainability of agricultural production. Even extensive agriculture involving the grazing of livestock can cause considerable landscape changes as a result of selective grazing by livestock, over grazing and soil erosion and other damages due to trampling by livestock.

Nevertheless, agricultural production is essential in order to meet basic human needs and therefore, some environmental costs are an acceptable and an unavoidable part of meeting human economic demands. The main problem is to ensure that socially excessive costs are not incurred as a result of agricultural development. Unfortunately, excessive social costs from agriculture can occur under free market conditions and in other circumstances.

Take a simple illustration. Suppose that two different techniques of agricultural production are available: techniques I and II. Technique I has a lower social marginal cost of production than technique II, but the latter has the lowest private marginal cost. In a free market, technique II, the one with the lowest private marginal cost, will be adopted, but this is not socially optimal. Public policies should be adopted to ensure that technique I is adopted rather than II.

For both types of techniques, negative spillovers will be present and they will continue to be present even if policy measures are adopted to bring the social marginal cost of production into equality with the extra value placed on the extra supply of agricultural produce. This is illustrated in Fig. 8.1. In Fig. 8.1, line *HJK* represents the private marginal

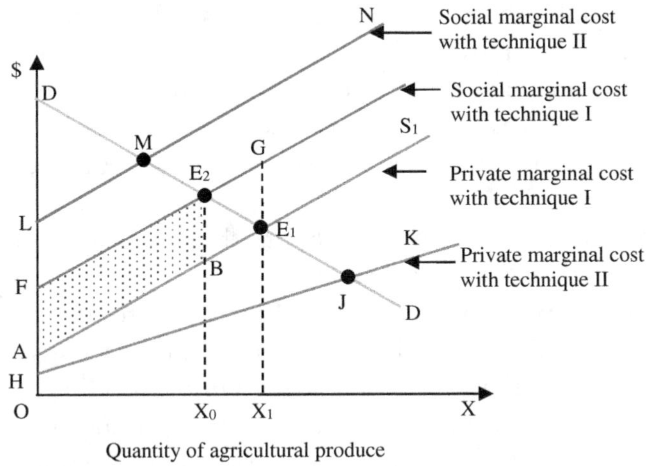

Fig. 8.1. Even after economically optimal policy responses are made to allow for the occurrence of environmental externalities generated by agriculture, environmental costs will still remain. In the case illustrated, there are marginal external environmental costs equal to AF once policies are adopted to disallow the use of technique II. After optimal policy responses, external environmental costs equivalent to the area of trapezium ABE_2F remain. Given the state of knowledge, these are unavoidable environmental costs of agricultural production.

cost of supplying X when technique II is adopted and line LMN is the corresponding social marginal cost of using this technique. In this figure, AS_1 represents the private marginal cost of supplying an agricultural product, X, if technique I is used; and line FG represents the corresponding social marginal cost of this supply. Line DD represents the demand for this agricultural product. The social economic costs of using technique I are considerably less than those from using technique II, even though private costs favor the use of technique II. It would be socially desirable not to allow the use of technique II. If only technique I is permitted, market equilibrium would be established at E_1. However, this is not socially ideal because a social deadweight loss equal to the area of triangle E_2E_1G occurs. Ideally, the level of agricultural production should be reduced from X_1 to X_0 (see Chapter 5). Suppose that this is achieved, for example, by imposing a tax equal to AF on each unit of agricultural production when technique I is adopted.

The market equilibrium is then established at E_2 and there is a Paretian ideal outcome. However, a total externality (environmental) cost equivalent to the area of trapezium ABE_2F still occurs. It would be necessary to stop all agricultural production in order to avoid environmental spillover costs in the case illustrated. This would clearly not be socially desirable.

Note by reference to Fig. 8.1, that as the demand for agricultural produce rises (that is as the demand curve for X shifts upwards), it will be economically optimal to bear higher environmental spillover costs even after optimal policy adjustment, other things remaining equal. This means that the area of trapezium ABE_2F is increased in size. Therefore, as the demand for agricultural produce rises, increasing environmental costs can be expected to occur even after socially optimal adjustment of the economic system.

8.2.2. *Demand for agricultural production expected to increase substantially*

The demand for agricultural produce is expected to increase substantially between now (2020) and 2050 and is anticipated continuing to rise until the end of this century. Rising demand will be partly driven by the growing level of global population. The UN estimates that, as at March 2020, the global population was 7.8 billion. It expects this population to increase by almost 2 billion by 2050 to reach a global level of 9.7 billion, that is to rise by almost a quarter. The largest increases are predicted for Africa and Asia. In order to keep pace with this population increase, agricultural supplies would also need to rise by almost 25%. A challenge is how to achieve this growth, to do so sustainably and minimize the ecological and environmental damage caused by agriculture.

As global demand for agricultural produce rises, public concern about the environmental impacts of agriculture and about the sustainability of agricultural production is bound to grow. Market failures may also magnify socially undesirable environmental impacts from agriculture and less sustainability of agricultural production than deemed to be socially desirable could become a serious problem. However, even in the absence of market failures, lack of agricultural sustainability can occur and can be a social concern. Let us consider these matters.

8.3. Market Failures Involving Agriculture and Their Implications for the Environment and Resource Use

8.3.1. *Background*

Socially undesirable use of the environment and natural resources may occur because of the presence of several types of market failures. These market failures are likely to lead to outcomes that do not minimize economic scarcity in the sense that the Paretian criterion is not satisfied. This implies that a change in resource use which results in a potential Paretian improvement would be possible, that is some individuals in society could be made better-off without any others being made worse off. These types of failures and their implications for economic scarcity were considered in depth in Chapter 3. Here, the focus is on their application to environments affected by agricultural development and their consequences for natural-resource use by agriculture. The discussion will concentrate on environmental spillovers involving agriculture, agriculture's open-access to resources and the consequences of agricultural development for the supply of commodities with the characteristics of public goods. These failures result in changed environmental conditions and can result in lack of sustainability of agricultural production.

8.3.2. *Environmental spillovers and agriculture*

Environmental spillovers (externalities) involving agriculture consist of a wide range of types. While they are often unfavorable, they are sometimes favorable. For example, clearing of vegetation for agricultural development is often regarded as having negative spillover effects. These can include reduced water quality, biodiversity loss and increased soil erosion as a result of the transport of soil by wind or water from agricultural sites with negative consequences for other neighborhoods. On the other hand, positive environmental spillovers are also possible.

Some types of agriculture may create favorable landscapes, reduce the threat of fires and lower the risks of attacks on humans, their crops and domesticated stock by forest-dwelling wildlife.

When an unfavorable environmental externality is generated by an agricultural activity (and it is Pareto relevant, see Tisdell, 1993, Chapters 2 and 3; 2005, Chapter 3) it will, as a rule, be over supplied in the sense that a reduction on its level would lead to a potential Paretian improvement. However, if a favorable externality is being generated by an agricultural activity, then it will be under supplied from the above point of view (assuming that the externality is Paretian relevant). Provided that the transaction costs of intervention are not too high, it can be economic to adopt policies that adjust for these influences, for example, impose charges or taxes to restrict negative externalities and pay subsidies to promote agricultural activities that generate positive environmental externalities.

Policies along these lines have been adopted in the European Union. Europe's new Common Agricultural Policy (CAP) provides economic incentives to farmers to adjust their economic activities in accordance with whether these activities are judged to create positive or negative environmental externalities (see, for example, Tisdell and Hartley, 2008, pp. 76–80).

Table 8.2 provides a list of some of the favorable and unfavorable environmental externalities that can be created by agricultural development. It should be noted that some of these environmental externalities can alter from being marginally favorable to being marginally unfavorable as their supply increases (Tisdell, 2009a). For example, there is often a demand for a particular mixture of landscapes rather than extensive areas of uniform landscape, for instance, mixed combinations of farmland and forested land. An optimal balance between land uses is required taking into account the external social values of each. In order to bring about a socially optimal result, policy needs to be targeted at increasing relative forest cover in some cases and reducing it in others.

A further possible complication is that social valuation of environmental impacts of agricultural activity can vary with the passage of time. Values are subject to historical change and institutional and social

Table 8.2. A list of some possible environmental spillovers generated by agricultural production.

Unfavorable externalities caused by agriculture

1. Increased *siltation of water bodies* as a result of greater soil erosion from rainfall. This can silt up rivers and ponds and adversely affect the spawning of some fish species. Siltation of dams accelerates.
2. In some cases, greater *wind-borne soil erosion* occurs thereby reducing visibility off-site and causing unwanted soil movements, including the spread of desertification.
3. *Water pollution* as a result of nutrient enrichment of water. This causes weed growth, algal bloom and eutrophication of water bodies. This can adversely affect fish stocks and algal bloom (blue–green algae) can result in water becoming toxic and unable to be consumed by humans and livestock. The problem is aggravated by the use of chemical fertilizers and high concentrations of animal excrement.
4. *Land subsidence* can occur over a wide area when agriculture draws water from underground aquifers for irrigation purposes. As a result, buildings in the neighborhood can suffer structural change, in some cases flooding of land becomes more likely, and if the land is near the sea, saltwater may intrude on it.
5. *Agricultural pesticides* which use toxic chemicals may drift in the wind and cause damage to nearby agricultural properties or the health of those in the environs. Some of these pesticides may kill bees.
6. Some farmers may grow crops that have adverse spillovers on others such as unwanted *cross pollination of genetically modified crops* with those that are not modified.
7. Some farmers may also fail to control *mobile pests* on their land and this has adverse external effects on other farmers.
8. In some regions (e.g. Australia), adverse external consequences involving *dryland salting* occur. Dryland salting occurs as the result of the removal of trees which allow the salt in some soils to rise towards the surface. This destroys much vegetation and the effects can spillover from one property to the next. Streams often become saline destroying aquatic life and becoming unfit for any normal use.
9. *Natural biodiversity is lost* due to transformation of habitats by agriculture. The available variety of niches for wildlife are reduced (Tisdell, 1999a, Chapter 4). This may have externality as well as public goods consequences.
10. In some cases, *landscapes may become less attractive* as a result of agricultural activity. For example, broadacre agriculture can result in a monotonous homogeneity of landscapes. Scars from increased soil erosion, for example, as in the loess area of China, can make the landscapes unattractive.

(*Continued*)

Table 8.2. (*Continued*)

Favorable externalities from agriculture

1. *Provision of landscapes that are aesthetically pleasing* to many individuals, for example, the moors in Yorkshire in England; mixed agricultural and other lands uses in mountainous parts of Switzerland; rice terraces in China and Japan.
2. *Animal pests reduced*. In some cases, agriculture eliminates or reduces greatly the population of wild animals that may attack human beings. This is regarded by some communities as positive spillover benefit.
3. In some cases, *agriculture reduces the risks of wild fires* by reducing the fuel available to feed such fires. However, clearing of land for the development of agriculture may add to the risk of wild fires, as in Kalimantan in Indonesia. There agricultural development has added to the risk of these fires, and has resulted in fires in peat soil. These fires have caused smoke to disperse over wide geographical areas with adverse consequences for human health.
4. *Nectar* supplied for bees *for honey*, but the bees also benefit farmers by assisting with the pollination of crops.
5. *Tree planting* and *hedge planting* by farmers can have several favorable environmental spillover impacts.

Note: It is not always possible to determine *a priori* whether an environmental externality should be regarded as favorable or unfavorable and different social groups may evaluate externalities differently. Also, as discussed in the text, an externality may alter from being favorable to being unfavorable depending on the scale of activity involved.

influences (see Chapter 2). This raises especially difficult issues when irreversible environmental change occurs and future social values are uncertain (Bishop, 1978; Krutilla and Fisher, 1975).

8.3.3. *Use by agriculturalists of open-access natural resources*

As demonstrated in Chapters 3 and 4, use of open-access resources by agriculturalists does, as a rule, give rise to several types of economic inefficiencies. Of particular concern in such cases is the failure to take into account user costs in economic decision-making. This is liable to result in unwanted lack of sustainability in the use of shared natural resources and can lead to eventual impoverishment of the users of such resources.

An example is the use of shared static or relatively static water bodies (e.g. underground aquifers, lakes). In the beginning, the returns of farmers from using the shared water resource may be high and this encourages greater use of water. Subsequently, its use may come to exceed the rate of recharge of the water body, and the costs of water extraction can be expected to rise with net returns from water use falling. Eventually, incomes may fall to subsistence level as water stocks dwindle. As pointed out by Tisdell (2009b), political action is unlikely to be taken to avert this problem. Once the problem develops, there is difficulty in developing countries to escape form the low-level income equilibrium that eventuates.

Sometimes, such problems can be reduced by presence of communal property (see Chapter 4). In such cases, the local community restricts water use by its members.

8.3.4. *Consequences of agricultural development for the supply of commodities with public goods attributes*

Agricultural development can reduce the supply of commodities that possess public goods characteristics or it can increase the supply of public bads. Agricultural development may, for example, extinguish wild species that possess the attributes of public goods. They may possess significant existence value, option value or bequest value. Examples include species that are present in tropical forests, but lose their habitat as a result of the extension of agriculture. These include the orangutan in Borneo which is not only threatened by extension of the cultivation of oil palm (Swarna Nantha and Tisdell, 2009), but also by the felling of tropical forests for timber.

The major problem for the conservation of many species dwelling in tropical forests is that although the global value of conserving them may be high, residents of the region and country where such species are present are able to appropriate little, if any, of this global economic value. Therefore, at very best, they have a weak economic incentive to conserve such species. On the other hand, they are able to appropriate most of the economic benefits from the extension of

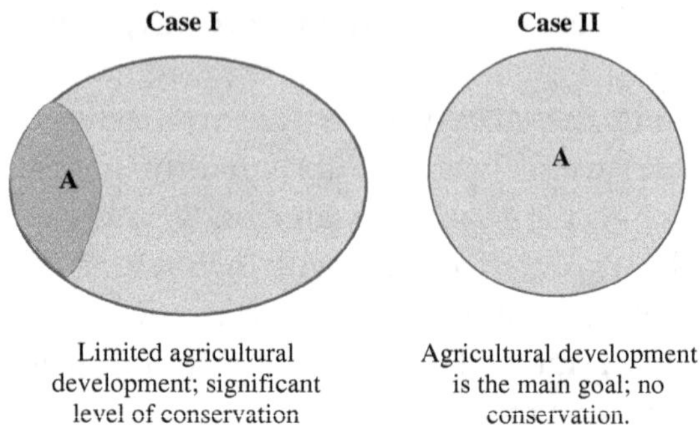

Fig. 8.2. An illustration of a case (Case II) in which emphasis on agricultural development benefits the region in which it occurs but reduces global economic benefits. Situation I above gives greater global benefits than II but situation II results in greater regional benefits.

agriculture because agricultural output is a pure private good. Therefore, local inhabitants are likely to prefer agriculture to nature conservation because, for them the opportunity cost of nature conservation is too high.

Thus, in Fig. 8.2 if a conservation strategy is adopted, let the area of set A (Case I) represent the benefit to a country, A, or region adopting this strategy, and let the area of set R be the benefit to the rest of the world. The area of A plus R represents global benefit. If, on the other hand, a strategy of agricultural development is adopted by country or region A, the area of the set on the right-hand side (Case II) might represent its benefits and the rest of the world may obtain no economic benefits. Total global economic benefits are lower in the latter case, but country or region A is better-off.

To avoid a global economic loss in such a situation, those who benefit from conservation would need to pay those who benefit from agricultural development the income they forgo by refraining from this activity. It is, however, not easy to arrange such transfers because of free-riding problems.

Agricultural extension and activity can also add to public bads such as the level of greenhouse gases in the atmosphere. Agricultural extension generally adds to land clearing and the destruction of trees which sequestrate carbon dioxide. The cultivation of soil for agriculture hastens the decomposition of organic matter in the soil which further adds to levels of greenhouse gas emissions. Livestock add to methane releases and the use of some artificial fertilizers accelerates greenhouse gas emissions. Fossil fuel use in agriculture further adds to agriculture's contribution to rising greenhouse gas levels. It is estimated that agriculture currently accounts for about one-eighth of global greenhouse gas emissions. However, most countries appear to be reluctant to regulate agriculture so as to reduce its greenhouse gas emissions. This is partly for political reasons. The regulation of emissions of greenhouse gas constitutes a collective prisoners' dilemma type of problem because individual self-interest and collective self-interest are in conflict (see Chapter 13).

8.4. Factors Leading to a Lack of Agricultural Sustainability

8.4.1. *Market factors as a source of lack of agricultural sustainability*

All the types of market failures discussed in the previous section can be sources that result in declining agricultural production. For example, adverse environmental spillovers from farming practices adopted by some farmers may reduce the production of other farmers affected by these spillovers. As previously demonstrated, open-access to natural resources can be expected to result eventually in falling levels of agricultural production until an equilibrium is established at a low-level of production. Rising levels of greenhouse gases in the atmosphere (to which agriculture contributes but is not the sole contributor) are likely to reduce global agricultural production in the long term, particularly if significant rises in the sea level occur. However, not all downward trends in agricultural production can be attributed to market failures.

8.4.2. *Lack of agricultural sustainability due to factors other than market failures*

Several factors other than market failures may result in failure to maintain levels of agricultural or production. Table 8.3 lists some of

Table 8.3. A list of factors that can contribute to lack of sustainability of agricultural productivity on individual landholdings due to internal rather than external causes. Some of these factors may also be subject to external influence.

1. *Loss of fertile topsoil* due to erosion. This is facilitated by natural vegetation removal, soil cultivation and over grazing by livestock. Soils vary in their proneness to erosion and with their location. For example, those on steep slopes are very prone to water erosion.
2. *Soil compaction* and other undesirable changes in the structure of the soil due to cultivation practices or trampling by livestock. The use of heavy farm machinery, such as heavy tractors, can result in an increase in soil compaction.
3. In some geographical regions, *dryland salting* of soil occurs as a result of tree removal. Only salt-tolerant plants will grow in such areas and often they become bare or almost bare of vegetation. In other areas, water from irrigation may bring salt into the topsoil with a similar effect.
4. Some soils are acidic and when cultivated their *acidity increases.* This can reduce their productivity.
5. Agricultural use of land may encourage the *growth of weeds* (or other pests) and this can result in a decline in agricultural productivity.
6. Agriculture results in *removal of nutrients from the soil* in produce sent off a property and accelerates leaching of nutrients from the soil. Lack of crop rotation and the practice of monoculture may result in deficiencies of particular nutrients occurring.

these factors which may result in agricultural productivity not being maintained.

Sometimes lack of agricultural sustainability occurs due to informed choices made by landholders but not always. On other occasions, lack of agricultural sustainability may occur due to ignorance. The long-term consequences of various types of farming practices for production may be poorly known and expectations may be overly optimistic. For example, many farmers may be unaware of the extent to which soil erosion will reduce their crop yields or the extent to which the structure of their soil will deteriorate with its continuing cultivation. In addition, they may lack knowledge about how to counteract these tendencies.

In competitive markets, farmers may find it difficult to adopt techniques that require foregoing considerable profit now to sustain productivity at a later stage, as in the case of organic farming. Many techniques that increase current profit also increase user costs. For example, adoption of large tractors adds to soil compaction which in many areas tends to reduce crop yields in the long term, but increases agricultural profit on broad acre farms in the shorter term (Mann, 2008).

In some cases, farmers may knowingly mine their land. For example, they may have a high preference for income now rather than in the future. They may, for instance, desire greater income now to educate their children, assist their children with migration or may wish to migrate themselves. They may, therefore, have little interest in the long-term productivity of their agricultural land, which may not always be easy to sell. Furthermore, in some cases, poor farmers who wish to sustain the productivity of their land may be unable to undertake investments to do this because of a shortage of investible funds and inadequate credit markets. This can be regarded as another case of market failure.

When lack of agricultural sustainability occurs as a result of informed decisions by farmers, there may not be a strong case for government intervention to counteract it unless it results in unfavorable externalities. But if this lack of agricultural activity occurs as a result of ignorance, then government intervention to improve knowledge can have economically beneficial results. However, we should also be aware that public authorities are not always well informed and sometimes have supported inferior agricultural choices.

8.5. Impacts of Agricultural Policies on the Environment and Natural-Resource Use

8.5.1. *Adverse environmental externalities from agriculture and government subsidies for agricultural production*

While some agricultural policies are designed to moderate adverse environmental spillovers from agriculture and support agriculture that has favorable externalities (such as the new CAP of the EU), many agricultural policies fail to do this or have failed to do it in the past. For example, when agricultural production having unfavorable spillovers is subsidized, this raises the environmental costs arising from agricultural production and increases the social deadweight loss from adopting a subsidization policy. This can also happen if quotas on imports of agricultural products or tariffs artificially raise the home prices of agricultural products that have negative production externalities. It aggravates environmental problems.

The inappropriate subsidization case is illustrated in Fig. 8.3. In this figure, the line *DD* represents the demand for an agricultural product, *X*, and *JS* is its supply curve (corresponding to private marginal costs in the absence of government intervention). However, this production generates an adverse environmental externality which involves an external marginal cost equal to *AJ*. Therefore, the social marginal cost of the production of *X* is represented by line *AF*. In the absence of

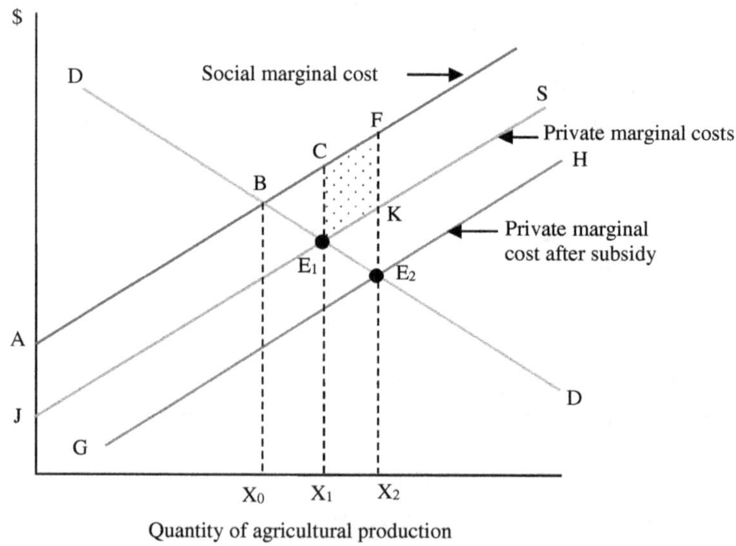

Fig. 8.3. An illustration of how subsidizing agricultural production magnifies the social economic loss incurred if agricultural production generates a negative environmental externality. In the case illustrated, subsidizing agricultural production adds an amount equivalent to the area of trapezium E_2KFC to environmental costs.

public intervention, a social deadweight loss equal to the area of triangle BE_1C occurs. Now suppose that the government decides to subsidize the supply of X so that the supply curve of agricultural producers after payment of the subsidy is GH. After the payment of the subsidy, the farmers have lower marginal costs of production. Market equilibrium is now established at E_2 rather than E_1. Consequently, the deadweight social loss increases from an amount equal to the area of triangle BE_1C to an amount equal to the area of triangle BE_2F, that is by an amount equal to the area of the quadrilateral E_1E_2FC. Environmental spillover costs increase by an amount equivalent to the area of trapezium E_1KFC (and resource misallocations costs rise by an amount equivalent to the area of triangle E_1E_2K) as a result of the subsidy. In this case, agricultural production is subsidized when it would be more appropriate from an economic efficiency point of view to tax it, for example, impose a tax on each unit of production equivalent to JA.

In some cases, governments subsidize or have subsidized the use of agricultural inputs which generate negative environmental spillovers. For example, the supply of chemical fertilizers has been subsidized. Sometimes agricultural externalities (for example, tree clearing) that result in negative environmental externalities have been subsidized or have qualified farmers for extra tax concessions thus encouraging these externalities. As well as causing a misallocation of resources, such policies add to the environmental costs associated with agricultural production. Consider, for example, a subsidy on chemical fertilizers.

This case is illustrated in Fig. 8.4. To make the exposition simple, assume that the price of agricultural produce is constant and let line ABC represent the net marginal value of using a chemical fertilizer for agricultural production. Then in the absence of externalities, it would be socially ideal from an economics point of view to use X_2 of the chemical fertilizer per period where X represents the quantity of fertilizer used. Suppose, however, that the use of this fertilizer generates a negative marginal externality equivalent to AD. Then the net social marginal value of chemical fertilizer used is as shown by line DEG. Consequently, the socially optimal use of this fertilizer would be X_1 not X_2 and ideally policies should be instituted to limit its use. Suppose, however, that chemical fertilizer is given a subsidy equivalent

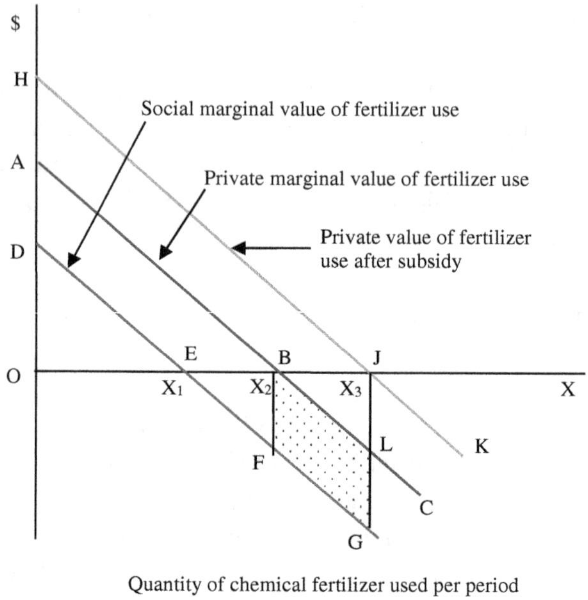

Fig. 8.4. An illustration of how a government subsidization of an agricultural input having an unfavorable externality adds to the social economic cost of agricultural production. In this case, a subsidy on chemical fertilizers increases the deadweight social economic cost of agricultural production from an amount equivalent to the area of triangle *EFB* to an amount equivalent to the area of triangle *EGJ*.

to *AH* per unit. After this subsidy is paid, the net private value of marginal product of chemical fertilizer use rises from line *AC* to line *HJK*. Hence, use of this fertilizer rises from X_2 to X_3. Whereas originally, in the absence of government intervention, the social economic loss from use of chemical fertilizer was equivalent to the area of triangle *EFB*, after the subsidy it rises to the equivalent of the area of triangle *EGJ*, an increase equivalent to the area of quadrilateral *BFGJ*. This increased social economic loss consists of two components — the increase in the environmental costs from spillovers from use of the fertilizer (which is equivalent to the area of quadrilateral *BFGL*) and the loss due to misallocation of resources in the absence of externalities, which is equivalent to the area of triangle *BLJ*. This type of government economic intervention can magnify the environmental costs of agricultural production.

8.5.2. *Favorable environmental spillovers from agriculture and public policy*

It is also desirable to realize that there can be some agricultural activities that generate favorable environmental externalities and that it can be desirable for governments to provide economic incentives for expanding the scale of these activities. For example, some types of agricultural activities create landscapes that are appealing to human beings or help to conserve wildlife favored by human beings. The logic for intervention in this case can be illustrated using a similar approach to that adopted in Fig. 8.4.

In Fig. 8.5, line *ABC* represents the net marginal private value to farmers of engaging in an environmentally favorable activity which has a marginal spillover benefit equivalent to *AH*. If farmers only pursue their private gain, they will engage in the activity to the extent X_1 although it is socially optimal to engage in the activity up to the level X_2.

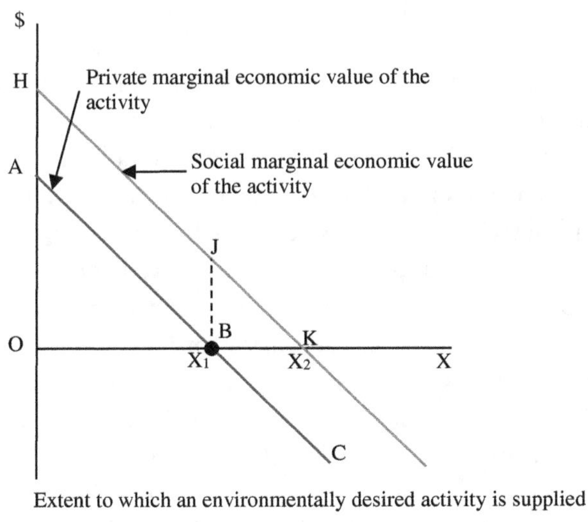

Fig. 8.5. An illustration that social economic gains are possible by intervening in agricultural activity if some agricultural activities generate favorable environmental spillovers. In the case shown, a social economic gain equivalent to the area of triangle *BKJ* can be attained if the level of the desirable agricultural activity can be increased from X_1 to X_2. In a free market, this activity would only be maintained at X_1.

An additional social economic benefit of an amount equivalent to the area of triangle *BKJ* can be obtained by this expansion in supply of the activity. The expansion could be achieved by subsidizing each unit of the desired activity by an amount *AH*. This, however, results in a higher payment to farmers than is necessary to bring about the desired result. If the marginal units of activity can be identified, then it is only necessary to subsidize marginal activity. For example, a subsidy of the equivalent of *AH* per unit of activity need only be paid on units of the desirable activity is in excess of X_1 in the case illustrated to bring about the result which maximizes the social value of the activity. Decisions about whether to pay the subsidy on the whole or the marginal part of the activity are likely to be influenced by desires to redistribute income in favor of farmers.

8.5.3. *Agricultural policy and the conservation of natural resources*

It was already mentioned that governments may fail to regulate open access to resources used by agriculturalists and there will be some more discussion of this matter in the next chapter. This failure may result in the socially unwanted reduction or depletion of natural resources. There has also been discussion of why governments at the national level or regional level are likely to fail to take action to regulate agricultural expansion and activity when this reduces the supply of global public goods. In particular, local governments are often keen to expand agricultural economic activity in their region even when this is detrimental to the environment and the conservation of natural resources because they are usually able to collect more public revenue as a result of the expansion of the level of local economic production, that is as a result of regional economic growth, rather than by engaging in conservation. Economic growth can mean higher salaries and perks for local government officials and can reduce political conflict with those interested in local economic development. While local or regional benefits may be maximized, global ones (or those of a wider community) are not.

On the other hand, in recent years, some governments (such as the Australian Government) have increasingly tried to inform farmers of practices that will increase the sustainability of their agricultural production and have provided financial support for the implementation of these practices. This may mean that society at large has a greater demand for agricultural sustainability than some farmers.

8.6. Agriculture and Climate Change

Agricultural production is sensitive to climatic conditions. It is predicted that increased global warming due to anthropocentric causes will result in substantial climatic change globally. The expected type of climatic changes are listed in Table 13.10 of this book. Rising temperatures will reduce the yields or result in no yields from some types of crops (e.g. wheat) in regions where they are now grown. This is because elevated temperatures restrict the ability of these crops to produce seeds (Ziska, 2011). In some areas, crop yields will fall due to changes in precipitation. Some regions will become drier and others wetter and this will change the areal pattern of agriculture.

There is still considerable uncertainty about the overall likely impacts of global warming on the global level of agricultural production. Mendelsohn and Dinar (1999, 2009) predict that the level of aggregate global output of agriculture will be little affected by global warming. This is because they believe that farmers will respond to climate change by altering the types of crops grown. For example, as temperatures rise, crops suited to temperate climates will be grown further away from the equator in cooler regions and will be replaced in those areas becoming hotter by crops that are more suited to warmer areas (Tisdell, 2017, Chapter 9). Also seasonal patterns of plantings may be altered. For example, the planting of crops that are less heat-tolerant may be delayed until cooler annual temperatures prevail. However, in many warm regions, the length of the annual cooler period could become so short as a result of global warming that this window of opportunity disappears.

Also it is not certain that the movement of agriculture towards the poles will compensate for the potentially reduced level of agricultural production elsewhere. This depends on sufficient agricultural land of suitable quality being available as agriculture moves towards the poles.

In the southern hemisphere, the land mass declines sharply as one moves away from the equator. Although the land mass may increase in the northern hemisphere as one moves north, it may be of reduced quality for agriculture. Furthermore, the possibility of multiple annual cropping might be reduced closer to the poles due to longer winter nights there and the reduced duration of sunlight in the winter. This would lower annual agricultural production.

Another reason to be skeptical of the prognosis of Mendelsohn and Dinar (1999, 2009) is that their modeling does not allow for sea-level rise as a result of climate change. Sea-level rise will reduce the total land mass and inundate low-lying alluvial soils in several parts of the world, thereby negatively impacting on global agricultural production. More freshwater could become saline as salt water moves upstream as a result of sea-level rise and as it seeps into some aquifers. Consequently, some water that is now used for irrigation will be rendered unsuitable for this purpose.

Although the modeling of the impact on agricultural production of climate change by Mendelsohn and Dinar (1999, 2009) is too simplistic, it does provide a useful starting point for discussing this impact. Matters requiring more attention are the consequences for agricultural production of the predicted increase in the frequency of extreme weather events and the greater variability of weather patterns as a result of climate change. If these changes are widespread, they may have a negative impact on the level of global agricultural output. This is because ambient weather conditions affect the yields of crops and the productivity of livestock. Although different types and varieties of crops (as well as different types and breeds of livestock) vary in their degree of tolerance to ambient weather conditions, none are impervious to these effects, as is evidenced by the biological law of tolerance (Tisdell, 1983). The tolerance of the yield of crops (and their varieties) can take different forms but a form similar to that shown in Fig. 8.6 might be common.

Figure 8.6 indicates that when extreme weather conditions occur, the yield of a particular crop variety falls to zero. For other weather conditions the relationship is of a reversed U-shape and is therefore, strictly concave. Given the type of relationship shown in Fig. 8.6,

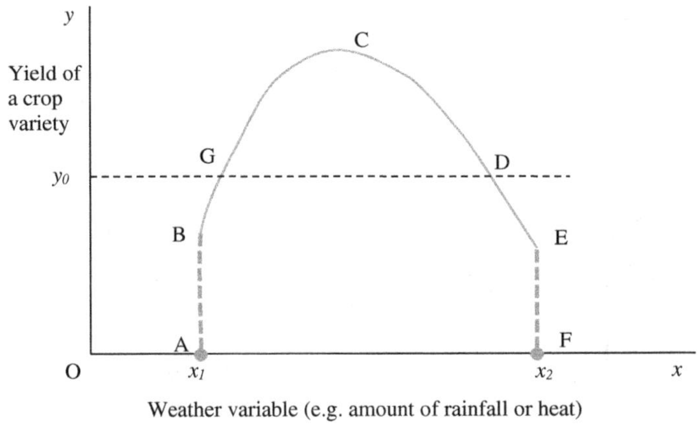

Fig. 8.6. A possible yield tolerance function for a crop variety. Given the nature of this function, yields on average are lower the greater is the variability of the weather and the more frequent is its extremes.

yields on average are lower the more frequent are extreme weather conditions, other things remaining unchanged. Even if extreme weather conditions do not occur, greater variability of weather conditions tends to lower average crop yields, because of the strict concavity of the assumed biological tolerance function. This mathematical relationship is implied by Karamata's inequality (Karamata, 1932).

In Fig. 8.6, the crop fails if $x \leq x_1$ (e.g. there is very low rainfall) or if $x \geq x_2$ (e.g. there is excessive rainfall). When weather conditions are in the range $x_1 < x < x_2$, yields are positive and attain the levels indicated by the curve BCDE. However, it may be uneconomic to harvest the crop if the yields are low (or of poor quality) due to unfavorable weather conditions. For instance, it may be uneconomic to harvest the crop if yields are less than y_0.

8.7. The Economics of Mitigating the Costs of Climate Change

It is frequently recommended that individual economic entities (including farmers) should adopt measures to mitigate the unfavorable effects of climate change. However, little attention is usually given to the

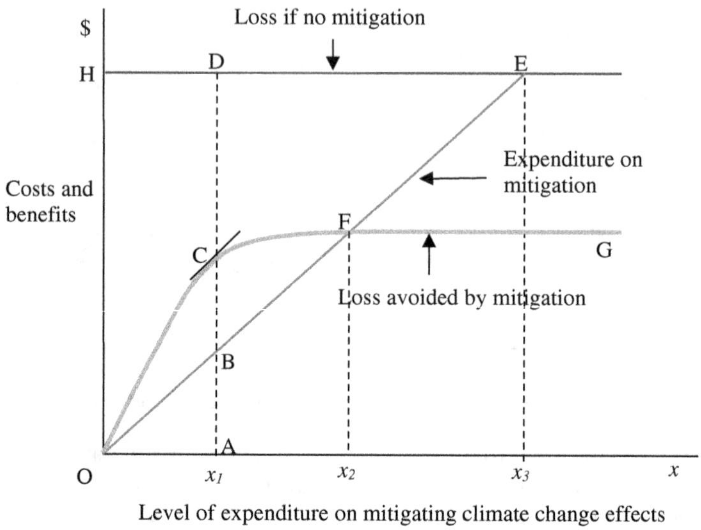

Fig. 8.7. An illustration of economic factors which should be taken into account by an economic entity (e.g. a farmer) in considering the mitigation of the effects of climate change.

economics of mitigation measures and the extent to which individuals are unable to limit the effects on themselves of climate change.

Figure 8.7 identifies economic factors which are relevant to determining the economic value to entities of climate mitigation. In this figure, OH (or line HE) indicates the loss in income (or profit) of a farmer (for example) if he/she does nothing to mitigate the effects of climate change. The curve marked OCFG shows the extent to which losses from climate change can be reduced by expenditure on the most cost effective means to do this. The 45 degree line, OFE, represents the total expenditure on mitigating the effects of climate change.

In the case shown in Fig. 8.7, the most economic expenditure on climate mitigation is x_1. At this level of expenditure, the marginal loss avoided from climate change equals the marginal expenditure on loss avoidance. The slope of the loss avoidance curve equals the slope of the expenditure line (which is also the cost line) at x_1. In fact, both have a slope of unity for an expenditure of x_1. When this choice is made, the remaining loss from climate change is equal to CD, and the total loss from climate change is equal to CD plus AB. The economic benefit obtained from the most profitable economic mitigation of climate change equals BC. However, mitigating the effects of climate change will only be worthwhile if after the optimal level of economic mitigation, the economic entity could still be profitable. In the case shown in Fig. 8.7, the reduction in total profit by AB + CD may be so large that the economic entity is no longer viable. Note that a break-even point in Fig. 8.7 occurs for an expenditure of x_2.

It is also possible that no mitigation of climate change is profitable. In that case, all of the loss avoidance curve is located below the expenditure curve. This can occur because of the high fixed cost (overheads) of adopting climate mitigation measures or because of the high variable costs involved in mitigation. When no mitigation of climate change is economic, a business entity may or may not remain profitable.

Given the above analysis, the following possible scenarios exist for a business enterprise (e.g. a farm enterprise) when climate change occurs and has adverse consequences for its profitability:

1. It may remain profitable without adjustment to climate change.
2. It may be more profitable if it is able to adjust to climate change.
3. It may only remain profitable after adjustment to this change.
4. There may be no climate mitigating options available to it which will enable it to remain profitable.

Note that not all farmers will be adversely affected by climate change. Some will benefit from it. However, most of this group will need to make agricultural adjustments in order to maximize their economic gain after they experience climate change.

8.8. Concluding Comments

There will be a substantial increase in the demand for agricultural production to meet the needs of a growing level of global population which is expected to rise by almost 30% in about two decades, and demand for fibers supplied by agriculture could also expected rise sharply. The ecological and environmental footprint of agriculture will become heavier. Even if environmental spillovers from agriculture are optimally controlled, its environmental and ecological costs can be expected to rise. In these circumstances, the social concerns about environmentally relevant market failures in agriculture, agricultural policies and the sustainability of its resource use can be expected to grow.

This chapter has outlined and analyzed factors that result in agricultural markets failing to allow adequately for environmental spillovers and for its not using natural resources in an efficient way. Furthermore, several social reasons for lack of agricultural sustainability have been identified. Some of these involve market failure but others do not. Government agricultural policies have been outlined and assessed in the light of these issues. It was found that some government policies exacerbate market failures, even though this is not always the case. Also, as discussed, climate change can be expected to have a substantial impact on the level of global agricultural production and the regional locations of agricultural activities. It will make it more difficult to sustain or increase this production in many locations. Most agriculturalists will have to adjust to climate change and they need to consider the economics of adjusting. Relevant factors influencing the economics of adjusting were outlined. The costs of mitigation of the adverse impacts of climate change could result in farm enterprises in some locations being less profitable or in their being no longer economically viable. There is further discussion of agricultural policy in the next chapter which concentrates on water management and the subsequent one which focuses on biodiversity conservation.

8.9. Keywords

Agricultural impact on natural-resource availability; agricultural impact on the environment; agricultural market failures and the environment; agricultural policies and environmental distortions; agricultural policies and natural-resource depletion; agricultural policies and the state of the environment; agricultural policies and the sustainability of resource use; agricultural sustainability; climate change and agriculture; environmental spillovers generated by agriculture; favorable environmental externalities from agriculture; lack of agricultural sustainability caused by market failures; lack of agricultural sustainability due to other than market failure; mitigation of climate change; open-access resources used by agriculture; public goods and agriculture; public bads and agricultural activity; regional versus global benefits from economic activity; trends in demand for agricultural produce; types of demand for agricultural supplies; unavoidable environmental externalities; unfavorable environmental externalities from agriculture.

8.10. Questions for Review and Discussion

1. Discuss the view that modern agriculture depends heavily on the use of natural resources many of which are nonrenewable and that it alters natural environments radically.
2. Humans require food for their existence and depend heavily on agriculture to supply it. Therefore, it is impossible to avoid all the environmental changes that agriculture generates. Nevertheless, steps should be taken to manage or limit the adverse environmental spillovers that agriculture generates. Discuss and illustrate.
3. Even if socially optimal adjustments have been made to regulate the adverse environmental externalities generated by agriculture, it is to be expected that agriculture production will still generate considerable external costs. Explain and illustrate.
4. Outline the type of general end uses of agricultural produce. The demand for greater agricultural production will rise substantially in the next few decades. Why? What consequence is this likely to have for the impact of agriculture on the availability and quality of natural environments?
5. List and explain the types of environmental spillovers that can be generated by agricultural production.
6. Why does the use of open-access natural resources by farmers usually result in economic inefficiency and sustainability problems?

7. Explain why many national and regional governments are unwilling to limit agricultural expansion when this results in a reduction of or complete loss of the supply of valued global public goods.
8. Why might farmers adopt policies which result in their agricultural incomes and yields not being maintained? List some of the agricultural sustainability problems that farmers may experience on their properties as a result of their *own* behavior.
9. Explain how some agricultural policies increase the social economic costs of unfavorable environmental agricultural spillovers. Illustrate your answer using a diagram.
10. Some agricultural activities generate positive environmental externalities. Discuss the economics of subsidizing such activities. Use a diagram to illustrate your answer.
11. If farmers choose not to adopt sustainable farming practices on their own land, do you think governments should intervene to try to alter their behavior? Give your reasons.
12. Mendelsohn and Dinar (1999, 2009) are of the view that the level of global agricultural production is likely to be little affected by climate change. Outline their view and consider its limitations, including its failure to take account of the predicted increase in the variability of weather conditions and the greater frequency of adverse weather events as a result of climate change.
13. What factors should be taken into account by a farming enterprise in assessing whether (and to what extent) it is economic for it to mitigate the adverse effects of climate change? Even after this mitigation, the profitability of the enterprise is liable to be reduced. Explain.

Readings and References

Bishop, R.C. (1978). Endangered species, irreversibility and uncertainty: The economics of a safe minimum standard, *American Journal of Agricultural Economics*, 60, 10–18. doi: 10.2307/1242715.

FAO (2007). *Food Outlook, Global Market Analysis*, FAO, Rome.

Ison, S., S. Peake and S. Wall (2002). *Environmental Issues and Policies*, Pearson Education, Harlow, Essex, UK [Chapters 8 and 11].

Kahn, J.R. (2005). *The Economic Approach to Environmental and Natural Resources*, 3rd edn. South-Western, Mason, Ohio, USA [Chapter 17].

Karamata, J. (1932). Sur une inégalité relative aux fonctions convexes, *Publications Mathematiques de l'Université de Belgrade*, 1, 145–148.

Kiers, E.T., R.R.B. Leakey, A.-M. Izac, J.A. Heinemann, E. Rosenthal, D. Nathan and J. Jiggins (2008). Agriculture at a crossroads, *Science*, 320, 320–321. doi: 10.1126/science.1158390.

Krutilla, J.V. and A.C. Fisher (1975). *The Economics of Natural Environments: Studies in the Valuation of Commodity and Amenity Resources*, Johns Hopkins University Press, Baltimore, USA.

Mann, C.C. (2008). Our good earth, *National Geographic*, 214, 80–107.

Mendelsohn, R. and A. Dinar (1999). Climate change, agriculture, and developing countries, *World Bank Research Observer*, 14, 277–293. doi: 10.1093/wbro/14.2.277.

Mendelsohn, R. and A. Dinar (2009). Land use and climate change interactions, *Annual Review of Resource Economics*, 1, 309–332. doi: 10.1146/annurev.resource.050708.144246.

Swarna Nantha, H. and C.A. Tisdell (2009). The orangutan-oil palm conflict: Economic constraints and opportunities for conservation, *Biodiversity Conservation*, 18, 487–502. doi: 10.1007/s10531-008-9512-3.

Tisdell, C.A. (1983). The biological law of tolerance, average biomass and production in a variable uncontrolled environment, *International Journal of Ecology and Environmental Sciences*, 9, 99–109. Reprinted in C.A. Tisdell (1983) *Economics and Ecology in Agriculture and Marine Production*, Edward Elgar Publishing, Cheltenham, UK and Northampton, MA, USA.

Tisdell, C.A. (1993). *Environmental Economics: Policies for Environmental Management and Sustainable Development*, Edward Elgar, Aldershot, UK and Brookfield, VT, USA.

Tisdell, C.A. (1999a). *Biodiversity, Conservation and Sustainable Development*, Edward Elgar, Cheltenham, UK and Northampton, MA, USA.

Tisdell, C.A. (1999b). Economics, aspects of ecology and sustainable agricultural production. In A.K. Dragun and C.A. Tisdell (Eds.), *Sustainable Agriculture and Environment*, 37–56. Edward Elgar, Cheltenham, UK and Northampton, MA, USA [Chapter 4].

Tisdell, C.A. (2005). *Economics of Environmental Conservation*, 2nd edn. Edward Elgar, Cheltenham, UK and Northampton, MA, USA.

Tisdell, C.A. (2009a). Complex policy choices regarding agricultural externalities: Efficiency, equity and acceptability In V. Beckmann and M. Padmanabhan (Eds.), *Institutions and Sustainability. Political Economy of Agriculture and the Environment — Essays in Honour of Konrad Hagedorn*, 83–106. Springer [Chapter 4].

Tisdell, C.A. (2009b). Poverty, policy reforms for resource-use and economic efficiency: Neglected issues, *Singapore Economic Review*, 54, 155–166.

Tisdell, C.A. (2017). *Economics and Environmental Change: The Challenges We Face*, Edward Elgar Publishing, Cheltenham, UK, and Northampton, MA, USA [Chapters 5 and 9].

Tisdell, C.A. and K. Hartley (2008). *Microeconomic Policy: A New Perspective*, Edward Elgar, Cheltenham, UK and Northampton, MA, USA.

Ziska, L.H. (2011). Climate change, carbon dioxide and global crop production: Food security and uncertainty. In A. Dinar and R. Mendelsohn (Eds.), *Handbook on Climate Change and Agriculture*, 9–13. Edward Elgar, Cheltenham, UK and Northampton, MA, USA.

Chapter 9

Water Management

9.1. Introduction

Water is essential for life. Freshwater is to a large extent a recirculating resource due to the hydrological cycle. In this cycle, water evaporates from the oceans, other water bodies and land areas to form clouds and water vapor. Subsequently, much of this evaporated water returns as rainfall or as other forms of precipitation to terrestrial areas (where it replenishes freshwater supplies) or falls into marine areas and other water bodies. Most freshwater is a flow resource in streams and rivers, but some water bodies are relatively stationary such as in lakes, ponds and some underground aquifers.

Kahn (2005, p. 515) suggests that, in general, water is most appropriately classified as a renewable natural resource. Nevertheless, he also points out that some water resources are virtually non-renewable. These include underground water bodies that have extremely slow rates of recharge and which have accumulated over millions of years. This water has been called "fossil" water. Although freshwater recirculates due to the flow of energy from the sun, it is not a self-reproducing natural resource, unlike a biological resource.

In fact, water is a very complex natural resource and occurs naturally as a liquid, ice or snow and vapor. On the whole, it has become an increasingly scarce resource as the level of global population has increased and demands to use it for human ends have grown. However, its relative scarcity (or abundance) varies with geographical regions and fluctuates usually with the passage of time. For example, in many regions, wet periods (in which water is in excess supply resulting in floods) alternate with dry periods in which water is scarce. Furthermore, regional water availability alters in the very long term as major geographical changes occur, for example, global warming and in an even longer time-frame, continental drift.

Furthermore, water quality varies and is increasingly affected by human activity. Most human uses of water reduce its quality. Poor management of water quality and poor allocation of available water can result in economic scarcity being greater than it needs to be. It is, therefore, important to consider administrative mechanisms that can improve the economic use of water and regulate its supply in an efficient manner.

In this chapter, the general problem of water scarcity is discussed first taking into account competing demands for the use of water. Subsequently, the efficiency of different managerial mechanisms for regulating the use of available water supplies are analyzed, and problems of controlling water quality are discussed. This is followed by a consideration of issues involved in managing the overall supply of freshwater such as water diversion, dams, weirs, control of evaporation and leakages, recycling of water and desalinization. Water-use is shown to involve important resource scarcity and environmental issues.

9.2. Scarcity and the Demand for the Available Quantity of Freshwater

Water is not always a scarce resource but it often is. The degree of its scarcity shows regional variation and can alter with the passage of time depending on its availability and the demand for it. This is illustrated in Fig. 9.1 assuming that water is a shared resource and that its use is rivalrous. In many instances, it is also a resource for which exclusion is possible. However, there are cases where it is either an open-access or a communal resource.

In the case illustrated in Fig. 9.1, assume that the demand for water per period of time is as shown by line D_1D_1 and that the rate of its

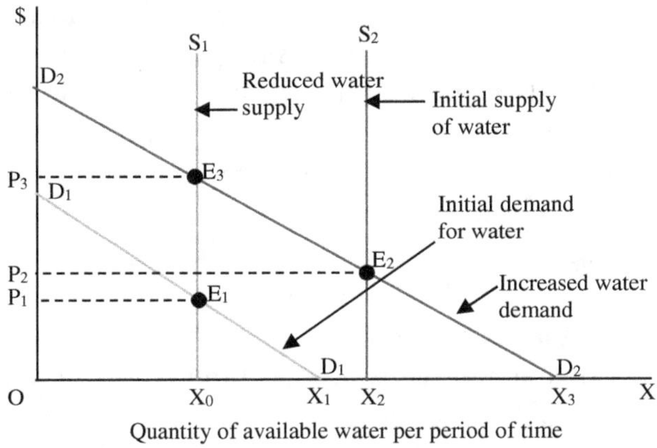

Fig. 9.1. Supply and demand factors influence the scarcity of water. In many regions of the world, water has become scarce and its scarcity has increased due to rising demand for water. In some regions of the world, this increased scarcity has been compounded by a reduction in the availability of water due to climate change.

natural supply per period of time is X_2. The vertical line identified by S_2 represents the natural supply of water. Assuming that accessing the natural water supply is costless, water is not scarce from an economic point of view in this case. If access to the available water is free, there is an excess supply of water of $X_2 - X_1$ per period of time. No economic problem arises in allowing open-access to the water resource assuming that the water is not used for waste disposal or emissions of pollutants.

Water becomes a scarce resource in the region under consideration if its supply remains unaltered but the demand for it rises substantially due, for example, to an increase in population and the expansion of water-using industries. This is so, for example, if the demand curve for water shifts up from D_1D_1 to D_2D_2 in Fig. 9.1. In that case if access to the available water remains free, there will be excess demand for water per period of time of $X_3 - X_2$. Methods for allocating the scarce resource will need to be considered. One method is to charge users of water a price of P_2 for each unit of water. This would ensure that available supply of water just equals the demand for it and would result in the available water being distributed to those who value water most, as indicated by their willingness to pay for it.

In the case illustrated in Fig. 9.1, water scarcity would also emerge if the availability of water fell from X_2 to X_0. This scarcity problem would be compounded if at the same time, the demand for water happened to increase, for example, the demand curve for water moved up from D_1D_1 to D_2D_2. In the former supply case, a price of P_1 per unit of water would be needed to allocate the available quantity of water efficiently and in the latter case, a price per unit of water of P_3.

In practice, the demand for water and its supply may fluctuate seasonally and during longer periods of time. This complicates the water management problem and dams may be built to help even out water supplies. This possibility is discussed later in this chapter.

Different regions relying on different sources of water supply frequently experience different degrees of economic scarcity of water. For example, in Fig. 9.1, let line D_1D_1 represent the demand for water in one region and let its supply be X_0. Assume that the line D_2D_2 represents the demand for water in another region and let X_2 be its supply. In this case, the economic scarcity of water is greater in the latter case than in the former case. If water happened to be priced so as to allocate the available supply in each region, the price of water would be higher in the latter region than in the former one; that is P_2 compared to P_1. Given the price differential, it may be economic to transport (divert) water from the region where it is less scarce to the region where it is scarce. However, the cost of the transfer of water needs to be taken into account. This aspect will be considered later in this chapter.

In most countries, the main users of water are agriculture, other industries (including some types of mining) and households. In many countries, agriculture accounts for more than half of anthropogenic water-use (see Chapter 8). In the United States, for example, agriculture is estimated to account for around 80% of anthropogenic water-use. Often pricing structures for the use of water distort the pattern of water-use by different users. For example, if agriculturalists do not fully pay the extra cost of their water supply (and in effect, have their water-use subsidized), this will encourage them to use excessive amounts of water from an economic point of view.

The withdrawal of water from natural water sources for human use usually has adverse environmental and ecological consequences which become increasingly evident as the volume of anthropogenic water-use rises. Both the quantity of water flows and fluctuations in these flows (all of which are affected by human use of water) have environmental spillover consequences. For example, human use of water can reduce the quantity of water entering wetlands and lakes and have negative effects on populations of water birds and if flooding is moderated in extent and frequency, this can reduce the reproduction of some wild species, for example, ducks, and some tree species that rely on flooding in order to germinate their seeds.

A problem is that markets do not normally exist for the general ecological and environmental services (ecosystem services) provided by supplies of water because environmental spillovers and attributes of public goods (or bads) are involved. An important question is how should water supplies be managed to take account of these factors? Should the allocation of water for general ecological and environmental purposes be decided by administrative or political means and if so, what types of problems may occur? For example, if the water allocation for ecological purposes is decided by political means, it may be set at a low level and during periods of drought may be lowered even further due to pressures by special interest groups of water-users. In some jurisdictions, little or no legal weight is placed on the availability of water for ecological and environmental purposes. For example, Kahn (2005, p. 525) reports that some western states of the United States do not regard uses of natural water bodies for recreational and ecological purposes as "beneficial uses" and therefore, do not provide for the legal protection of natural water bodies for these purposes.

9.3. Economic Failures in Allocating Scarce Water Resources

9.3.1. *Background*

When shared water resources are scarce, an important social goal can be to ensure that they are allocated in a manner which maximizes the (social) economic value obtained from their use. This problem can usually be subdivided into two subsidiary problems: (1) distributing the quantity of water allocated at any point of time so as to maximize its economic value and (2) when water is storable, making sure that its intertemporal allocation is optimized. Economic failure in utilizing this scarce resource occurs if these goals are not satisfied.

These goals may not be satisfied for several reasons. For example, where water is a flowing shared resource and access to it is not regulated, those who first have access to it (for example, in the headwaters of a river) take no account of those who have later access to the flow of water. This can result in those who have initial access to the flow of water using an amount of water that reduces the quantity available to those who have later access to the flow of water. This can occur to such an extent that the overall economic value of the water resource is not maximized. Or again in some cases, public policies may allocate the shared water between users (and uses) in a manner that does not maximize the economic value of its allocation.

If shared water resources are storable, intertemporal economic failure can also occur. For example, if there is open-access to a stored water body, those who use the water now will take no account of the possible future costs of using the available stock of water (see Chapter 3). They fail to take account of user costs. This becomes an economic problem once the rate of use of water from a water body (a pool of water) exceeds its rate of recharge. Pools of water can include ponds, dams and underground water bodies, including aquifers that recharge slowly. It is worthwhile using a couple of diagrams to illustrate the economic nature of both the temporal and the intemporal allocation of water.

9.3.2. *The most economic allocation of water in any time period*

If the aggregate economic value of water available for allocation between alternative uses (or users) is to be maximized, then it is necessary that it is be allocated so that its (social) marginal economic value is equal in all of its uses (or for all of its users). If this condition is not satisfied, it is possible to increase the total economic value obtained from a shared water resource by making sure that it is fulfilled. This

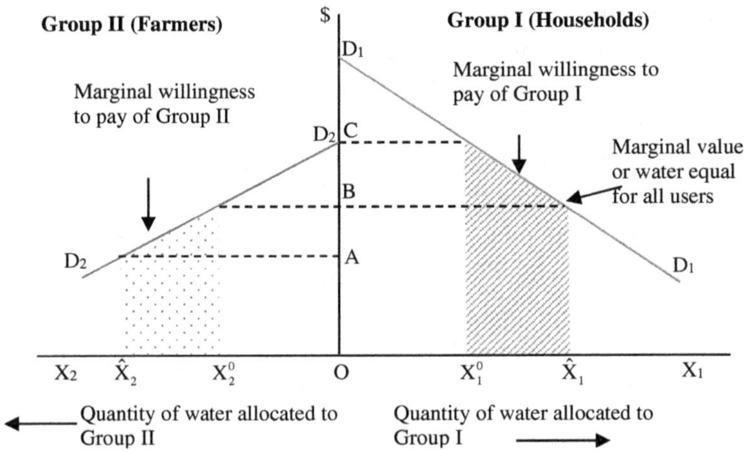

Fig. 9.2. An illustration that the overall economic value of water-use is not maximized unless water is allocated to ensure that its marginal economic value is equal in all of its alternative uses. In the case illustrated, marginal willingness to pay for water indicates its value to alternative users. In the example (specified in the text), the total economic value of water-use is maximized where $\hat{X}_1$ of it is allocated to Group I and X_2^0 of it is distributed to Group II. The marginal value of water is then equal to *OB* for each of the groups.

is illustrated in Fig. 9.2, supposing that the private marginal value of water-use does not diverge from its social marginal value. Cases in which divergence occurs will be explored later in this chapter.

In Fig. 9.2, it is assumed that there are two sets of users (or uses) of a shared water resource. Group I might consist of households and Group II of farmers. In Fig. 9.2, line D_1D_1 shows the demand of Group I for water and D_2D_2 specifies the demand for Group II for water. These lines indicate the marginal willingness to pay of the different groups for access to extra water supplies and therefore, can be regarded as indicators of the economic value of water in its alternative uses. If X represents the quantity of water, let X_1 indicate the amount of water allocated to Group I and let X_2 measure the quantity of water distributed to Group II. Furthermore, suppose that $X = \bar{X}$ is the total available quantity of water to be distributed. Then assuming that there are no costs in distributing the water (except opportunity costs), the maximum economic value from water use is obtained when it is allocated to ensure that the marginal willingness to pay off Group I for water is equal to that for Group II. This is achieved when $\hat{X}_1$ of water is allocated to Group I and X_2^0 of water is distributed to Group II. It is easy to see that if this necessary mathematical condition for a maximum of total economic value is not satisfied, then economic scarcity is greater than it needs to be. For example, if X_1^0 of water is supplied to Group I and $\hat{X}_2$ to Group II (where $X_1^0 + \hat{X}_2 = \bar{X}$), the economic value of water (compared to the allocation which maximizes economic value) used by Group I is reduced by the equivalent of the area of the hatched quadrilateral in Fig. 9.2 and that for Group II is increased by the equivalent of the dotted quadrilateral. Given that $\hat{X}_1 - X_1^0 = \hat{X}_2 - X_2^0$, the area of the hatched quadrilateral is greater than that of the dotted one. Hence, this allocation of water would fail to maximize the overall economic value of water use. Similarly, if more than $\hat{X}_1$ of the available water is allocated to Group I and hence, less than X_2^0 to Group II, the overall economic value of water use is reduced.

9.3.3. *The intertemporal allocation of water*

Consider now the intertemporal allocation of water. Suppose that D_1D_1 in Fig. 9.3 represents the demand for water in the current period and that X_3 is the available supply of water. If access to the available water is free (open-access), X_2 of it will be used in the current period. If the water can be stored and is likely to be in short supply subsequently, this is likely to be an excessive use of the available water. For example, suppose that $OABC$ represents the marginal user costs of consuming water now. It shows the future economic benefits that are forgone by using water now rather than storing it for later use. If the current use of the water is X_0 or less, no future economic benefits are forgone as a result of its use, but greater use results in future economic benefits being forgone. Given the marginal user cost curve shown in Fig. 9.3, net economic benefit will be maximized when X_1 of water is used now and $X_3 - X_1$ of water is saved for future uses. The optimal allocation occurs when the marginal economic benefit from current water-use equals its marginal user cost. Should there be open-access to water in the initial period, an economic benefit equivalent to the area of the

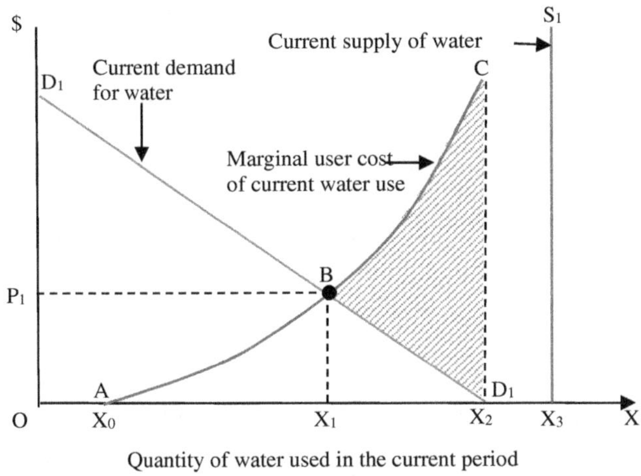

Fig. 9.3. When water can be stored, future economic benefits may be forgone be its current use. The user costs incurred will then need to be compared with the current economic benefits from use of the available water. Usually, the most economic allocation will occur when the marginal economic benefit from current water-use is equated to its marginal user costs. This occurs in the above case when X_1 of water is used in the initial period and $X_3 - X_1$ is stored for future use.

hatched triangular figure would be forgone as a result of excessive use of water in the current period. When open-access to a resource occurs, users of it take no account of user costs (see Chapter 5).

The above is a simplified exposition. User costs are frequently uncertain because the amount of replenishment of water stocks (for instance, in dams or similar bodies) depends on variations in weather patterns and these are not perfectly predictable. This does not mean that no rational decision can be made about economic levels of water-use.

In order to illustrate this, assume the same type of situation as in Fig. 9.3, but that marginal user costs are now uncertain. However, suppose that it is certain that marginal user costs would be at their highest as shown by relationship $OA'B'C'$ in Fig. 9.4, and at their lowest as indicated by relationship $OABC$.

In the above circumstances, it will never be economic to use less than X_1' of water in the current period nor more than X_1 of it. To do

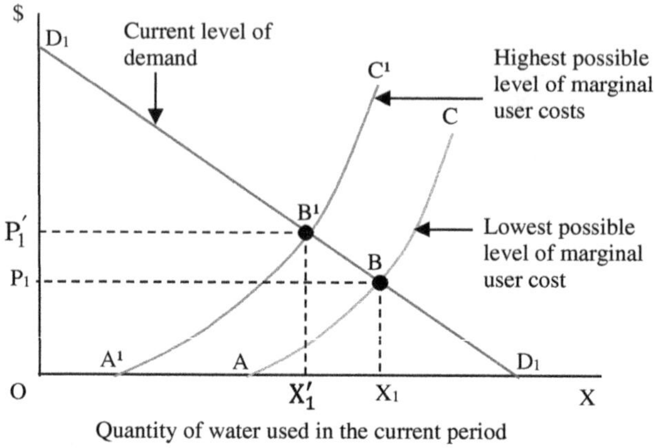

Fig. 9.4. In the case illustrated, marginal user costs are uncertain and may vary between a high shown by relationship OA'B'C' and a low indicated by OABC. In these circumstances, it will never be economic to use more than X_1 of water and less than X_1' of water in the current period.

so would be irrational. The optimal initial quantity of water-use within the range $X_1' \leq X \leq X_1$ will depend on the attitude of the decision-maker towards risk-taking. Furthermore, the demand for water in the current period may not be perfectly known and that would also have to be factored into water management. Nevertheless, it is once again true that such uncertainty does not completely rule out scope for rational choice.

9.4. Mechanisms for the Management of the Available Quantity of Water

9.4.1. *Background*

When available shared water resources are in short supply, unregulated access to these is unlikely to result in their most economic use from a social point of view. Social mechanisms to manage the use of water can potentially increase the collective economic benefits obtained from shared water resources. The managerial mechanisms that can be adopted are varied. These mechanisms include:

(1) administrative control of the quantities of water used by different users and for different purposes;
(2) control by adopting administered prices for water-use; and
(3) tradable permit systems for water consumption.

Furthermore, features of these different approaches may be combined in some management strategies. In addition, social customs, codes and moral persuasion may sometimes be used to influence water consumption. Consequently, complex systems for the social control of the shared water resources can emerge. Let us consider each of the main managerial systems mentioned above and their limitations.

9.4.2. *Administrative control of the quantity of water used by different entities or for different purposes*

Some systems for regulating water-use involve command-and-control. For example, some supreme authority may dictate the quantity of water that can be used by each entity in each period of time and the purposes for which the water may be used. Furthermore, the days and times at which water may be used for particular purposes may be specified. The regulating authority can be appointed democratically or by other means. Particularly, if the geographical area in which water-use is to be managed is large, a hierarchal administrative structure may be adopted with administrators at different levels having different functions and degrees of responsibility for water management.

Such systems can involve considerable agency costs; that is costs of funding the bureaucracy that regulates water-use and can be economically very inefficient in allocating the available quantities of water. Even if the regulating authority aims to maximize the overall economic value of water-use by regulating quantities of water consumed by users, it is likely to have insufficient information to achieve this goal and it may have difficulty in enforcing its regulations. Consequently, this can be an inefficient mechanism for the social management of water-use. It is unlikely to result in the value of the marginal product of water (or the marginal willingness of users to pay for water) being equalized even when this is the appropriate rule for maximizing the overall economic value from water-use. This failure may occur because of the water authority's limited knowledge and because political factors influence the decisions of bureaucrats allocating water resources.

9.4.3. *Administered prices for water-use*

Authorities managing shared water resources may determine prices for water consumption. These administered prices may be employed to regulate the quantity of water used by consumers, or they may be used primarily to raise revenue, or they may serve the dual function of regulating water-use and raising revenue. They may be imposed in conjunction with measures to control directly the quantity of water used by individuals, regulate its purpose and the timing of this use. In this case, the price for water is usually less than that which equates the demand for water with its available supply. However, initially, let us explore the scope for employing the price of water as a rationing mechanism.

Take a case like the one illustrated by Fig. 9.5 in which water is a scarce economic resource. Assume that the demand relationship for water is D_1D_1 and its available supply is X_0 per period as illustrated in Fig. 9.5. If the regulated price of water is P_1, this allocates the available quantity of water exactly. Assuming that the price of water is the same for all users, this price would also result in the overall economic value of water-use being maximized (given the absence of externalities) because it would ensure equality in the marginal willingness of each buyer to pay for water.

However, if the demand for and the supply of water are variable, it can be difficult for administrators to determine the price that will exactly equilibrate the demand for water with its supply. For example, if the supply of water is predicted to be X_1' and its price is fixed at P_0, there will be excess demand for water if the available supply of water turns out to be X_0. If the price of water is fixed at a level higher than P_1, excess supply of water eventuates. Nevertheless, in the face of uncertainty, the authority may set the price of water on the high side in order to avoid the possibility of excess demand.

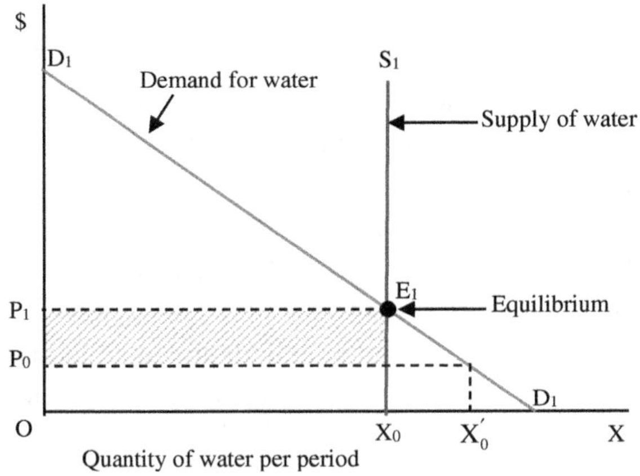

Fig. 9.5. Water pricing provides one way of allocating available water supplies. In the case illustrated, a price of P_1 exactly allocates the available supply and results in an allocation between users that maximizes the economic value of water.

In the case illustrated in Fig. 9.2, a price equal to *OB* for both groups of water-users ensures that the available quality of water is allocated so that its economic value is maximized. However, for political or other reasons, one group of water-users may buy water at a lower price than others. For example, Group II (farmers) may pay *OA* per unit of water whereas Group I (households) may be required to pay *OC* per unit of water. As a result, the quantity of water used is not allocated in a way which maximizes its overall economic value.

Furthermore, observe that water pricing can be used to ensure that adequate account is taken of the marginal user cost of water. For example, in the case illustrated by Fig. 9.3, if the price of water in the current period is fixed at P_1 per unit, marginal user costs are fully accounted for by water consumers.

Because of the income distributional consequences of the pricing of water and political considerations, water pricing may not be relied on entirely by public authorities to allocate water-use. For example, in the situation illustrated in Fig. 9.5, assuming that X_0 is the supply of water, the price of water may be set at a level below P_1, say P_0, on distributional grounds and direct controls on the quantity of water to be used by individual buyers may be introduced to ensure that the demand for water does not exceed its supply. As a result, $P_0 X_0$ will be collected in revenue by the water authority and the income of buyers can be expected to be greater than if P_1 per unit is charged for water. The income of buyers *could* be higher by an amount up to the equivalent of the hatched area, that is by $(P_1 - P_0)X_0$.

Another possibility is to adopt a stepped or tiered approach to water pricing. If this method is adopted, the marginal price of water to buyers of water rises with the quantity purchased by them. This method can be used to moderate reductions in income resulting from water payments and ensure that water prices efficiently ration and allocate water supplies.

A simple example of this tiered price system is illustrated in Fig. 9.6. There the line $d_1 d_1$ shows the demand of an individual consumer for water. The tiered price system may require payment of P_0 per unit of water for the first x_0 units used and P_1 per unit thereafter. Given this pricing system, the buyer purchases x_1 units of water per period. However, instead of paying $P_1 x_1$ for the quantity of water used, the buyer pays an amount that is smaller by the amount $(P_1 - P_0)\, x_0$ which is equal to the hatched rectangle.

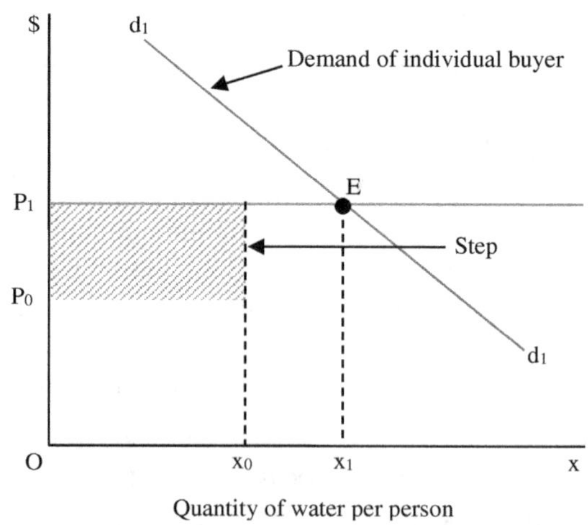

Fig. 9.6. An illustration of tiered (stepped) water pricing. In the case illustrated, the buyer pays P_0 for each unit of water consumed per period for up to x_0 units of water and P_1 on each additional unit of water purchased.

Furthermore, if all buyers pay P_1 for their marginal purchases of water, then given the situation illustrated by Fig. 9.5, the demand for water will be brought into equality with its supply (if the income effect on the demand for water is assumed to be zero). Moreover, assuming the absence of externalities, the supply of water will be allocated efficiently between users because all purchasers of water pay the same price for their marginal use of water. This price parity results in the marginal value of water use being equalized for all users. Nevertheless, administering the marginal price of water in a way that ensures that the pricing system is efficient is not easy if uncertainties exist about supply and demand relationships.

9.4.4. *Tradable permit systems for water-use*

There has been increasing interest in using tradable permit systems for water allocation and they have been adopted in some jurisdictions for allocating water for agricultural use. The general benefits and limitations of tradable permit systems as a method of managing the use of shared natural resources were outlined in Chapter 5. These observations are applicable to water use. However, it is worthwhile considering some special aspects of their relevance to water consumption.

Often tradable permit systems for water can be very efficient, but not in all cases. For these systems to be efficient, users within areas where the permits can be traded need to share the same water body. Furthermore, trading of permits should be limited to areas where the same water body is shared. For example, if there are two separate pools or sources of water, water may be scarcer in one source than the other relative to demand. Therefore, the efficient allocation of the available water will require that the price of water be higher in the area where it is scarcer relative to demand. For example, suppose two separate water bodies, A and B. In Fig. 9.7, let the left-hand diagram represent the supply and demand for water from water body A and let the right-hand diagram depicts that for water body B. The demand for water in A is represented by line $D_A D_A$ and in area B by the line marked $D_B D_B$. The supply of shared water from source A is shown by the line marked $S_A S_A$ and from source B by the line $S_B S_B$. Given that the water

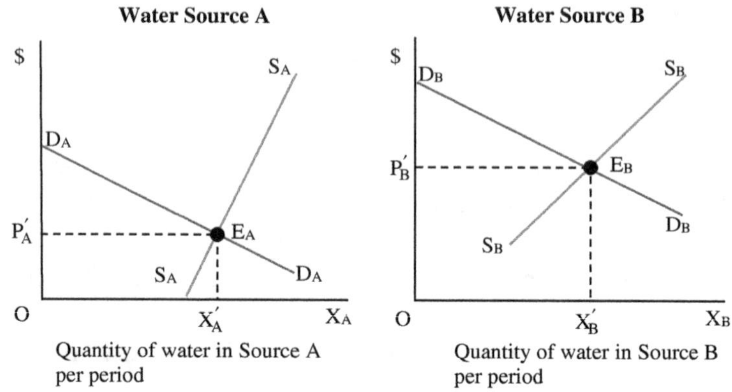

Fig. 9.7. Trading of permits for water use between separated water sources is not likely to be economically efficient. In the case illustrated, water sources A and B are separated and it is efficient for the price of water (or permits for water use) to be P'_A for water from source A and P'_B for water from source B.

sources are separated and are in different regions, economic scarcity will be minimized when X'_A of water is used in area A and X'_B is consumed in area B. This could be achieved by having an administered price in area A of P'_A and in area B of P'_B or by issuing tradable permits for total entitlements for water use in area A of X'_A and in area B of X'_B with entitlements being restricted to each of these respective areas. Should permits be able to be freely traded between areas, this would result in some permits issued to those in area A being sold to water-consumers in area B and trading of permits would take place until their price was the same in both areas. As a result of this trading, a greater quality of water than X'_B would be used in area B and less than X'_A would be used in area A. Consequently, the marginal cost of increased water use in region B would exceed its extra value and the reverse would be so in region A. There is insufficient economic use of water in region A and excessive economic consumption of water in region B, and inter-regional trading of water permits reduces economic efficiency in this case.

If externalities arise from water withdrawals, then even when water-users draw on the same water body, uniform prices for water need not be ideal. Consequently, if a tradable permit system is adopted, zoning

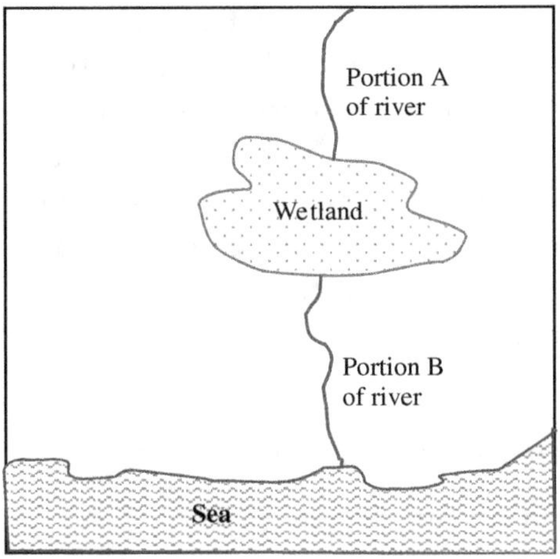

Fig. 9.8. A hypothetical case designed to illustrate a difficulty involved in managing shared water-use when the social economic value of water varies at different locations. This can require zoning of areas in which tradable water-use permits can be transferred within the same water body.

of areas within the same water body in which trading may take place can be required. This may occur if differences exist in environmental externalities from water consumption at different locations of the water body. Consider, for example, the hypothetical case illustrated in Fig. 9.8. Here a river with a single branch is shown as flowing through a wetland and then eventually to the sea. Suppose that the wetland is considered to have ecological value and that the government decides that a particular quantity of the flow of water from above the wetland should be reserved for maintaining the wetland. Below the wetland, there may be no such demand for reservation of water for ecological purposes. Relative to the demand for water, the socially optimal price of water above the wetland is likely to be higher than below the wetland. This differential pricing is likely to be needed to ensure that sufficient water is reserved to meet collective demand for ecological services provided by the wetland.

In the case of an administered price system designed to allocate the available water efficiently, a different price for water should normally prevail above and below the wetland. In the case of tradable permits, a different set of permits would need to be issued for trading water below the wetland to those for trading water above the wetland, and the trading of each set would need to be limited to its own zone. There may also be other non-market factors that cause water in the same water body to have different levels of economic value at different points; for example, sufficient waterflows may be required at different points in a river to support navigation, recreational activities, or to prevent salt intrusion from the ocean.

9.5. Transboundary Use of Water

Water often flows through different nations, states or provinces with separate jurisdictions and similarly, some underground water supplies may be shared by different countries, states or provinces. This can create problems for the efficient economic management of the shared water resources. The various jurisdictions sharing the water need to cooperate to enable an efficient economic pattern of water-use to be achieved.

In cases where one nation or state has prior access to available water supplies, it has no economic incentive to conserve water for the use subsequently of nations or states located downstream, unless it is paid (or in some other way compensated) for this action. However, compensation involves a transfer of income from nations downstream to those upstream. The equity of such payments is likely to be questioned by downstream states and interstate conflict emerges.

In the absence of cooperation, the value of marginal use of water by upstream states is likely to become less than the value of the marginal use of water by downstream states. Consequently, the overall economic value obtained from use of the available water is not maximized.

This is illustrated in Fig. 9.9. This is a similar diagram to that in Fig. 9.2, but now the right-hand side of the diagram relates to an upstream state and the left-hand side to a downstream state. The line D_1D_1 is the marginal value of water in the upstream state and D_2D_2 is the demand for water in the downstream state. Suppose that the natural flow of water in a shared river is $\bar{X}_1$. In absence of cooperation, the upstream state will use $\hat{X}_1$ of water per period of time and only leave

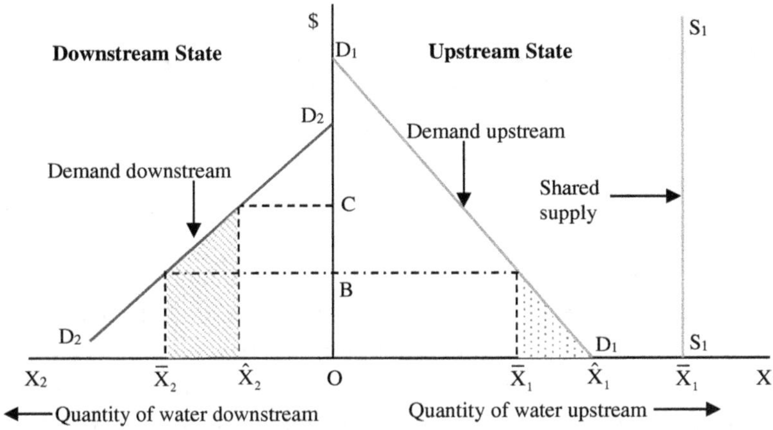

Fig. 9.9. An upstream state may use so much water that the aggregate economic value of water shared with a downstream state is not maximized. This is explained in the text.

$\bar{X}_1 - \hat{X}_1$ for use by the downstream state. The downstream state will use all of its available water, that is $\bar{X}_1 - \hat{X}_1 = \hat{X}_2$. Consequently, while the marginal value of water consumed in the upstream state is zero, in the downstream state it is *OC*. By reallocating the available water, the total value of water-use can be increased. The total value of water consumption is maximized when the marginal value of water consumption is equal in both states. This occurs in this example when $\bar{X}_1$ of water is consumed by the upstream state and $\bar{X}_2$ by the downstream state. The increase in the aggregate value of water-use is equal to the area of the hatched quadrilateral less the area of the dotted triangle. Note that it is possible for the demand to be so high in the upstream state that no water remains for the downstream state. In that case, the line $D_1 D_1$ crosses line $S_1 S_1$. For example, the USA uses so much water from the Colorado River that none is left when the river bed enters Mexico.

In addition, if water pollution originating in upstream states mostly adversely affects downstream states, upstream states have no economic incentive to moderate this pollution. In general, upstream states have no economic incentive to moderate any shortcomings of their water management policies which primarily affect downstream states unless they are compensated for any conservation action which they adopt.

An example of international cooperation to improve the management of use of shared water resources is the Mekong River Commission. It was formed in 1995 as a result of an agreement between Cambodia, Laos, Thailand and Vietnam and in 1996, China and Myanmar became dialog partners. China's cooperation is important because much of the length of the Mekong River is in China where it is known as the Lancang River. The main purpose of this commission is to foster the joint management of the shared water resources in the Mekong River Basin and to develop the economic potential of the river (Anon, 2020). How efficient this joint management has been is not clear. In Australia, the Murray-Darling Basin Commission tries to coordinate the joint management of freshwater in this inland river system which is shared by several Australian states. In the past, the Commission has had limited success in improving the economic management of these shared water resources. For example, there has been a tendency for the available supplies of water to be over allocated for human end uses. Consequently, South Australia (at the lower end of this water system) is often deprived of water and marked negative impacts on ecological systems are observed, particularly in the lower reaches of the Murray River.

9.6. Water for Nature Conservation and for Non-marketed Uses

The management of shared water resources is complicated by demands for their use for non-marketed purposes such as for nature conservation, recreational use and sometimes, water availability for transport purposes. How should these demands be allowed for? Should, for example, these demands be estimated and responded to by employing the techniques outlined in Chapter 6? This is a possibility, but not everyone accepts that nature conservation goals should be determined merely by economic valuation.

Nevertheless, if this economic valuation approach is adopted, then its implications can be illustrated by reference to Fig. 9.10. There the line $D_M D_M$ represents the demand for water for marketable uses and the difference between line DD and $D_M D_M$ represent the overall

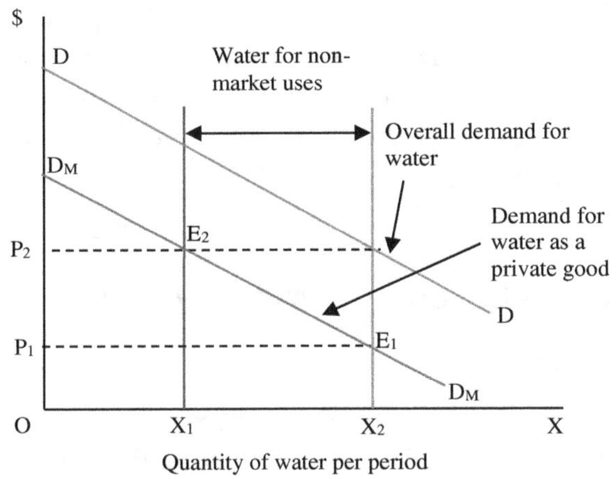

Fig. 9.10. Water often has dual values. It is valued as a private good and as a collective good. Its use for collective purposes is usually not marketed. This may result in it being under supplied for collective uses. In the case discussed, it is economically optimal to allocate $X_2 - X_1$ of water for collective use and X_1 of it for private use.

willingness of individuals to pay for the allocation of water for non-market purposes, such as for nature conservation. Let X_2 be the available supply of water per period of time. Then, using willingness to pay as an indicator of the non-market value of water, $X_2 - X_1$ of water should be reserved for non-market use with X_1 being made available for market use. This non-market allocation will raise the price of water to those for whom water is a private good from P_1 to P_2 per unit (if water is sold to clear the available supply) compared to the situation in which no water is reserved for non-marketed uses. Therefore, water allocation for non-marketed uses is unlikely to be welcomed by those who consume water as a private good.

In reality, decisions on the allocation of shared water resources are rarely made using the techniques illustrated by Fig. 9.10. Political considerations and procedures are the main influence. As a result, less water may be allocated to nature conservation and other non-market uses of water than is economically ideal in terms of economic valuations based on non-market uses of water. This is likely to occur if those who use water as a private good are a more effective political lobby group than those who use water for non-market purposes. In addition, it is often the case that when the supply of water becomes scarce (for example, due to drought) political expediency results in most of the reduction in water availability being borne by water allocated for non-market uses.

9.7. Water Pollution and Water Quality

9.7.1. *General aspects*

Water quality is important both for the use of water as a private good and for its uses as a collective non-marketed commodity. Poor quality and polluted water poses a risk to human health and to the health of animals, and when used to irrigate crops may reduce their yields or in extreme cases, kill crops, for example, where the water contains high levels of salt. Population of wild species can also be adversely affected by polluted water. In Kenya, for example, flamingo populations have declined because industrial pollutants are disposed of in streams that flow into lakes where the flamingos congregate and feed. Polluted water bodies often become unsuitable for recreational activities such as swimming, boating and fishing. Fish and other aquatic animals may become contaminated (for example, by heavy metals) thereby making them unsuitable for human consumption. Many different types of pollutants can be transported by water.

Note also that the quality of a water body can be adversely affected by the quantity of water extracted from it. For example, salt intrusion can occur in river estuaries as water consumption rises upstream, salt may enter underground aquifers when they are near the sea if the volume of water extracted from them is too high and irrigation of saline soils may result in salt accumulating in water runoff to rivers. Apart from this, other environmental ill-effects can occur, such as land subsidence when water is drained from aquifers. This may damage buildings and infrastructure, and result in seawater intrusion, as has happened in Taiwan. Land collapses may permanently lower the underground storage capacity of aquifers, and create new (inland) drainage basins. Such a basin has formed, for example, in the lower San Joaquin valley,

California and the water in it no longer drains to ocean but has become saline (personal communication, Darwin Hall, April 12, 2009).

9.7.2. *Controlling water pollution and managing water quality*

Pollutants may enter water at one or a few distinct points, such as through effluent pipes from factories, or they may enter the water in a broad band. Often the former situation is referred to as involving *single point pollution*. It is usually easier to monitor and regulate pollution emissions that enter water bodies at single identifiable points. The types of economic regulations outlined in Chapter 6 can be applied in the case of pollutants that enter water at single points.

Regulating pollution which has a broad band of emissions is more difficult than controlling point pollution. Broad plumes of water pollution may arise, for example, from agricultural activity, some types of silviculture, urban lawns and gardens and golf courses. As a result of these land uses, chemicals often leak into waterways, particularly if artificial fertilizers are applied, and some pesticides can be transported by water.

In order to regulate spillover effects from such activities, restrictions may be placed on the type of land uses allowed in particular locations. For example, only particular types of agriculture may be allowed in specified areas. If use of a chemical fertilizer is believed to be a major source of water pollution, then its sales may be taxed in order to reduce the economic incentive to use it. Its use should certainly not be subsidized (see Fig. 8.5 and the surrounding discussion of it). Furthermore, the development of techniques that reduce spillovers may be encouraged, for example application of slow-release chemical fertilizers, and if use of fertilizers is regulated by taxes, these slow-release fertilizers may be taxed at a lower rate than more soluble fertilizers. Landholders may also be made more aware of the spillover impacts of the different methods of land use available to them.

Many diseases that affect humans are water-borne. Considerable reductions in morbidity and mortality can and have been achieved by treating water to make it safer for human consumption, for example, the addition of chlorine to municipal water supplies to kill some pathogens. In this regard, it might be noticed that there is usually an economic trade-off between the cost of treating natural supplies of water prior to specific uses and the quality of these supplies. The less polluted (or the better is the quality) is the natural supply of water, the lower normally is the cost of its necessary treatment prior to human use. Sometimes, it may be cheaper to vary natural environmental conditions in order to improve water quality than to incur the extra costs of treating water prior to its use by humans so that it reaches a particular level of quality. As mentioned previously in this book, the New York City water authority came to the conclusion that the cost to it of making revegetation agreements with landholders in its water catchment area (which improved the quality of its water supplies) was less than the extra cost it would incur to treat its water supplies to reach its mandatory standard of water quality in the absence of such agreements. In most cases, the defensive costs of reacting to pollution emissions need to be compared with the costs of preventing or reducing the levels of pollution emissions to determine the least cost combination of these activities.

This can be illustrated by the case shown in Fig. 9.11. There line *ABC* represents the marginal economic benefit to polluters of being able to release a pollutant into waterways and line *OBD* represents the amount of marginal defensive expenditure that is required to bring the water to a specified standard prior to its use by humans. X indicates the quantity of pollutant emitted into the water. In the absence of any institutional control of the emissions, X_2 of the pollutant would enter the waterway and total (variable) costs equal to the area of triangle *ODC* would be incurred in treating the water. This does not, however, minimize the social cost of providing water that meets the required quality standard. This would be achieved when X_1 of the pollutant enters the waterway. This outcome might be achieved by a bargained solution. For example, as in the case of New York City, a water authority may pay landholders in its water catchment area to alter their land-use patterns to reduce pollution emissions. For instance, in the case shown, the water authority might pay landholders an amount

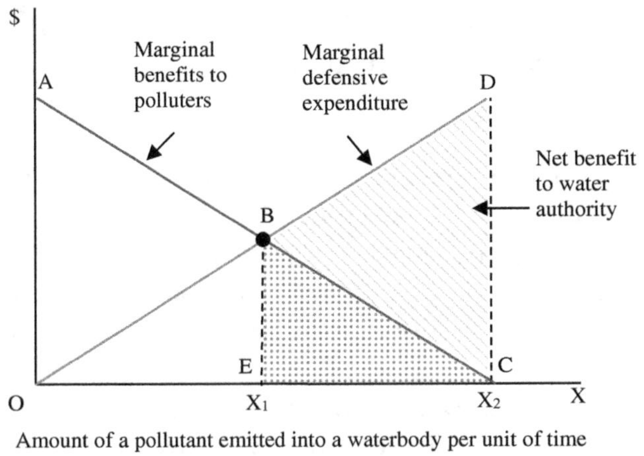

Fig. 9.11. In order to minimize the costs of supplying water for human use so that it reaches a prescribed standard, the options of treating the water and of reducing the emission of pollutants entering the water need to be considered. In the case illustrated, the overall cost of supplying water of the prescribed standard is reduced if the level of pollution emissions is lowered from X_2 to X_1.

equivalent to the dotted area of triangle *ECB* to reduce their total emission of the pollutant from X_2 to X_1. This would then result in a net reduction in the water treatment costs of the authority by an amount equivalent to the area of the hatched triangle *BCD*. As a result of the reduction in emission of the pollutant to level X_1, the water authorities cost of treating water would be reduced to an amount equivalent to the area of triangle *OBE*. Other types of policy interventions of the kind outlined in Chapter 5 can also be considered and evaluated.

Often the acceptable quality of water for different end uses varies. For example, the quality of water required for drinking is higher than that required for the operation of power stations. Up to a point, it can be economic to separate water of different quality and allocate it accordingly to different end users depending on its quality, or vary the extent of its treatment depending on its end use. Recycled water is likely, for example, to need less treatment for some industrial uses. All of these options call for consideration of economics.

9.8. The Economics of Investments to Supplement Available Water Supplies

9.8.1. *General aspects*

Water supplies can be supplemented in a variety of ways. These include recycling of water, its desalinization, its diversion from one watershed to another and the sharing or pooling of water from different sources. In addition, dams and weirs may be constructed on rivers to enable intertemporal allocation of available water supplies to be improved.

Water leakages and evaporation from water delivery systems can be reduced. However, all these methods have economic costs and environmental consequences. Let us consider in turn these methods of supplementing water supplies.

9.8.2. *Water recycling and desalinization*

As water supplies become increasingly scarce, one possible option is to recycle water used in urban areas. Once the demand for water rises sufficiently, it can become economic to recycle wastewater from urban areas. A simple illustration is provided by reference to Fig. 9.12.

In this figure, X_1 is the per period supply of water from natural sources which is assumed, for simplicity, to be available at zero cost. Initially, the demand for water is as shown by line D_1D_1. If price is used to allocate the available quantity of water, its price is P_1 per unit. Now suppose that the demand for water rises so that the demand for water is as shown by line D_2D_2. Given that the available supply of water remains unchanged at X_1, the equilibrium price of water rises to P_3. But suppose that water can be recycled at a cost per unit of AB. Then the marginal cost of recycling water is as shown by line BCE. It is economic to recycle water because the demand for water exceeds the marginal cost of recycling water. In the case illustrated, it will be economic to provide $X_2 - X_1$ of water by recycling it, assuming that the total economic benefits from recycling exceed its total costs. As a result, the equilibrium price of water per unit would be reduced from P_3 to P_2 and a net economic gain equivalent to the area of the dotted

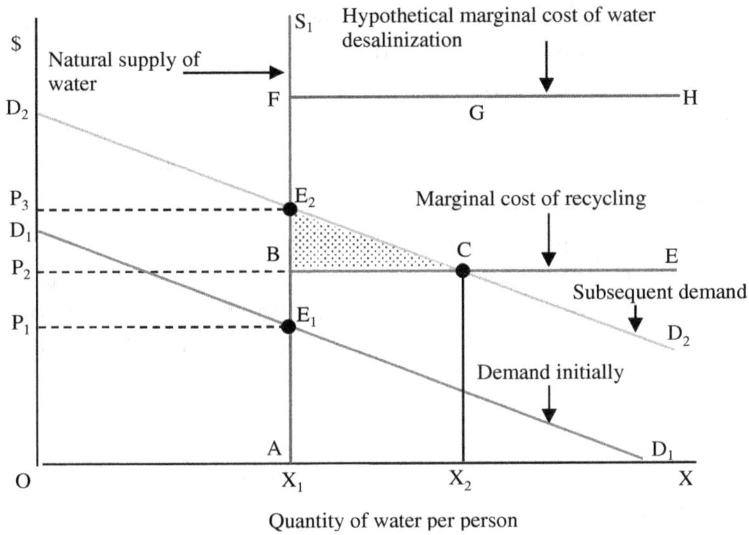

Fig. 9.12. If water becomes scarce enough, it may be economic to recycle it or desalinate salty water to supplement supplies. If the marginal cost of recycling water is *AB*, then in the case illustrated, it is economic to recycle $X_2 - X_1$ of water. But recycling is uneconomic if the marginal cost of this is *AF*. Similar observations apply to supplying freshwater by desalinization.

triangle results. Buyers of water are better off by an amount equivalent to the area of this triangle plus the area of rectangle $P_2BE_2P_3$.

However, recycling is not always economic. For example, if the cost per unit of recycling water is *AF* and the marginal cost of recycling as indicated by line *FGH*, it is not economic to recycle water in the area illustrated. In practice, there are likely to be limits on the amount of water that can be recycled and the marginal costs of recycling water may eventually rise with the amount of water to be recycled. There may also be environmental costs because the amount of water returning to natural outlets may be reduced as the extent of recycling rises.

In some geographical areas, desalinization of seawater is an option for supplying freshwater. Whether it is economic depends on the costs of the conversion relative to the demand for water. In the case, illustrated, if recycling of water is ruled out, desalinization is economic if its marginal cost is *AB* but not if it is *AF* and total benefits of desalinization exceed total costs. Provided that the marginal costs of recycling water or its desalinization is less than P_3 then these activities can be economic, but not if marginal costs are higher than P_3. The cheaper alternative for supplementing water supply should be pursued first until the marginal cost from this source reaches that of the next available source of supplementary supplies. Thus, the scope for economic recycling may be exploited first and then desalinization may be used to further supplement supplies if the equilibrium price of water exceeds the marginal cost of desalinization. Methods for desalinizing water can be quite energy intensive; so, any consequential environmental effects should also be taken into account.

9.8.3. *Diversion of water and the pooling of water resources*

Sometimes, it is economic to transport water from a source where it is less scarce to one where it is quite scarce. The economics of this depends on the cost of the diversion of the water. If, for example, the equilibrium price of water in one region is P_1 and at a higher level, P_2 in another region and water can be transported at a per unit cost of less than $P_2 - P_1$ from the former to the latter region, it is economic to transfer water until the equilibrium price of water in the latter region equals that in the former region *plus* the marginal cost of transporting water. However, the environmental costs of water diversion also need to be taken into account. If the environmental costs of diversion in terms of reduced nature conservation are very high, water diversion may be forgone as an option even though it is otherwise economic.

Another strategy sometimes used to smooth out the availability of water is to link various supply sources such as dams in different regions or water grids. This enables areas that may seasonally have plenty of water to augment the supplies of areas that temporarily have water shortages. Also taking measures to reduce leakages of water from water distribution systems can also effectively increase supplies of water. The costs and effectiveness of these alternative means of supplementing water supplies needs to be assessed and the least cost combination of strategies should be adopted. Similarly, in some cases, it may be economic to reduce water evaporation by replacing open water channels by pipes.

9.8.4. *The provision of dams and weirs*

Dams and weirs are often built to improve the intertemporal availability of water to users. In some cases, they have multiple uses. For example, dams may be used to generate electricity and weirs may be utilized to facilitate navigation. Dams may also be utilized for flood mitigation, weirs are often used to raise water levels to facilitate the irrigation of nearby land and to aid navigation, and in some instances, barrages (barriers) are built to prevent saltwater moving upstream from the sea, thereby preventing freshwater becoming saline in the lower reaches of rivers or entering underground aquifers. Assessing the costs and benefits of such projects is complex. The overall value of the net addition made to the supply of private goods as a result of such projects may overestimate the social net value of such projects. This will be so if there is considerable loss of non-marketed commodities as a result of these projects.

In the past, a number of these water-related projects were undertaken even when the return on the investment was very low based on their impacts on the supply of marketed commodities. These projects were often undertaken by the state with no intention to recover the full costs from the beneficiaries, such as agriculturalists using the water to irrigate their crops. Consequently, an indirect subsidy was provided to beneficiaries of these projects for political reasons, for example, to seek votes in marginal rural electorates.

The time-trend in the total storage capacity of major dams appears to have followed a logistic pattern, at first increasing at an increasing rate then at a declining rate and converging towards a constant value. Several factors have contributed to this trend:

(1) The total amount of water available for storage in any river catchment area is limited and in many catchment areas, this constraint is being approached.
(2) The most suitable sites for building dams are likely to be utilized early in the process of building dams and only inferior sites for potential dams remain.

(3) There has been increasing social opposition to the building of dams on environmental grounds.

A further problem is that dams often silt up and become wasting assets or with climate change, fail to fill to their designed capacity. They also can have negative ecological consequences, some of which were indicated in Section 9.2. They impede the movement and reproduction of several aquatic species, e.g. salmon but not just salmon.

9.9. Concluding Comments

This chapter reveals that the management of shared water resources raises complex economic issues, and that social conflicts about the use and allocation of water resources becomes more intense as water scarcity increases. As demonstrated, increasing demand for water and/or a reduction in its natural supply can transform situations in which water is plentiful to one in which it becomes scarce and its economical use becomes a major issue. Nevertheless, there may still be failures to use water in an economical manner. As shown, misallocation of water can occur between current users and in the intertemporal allocation of water. Various social mechanisms for allocating shared water resources were discussed. There included restrictions on the quantity of water to be used, systems of administered prices for water and tradable water permits. The advantages and limitations of methods of social management of water allocations were considered.

Other important matters which were investigated included the economics of regulating water pollution and managing water quality as well as the economics of investments in order to supplement available water supplies and in order to physically control the timing of available stocks of water. Although many different dimensions of the economics of utilizing shared water resources have been examined in this chapter and significant economic issues have been identified, this chapter should be regarded as merely as an introduction to this subject. Because water is primarily a shared communal resource in short supply, its use is subject to political debate and social conflict. Often there is a lack of political support for Paretian efficient policies for its management, as demonstrated, for example, by Darwin Hall (2009). Politics plays a major role in determining whether economic policies for reducing collective economic scarcity can be implemented. Therefore, from an applied point of view, decision-making about public policies designed to reduce economic scarcity need to take into account the political acceptability of alternative policies (Tisdell, 2009). In general, the nature of institutions, types of political systems, as well as cultural factors, influence the possibility and social acceptability of implementing public policies designed to improve the economic use of natural resources and the environment.

9.10. Keywords

Administered water prices; administrative regulation of the volume of water used; broad band pollution; defensive water management; desalinization of water; economic allocation of current water-use; efficient intertemporal water allocation; equality of the marginal value of water-use; multiple point pollution; multiple uses of dams and water storage facilities; non-market purposes of water-use; pollution prevention; pooled water resources; private (appropriated) net benefits from water projects; recycling of water; single point pollution; tiered water prices; social net benefits from water projects; transboundary water-use; user costs of water; water as a natural resource; water diversion; water scarcity.

9.11. Questions for Review and Discussion

1. Explain and illustrate the circumstances in which freshwater is not a scarce economic commodity and those in which it is. Do you think the economic scarcity of freshwater is likely to increase in the future? Why?
2. For what purposes are supplies of freshwater mostly used? Why do these uses result in environmental and ecological problems? How do market systems and some institutional systems involving water rights contribute to environmental deterioration?

3. Outline the general types of economic failures that can occur in allocating shared water resources taking into account current and intertemporal allocation of available water resources.
4. Why (and when) should the marginal value of the use of water be the same in all uses? Illustrate your answer.
5. Ideally available water supplies should be allocated in a manner that makes the *social* marginal value of water equal everywhere. Equating the *private* marginal value of water-use will, as a rule, only achieve the goal if there is no divergence between private and social marginal values of water-use. Do you agree? What factors may cause the social value of water-use to diverge from its private value?
6. How can marginal user costs be used to help manage the intertemporal allocation of water? Use a diagram to illustrate your answer.
7. Do you agree with the view that the "efficient" management of shared water resources is impossible because water supplies and, to some extent, demands are uncertain? Explain and illustrate your answer.
8. Outline the main managerial measures that may be used to allocate scarce supplies of water. Can they be combined, to some extent, and supplemented by other social means of controlling water-use?
9. Why might administrative controls on the quantity of water used by water-users give uneconomic results?
10. What types of functions can administered prices for water perform? Why are administered prices for water not relied on entirely by many public authorities to allocate water supplies?
11. Why do different water-users often pay different prices for water obtained from the same source? Why is this likely to be economically inefficient?
12. What are the advantages of using a tiered pricing system for charging for water-use? In your answer, explain the rationale for such a system.
13. What are the possible advantages and disadvantages of using a tradable permit system for water-use? Why is it usually necessary to zone the areas in which water permits can be traded?

14. Explain what types of transboundary problems occur in the use of water and why they occur.
15. How and why is the management of shared water resources complicated by demands for water availability for nature conservation and other non-market uses? Explain why there is likely to be an under allocation of shared water resources for non-market purposes. Why might governing bodies not be guided, to a great extent, by economic valuations of the demand for water for collective purposes?
16. Controlling water pollution at its source is made more difficult when it does not occur at a single point or a few single points. Pollution which occurs at numerous emissions in broad band is difficult and very costly to monitor thereby making pollution emission fees impractical. Therefore, alternative policies to charging fees based on levels of pollution emission need to be considered to control pollution. What types of policies may be adopted to control water pollution in such cases?
17. To what extent is it economic to combine defensive treatment of water for human use with reductions in pollution of a water source? Illustrate your answer using a diagram.
18. In what circumstances can it be economic to recycle or desalinate water? Use a diagram to illustrate your answer.
19. To what extent is it likely to be economic to direct water from one area to another? Why is it important to take account of environmental issues in such cases? What are the possible advantages of pooling water from different sources? Are there any possible disadvantages?
20. Dams often have multiple uses and can have net economic benefits. Explain. However, the building of dams involves environmental and other costs. What types of costs may be involved?
21. Dams have been built (and some may still be supplied) when their net social economic benefit is low or even negative. Why does this occur?
22. Expansion in the total capacity of dams in most countries has slowed in recent times and in many cases, there is close to zero expansion in total capacity. Why do you think this has happened?

Readings and References

Anon (2020). *The Mekong River Commission*, http://www.mrcmekong.org/ [Accessed 15 June 2020].

Bergstrom, J.C., K.J. Boyle and G.L. Poe (2007). *The Economic Value of Water Quality*, Edward Elgar, Cheltenham, UK and Northampton, MA, USA.

Bjornlund, H. and J. McKay (2002). Aspects of water markets for developing countries: Experiences from Australia, Chile, and the US, *Environment and Development Economics*, 7, 769–795. doi: 10.1017/S1355770X02000463.

Doughman, P.M., J. Blaster and H. Ingram (2007). *Reflections on Water: New Approaches to Transboundary Conflicts and Co-operation*, MIT Press, Cambridge, MA, USA.

Hall, D.C. (2009). Politically feasible, revenue sufficient, and economically efficient municipal water rates, *Contemporary Economic Policy*, 27, 539–554. doi: 10.1111/j.1465-7287.2009.00164.x.

Kahn, J.R. (2005). *The Economic Approach to Environmental and Natural Resources*, 3rd edn. South-Western, Mason, Ohio, USA [Chapter 15].

Organization for Economic Cooperative and Development (2003). Improving Water Management: Recent OECD Experience [Online] OECD, Paris. [https://doi.org/10.1787/9789264099500-en [Accessed 15 June, 2020].

Tietenberg, T. and L. Lewis (2018). *Environmental and Natural Resource Economics*, 11th edn. Routledge, New York and Abingdon, Oxon, UK [Chapter 9].

Tisdell, C.A. (2009). Complex policy choices regarding agricultural externalities: Efficiency, equity and acceptability. In V. Beckmann and M. Padmanabhan (Eds.), *Institutions and Sustainability. Political Economy of Agriculture and the Environment — Essays in Honour of Konrad Hagedorn*, 83–106. Springer.

Chapter 10

Biodiversity Conservation

10.1. An Introduction to the Relationship between Biodiversity and Economics

Economics is relevant to biological conservation in several ways. First, the composition of the stock of living things is substantially influenced by the nature of economic activities and economic growth. For example, economic growth results in the loss of habitat required for the survival of some species but at the same time, may result in alterations in available habitats that favor populations of other species. The operation of economic systems nowadays is the major influence on changes in the composition of biological diversity and this has been so for a considerable period of time (see for example, Harting, 1880, especially p. 209). Moreover, human impacts on biological diversity have grown in comparative importance with the passage of time and now greatly exceed non-anthropogenic influences. Given the large and continuing loss in biodiversity due to anthropogenic causes, there are concerns that this loss will eventually become a threat to economic sustainability. Therefore, one can study the relationships between economic activity and economic growth and their consequences for biodiversity conservation and genetic diversity and the implications of this for economic welfare and economic sustainability.

Second, one can consider whether alternative types of economic systems promote economically desirable patterns of biological conservation and genetic development, and if they fail to do this, why this happens. Third, possible policies to rectify any such failures can be assessed. However, complex issues are involved. Ethical conflict and differences in values held by individual human-beings complicate policy choices. For example, not everyone is convinced that human wants should be the sole of arbiter of whether individual species and natural environments should continue to exist.

Some individuals and philosophers believe that humans have a moral obligation to help conserve biodiversity and the natural webs of life. For example, John Passmore (1974) has argued that humankind has an ethical responsibility to help conserve nature and Aldo Leopold (1933, 1966) has expounded the view (in his land ethic) that humans have a moral duty to conserve webs of life; that is collections of interdependent species and their ecosystems. Nevertheless, these ecocentric views do not mean that the economic issues mentioned above should not be considered. Furthermore, human wants cannot be ignored completely. For example, it can be important to achieve ecocentric goals (or more realistically, anthropocentric goals modified to take account of ecocentric objectives) at minimum economic cost.

The discussion in this chapter begins by considering the concept of biodiversity and its measurement, and why biodiversity has economic value. Then factors (both non-anthropogenic, and anthropogenic) are identified which cause changes in biodiversity with particular attention being paid to economic factors that bring about alterations in biodiversity. The question is posed of whether economic mechanisms produce an ideal achievable stock of living things, including their diversity, when the ideal is assessed from an economic point of view as well as other viewpoints. Several shortcomings of economic mechanisms as influences on the development of the biological stock are identified and policies that can help to rectify are outlined.

Humankind has been very active in creating human-modified and human-regulated ecosystems and new forms of living things. Selective breeding, the development of genetically modified organisms (GMOs) and different forms of farming systems influence the nature and composition of the biological world. Therefore, the ecological and economic consequences of these anthropogenic developments are given particular attention in the latter part of this chapter.

10.2. The Concept of Biodiversity and the Measurement of Biodiversity

Biological diversity has many dimensions and its extent cannot be satisfactorily portrayed by a single measure (see for example, Nunes *et al.*, 2003; Gaston and Spicer, 2004, Section 1.4). Nevertheless, it is clear that human activities have resulted in reduced biodiversity in virtually all of its dimensions. As a result of human activity, the extent of genetic diversity within species has declined and there has also been a fall in species diversity and reduced diversity of ecosystems (see Pearce and Moran, 1994, Chapter 1).

Although an overall decline in biological diversity has occurred in recent centuries due to human activities, at the same time human beings have developed new varieties of living things by selective breeding and more recently, by genetic engineering. Human interaction with undomesticated or uncultivated species has also had some influence on the evolution of genetic diversity in the wild by favoring some biological varieties and organisms and not others.

The stock of biodiversity of species and of their varieties may be divided into the wild stock and into the domesticated or cultivated stock of living things. This, however, is a simplification because the borders between the two sets are fuzzy. These genetic stocks are in a process of constant change. With the passage of time, some of the stock is lost, some portion is retained and some part is added. In Fig. 10.1, for example, the set A might represent the genetic stock lost compared to the initial situation, the set B might represent the genetic stock retained and C may be stock added. Human activities can result in A being relatively large and C being comparatively small as far as the wild stock is concerned.

While much attention has been given to the extent of biological diversity, including genetic diversity in the wild, it should also be kept in mind that the stock of genetic diversity of domesticated

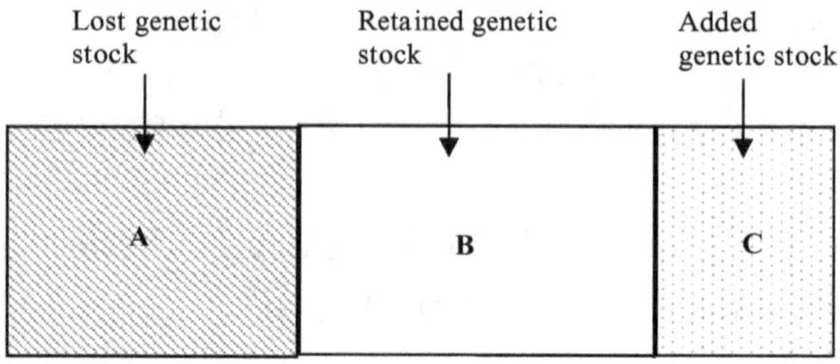

Fig. 10.1. The world's genetic stock is not constant but is subject to continual change. With the passage some of the stock is added to, some is retained and some is lost. Nevertheless, there has been a net decline in the diversity of the stock in modern times as a result of human activity.

or cultivated species is an important economic asset. Economic and social change has led to considerable loss in the extent of this type of genetic diversity and further losses seem probable in developing countries as they become more integrated with the global economy (Tisdell, 2003). Furthermore, the continuation of selective breeding and more widespread application of genetic engineering are likely to add to these losses. There is no doubt that genetic engineering poses new challenges for the conservation of biodiversity.

10.3. Why Does Biodiversity Have Economic Value?

There are several reasons why biodiversity can have economic value. Firstly, many individuals value the diversity of life forms themselves and some feel that humankind has an ethical or moral responsibility to try to conserve that biodiversity. Some individuals are willing to pay for the conservation of biodiversity for these reasons. Second, biodiversity may be seen as providing consequential economic benefits. Several types of consequential economic benefits can be envisaged.

Biodiversity "hotspots" may attract tourists and this may provide economic benefits to local communities. For instance, many individuals like seeing diverse creatures and place an economic value on that. To take an extreme example, keen bird-watchers (twitchers) highly value being able to see a large variety of birds. In addition, biodiversity may sustain or add to consumptive economic benefits obtained by humans. It can do this, for example, because greater biodiversity usually keeps open a wider range of options for humans than would otherwise occur. Because we cannot be sure now what genetic material will have economic value in the future and do not know the relative value of different types of genetic material in the distant future, it is normally rational to err on the side of conserving a diversity of genetic material. In a variety of circumstances, this is a rational response to the presence of uncertainty and to our ability to discover new economic applications for living things in the future. Furthermore, it can be a rational form of behavior even if individuals are not risk- or uncertainty-averse and want to maximize their expected economic gains (Krutilla, 1967; Tisdell, 1970, 1996, Chapter 5).

Ciriacy-Wantrup (1968) argues that there is a strong case for conserving biodiversity because the cost of conserving many species at a safe minimum level of population (that is a minimum viable population) is low relative to their *potential* future economic benefit. Therefore, there is likely to be a net economic benefit of erring in favor of the conservation of biodiversity. Observe that the lower the cost of conservation in relation to its possible economic benefits, the more likely is conservation to be a beneficial economic strategy. On the other hand, if the current costs of saving a species from extinction (that is, the opportunity costs of conserving the species based on the economic benefits forgone as a result of conserving it) are high relative to the potential economic benefits of its conservation, saving the species is (unfortunately) likely to be uneconomic. In such cases, one has to consider whether economics should be the sole arbiter of the survival of the species.

The work of Bishop (1978) suggests that aversion to risk-bearing or to uncertainty is also likely to favor greater conservation of biodiversity. However, as pointed out in Chapter 2, risk-aversion does not in itself foster conservation. Whether it does so depends on the type of criterion adopted for choice under uncertainty and the structure of the payoffs available. This can be made clear by a couple of examples.

Suppose that two strategies are available: one, α_1, is to conserve all those species that are currently of economic value (set A) (but no others) and the second strategy, α_2, is to conserve set A plus a minimum

Table 10.1. A game theory matrix to consider whether biodiversity conservation is an economically beneficial strategy. In this case, the maximin gain strategy does not favor biodiversity conservation.

		State of nature		
		s_1	s_2	
Conserve set A	α_1	10	10	10*
Conserve sets A & B	α_2	8	14	8

viable populations of a set of species (set *B*) that are not currently of economic value, but which could be of value in the future. Adoption of strategy α_2 involves the conservation of greater biodiversity than strategy α_1. Hypothetical payoffs are shown in the body of the matrix specified as Table 10.1. If state of nature s_1, prevails, and if strategy α_2 (biodiversity conservation) is adopted, biodiversity conservation reduces economic value, but if s_2 prevails it adds to economic wealth considerably. It is assumed that if strategy α_1 is adopted, the payoff is the same whether or not state of nature s_1 or s_2 prevails.

Assume that decision-makers are so risk-averse that they want to be prepared for the worst state of nature. This means that they want to maximize their minimum possible gain from whatever strategy they adopt (or to minimize their maximum possible loss). Given the payoffs shown in matrix in Table 10.1, the minimum possible gain if strategy α_1 is adopted is 10 and if α_2 is adopted, it is 8. Therefore, strategy *A* is the optimal strategy in this case. Conserving biodiversity (strategy α_2) is an inferior choice. On the other hand, if the minimax regret criterion is adopted for decision-making under uncertainty, α_2 becomes the optimal choice given the payoffs shown in Table 10.1. Table 10.2 shows the regret matrix corresponding to Table 10.1. The maximum regret (benefits forgone) is 4 when α_1 is adopted and is 2 when α_2 is adopted. Therefore, in this case, α_2 is the optimal strategy. The strategy conserving greater biodiversity is favored.

Nevertheless, the maximin gain strategy does not always reject biodiversity conservation. For example, if the payoffs shown in the matrix

Table 10.2. The regret matrix corresponding to the matrix in Table 10.1. In this case, the minimax regret criterion favors biodiversity conservation which differs from the result for the maximin gain criterion for the example in Table 10.1.

		State of nature		
		s_1	s_2	
Conserve set *A*	α_1	0	4	4
Conserve sets *A* & *B*	α_2	2	0	2*

Table 10.3. An illustration of a case where the maximin gain strategy favors biodiversity conservation. This contrasts with the case in Table 10.1.

		State of nature		
		s_1	s_2	
Conserve set *A*	α_1	10	4	4
Conserve sets *A* & *B*	α_2	8	7	7*

in Table 10.3 apply and the available strategies and states of nature are as before, strategy α_2 is the optimal maximin strategy. In the case shown in Table 10.3, the genetic set, *A*, fails to retain its economic value if state of nature, s_2, prevails. Set *A* may fail to maintain its economic value because it becomes less resistant to diseases with the passage of time, or a new disease may evolve against which it is not resistant. Many scientists believe that these scenarios are quite likely to occur. Note that the minimax regret criterion would also favor biodiversity conservation in the case illustrated. However, the minimax regret criterion does not always favor conservation when the maximin gain criterion favors it. For example, if the entry in the top right-hand corner of the matrix in Table 10.3 is 6 rather than 5, α_1 is the minimax regret strategy but α_2 remains the maximin gain strategy. It can also be shown that the minimax regret criterion does not always favor biodiversity conservation.

There are other criteria for choice under uncertainty and their application can yield a variety of results. Nevertheless, it is still true that even if choices are made to maximize expected economic gains, it is normally optimal to err in favor of conserving biodiversity because flexibility is retained for using genetic material in the future.

Other factors may also favor the retention of biodiversity. Firstly, diversity usually reduces risks. If benefits from conserving the individual components (species and their variants) of living organisms are uncorrelated or positively correlated, their diversity will reduce the economic risks from biological conservation because it lowers the variance of total benefit about its average. It is likely that positive complementarity or correlation of benefits occurs. Second, there can be economies in the cost of conserving biodiversity. For example, as the size of a protracted area is increased, the number of different species conserved may rise at an increasing rate *up to a point*, and the cost of extension of the size of this protected area may rise at a slower rate. Consequently, the cost per species conserved is likely to fall (*up to a point*) as the size of a protected area increases and a larger range of species are conserved. Given the above observations (which imply the existence of economic *synergies* in the conservation of biodiversity), it follows that the economic value of a group of diverse species (or a diverse set of living things) is greater than the sum total of the value of each species (or each component of the living mosaic) assessed in isolation. This provides a strong economic argument in favor of biodiversity conservation. Yet, at the same time, it should be recognized that most species and components of the living world cannot be valued in complete isolation because their very existence depends on the existence of other species and on components of an interdependent ecological web. In order to conserve most species, several other species and a variety of environments have, as a rule, to be conserved also.

As is well known, the operations of market mechanisms do not take into account the total economic values of the continuing existence of many species and life forms. This is because several types of market failures occur in relation to the conservation of living things.

The overall consequence of these market failures is that less biodiversity is sustained than is desired from an economic point of view. Nevertheless, even when markets operate efficiently, their operation and their geographical extension can be a source of substantial biodiversity loss, particularly in relation to organisms cultured by human beings (Tisdell, 2017, Chapters 5 and 6). Let us therefore, consider both non-anthropogenic and anthropogenic factors that cause changes in biological diversity.

10.4. Factors Causing Changes in Biodiversity

10.4.1. *General aspects*

The diversity of living things is subject to constant change. In some past periods, biodiversity has declined very rapidly due to non-anthropogenic causes (for general information on these mass extinctions see, for example, Kretsch III *et al.*, 2004, p. 129) and there have been periods in which a substantial expansion in biodiversity has occurred naturally. A hallmark of the current era is the substantial decline in biodiversity occurring as a result of human activities. This is a cause for considerable concern because the *normal* rate of extinction of species is about one species per million species per year whereas the current rate (due mainly to human impacts) is hundreds of times higher (Kretsch III *et al.*, 2004, p. 129). This is leading to the impoverishment of the stock of biodiversity and is considered to be a potential threat to economic sustainability (see, for example, Balmford *et al.*, 2002). Nevertheless, at the same time, as humans are reducing the overall extent of biodiversity, they are also bringing into existence new organisms that would not have emerged without their efforts to create these. These organisms are created, for example, by selective breeding and by the creation of GMOs. However, these additions are miniscule in comparison to the rate of loss of biodiversity otherwise. Furthermore, anthropogenic changes to natural environments increasingly influence the evolution and survival of wild species, that is speciation.

Economists have mostly given attention to the economic causes of the loss of genetic diversity in the wild (Ninan, 2007). However, there has also been substantial loss of biodiversity of cultured organisms, partly (but not entirely) because economically superior organisms have been developed by human beings (see Fig. 10.1). Concern also exists about these losses, for example, the prospect that they will result in the long run in economic impoverishment rather than maintain economic wealth. Let us consider in turn non-anthropogenic factors that can affect biodiversity, anthropogenic factors that alter biodiversity in the wild and those anthropogenic influences that determine the biodiversity of cultured organisms.

10.4.2. *Non-anthropogenic causes of alterations in biodiversity*

The geophysical world helps to shape the composition of the living world and it is normal for some species or varieties of species to disappear with the passing of time and for new species and variants of species to occur. In the past, mass extinctions of species have sometimes taken place in a short time-period as a result of major geophysical changes, such as climate change, asteroids or comets striking the earth and the upwelling of volcanic activity (Ochoa, 2007, Chapter 8). The current phase of global warming (which is due to human activity) is expected to result in mass extinctions (Ochoa, 2007, p. 131).

Most global alterations in biological diversity occur gradually as a result of natural selection of species (and their variants) in response to genetic mutation. Most variations in life forms arising from genetic mutation fail to persist; but some forms are fitter for survival than their rivals lacking the mutation. They, therefore, outcompete their rivals and become dominant in their species or they may become dominant in particular niches where they are fitter than their rivals. Mutations allow adaptive radiation of living things to different niches and environments. This leads to a natural increase in biological diversity (speciation) over long periods of time in the absence of cataclysmic events, which (for a time) reduce biodiversity. The extent and rapidity with which adaptive radiation (speciation) occurs depends on the frequency and nature of mutations and the variety of different niches or natural environments available. Consequently, if the variety of environments increases and persists for a sufficient length of time, the extent of biodiversity should also increase. The converse can also be expected to hold.

Patterns of genetic evolution are not completely predictable. Small random variations in events and in environments are capable of significantly influencing the composition of life forms in the long run, as has been argued by Gould (1989, 1990) The pattern of evolution of biological systems may be very sensitive to variations in their initial conditions or to variations at crucial times in their development. This complicates the theory of ecological evolution.

10.4.3. *Anthropogenic (mainly economic) impacts on the biological diversity of wild organisms*

Many human activities contribute significantly to the loss of biodiversity in the wild and most are the result of the quest by human beings to better their economic situation. A list of the proximate anthropogenic causes of biodiversity loss (together with some relevant observations) is given in Table 10.4. This is not an exhaustive list, but it is relatively complete. In the recent economic literature, most attention has been focused on habitat loss as a source of biodiversity loss in the wild (Swanson, 1994, 1997). While it appears to be the main proximate cause of biodiversity loss in the wild, other contributors to that loss should not be ignored because they can have a substantial impact overall.

Observe that while many of the factors causing biodiversity loss in the wild can be attributed to market failures, this is not true of all. Furthermore, in some cases, the extinction of some species may be desired from a purely economic or anthropogenic point of view, for example in cases 3 and 5 listed in Table 10.4. Most individuals would for instance, agree that the eradication of smallpox in the wild has been a desirable achievement from an anthropogenic viewpoint. There are, however, conflicting views about the local eradications of some species, such as the wolf.

10.4.4. *Anthropogenic impacts on the biodiversity of cultured organisms*

As mentioned above, the diversity of cultured organisms is an important economic asset. Cultured organisms have been selected or

Table 10.4. A list of proximate anthropogenic causes of loss of biodiversity in the wild.

	Causal factors	Observations
1.	*Habitat loss* due to its conversion for human use.	This reduces the availability and variety of natural habitats. Conversion is motivated by higher private returns from transformed habitats than wild ones.
2.	Over hunting of wild species due to open-access.	Lack of property rights can contribute to extinctions (see Chapter 4).
3.	*Substitution* (replacement) *of* some wild *species* by other species that give higher private economic returns.	For example, slow growing stands of natural forest may be replaced by faster growing plantation species. This can happen in the absence of market failure.
4.	*Deliberate or coincidental introduction of exotic or new organisms* that outcompete existing organisms or to which indigenous organisms show little biological resistance.	Humans have continued to contribute to the geographical speed of exotic organisms. Humans also introduce new organisms or substantially modified organisms via human selection of biological material.
5.	Eradication of wild species as pests.	Wild species are often viewed by humans as being pests and attempts are made to eradicate them. They may be seen as pests because of their negative impact on economic activity or because they threaten human well-being, health or survival.
6.	*Negative environmental spillovers* from human activity that eliminate life-support systems of wild species. These include negative effects of *climate change*.	These effects can be varied. They include spillovers from water and air pollution and changes in the quality of these resources.

Table 10.4. (*Continued*)

Causal factors	Observations
	Alterations in water availability and the reliability of supplies are consequential for the survival of some wild species e.g. water for wetlands (see Chapter 9).
7. *Direct competition of humans* with wild species for natural resources such as food obtained from the wild.	There is a risk that the harvesting by humans of wild species on the lower end of the food chain may cause species extinction higher up the food chain.

developed by human intervention because they have valuable traits from an anthropogenic perspective. The diversity of the stock of cultured organism is constantly changing. As new organisms are added to this stock, many existing cultured organisms in the stock disappear. Despite additions to this stock (and sometimes because of these additions), there has been a considerable decline in the diversity of the stock of cultured organisms in recent centuries. This has led to concern amongst scientists that economic production dependent on the use of cultured organisms may prove to be unsustainable because of the risks associated with genetic erosion; a risk which is compounded by the loss of the wild relatives of cultured organisms. Currently, production from some of the major crops, such as wheat, depends on a very limited number of wheat varieties. There is a risk that these will fail because of the evolution of or spread of new diseases. A more diverse genetic base for wheat (and other crops) increases the chances of being able to breed new varieties which resist a new disease. Varieties and breeds of cultured organisms which appear at some point to be no longer of economic value may subsequently prove valuable as possibilities alter. For example, the Cornish hen (which is relatively square) almost went out of existence, but later its shape was found to be valuable for breeding chickens for freezing and subsequent packing.

Table 10.5 lists several functions that may cause varieties of cultured organisms to disappear. The efficient extension of markets and growing globalization and powerful forces tends to reduce the biodiversity of cultured organisms (Tisdell, 2017, Chapters 5 and 6). Several types of economic mechanisms and processes lead to this result. They include regional and international specialization in production (as promoted by market competition and the pursuit of comparative economic advantage) as well as the decoupling of agriculture and other cultured organisms from local conditions. The latter is facilitated by interregional and international trade. As a result of market extension, inputs into agriculture and similar economic activities no longer depend solely on the availability of local supplies. This together with new technologies makes the culture of organisms less dependent on local environmental conditions. Therefore, varieties or breeds of organisms that are particularly well adapted to local natural environmental conditions may be displaced by others that are not but which are more suited to the environmental conditions that can now be established and managed by farmers.

Furthermore, with improvements in transport and communication, knowledge about exotic varieties of crops and breeds of livestock that can prove to be more economically valuable than indigenous ones is now diffused more widely and quickly than in earlier times. The costs of transporting genetic material from one place to another have also decreased in real terms and expertise in relocating genetic material has improved. This accelerates the rate at which many indigenous varieties of cultured organisms are displaced by exotic varieties.

While the stock of diverse cultured cultivated organisms developed by humans has benefited humankind, it is not necessarily the best stock that could have been developed from an economic point of view. This is because (for all intents and purposes) it has been developed in a piecemeal and uncoordinated way and has often involved chance elements typical of processes involving creativity. At the same time, selection processes for new organisms do bring benefits to their developers, at least in the short run. Usually, the long term and global consequences of such developments are uncertain, as are the holistic ecological impacts

Table 10.5. Anthropogenic (mostly economic) causes of losses of biodiversity of cultured organisms with observations about the proceeds involved.

	Causal factors	Observations
1.	Displacement of existing varieties of cultured organisms by new ones considered to be of greater economic value	New varieties may appear as a result of selective breeding, chance, or genetic engineering.
2.	Introduction of new varieties of cultured organisms from abroad or elsewhere	As a result, indigenous varieties of cultured organisms may be replaced.
3.	International specialization in production	As a result of this, local production of a biological commodity using an indigenous variety of a cultured organism may cease and this variety then disappears.
4.	Imports of materials for culturing organisms	As imports become more economic, the culture of organisms becomes less dependent on local natural resources and environmental conditions. Therefore, local varieties of cultured organisms may become less economic than exotic varieties.
5.	*New technologies* for the culture of living things provide a controlled environmental package	These technologies improve the environment for cultured organisms and increase the control of it. Fewer varieties are, therefore, required to ensure maximum economic benefit.
6.	Changing tastes	Changes in tastes can lead to the demise of some cultured varieties of organisms. Increased demand for less fatty pork, for example, threatens some breeds of pigs that produce fatty meat.

of such changes. The significance of such issues have been highlighted by innovations involving the introduction of GMOs.

While the development of diverse cultured organisms is less fluid or chaotic than the evolution of the stock of wild organisms, it still appears to involve very imperfect processes. Imperfection in such processes seems unavoidable because of the bounded rationality of human beings, interdependence, and the complexity of the problem (compare Parker and Stacey, 1995, p. 5). The best that one might hope to do from a policy point of view is to reduce the imperfections involved. It is a fantasy to believe that all imperfections in human regulated or influenced systems can be eliminated. It is appropriate now to assess policies that governments and the international community have adopted to regulate the conservation of biodiversity and then explore some of the special issues raised by the advent of genetic engineering.

10.5. Policies to Promote Biodiversity Conservation

10.5.1. *An overview*

Policies to conserve particular species and specific biological types (as well as biodiversity) vary considerably. Some are designed to promote conservation in natural settings (*in situ*) whereas others are for conservation in human-regulated environments (that is, *ex situ*). The former includes protection of nature in national parks and the controlled use of nature in the wild and the latter covers conservation by means of zoos, seed banks and the farming or culture of species.

Three broadly different policy approaches to the conservation of a particular species and the biodiversity can be identified. These are:

- The restriction of market operations or of their use in order to foster biological conservation.
- The promotion of market operations and the use of species to provide incentives for biological conservation.
- Measures that make biological conservation independent of market forces, or virtually so.

Globally, the Convention on International Trade in Endangered Species (CITES) follows the first-mentioned approach whereas the more recent Convention on Biological Diversity embraces the second approach. In many countries, the third approach is adopted in conserving biodiversity in national parks and protected areas. To some extent, the philosophies and theories underlying these different policies appear to be in conflict. However, in reality, the types of policies that are likely to be effective in biological conservation vary with prevailing conditions. No single one of the above-mentioned policies is effective in promoting biological conservation in all circumstances. For example, promoting market operations will, as a whole, be ineffective if it is impossible or too costly to prevent open-access to a species to be conserved or if the species intrinsically has little or no marketable value. Let us briefly evaluate each of the basic policy approaches to biological conservation.

10.5.2. *Restriction of market operations as a conservation measure*

If a species (or products derived from it) have commercial value and there is open-access to its harvest, then there is a possibility of it being harvested to extinction, especially if it is a slowly reproducing species, such as many species of marine mammal are, for instance, species of whales. Due to either a substantial increase in demand for consumptive use of such a species or a sharp reduction in the per unit costs of harvesting it (due for example to technological progress), a bionomic disequilibrium can occur and the species can be harvested to extinction. In such cases, measures to reduce market demand for consumptive use of the species or to limit harvesting effort may prove to be effective conservation measures. The policy approach adopted in CITES is to limit demand for the consumptive use of endangered species by restricting their export and the export of products derived from them. National governments may also restrict harvesting effort by imposing quotas on the catch or harvest of such species. These may or may not be tradable. Restrictions on the harvest may also be part of a general scheme

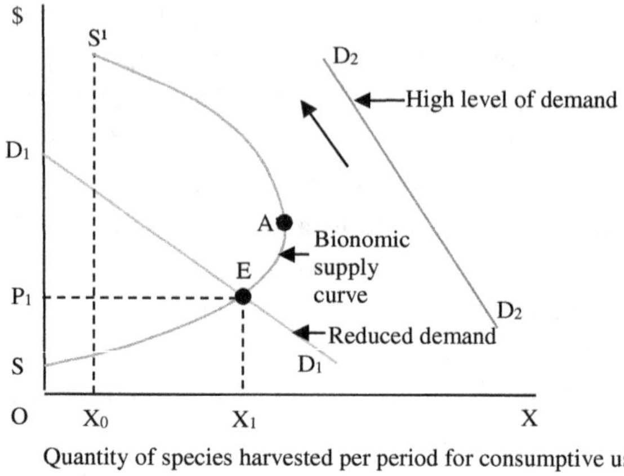

Fig. 10.2. A high level of demand for consumptive use of a species to which there is open-access may result in its extinction. Measures that reduce demand in such circumstances may save it from extinction. In the case illustrated, measures that shift the demand curve down from D_2D_2 to D_1D_1 are effective in saving the species from extinction.

to increase the economic efficiency of harvesting open-access species that have consumptive value (see Chapter 5) or harvesting may be controlled by the government to help placate those who are opposed to wildlife harvesting.

Figure 10.2 provides some insights into this issue. The backward-bending curve marked SAS^1 represents the rate of sustainable harvest of a wild species given the population dynamics of the species (Tisdell, 2005, pp. 137–140). The maximum sustainable yield per period of time from the species is X_2 per period of time and this corresponds to point A. Should harvesting effort increase further in an attempt to increase the yield, the yield will fall as the population of the species continues to decline. Eventually with heightened effort, yield may fall to X_0 and a further increase in effort can lead to extinction of the species. The species becomes more vulnerable to extinction as its population approaches low levels and at very low levels, extinction becomes certain. If in the case shown, demand for the consumptive use of the species is as shown by line D_2D_2, extinction of the species is certain in the absence of intervention. This is because demand for consumptive use of the species exceeds the cost of its supply at every level. The high level of demand stimulates extra harvesting pressure on the species which eventually results in its extinction. However, if the demand for consumptive use of the species can be reduced to a level like that shown by the curve marked $D_1 D_1$, the equilibrium harvest corresponds to point E and extinction of the species is avoided. Alternatively, or as well, governments sometimes try to ban or limit the harvesting of a wild species that is considered to be endangered. In such cases, remaining demand for the consumptive use of the species is likely to exceed supply and this may encourage illegal harvesting of the species and the development of black markets in trading of the species. Nevertheless, government restrictions may still have a net beneficial conservation impact.

10.5.3. *Fostering market operations in order to conserve species*

If a species has sufficient commercial value and if those who possess stocks of the species can maintain adequate property rights economically in their stocks, then it can be profitable to sustain the species as a result of market operations. Nevertheless, the mere fact that it is profitable to possess stocks of a species does not ensure its survival. If there is a competitive species using the same resources and this species is more profitable, economic motivation will result in the more profitable species replacing the less profitable one.

Secondly, in many cases, the commercial value of a species differs significantly from its economic value. Some species have the characteristics of public goods or involve a mixture of private goods plus public good attributes. Hence, their commercial value is less than their economic value. Consequently, market mechanisms can fail to conserve species that are highly valued from an economic point of view, but have little commercial value.

Sometimes, private ownership (or similar ownership by an entity) of stocks of species results in their culture. Farming is a common form of this. While this favors the survival of the cultured species, this is generally at the expense of other species, particularly wild species.

For example, habitats are likely to be altered to favor the cultured species and its biological competitors harassed or killed by humans as pests. While the cultured species benefit, many other species are disadvantaged and the consequence can be a net loss of biodiversity.

This is not to say that systems of private (or similar) property rights combined with market operations can never be effective in helping to conserve biodiversity. Sometimes such systems help to save an endangered species and there is no loss (or no significant loss) in biodiversity. For example, safari farms in South Africa have been credited with saving the black rhinoceros from extinction. In New Zealand, the Otago Peninsula Trust protects a rookery near Dunedin of a species of royal albatross and finances this to a large extent by fees paid for by visitors in order to view the albatross. The area of land set aside for this conservation effort is relatively small, but the contribution made to the survival of this species of albatross is positive (for more information see Tisdell and Wilson, 2012, Chapter 13).

Another case to consider is that of the African elephant. Apart from its non-consumptive value for tourism purposes, it has consumptive value for its ivory, meat and hides. It has been commercially harvested in some national parks in Africa, for example, Kruger National Park. This was done to prevent the population of elephants exceeding the carrying capacity of Kruger National Park and to provide revenue to help fund park management. This funding contributed positively to the conservation biodiversity in national parks and South Africa had an incentive to sustain elephant stocks because of their economic value. Economic motivation for this conservation was undermined in the 1990s when CITES imposed bans on international trade in products derived from elephants.

While the policies adopted as a result of CITES can have positive consequences for biological conservation, this is not always the case as the African elephant problem indicates. In the case of the African elephant, weak state property rights existed in some African countries and illegal de facto open-access to the killing of elephants has occurred. However, in other African nations, state property rights in elephants in national parks were relatively secure and their commercial use contributed to conservation of the African elephant and to biodiversity.

Regulations imposed by CITES can sometimes create barriers to new initiatives to conserve species. For example, attempts to farm marine turtles face trade restrictions which reduce the economic attractiveness of such initiatives. This was so for the farming of green turtles and similar problems have arisen for those attempting to develop a closed-cycle for the culture of hawksbill turtles (Tisdell *et al.*, 2007).

10.5.4. *Measures designed to make biodiversity conservation independent of market forces*

Even when developed to a high level, market mechanisms are incapable of conserving *all* species and *all* biodiversity because of some inescapable market failures and because some species are not commercially or economically valuable enough to warrant their conservation from an anthropogenic perspective. Therefore, market systems cannot be relied on entirely as mechanisms to ensure biodiversity conservation. Note that, nevertheless, this observation is consistent with the view that improvements in market operations can be effective in some instances in promoting conservation goals, such as the conservation of particular species.

Various nonmarket mechanisms play a role in biodiversity conservation. These include the provision of national parks and protected areas by the state which are to a large extent funded from government revenues. These often protect life forms that no private enterprise would find it profitable to conserve. This is because a large portion of the economic benefits from protecting those life forms are obtained offsite due to the presence of living things with the characteristics of public goods.

Furthermore, non-government organizations (NGOs) often contribute to biodiversity conservation by generating political pressure in its favor and also by directly acquiring areas for nature protection or otherwise providing support for nature conservation. These are voluntary bodies relying to a large extent on charitable donations. While they make an important contribution to biodiversity conservation, they are not a perfect answer to market failure in nature conservation. For example, to the extent that conservation NGOs provide public goods, they are subject to free-riding. The latter results in some individuals not contributing funds for the supply of the good (even though they have a demand for it) because they will be able to benefit from the contribution of others (see Chapter 3).

Legal restrictions are frequently imposed by governments on private use of natural resources in order to promote nature conservation. For example, as already noted, bans may be placed on the sale and use of particular species as well as the killing of them in an attempt to conserve them. However, this will be ineffective if it does not address the fundamental cause of their disappearance. For example, a ban on the killing of koalas, pandas or orangutans will be ineffective as a conservation measure if the fundamental cause of their endangerment is the destruction of their habitat to make way for economic developments. On the other hand, legal restrictions on tree clearing on private property can be effective in helping to conserve particular wild species.

The question should also to be considered of whether market mechanisms result in the best achievable pattern of conservation of desired cultured organisms (including their wild relatives) and whether there is a case for supplementing this conservation of cultured organisms by nonmarket mechanisms. In practice, some supplementation already occurs. For example, an internationally funded seed bank has been set up in Greenland to help conserve the genetic diversity of plants and some subsidies are provided in the European Union to help conserve rare breeds of livestock. The economic value of such policies is hard to determine given the uncertainties of future benefits. However, these policies appear to be a reaction to possible private failures in conservation. These failures can arise due to uncertainty, the high cost and difficulties involved in enforcing property rights in any genetic material conserved, and the existence of synergies in biodiversity conservation. The latter implies that the economic benefits from conserving a diversity of life forms is greater than the sum of the benefits that can be appropriated by individual conservationists from each of these forms. It is also greater than the sum of the benefits from conserving individual species or varieties of life forms. This synergy makes managing biodiversity conservation a very complex problem indeed.

10.5.5. *An overall perspective*

A clear message from the above analysis is that the management of biodiversity conservation in order to attain economic or other anthropogenic ends is complex and uncertain. It is also apparent that biodiversity conservation cannot be effectively addressed by a single type of policy, such as relying just on the strengthening of market mechanisms. A mixed (heterodox) policy approach is needed which relies on the use of both market and nonmarket mechanisms. However, it is unrealistic to expect that humankind will find an optimal policy solution to biodiversity management as the problem is too complex. Possibly the best that can be hoped for is to avoid some of the worst outcomes that could eventuate if no conscious human effort is made to conserve biodiversity.

10.6. Human Development of the Cultured Genetic Stock Including Genetically Engineered Organisms

10.6.1. *General features*

At the same time as humans have been responsible for the loss of a major part of the global genetic stock, they have also developed new genetic material (which is unlikely to have come into existence without human intervention). This feature was highlighted by Fig. 10.1. Furthermore, human activities have caused genetic changes in the wild stock which would have otherwise not occurred, or which would have occurred at a slower rate in the absence of human activities.

Over a very long period, humans have domesticated and cultured wild biological stock that appeared to be amenable to this process and have by selective breeding obtained variations in this stock which have increased its suitability for culture as judged by human desires. This has been a relatively slow process. At the same time as this has occurred, humans have modified environmental and resource conditions to better suit the cultured organisms they have produced and they have developed an array of techniques to support their culture. These changes have on the whole been far reaching because they have in turn often altered human cultural and social relationships. Consequently, interdependence has occurred between the pattern of ecological change or biological evolution and the nature of human societies. In other words, coevolution has occurred (Norgaard, 1994). In the past, the processes of coevolutionary change appear to have been fairly gradual, but they have accelerated in modern times. This has created fears that due to larger ecological leaps in shorter periods of time, the outcome could be one of ecological disaster accompanied by traumatic social impacts (Norgaard, 1994; Tisdell, 2000).

The advent of genetic engineering has fanned these fears. The creation of a GMO involves, as a rule, a major leap in the stock of genetic material and often involves genetic changes that would have had virtually no chance of evolving naturally. GMOs are created in laboratories and highly controlled environments. Outside these environments, there is often considerable uncertainty about their potential impacts, particularly in the long run. Furthermore, the introduction of GMOs can contribute to societal changes by favoring the development of large agricultural enterprises involved in factory-type farming serviced by large biotechnology companies. However, the nature of their developments depends on the type of institutional arrangements made for the development and use of GMOs, for example, the type of property rights in GMOs. This aspect is discussed below.

It is useful to consider the general relationship between human-activated environmental change and alterations in the stock of living things. This is illustrated in Fig. 10.3. Human changes to environments (which include biological changes as well as physical ones, including chemical ones) result in reactions by the existing stock of living things (cultured or non-cultured). This is because their set of environmental opportunities creates an initial disequilibrium (or variation in the path of dynamic change) and subsequently leads to alterations in the stock of living things. A new set of living things evolves or comes into existence. This interdependence is unavoidable and arises both for human selection of organisms and for their genetic engineering, except that the speed and extent of environmental change is much greater in the latter case than in the former one. In the case of biological organisms developed by humans or extensively used by them,

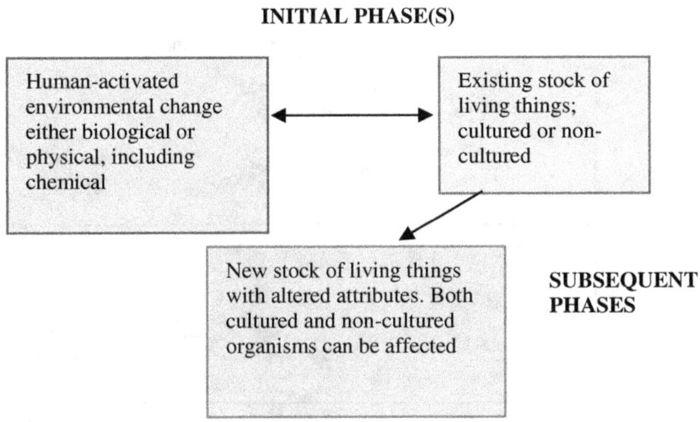

Fig. 10.3. Changed environmental conditions brought about by human activity (either of a biological or a non-biological nature) trigger alterations in the biological stock and its attributes. Human environmental impacts cannot be divorced from changes in the biological world and often have uncertain long-term consequences.

their efficiency or effectiveness tends to decline with the passage of time as they are increasingly exposed to other organisms which react to their abundance. For example, increased use of antibiotics leads to increasing disease resistance because of natural selection for the more resistant germs and new openings are also provided for mutations of germs.

Although humans can and have altered the biological world, there are limits on what they can achieve and on the economic optimality of the new life forms they can create. This is just as true for genetic engineering of organisms as for their human selection by means of purposive breeding. In both instances, what can be achieved depends on the stock of available genetic material and on scientific constraints. Usually, an economics type of problem is also encountered.

The type of economic problem that is likely to be encountered can be illustrated in Fig. 10.4. In this example, line *ABCD* represents changes in the traits of a species of tree used for paper production (for instance, a poplar species in China), that can be achieved by genetic manipulation. Trait y (the lignin content of the trees) can be reduced, but this results in an increase in an undesirable trait, x, which may be

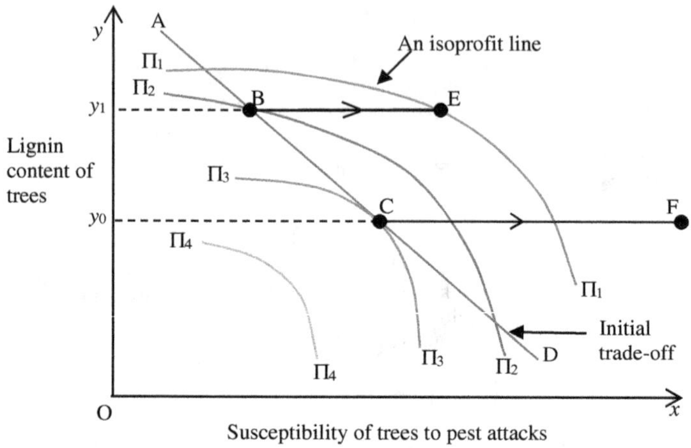

Fig. 10.4. By genetic engineering or other means, it may be initially possible to make the trade-off in traits indicated by line *ACD*. Given the isoprofit indicated, the combination at *C* would initially seem to be optimal. But this may not be biologically sustainable since it is achieved by changing the nature of the tree stock. With the passage of time, pests may adapt to this environmental change and in subsequent periods, a dynamic shift from *C* to *F* may occur. In the long run, the situation is less economic than originally, less profit is to be earned at *F* than *B*.

the susceptibility of the trees to insect damage or wind damage. Other things held equal, a reduction in lignin content is desirable because it lowers the cost of paper production. Suppose that the initial lignin content of the trees and their susceptibility to pests corresponds to point *B*. Taking into account the economic benefits of lowered lignin content and the costs of lower pest resistance of the trees, it would be most economic if the trade-off relationship *ABD* applies and the cost of genetic manipulation itself is ignored, to lower the lignin content of trees from y_1 to y_0. The optimum economic combination corresponds to point *C* given that the curves designated by $\Pi_1\Pi_1$, $\Pi_2\Pi_2$, $\Pi_3\Pi_3$, and $\Pi_4\Pi_4$ are isoprofit curves. Profits are higher for movements toward the origin of this figure.

However, the initial trade-off is likely to be unsustainable because of environmental change. In subsequent periods, pests may adapt to the lower lignin content of trees and eventually a shift from point *C* to *F* may occur. Profitability is then lower than at the original point *B*.

Even if there happened to be some increase in pestilence with the lignin content held constant at y_1 (say resulting in a shift from B to E with the passage of time) the eventual consequence of the genetic manipulation would be reduced profitability, compared to a situation of no manipulation. Now it might be claimed that it would always be possible to revert to situation where trees have lignin content corresponding to y_1 if some of the trees were retained. Yet that is by no means certain because, for example, the change may have resulted in the evolution of pests more able to attack wood with a higher lignin content. The problem of path dependence limits reversibility. That is not to say that irreversibility will always be a problem, but to emphasize that the issues involved are more complex than appears to be the case at first sight.

10.6.2. *Property rights in genetic material and in methods of engineering genetic material*

In the absence of legal protection of rights to use genetic material and in techniques to produce new genetic material, excluding others from their use is extremely difficult to achieve, even though sometimes secrecy may provide protection for a time to those who possess these things. Because property rights in biological material are insecure in the absence of legal protection, economic incentives to conserve and develop this material are weak. Therefore, in modern times greater legal protection has been given to such material with the aim of helping in some cases to conserve it and in other cases, to encourage the development of new genetic material.

Legal rights granted in such material and methods for the production of GMOs vary with jurisdictions. Two common methods of protection are laws for plant variety protection and patent laws. Usually, protection of new plant varieties applies to new varieties developed by human selection and the period of property rights is for a relatively short period of time. Patent protection is normally for a longer period and usually applies to techniques used to produce GMOs. However, in some jurisdictions the exclusive property rights granted by a patent for GMOs not only applies to new techniques developed for their production, but also extends to the seeds or propagules able to be produced by the use of the technique. This is the position in the United States, for example, but in China patent rights only apply to techniques for the production of GMOs not the seeds produced. The degree of monopoly power provided by plant variety rights is much weaker than in the case of patents. Monopoly powers bestowed on patentees can be particularly strong where they have property rights both to techniques for producing GMOs and the propagators produced by their application, as in the United States.

The economic rationale for such legal systems of protection varies. One view is that the granting of a temporary monopoly is necessary to provide economic incentives for research and development and innovation, and that progress in these areas will bring economic benefits exceeding any loss in economic benefits due to the granting of monopoly for a limited duration. However, this favorable result is by no means guaranteed. Patents for GMOs may lead to economic exploitation by patentees, favor large multinational companies and alter societal structures in undesirable ways as well as increasing ecological hazards and health problems. Gradual coevolution can be disrupted and social conflict can escalate, for example, due to adverse externalities between farmers growing GM crops and those cultivating non-GM crops. It is not possible to discuss all these views here, but see Tisdell (2008) for some further discussion.

The potential for monopoly pricing of GM seed can be illustrated by reference to Fig. 10.5. There the line marked DD represents the demand for a GM variety of seed given the alternative types of seed available. The line identified by MR is its corresponding marginal revenue line. Let the line P_1BC represent the per unit cost of supplying GM seed. Then a patentee of this seed will (in the absence of price discrimination) maximize profit by charging P_2 per unit of GM seed sold. Consequently, X_1 of this seed will be sold per unit of time. The patentee's profit per period is equal to the area of rectangle P_1BAP_2. This, however, is not ideal from an economics point of view. Collective economic benefit could be increased in principle by supplying X_2 of the GM seed and selling it at P_1. This would result in an increased benefit to buyers of the seed of an amount equivalent to the area of the dotted triangle BKA. In principle, a potential Paretian improvement

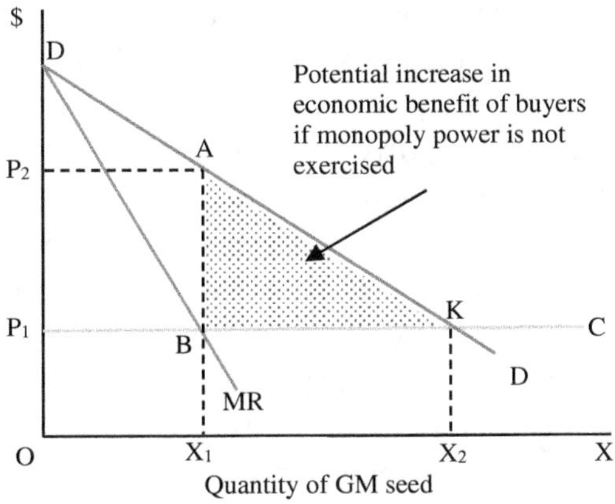

Fig. 10.5. Although the patent system provides an economic incentive for technical progress and innovation, it does not *minimize* economic scarcity, even though paradoxically it may reduce economic scarcity. In the case illustrated, a patent for GM seed results in it being priced at P_2 per unit because of market power bestowed by the patent. Given the *existence* of the GM seed, economic scarcity can be potentially reduced by an amount equivalent to the dotted area. However, most policies which would achieve this would remove all incentive to develop the GM seed.

is possible because buyers could compensate the patentee for the extra cost of supplying X_2 rather than X_1 of the seed and be better-off after having done so.

It could, however, be argued that while the situation illustrated in Fig. 10.5 in which the patentee exercises his/her monopoly power is not ideal economically, it is nevertheless economically preferable to a situation in which the GM seed does not exist. It may only be as a result of offering the possibility of above normal profits that sufficient economic incentive is given to develop the GM product and market it. Furthermore, it could be argued that after all, farmers have the free choice of using existing seed or the new GM seed. If they choose the GM seed, then they consider this to be a better economic choice. While this can be accepted, there are still potential problems. First, all farmers may switch to GM seed and the alternative seed may be lost permanently. Secondly, the patentee could engage in predatory pricing thereby driving substitutes out of existence and subsequently strengthening his or her monopoly. The loss of traditional varieties of crops due to inroads made by the advent of GM varieties may result in long-term lack of agricultural sustainability as GM varieties become less fit biologically with the passage of time.

Given the legal costs involved in the enforcement of patents and the cost of enforcing rights generally in patented biological materials and methods, the patent system usually favors larger sized companies rather than small- or medium-sized enterprises. Patentees of GM seeds also usually find it most economic to contract with larger sized farming units because this lowers their per unit transaction costs (Tisdell, 2008). Therefore, this system of granting property rights influences the industrial structure of societies and this in turn, impacts on social relationships. Furthermore, given that GMOs can give rise to significant environmental spillovers and *may* have adverse health impacts, it is hazardous to leave their development and use solely in private hands. For this reason, most governments regulate the development and use of GMOs to some extent.

10.7. Concluding Observations

Although the concept of biodiversity is multidimensional and, therefore, difficult to measure precisely, there is no doubt that the net impact of economic changes and activity has been to reduce biodiversity significantly, particularly in modern times. At the same time as there has been a loss in overall biodiversity, humans have developed new life forms by engaging in human (rather than natural) selection and more recently, in genetic engineering.

It was not until 1982 that the first product from genetic engineering was marketed. This was human insulin used for treating diabetes and was produced by a genetically engineered bacteria (Ochoa, 2007, p. 28). Many other genetically engineered products have followed such as herbicide-resistant soy beans and canola (rape), and insect-resistant maize and cotton, and others are in the pipeline. Therefore, human activity is now shaping the nature of the biological world to a larger extent than before; some might even suggest to an alarming extent. Apart from studying how human actions, including economic activity, alter biodiversity and the nature of the living world, it is also important to consider how human beings *should* act in relation to other living things. Should human beings be guided in their actions only by their own narrow economic self-interest, or should they be guided by broader principles? Many philosophers argue in favor of less human-centered views than have commonly been advocated in economics. However, if an anthropogenic stance is taken, several issues arise. These include the following: What is the possible economic value of maintaining biodiversity? Taking into account anthropogenic factors that cause changes in biodiversity (in the biological stock generally), are there reasons to expect that economic systems will lead to economically desirable alterations in the biological stock? Several reasons why economic activity may fail to achieve this end have been outlined. Three types of policy approaches to promoting biodiversity conservation have been identified, namely policies to restrict market operations policies to encourage market operations and policies to make biological conservation independent of market operations. As shown, depending on the underlying circumstances, each of these approaches is economically appropriate. Therefore, in practice, one might expect a mixed portfolio of these policies to be most appropriate for promoting biodiversity conservation.

Rational human development of the genetic stock raises many difficult issues not least of which is uncertainty about the long-term biological consequences of this development given the complexities of the interactions involved. Environmental changes of a biological or non-biological nature brought about by humans normally lead to uncertain variations in the biological stock, particularly in the long run. This reduces the scope for rational human choices and has heightened fears about the possible consequences of new GMOs.

While genetic engineering can provide substantial anthropogenic benefits (as the development of methods for supplying insulin indicates), the potential for genetic engineering is subject to constraints as was demonstrated. For example, in developing one or several desirable traits of an organism, other desirable trait may have to be forgone. Consequently, problems of economic choice are involved. These choices are made difficult by the fact that the value of new traits may alter as other organisms react to the presence of the new engineered organism in the environment.

The development of genetic materials by humans is extremely dependent on the institutional framework of society because this affects the economic incentive for such development. In turn, this framework influences how the nature and structure of society itself evolves. Plant variety rights and patent protection are two social mechanisms that have been used in recent decades to provide economic incentives for the development of new genetic material (see Tisdell, 2017, Chapter 10). Patent protection for individuals or organizations that develop new GMOs and methods for the production of GMOs can have far reaching economic and social consequences, as well as cause substantial alterations in the global biological stock. It was pointed out that use of the patent system involves a dilemma because while it does not minimize economic scarcity, its operation may result in less scarcity than would otherwise exist. However, there are features associated with the granting of patents for GMOs that raise particular concerns. These include the possibility that they may be used in some cases as a means for predatory monopolization and the system may accelerate socially undesirable biodiversity loss. Other social issues can include lack of attention to negative environmental externalities; lack of harmonious coevolution due to the speed and magnitude of the changes involved; alterations in industrial structure believed by some to be socially undesirable, such as greater business concentration in the supply of biological materials accompanied by higher barriers to entry into the relevant industries, and the extension of factory-type farming. The above discussion indicates that while economic benefits can be obtained by developing the biological stock and managing biodiversity conservation, human beings are limited in their capacity to do this rationally. This is because of the occurrence of long-term uncertainties generated by environmental change, including biological developments. While reason is still valuable in considering the possible consequences of such changes, it would be foolish to believe that it will yield perfect answers about the long-term biological consequences of such changes and their economic implications.

10.8. Keywords

Anthropogenic effects on the biodiversity of cultured organisms; biodiversity; biodiversity and flexibility; biodiversity and options; biodiversity conservation policies divorced from markets; biodiversity measurement; CITES; coevolution; components of the genetic stock; convention on biological diversity; ecocentric objectives; genetically engineered organisms; GMOs; human selection of organisms by breeding; land ethic; market-limiting policies for biodiversity conservation; minimax gain; minimax regret; non-anthropogenic sources of biodiversity change; patents for GMOs; plant variety rights; pro-market policies for biodiversity conservation; safe minimum population of a species; safe minimum standard; synergies in conservation; trade-offs of traits in genetic engineering; variations in the genetic stock.

10.9. Questions for Review and Discussion

1. How do the operations of economic systems broadly influence the conservation of biodiversity? Why does the relationship between economics and biodiversity merit study?
2. What is biodiversity and what are the difficulties involved in measuring its extent?
3. The genetic stock consists of two main components. What are they? Do these components change with the passage of time?
4. Why can biodiversity have economic value? Is it always economically valuable?
5. Does uncertainty about the future economic value of organisms always favor the conservation of biodiversity? Discuss and in doing so, take into account game-theoretical models for decision-making under uncertainty.
6. Why do synergies between the diversity of living things increase the likelihood that market systems will be deficient in conserving biodiversity?

7. What types of non-anthropogenic factors can cause biodiversity to alter? Why are the biodiversity consequences of these factors difficult to predict?
8. Humans have had major impacts on the biological diversity of wild organisms. What have been the anthropogenic causes of this and to what extent has the loss of biological diversity been motivated by economic factors?
9. In what circumstances would it be appropriate to restrict market operations in order to promote biological conservation? What are the limitations of this policy?
10. In what circumstances can pro-market policies be beneficial in promoting biological conservation? What are the limitations of this approach?
11. Why are biodiversity conservation measures adopted that do not rely on market forces? Give examples.
12. Do you think that the market mechanism results in the best achievable pattern of ecological conservation? Why? Why is a mixed portfolio of policies likely to be required to promote biodiversity conservation?
13. Norgaard (1994) argues that coevolution is important? What did he have in mind? How might genetic engineering disrupt coevolution?
14. Explain how human-activated environmental change (whether biological or non-biological) may result in variations in the genetic composition of the biological stock. To what extent are the long-term consequences for biodiversity likely to be uncertain?
15. Discuss critically the view that the economic potential of genetic engineering is virtually unlimited. Why does genetic engineering raise issues involving economic choices?
16. Property rights in new genetic material are essential if private bodies are to be motivated to produce and market new genetic material. At the same time as such rights may result in a reduction in economic scarcity, they fail to minimize economic scarcity. How can this statement be explained?

17. What types of economic and biological dangers can potentially arise from granting patents for GMOs or for techniques to produce GMOs?
18. Humans are limited in their ability to rationally manage biodiversity. Why?

Readings and References

Balmford, A., A. Bruner, P. Cooper, R. Costanza, S. Farber, R.E. Green, M. Jenkins, P. Jefferiss, V. Jessamy, J. Madden, K. Munro, N. Myers, S. Naeem, J. Paavola, M. Rayment, S. Rosendo, J. Roughgarden, K. Trumper and R.K. Turner (2002). Economic reasons for conserving wild nature, *Science*, 297, 950. doi: 10.1126/science.1073947.

Bishop, R.C. (1978). Endangered species, irreversibility and uncertainty: The economics of a safe minimum standard, *American Journal of Agricultural Economics*, 60, 10–18. doi: 10.2307/1242715.

Ciriacy-Wantrup, S.V. (1968). *Resource Conservation: Economics and Policies*, 3rd edn. Division of Agricultural Science, University of California, Berkely, CA.

Gaston, K.J. and J.I. Spicer (2004). *Biodiversity: An Introduction*, Blackwell, Malden, MA.

Gould, S.J. (1989). *Wonderful Life: The Burgess Shale and the Nature of History*, Norton, New York.

Gould, S.J. (1990). *The Individuals in Darwin's World*, Edinburgh University Press, Edinburgh.

Gowdy, J.M. (1997). The value of biodiversity: Markets, society, and ecosystems, *Land Economics*, 73, 25–41. doi: 10.2307/3147075.

Harting, J.E. (1880). *British Animals Extinct Within Historic Times*, Trubner & Co., Ludgate Hill, London.

Kahn, J.R. (2005). *The Economic Approach to Environmental and Natural Resources*, 3rd edn. South-Western, Mason, Ohio, USA [Chapter 14].

Kretsch III, S., J.R. McNeill and C. Merchant (2004). *Encyclopedia of World Environmental History: A-E*, Routledge, New York.

Krutilla, J.V. (1967). Conservation reconsidered, *The American Economic Review*, 57, 777–786. doi: https://www.jstor.org/stable/1815368.

Leopold, A. (1933). *Game Management*, Scribner, New York.

Leopold, A. (1966). *A Sand County Almanac: With Other Essays on Conservation from Round River*, Oxford University Press, New York.

Ninan, K. (2007). *The Economics of Biodiversity Conservation*, Earthscan, London, Sterling, VA [Chapter 1].

Norgaard, R.B. (1994). *Development Betrayed*, Routledge, London.

Nunes, P.A.I.D., J.C.J.M. van den Bergh and P. Nijkamp (2003). *The Ecological Economics of Biodiversity: Methods and Applications*, Cheltenham, UK and Northampton, MA, USA.

Ochoa, G. (2007). *Science 101: Biology*, Harper Collins, New York.

Parker, D.M. and R. Stacey (1995). *Chaos, Management and Economics: The Implications of Non-Linear Thinking*, The Centre for Independent Studies, St Leonards, NSW, Australia.

Passmore, J.A. (1974). *Man's Responsibility for Nature: Ecological Problems and Western Traditions*, Duckworth, London.

Pearce, D. and D. Moran (1994). *The Economic Value of Biodiversity*, Earthscan, London [Chapter 1].

Swanson, T. (1994). *The International Regulation of Extinction*, New York University Press, New York.

Swanson, T. (1997). *Global Action for Biodiversity*, Earthscan, London.

Tietenberg, T. and L. Lewis (2018). *Environmental and Natural Resource Economics*, 11th edn. Routledge, New York and Abingdon, Oxon, UK [Chapter 13].

Tisdell, C.A. (1970). Implications of learning for economic planning, *Economic Planning* 10, 177–192. Reprinted in C.A. Tisdell (1996) Bounded Rationality and Economic Evolution. Edward Elgar, Cheltenham, UK and Brookfield, USA [Chapter 5].

Tisdell, C.A. (1996). *Bounded Rationality and Economic Evolution*, Edward Elgar, Cheltenham, UK and Brookfield, VT, USA.

Tisdell, C.A. (2000). Coevolution, agricultural practices and sustainability: Some major social and ecological issues, *International Journal of Agricultural Resources, Governance and Ecology*, 1, 6–16. doi: https://doi.org/10.1504/IJARGE.2000.000005.

Tisdell, C.A. (2003). Socioeconomic causes of loss of animal genetic diversity: Analysis and assessment, *Ecological Economics*, 45, 365–376. doi: 10.1016/S0921-8009(03)00091-0.

Tisdell, C.A. (2005). *Economics of Environmental Conservation*, 2nd edn. Edward Elgar, Cheltenham, UK and Northampton, MA, USA.

Tisdell, C.A. (2008). Economics, ecology and the development and use of GMOs: General considerations and biosafety issues, *Economics, Ecology and the Environment*, Working Paper No. 163. School of Economics, The University of Queensland, Brisbane, QLD, Australia.

Tisdell, C.A. (2015). *Sustaining Biodiversity and Ecosystem Functions: Economic Issues*, Edward Elgar, Cheltenham, UK and Northampton, MA, USA.

Tisdell, C.A. (2017). *Economics and Environmental Change: The Challenges We Face*, Edward Elgar, Cheltenham, UK, Northampton, MA, USA [Chapter 7].

Tisdell, C.A. and C. Wilson (2012). *Nature-based Tourism and Conservation: New Economic Insights and Case Studies*, Edward Elgar Publishing, Cheltenham, UK and Northampton, MA, USA.

Tisdell, C.A., H. Swarna Nantha and C. Wilson (2007). Conservation and use of the Hawksbill Turtle — public valuation and attitudes: An Australian case study, *Pacific Conservation Biology*, 13, 35–46.

Chapter 11

Problems Involving the Availability of Natural Resource Stocks and Flows

11.1. Introduction

The use and the availability of both natural resource stocks and flows make a major contribution to economic production, its sustainability and the well-being of humankind. Collectively, natural resource stocks constitute natural capital but they vary considerably in their nature. Some are depleted by their economic use and are not renewable (for example, mineral deposits) whereas others (for example, living resources) have the ability to regenerate subject to ecological limits. For example, humans can extinguish wild species by destroying their habitats or by over harvesting them. The activities of humans have been instrumental in the extermination of many wild species and these biodiversity losses are continuing.

To date, the economic literature has paid more attention to natural resource stocks (natural capital) than to natural resource flows. However, more attention should be given to physical resource flows (such as rainfall, water flows, the amount of sunlight, wind and temperatures) because they are major influences (or potential influences) on the level of economic production, its sustainability and human welfare. These flows are of particular economic interest today because of increasing demand to use them and some are becoming economically scarce, e.g. water flows. In addition, human-induced climate change is altering the nature and availability of these flows with potentially negative economic consequences.

This chapter (which supplements material in Chapters 6, 7 and 10) begins by briefly considering how historically economists have altered their emphasis on natural resources as important contributors to economic production, and then outlines (in general terms) how the reliance of humankind on natural resources for economic activities has altered over the ages. Subsequently, scarcity issues involving the following are raised and analyzed in turn:

- flows and stocks of natural biotic resources;
- flows of natural abiotic resources; and
- stocks of non-renewing abiotic resource stocks, e.g. minerals.

Natural resource stocks and flows are quite diverse. From a sustainability point of view, there are many different issues that need to be resolved in assessing their availability and their economic worth. Questions which need to be considered include the following. How scarce are individual types of natural stocks and flows? How is that scarcity to be measured? How accurate are the available measurements? What is likely to be their future availability and scarcity? What is their relative economic value? Economic assessment of their worth requires both their quantities and their economic values to be taken into account. Answers to the above questions vary with the type of natural resource being considered.

11.2. The Emphasis of Economists on the Economic Importance of Natural Resources has Varied Historically

Economists have varied in the amount of attention they have given to natural resources as contributors to economic production and its sustainability, as well as to ways in which non-consumptive natural resources (such as those present in national parks) can enhance well-being. Even today, economic opinions differ about the economic importance of conserving natural resources and natural environments.

Particularly during the 20th century, mainstream economists paid little or no attention to the role played by natural resources in economic activity and its sustainability. Some prominent economic models focused only on labor and man-made capital as contributors to economic production and growth (Solow, 1956; Swan, 1956). At a later stage, technological progress was added to these models as a significant influence on economic growth (Solow, 1957).

In these models, the fact is overlooked that the manufacture of man-made capital depends to a major extent on the supply of natural resources. In addition, the supply of labor (which is partly a function of the level of population) also ultimately relies on the availability of natural resources. This is because the use of some natural resources are essential for food production (they are critical resources) and they influence the quantity and quality of food supplies. This is true even though human knowledge and man-made capital play a major role in agricultural food production today. The supply of chemical fertilizers used in modern agriculture, water and agricultural man-made equipment as well as energy supplies all depend on the availability of natural resources.

Despite the lack of attention of mainstream economists in the 20th century to the availability of natural resources (including the quality of natural environments), ecological economists and others began to express concerns in the second half of the 20th century about the depletion of these resources and their environmental deterioration. Furthermore, the United Nations began to explore the possibility that natural resource depletion and destruction, as well as deteriorating natural environments, could threaten sustainable economic development and human well-being. This issue was considered by the first UN Conference on Sustainable Development held in Stockholm in 1972 which was followed by the UN commissioned Brundtland Report, *Our Common Future* (*World Commission on Environment and Development, 1987*). This, and several subsequent publications and activities of the United Nations, have helped to keep the spotlight on the importance of natural resources (in all their diverse forms) as significant contributors to the level and sustainability of economic production and as influences on human well-being. Diverse forms of natural resources include biological resources and the natural environments on which they depend, as well as physical natural resources.

11.3. The Nature and the Extent of Economic Reliance on Natural Resources has Varied Historically

Since *Homo sapiens* evolved in Africa, some 200,000 years ago, the nature and extent of the contributions of natural resources to the economies of humans have varied considerably. The economies of hunter and gatherers depended heavily on the use of living natural resources. The nature and the extent of this dependence began to alter once agricultural production started to develop at first in Asia Minor some 10,000 years ago and later elsewhere. Subsequently, metal production developed (for instance, the production of copper and bronze, silver and iron) prior to the first century BC. Economic reliance on the use of non-renewable resources began to accelerate once metal production started.

This trend was magnified when the Industrial Revolution commenced. Demand for metals increased greatly as did the demand for fossil fuels (coal and then oil and later natural gas). Industrial economies found it increasingly difficult to meet their energy needs by relying on renewable non-fossil sources of energy and found that it was more economic to increase their dependence on natural non-renewable fossil energy resources compared to fuels such as wood. As well, the use of wind and flowing water power declined.

The massive increase in economic production which began around 300 years ago as a result of the Industrial Revolution (which was made possible by technological innovations and advances in knowledge) may have led to the belief that the limited availability of natural resources (and natural environments) is not a significant constraint on economic production and its sustainability. Hence, this may explain the development of economic growth models (of the type noted above) that do not consider the availability of natural resources and the state of natural environments (such as natural ecosystems, which can also be regarded as natural resources) as significant influences on the possibility of economic growth. It is now clear that the environmental effects of many current economic growth patterns are making it increasingly challenging to sustain economic production and growth (for example, as a result of human-induced climate change) and that there is growing scarcity of natural resources in many parts of the world, such as water.

Furthermore, even if fossil fuels, such as coal, are not in short supply, their use impacts negatively and substantially on the quality of natural environments, thereby threatening the quality of life and the long-term sustainability of economic production.

11.4. Stocks and Flows of Natural Biotic Resources: Initial Perspectives

11.4.1. *Biological natural resources and the multiple dimensions of natural resource stocks and flows*

Let us begin by considering the stocks and flows of natural living resources. The stocks of biological natural resources depend on the natural environments in which they are embedded. These natural environments include the stock of physical resources, the flow of resources such as sunlight and rainfall, as well as the array of living resources of which they are a part. In other words, they depend on the natural ecosystems to which they belong. When these ecosystems alter, this usually alters the natural biodiversity within them. For example, substantial changes in climate in a region can be expected to result in the loss of some wild species and their replacement by others. Widespread and rapid climate change can be expected to result in an overall loss in biodiversity.

Stocks of wild organisms depend both on natural resource stocks and flows. In addition, there is another important connection between the stocks and flows of living resources which has been emphasized by natural scientists. This involves the relationship between the rate of growth of the biomass of these species (a flow) and their population levels (a stock). For some species (for example, fish species), this can

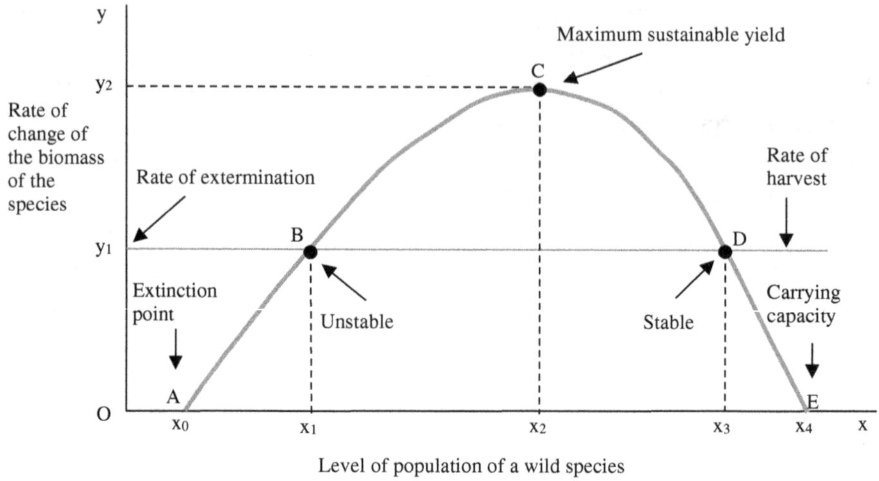

Fig. 11.1. A simple model to illustrate the renewability attributes of the population of a wild species, e.g. a species of fish.

be represented by a unimodal function (frequently a quadratic one) similar to that shown in Fig. 11.1 by the curve ABCDE, assuming a stable environment.

11.4.2. *The rate of change of the biomass of wild species as a function of their level of population*

The type of relationship shown in Fig. 11.1 should only be regarded as providing a preliminary introduction to this subject. Given the relationship shown, the maximum sustainable yield of a species (such as a fish species), if it is harvested, is y_2 and occurs when its level of population is x_2. The maximum level of the population that the environment is able to support (its carrying capacity) is x_4. Furthermore, this relationship indicates that if the level of population of the species is reduced to x_0 or to less than this, it fails to regenerate and becomes extinct.

The following additional observations can be made by reference to Fig. 11.1. The maximum rate of increase in the biomass of the focal species is y_2 and occurs when the population of the species is reduced from x_4 to x_2. If the species is being harvested (or efforts are being made to exterminate it) at the rate of y_1 per period of time, a stable and an unstable equilibrium exists. The equilibrium at D is stable. After any small deviation from it, the population will return to x_3 or if multiple small deviations occur, it will fluctuate around x_3. On the other hand, if the system arrives at point B, the system is unstable. A small reduction in the population of the focal species, which results in its population being less than x_1, will result in it being extinguished if the rate of extermination or harvest remains at y_1. On the other hand, a small increase in the population of the species when the system is at point B will result in the population of the species increasing, gravitating towards the stable equilibrium D.

If a species is valued only for its physical (tangible) yield (as is basically true of some wild fish stocks, for instance, tuna, but not all marine animals, for example, whales), then it can be inferred from Fig. 11.1 that if the effort in exploiting the species is such that its population is reduced to less than x_2, this results in a less economic outcome than if this effort is not so great and the population of the species exceeds x_2. For example, suppose that as a result of harvesting effort, the population of a species is reduced from x_3 to x_1. The yield from the species in both situations (D and B) is the same (y_1) but the cost of the harvest is lower in the former case than in the latter. This is because if the species is mobile (for example, a fish species), its density on average is higher in the former case than in the latter case. As pointed out in Chapter 4, open access to the exploitation of a species can result in its population being driven below x_2. The cost of harvesting the resource in relation to its yield is consequently higher than it need be. Hence, in these circumstances, an institutional economic failure occurs.

Note also that the value and nature of the yield and the rate of increase in the biomass of a harvested species is affected in most cases by the effort in harvesting. For example, larger and more mature fish may be removed first as a result of harvesting effort. As a result, the proportion of small (undersized) and immature fish in the population is liable to increase. These smaller fish can be expected to be of lower commercial value than larger fish and the biomass of the species is likely to be less prolific in its reproduction. Furthermore, if the growth rate of individual members of the exploited species as a function of their age is of a reversed U-shape, increasing the proportion of juveniles in the population can reduce the growth rate of the biomass below its maximum attainable level. Therefore, the rate of change in the biomass of the species (and its value of its flow) is likely to be skewed declining more sharply to the left of its maximum point C in Fig. 11.1 compared to its rate of decline to the right of this point. The composition of the biomass alters as effort increases and so too does its rate of change.

The relationship shown in Fig. 11.1 gives rise to a backward bending supply curve like the one shown in Fig. 10.2 if there is open access to the harvesting of a species. As discussed in relation to Fig. 10.2, a high level of commercial demand for a species is liable to lead to its extinction rather than to its conservation in this case. The market reaction is a perverse one due to the presence of open access to the resource.

Note that the analysis based on Fig. 11.1 assumes that the curve of the rate of growth in the biomass of the focal species does not shift. However, it may shift periodically or relatively permanently for several reasons, all of which are a consequence of environmental changes altering its available habitat. These may be due to natural changes or due to human activities. As a result, the level of the minimum viable population (MVP) of the species (which arguably is a level of population in Fig. 11.1 slightly in excess of x_0) is liable to alter. If the environment becomes less favorable for a species, its MVP could increase and the species may require greater availability of suitable habitat for its survival. In fact, in the worst-case scenario, the species could even disappear because the changed available environment is too inhospitable for its survival. For example, due to permanent climate change, no habitat may remain where it is able to survive.

11.5. Stocks and Flows of Natural Biological Resources: Further Perspectives

11.5.1. *Natural biological stocks are not solely valued for their flow of physical (tangible) products*

Some textbooks on natural resource economics (particularly those published in the 20th century) focus mainly on the physical yields that natural biological resources are able to supply and their market value. It is widely recognized today that the perspective is too narrow because it only considers their consumptive direct use value. The analysis in the previous section based on Fig. 11.1 reflects this type of approach to the assessment of natural biological resource stocks. Although this 'traditional' approach is useful for considering some very important issues involving the conservation of natural resource stocks, it fails to take account of values other than direct consumptive use value, many of which have increased in economic and social importance in modern times. In other words, the traditional approach does not take account of the varied types of values placed on the conservation of living resources, as well as in some cases, the conservation of natural landforms. In this regard, the total economic valuation framework provides a more comprehensive guide for valuing natural resources.

11.5.2. *An outline of the total economic valuation framework for valuing natural biological resources*

Table 11.1 sets out the main components of the total economic valuation framework for valuing natural biotic resources (see, for example, Pascual *et al.*, 2010). It can, however, be applied to the stocks of other types of resources, including the conservation of human-developed heritage resources and valued landforms. As far as natural biological resources are concerned, the relevance of the different types of values can be expected to vary with the type or types of species or ecosystems being assessed for conservation. Furthermore, all of these types of values should be kept in mind when assessing the worth of conserving natural resources even if all are not susceptible to (reliable) monetary valuation, or if the relevance of monetary valuations are contested.

Direct consumptive use values of biological natural resources seem to be most closely related to the flows they generate whereas direct non-consumptive use values of these resources seem to depend to a considerable extent only on their stocks. On the other hand, indirect use values of abiotic resources appear to be influenced both by their stocks and by the flows they generate. Option values basically relate to stocks, that is to the conservation of biota and natural resources stocks for potential future use. Bequest and other altruistic values may relate to both natural resource stocks and their flows. Existence values seem to relate primarily to the conservation of stocks.

The categorization of values listed in Table 11.1 may give the impression that they are exclusive entities or nearly so. However, this should not be inferred. For example, individuals may obtain value (satisfaction) from the direct and the indirect use of a living natural resource and as well gain satisfaction from knowing that this conservation will benefit others alive now or expected to live in the future. Various combinations of the types of values listed in Table 11.1 can contribute to the total (economic) value of a living natural resource.

In addition, note that the distinction between the consumptive and non-consumptive use of living natural resources is not discrete. For example, non-consumptive nature-based tourism or recreation (which may seem to be passive) can have negative effects on the conservation of the natural environmental resource-base on which these living resources depend. For instance, inadequately regulated tourism based on the viewing of marine turtles and their hatchlings can be detrimental to the conservation of sea turtle populations. For example, lights from tourist activities generated by turtle-based tourism development can result in turtle hatchlings moving inland (where they perish) rather than going to the ocean.

11.5.3. *The economic relevance of the minimum viable population of a species*

The concept of the MVPs of a species (the minimum population levels considered to be necessary for their survival) is widely used by ecologists as a guide to decisions about conserving wild species. These values are considered to be tipping points for the survival or extinction of wild species. Once the level of population of a species falls below its MVP, its extinction is posited to occur. Often sustaining the MVP of a species is seen as both necessary and sufficient for its survival. Ciriacy-Wantrup (1968) argued that a strong economic case exists for conserving all wild species (at least) at the safe minimum of their populations. He argued that the cost of conserving a safe minimum population of each

Table 11.1. The total economic value framework for assessing the worth of conserving a natural biological resource.

Type of values	Attributes and examples
USE VALUES	
Direct use values	
• **Consumptive**	Resource extracted from natural ecosystems and consumed or utilized by humans e.g. wild caught fish.
• **Non-consumptive**	Passive (non-extractive) use of natural resources e.g. passive nature-based tourism and recreation in national parks and protected areas; spiritual/cultural worth, contribution to knowledge.
Indirect use value	The valued ecological and environmental consequences of the presence of the natural resource, e.g. the value of an individual wild species or group of species in providing sustenance or habitats for other valued wild species, the role of natural ecosystems in providing environmental services.
Option value	The benefits that may be derived from using a natural resource in the future if it is conserved. Its potential future use value, e.g. the possible future use of natural flora for medicinal purposes if this flora is conserved or its potential value for providing genetic material for development of crops.
NON-USE VALUES	
Bequest value	The value to those alive now of knowing that future individuals will have access to a natural resource if it is conserved. This is a purely altruistic motive because the beneficiaries are individuals who will benefit after the valuers are dead.

(*Continued*)

Table 11.1. (*Continued*)

Type of values	Attributes and examples
The value of altruism towards those alive now (Altruistic value)	The value of knowing that others alive now will enjoy the resource or its benefits if it is conserved. This may involve only partial altruism because individuals may use the resource themselves but get extra benefit (utility) from knowing that others benefit from its availability.
Existence value	The value obtained purely from knowing that a living natural resource exists independently of its use or of other values. For example, it may reflect the view that other species have the right to exist independently of their value to human beings.

species is relatively low in relation to the potential economic benefits of doing so. This view (if accepted) provides a strong economic case for conserving nature. Nevertheless, there are limitations to this approach.

First, the safe minimum population level (or the MVP) of a species is not unique. There may be some levels at which the species will disappear for certain but at higher levels, its survival is of a probabilistic nature (Hohl and Tisdell, 1993). Second, it is not always the case that the (opportunity) cost of conserving a species in the wild is low. In addition, the likely economic benefit of conserving some of these species could be low. For example, orangutans need a very large natural territory to support their estimated MVP and in some cases, the opportunity cost of preserving this territory (in terms of the net value of crops and forestry forgone) can be high. Consequently, given the economic analysis of Ciriacy-Wantrup, the economic argument for their conservation can be weak. Therefore, it is necessary in such cases to depend on non-economic arguments to bolster the case for their conservation.

Although some formal attention was paid to the view of Ciriacy-Wantrup in Section 10.3 of this book using a simple game-theory approach in order to discuss the economics of biodiversity conservation, it is worthwhile exploring this approach further in the present context. This is because Ciriacy-Wantrup's analysis provides one type of application of the **precautionary principle**. It is often asserted that the precautionary motive provides a strong reason for conserving natural biota. However, analysis indicates that the desirability of doing this is not straightforward. This matter involves decision-making under conditions of uncertainty. It can be shown that being precautious does not necessarily favor conservation. Whether it does or not, depends on the structure of the possible payoff (net benefits) from conserving or not conserving as well as the goals (objectives) adopted for choice under conditions of uncertainty. This can be illustrated by a simple example.

Assume that a society has two alternative strategies, a_1 and a_2. Strategy a_1 is to conserve the safe minimum population of a wild species by providing it with adequate habitat for this purpose. Strategy a_2 is not to conserve the MVP of the species and to alter its habitat for the purpose of economic development. Two possible future states of nature, s_1 and s_2, are considered to be possible. If s_1 prevails, the economic benefit from conserving the species exceeds the benefit from not doing so. If s_2 prevails, the economic benefit from conserving the species is less than if its habitat is destroyed for economic development to occur. An example of this set of possibilities is given in Table 11.2 which shows the hypothetical net benefits (payoffs) to a society of its alternative conservation choices (a_1 and a_2) and the different states of nature which may prevail.

In the case shown in Table 11.2, the maximum **possible** economic benefit from conserving the focal species (a_1) is much higher than that for destroying its habitat to make way for economic development (a_2). On the other hand, it is also possible that the economic benefit from choosing a_1 could be lower than if a_2 is chosen. In these circumstances, if a society wants to minimize its economic risk (is very cautious or risk-averse), it should opt for using the available habitat for development purposes, that is choose strategy a_2. This is the maximin gain strategy,

Table 11.2. A matrix of the various payoffs that a society is assumed to obtain depending on its choice of strategy (a_1 or a_2) for conserving a species and whether state of nature s_1 or s_2 prevails.

	s_1	s_2	
(Conserve species) a_1	10	1	1
(Do not conserve) a_2	3	3	3*

that is the one that maximizes the minimum possible gain from each of its available strategies. This choice results in a certain payoff of 3 in this case. Consequently, Ciriacy-Wantrup's assumptions and the precautionary principle do not favor the conservation of nature in the cases just analyzed.

However, it is also possible that a society might be guided by the opportunity cost or regret it will experience if it does not conserve a species or a similar resource. If so, given the possibilities listed in Table 11.2, the outcome is now supportive of Ciriacy-Wantrup's recommendation and the precautionary principle if a minimax regret strategy is adopted.

The values in the regret matrix shown in Table 11.3 are the possible opportunity costs corresponding to the choices of strategies in Table 11.2. A society might want to make a choice which minimizes the maximum of its possible regret, that is adopt a minimax regret strategy. In the case shown in Table 11.3, this happens if it decides to conserve the focal species. This is because the level of its maximum possible regret (its opportunity cost) is 7 when it does not make this choice but only 2 if it does make this choice. Hence, the optimal choice about conservation and economic development is the opposite in this case to that in the previous case.

Decision making about the desirability of nature conservation under conditions of uncertainty is sensitive to the types of criteria that are adopted, as well as payoff structures. Empirical information needs to be gathered about the types of criteria that societies want to adopt. Many additional criteria for decision making under uncertainty have

Table 11.3. The regret (opportunity cost) matrix corresponding to the matrix in Table 11.2.

	s_1	s_2	
(Conserve species) a_1	0	2	2*
(Do not conserve) a_2	7	0	7

been considered in the economic literature. These (along with their limitations) are briefly reviewed in Tisdell (1968, Chapter 2).

Note that in practice, the opportunity cost of not conserving a species or a natural environment may never be really known. This is because its loss may mean that the value of not having it cannot be assessed. There is also the problem that the existence of many naturally occurring species is still unknown and yet their future value could be considerable. This can provide a basis for being more favorable to the conservation of whole natural ecosystems than otherwise. This is because the expected value of conserving these systems is greater than would be assessed on the basis of their known species and the possible value of conserving solely these known species.

11.5.4. *A simple model illustrating the relevance of the opportunity cost of conserving wild species by preserving their habitat*

The opportunity costs of conserving wild species and natural ecosystems are often neglected in ecological studies advocating their conservation. However, rational choice about nature conservation requires that the trade-offs involved in conserving species and ecosystems needs to be taken into account. This can be illustrated by the simple model shown in Fig. 11.2.

Suppose initially that the population level of a wild species is y_2 and that it is supported by an area of suitable habitat of x_3. The population carrying capacity of the available habitat is y_2. However, this habitat may be altered for economic development.

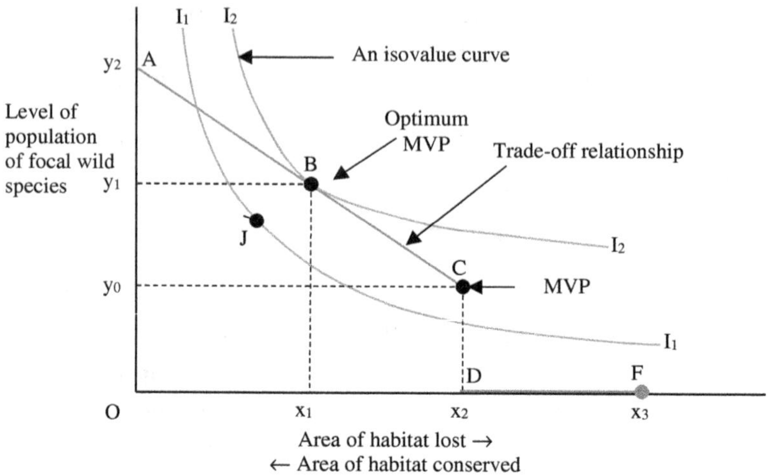

Fig. 11.2. An illustration of a choice problem involving the conservation of a species given that its conservation incurs an opportunity cost.

This alteration results in a loss of habitat and reduces the level of the population of the focal species. The relationship between the level of the population of the focal species and the loss in the area of its available habitat (initially, x_3) might be like that represented by the discontinuous relationship ABCDF. In this case, y_0 is the MVP of the focal species and corresponds to $x = x_2$. For $x > x_2$, $y = 0$. The species becomes extinct when more than x_2 of its habitat is destroyed.

In order to make an informed choice about conserving the focal species, it is necessary to consider the value placed on its conservation compared to depriving it of habitat for the purposes of economic development. The valuation function involved is represented by a series of isovalue curves, that is indifference curves of which two possible ones are illustrated by the curves identified by $I_1 I_1$ and $I_2 I_2$ in Fig. 11.2. It is assumed that a relevant society would like to have a greater population of the focal species as well as use more of its habitat for development purposes. Consequently, any point to the right of that on $I_1 I_1$ is preferred by this society. For example, the combination B is preferred to J. Combinations on the isovalue curve $I_2 I_2$ are preferred to those on $I_1 I_1$. The curves are strictly convex indicating that there is a reduction in the marginal willingness to accept a decline in the population of the focal species as the amount of its available habitat is reduced for the purpose of economic development, and vice versa.

In the case shown, it is optimal to conserve a population of y_1 of the focal species. This requires $x_3 - x_1$ of the area of its habitat to be conserved. It is also optimal to use x_1 of the species' habitat for economic development. However, there is no guarantee that the optimal choice will be made. Market failures and failures in governance can result in more than x_1 of the species' habitat being destroyed. The area destroyed could even exceed x_2, in which case the species would disappear.

Note that if the conservation of the focal species is valued very highly relative to the worth of using its habitat for incompatible economic development purposes, this can result in a corner-point solution to this conservation problem. The optimum then occurs at point A and no loss of the species habitat is optimal. Conversely, if the economic value of using the species habitat for economic purposes is very high, then the optimal loss of habitat may exceed x_2. In this case, it is optimal to allow the species to become extinct, given the valuation system used.

How this valuation system is decided on has not been discussed above. Different social groups and individuals may differ in their valuations. In some cases, they may be able to reach a compromise on the valuation to be adopted or it may be imposed politically in a dictatorial fashion. Sometimes, no societal valuation function may be established. Nevertheless, societies need to be aware that they need to consider the opportunity costs of forgoing the conservation of wild species when depriving them of their habitat in order to facilitate economic development. While there may be instances in which these opportunity costs are zero, there are many cases in which this is not so. However, because of market failures and deficiencies in governance, there is likely to be less conservation of wild species on the whole than is socially desirable.

11.5.5. *Trade-offs and opportunity costs involved in the conservation of natural ecosystems*

Scientific studies often highlight the valuable functions performed by natural ecosystems and point out that the value of the many services they provide are frequently overlooked in economic development

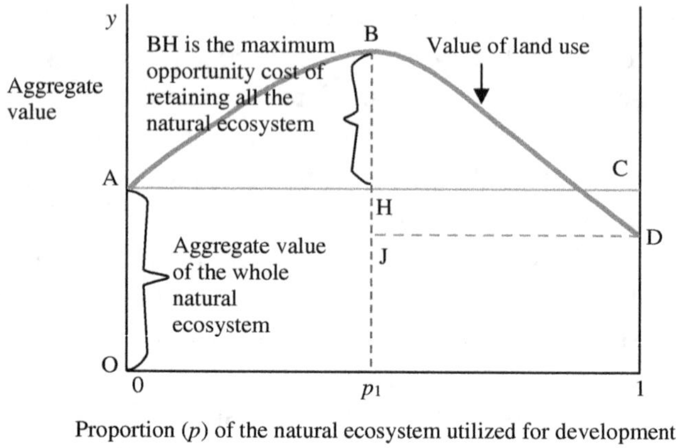

Fig. 11.3. Another illustration of the importance of considering opportunity costs in making conservation versus economic development decisions.

decisions that damage or destroy these functions. While this is true, such studies can fail to give enough attention to the trade-offs or opportunity costs associated with the conservation of natural ecosystems. The total economic value (TEV) of conserving natural ecosystems needs to be compared with the TEV of their alternative uses, e.g. for agriculture. Or comparisons need to be made using alternative valuation systems to an economic one. The importance of taking account of trade-offs when making decisions about the conservation of natural ecosystems can be illustrated by a couple of examples.

Consider two theoretical cases in which some transformation of a natural ecosystem is optimal taking into account both the value of its conservation and of its transformation. The first case is illustrated in Fig. 11.3. The aggregate value of a land area (spatial area) is supposed to depend on the proportion (p) of its area transformed for development purposes. If the relationship *ABCD* shown in Fig. 11.3 applies, then the aggregate value of land use is maximized when the proportion p_1 of the natural ecosystem is transformed for development purposes, and the proportion $1 - p_1$ is left in its natural state. If all the area is left in a natural state, the opportunity cost of doing this is equivalent to HB because the aggregate value of conserving the whole ecosystem is equivalent to OA. HB represents the maximum increase in aggregate

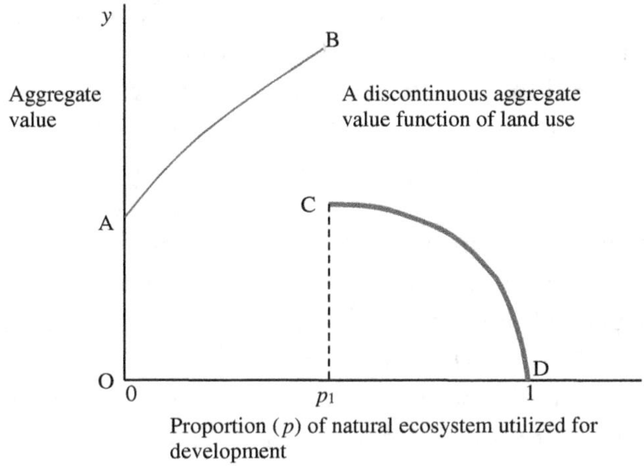

Fig. 11.4. A discontinuous aggregate value curve showing a sharp drop in the aggregate value if more than the proportion of p_1 of the natural ecosystem is lost due to economic development.

value that can be obtained by transforming the natural ecosystem. The maximum benefit forgone by completely transforming this system is even greater. It is higher by an amount equivalent to DC = JH.

We should, however, also allow for the possibility that the aggregate value function is not a smooth unimodal one like that shown in Fig. 11.3. It may, for example, decline sharply when some level of transformation of the natural environment occurs. In Fig. 11.4 for example, a major decline in the value of land use occurs if more than p_1 of its area is transformed for development purposes. Many other possibilities exist. The decline may not be as sharp as shown in Fig. 11.4 but it still could be very rapid. The aggregate value function may also have a scalloped or saw-toothed pattern and multiple local maxima may occur. Furthermore, alterations in the natural ecosystem may result in changes in aggregate value that are not reversible or only partially reversible.

A practical difficulty in determining the maxima of the aggregate value of the type of functions discussed is that their characteristics are likely to be poorly known. Furthermore, determining their nature by trial and error can be risky if losses in natural ecosystems cannot be reversed, are costly to reverse or are feasible only to a limited extent. This is particularly so in cases like that shown in Fig. 11.4 where a small transformation in a natural ecosystem in excess of p_1 results in a major drop in the aggregate value of land use. Furthermore, the consequences of transforming natural ecosystems may be delayed. As a result, the lagged signs of a long-term reduction in the aggregate value of land use may result in inferior decision being made about its use. These cases call for extra care when transforming natural ecosystems.

Note that the above models only provide an introduction to problems that can arise in deciding whether to conserve natural living resource stocks or whether to deplete these to make way for economic development. More specific modeling is required for particular cases. Nevertheless, in all cases, rational conservation versus economic development decisions involving natural ecosystems require account to be taken of opportunity costs.

11.6. Flows of Abiotic Natural Resources

Many natural resources only exist as stocks, e.g. minerals such as coal, oil and iron ore, whereas some only occur as flows. Flow natural resources include sunlight, rainfall and the power of wind and tides. Stocks of living resources are highly dependent on the availability of sunlight and water. These are essential for the growth of plants which in turn support other life forms. Rainfall can result in a combination of water flows (running streams) and stocks of water (e.g. natural lakes). Mankind has harnessed these resources for many economic uses and has created artificial stores of water (e.g. by building dams). The human use of water resources has important ecological consequences given the scale on which it occurs today and its use has significant implications for economic scarcity. Furthermore, alterations in rainfall patterns due to climate change have major economic and ecological implications. Important aspects of the management and availability of water resources were discussed in Chapter 9.

Sunlight is another flow resource, the energy of which is captured to some extent by plants, which release this energy when burnt. Whereas water resources tend to be recycled globally, some of the light and heat originating from the sun is radiated back into the atmosphere. Global warming occurs when this radiation process is partially blocked by the presence of greenhouse gases in the atmosphere.

Wind power appears to be a pure flow resource and so is tidal power. Humankind has devised (and is still developing) ways to convert these sources of energy into stocks for supplying power for economic use, for instance by storing electricity generated by wind turbines in lithium batteries. This is also happening with the generation of electricity from solar power. Storage of solar and wind power (as well as other sources of energy) may also be achieved by other means, such as by pumping water to storages at higher elevations when the demand for electricity is low to be subsequently released to produce hydro-electricity during periods of high demand for electricity. The proportion of global electricity being supplied by solar and wind power is rising significantly and this upward trend is expected to continue (see Chapter 13). It is, therefore, appropriate that greater attention be paid to the economics of the use of these natural resource flows than has been the case in the past.

11.7. Natural Abiotic Resource Stocks that are Incapable of Renewal, For Example, Minerals

11.7.1. *The economic importance of these natural resource stocks*

Abiotic natural resource stocks are depleted once used and basically are not being added to. They include raw materials such as iron ore, bauxite, copper, lithium and rare earths as well as fossil fuels. With the passage of time, humans have become more dependent on a greater range of these resources to improve and sustain their standard of living. Their increased use has enabled the globe to support a much larger human population at a higher standard of living that would have otherwise been achievable. Many of these resources have indirectly increased food availability. Iron has been substituted for example, for wood in many of its previous uses, as has the production of some plastics derived from oil. Fibers, such as polyester (derived from petrochemicals) have substituted for natural fibers. As a result of substitution of this nature, more land is available for food production and consequently, it ought to be possible to conserve more forested land. Rare earths play a vital role in supporting the information technology revolution.

Given the current size of the human population, if the availability of non-renewing natural resource stocks became quite scarce, it would be impossible or extremely difficult to maintain this level of the global population by relying mainly on living resources. This is one reason why there is interest in determining how long these stocks will last. Both pessimistic and optimistic views exist about the length of time for which these non-renewable resources are likely to be available. Optimists generally argue that these resources are more abundant than pessimists, that there is a high degree of substitutability between many of these resources, and that scientific advances will be able to effectively address increasing shortages of some of these resources, the abundance of which varies greatly.

In considering the long-term availability of these resources, one must take into account their substitutes and the scope for recycling materials derived from these resources as well as the economics involved in substituting and recycling them. Even if recycling is feasible, it may not be economic (see Chapter 14) and entropy is likely to occur in the process of recycling and in the use of stocks of minerals. Furthermore, it can also be quite difficult to predict the types of natural resources which may be substituted for other types. For example, in the last century, the extent to which solar energy and wind power could be substituted for fossil fuels to produce electricity was not commonly realized. However, today an increasing proportion of electricity production is being met by the use of solar energy and wind power and the proportion attributable to the use of fossil fuels is falling (see Chapter 13). With these processes in mind, let us consider various methods that have been used to measure the long-term availability of non-renewing natural resource stocks, principally stocks of minerals.

11.7.2. *Measuring the long-term availability of non-renewing natural resource stocks, mainly minerals*

Measures of the availability of non-renewing natural resources stocks are imprecise. The estimated amounts of mineral deposits are sometimes divided into reserves and resources. **Reserves** constitute known mineral deposits that can be profitably mined at the time of the assessment. **Resources** constitute known deposits with a reasonable prospect of economic extraction in the future. There are however, several other definitions and classifications of the availability of non-renewing resources. Note that in the above definition of resources, the concept of what constitutes reasonable prospects of economic extraction is imprecise.

Observe that three main factors need to be considered in assessing the available stock of non-renewing mineral resources. These are:

- Their size classified according to the degree of knowledge about their availability. This can range from the portion of stocks which are known perfectly (or almost so), through different degrees of probability of their existence, to those that are merely inferred.
- The size of stocks classified according to the economics of their exploitation. For example, known reserves can be classified according to whether they would be economic to mine given the current profitability of doing this. Those that would not be profitable to mine given current economic conditions can be classified according to the economic circumstances in which they would become profitable to mine.
- In addition, the scope for economically recycling the use of non-renewing resources can be relevant. For some, there is little or no scope for this but for others (mostly metals), significant recycling possibilities exist.

The profitability of mining minerals depends on the prices obtained for them and the costs of their extraction and preparation for the market. Other things being held constant, a rise in the price of a metal or mineral will make its mining more profitable. Similarly, a reduction in the cost of its extraction will do likewise. The latter depends on several factors such as available technologies, the grade of the available ore, the level of variable costs and the magnitude of overhead costs. In addition, economic developments along the whole product chain affect the economics of mining a mineral. Economic complexities make it very difficult to predict accurately the long-term availability of mineral stocks and the economics of mining them. Furthermore, the demand for minerals and their derivatives fluctuates considerably with (cyclical) variations in the level of aggregate economic activity. This can influence predictions about their long-term availability. Nevertheless, various simplistic models have been employed to give an idea of the economic scarcity of different types of minerals and how long their use will last. Let us consider these.

11.7.3. *Simple models used to estimate the long-term availability of mineral stocks*

Reserve-production ratios, and resource-production ratios are rather routinely estimated to provide a rough indication of the long-term availability of mineral stocks. The former ratio is equal to the estimate of the available reserves of the mineral divided by the output of the mineral in the year of its assessment. It gives the years to depletion of current reserves at the end of the year, based on the level of production of the material in the year of the assessment. Similarly, the resource-production former ratio is equal to the stock of resources of the mineral divided by output of this material in the year of assessment. Added together, they give the total number of years for which reserves plus resources can be "reasonably" expected to last given current production levels. However, this approach is very mechanical because it does not take account of the economic complexities mentioned above. Nevertheless, it is worthwhile considering the application of this approach to a specific metal, namely tin, drawing on the 2016 Report on Global Tin Resources of the International Tin Resources Institute (ITRI 2016).

The relevant information is provided in Table 11.4. This shows the various estimates of global tin reserves and of tin resources as at the end of 2015 and the number of years that it would take to exhaust these stocks if the annual rate of mined production was the same as

Table 11.4. Estimates at the end of 2015 of global stocks of tin in Mt and years availability based on the estimated mined production level in 2014 of 306 ktpa.

Estimates	Stocks in Mt	Years stocks available[(a)]
Reserves		
ITRI	2.2	7
US Geological Survey	4.8	16
Resources		
ITRI	11.7	38
United Nations Environment Program	220	720

Note: (a) Rounded to the nearest year.
Source: Based on ITRI (2016, p. 17) data.

in 2014. The amount of mined output of tin was estimated to be 306,000 tonnes. It can be seen that there are significant differences in estimates by different organizations of the stocks of tin. Table 11.4 underlines the point that determining the availability of stocks of minerals is subject to considerable error. Furthermore, predictions about how long they will last become more uncertain if detailed account is taken of economic considerations.

Despite what seems to be a relatively short life-span for the availability of tin reserves, the ITRI (2016, p. 17) concluded that "there is no reason to suggest that remaining [global] tin deposits will be unable to sustain a long-term gradual upward trend in primary tin production well into the future". The proving and exploration for tin deposits depends on the economics of supplying tin and is basically demand-driven (see subsection 7.3.4). Also, as existing mines become exhausted, search takes place for new tin deposits which can be profitably mined. Consequently, new additions are being made to tin reserves with the passage of time as well as to estimates of resource stocks.

Another feature of significance in the supply of tin is the amount provided by recycling. In recent years, this has amounted to around

18% of total supply. Consequently, the economics of recycling affects the total supply of tin. ITRI (2016, p. 17) points out that "whether the market share of secondary refined tin will grow or decline will depend on the balance between improvement in tin recycling technology and economics versus the falling concentrations of tin in end-of-life products as a result of economization [that is due to economizing on the use of tin in end-of-life products]".

The above method of estimating the availability of minerals assumes a constant rate of mine production until all reserves are exhausted, and is therefore a linear model of their availability. Hubbert (1956) has suggested an alternative simplistic model in which the annual production of a mineral in relation to time is a bell-shaped (Gaussian) function and consequently, the cumulative level of the production of the mineral as a function of time passes is logistic-like. Historically, however, the production of most minerals does not accord well with this Gaussian relationship. Production is often sustained or even increases beyond the peaks of fitted Hubbert functions due primarily to finds of new deposits of a mineral or because their extraction becomes economic from a wider range of sources such as oil from shale in the United States (Ritchie and Roser, 2019). In practice, most applications of Hubbert's modeling have historically provided overly pessimistic estimates of the long-term economic availability of minerals. This is also true of the modeling used by the Club of Rome (Meadows *et al.*, 1972) which will be considered in the next section.

11.8. Discussion

11.8.1. *The Club of Rome's prediction of impending economic collapse due to the depletion of minerals*

In 1972, the Club of Rome (a group of concerned scientists) issued a warning that the global economy would collapse in a rather short period of time due to the depletion of vital stocks of minerals (Meadows *et al.*, 1972). Members of this club predicted that this collapse would occur in 2020. However, we know now that their prediction was

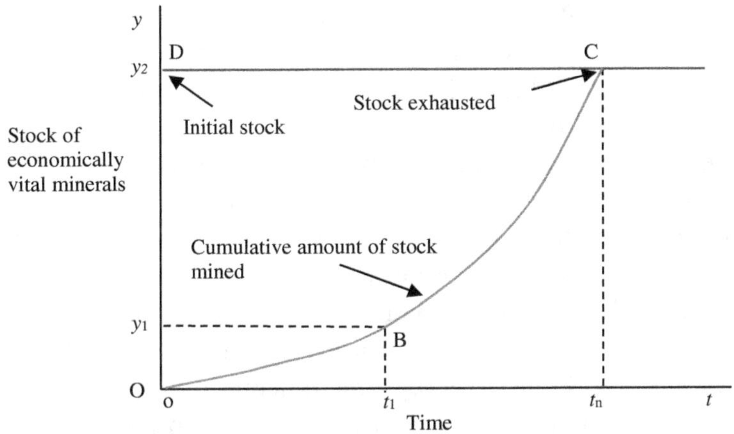

Fig. 11.5. A simple diagram to illustrate the nature of the Club of Rome's catastrophe theory of mineral depletion.

incorrect because they relied on a static model for their predictions. They failed to take account of the possibilities for resource substitution and they did not allow for continuing new discoveries of mineral deposits. In addition, their model did not factor in scientific and technological advances in mining and in the economies of mineral production. Although their view has turned out to be too pessimistic, it should not be concluded that reductions in some important stocks of minerals will never be an impediment to sustaining economic activity.

The gist of the approach of the Club of Rome can be illustrated by Fig. 11.5. In this figure, y_2 is the initial stock of vital minerals that can be economically mined. It is assumed that this stock is mined at an accelerating rate as a function of time. Hence, the cumulative amount of the stock mined might be as shown by the strictly convex relationship OBC. The distance between function OBC and line DC indicates the remaining amount of the vital mineral stock left as mining proceeds. Consequently, at time t_n, the stock of all the economically vital minerals is exhausted. The result is an economic catastrophe.

According to Meadows *et al.* (1972), society may fail to appreciate this looming disaster early enough to adopt policies to avert or moderate it. This is because the rate of extraction of the vital minerals occurs at an accelerating rate. Therefore, the stock may appear to be abundant until it is nearly exhausted. For example, halfway through the process of exhaustion of the stock, the remaining stock of these vital minerals still seems to be plentiful.

For example, in the case shown in Fig. 11.5, at $t_1 = 0.5\ t_n$, the remaining stock amounts to $y_2 - y_1$ which is well over half of the initial amount of the stock. However, this argument does not hold if the stocks of minerals are depleted at a decreasing rate. In this case, the cumulative depletion curve in Fig. 11.5 is strictly concave rather than strictly convex. At the halfway point in the period of time involved in totally exhausting the stock of the vital minerals, more than half of their initial stock is depleted. This could trigger alarm and political pressure for greater conservation of these resources well before their stocks are exhausted.

The Club of Rome's model places little faith in the ability of the market system to conserve mineral stocks as they become scarcer. Because increasing scarcity of these stocks might normally be expected to lead producers to predict rising future prices for the minerals involved, this should provide an economic incentive for miners to conserve these as they become scarcer. Therefore, the rate of their extractions might be expected to taper-off as they become scarcer, other things being held constant. Thereby, their complete exhaustion is avoided. Although, markets do not operate as perfect resource allocation mechanisms, the way in which they operate should not be neglected, as has been done in the modeling by the Club of Rome. While the modeling of the Club of Rome is too simplistic, it highlights the importance of the activity stocks of minerals for the sustainability of modern economic activity.

11.8.2. *Entropy and natural resource use and depletion*

Georgescu-Roegen (1974) has emphasized that economic use of non-renewing mineral resources results in their entropy, that is in their widespread dispersal and in some cases, in their physical transformation to forms that make their re-use impossible. Consequently, physical and economic possibilities for recycling natural resources utilized in economic production are limited. His concern is that the increased entropy of mineral resources as a result of economic activity will eventually limit the sustainability of economic activity.

Consider the following examples. Fossil fuels once combusted cannot be returned to their original form. They are not recyclable, even though the extra CO_2 produced by their use can stimulate plant growth and this extra growth could be used as a fuel source. However, this extra growth will be insufficient to compensate for the fossil fuel loss. On the other hand, many metals can be recycled. However, complete recovery of metals is impossible and there are limits to the economics of their recycling. Most metals oxidize or otherwise lose mass after their manufacture and in their end uses. They may also be present in end-products in such small quantities or incorporated in products in such a way that it is too costly to recover them for recycling. Similar problems arise with several products derived from oil, such as plastics and artificial fibers.

Soils utilized for agriculture are also subject to entropy, that is the dispersal of their materials and the destruction of organic matter, both as a result of cultivation methods and the loss of these items in produce being sent off farms to consumers. Soils are subject to mining and degradation as a result of agriculture. This can be compensated to some extent by the use of artificial fertilizers but their supply is dependent to a large extent on non-renewing natural resources which are subject to entropy.

The relevance of the economic sustainability perspective of Georgescu-Roegen is to bring attention to the limited physical and economic scope for recycling non-renewing natural resources, even though he does not closely examine these aspects. Recycling issues are discussed in Chapter 14.

11.8.3. *The impact on natural resource depletion and deterioration of social embedding in the economic system*

The over-riding desire for economic growth in modern economies, especially market-driven ones, is the major contributor to natural resource depletion and environmental deterioration of natural resources. This is because economic growth is the principal force for maintaining and increasing employment, enables per capita levels of consumption to be increased, and raises or helps to sustain the level of profits and rents. Consequently, in today's market-driven economies, economic growth is a priority for most social groups. These groups include employees, employers and investors. Furthermore, it is from the supply of marketable commodities that these groups mainly benefit economically. As a result, individuals are socially embedded in the market system and have little option but to support policies that promote economic growth. Because economic growth is primarily registered in terms of the increased production of marketable commodities, excess exploitation and deterioration of natural resources is a common consequence. This can result in the negative environmental externalities generated by the use of some natural resources, (such as fossil fuels) ignored or being given inadequate attention. As well, natural resources may be depleted at a faster rate than is desirable from a sustainable development point of view.

The strong desire for economic growth can also influence population policies. One of the arguments that has underpinned Australia's policy of favoring continuing immigration is that it is an important contributor to economic growth. China has abandoned its one-child policy and this may partly be due to economic growth considerations. Other countries, which are experiencing a decline in their natural birth rate (such as Singapore, some European countries and Japan), have adopted policies to counteract or offset this decline. Other things unchanged, increasing populations place increased demands on the use of natural resources and are liable to generate negative environmental effects.

Given the nature of social embedding in the modern economic system, there is little or no political appetite for implementing proposals for establishing steady state economies (SSEs) involving zero population growth (ZPG) and restricting increases in the amount of per capita consumption. There would be even less social support for reducing levels of per capita consumption. It follows that the study of the depletion and deterioration of natural resources cannot be divorced from the social and political consequences of the operation of economic systems. These aspects are interdependent. Economic systems do not exist in a vacuum.

11.9. Concluding Comments

Natural resources, as well as heritage resources (such as the stock of knowledge and human-developed genetic material), are the basic building blocks of economic activity. It is important to manage rationally the use and conservation of these resources to meet future human needs and to ensure desired sustainability outcomes. Appropriately classifying natural resources and increasing our knowledge about their nature are significant first steps towards meeting this objective.

In this chapter, it has been argued that it is more useful to consider a tripartite classification of natural resources than the bipartite one commonly adopted in text books. The tripartite dimension of natural resources covers three categories: (1) biological resources that are renewable but also able to be extinguished, (2) flow resources, and (3) abiotic natural resources which (for all practical purposes) do not renew themselves. Most texts do not identify flow natural resources as a separate category of natural resources. However, they are of considerable and growing economic importance and are increasing in economic value. They include resources such as solar energy, rainfall and water flows, and wind power.

The economic sustainability concerns raised in this chapter arise from the possible exhaustion or excessive decline in natural resource stocks as a result of human economic activity. The main concern is that their depletion might threaten the sustainability of economic activity and development. However, the available evidence suggests that for the foreseeable future, shortages of non-renewing natural resource stocks are unlikely to be an obstacle to maintaining economic activity and economic development. Nevertheless, this possibility cannot be ruled out in the very long-term. Loss of stocks of biological resources could pose a more immediate and insidious threat than shortages of non-renewing natural resources.

The most immediate threat to sustaining human welfare, to maintaining economic activity and to ensuring lasting economic development is the deterioration in the natural environment caused by increased economic activity. This environmental deterioration principally stems from the exploitation and use of non-renewing material resources and from the loss of biotic natural resources, such as natural ecosystems. Therefore, the next chapter and the subsequent chapter will pay particular attention to the environmental consequences of the exploitation and use of non-renewing resources, primarily minerals.

11.10. Keywords

Altruistic value; bequest value; carrying capacity; Club of Rome's model of mineral availability; Hubbert model of mineral extraction; maximum sustainable yield; minimum viable population of a species (MVP); natural capital; natural resource flows; natural resource stocks; non-use values; opportunity costs of conserving natural resources stocks; option value; precautionary principle; regret (opportunity cost) matrix; reserve-production ratios of minerals; resource-production ratios of minerals; safe minimum population of a species; social embedding in the economic system; total economic value (TEV); use values.

11.11. Questions for Review and Discussion

1. Explain each of the concepts listed in Section 11.10.
2. Distinguish between natural resources which only occur as flows and those that only exist as stocks. Give examples. On the other hand, some natural resources consist of both stocks and flows. Identify these.
3. In the 20th century, mainstream economists did not include natural resources in their economic growth models. In your view, does this limit the relevance of their models to current issues involving economic growth? Why do you think natural resources were excluded from these models? Do you think the development of these models might have been influenced by social embedding? Explain.

4. How has the extent of economic reliance on non-renewing natural resources varied with the passage of time?
5. Increased economic production based on greater utilization of abiotic non-renewing resources has enabled products obtained from these sources to be substituted for the use of biotic resources. As a result, the globe is able to support a higher level of human population than otherwise. Explain giving examples of the types of product substitution that have occurred.
6. What types of questions and general issues need to be considered in assessing the scarcity of natural resources and their economic worth?
7. The rate of growth in the biomass of a species is related to the level of its population. What does this relationship typically look like? Why do you think this type of relationship is typical?
8. The harvesting of a wild species (for example, fish species) can result in a stable or unstable equilibrium of its biomass. Nevertheless, in most cases habitat loss or habitat change is the greatest threat to the survival of wild species. Explain and discuss.
9. Give reasons why the MVP of a species is unlikely to be a constant value. Why is it a relatively imprecise concept?
10. The total economic value of natural biotic systems can be comprised of several different types of values. Identify and explain each of these values. Why is the concept of total economic value important?
11. Does the precautionary principle (despite the claim of Ciriacy-Wantrup) always support the conservation of a safe minimum population of all wild species? Explain and discuss.
12. Opportunity cost is an important concept for helping to determine the optimal allocation of resources. How might it be applied (in principle) to determining the optimal population of a wild species taking into account its habitat requirements.
13. Conserving whole natural ecosystems is often uneconomic. On the other hand, in many cases, there is insufficient conservation of such systems. Explain and discuss paying attention to opportunity costs.

14. Give examples of natural abiotic resources that only exist as flows. How important are these flow resources? Consider the economic value of these resources and factors that alter their supply.
15. What are the three main factors that need to be considered in assessing the stock of mineral resources?
16. Outline the types of models (mostly used by geologists) that have been employed to determine the long-term availability of minerals. What are their limitations?
17. The Club of Rome predicted in 1972 that stocks of vital mineral resources would be so depleted by 2020 that this would result in an economic collapse. Why has this not happened? What was wrong with this modeling?
18. Georgescu-Roegen has pointed out that the economic utilization of natural resources results in their entropy and claims that this limits the possibilities for long-term economic growth. Discuss his view. Why does this entropy limit the scope for recycling the products and materials produced by the economic utilization of natural resources?
19. The deterioration of the natural environment as a result of natural resource use is a greater threat to economic sustainability than the depletion of mineral resources. Discuss.

Readings and References

Ciriacy-Wantrup, S.V. (1968). *Resource Conservation: Economics and Policies,* 3rd edn. Division of Agricultural Science, University of California, Berkely, CA.

Georgescu-Roegen, N. (1974). *The Entropy Law and The Economic Process,* Harvard University Press, Cambridge, MA, USA.

Hohl, A. and C.A. Tisdell (1993). How useful are environmental safety standards in economics? — The example of safe minimum standards for protection of species, *Biodiversity and Conservation,* 2, 168–181. doi: 10.1007/bf00056132.

Hubbert, M.K. (1956). Nuclear Energy and the Fossil Fuel, *Drilling and Production Practice* [Online] American Petroleum Institute, New York, New York, 19. https://www.onepetro.org/conference-paper/API-56-007 [Accessed 15 August, 2019].

International Tin Research Institute (2016). 2016 *Report on Global Tin Resources and Reserves–Security of Long-term Tin Supply* [Online] International Tin Association. https://www.internationaltin.org/reports/2016-report-on-global-tin-resources-reserves/ [Accessed 31 July 2019].

Meadows, D. H., J. Ronders and W. Behrens (1972). *The Limits of Growth: A Report for the Club of Rome's Project on the Predicament of Mankind,* Universe Books, New York.

Pascual, U., R. Muradian and L. Brander, *et al.*, (2010). The economics of valuing ecosystem services and biodiversity. *The Economics of Ecosystems and Biodiversity: Ecological and Economic Foundations.* P. Kumar Earthscan (ed.), London and Washington DC. 183–256 Chapter 5. http://www.teebweb.org/our-publications/teeb-study-reports/ecological-and-economic-foundations/.

Ritchie, H. and M. Roser (2019). *Fossil fuels,* Our World in Data, https://ourworldindata.org/fossil-fuels [Accessed 13 August 2019].

Solow, R.M. (1956). A contribution to the theory of economic growth, *Quarterly Journal of Economics,* 70, 65–74. doi: https://doi.org/10.2307/1884513.

Solow, R.M. (1957). Technical change and the aggregate production function, *The Review of Economics and Statistics,* 39, 312–320. doi: 10.2307/1926047.

Swan, T.W. (1956). Economic growth and capital accumulation, *Economic Record,* 32, 334–361. doi: https://doi.org/10.1111/j.1475-4932.1956.tb00434.x.

Tietenberg, T. and L. Lewis (2018). *Environmental and Natural Resource Economics,* 11th edn. Routledge, New York and Abingdon, Oxon, UK [Chapter 12].

Tisdell, C.A. (1968). *The Theory of Price Uncertainty, Production and Profit,* Princeton University Press, Princeton, NJ. (Chapter 2: Some theories of decision-making). Reprinted, 2015.

Tisdell, C.A. (2005). *Economics of Environmental Conservation,* 2nd edn. Edward Elgar, Cheltenham, UK and Northampton, MA, USA.

Tisdell, C.A. (2015). *Sustaining Biodiversity and Ecosystem Functions: Economic Issues,* Edward Elgar, Cheltenham, UK and Northampton, MA, USA. [Chapters 12 and 16].

World Commission on Environment and Development (1987). *Our Common Future,* Oxford University Press, Oxford.

Chapter 12

More on Mineral Resources: Their Economic Significance, Sustainability, and Environmental Issues

12.1. Introduction

Humankind's utilization of minerals has made (and continues to make) a major contribution to economic growth and to the way in which civilizations have developed. Their utilization has resulted in the globe supporting a larger population with higher standards of living than could otherwise have been achieved. Nevertheless, our heavy reliance on the utilization of minerals for our economic welfare raises several serious sustainability and environmental concerns. These concerns are examined in this chapter which also considers policies for responding to these concerns.

Several important aspects of the use of minerals could not be covered in the previous chapter. These include the significance of their use for economic growth, development and standards of living. Furthermore, trends in the real prices of minerals need to be considered in addition to alterations in their reserve-production ratios as indicators of changes in their economic scarcity. The effectiveness of the market mechanism in conserving the stock of minerals also requires discussion. In addition, adverse environmental spillovers from the use of minerals must be taken into account. These externalities can have negative sustainability effects as well as adverse economic efficiency consequences. The latter results in an inferior allocation of resources and creates greater economic scarcity than need be the case.

In summary, the main topics addressed in this chapter are:

1. the increasing economic dependence of hominids on the use of minerals;
2. trends in the real price of minerals as an indicator of their changing economic scarcity;
3. the impact of the market mechanism on the conservation of the stock of minerals;
4. environmental effects from mining and the use of minerals and market failure;
5. policies to address market failures arising from the utilization of minerals; and
6. social conflicts and aspects of economic inequality associated with mining.

12.2. The Increasing Economic Dependence of Humankind on the Utilization of Minerals

12.2.1. *General historical context*

The commencement of agriculture (which has happened only in the last 10,000 years, see for example, Renfrew, 2007 for some details) has been identified as an episodic catalyst for accelerating economic growth and social change. Childe (1965) describes it as a revolution (the Agricultural Revolution) which subsequently supported the growth of cities and urban centers (the Urban Revolution). The initial development of agriculture occurred in the Neolithic period, the last Stone Age period. Many later initiatives contributed to the momentum for economic growth, including the development of metallurgy. The evolution of bronze and subsequently iron production have been identified by some writers as revolutionary steps in economic development. In practice, a complex and long chain of interacting innovations and historical events have shaped today's economic systems and the nature of societies. In the case of agriculture, there have been continuing innovations of considerable socio-economic importance (Mazoyer and Roudart, 2006), and this has also happened in the case of the utilization of minerals. It is not possible here to consider all the major innovations that have shaped our modern world. In relation to this chapter, the main point to keep in mind is that modern economies rely heavily on the utilization of minerals for the supply of material goods and for the supply of energy and heating. This economic dependence has increased with the passage of time. We are now extremely dependent on these resources for sustaining our economic welfare.

12.2.2. *Classification of different types of minerals and trends in their utilization*

For all practical purposes, minerals are non-renewable (non-regenerating) resources. They vary considerably in their availability and in their attributes. Table 12.1 provides an indication of the range of minerals used for economic purposes. All non-metallic ores are used to supply physical commodities and this is true of nearly all metallic ores. An exception, for example, is uranium, which is used to supply heat in nuclear reactors for the production of electricity. Mineral fuels are mostly used to produce heat and energy. However, oil is also utilized to supply physical products, e.g. plastics and artificial fibers.

Initially, hominids made use of various types of stones for economic purposes, namely the production of stone implements. Subsequently, much later, in some parts of the world, clay began to be used for the supply of clay pots. The melting and use of metallic ores began at an even later stage in the development of ancient economies. Archaeologists, anthropologists and economic historians have singled out the early development and spread of bronze production as an important contributor to the pattern of socioeconomic development, and also the subsequent production of iron which occurred a few centuries before the first millennium. This led to the classification of the early economic development of hominids into three stages, namely the Stone Age, the Bronze Age and the Iron Age. However, many other innovations occurred within these specified ages which also contributed to

Table 12.1. A list of the main categories of minerals used for economic purposes.

Non-Metallic Ores	These include stones, clay, kaolin, sand and gravel, chemical and fertilizer minerals, gemstones
Metallic Ores	• Base metals, e.g. copper, lead and zinc • Precious metals, e.g. gold, silver and platinum • Lightweight minerals, e.g. aluminum • Radioactive minerals, e.g. uranium • Rare earth minerals
Mineral Fuels (Fossil Fuels)	• Peat • Coal, e.g. brown coal, anthracite (hard coal), bituminous coal (soft coal) • Oil, e.g. oil, shale oil • Natural gas, e.g. methane deposits, methane extracted from coal deposits by fracking

Source: Based on information in Spitz and Trudinger (2009, Table 5.1, p. 223).

economic growth. A useful chronology of the evolution of mining and metal production is available in Spitz and Trudinger (2009, Chapter 1, see especially Table 1.1).

With the passage of time, the importance of minerals as a basis for economic production has increased greatly. Both the quantity and the range of minerals used for economic purposes has risen tremendously. The Industrial Revolution (and the subsequent economic growth which it facilitated) resulted in the accelerating use of fossil fuels and the growing use of most metallic minerals, particularly iron ore. Although the amount of fossil fuel used now appears to be tapering off (see Chapter 13), it still remains high. Furthermore, the development of digital technologies and information and communication technology (ICT) has resulted in the rising demand for the use of rare earth minerals. Moreover, the demand for batteries to improve the storage and dispatchability of electricity supplies obtained from solar and wind power has led to increasing demand for relatively scarce minerals, such as lithium. Supplies of rare earth minerals are essential to produce equipment used in our Digital Age. In addition, the availability of lithium batteries is starting to reduce the dependence of economic activity on fossil fuels for supplying a flexible supply of heat and energy. The adoption of these batteries increases the social acceptability of generating electricity from solar and wind power rather than from fossil fuels. Consequently, greenhouse gas emissions can be reduced and the extent of climate change can be moderated. These are important examples of how previously unused or little used minerals are helping to underpin modern economic developments.

12.2.3. *Basic trends in the utilization of minerals and their role in increasing product substitution*

The long-term socioeconomic development of humankind has been positively associated with

1. an increase globally in the quantity of minerals used in economic production;
2. the employment for economic purposes of an ever expanding variety of minerals; and
3. a substantial increase in the range of products supplied by using minerals.

Both the expansion in the range of minerals used and the range of products able to be manufactured by their use has resulted in greater substitutability between different types of minerals in economic production. For example, in some uses, aluminum, steel, glass and plastics are substitutes. In addition, mineral-based products provide substitutes for many non-food products obtained from living resources. For example, artificial fibers and plastics obtained from oil provide replacements for natural fibers and leather, and in buildings, mineral-based products substitute for wood and other organic building materials, fossil fuels replace wood for heating, and machines using fossil fuels (either directly or indirectly) provide a substitute for animal and human motive power. There are many such substitutes and their number has increased with the passage of time.

12.2.4. *The increased human carrying capacity of the globe and mineral use*

The increased economic use of minerals has enabled a larger human population to exist at a higher per capita (average) level of material wealth than would otherwise have been possible. Increased mineral use has indirectly contributed to greater food production than otherwise could be achieved. It has done this by

1. providing mineral-based substitutes for non-food crops and items derived from natural living products;
2. by making it easier and less costly to transform natural ecosystems to ones that are more productive for food production; and
3. by enabling the range of commodities available to humankind to be increased substantially.

Potentially, the increased use of mineral resources might have been used (and still could be employed) to ensure more conservation of natural ecosystems. In practice, however, this has not happened. The global area of natural biomass has declined as the utilization of mineral resources has risen and the economic benefits from greater use of minerals have been utilized to support an increasing world population and to achieve, on average, a rising level of per capita material consumption. The capacity of the earth to support its human population has been elevated by the growing use of minerals. Although this carrying capacity has not been fully exploited by an increase in the level of population of *Homo sapiens*, a large amount of the economic surplus generated has been utilized to support a major rise in the level of human population globally and its demands for higher levels per capita of material consumption. We have now reached a situation where the global level of human population and the amount of its material production could not be maintained if the economic supply of mineral resources was to become much scarcer than today. This would undoubtedly result in economic catastrophe. However, given continuing technological progress, more economical use of minerals in product chains and the widening range for substitution of different types of minerals in economic production, there appears to be little possibility of such a resource scarcity catastrophe occurring in the foreseeable future, e.g. in this century. Trends in the real price of minerals may provide an indication of likely changes in their economic scarcity in the foreseeable future. Let us now consider these trends.

12.3. Trends in the Real Price of Minerals

12.3.1. *Empirical evidence and economic theories*

Empirical evidence indicates that the real prices of most minerals have not increased since the late 19th century or since the start of the 20th century. In fact, the real level of the prices of the majority have fallen and the increases in the prices of those that have risen are modest. While the trend in the real prices of most minerals has mostly been downwards, some have displayed a slight upward trend whereas others have a U-shaped trend but with no substantial increase in their real price.

Barnett and Morse (1963) initially examined trends in the real prices of selected minerals and their analysis was updated by Baumol and Oates (1979). Baumol and Oates identified trends in the prices of fifteen minerals relative to a wholesale price index using nine-year moving averages based on data from 1900 to 1975. They found that there was a long-run tendency for the real prices of seven of these 15 minerals to fall. However, some did exhibit a rising trend and a few displayed a U-shaped pattern. Nevertheless, even in these latter cases, the rise in their real prices was slight. They concluded, as had Barnett and Morse (1963), that there are no signs of imminent economic catastrophe due to the economic exhaustion of mineral reserves.

A more recent study by Cuddington and Nülle (2014) covering an even longer period (mainly 1900–2010), investigated trends in the real prices of 102 minerals listed in the United States Geological Survey. It basically supports the same conclusion as that of the above mentioned authors but employed a different statistical technique to distinguish between cycles in the real prices of minerals and their long-term trends. Their analysis employs low-frequency band-pass filters to distinguish between cycles in the real price of minerals and in their trends. Mineral prices are subject to a variety of cycles and are quite sensitive, for example, to business cycles because they are important constituents in capital formation, that is investment in real capital. In practice, it is difficult to distinguish between the long-term cycles in the real prices of most minerals and their trends.

The method of statistical analysis used by Cuddington and Nülle allows for a change in trends. Applying their method, they observe a variety of trends for the real prices of the 102 minerals. While the majority (more than two-thirds) displayed average negative trends in their real prices (e.g. aluminum, bauxite, industrial, diamonds and zinc) a few (e.g. gold, iron ore and silicon) exhibited average rising trends. Several showed one to three alterations in trends over the time-periods considered. Some exhibited a U-shape but not those that had more than one turning point or no turning point at all. Those for which the long-run price trends exhibited a U-shaped pattern included chromium, gold, graphite and rare earths. The average growth rate in the trend in the real prices of those minerals showing a rise was modest. For example, for iron ore, it was 0.005 on average per annum (five thousands of one percent) and for silicon the same.

Cuddington and Nülle (2014, p. 234) point out that economists have predicted three different trends in the real prices of minerals based on their economic theories. These are a rising trend (Hotelling, 1931), a falling trend (Prebisch, 1962; Singer, 1950) and a U-shaped relationship (Heal, 1981; Levhari and Pindyck, 1981; Slade, 1982). The empirical evidence indicates that none of these patterns are observed for the long-term prices of all minerals. These relationships are heterogeneous (and complex) but negative trends predominate. While Cuddington and Nülle attribute the nature of long-term trends in mineral prices to the ongoing tug-of-war between mineral exploration, depletion and technological change (supply-side market factors), demand-side factors also influence variations in these price patterns. Examples of demand-side influences include:

1. Innovations that alter the demand for particular minerals. For example, digital technologies and ICT have increased the demand for rare earth minerals. The increased use of solar and wind power to generate electricity is raising the demand for lithium batteries to store electricity. All electric vehicles also increase the demand for such batteries.
2. Increased substitutability of minerals and other resources in their economic uses is also important. For example, solar and wind power in some countries is substituting for the use of fossil fuel. This is one factor reducing the demand for steaming coal.
3. The extent to which some metals are recycled influences trends in their long-term real prices. Other things unchanged, greater recycling of metals and plastics lowers the demand for the minerals from which they are derived.
4. In many cases, the amount of metal used to produce particular products has been reduced without lowering their functionality. Other things constant, this reduces the demand for the minerals from which they are obtained.

Nevertheless, it is also true that the supply-side influences on real mineral prices mentioned by Cuddington and Nülle are important. For example, modern mining technologies and equipment have permitted the economical mining of many lower grades of minerals that would otherwise have been uneconomic to mine. For example, whereas in the early part of the 20th century, grades of around 1.8% copper were being mined, by the early part of this century, this percentage had dropped to around 0.7% (see Spitz and Trudinger, 2009, Fig. 12.1, p. 6).

Both future short-term variations in mineral prices and their long-term trends are very difficult to predict. The prices of many minerals in the short- to medium-term are quite volatile. As a result, the price of shares (stocks) in mining companies tend to be relatively volatile also. Even distinguishing past trends in mineral prices from cyclical changes in their values is far from straightforward, as the study by Cuddington and Nülle (2014) reveals.

12.3.2. *Comparative static market analysis and changes in mineral prices*

Comparative static market analysis is useful for comprehending the way changes in the markets for minerals alter their real prices. Shifts in market supply and demand schedules for individual minerals are the dominant influences on alterations in their prices. The price elasticity of these schedules is also relevant. A couple of examples are given to illustrate these points.

In Fig. 12.1, a case is illustrated in which the relative shifts in the demand and supply schedules of a mineral result in a decline in its market equilibrium price. In this case, the shift to the right of its supply curve, a change from S_1S_1 to S_2S_2, is larger than the shift to the right of its demand curve, a change from D_1D_1 to D_2D_2. The market equilibrium alters from E_1 to E_2 as a result, and the equilibrium price of the mineral falls from P_1 to P_0. New mining technologies and favorable discoveries of new mineral deposits may cause the supply curve of a mineral to shift to the right, that is downwards.

Consider a different case in which the market equilibrium price of a mineral declines due to a fall in the demand for it. This is illustrated

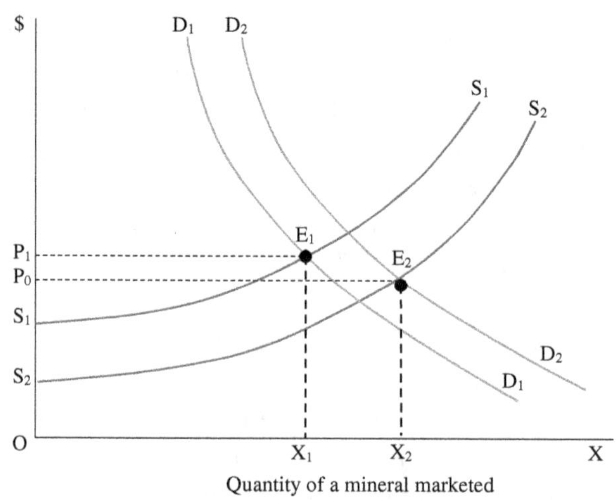

Fig. 12.1. An example of a changing combination of market demand and supply conditions leading to a decline in the market price of a mineral. In this case, the extra supply of the mineral outpaces the increased demand for it.

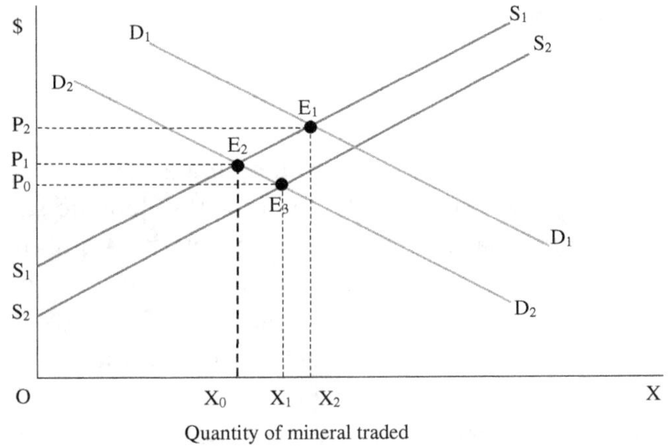

Fig. 12.2. Another illustration of how alterations in the market demand and supply schedules for a mineral can influence changes (trends) in its price.

by Fig. 12.2. In this case, the demand schedule for a mineral shifts to the left (from D_1D_1 to D_2D_2) and a smaller quantity of the mineral is demanded than previously. Indications are, for example, that the demand for coal is declining due to the greater availability and falling prices of substitutes (such as solar and wind power) as well as because of the climate change policies of some nations wanting to reduce their carbon dioxide emissions. Other things held constant, this decline in the demand for a mineral reduces its market equilibrium price. For example, if the supply curve of the mineral remains unchanged at S_1S_1, the market equilibrium for the mineral changes from E_1 to E_2. Both the equilibrium price and quantity traded of the mineral decline. This outcome, however, is affected if the supply curve of the mineral also shifts to the left. Other things unchanged, the equilibrium price of the mineral still declines but the extent of the alteration in its equilibrium quantity traded depends on how far to the right the supply schedule for the mineral shifts. In the case illustrated in Fig. 12.2, a shift in the supply curve from S_1S_1 to S_2S_2 results in the market equilibrium changing from E_1 to E_3. The equilibrium price of the mineral still falls but there is only a slight reduction in its equilibrium quantity traded. A large shift of the supply schedule to the right, other things unchanged, would move its equilibrium price further downwards and result in an increase in the equilibrium quantity traded of the mineral.

The sequence of shifts in the supply and demand schedules in Fig. 12.2 could occur in the opposite order to that just considered. For example, an increase in the cost of producing a mineral could cause its supply schedule to rise from S_2S_2 to S_1S_1. If the demand schedule for the mineral remains unaltered at D_2D_2, the market equilibrium price of the mineral rises and the quantity mined declines. If the demand schedule for the mineral rises (for example, from D_2D_2 to D_1D_1), the market equilibrium price of the mineral rises even more. Whether or not the quantity mined and traded of the mineral rises or falls depends on how much the demand for it increases. In the reverse sequence of events, the market quantity of the mineral traded, increases compared to the initial situation. It rises from X_1 to X_2.

The application of economic supply and demand analysis indicates that a large range of possible patterns exist for possible changes in the market equilibrium prices of minerals. Basically, the alteration in the price of a mineral is more the result of a tug-of-war between supply and demand conditions rather than the three supply-side factors (exploration, depletion and technological change) which Cuddington and Nülle (2014) mention. Furthermore, economic theory indicates that the short-run and long-run changes in these values normally differ. Empirical evidence is required to determine for individual minerals the nature of alterations in market demand and supply schedules which change their market equilibria. Consideration of traditional economic market analysis (based on comparative statics) can be helpful in initially investigating changes in the market values of individual minerals. It can be profitably considered as a prelude to deeper investigations.

12.4. How Well Does the Market System Conserve Mineral Stocks?

12.4.1. *Preliminary considerations*

The answer to the question of how well does the market system conserve minerals for future use is not straightforward. This is so for at least, two reasons:

1. it requires us to have a criterion of what would be an ideal (or at least what would be a satisfactory) time-related pattern of the conservation of mineral stocks; and
2. to allow for limitations in the operation of market systems, some of which are due to institutional factors and the presence of unavoidable uncertainties about the economic future.

In relation to the first factor, one could adopt the goal that current generations should ensure future generations of sufficient stocks of minerals to enable them to maintain a specific level of income or standard of living. A major problem, however, in satisfying this goal is the uncertain level of mineral stocks (given technological change and other factors) needed to ensure this.

In relation to the second factor, mineral markets do not operate perfectly. They are impacted by uncertainty about the future prices of minerals and other uncertainties. Furthermore, in most countries, mineral deposits are the property of their governments (that is the state) and access to them is controlled by these governments. Royalties are charged by governments for their extraction by mining companies. In most cases, access to minerals and the level of royalties are only partially influenced by competitive market forces. Furthermore, large companies dominate the supply of some minerals, e.g. iron ore supplies, and this could reduce their competitiveness.

12.4.2. *The effectiveness of markets in conserving minerals according to traditional (neoclassical) economic theory*

Baumol and Oates (1979, p. 115) explain in simple terms how a perfect or near perfect mineral market would increase the conservation of the stock of a mineral in response to growing economic scarcity of the mineral and its rising future market price. Their argument is based on the view that firms will try to maximize their capitalized value or the net present value of their stream of profits; the theory of which is outlined in detail by John Hicks (1946). In practice, however, the market mechanism is subject to imperfections which limit its effectiveness in allocating the time-dependent supply of minerals, even though this

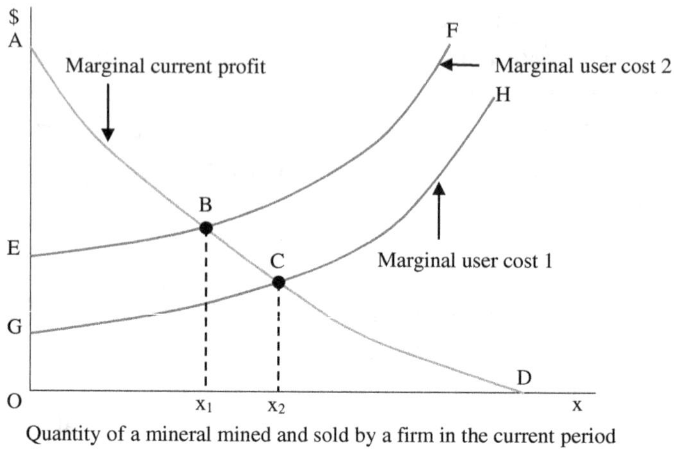

Fig. 12.3. This diagram illustrates, on the basis of traditional (neoclassical) economic analysis, how a mining firm reacts to a rise in the future price of a mineral mined by it. A rising price would signal growing economic scarcity of the mineral.

mechanism does display responsiveness to price variations and expected changes in prices. The responses are not always of the type predicted by theories of perfect competition (or near perfect competition) or more generally, neoclassical economic theories of market operation.

Applying traditional (neoclassical) economic theory, Fig. 12.3 provides a simplified illustration of how a profit-maximizing mining firm (intent on maximizing its capitalized value) would react to rises in the future prices of the mineral mined by it. Line ABCD represents its marginal profit from mining its stock of mineral (or minerals) in the current period. Line GCH is the marginal capitalized value of saving this stock for mining in the future. It represents the marginal opportunity cost or marginal user cost of mining its mineral or minerals in the current period, that is, its marginal future (discounted) profit which is forgone.

In this case, given GCH, the capitalized value of the stream of profits of the mining firm is achieved when it mines x_2 of its mineral stock in the current period. Now suppose the future prices of the mineral are forecast to increase, everything else unchanged. This pushes the firm's marginal opportunity cost or marginal user cost of mining and selling its mineral in the current period upwards so that, for example, its marginal user cost curve becomes EBF. The firm now maximizes its capitalized value by mining and selling x_1 of the mineral in the current period, and the stock of the mineral conserved for future use is increased by $x_2 - x_1$. Given this analysis, markets react to growing economic scarcity of a mineral by conserving more of it.

12.4.3. *Limitations of markets as mechanisms for conserving mineral resources*

Markets do not operate as perfectly as predicted by neoclassical economic theory. Uncertainty about future economic conditions, a high degree of preference for extracting profit in the near future as well as the nature of managerial economic rewards can reduce the willingness of firms to conserve their mineral resources. Consider each of these aspects in concern.

A firm's uncertainty about the profitability of conserving its mineral resources for future use tends to reduce its willingness to conserve these if it is risk-averse. This effect depends on how risk-averse the firm is and how great is its uncertainty about the profitability of conserving its mineral resources for future use. A wide range of risk-averse reactions to uncertainty are possible (Tisdell, 1968, Chapter 2). However, just consider a single case here.

Suppose that a mining firm is uncertain about its marginal user costs. Then suppose that line EBF in Fig. 12.3 represents the set of the highest marginal user costs it believes to be possible and that the line GCH represents its lowest estimated values for these costs. GCH represents its most pessimistic prediction about the value of conserving its stock of the mineral for future production. If a mining firm is highly risk-averse and it adopts a minimax gain strategy (aims to maximize its profitability given the most pessimistic scenario), it will utilize x_2 of its resource in the current period. A higher level of uncertainty will result in less conservation. For example, if EBF in Fig. 12.3 is higher and GCH is lower (indicating increased uncertainty), this risk-averse (minimax) criterion results in greater use of the mineral resource in the current period. Other risk-aversion criteria yield a similar result.

If the owners of a mining firm have a strong preference for current profit rather than for delayed profit (which would maximize the capitalized value of their business), this also reduces their willingness to conserve their mineral resource. For example, suppose in Fig. 12.3 that line EBF represents the marginal capitalized profit forgone by the firm by mining its stock of its mineral in the current period. If the firm wants to maximize its capitalized value, then it should mine x_1 of the resource in the current period. However, the owners of the firm may be impatient to extract a larger amount of current profit from their business. Consequently, they might act as if curve GCH is their marginal user cost curve. Hence, they would mine x_2 of their stock in the current period. Compared to the situation in which the firm maximizes its capitalized value, the amount mined of the resource increases by $x_2 - x_1$, less if the mineral is conserved for future use.

The way in which economic rewards are offered to managers of mining companies can also affect their conservation of mineral stocks. If managerial economic bonuses are based on the increased returns on the assets of their firm during their term of office, managers have an incentive to increase the profitability of the business during their time of office at the expense of its profit at a later time. If, for example, managers of publicly listed companies are rewarded with rights to shares in it, the amount of which depends on its economic performance during their term of office, this can have this effect; especially if the value of shares on the stock market is dependent on the short-rather than the long-term profitability of the company. As a result, managers of mining companies are less likely to forgo profits during their term of office in favor of profits later on. Hence, they are less likely to conserve mineral stock for future use.

Also note that since it is difficult for experts such as Cuddington and Nülle (2014) to distinguish between trends and cycles in mineral prices, it is probably even more difficult for investors to do likewise. This could result in many markets exhibiting cobweb-like responses to changing mineral prices.

12.5. Environmental Effects from Mining, Processing and Using Minerals and Market Failures

12.5.1. *Negative environmental effects associated with the mining, processing and use of minerals*

Adverse environmental effects can occur at the different stages involved in the extraction, processing and use of minerals. They vary with the variety of factors, for example, with the type of mineral being utilized and its attributes, the types of production techniques used at different stages in its utilization and even with the location where these activities occur. Detailed information about relationships between mining and the environment can be found in Spitz and Trudinger (2009). Some of the adverse environmental effects which are directly associated with different types of mining are listed in Table 12.2 with accompanying comments.

Note that just because a mine (or the processing or use of minerals) has negative environmental effects, it should not be concluded that these activities are undesirable from a social economic point of view. The social economic benefit from these activities can still be positive even if they generate adverse environmental externalities. Nevertheless, sometimes the environmental costs of these activities will outweigh their social benefits and these activities will be socially undesirable. This case is illustrated in Fig. 12.4 below. However, the opposite is probably most common. Nevertheless, market failures are liable to result in socially inadequate private management of environmental spillovers. For instance, in the cases illustrated by Figs. 12.5 and 12.6 in the next subsection, mining is socially advantageous from an economic point of view, but profit-maximizing mines do make socially optimal economic choices given the presence of environmental spillovers.

12.5.2. *Simple illustrations of market failures due to environmental spillovers from mining*

Mining firms and those utilizing minerals may not be required to pay (or may only partially pay) for the environmental costs imposed on

Table 12.2. A list of adverse environmental effects which can be caused by different types of mining.

Type of environmental effect	Comments and examples
Water pollution	For example, from chemicals and substances used in mining operations; leaking of chemicals from disturbed mineral deposits (for instance, copper mines and abandoned mining sites), acidic water, dirty water.
Air pollution	For example, dust and other particulate matter from mining operations having negative environmental impacts on surrounding areas. Some contribution to greenhouse gas emissions as a result of fossil fuel use to operate mining equipment. This use may be direct or indirect.
Soil contamination	In some cases, for instance, from fracking to obtain natural gas.
Solid wastes	Soil, rocks and other solid residue from mining.
Land subsidence	From underground mining, e.g. of coal, resulting in damage to buildings and infrastructure.
Loss of natural biodiversity	As a result of open cut mining removing habitat utilized by endangered species and as a consequences of water pollution adversely affecting aquatic species and water sources used by threatened species.
Loss of agricultural land and land with alternative commercial or other uses. Loss of visual amenity.	The loss is usually a result of open cut mining. The length and extent of the loss varies with rehabilitation efforts.
Increased water scarcity	Some types of mining use considerable amounts of water in their mining operations and this may deprive other users of water. Market failure occurs if miners have open access to shared water bodies or do not pay the opportunity cost of their water use.
Potential environmental disasters associated with mining	These include the possible collapse of tailing dams used to dispose of wastes from mining. These collapses can cause flash flooding downstream, siltation, and serious water pollution as well as loss of human and other life, and destruction to property.

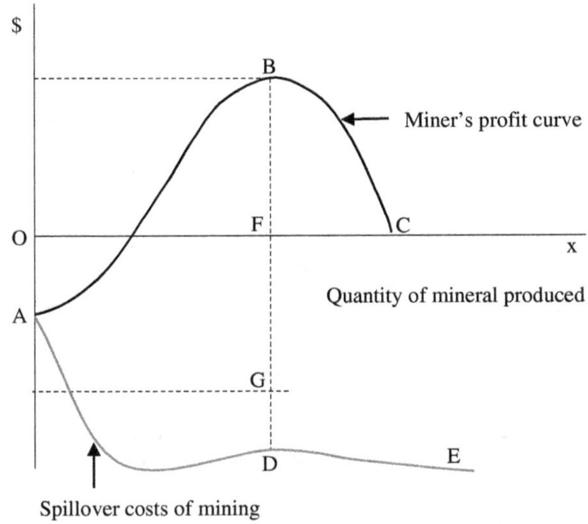

Fig. 12.4. A case in which the negative social value of operating a mine exceeds the private profitability of doing so because of the presence of negative environmental spillovers.

others by their activities. As a result, several types of market failure may occur. For instance,

1. mines and mineral-based businesses which are privately profitable may be of negative value from a social point of view;
2. if the marginal external environmental costs of mineral production are a positive function of the level of economic activity (value of production), the level of private economic activity is likely to be socially excessive;
3. there can be a private incentive to utilize grades of minerals which are more damaging to the environment rather than less environmentally damaging grades; and
4. the socially optimal technique of production (taking into account environmental costs) may not be adopted.

Diagrams can be used to illustrate the nature of these four types of market failure.

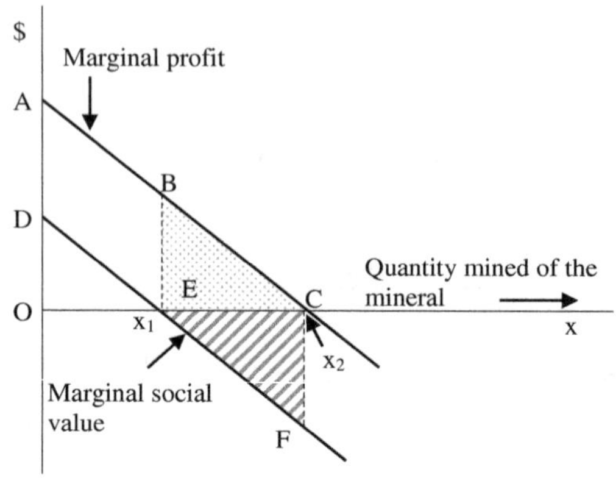

Fig. 12.5. The marginal environmental spillover costs from the operation of this hypothetical mine are negative. Hence, the marginal profit obtained from mining exceeds its marginal value. Consequently, the quantity of the mineral mined is excessive from a social point of view if the miner is a profit-maximizer.

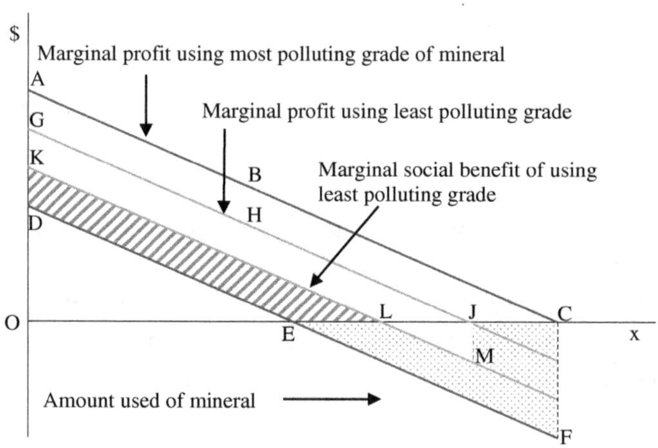

Fig. 12.6. A diagram used to illustrate market failure (due to the presence of environmental spillovers) resulting from the utilization of a more polluting grade of mineral than is socially desirable. This diagram is also re-interpreted to show how market failure can result in the adoption of a more environmentally damaging mining technique of production being adopted than is socially desirable.

Figure 12.4 illustrates the case where mining is privately profitable for a miner but the social value of its production is negative and exceeds its profitability for all levels of its production. The relationship ABC represents the firm's profit possibilities and that marked ADE represents the environmental spillover costs of the firm's production. The social value of the firm's production is negative and exceeds the firm's profit for all of its possible levels of production. If the mining firm operates to maximize its profit, its maximum profit is equivalent to BF. Therefore, since the distance FG is equivalent to BF, society suffers a net economic loss equivalent to GD. A potential Paretian improvement (sometimes called a Kaldor-Hicks gain) would be possible (in principle) because those suffering environmental damage from the mine would (after paying BF = FG to the miner not to operate the mine) be better off by an amount equivalent to GD. In this particular case, any level of mining operations imposes a net economic burden on society.

Now consider the second case in which social marginal costs of operating a mine exceed the miner's private marginal costs due to environmental spillovers. This results in the marginal profitability of operating the mine exceeding the marginal social value of doing so. Consequently, from a social point of view, this results in an excessive rate of extraction of the mineral if the miner is a profit-maximizer. This case is illustrated in Fig. 12.5. In this case, line ABC represents the marginal level of profit obtained by a miner from mining. Line DEF is the marginal social value of that mining after allowing for the negative environmental spillovers generated by it. A profit-maximizing miner would mine x_2 of the mineral. However, x_1 is the socially optimal amount which ought to be mined if the potential Paretian improvement criterion is applied. The difference between line ABC and DEF measures the external environmental costs associated with the mining of the mineral.

In Fig. 12.5, the deadweight social loss from mining operations is equivalent to the area of the hatched triangle EFC and the output of the mine is socially excessive by the amount $x_2 - x_1$. This is so if the miner maximizes profit (by producing x_1 of the mineral) and the potential Paretian improvement principle is applied. Those damaged by the environmental spillovers would be potentially better off if they paid an amount equivalent to the dotted area of triangle BEC to the miner to reduce its rate of extraction of the mineral from x_2 to x_1. The miner would then be no worse off economically than otherwise, and environmental victims would be better off by an amount equivalent to the area of triangle EFC. Note that this does not imply from a policy point of view that the environmental victims should pay. It may be more equitable to impose a levy on the miner which internalizes the miner's environmental spillover costs, that is to apply the environmental user pays principle. A levy of DA on each unit of production would, for example achieve this result.

Figure 12.6 can be used to illustrate points (3) and (4) above. In relation to point (3), suppose that a firm has an option of utilizing the grade of a mineral that is more polluting than an alternative grade but which yields it greater profit, for example, high sulfur coal rather than low sulfur coal. If the social disbenefit of using the more polluting grade of mineral is higher than for the less polluting grade then a social economic gain can be achieved by banning the use of the more polluting grade of the mineral.

In Fig. 12.6, let line ABC represent the firm's marginal profitability of using the more polluting grade of the mineral and line DEF represent the corresponding marginal social benefit of its use. The difference between these two lines represents the marginal external environmental cost associated with the use of this grade of the mineral. Similarly, let line GHJ represent this firm's profit from utilizing the less polluting mineral and let line KLM be the corresponding marginal social value of doing so. If there is no technique for adequately reducing the environmental spillovers for the use of the more polluting minerals, then banning its use is socially beneficial. If the quantity used of the mineral is unregulated, the social value of preventing the use of the most polluting mineral will be equal to the hatched area plus the dotted area in Fig. 12.6, assuming that the firm is a profit-maximizer. If for both grades of the mineral the quantity used is regulated so as to ensure that the social marginal value of their utilization is zero (that is, the total social value of their use is maximized), then the gain in economic benefit from stopping the use of the polluting grade of the mineral is equivalent to the hatched area in Fig. 12.6. However, it should be noted that in some circumstances, it can be a superior policy to impose an appropriate levy on the level of polluting emissions rather than banning the use of more polluting grades of a mineral. No matter what policy is used to address this problem, it is clear that in the illustrated case, market failure results in the social economic benefit of utilizing the mineral being less than it could be if the less polluting grade of the mineral is utilized.

Figure 12.6 can also be re-interpreted to illustrate how (due to the presence of environmental externalities) a profit-maximizing miner or processor of a mineral can fail to adopt a socially optimal technique of production. Suppose that two alternative techniques of production are available and suppose that the X-axis in Fig. 12.6 represents the quantity of output of a mine or a mineral processor. Let line ABC represent the firm's marginal profit from employing the technique generating the most costly negative externalities. After allowing for these externality costs, assume that marginal social benefit of the least environmentally friendly production technique is as shown by line DEF. Let line GHJ indicate the firm's marginal profit when it uses the most environmentally friendly technique of production and suppose that line KLM represents the marginal social benefit of production given this choice of technique. The firm has no profit incentive to adopt the most environmentally friendly technique ever even though doing so is of the greatest social benefit. This hatched area plus the dotted area in Fig. 12.6 provides a monetary measure of the increased social benefit obtained when the more environmentally friendly technique rather than the less friendly one is adopted, and the firm's level of production is unregulated. When the firm's level of output is adjusted to ensure that the marginal social benefit of its production is zero whichever technique is adopted, the increase in the monetized value of the social benefit by using the most, rather than the least environmentally friendly technique of production, is equivalent to the hatched area in Fig. 12.6.

12.5.3. *The desirability of the holistic consideration of the environmental effects of mining and of the utilization of minerals*

When assessing the environmental effects of mining and its social economic value and the formulation of policies to address unfavorable spillovers generated by mining, it is desirable to consider a wider range of impacts than those typically taken into account in standard economic modeling, for example, of the type outlined in Chapter 5 and in the previous subsection. Particularly in market economies, the mining industry does not exist in economic isolation. It is connected to the rest of the economy by backward and forward economic linkages, that is by its use of inputs supplied by other industries and by the utilization of its production of minerals by other sectors of the economy. These linkages (or industrial networks) result in most cases in the generation of added environmental spillovers beyond the immediate mining sphere. Therefore, a more holistic picture of the total environmental effects of mineral production and utilization of minerals can be obtained when their economy-wide environmental spillovers are accounted for. Input-output analysis can provide an initial step in accounting for these spillovers. For example, it can help to quantify the extent of the economic linkages and the environmental effects associated with each of these linkages can be identified and their environmental consequences could be measured to provide an overall picture of environmental effects. However, this exercise can be costly; available information may be limited and obtaining funding for this type of research may not be easy.

Furthermore, in assessing the environmental consequences of economic projects associated with mining and the use of minerals, it is important to consider their whole-of-life environmental consequences. For example, at the end of their economic life, equipment for solar and wind power generation will need to be disposed of. The environmental effects of doing so (or failing to do this) should be considered. This type of problem seems to be acute in the case of nuclear power generation. In this case, spent nuclear fuels needs to be disposed of and at the end of their useful economic life, and nuclear power plants need to be decommissioned taking into account the environmental consequences of doing this.

Many current assessments of the environmental effects of mining and mineral utilization are insufficiently holistic.

12.6. Policies for Regulating the Environmental Impacts of Mining and the Possible Future Scarcity of Minerals

12.6.1. *Preliminary points*

Chapter 5 provides an in-depth discussion of the major types of policies considered by economists for regulating adverse environmental spillovers and other environmental deficiencies generated by market failures. These have been applied in some jurisdictions to regulate negative environmental externalities involving the utilization of minerals, for example, carbon-trading schemes designed to limit CO_2 emissions. These schemes are intended to limit greenhouse gas emissions in order to reduce the rate of human-induced climate change. The detailed coverage in Chapter 5 of economic instruments for regulating adverse environmental externalities will not be repeated here. Instead, new aspects of particular relevance to mining will be discussed.

It should be borne in mind that using economic instruments to control adverse environmental externalities is not costless. For example, market transaction costs are involved in the trading of pollution rights and these markets need not work perfectly. Governments usually incur costs in regulating adverse environmental spillovers and in limiting resource use, these agency or transaction costs diminish the social value of government intervention. Sometimes these costs exceed the social benefits that would otherwise be obtained by government intervention. In addition, environmental regulation results in businesses incurring extra administrative costs. These costs also reduce the social benefits of environmental regulation. The estimated social economic gains from any type of environmental regulation need to be adjusted to allow for such factors.

Another important economic issue is the extent to which controlling one adverse environmental externality can result in a reduction in other types of negative externalities. For example, the control of one type of negative environmental spillover may indirectly reduce that of another or other environmental spillovers. Considerations of side effects of this type should ideally be factored into decision-making about environmental regulation. Because it is likely to be uneconomic to regulate all the multiple types of adverse environmental externalities caused by an economic activity (including mining and the utilization of minerals), the above-mentioned synergies should be taken into account in determining and prioritizing the types of environmental spillovers that ought to be regulated. It is also possible that when one adverse externality is moderated, another negative one becomes more marked. This possibility should also be considered.

12.6.2. *Legal actions and remedies as a way of regulating adverse environmental externalities from mining*

The way in which laws are used to regulate environmental damages or to limit the risks of such damages varies with jurisdictions. Environmental laws also vary considerably in their nature and in their content. In addressing this subject, one needs to consider the role of the state (government bodies) in formulating and enforcing environmental laws (statutory law) and the nature of these laws. However, in some jurisdictions common law is also relevant. It is an important component of the law of torts, for example, in the United Kingdom.

It is not possible here to provide an in-depth economic coverage of environmental law. Additional relevant aspects are covered, for instance, in Tisdell (1983). The focus here is on economic limitations of utilizing the legal system to manage the occurrence of adverse environmental spillovers from mining activity as well as controlling the risks of such spillovers. Consideration is given first to factors which limit the ability of state authorities to utilize statutory environmental laws to manage unwanted environmental consequences of mining.

Subsequently, attention will be paid to the economic consequences of the ability of victims of adverse environmental spillovers from mining to sue perpetrator(s) of these for compensation and/or to obtain court orders requiring the perpetrator(s) to desist from such actions. In addition, some consideration will be given to the economics of legal action that might be taken by legal entities at risk of adverse environmental spillovers from possible mining disasters. The discussion will focus on the limited ability of the legal system to regulate the environmental risks and damages in a socially beneficial economic manner.

Several factors can limit the ability of state authorities to enforce statutory environmental laws, and to effectively control adverse (actual or potential) environmental spillovers. These can include their limited ability to detect breaches of the law and a low-level of motivation to enforce the law. Furthermore, the economic gain to those flaunting environmental law, in some cases, can be well in excess of the penalties for breaking the law. To be more specific, the economic gains from ignoring environmental laws can be well in excess of the expected penalty (cost) from doing this, that is, the probability of detection times the probable size of the fine. The greater the net anticipated economic gains involved, the greater is the economic temptation of those subject to environmental laws to disregard them or to diminish their compliance with them.

A second issue of particular relevance to mining is the ability of a mining entity to pay financial penalties for breaches of environmental law, including environmental disasters for which it is legally responsible. If a miner becomes financially bankrupt or insolvent, it will be unable to comply with legal environmental regulations, pay fines for environmental damage or pay compensation to victims of adverse environmental spillovers. Sometimes, large mining companies deliberately create subsidiary companies to limit or escape their legal responsibility for dealing with environmental damage. For example, a parent company might establish subsidiary mining companies (each with limited liability) in developing countries. Hence, the parent company may escape paying should environmental disasters occur. Also, most of the profits from these subsidiaries might be paid to the parent company.

Consequently, on the closure of these mines, little or no funds may be left with these subsidiaries to ensure the environmental integrity of their mining sites or to undertake any restoration work.

It also follows that when the law permits those damaged to claim compensation from a perpetrator for adverse from environmental spillovers, this will be of little avail if the perpetrator has insufficient funds to pay. Furthermore, legal action to sue for damages can be costly and the outcome uncertain. This can be expected to deter many of those who are adversely affected by environmental spillovers from pursuing their legal rights. On the other hand, class actions organized by legal firms on a no win/no fee basis increase the likelihood of such action being taken.

Nevertheless, the possibility of class actions does not provide a perfect solution to the above-mentioned problem. Legal firms are only likely to institute class actions if their anticipated economic returns from doing so are sufficiently high. They can be expected to be selective in the cases they are willing to pursue. As a result, some deserving cases will not be pursued. Furthermore, depending upon the fees of legal firms acting on behalf of plaintiffs and the award of court costs (if an environmental dispute goes to court), the victims of environmental spillovers can be left with little compensation. In addition, the relevant legal process of attaining compensation is of no economic value in itself — in fact, it would be an economic advantage to society if the costs involved could be avoided or reduced.

Class actions are less likely to be pursued to reduce the likelihood of environmental damages (or to obtain compensation for exposure to the risk of these damages) than following the occurrence of actual environmental damages. In cases involving only the risk of environmental damage, there is unlikely to be a payout to plaintiffs. It also may be difficult for those at risk of environmental damage to collect any or sufficient convincing evidence about the risks to them of environmental damage.

If the state sets environmental standards and these are flouted by miners, this may make it easier to mount a successful case against them if the standards are breached. On the other hand, if these standards are low, this can protect miners from claims for damages in those cases where the standards are met but environmental damages are considerable.

12.6.3. *Bonds as a means of ensuring environmental compliance*

Given that mining companies may be involved in ventures that prove to be uneconomic, it has been suggested that they might be required to lodge bonds (a quantity of funds) with the state or some state body to cover the possibility that they may be unable to comply with their environmental obligations or to pay penalties for non-compliance. Any excess of funds can be returned to the miner on the closure of a mine, provided all environmental obligations are met, for example, after all required site remediation has been completed.

This approach, however, creates a financial burden for mining companies and is likely to have a negative effect on economic growth, especially if the size of the bond is large. On the other hand, if the size of the bond is small, it may be insufficient to cover the environmental obligations of the company such as site restoration. The company may then find it economic to forgo repayment of the bond and not undertake the required measures to remediate a mining site. McCullough *et al.* (2009) state that usually the size of mining bonds is inadequate to cover the cost of rehabilitating abandoned mining sites.

The question is also relevant of how much a mining site should be restored to its original state, and to what extent future environmental spillovers (or risks of these) should be mitigated. Social cost-benefit analysis may provide some guidance in that regard.

12.6.4. *Policies to limit the extraction of minerals on economic sustainability grounds*

Daly (1980) has raised the possibility that the depletion of the stock of minerals is occurring at a faster rate than is socially desirable from an economic sustainability point of view. He has proposed that governments introduce aggregate quotas to reduce the amount of each type of mineral mined annually so that this amount is less than otherwise would prevail. Daly (1980) envisages that mining permits would be

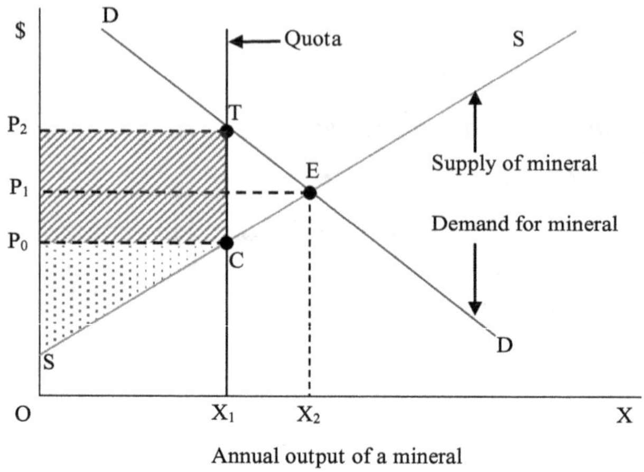

Fig. 12.7. A diagram similar to that used by Daly (1980) to illustrate how a government quota restricting the production of a mineral would work.

auctioned so as to allocate quotas and illustrates his policy proposal by a diagram similar to that in Fig. 12.7. In that figure, line SS represents the market supply schedule of a mineral and the line marked DD indicates its market demand schedule. Based on market demand and supply analysis, the market equilibrium of this mineral would be established at point E. The aggregate output of the mineral would be X_2 and its price per unit would be P_1. Daly believes that for economic sustainability reasons, actual rates of mining of minerals are typically too high. To counteract this, he recommends that a quota be imposed by the government to restrict mineral production, for example, to an output of X_1 in the case illustrated in Fig. 12.7. In a competitive market, mining permits for each unit of the mineral would sell for P_0 if auctioned and the price of each unit of the mineral would rise from P_0 to P_2. Furthermore, as a result of auctioning mining permits, the government would obtain revenue equivalent to the hatched area in Fig. 12.7. The rents (economic surplus) of miners would be reduced by an amount equivalent to the area of trapezium P_0CEP$_1$. They would be left with an economic surplus equivalent to the dotted triangle.

Daly's outline of his policy approach is incomplete. Just how much he believes the output of minerals should be reduced is not specified.

Presumably, a permit system for mining production would need to specify the allowable production for several years not just one and permits ought to be tradable (see Chapter 5). The permits could also have an in-built adjustment factor as time passes and circumstances change. Daly does not give much guidance in this regard. However, several relevant issues involving the use of tradeable permits are discussed in Chapter 5.

It is also relevant to note that in principle, point T in Fig. 12.7 could be obtained by imposing a tax, levy or royalty payment on the production of the mineral which raises its supply schedule so that it passes through point T (see Chapter 5).

Even if restricting mineral output is desirable, implementing policies to achieve this nationally can be difficult. For example, nations often compete with one another to obtain (foreign) investment in mining. This can restrict the willingness of individual nations to deter such investment by limiting the allowable output of miners and imposing high taxes or levies on their output. Corruption can also result in under payment of mineral royalties and in the understatement of mineral output. Furthermore, future economic scarcity of individual minerals is difficult to predict. This uncertainty makes it challenging to determine how much current mineral production should be restricted on sustainability grounds, for example, how much precaution should be exercised in depleting mineral stocks.

12.7. Social Conflict, Mining and the Environment

Mining is frequently a source of social conflict. Temper *et al.* (2015) have mapped the incidence of social conflicts and their nature, many of which involve mining. Many (but not all) of these conflicts arise because of the adverse environmental impacts of mining. Local communities experiencing a decline in the quality of their life due to the environmental consequences of mining operations or which find their livelihoods suffer as a result of environmental spillovers from mining (for which miners do not compensate them or acceptably so in the opinion of members of these communities) may oppose mining and protest against it. In addition, "green" groups not belonging to these local communities may oppose mining, as has become more common in the case of coal mining because coal production is seen as making a major downstream contribution to greenhouse gas emissions and hence, adds significantly to global warming. On the other hand, these green groups may come into conflict with local individuals who have gained or expect to gain employment in coal mining and thereby benefit from it economically. The parties to such conflicts can be quite varied. Both members of local communities and of wider communities can be very divided about the desirability of mining operations and the basis of these social conflicts can vary considerably.

The distribution of rents (returns) from profitable mining operations can generate social conflict. Sometimes, regions where profitable mining takes place demand a greater slice of the public revenue obtained from it and agitate for autonomy from centralized governments. Another possible source of contention is the extent to which locals are employed in mining. In some instances, little or no employment of locals may occur, particularly where there is a lack of local labor having skills required in the type of mining being undertaken. Especially in some developing countries, some types of mining can have the attributes of an enclave industry, that is, they have little or no economic interdependence with the rest of the national economy. Hence, circumstances can occur in which mining operations generate little employment of nationals either directly or indirectly. A similar situation can occur regionally within nations, that is a low level of employment of locals in mining and little interaction with the local economy. Nevertheless, care should be taken not to generalize because the social political and economic conditions faced by miners vary. The economic consequences of new mining ventures in remote areas can, for example, differ significantly from those in regions where mining has been established for a long period of time.

Mining also raises several types of sustainability issues. It can disrupt traditional cultures and ways of life, particularly of indigenous people. In addition, mines usually have a limited length of economic life; the length of which can be uncertain. This often leads to the lack of sustainability of local communities which depend on mining. Furthermore, some nations that rely heavily on mining for incomes (such as oil and natural gas dependent states in the Middle East and Brunei in Southeast Asia) face the future prospect of diminishing economic reserves of these fossil fuels and possibly, in the long-term, reduced demand for their output. If their rental income from production of oil and natural gas falls (or grows at a slower pace than the rate of increase of their population), they face the challenge of finding new ways to maintain or limit the reduction in their income levels. Their scope for developing alternative industries (diversifying) in order to sustain their high levels of incomes may be limited and a reduction in their income levels may eventually be inevitable. It follows that economic dependence on mining can raise significant sustainability challenges both at the national and at the local level.

A pertinent question is whether it is socially just to determine the desirability of mining ventures purely on the basis of the Kaldor-Hicks (potential Paretian improvement) criterion. Posner (1981) has argued that this criterion ought to prevail in determining whether an economic change is justified (see Chapter 4). The basis of his view is that application of this criterion will promote economic growth, and all will subsequently gain as a result of greater economic growth. Even those who initially lose will benefit eventually according to this view. However, in practice, there is no guarantee that this will happen. Individuals can experience permanent economic damage as a result of mining developments. Moreover, the question of how fairly or unfairly the economic benefits of mining are distributed needs to be considered (see, for example, Martinez-Alier, 2002). Furthermore, ignoring the distributional consequences of mining can be costly (for instance, it can have a negative effect on economic growth) if it results in disruptive demonstrations or, for example, in armed rebellion as happened in the case of the Bougainville copper mine in Papua New Guinea. Because of armed local opposition to the copper mine, it had to be closed. This development also led to agitation for Bougainville to become politically independent of Papua New Guinea. Local resistance to the mine stemmed from its adverse effects on the local environment and because residents of Bougainville felt that they did not obtain a fair share of the economic benefits from its operation.

Governments can also have a vested interest in allowing mining to occur because royalties and taxes received from mining add to government revenue. Public servants may have an interest in greater public revenue because it can increase the level of employment and salaries in the public sector. Furthermore, politicians may welcome greater public revenue since this can enable them to fund political promises. It is also pertinent to note that most of the public revenue from mining may be spent in urban areas where public servants are mainly employed and in most cases, the majority of electors reside. This can result in urban bias in economic development.

Another important sustainability aspect is the availability of minerals and metals needed for national defense. Since ancient times, ensuring sufficient supplies of minerals and metals essential for defense and wars has been a strategic concern of states wanting to maintain their sovereignty or to expand their territorial influence. This concern can shape the foreign policies of nations and their economic support for industries considered to be vital in times of war as well as the stockpiling of materials limited in availability in a country but required in the case of war.

12.8. Concluding Comments

In this chapter, two important aspects of mining have been discussed, namely the long-term economic availability of supplies of minerals (as indicated by trends in their real prices) and the negative environmental externalities associated with the mining and utilization of minerals. Both of these aspects (as was demonstrated) have important sustainability consequences. The first matter is of particular relevance to the ability of humankind to sustain its level of material production and maintain its economic prosperity. In addition, localities and nations which rely heavily on mining for their economic prosperity can find it difficult or impossible to maintain their income levels in the long run because of the limited economic life of the mining operations.

As for the second matter mentioned above, environmental externalities from mining can have both adverse sustainability consequences as well as negative effects on the economic allocation of resources. These negative environmental externalities result in the private value of production by firms exceeding its social value. In these circumstances, the market system is unlikely to allocate resources to mining so as to maximize the social value of production, and the market system may fail to result in the choice of socially optimal techniques for mining production. Indeed, economic activity can have a much lower economic value than is theoretically socially desirable due to the presence of unfavorable environmental spillovers and a lower social value than that which might be attained by some government intervention in the working of the market system. Some public policies and legal actions to address the above-mentioned economic failures were discussed in this chapter with particular reference to mining.

Note that the existence of sustainability problems and negative spillovers associated with mining and the utilization of minerals does not imply that it would be a social economic advantage to stop these activities. Even activities that have unfavorable negative spillovers can have a positive social economic value. In addition, it seems pointless to forego the use of many types of minerals in perpetuity on the grounds that they are not renewable. Furthermore, it should be borne in mind that given current global population and consumption levels, a major reduction in the allowable level of production of minerals would result in a substantial decline in incomes. While some of this reduced availability of minerals might be offset by substitutes obtained from renewables, such as the substitution of wood for some metals and natural fibers for artificial fibers, this is likely to be at the expense of food output. The current capacity of the planet to support existing humans could, as a result, fall significantly resulting in a catastrophe. The sustainability of a policy of substantially raising the quantities of minerals conserved is likely to depend on reducing the level of the human population and the levels of their material consumption. Politically, these policies would be difficult to implement. However, the use of some minerals may be phased out or significantly reduced with the passage of time as new and more sustainable substitutes with fewer negative spillovers become available and are more economic to supply.

As pointed out in the next chapter, this is already happening in the case of fossil fuels — energy from wind and solar power is being increasingly substituted for the use of fossil fuels, especially coal.

12.9. Keywords

Bonds and mining; economic growth and mining; economic inequality and mining; economic scarcity of minerals; environmental laws and mining; limiting mining output for sustainability; minerals and economic development; mining and sustainability; mining; negative environmental externalities from mining; social conflict and mining; trends in real prices of minerals; types of minerals; user costs.

12.10. Questions for Review and Discussion

1. How has the increased utilization of minerals contributed to economic development? Has this contribution been, in your view, beneficial for humankind? Why?
2. Do you agree with the view that the increased utilization of minerals has enabled the earth to support a higher level of human population at a higher standard of living than otherwise would have been achieved? Explain your answer. What would happen to the level of global population and living standards if the supply of minerals was substantially and rapidly reduced? Why would this happen?
3. Trends in the real prices of minerals have not been uniform. What types of basic trends have been observed? Which trends appear to predominate? Can we expect these predominant trends to continue in the future or should we be cautious in this regard? Why?
4. Explain how the use of comparative static market analysis can help explain changes in mineral prices.
5. Critically assess the effectiveness of the market system as a mechanism for conserving the stock of minerals. Under what conditions would it be a relatively effective mechanism for conserving these stocks. What factors reduce its effectiveness in this regard?

6. What types of adverse environmental effects can be caused by mining? Is the existence of these effects sufficient to warrant the banning of mining? Discuss.
7. The nature of market failures due to environmental spillovers from mining varies. Outline and discuss the four types of market failures that can occur. How might governments interfere to regulate these spillovers?
8. Do you believe that the economy-wide environmental spillovers stemming from mining ought to be taken into account in formulating environmental policy? Why? Why is it important in assessing the social economic value of mining to consider the whole-of-life environmental impacts of mining?
9. To what extent is the legal system likely to be effective in regulating the possible adverse environmental consequences from mining?
10. What are the possible advantages and disadvantages of using bonds to motivate mining firms to comply with environmental regulations?
11. Daly has argued that the extraction of minerals should be restricted by governments for sustainability reasons. Do you agree with his point of view? Explain. What problems are likely to arise in implementing this type of policy?
12. What types of social conflicts can arise as a result of mining?
13. Is it socially just to determine the desirability of mining projects only on the basis of the Paretian improvement criterion? Furthermore, in what circumstances might application of this principle hinder economic growth rather than foster it?
14. The types of sustainability issues involving mining are quite varied. Outline and discuss these issues. In doing so, pay attention to local, national and global sustainability issues.

Readings and References

Barnett, H.J. and C. Morse (1963). *Scarcity and Growth,* The Johns Hopkins University Press for Resources for the Future, Baltimore, MD, USA.

Baumol, W.J. and W. Oates (1979). Are we running out of resources? *Economics, Environmental Policy and the Quality of Life,* Prentice-Hall, Englewood Cliffs, NJ, USA.

Childe, V.G. (1965). *Man Makes Himself,* 4th edn. (first published 1936), Collins, London. First published 1936. London, Watts.

Cuddington, J.T. and G. Nülle (2014). Variable long-term trends in mineral prices: The ongoing tug-of-war between exploration, depletion, and technological change, *Journal of International Money and Finance,* 42, 224–252. doi: https://doi.org/10.1016/j.jimonfin.2013.08.013.

Daly, H.E. (1980). The steady-state economy: Toward a political economy of biophysical and moral growth. In H.E. Daly (Ed.) *Economics, Ecology, Ethics: Essays Toward a Steady-State Economy,* 324–356. W.H. Freeman & Co, San Francisco.

Heal, G. (1981). Scarcity, efficiency and disequilibrium in resource markets, *The Scandinavian Journal of Economics,* 83, 334–351. doi: 10.2307/3439904.

Hicks, J.R. (1946). *Value and Capital,* Clarendon Press, Oxford.

Hotelling, H. (1931). The economics of exhaustible resources, *Journal of Political Economy,* 39, 137–175.

Levhari, D. and R.S. Pindyck (1981). The pricing of durable exhaustible resources, *The Quarterly Journal of Economics,* 96, 366–377. doi: 10.2307/1882678.

Martinez-Alier, J. (2002). *The Environmentalism of the Poor: A Study of Ecological Conflict and Valuation,* Edward Elgar Publishing Cheltenham, UK and Northampton, MA, USA.

Mazoyer, M. and L. Roudart (2006). *A History of World Agriculture: From the Neolithic Age to the Current Crisis,* J.H. Membrez [trans.], Earthscan, London and Sterling, V.A.

McCullough, C., D. Hunt and L. Evans (2009). Sustainable development of open pit mines: creating beneficial uses for pit lakes. In DN Castendyk and L.E. Early (Eds.), *Mine Pit Lakes: Characteristics, Predictive Modelling and Sustainability,* Vol. 3, 249–267. SME Society for Mining, Metallurgy and Exploration, Littleton, Colorado, USA.

Posner, R.A. (1981). *The Economics of Justice,* Harvard University Press, Cambridge, MA, and London, UK.

Prebisch, R. (1962). The economic development of Latin America and its principal problems, *Economic Bulletin for Latin America,* 7, 1–22.

Renfrew, C. (2007). *Prehistory: The Making of the Human Mind,* Weidenfeld and Nicolson, London.

Singer, H.W. (1950). The distribution of gains between investing and borrowing countries, *The American Economic Review,* 40, 473–485.

Slade, M.E. (1982). Trends in natural-resource commodity prices: An analysis of the time domain, *Journal of Environmental Economics and Management,* 9, 122–137. doi: https://doi.org/10.1016/0095-0696(82)90017-1.

Spitz, K. and J. Trudinger (2009). *Mining and the Environment: From Ore to Metal,* CRC Press, Lieden, The Netherlands.

Temper, L., D. del Bene and J. Martinez-Alier (2015). Mapping the frontiers and front lines of global environmental justice: The EJAtlas, *Journal of Political Economy,* 22, 255–278. doi: https://doi.org/10.2458/v22i1.21108.

Tietenberg, T. and L. Lewis (2018). *Environmental and Natural Resource Economics,* 11th edn. Routledge, New York and Abingdon, Oxon, UK [Chapters 6 and 8].

Tisdell, C.A. (1968). *The Theory of Price Uncertainty, Production and Profit,* Princeton University Press, Princeton, NJ. (Chapter 2: Some theories of decision-making). Reprinted, 2015.

Tisdell, C.A. (1983). Law, economics and risk-taking, *Kyklos,* 36, 3–20.

Chapter 13

Energy Use, Global Warming, and Air Pollution

13.1. Introduction

Currently, energy use is the major (but not the only) source of reduced air quality. It is the main cause of global warming, a source of acid rain in some parts of the world, and often results in emissions of smoke, particulate matter and noxious gases resulting in ill health and poor visibility. In addition, excessive noise is frequently generated by energy use, such as noise from road, rail and air transport. As a result of economic changes that started with the Industrial Revolution, combustion of fossil fuels (coal, oil and natural gas) to produce energy has become the major source of reduced air quality. The Industrial Revolution stimulated the demand for coal and further technological advances reinforced the upward trend in demand for coal as an energy source. Subsequently, demand for other fossil fuels accelerated because the invention of the combustion engine greatly expanded the demand for oil and more recently, the demand for natural gas has grown substantially. While fossil fuels are the major contributors to global human-generated supplies of energy, use of other sources (such as hydro, wind and solar power) has increased in recent years. Use of these energy sources (discussed below) also can have adverse environmental consequences.

The use by humans of fossil fuels following the Industrial Revolution meant that humankind was much less reliant on human energy and energy supplied by animals (such as horses and oxen). This heralded a substantial economic advance resulting in a significant rise in standards of living in countries that adopted the new technologies. It may also have contributed to the end of slavery in more developed countries and their colonies.

However, these economic benefits were secured at a cost. They appear to have resulted initially in considerable social stress, as observed by Karl Marx (1967, Chapter 28), and in severe environmental problems as predicted by the environmental Kuznets relationship (see Subsection 7.2.4). In the initial phases of industrialization, most of these negative environmental impacts were probably of a local and regional nature but were nevertheless, very damaging to human health. The long-term environmental costs of dependence on fossil fuels, particularly the potential costs associated with global warming were not evident. It is only in recent decades that the potential magnitude of the environmental costs associated with global warming have become of concern. Global warming threatens economic sustainability and is predicted to wipe out some human communities (such as those located on low maritime islands and on coastal estuaries) as a result of projected rises in sea level. Furthermore, communities in some other regions may no longer be economically viable because of climate change, for example, resulting in the onset of recurrent drought and desertification.

This is a long chapter. It has therefore, been divided into two parts. Part A (Sections 13.2 and 13.3) concentrate on electricity, heat production and greenhouse gas (GHG) emissions. The production of electricity plus heat is a major source of GHG emissions and therefore, merits special attention. Part A examines trends in the global amount of electricity and heat produced, identifies changes in the quantities of different natural resources utilized for this production and considers the implications of these changes for the level of GHG emissions. As well, it outlines the infant industry case for subsidizing the development and use of "green" electricity.

Part B (Sections 13.4 to 13.9) focuses on additional issues involving air quality. Its coverage includes the analysis of barriers to collective action designed to reduce the deterioration of global air quality, ozone layer depletion and important economic aspects of global warming such as estimates of its economic costs. The nature and shortcomings of international agreements to limit global warming are also considered. In addition, economic measures for regulating the level of GHG emissions are given specific attention in Part B. Subsequently, the economic analysis of local and regional air pollution as well as transboundary pollution is given attention. The concluding section provides a retrospective perspective on the coverage of the whole of this chapter. Each section (and most subsections of this chapter) can be read independently.

Part A: Production of Electricity and Heat: Trends, Changes in Natural Resource Use and their Consequences for GHG Emissions

13.2. Sources of Energy Supply for Electricity and Heat Production and the Global Consumption of These Sources

13.2.1. *The basics*

The sun is the prime source of energy on earth. Nearly all living things depend directly or indirectly on the sun in order to sustain their life processes. The sun has made possible the occurrence of fossil fuels (such as coal, oil and natural gas) which have stored this energy. Fossil fuels consist of ancient deposits of dead plant material (and its derivatives, such as natural gas) and contain carbon and other volatile substances which the plants (and plant-like single-celled organisms) accumulated during their life-time by photosynthesis made possible by sunlight. Fossil fuels provide a large source of (virtually) non-renewable energy supplies. Plants continue to absorb and store energy from the sun and non-fossil organic fuels, such as wood, and were the earliest sources of inanimate energy resources used by mankind to provide heat and light.

Today, plant material is being used to supply biofuels such as biodiesel and ethanol. However, non-fossil organic materials only account for a small proportion of fuel used today, except in some developing countries. Globally the use of fossil fuels as an energy source continues to expand prompting fears that economic sustainability will be jeopardized. This is because of their impacts on air pollution, their cumulative consequences for global warming, and the prospects of depletion of some fossil fuels, such as oil (see Chapter 7).

The importance of the sun as an energy source is not limited to its contribution to the growth of plants and those single-celled organisms which rely on photosynthesis to survive but also plays an important role in the hydrological cycle, in air movements and in the pattern of water currents. Consequently, it contributes indirectly to the supply of hydro-power and wind as power-sources. Solar energy can also be used directly by humans. Nevertheless, as pointed out in Chapter 7, the sun is not the only source of energy on the earth. Other sources include energy stored in the earth's core, radioactive substances such as uranium, and gravitational forces which, for instance, give rise to tidal movements.

13.2.2. *The quantity of electricity produced globally by utilizing different natural resources*

Electricity generation accounts for a large share of energy use globally and is a major contributor to CO_2 emissions. Tables 13.1 and 13.2 present information on the sources of global energy production in 2005 and 2017 and changes in these sources between 2005 and 2017. Coal and gas were the main sources of electricity production in both 2005 and 2017. Fossil fuels (coal and gas plus oil) accounted for 66% of electricity production in 2005 and in 2017, this fell slightly to 65%. Increased utilization of coal made the largest contribution to the rising volume of electricity production followed by gas. Even though the utilization of oil for electricity production fell, the overall increase in the utilization of fossil fuels increased substantially. As a result, the electricity sector added considerably to the volume of GHG emissions, especially of CO_2.

Table 13.1. The amounts contributed to global electricity production by different sources in 2005 and 2017 and changes in these.

Rank 2005	Rank 2017	Production source	Electricity (Unit: GWh) 2005	Electricity (Unit: GWh) 2017	Change in source(GWh)	Percentage change in source
1	1	Coal	7321697	9863339	+2541642	34.713
2	2	Gas	3704141	5882825	+2178684	58.817
3	3	Hydro	3019502	4197299	+1177797	39.006
4	4	Nuclear	2767952	2636030	−131922	−4.766
5	6	Oil	1135309	841878	−293431	−10.601
6	7	Biofuels	170875	482529	+311654	182.387
7	5	Wind	103922	1127319	+1023397	984.774
8	9	Waste	57821	114043	+56222	97.234
9	10	Geothermal	58284	85348	+27064	46.434
11	8	Solar PV	3929	443554	+439625	11189.233
12	12	Solar thermal	597	10848	+10251	1717.085
13	13	Tide	516	1044	+528	102.325
10	11	Other	33309	36022	+2713	8.144
		Total Production	18377852	25721050	+7343198	39.956

Source: Based on an International Energy Agency (2005) table entitled "Electricity/Heat in World in 2005" and 2017 Based on International Energy Agency (2017a) table entitled "Electricity and Heat/World/2017".

The rising quantities of electricity generated by coal and gas since 1990 are illustrated in Fig. 13.1. Generation of electricity using gas has accelerated in recent years whereas the rate of use of coal (while still positive) has declined. Figure 13.2 shows the total amount of electricity generated globally by the utilization of fossil fuels. This displays a positive trend.

As for other sources of global electricity production, hydro made the third largest contribution in 2005 and 2017 and nuclear was in fourth place. Nuclear displayed almost a 5% decline in its contribution, probably as a reaction to the nuclear disaster in Fukushima, Japan in 2011.

Table 13.2. Percentage contributions to total global electricity production by sources in 2005 and 2017 and differences in these.

Production source	Percentage of total electricity production		Difference in percentage contribution
	2005	2017	
Coal	39.839	38.347	−1.492
Gas	20.155	22.871	+2.716
Hydro	16.430	16.318	−0.112
Nuclear	15.061	10.248	−4.813
Oil	6.177	3.273	−2.904
Biofuels	0.929	1.872	+0.943
Wind	0.565	4.382	+3.817
Waste	0.314	0.443	+0.129
Geothermal	0.317	0.331	+0.014
Solar PV	0.021	1.724	+1.703
Solar thermal	0.003	0.042	+0.039
Tide	0.002	0.004	+0.002
Other sources	0.181	0.140	−0.041
Total Production	100	100	

Source: Based on Table 13.1.

Solar (photovoltaic and thermal) followed by wind, registered the greatest percentage increase in supplying electricity between 2005 and 2017. The amount of extra electricity supplied by wind power was almost equal to the additional amount provided by hydro. However, in 2017, wind and solar PV still only accounted for around 6% of global electricity production. Their share is likely to increase in coming years. This is because the production of electricity using these technologies is becoming more competitive with the production using coal and gas. The International Energy Agency (2017b, p. 1) reported that since 2010 the costs of new solar PV electricity generation had fallen by 70%, wind by 25% and battery costs were down by 40%. Further declines in these costs are anticipated. The International Energy Agency (2017b, p. 2) anticipates that by 2040 the share of all renewables in total electricity generation might reach 40%.

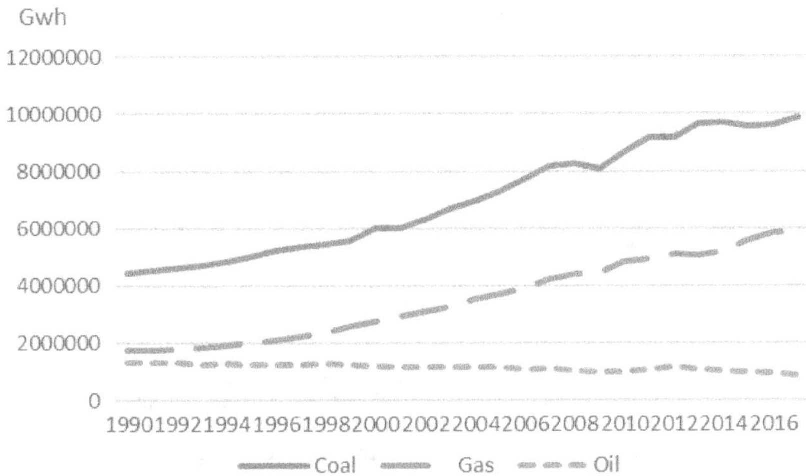

Fig. 13.1. The annual amount of global electricity production generated by the use of coal, gas and oil in the period 1990–2017.
Source: Based on data in International Energy Agency (2017a).

If this happens, the electricity sector will still continue to make a substantial contribution to GHG emissions because up to 60% of electricity production would still be obtained by using fossil fuels. In addition, because the demand for and supply of electricity is predicted to increase substantially by 2040 (International Energy Agency, 2017b) this will have an elevating effect on GHG emissions from fossil fuel uses in the electricity sector. Furthermore, when backward and forward linkages are taken into account (as well as life-cycle considerations) even the use of "renewable" resources for the production of electricity results in some emission of GHGs, albeit on a much smaller scale than the utilization of fossil fuels.

Some of the factors that are expected to elevate the demand for electricity in coming years include

- increased reliance on electric vehicles for transport;
- greater use of air conditioning units for cooling and heating;
- growing electricity use involving digital technologies (see International Energy Agency, 2017b, pp. 2–3).

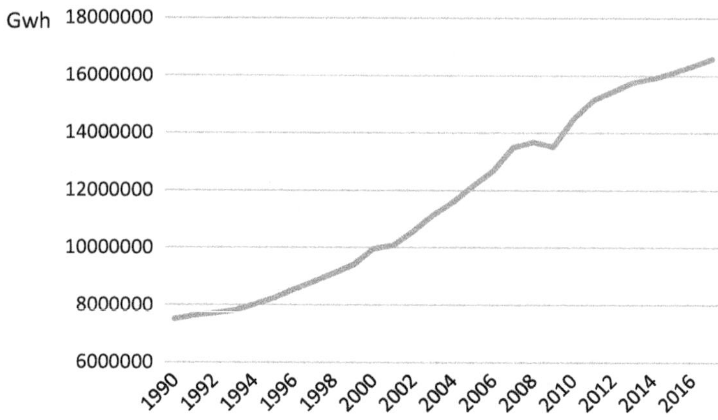

Fig. 13.2. The annual amount of global electricity generated by the use of fossil fuels (coal, gas, and oil) 1990–2017.
Source:Based on data in International Energy Agency (2017a).

13.2.3. *The quantity of heat produced globally by utilizing different natural resources*

Substantial amounts of natural resources are utilized for producing heat globally other than for the purpose of generating electricity. Table 13.3 sets out the amounts different sources contributed to total heat production in 2005 and 2017 and Table 13.4 lists the percentage contribution of each source. It can be seen from Table 13.1 that the percentage increase in production of electricity between 2005 and 2017 (almost 40%) significantly outstripped the percentage rise in the total production of heat in this time-span which (as specified in Table 13.3) was 7.6%. There has been a long-term tendency for heat provided by electricity to replace that supplied directly from other sources.

Fossil fuels account for the bulk of total heat supplied directly to end users. In 2005, fossil fuels (gas, coal and oil) accounted for 92.33% of global heat production and in 2017, 88.5%. In that time-span, coal increased its contribution from 35.6% to 41.6%. Relative reliance on both gas and oil fell. The differences in percentages of heat produced by the use of gas and oil were 6.6% lower for the former and 3.57%

Table 13.3. The amounts contributed to global heat production by different sources in 2005 and 2017 and changes in these.

Rank 2005	Rank 2017	Production source	Heat (Unit: TJ) 2005	Heat (Unit: TJ) 2017	Change in source (TJ)	Percentage change in source
1	1	Gas	6619936	6175340	−444596	−6.716
2	2	Coal	4752119	5978057	+1225938	25.797
3	5	Oil	965171	526230	−438941	−45.478
5	3	Biofuels	295019	627335	+332316	112.642
6	6	Waste	235260	454656	+219396	93.256
7	7	Geothermal	23811	39910	+16099	67.611
8	8	Nuclear	20534	26771	+6237	30.374
9	9	Solar thermal	55	1815	+1760	3200
4	4	Other sources	440858	537483	+96625	21.917
		Total Production	13352762	14367598	+1014836	7.6

Source: Based on an International Energy Agency (2005) table entitled "Electricity/Heat in World in 2005" and 2017 based on International Energy Agency (2017a) table entitled "Electricity and Heat/World/2017".

lower for the latter in 2017 compared to 2005. The increase in the use of coal probably reflects its increased use for smelting minerals, especially iron ore. The substantial decline in the amount of oil utilized for heating may partly be a result of the rising use of electricity and gas for the provision of household heating.

It is clear that fossil fuels still continue to make a substantial contribution to the global production of heat and consequently, to GHG emissions, even though the proportion of heat supplied by the use of fossil fuels fell in 2017 compared to 2005. Note also that the growing use of biofuels (such as firewood) is also likely to make an increased contribution to global warming, for example, as a result of greater deforestation to supply firewood in some less developed countries, such as Madagascar. Furthermore, the production of biofuels using palm oil has reduced tropical forest cover. These developments reduce the

Table 13.4. Percentage contribution to total global heat production by different sources in 2005 and 2017 and differences in these.

Production source	Percentage of total heat production 2005	Percentage of total heat production 2017	Difference in percentage contribution
Gas	49.577	42.981	−6.596
Coal	35.589	41.607	+6.018
Oil	7.228	3.662	−3.566
Biofuels	2.209	4.366	+2.157
Waste	1.761	3.164	+1.403
Nuclear	0.153	0.186	+0.033
Geothermal	0.178	0.277	+0.099
Solar thermal	0.001	0.012	+0.011
Other sources	3.301	3.740	+0.439
Total Production	100	100	

Source: Based on Table 13.3.

capacity of forests to store carbon dioxide, add to the presence of CO_2 in the atmosphere and have other adverse environmental consequences.

13.2.4. *Further comments on the provision and use of electricity and heat as energy sources*

Tables 13.5 and 13.6 list the amounts of global consumption respectively of electricity and heat by sector (and in total) in 2005 and 2017. It can be seen that total electricity consumption increased in this period by almost 41%. On the other hand, the final global consumption of heat only rose by 1.88%. This reflects the growing preference for using electricity as a source of energy and heat rather than the direct utilization of heat. It can be deduced from Table 13.5 that in 2005 residential consumption of electricity accounted for 27.818% of total electricity consumption, and the non-residential share of this consumption was 72.182%. In 2017, these statistics were similar, namely 27.022% and 72.978%. Non-residential use of electricity accounted for the lion's share of electricity consumption and its share increased slightly in

Table 13.5. Global consumption of electricity by sector, 2005 and 2017 and changes in these quantities.

Rank 2005	Rank 2017	Sector	Consumption of Electricity (Unit: GWh) 2005	2017	Change in GWh	Percentage change by sector
1	1	Industry	6271220	8944697	+2673477	+42.630
2	2	Residential	4218567	5775265	+1556698	+36.901
3	3	Commercial and Public Services	3553866	4637213	+1083347	+30.483
5	5	Agriculture/Forestry	410309	641749	+231440	+56.406
6	6	Transport	260285	363664	+103379	+39.717
7	7	Fishing	4193	7592	+3399	+81.063
4	4	Other Non-Specified	446010	1001576	+555566	+124.563
		Total Final	15164450	21371756	+6207306	+40.933

Source: Based on an International Energy Agency (2005) table entitled "Electricity/Heat in world in 2005" and 2017 based on International Energy Agency (2017a) table entitled "Electricity and Heat/World/2017".

2017 compared to 2005. From Table 13.6, it can be calculated that in 2005, residential consumption of heat amounted to 35.40% of its global total, and non-residential use was equal to 64.60% of this total. Again these figures were similar in 2017, namely 35.07% and 64.93% respectively.

Increases in the quantity of electricity consumed and produced by nations depends to a considerable extent on their stage of economic growth. In less developed slowly growing or stagnant economies, there is little increase in their level of electricity consumption and production. However, once they enter a rapid economic growth phase, their production and consumption of electricity rises rapidly. When an economy eventually matures and becomes relatively developed and its rate of economic growth starts to decline, so too does the rate of increase in its production and consumption of electricity. A hypothesized relationship similar to that shown in Fig. 13.3 may apply.

Table 13.6. Global consumption of heat supply by sector, 2005 and 2017 and changes in these quantities.

Rank 2005	Rank 2017	Sector	Consumption of Heat (Unit: TJ) 2005	Consumption of Heat (Unit: TJ) 2017	Change in TJ	Change of sector %
1	1	Industry	4742229	5763694	+1021465	+21.539
2	2	Residential	4216339	4243538	+27199	+0.645
3	3	Commercial and Public Services	1327422	1633459	+306037	+23.054
5	5	Agriculture/Forestry	159448	145183	−14265	−8.946
6	6	Fishing	678	2374	+1696	+250.147
7	7	Transport	—	—	—	—
4	4	Other Non-Specified	1464541	332015	−1132526	−77.329
		Total Final	11910657	12120263	+209606	+1.759

Source: Based on an International Energy Agency (2005) table entitled "Electricity/Heat in World in 2005" and 2017 based on International Energy Agency (2017a) table entitled "Electricity and Heat/World/2017".

The relationship shown in Fig. 13.3 is compatible with trends in the production and consumption of electricity in Organisation for Economic Co-operation and Development OECD countries compared to non-OECD nations. Rapid economic growth in non-OECD nations resulted in their production of electricity exceeding that of OECD countries in 2011 (International Energy Agency, 2019, p. 3). The rate of economic growth of non-OECD countries in recent times has been much faster than that of the relatively mature OECD nations. As a result, electricity production has risen at a much slower rate in the latter countries compared to the former ones.

The demand for electricity is quite sensitive to the variations in the level of economic activity. A decline in the level of economic activity is usually associated with a fall in electricity production and in turn, this reduces the demand for resources which produce it. For example, the dip in the global production of electricity utilizing fossil fuels (evident from Fig. 13.2) which occurred in 2007–2009 was mainly due to the

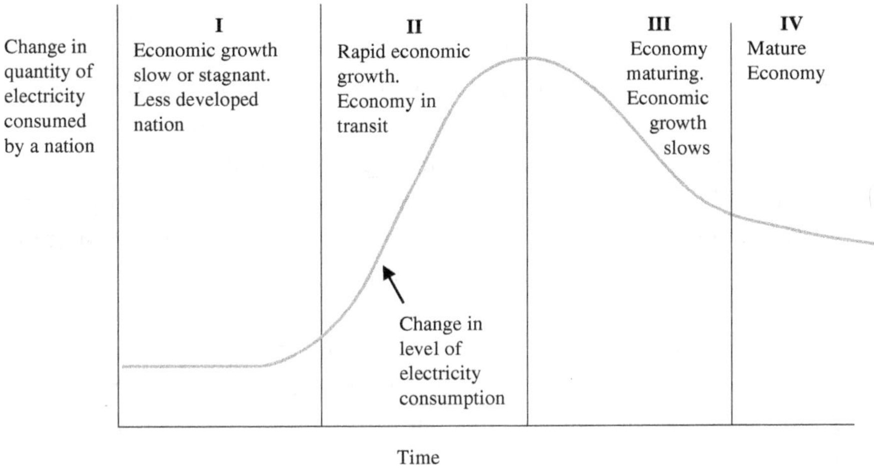

Fig. 13.3. As suggested in the text, an illustration of possible changes in a nation's consumption of electricity in relation to its stage of economic development.

fall in economic activity following the Global Financial Crisis. The novel coronavirus (COVID-19) resulted in a pandemic in 2020 and led to a substantial fall in the level of economic activity. Consequently, there was a marked dip in the global consumption of electricity and in the amount of energy utilized for other purposes, e.g. transport. Hence, the demand for resources required for energy production also exhibited a fall.

13.3. Issues Involved in Managing and Developing Electricity and Energy Supplies

13.3.1. *Preliminary points*

There are several different methods of producing energy and supplying energy to users. Fuel may be supplied directly to customers for combustion as mostly is the case for gasoline (petrol), diesel and gas, or it may be processed indirectly to supply electricity to users. Considerable economies of scale occur in the supply of most types of energy. This is probably one of the reasons why the petroleum industry is dominated by a few large multinational companies. Furthermore, because oil and natural gas have multiple uses (for example, in addition to providing a source of power, they can be used to produce plastics, artificial fibers, chemicals and detergents), economies of scope (that is economies from producing more than a single commodity) favor business concentration in this industry. Also, economies of scale occur in the supply of electricity. The total per unit costs of producing electricity tend to fall as the size of power plants increases, and the per unit costs of distributing electricity to customers are lower if distribution networks are not duplicated.

The above factors create barriers to entry in the supply of energy and are a source of market power for energy suppliers. Local monopolies, therefore, frequently occur in the supply of some energy sources, such as electricity. Three types of economic policy responses to this phenomenon can be observed:

(1) Supply of electricity by the state.
(2) Supply of electricity by private enterprise with the state regulating its price to buyers.
(3) Supply of electricity by privately owned power plants with its distribution via state-owned networks or non-duplicated networks under private ownership but subject to state regulation.

In recent times, as a result of growing political support for economic liberalization, there has been reduced emphasis on the supply and distribution of electricity by the state and greater emphasis on trying to increase private involvement in and business competition in the supply of electricity (Tisdell and Hartley, 2008, Chapter 10).

In pursuing this privatization goal, the following procedures have been broadly followed. Multiple private firms have emerged to supply electricity and they have been guaranteed access to electricity distribution grids on "reasonable" and equal terms to sell their electricity to end-users. In addition, electricity grids in different geographical areas have been linked to increase the scope for price competition between suppliers, for example, interstate links in the electricity grid have been established in Australia. Further reasons for increasing the interlinking of electricity grids are to guard against fluctuations in supplies from individual electricity plants, and to enable the cheapest sources of energy supply to be tapped, taking into account the fact that electricity demand fluctuates throughout the day and seasonally.

These fluctuations have implications for the appropriate mixture or portfolio of sources of electricity supply required to provide continuous availability of electricity at minimum cost. For example, while the volume of supplies of electricity from power stations using fossil fuels can be varied without undue difficulty, electricity from nuclear power stations is generated at a constant (non-variable) rate. This makes nuclear power stations more suitable for supplying base loads of electricity than for meeting peak-load demands. Therefore, it is **unlikely** to be helpful from the point of view of managing the availability of electricity supplies to rely on nuclear plants to generate a **very** high proportion of electricity needs. Depending upon the resources available in different geographical regions and countries, the optimal mixture of sources of energy supply can be expected to vary. It should also be noted that supplies of electricity from solar power are variable and cannot be completely controlled, nor can supplies obtained by using wind power. Furthermore, the availability of hydro-electricity depends on available water supplies and these can alter seasonally and for other reasons. The optimal composition of sources of electricity, therefore, needs to be considered in an integrated manner.

Apart from managing the sources of electricity supply in order to cope with fluctuations in supply and demand, variations in price of electricity supply can be used to prevent situations of excess demand occurring. For example, prices for electricity can be lower during periods of off-peak demand and higher during periods of peak demand. Because the availability of electricity is now considered in many countries to be a necessity, governments are under political pressure to keep electricity tariffs low when they are able to regulate electricity prices. However, very low prices for electricity can contribute to blackouts and brown outs and reduce incentives to invest in extra electricity capacity. Prices below market equilibrium result in the demand for electricity exceeding its supply.

Very often negative environmental externalities are not taken into account (or are only taken into account to a limited extent) in managing electricity and other energy supplies. Furthermore, if they are taken into account, they may only be allowed for in developing policy for one portion of the energy production chain. However, externalities throughout the **whole** production chain ought to be considered if the goal is to maximize social welfare. For example, one should not only take into account the pollution and reduction in air quality caused by the combustion of fossil fuels but the negative (or potentially negative) externalities from the mining and transport of fossil fuels should also be allowed for. In the case of oil, this includes possible oil spills, for instance, as a result of oil tankers running aground. In the case of coal, open-cut mining scars the countryside, results in the spread of dust and coal particles to nearby properties with negative economic consequences, and may create external noise. Dust from coal is also a problem in its transport. At some ports from which coal is shipped in Australia, residents in their vicinity suffer significant damage from coal dust. Subsequently, coal combustion adds to air pollution and adds to GHG emissions. In virtually all cases, users of commodities produced by using coal and suppliers of coal do not pay for the full external environmental costs generated by their activities.

This may also be the case for several other sources of energy. For example, biofuels appear at first glance to be an environmentally friendly alternative to the use of mineral oil for combustion because of the lower emissions of GHGs involved. But in some cases, forests are destroyed to grow crops to supply biofuel. As a result less carbon is stored in plant material and the cultivation of the soil hastens decomposition of organic matter in the soil, thereby adding to GHG emissions. Loss of biodiversity in the wild is also accelerated. For example, the expansion of palm oil plantations in Borneo has to a large extent been achieved by clearing rainforests and this is resulting in loss of tropical diversity (Swarna Nantha and Tisdell, 2009). One of the end-uses for palm oil is to produce biodiesel.

Two issues: concerning biofuels are worth noting. First, life-cycle analysis of the GHG emissions of biofuels shows that in some cases, for example in ethanol production from corn in the United States, fossil fuels are used not only in the growing of the corn but also to power ethanol plants, thereby reducing net GHG savings considerably (Wang *et al.*, 2007). Second, the switch to biofuels in the US and EU pushed up world prices for grains and cooking oils resulting in the acceleration of clearing of tropical rainforests and the release of GHGs (Searchinger *et al.*, 2008).

13.3.2. *Aspects of the availability of energy sources nationally and regionally*

Nations and regions vary in the extent to which they have locally available energy sources. Although many of these sources, such as coal or natural gas, can be imported, renewables such as solar and wind power cannot. They may, however, be converted into electricity and this may be exported. The economics of this depends on the cost of establishing transmission lines and account needs to be taken of lost electricity in transmission. Another more recent possibility is to use the electricity from these sources to produce hydrogen fuel which could then be exported. The economics of this is yet to be determined.

Not all regions have adequate wind resources to use these economically to supply electricity. Given the long winters and short winter days in some parts of the world, electricity generation from solar power may not be a viable economic option. Furthermore, the remoteness and small size of settlements in some of these areas can rule out the economic extension of electricity grids to serve them.

Lack of domestic sources of energy can make nations vulnerable to disruptions in the availability of energy exports. Some nations hold oil reserves as a hedge against these possible disruptions. Another rational long-term strategy is to develop energy sources domestically that can be substituted for imports. For example, China is developing and increasing its production of electric cars. This will reduce its dependence on imported oil. China is short of domestic supplies of oil.

13.3.3. *The dispatchability of (flexibility in) the supply of electricity and the development of new sources of energy*

Matching the demand for electricity with its supply can be quite challenging. The process of doing this is easier when the flexibility or the dispatchability in electricity supplies is greater. This depends on the extent to which these supplies can be controlled or managed. For example, the amount of electricity which can be generated by wind power is variable and to some extent uncertain. Solar power is not available at night, depends on the length of the day and on the amounts of cloud cover. Both electricity from wind and solar power are not very adaptable to electricity demands. However, the progress made in developing lithium batteries provides a new means of storing this electricity and increasing its dispatchability. The use of pumped hydro storage is another possibility. However, in many regions, pumped hydro is not an option because of the lack of available water or because of the unavailability of sufficiently elevated sites for water storage ponds or reservoirs. In suitable locations, pumped hydro can also be used to increase the flexibility of supplying electricity obtained from other sources, e.g. nuclear energy.

In considering the extent to which electricity supplies can be varied, the time-period and circumstances in which variations in electricity availability are demanded should be taken into account. Seasonal and daily variations in the demand due to changing weather conditions, and so on are all relevant. Some of these variations are predictable but others cannot be easily predicted. Some methods of supplying electricity are relatively unresponsive to short-term changes in the demand for electricity (e.g. electricity from nuclear power plants) whereas others can be very responsive, e.g. hydroelectricity and electrical power stored in batteries. During seasonal lows in demand for electricity, some plants can be closed, e.g. coal-fired and natural gas reliant plants. Flexibility in the overall supply of electricity depends on the ability of individual supply units altering their supply as well as (in a connected electricity grid) on the ease with which individual units can stop or start their operations. Buyers of electricity seem to have a strong preference for stable electricity prices and for having their demands satisfied at these prices. This is one reason why the dispatchability of electricity merits attention.

13.3.4. *GHG emissions and alternative sources of energy production*

Although the accumulation of carbon dioxide (CO_2) is considered to be the main contributor to the build-up of GHGs in the atmosphere, several other gases emitted as a result of human activity (including by processes involved in supplying electricity) also add to the build-up. Different energy sources and processes for energy supply and use produce different amounts of GHGs. The carbon dioxide equivalent of the GHGs (CO_2e) emitted by each source of electricity production is its equivalent amount of CO_2 emission that would result in the same degree of global warming. Using CO_2e as the common denominator, the Intergovernmental Panel on Climate Change (IPCC, 2011, Chapter 9) has provided estimates of the lifecycle emissions of greenhouse goals per kWh of electricity produced by alternative sources of electricity production.

As might be expected, this panel's estimates of CO_2e/kWh emissions were highest for the use of fossil fuels. Fig. 13.4 provides an indication of the relative contributions to GHG emissions of different sources used for generating electricity. It shows their approximate

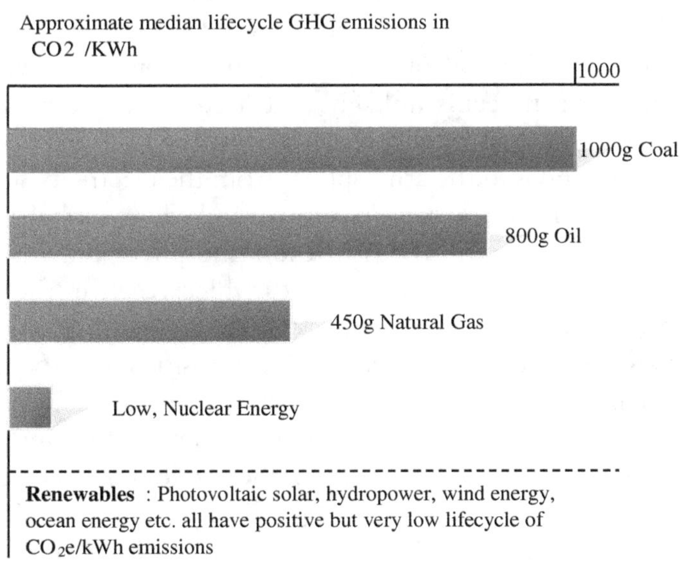

Fig. 13.4. Estimates of approximate median levels of carbon dioxide equivalent emissions for kWh of different sources of electricity production.
Source: Based on data in the Intergovernmental Panel on Climate Change Report, (2011, Chapter 9).

median values of CO_2e/kWh. The ranges in the values for coal, oil and natural gas are also wide. Nevertheless, even at the bottom of their ranges, levels of GHG emissions of fossil fuel use are much larger than for alternative sources of electricity generation. The range in the GHG emission values for coal is the largest because these emissions vary with the type of coal used as well as with the efficiency of different coal-fired power stations.

The approximate IPCC figures shown in Fig. 13.4 may not provide a complete inventory of CO_2e/kWh emissions resulting from generating electricity from alternative sources. All emissions due to economic backward and forward linkages do not seem to be accounted for. Nevertheless, they are a useful indicator of the comparative contributions to GHGs of the alternative sources of electricity production.

It would also be desirable to take into account extra GHG emissions associated with increasing the dispatchability of electricity obtained from different sources. At present, the supply of lithium batteries utilized to increase the flexibility of electricity obtained from PVA (photovoltaic) solar does, for example, add to GHG emissions.

At present, no method of generating and supplying electricity is GHG neutral and it seems unlikely that a completely neutral GHG system will be developed in the foreseeable future. Therefore, additions to the stock of GHGs in the atmosphere from the electricity sector can be predicted to continue to remain positive and add to global warming. However, the increase in GHGs in the atmosphere can be reduced by making greater use of energy sources which result in the smallest contributions to emissions of GHG.

It is also relevant to note that GHG emissions are not the only negative environmental spillovers and environmental challenges from the generation and supply of electricity. For example, PVA installations have a finite economic life. Disposing of their solid wastes can be problematic. The same is true for the disposal of lithium batteries at the end of their useful life. Furthermore, the use of different sources for supplying electricity utilize different quantities of water. In general, generating electricity by using mineral energy sources is much more demanding of water than its provision by the utilization of renewables e.g. its PVA production and its supply by harnessing wind power.

No water is needed in the operation of PVA and wind-based systems but it is required in the production of equipment for such systems. Nevertheless, these systems are much more water efficient overall than electricity systems based on the use of fossil fuels. Given that water is increasingly in short supply in many parts of the world, the water efficiency of different methods of supplying electricity can be an important consideration in choosing an electrical system.

13.3.5. *A discussion of government initiatives to support the supply and use of low GHG electricity and energy*

Two basically different types of policies can be adopted by governments to encourage the development, supply and use of low GHG electricity or energy. On the one hand, the polluter pays principle may be applied. The aim of this approach is to favor low GHG electricity providers by taxing the level of GHG emissions or by adopting a tradable permit system, for instance, schemes for trading entitlements to emit CO_2. These policies were discussed in Chapter 5 in general terms and are more specifically covered in relation to GHG emissions in subsections 13.6.2 and 13.6.3.

On the other hand, governments can subsidize the development, use, and supply of low GHG electricity. Some governments have done this to accelerate the supply and use of low GHG electricity, such as that relying on PVA solar and electricity derived from wind power. While applying the polluter pays principle should encourage the development and increased supply and use of low CO_2 intensive electricity, it may do so at a much slower rate than would be achieved by subsidizing sections of the electricity industry which emit low levels of GHGs per kWh. Given our perceived climate emergency, adopting a subsidization approach to reducing GHG emissions might be preferred to the polluter pays option, or these types of policies could be adopted in tandem.

An additional dynamic argument favoring the subsidization of some industrial sectors producing 'green' energy is that some may qualify as infant industries. If they are subsidized in their infancy, this may enable them to subsequently become economically self-reliant, that is able to survive without government support. Without initial government support, they may fail to develop or it may take them much longer to become self-reliant. In the early stages of their development, sectors producing PVA solar electricity and electricity based on wind power most likely qualified as 'infants'. More recently the development of hydrogen-based energy supplies appears to be at an infant stage in its development.

Economic arguments in favor of government support for infant industries were first put forward by List (1841 [1856]). A minimum economic requirement for justifying government support for such industries is that they should be able to survive (in due course) without continued government assistance. Suppliers of PVA solar electricity and electricity based on wind power have reached or may be approaching this stage in their development. In fact, in some regions, the cost of supplying electricity from these sources is now lower than its costs of supply using fossil fuels. In all probability, this outcome would have taken longer to achieve without initial government support for these fledgling green sectors, or may not have ever happened at all.

Although there are several types of impediments that have to be overcome by emerging infant industries, possibly the major hurdle occurs in the case of industries for which the level of costs of individual firms declines with the level of production of the whole industry. These industries exhibit decreasing industry long-run supply curves because the costs of firms in the industry fall with the increase in volume of production of the whole industry. Factors contributing to this include the process of learning by doing and increasing specialization in production as an industry expands, as has been pointed out by Alfred Marshall (1890). In these circumstances, the level of production of an industry must sometimes reach a threshold level of production before the industry can sustain itself economically.

The essence of this situation can be illustrated by Fig. 13.5. In that case, the development of PVA based electricity is used as a hypothetical illustrative example. The long-run supply curve for solar electricity (marked SS) is assumed to be declining because the per unit costs of

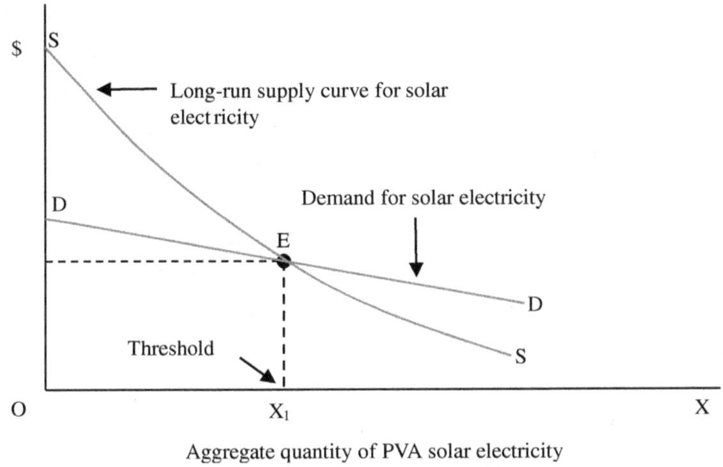

Fig. 13.5. An illustration of why the nascent PVA solar electricity sector could qualify as an infant industry.

producing this electricity falls with the aggregate output of this electricity. This decline is due to cost economies external to individual firms rather than cost economies available to individual firms by increasing their own output. The demand schedule for solar electricity is identified in Fig. 13.5 by DD. In this illustration (which relies on static analysis), the commercial supply of solar electricity is not economically viable until its aggregate production per unit of time reaches the threshold X_1. At this level of production, the solar electricity sector is commercially viable and needs no government assistance for its economic survival. On the other hand, until the total production of this sector reaches X_1, this sector requires government subsidization to survive and to develop because its per unit cost of supplying electricity exceeds the price buyers are willing to pay for it.

Employing comparative static analysis, the type of factors that alter the threshold for the independent survival of an infant industry can be discerned from Fig. 13.5. For example, other things being held constant, if the supply curve SS shifts downward, the threshold level of aggregate output is lowered. This change might come about because research and development (R&D) lowers the per unit costs of supply of solar electricity. Governments (as some have done) may subsidize this type of R&D in order to achieve this result. Furthermore, if the demand schedule for solar electricity shifts upwards, other things unchanged, the threshold of total production of solar electricity needed for the independent survival of the solar electricity sector declines. An upward shift in this demand curve might occur if buyers feel an increased moral responsibility to buy green electricity, or if the government subsidizes its purchase, or if the public sector buys this type of electricity for its own use. All of these measures have been adopted by some governments to boost the demand for green electricity and have contributed to its economic development.

The equilibrium point E shown in Fig. 13.5 is unstable if the following type of behavior occurs: suppliers of solar electricity increase their supplies when buyers are prepared to pay more than its costs of production, and reduce their supplies when buyers are unwilling to pay the cost of producing solar electricity. However, infant industries usually have more than one equilibrium. They mostly have two. This is because once high volumes of collective output occur the relevant long-run supply curve (for the supply of solar electricity in this case) can be expected to turn upwards. This is due to a rise in the collective per unit costs of production. Therefore, a U-shaped long-run supply curve like that shown in Fig. 13.6 emerges. Given the demand schedule marked DD, two equilibrium points now exist, namely one at E_1 and another at E_2. Equilibrium E_1 is unstable but equilibrium E_2 is stable given the dynamic reactions of suppliers stated above.

It is also pertinent to note that in a dynamic context, the demand for solar electricity (or green electricity generally) is liable to alter as it increases its market share. The demand for this electricity is liable to become less elastic if it becomes a low-cost source of supply and eliminates most competing sources for supplying electricity.

Let us now consider policy responses to a reduction in global air quality and discuss the economics of global warming. Bear in mind that electricity production and energy consumption are not the only sources of changes in air quality and influences on global warming.

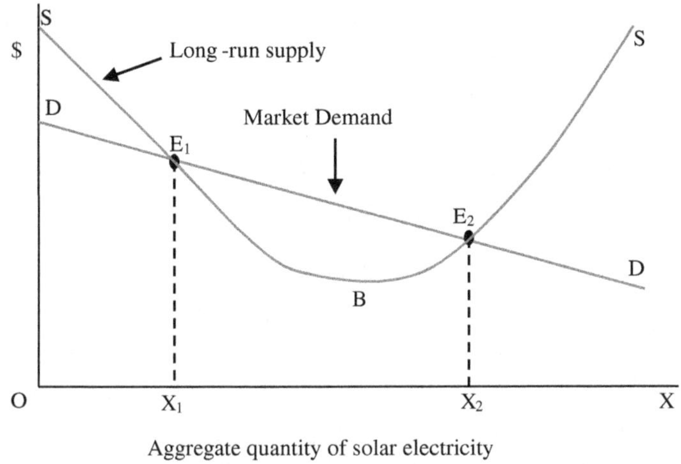

Fig. 13.6. An illustration of the eventual achievement of the economic stability of an infant industry once its aggregate production results in a rise in its collective per unit costs of supply. This causes its long-run supply curve to eventually slope upwards. The supply of solar electricity is used for illustrative purposes.

Part B: Reduced Air Quality: Global, Local and Regional Air Pollution, Climate Change and Ozone Depletion

13.4. Global Deterioration in Air Quality — Barriers to Collective Action, Ozone Layer Depletion, and Global Warming

13.4.1. *General observations*

Some types of reduction in air quality are so widespread that they have direct impacts on the whole globe. Ozone layer depletion and global warming caused by GHG emissions fall into this category. They are, therefore, of concern to everyone. On the other hand, it is also the case that some non-global forms of pollution indirectly have global consequences. For example, acid rains (which are a result of some anthropogenic air pollutants) can result in the loss of wild species in the regions where they occur and, consequently, a global loss of biodiversity. This may be regarded as a negative effect even by those not resident in the region affected.

13.4.2. *Do global reductions in air quality due to human activity provide incentives for collective regulatory action?*

The answer to the above question depends on the nature of the choice problem faced by individual nations. This can be illustrated by means of three different hypothetical models (cases). These are set out below by using matrices of the type employed in game theory. In case 1 (Table 13.7), each country has an incentive to reduce its emission of a global pollutant **irrespective** of what the others do. **No co-ordination is needed**. In that case, all countries reduce their emissions and the best possible outcome is achieved. This outcome is stable. In case 2 (Table 13.8), all nations must agree to co-ordinate to reduce their global emissions in order to achieve the best outcome for all. If they do this, the outcome is stable — there is no incentive to renege on the agreement. In case 3 (Table 13.9) each nation can gain if all nations agree to reduce their emissions of a global pollutant but the outcome is unstable. Each has an incentive to dishonor the agreement in this case. Furthermore, if some nations believe that other nations cannot be trusted to comply with an agreement of this type, no collective agreement may be reached. Or, if there is limited trust, each nation may commit itself to a smaller reduction in its emission of a global pollutant than is necessary to improve the outcome for all to the best extent possible. The illustrative cases are highly simplified possibilities.

In order to illustrate case 1, consider two countries, I and II, and for simplicity assume that they constitute all the countries in the world. Each is supposed to be the source of a global air pollutant and each has two strategies: they may either do nothing to reduce their emissions of the global air pollutant or they may each reduce its emission to a particular level. Let α_1 and β_1 represent "the do nothing" strategy of country I and country II respectively, and let α_2 and β_2 represent respectively the strategy of each of these nations reducing their

Table 13.7. A case in which the individual self-interest of nations results in the optimal control of a global pollutant.

		Strategies of Country II	
		β_1	β_2
Strategies of Country I	α_1	(2, 2)	(4, 3)
	α_2	(3, 4)	(5, 5)

Table 13.8. A more complex case than that illustrated by Table 13.7. Both countries have a strong incentive to abate global pollution but both must do it in order for each to gain. They may achieve this outcome by agreement or if one shows initial leadership in abating its pollution emissions, the other has a strong incentive to follow if the 'game' is replicated.

		Country II's strategies	
		β_1	β_2
Country I's strategies	α_1	(2, 2)	(2, 1)
	α_2	(1, 2)	(4, 4)

emissions. Given the distribution of payoffs shown in the matrix in Table 13.7, the self-interest of each nation will lead it to restrict emissions of the global pollutant. Country I would adopt strategy α_2 and country II would adopt β_2. As a result, the best possible payoff will emerge. In this case, the pursuit of the individual self-interest of each nation results in a "win-win" outcome. No coordination is needed. The outcome is stable.

In the case shown in Table 13.8, coordinated action is required to reduce the emission of the global pollutant is required. Both countries will gain if both lower their emission of the pollutant, but if only one nation does this, it is worse off and the other country is no better off. This may be because a minimum total reduction in the level of emissions is required before any significant reduction in environmental damages occurs. One country alone cannot reach the required threshold but if both co-operate, they can. There is a strong incentive to co-operate in this case and the outcome is stable. If the "game" is a replicated one,

Table 13.9. A challenging case in which the blind pursuit by nations of their own self-interest results in none abating their emissions of global pollutants. As a result, all are less well-off than they could have been if all nations had restricted their emissions.

		Country II's strategies	
		β_1	β_2
Country I's strategies	α_1	(2, 2)	(5, 1)
	α_2	(1, 5)	(4, 4)

then if in one period, one of the countries shows leadership and adopts the pollution abatement strategy, then the other has an incentive to follow its lead.

The case illustrated in Table 13.9 is relatively unfavorable to the lowering of the emissions of global pollutants although it is in the interest of all countries to abate global pollution — the pursuit of self-interest by each nation has perverse consequences. In this case, if each country follows its own selfish interest, it makes the maximum possible gain irrespective of what the other country does. The result is that neither country abates its pollution emissions and they fail to achieve a situation in which both would be better off by abating their emissions. The inferior outcome where both do not abate their emissions corresponds to a stable equilibrium (a Nash equilibrium) whereas the situation in which both nations abate their emissions is unstable. This case involves a prisoners' dilemma problem. This name reflects the example that was originally used to illustrate it. The structure of the choice problem is such that there is a high probability that it will result in a Paretian inferior outcome.

It has been suggested that the problem of abating GHG emissions has the type of (prisoners' dilemma) structure illustrated by the case in Table 13.9. This makes it difficult to obtain a binding international agreement to abate these emissions. This is because each country acting alone calculates that it is better off doing as little as possible to reduce these emissions no matter what other countries do. This makes binding international agreements difficult but very necessary in that each country needs to be confident that commensurate efforts will be made by other countries. In the case of international agreements and protocols, their enforcement is problematic and monitoring compliance within the borders of sovereign nations is sometimes impossible or difficult. These factors can contribute to the types of Paretian inferior social outcome illustrated in Table 13.9 (Tisdell, 1966).

In reality, the situation as far as global pollution is concerned is even more complicated than the above cases indicate. For example, multiple choices rather than binary choices about the abatement of emissions can be made. It is not just a question of whether or not to abate but by how much each country should (or can) abate its emissions of global pollutants. This leads to international disputes about how much effort each country should make to reduce its emissions. This is a distributional problem. A further complication is uncertainty about the extent, nature, reversibility and timing of environmental damages likely to be caused by emissions of global pollutants. Consequently, the obstacles to obtaining international cooperation in order to reduce emissions of global pollutants can be formidable.

13.4.3. *Ozone layer depletion*

Let us now consider some specific cases involving global air pollution. The first involves the depletion of ozone in the upper atmosphere and the second involves emissions of GHGs which contribute to global warming.

Ozone is present in small quantities in the air. In the upper atmosphere, ozone performs the function of reducing the amount of ultraviolet (UV) rays reaching the earth. An increase in the amount of UV rays reaching the earth has several deleterious consequences. For example, it increases the incidence of skin cancer and cataracts, accelerates the corrosion of some materials (such as plastics and paints) and reduces the yield of many crops. Some air-borne chemicals have the capacity to facilitate destruction of ozone molecules in the upper atmosphere (stratosphere). These include chlorofluorocarbons (CFLs) which have been used in aerosols and as refrigerants. Their ability to deplete the ozone layer is very long-lasting. Ozone destroying agents are more active in higher altitudes than in lower altitudes and consequently, there is greater thinning of the ozone layer towards the Poles than nearer the Equator. The presence of ice-particles in the stratosphere closer to the Poles facilitates the catalytic action of the ozone-destructive chemicals in the stratosphere. This also means that the damaging impacts of ozone depletion are unevenly distributed by geographical areas – damages tend to be higher in Alaska, Australia and South Africa than in say, Malaysia or Hawaii. The long-life of ozone-depleting agents in the stratosphere is a cause for concern.

In 1987, most countries signed the Montreal Protocol on Substances that Deplete the Ozone Layer with the intention of phasing out the use of CFCs. As a result of further amendments to the Protocol, plans to phase out CFCs were accelerated with the intention of eliminating the use of CFCs in developed nations by 1998 and in developing countries by 2010. The phase out of CFCs has been facilitated by the availability of substitutes for CFCs involving comparable costs of supply. However, while the substitutes for CFCs (hydro chlorofluorocarbons HCFCs, and hydro fluorocarbons HFCs) deplete the ozone layer at a slower rate than CFCs, their length of life in the stratosphere is longer and they are potent GHGs. Therefore, this is a continuing concern.

There would, therefore, still be a case for further restricting the use of these ozone-depleting substances, for example, by imposing a tax on their sales or by instituting a tradable permit system (see Chapter 5 and also Kahn, 2005, p. 223). Kahn (2005, p. 224) argues that it was relatively easy to obtain international agreement on the phasing out of CFCs because the cost of their phase out was relatively low, given available substitutes, and there was widespread scientific agreement about their effects. Furthermore, a multinational company, DuPont, holding patent rights to CFC technology was supportive. This was probably because it had developed substitute technologies and in due course, its patents on CFCs would have expired. Consequently, after the expiry of Du Pont's relevant patents, a ban on CFCs would have removed future potential competition with it from others using CFCs.

13.4.4. *Global warming — its basic causes and its predicted consequences*

Most natural scientists agree that global warming is occurring because of the accumulation of GHGs in the earth's atmosphere. Loss of vegetation that helps store some of these gases, such as carbon dioxide, and the burning of carbon-based fuels are among the factors contributing to global warming. The current upward trend in global temperatures (which has happened following the Industrial Revolution) is unique because it is a result of human economic activity rather than natural causes.

Although carbon dioxide, CO_2, is the most widely known GHG, several other gases also contribute to global warming. These include nitrous oxide, N_2O, methane, CH_4, and various fluorocarbons — CFCs, HCFCs and HFCs. GHGs in the atmosphere reduce the radiation of the heat from the earth back to space. This effect intensifies as the density of GHGs increases in the atmosphere. Scientists have found that atmospheric density of GHGs has increased in the last 200 years or so due to human activity and global air temperatures have risen (IPCC, 2007a). Unless radical changes are made in the nature of economic activity, substantial further increases in GHG concentrations in the atmosphere and in global air temperatures are predicted to occur in this century (IPCC, 2007a).

The IPCC (2014, p. 44) has pointed out that concentrations of GHGs in the atmosphere are now their highest level for at least the last 800,000 years. There has been a rapid rate of rise in these concentrations since 1850 when the Industrial Revolution was taking off. Annual global GHG emissions have increased most rapidly since 1950 (see IPCC, 2014, pp. 44–45, Figs. 1.3 and 1.5). Global anthropogenic GHG emissions in terms of CO2e rose by an average of 1.3% annually in the period 1970 to 2000, and then by 2.2% annually in the period 2000–2010 (IPCC, 2014, p. 5). This is accelerating the rate of climate change. Rising atmospheric temperatures are expected to result in substantial climate changes (some regions will, for example, become drier and others will become wetter), sea levels are expected to rise due to the melting of snow and ice cover, temperatures of water bodies will increase, ocean currents may alter and, in many places, weather patterns are likely to become more variable. Consequential adverse impacts on agricultural productivity, human health, biodiversity and economic productivity generally are anticipated to occur. Natural water bodies (such as the seas) are expected to become warmer and more acidic with adverse consequences for some aquatic organisms, such as corals. Sea level rise is also predicted.

Estimates by natural scientists of the biophysical consequences of GHG emissions are subject to some uncertainty. The Intergovernmental Panel on Climate Change (IPCC, 2007b) which was established by the United Nations to monitor and predict the consequences of climate change (following the United Nations Conference on Environmental Development held in Rio de Janeiro in 1992), usually provides a range of estimates for the likelihood of predicted occurrences. For example, if there are no dramatic reductions in GHG emissions, the IPCC has estimated that the likelihood of different types of climate changes occurring (in this century) are as set out in Table 13.10. For those changes stated to be "very likely", the effects correspond to a 90% or greater probability of occurrence and for those variations said to be "likely", the consequences correspond (according to the IPCC's measures) to a 90% or more chance of occurrence. "Virtually certain" corresponds to a probability of 99% or higher.

Even if the extent of global warming is limited to 2°C (the upper target of the Paris Agreement on climate change) above pre-industrial levels, there will be a high risk of the extreme weather events of the type listed in Table 13.10 occurring and of the loss of unique and threatened ecosystems (IPCC, 2014, p. 18). These risks are still high (even if somewhat smaller) if the rise in global temperature is limited to 1.5°C (IPCC, 2014), the proposed target mentioned in the Paris Agreement on Climate Change. As discussed in subsection 13.5.2, there is still a real risk that anthropogenic behaviors will fail to limit global warming in this century to less than a rise of 2°C above pre-industrial levels.

It is unlikely that most nations will be prepared to forego significant current economic growth in order to reduce global warming (Tisdell, 2017, Chapters 5 and 8). However, if technologies become available

Table 13.10. Projected changes in weather events and sea levels in this century as a result of global warming.

Changes in weather patterns	Likelihood (a)
Higher maximum temperatures and more hot days over most land areas	Virtually certain
Higher minimum temperatures over most land areas	Virtually certain
More intense precipitation events	Very likely
Increased risk of drought	Likely
Increased intensity of tropical cyclones	Likely
Increased incidence of extreme high sea level	Likely

Note: (a) **Virtually certain** implies >99% probable **Very likely** implies >90% probable **Likely** implies >66% probable.
Source: Based on IPCC (2007b, Table 3.2, p. 58)

that are more climate friendly, economical and which are growth promoting, these are likely to be adopted given the nature of market economies. Their availability would improve the prospects of reducing anthropogenic GHG emissions and slowing global warming.

To predict the time-path likely to be followed by global temperature changes and by sea-level rises is even more difficult than predicting the qualitative impacts listed in Table 13.10. Furthermore, estimates become more uncertain the further into the future projections are made. It is estimated that by the end of this century, global temperatures could rise by up to 6°C and sea levels by about 80 cm although the average prediction is for a rise of 4–5°C in temperature and a rise of about 40 cm in the sea level, if business continues as usual. If effective measures are taken to curb global GHG emissions, there is likely to be a significant delay before GHG concentrations in the atmosphere decline. This means the reversibility of GHG concentrations takes some time and during that time, growing adverse environmental consequences from past emissions of these gases will continue to be experienced.

Predictions by scientists about the biophysical consequences of increasing concentrations of GHGs in the atmosphere are based on complex simulation models and are estimated for several scenarios.

Although considerable uncertainties exist, the weight of evidence indicates that significant global warming can be expected in this century together with sea level rises with consequences of the type listed in Table 13.10. John Quiggin (2008) argues persuasively that this uncertainty should not be used as an excuse for not mitigating global warming.

As mentioned above, several gases contribute to global warming of which CO_2 is just one. These gases have different lengths of life in the atmosphere. Some last for a relatively short time but others have a long life. Some, for example, have a lower level of radiation forcing but are present for a much longer period of time. A problem is how to estimate their relative global warming potential. The IPCC has developed indices for this (Kahn, 2005, pp. 239–243) but the economic implications of these indices have not been clarified.

13.5. Estimates of the Economic Impacts of Global Warming

13.5.1. *Estimating the economic costs of global warming and the net benefits of controlling it*

Estimation of the economic costs of global warming and the economic benefits of moderating global warming are extremely challenging because of uncertainties about the biophysical dynamics of global warming and because of additional uncertainties about future socio-economic conditions. This is so because of the lengthy periods for which estimates are required — some economic projections have been made for up to 200 years into the future. Nevertheless, given the potential magnitude of the adverse consequences of global warming, it is necessary to address the problem.

At least three different methods have been used to estimate the economic costs of climate change with varying degrees of attention to its non-economic social consequences. One approach has been to identify the major anticipated socio-economic impacts of climate change and where appropriate, assign economic values to these. This can be regarded as a form of Environmental Impact Assessment. These impacts include consequences for the level of agricultural production, for human health and comfort, for forced migration due to climate change and for sea level rise, as well as for loss of and damage to infrastructure. Monetary values might be assigned to some of these impacts. However, monetary values would give a limited measure of the costs of some of them. For example, monetary values are unlikely to account fully for the trauma and problems some people may face as a result of forced migration and the difficulties of becoming settled again.

A second economic approach (which to some extent can be regarded as an extension of the one just mentioned) is to estimate the social economic cost of carbon dioxide (or more generally, GHG) emissions. Not surprisingly, estimates of these costs vary widely. The IPCC (2007b) found from a survey of 100 estimates of these costs that they ranged from the equivalent of US$3 per tonne of carbon dioxide to US$95 per tonne of CO_2 with their average being US$12 per tonne (Anon, 2020a). Tol (2008) reviewed 211 published estimates of the marginal social cost of the emission of a tonne of CO_2 equivalent and also found huge variations in the estimates. These variations are greatly influenced by the nature of the assumptions made about the biophysical impacts of global warming and the discount rate applied to future costs. The higher the discount rate used, the lower is the computed social costs of the emissions. For example, if the social marginal cost associated with the emission of an extra tonne of CO_2 now is $100 in 100 years time, this contributes $100 to the stream of marginal cost from this emission if no discount rate is applied. However, if a discount rate of say 4% is applied, the contribution is only $1.98. Furthermore, if the costs include a weighting which assumes that a dollar cost to the poor is equivalent to more than a dollar loss to the rich, this will inflate the cost estimates. In addition, most of the estimates are for average social costs per unit of CO_2 emitted, not marginal costs. If the marginal cost of CO_2 emissions increases as a function of their level, marginal cost as a function of increased CO_2 emissions will exceed the average cost of extra emissions of CO_2. Therefore, average cost will underestimate the relevant marginal cost of a rise in CO_2 emissions. Furthermore, the marginal cost of GHG can be expected to alter with the concentration of GHGs already in the atmosphere. For example, at

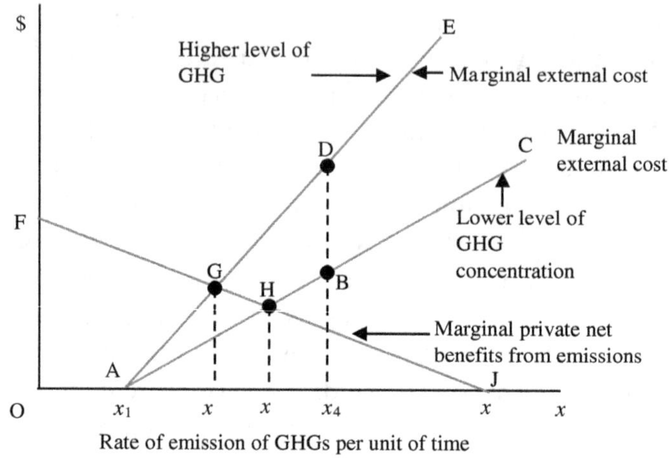

Fig. 13.7. The social marginal external cost of GHG emissions is likely to alter with the rate of emissions and with the extent of their concentration in the atmosphere.

higher levels of GHG concentrations in the atmosphere, the marginal social external cost of a particular level of GHG emissions per period is likely to be higher than at a lower level of this concentration. However, there may be some threshold of emissions below which no accumulation of GHGs occurs. From the global warming perspective, the social external marginal costs of increased emissions below this threshold are zero.

This possibility can be illustrated by Fig. 13.7. There, x represents the level of emissions of GHGs per period. Two different levels of GHG concentration in the atmosphere are considered. For the lower level of concentration, the social marginal external cost curve OABC is assumed to apply and for the higher level of concentration, social marginal external cost curve OADE is supposed to apply. Social marginal external costs are likely to become positive once the rate of emissions exceeds some threshold, which in this case is x_1. Whether these marginal costs will increase at an increasing or decreasing rate is unclear. However, if the emissions exceed the threshold, x_1, then the concentration of GHGs in the atmosphere increases. Therefore, if the rate of emission of GHGs is x_4 per period initially, then marginal external cost will correspond to point B but eventually at this rate of emission, the concentration of GHGs in the atmosphere may rise because their rate of emissions exceeds environmental absorption levels. Consequently, the social marginal cost associated with the rate of emissions of GHGs, x_4, rises as time passes to a level corresponding to point D. If the private net marginal benefits from GHG emissions are as indicated by line FJ, then in the absence of regulation, emissions equivalent to x_5 would occur per period. At the lower level of GHG concentration in the atmosphere, it would, therefore, be socially optimal to reduce GHG emissions to x_3 per period. At the higher level of GHG concentration, it is optimal to reduce these emissions to x_2. Greater reductions in GHG emissions are required as the level of GHG concentration in the atmosphere rises. This also implies that the longer reductions in emissions are delayed, the greater is the necessary adjustment. However, this illustration needs to be interpreted cautiously given the uncertainties of the relationships involved. The very long-period for which possible marginal external costs associated with extra units of GHG emissions need to be estimated results in these estimates being subject to considerable uncertainty. This is because these costs are influenced both by social change and biophysical factors, the long-term dynamics of which are imperfectly predictable.

A third approach to estimating the economic consequences of GHG emissions is to consider their macroeconomic implications. This usually involves considering their likely impacts on the gross level of global production. This approach (together with the other methods mentioned above) was adopted in the Stern review of the economics of climate change (Stern, 2007a). This comprehensive review was undertaken for the British Government using an integrated model which took into account general economic relationships as well as the climate predictions in the 2001 report of the IPCC. The review estimated that the total cost over the next two centuries of climate change if global emissions of GHGs continue to rise without abatement to be equivalent to an average reduction in per-capita global consumption of **at least** 5% compared to what they would have been in the absence of global warming (Stern, 2007b).

However, as pointed out by Stern, this is a conservative indicator of the likely economic loss because it is based on market-related losses. As is well known, traditional macroeconomic models and standard computable general equilibrium (CGE) models of economies do not allow for the economic value of non-marketed environmental amenities which are, nevertheless, valued (see Chapter 6). Furthermore, some macroeconomic indicators, such as gross product, can actually rise at the same time as economic welfare demonstrably declines. For example, if health costs increase and if expenditure to avert environmental damage or to repair such damage rises, gross product and recorded levels of consumption per head may actually rise even though economic welfare clearly declines. Stern believes that when such factors are taken into account, the reduction in global per-capita consumption would increase from 5% to the equivalent of 11%. Yet even this could be, in his view, a conservative estimate because the actual extent of global warming might be greater than allowed for in these estimates. Allowing for this possibility, it is likely that per capita global consumption will fall by 7% (rather than 5%) if market transactions only are taken into account, and by 14% (rather than 11%) if non-market losses are taken into account as well. However, if extra weight is given to the loss in per-capita consumption in developing countries, Stern finds that there would be the equivalent of approximately a 20% reduction in per capita consumption over the next two centuries. These losses are likely to be irreversible.

Note that as extra components of the economic losses estimated by Stern are added, his estimates become subject to greater controversy. For example, will global warming be towards the upper end of the range predicted by the IPCC? How much weight should be given to reductions in levels of per capita consumption in developing countries compared to the more developed ones? It should also be observed that Stern's estimates of economic loss are considerably higher than those of earlier economic studies. Most earlier studies suggested that the permanent loss in global world output would be of the order of 0–3% but they were based on a lower degree of global warming than is now considered likely and did not allow for non-market factors and make an allowance for income distribution considerations. However,

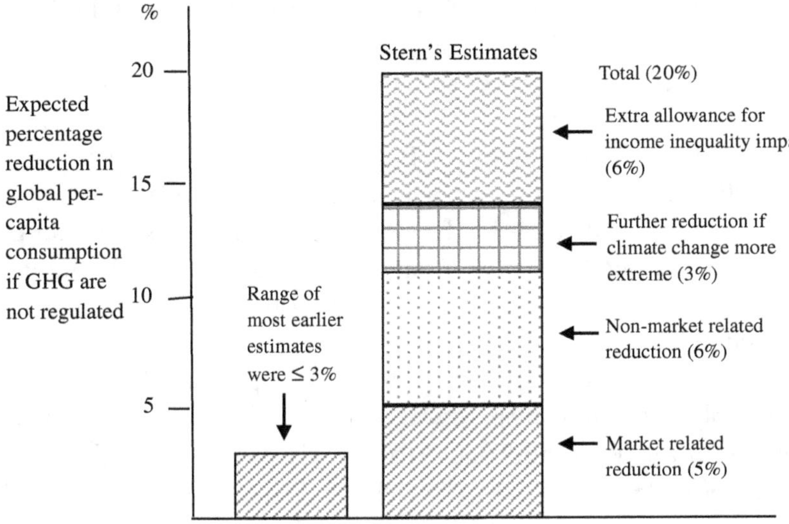

Fig. 13.8. A bar chart illustrating Stern's expected losses in global per capita consumption over the next two centuries if GHG emissions continue unabated. As one moves up the chart, the size of the components are likely to be subject to increasing controversy. Most earlier estimates were for a 0–3% reduction in global product per capita.

it could also be the case that the Stern review presents a very favorable case for controlling GHG emissions because it is a document intending to promote action. Nevertheless, even taking this aspect into account, it does establish a more persuasive economic case for regulating global GHG emissions than previously.

The main findings of the Stern review about the expected loss in per capita global consumption over the next two centuries if nothing is done to curb emissions of GHGs are summarized in Fig. 13.8. As one moves up the bar chart highlighting Stern's estimates, his estimates become more debatable.

One valuation issue is how to allow for the loss of income of future generations due to GHG emissions. The average level of global per capita income could fall in the future if GHG emissions continue unabated. Sustainability and welfare issues of the type raised in Chapter 7 therefore need to be considered.

The Stern review stated that very large reductions in GHG emissions compared to their levels in 2006 would be required in order to stabilize their concentrations in the atmosphere and consequently avoid serious economic harm. In fact, the review points out that in order to stabilize atmospheric GHG concentrations at levels prevailing in 2006 or thereabouts (a level of 450 ppm CO_2 equivalent), an eventual reduction of 80% in the amount of emissions prevailing in 2006 would be needed. Stern emphasized that the longer the delay in reducing GHG emissions the greater will be the economic cost of climate change.

Stern concluded that stabilization at 450 ppm of CO_2 equivalent was probably not politically practical (because of the high upfront costs involved in mitigation) and opted for a higher level of stabilization at 550 ppm of CO_2 equivalent to be achieved by 2050. To achieve this target he estimates that **most likely** 1% of global gross product would need to be forgone in the initial control period involving mitigation ending in 2050. However, the exact figure is uncertain and depends on the pathway for mitigation enforced by governments. Nevertheless, Stern is confident that the long-run economic benefits (in terms of the avoided reductions in future global gross product) of his proposed CO_2 equivalent stabilization policy would substantially exceed its upfront costs (and any continuing costs) in terms of the amount of global gross product sacrificed to achieve his proposed target.

There is no recent study of the type of economic review of climate change which was completed by Stern. However, the issues he raises and the various types of economic costs which he considers still remain relevant.

Depending on the time-path for compliance with mitigation requirements, significant economic costs may be experienced initially as a result of regulation of greenhouse emissions. This is so because adjustment of economies takes time and there is less responsiveness in the short-term than in the long-term to economic signals to alter resource-use. If upfront costs of mitigating GHG emissions are to be minimized, considerable attention needs to be given to the time-path for phasing in such measures and policy intentions should be announced well in advance of their implementation to allow for forward planning by businesses. Furthermore, uncertainties about policy implementation ought desirably to be minimized. In practice, however, these policy objectives are difficult to achieve given the limited terms in office of most governments, political popularism and the re-election ambitions of most political parties. These tend to favor myopic policy responses and "rubbery" policy proposals.

13.6. International Agreements and Global Warming

Effective control of the process of global warming requires cooperation by all nations that are major contributors to the occurrence of global warming. However, obtaining effective international agreements to control this process is not easy. This is because the decision-making problem can have the type of structure shown in Table 13.9 the implications of which are discussed in the text surrounding this table. Given this structure, it is in the self-interest of individual nations not to reduce their GHG emissions or to do so as little as possible, no matter what other nations do. Furthermore, there is usually a conflict of interest between nations about how the economic costs of reducing global warming should be shared between them. The distribution of these costs impact on international income inequality and on the relative global political/military power of individual nations. For example, if all nations are allocated the same level of per capita GHG emissions, China would benefit substantially relative to the United States. Economic conditions would most likely worsen considerably in the United States and its international political influence would decline, given current technologies.

A further challenge is how to deal internationally with land use changes, such as deforestation, that contribute to global warming. Of particular concern is the continuing loss of tropical forests due to agricultural expansion and forestry. This adds to the concentration of GHGs in the atmosphere. On the other hand, most of these forests are situated in developing countries and the economic opportunity cost to them of forgoing changed land use is considerable. Unless they receive adequate economic compensation from higher income nations, they are unlikely to forgo the economic benefits they can obtain from land clearing. Despite such difficulties, there has, nevertheless, been some international progress in addressing the issue of global warming but not enough progress yet to solve the problem.

In 1990, several world leaders brought attention to the problem and saw the need for international action to address it. Their concern was followed up at the United Nations Conference on Environmental Development (UNCED) held in Rio de Janeiro in 1992. At this conference, national leaders endorsed an agreement intended to provide an international structure for addressing climate change. They agreed to the *United Nations Framework Convention on Climate Change* (UNFCCC) and this convention came into effect in 1994. This convention established the Intergovernmental Panel on Climate Change (IPCC), the main function of which is to provide scientific information about GHG emissions. This convention also provided a basis for the negotiation of the Kyoto Protocol. This international treaty came into full force in 2005 but many developed countries had agreed to it earlier. The stated purpose of the Kyoto Protocol was to achieve "stabilization of GHG concentrations in the atmosphere at a level that would prevent dangerous anthropogenic interference with the climate system".

Although each of the Annex I states (higher income nations) signing the Kyoto Protocol agreed to reduce their GHG emissions in the period 2005–2012 by at least 5% of their level of 1990, the majority failed to do so, and in fact, many increased their emissions. As predicted by the prisoners' dilemma game model (see the matrix in Table 13.9), many nations acted in their individual self-interest rather than the collective global interest. The reasons given by individual developed nations for not meeting their commitments are outlined and discussed in Napoli (2012). Developing nations (named Annex-II countries) such as China (a major emitter of GHGs) were exempt from the obligations of the Kyoto Protocol and they also increased their GHG emissions. While the Kyoto Protocol probably resulted in fewer GHG emissions than would have occurred otherwise, globally the level of these emissions continued to rise dangerously from a global warming perspective despite the Kyoto Protocol.

The successor to the Kyoto Protocol is the Paris Agreement, a useful overview of which is available in Anon (2020b). It aims to limit global warming to not more than 2°C by the second half of this century but if possible by not more than 1.5°C. Nearly all nations have signed this agreement including most developing countries. The latter includes China and India. Each country sets its own targets for lowering its GHG emissions and each is expected to reduce these emissions progressively with the passage of time. Each is to report its progress in this regard every five years.

It is unclear whether the aims of the Paris Agreement on Climate Change will be met. It is feared that the sum of the pledges made by individual nations to reduce their GHG emissions will be inadequate to limit global warming to a rise of 2°C or less (Rogelj *et al.*, 2016) and furthermore, it appears that many countries are not meeting their pledges (Victor *et al.*, 2017). Moreover, the former US President, Donald Trump, withdrew the United States from this agreement and he began earlier to adopt policies at variance with the agreement, such as providing greater support for the use of fossil fuels in the US. His decision was made in order to pursue his perception of the self-interest of the US, and the adoption of his "America First" policy. President Biden has reversed this decision.

The pursuit of national self-interest still continues to be an obstacle to obtaining effective collective action on limiting climate change. Fortunately, national self-interest can change. For example, low GHG emissions technologies for supplying electricity are becoming more economic sources of supply than using fossil fuels and this could change the self-interest of some nations, such as Australia, in using and promoting the export of fossil fuels, as has been argued by Garnaut (2019). Also China, for example, seems to be making a strong effort to reduce its GHG emissions by increasingly substituting low GHG emitting sources of energy supplies for those with high levels of emissions. This may now be in its national self-interest, for example, as a means for reducing the prevalence of air pollution in China and the extent of its dependence on imported fossil fuels. The production and use of hydrogen fuel obtained by utilizing electricity obtained from low GHG sources may also become economical and provide an additional avenue for lowering GHG emissions.

13.7. Economic Methods for Reducing GHG Emissions and Global Warming

13.7.1. *Mitigation versus adjustment and other general issues*

In responding to the problem of global warming, policies can be adopted to reduce the development of global warming (for example, policies that reduce GHG emissions and encourage land-use activities that sequester carbon) and measures may be taken to foster optimal adjustments to global warming. Both mitigation and adjustment involve economic considerations. One of the economic advantages of reducing the extent of global warming is that the cost of adjusting to it is diminished. Because, it is unlikely that policies will be adopted in the foreseeable future to completely halt global warming. Therefore, in coming years, it will be necessary to determine how social adjustments to global warming can be made in the most economical manner. This may, for example, involve anticipatory behavior, for instance, disallowing urban development in low-lying coastal areas and relocating infrastructure to higher ground. As a result of changing climate, some communities may no longer be economically viable in their current locations and collective assistance may be required to resettle these communities (see, for example, Tisdell, 2008).

In order to reach particular levels of reduction in aggregate GHG emissions, the cost to individual entities is likely to be lower the more widely the burden of the reduction is shared. Concessions or exceptions for particular entities in reducing their GHG emissions increase the economic burden imposed on others by adjustment. Again, the costs of mitigation of emissions are likely to be lower if economic entities are advised well in advance of policy intentions. At an early stage, there is usually considerable flexibility in plans, and compliance with new regulations to reduce GHG emissions can be obtained at lower cost than if short-form notice is given of such regulations. The way in which regulations are phased in is of economic importance.

Some countries are giving concessions to producers who are major emitters of GHGs because it is believed that they will move offshore to other countries, particularly developing countries, where the emissions will not be restricted. This can occur if they are in footloose industries or if the relative economic benefit of staying in the country where they are currently located is slight. This creates a problem because if such movement occurs, the producers involved will not reduce their GHG emissions and their contribution to global emissions will basically remain unaltered. It may also be that their products are mostly consumed in more developed countries. Thus the location of the source of emissions is merely shifted with no reduction in the level of global emissions. However, an import tax (tariff) on goods of this nature, if imposed by developed countries, would help to rectify the problem.

Some industries are looking for a "technological fix" in order to solve the problem of GHG emissions. For example, coal producers and users are stressing the possibility of storing carbon dioxide emissions underground. But the technology is not yet developed. Politically, it may be a way to defer policies intended to reduce GHG emissions. On the other hand, it can be argued that taxes on GHG emissions or a tradable permit system for these emissions would increase incentives for technological changes of this kind. Nevertheless, as pointed out in subsection 13.3.5, there can be a case for subsidizing the development of infant industries which are low emitters of GHGs.

13.7.2. *Taxes on GHG emissions*

Most of the policy measures outlined in Chapter 5 can be adopted to control GHG emissions. Currently, policy-makers appear to have a preference for using tradable permit systems for this purpose but taxes on these emissions are also a possibility. Kahn (2005, p. 253) argues that taxes on carbon emissions are likely to be relatively efficient as controls provided that they are indexed for inflation.

Because GHGs are a global pollutant, taxes on their emissions should be uniform everywhere if GHGs are to be abated to achieve minimum overall cost (Kahn, 2005) . However, some modifications to this policy are required. First, GHGs can have negative local or regional pollution impacts, apart from contributing to global warming. For example, nitrous oxide emissions contribute to global warming as well as to the occurrence of acid rain in some regions. They should therefore, be taxed at a higher rate in localities or regions where this happens. Secondly, the global economic system is not in economic equilibrium and the geographical pattern of global production is changing. For example the share of global production accounted for by newly industrializing developing countries (such as China, India and Brazil) has risen. A lower rate of taxation of GHGs in these countries compared to more developed countries would help accelerate adjustment of the world economy in its transition. Furthermore, many of these countries argue that their emission of GHGs is low relative to their population and that equity considerations imply that they should be allowed to increase their share of GHG emissions compared to that of developed countries.

As pointed out in Chapter 5, taxes are not politically popular as means for regulating environmental externalities because they redistribute income, add to government revenue and add to the economic power of the state. The full impacts of such policies can only be evaluated by taking into account the use which governments make of the extra public revenue collected and the way in which they adjust their budgets and fiscal policies in the light of this extra source of income. For example, will the extra tax revenue be used to provide income support to the poor who might be adversely affected by taxes on GHG emissions because of rising electricity or fuel costs, and how will that assistance be provided? If the assistance is provided by subsidizing the use by the poor of products that are GHG intensive, then it will be, to some extent, counterproductive in providing incentives for a reduction in the consumption of greenhouse intensive goods. A rebate for the poor unrelated to their quantity of use of such products or a lump sum income transfer to them would be more effective in compensating the poor and would provide less economic incentive for them to use products that add to GHG emissions.

13.7.3. *Tradable permits for GHG emissions*

As pointed out in Chapter 5, tradable or marketable permit systems can take a wide variety of forms and their economic consequences can be very different depending on the type of system adopted. Such systems are sometimes described as cap and trade systems where the term "cap" refers to the total or aggregate allowable quantity of a pollutant that can be emitted and traded. If the government charges an annual fee to those who hold permits, the system can have similar consequences to taxes on emissions and similar issues can arise. However, a difference is the presence of a cap in the case of a tradable permit scheme. There is no such regulation on the quantity of emissions if taxes are imposed on emissions.

Figure 13.9 provides a useful economic comparison between a simplified tradable permit system for GHGs and one that imposes a uniform tax on the quantity of these emissions. In this figure, the line marked DD represents the aggregate demand for GHG emissions in a period of time. Suppose that the government decides to introduce a tradable permit system which caps the level of GHG emissions at X_1 in this period. This means that the supply of permits in this period will correspond to the vertical line identified by S. Observe that given this demand and supply situation, a market equilibrium for the price of permits would correspond to point E, and the equilibrium market price of tradable or marketed permits will be P_1.

If the government imposes a tax of P_1 on each unit of GHG during the relevant period, this will result exactly in X_1 emissions. The government will raise P_1X_1 in revenue. Consequently, the reduction in the level of emissions would be the same as in the tradable permit case. However, the level of demand for GHG emissions may be uncertain. If for example, demand is higher than that shown by the line DD, at a tax rate of P_1, per unit of emission of GHG, the level of emissions will exceed X_1. Therefore, if it is considered (for political or other reasons) that a cap of X_1 of emissions should not be exceeded, then the tradable permit system will be preferred to taxing emissions.

The economic consequences of a tradable permit system for GHGs depend partly on how the permits are distributed to those who want

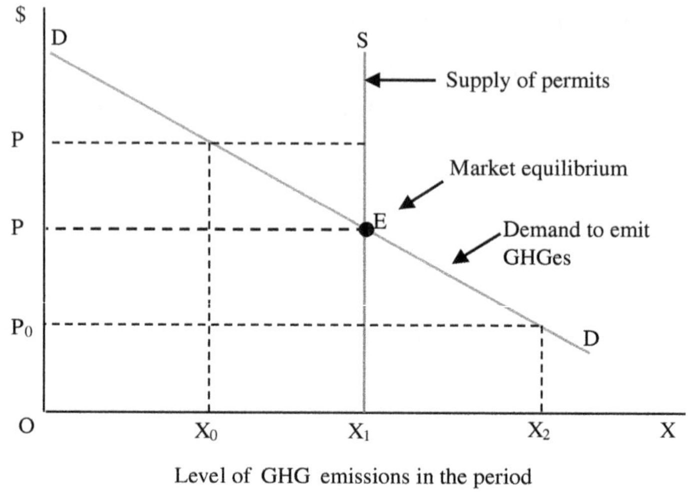

Fig. 13.9. An illustration designed to compare a scheme for trading GHG emissions with the taxation of these emissions. In the case illustrated, if a tradable permit scheme is adopted, X_1 is the cap on emissions of GHGs in the period.

to use them. If the government determines the price for each permit, and if it is uniform for all entities allocated permits and if the price per permit is less than P_1, the equilibrium price in Fig. 13.9, the demand for permits will exceed their supply. Some mechanism in addition to their price will be required in this case to allocate the available quantity of permits. If for example, the price for each permit (which is assumed to give entitlement to emit a specific quantity of GHG) is P_0, X_2 permits will be demanded but only X_1 are available. Excess demand is equal to $X_2 - X_1$. Those who are allocated the permits could earn a rent of up to $(P_1 - P_0)\, X_1$ from their allocation. If permits for X_1 emissions are issued free of charge (for example, by the process of grandfathering) those allocated the permits could obtain a "windfall" gain as a group of P_1X_1. On the other hand, if the government misjudges the demand for permits and say charges a price of P_2 for these, their availability exceeds the demand for them and the cap is not reached.

The revenue transfer to the government is P_0X_1 if P_0 is charged for each permit and P_1X_1 if P_1 is charged. In the latter case, this is the same as when a tax rate of P_1 on emissions is applied.

The question arises of whether permits should be tradable internationally. This is favored by some economists on economic efficiency grounds and should result in global uniformity for the price of permits. However, similar problems arise to those mentioned above in the case of globally uniform taxes on GHG emissions. Nevertheless, hybrid regulatory systems are possible. For example, rights to emit gases that cause global warming based on CO_2 equivalents might be traded internationally with appropriate levels of taxation being also imposed on those emissions which give rise to adverse regional environmental externalities, for instance acid rains (see Section 13.8).

13.7.4. *Who pays for reductions in emissions of GHGs?*

It should be noted that the economic incidence of measures imposed by governments on suppliers of products in order to reduce their GHG emissions need not fall primarily on them. Depending on the degree of inelasticity of demand for these products, a portion of the costs of meeting emission targets will be passed on to buyers. Other things equal, the more inelastic is the demand for such products the greater will be the proportion of these costs passed on to buyers. Nevertheless, substitution of inputs which reduce the emission of GHGs will be encouraged. However, this substitution is likely to be more of a long-term process than a short-term response. There is less economic flexibility in changing production decisions in the short-run than in the long-run.

13.8. Local and Regional Air Pollution, Including Transboundary Pollution

13.8.1. *Background*

The main focus in this chapter so far has been on global air quality. However, the occurrence of air pollution at the local level and its spread to regional areas are also of economic importance. Much local and regional air pollution is generated by the use of fossil fuels and by industrial activities, such as the smelting and refining of minerals, but they are not its only sources of air pollution. For example, forest fires have been a serious source of air pollution. Forest fires in Indonesia have, for instance, resulted in smoke and haze in nearby countries. Agricultural practices in arid or semi-arid areas sometimes contribute to dust storms which spread over long distances. Offensive smells from intensive livestock production (such as from piggeries, poultry farms and cattle lots) are a source of local air pollution. Furthermore, pesticides from agricultural properties may drift in the air to nearby properties and pollen from some genetically modified crops may drift in the air and cross pollinate with other crops.

In many cases, a reduction in the use of fossil fuels (other things unchanged) would not only reduce the level of emission of GHGs but would reduce the extent of local and regional air pollution as well. Nordhaus (1994, 1998) has pointed out that this would be a side-benefit from reducing fossil fuel use in order to lower the rate of global warming. He also points out that when these side-benefits are taken into account, the economic benefit from reducing GHG emissions is increased substantially.

13.8.2. *Local air pollution*

Some air pollutants do not travel far away from where they are emitted and are responsible for local air pollution. This is likely to be the case for some types of particulate matter, noxious smells and some heavy metal particles such as lead from smelting works. The geographical pattern of distribution of air pollutants released from chimneys depends on the height of these and the prevailing winds and air currents. Social economic choices can be made about where it is best to locate economic activities that emit air pollutants and whether or not to allow their emissions to be deposited locally or further afield. Aspects of these choices were discussed in Section 5.7 of this volume.

Sometimes options exist to reduce the emissions of air pollutants by using technologies which collect the emissions as solid waste which can then be disposed of. The private cost of installing technologies and equipment to do this may be lower than the extra social economic benefits obtained, for example, as a result of improvements in human health. Hong *et al.* (1991) found this to be so for cadmium smelting in a local area in China.

Although local residents may suffer economic losses from local air pollution, they do not always have the political will and ability to stop it or to regulate it. There are several reasons for this, including some of an institutional nature. For example, the victims may be economically weak compared to the local polluters and free riding in relation to political action may occur amongst the victims. Political action requires an economic investment. Secondly, locals may judge that the economic benefits they obtain from the occurrence of a polluting economic activity (e.g. their local employment and work as a result of it) outweigh its economic cost to them. If this is **not** so, local residents may still be powerless to change the situation because politically influential individuals outside the local area may obtain an economic benefit if the local pollution is allowed. They may, therefore, successfully oppose attempts of the local community to curb this pollution.

13.8.3. *Regional air pollution including transboundary or transfrontier air pollution*

Some air pollutants are able to travel long distances and can result in pollution in regions far away from where they are emitted. In some parts of the world, acid rains and other forms of acidic precipitation occur in regions well away from areas where the precursors (namely sulfur dioxide and nitrous oxide) are released into the air. For example, as a result of release of these substances in the United Kingdom, acid precipitation occurs in Scandinavia; their release in the US mid-west results in this type of precipitation in Canada, and Japan and Korea experience acid precipitation as a result of economic activity in China. These are international effects but in large countries, such as India, some regions that do not emit the precursors for acid precipitation also experience acid rains.

Power stations burning fossil fuels, particularly those using coal with high sulfur content, are major sources of acid precipitation. However, car emissions also add to the problem. Switching to the use of low sulfur coal and more efficient power stations helps to reduce the problem created by fossil-fueled power stations.

Acid precipitation can reduce agricultural productivity and the growth of forests, increase the acidification of water with negative impacts on aquatic life, increase the rate at which some buildings corrode and have some adverse consequences for human health. Beginning in the 1990s, the United States introduced legislation (the *Clean Air Act 1990 Amendment*) which helped to reduce sulfur dioxide emissions in the United States (Kahn, 2005, pp. 306–312). A cap and trade system for sulfur dioxide was introduced for power plants in the midwest of the United States. It was most likely motivated by concerns to reduce acid deforestation in the United States rather than to reduce the spillover of acid deposition in Canada from precursors emitted in the United States. If nations follow their own self-interest in environmental policy formulation, then they will not take into account their environmental spillovers on other nations if the spillovers are not reciprocal or sufficiently so. If the adverse spillovers are reciprocal, it can be in the interest of all nations involved to agree to a reduction in their adverse spillovers. Nevertheless, as shown in Section 13.4.2, this does not necessarily mean that nations will act in their common interest. Let us, however, consider the situation where an adverse international environmental externality occurs in only one direction; that is from one nation to another or others. Air pollution, such as acid deposition, is often of this nature.

In order to simplify the analysis, assume just two nations, for example, China and Japan. One nation is the source of air pollution in the other, (for example, acid precipitation) and the effect is assumed to be unidirectional. In Fig. 13.9, let line ABCD represent the marginal benefit to the emitting country (Country I) of being able to emit the air pollutant and let line OCG represent the marginal cost of damages within this country from emissions of its air pollutant. In the absence of control, x_3 of the air pollutant would be emitted per period of time by Country I but the **national** net benefit of Country I is maximized by reducing the level of emissions to x_2 because this country is adversely affected by the pollutant. The external marginal costs experienced by Country II are assumed to be equivalent to the difference

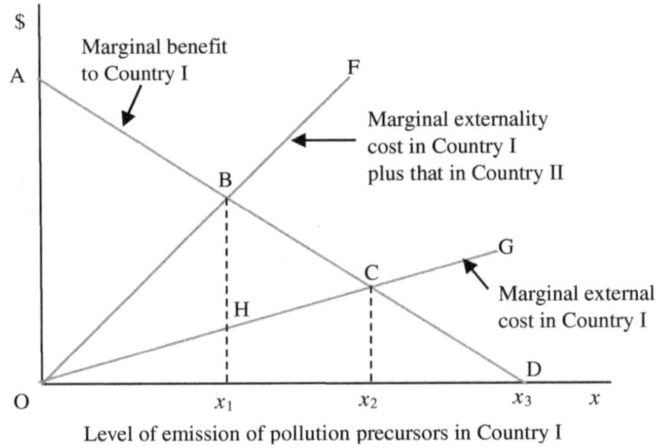

Fig. 13.10. In the case illustrated, international air pollution occurs but Country I which is the source of the pollutant only has an economic incentive to take into account its own economic benefits from reduction of emissions. Therefore, while Country I benefits from reducing its emissions from x_3 to x_2 per period, it has no incentive to reduce these further even though the marginal external costs imposed on Country II exceed the marginal net benefit obtained by Country I from polluting.

between lines OBF and OCG in Fig. 13.10. When this is taken into account, the aggregate net economic benefit of both countries considered together is maximized when the emission of the pollutant in Country I is reduced to x_1 per period. At this point, the combined marginal external cost experienced by the countries as a result of the emission of the air pollutant in Country I, equals the marginal benefit to Country I of being able to emit this pollutant. However, Country I has no economic interest in reducing its level of emissions to this extent unless it receives an economic inducement from Country II to do so.

Figure 13.11 can be used to further clarify the situation. There the line JKM represents the marginal **net** benefit to Country I of being able to emit air pollutants. It is equal to the difference between the marginal benefit of Country I being able to pollute and the marginal external costs experienced by Country I from this pollution. Line OKP represents marginal external environmental costs imposed on Country II as a result of the emission of the air pollutant in Country I. Considering

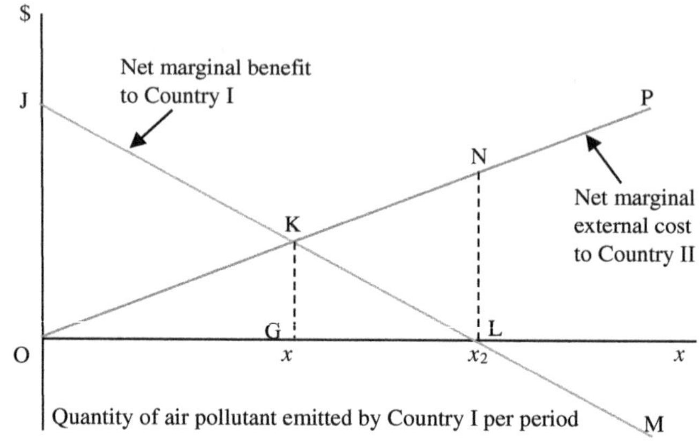

Fig. 13.11. An illustration based on Fig. 13.9 of a problem involving external environmental costs imposed on Country II of air pollution originating in Country I. Bargaining combined with payments to Country I by Country II may be used to improve the economic outcome, as is explained in the text.

its self-interest, Country I has an economic incentive to limit its emission of air pollutants to x_2. However, when the external environmental costs of this on Country II are taken into account, this situation does not maximize overall economic gain. Overall, economic gain would be maximized when Country I's level of emissions is restricted to x_1 because at this level the marginal net economic benefit to Country I of being able to pollute is just equal to the marginal external costs which it imposes on Country II.

Note that it would be in the economic interest of Country II to make a payment to Country I to reduce the level of its air pollutants from x_2 to x_1; given the situation illustrated in Fig. 13.11. The maximum amount Country II would be prepared to pay for this reduction would be equivalent to the area of quadrilateral GLNK and the minimum that Country II would accept for such a reduction would be equivalent to the area of triangle GLK. Therefore, both countries can gain from a bargained solution to the problem. The payment to Country I by Country II could, for example, be in the form of foreign aid. Japan has, for example, provided foreign aid to China to increase the efficiency of its coal-fired power stations and this may help to reduce acid precipitation in Japan originating from sources in China. Nevertheless, bargaining need not result in an optimal outcome from an economic efficiency point of view. Bilateral bargaining about how to share the economic gains from co-operation can result in political stalemate. For example, Country I may not be satisfied to accept an amount equal to the area of triangle KGL in Fig. 13.11 and it may demand a portion of the amount indicated by the area of triangle KLN. Country I may refuse to agree to this or to the sum requested. Hence, there is a political stalemate.

13.9. Concluding Comments

The increasing use of inanimate sources of energy (particularly fossil fuels) since the beginning of the Industrial Revolution has contributed greatly to rising standards of living worldwide. Globally fossil fuels are still the main source of electricity production and by far, the major source for the anthropogenic production of heat. However, some other sources of electricity production (notably solar and wind power) which only make a very small addition to global warming are increasing in their relative importance as contributors to electricity supply. The bulk of electricity and heat is used outside residences, mainly for economic production.

The management of electricity and heat supplies was found to involve complex issues. For instance, decisions have to be made by governments about whether electricity should be supplied by the state or privately owned enterprises (or by a mixture of these) and about competition and pricing in the electricity industry. These decisions are complicated by the presence of economies of scale, diseconomies of duplication of networks, periodic variations in demand for electricity and differences in the degree of flexibility in varying supplies of electricity produced from different sources. For example, there is more scope to vary electricity supplies obtained by using natural gas and other fossil fueled power stations than from nuclear ones. Altering the supply of electricity obtained from solar and wind sources can also be a problem. However, the supply of electricity from solar and wind power is becoming more competitive with its supply from other sources and its dispatchability has increased due to the use of lithium batteries. A benefit of using these technologies is their low contribution to GHG emissions. Infant industry arguments for governments subsidizing the development and use of these technologies were outlined.

The need to vary electricity supplies as the demand for supply of electricity fluctuates is one factor that affects the optimal mixture of sources of electricity supplied to an electricity grid. Furthermore, the production of electricity and heat production generally produces significant negative environmental externalities. These externalities ought to be taken into account from a social economic point of view. The use of fossil fuels has negative impacts on local and regional air quality and is a major contributor to global warming. However, the negative environmental consequences of the use of many fossil fuels are not limited to their reduction of air quality. The supply of those fuels can reduce water and soil quality. In assessing environmental impacts, the whole chain of fuel production and use should be taken into account.

Reductions in global air quality (as a result of human activities) have become a major issue. Ozone layer depletion and global warming are particular concerns. As demonstrated in this chapter by using some simple game-like models, the pursuit of national self-interest may not lead nations to regulate their emissions of air pollutants even when it is in their collective interest to do so. The outcome was shown to depend on the structure of the strategic situation being faced by nations. If the relevant biophysical relationships involve thresholds, jumps and irreversibilities as well as uncertainties, this adds to the difficulty of achieving a collectively optimal behavioral outcome. These complexities are relevant to the prospects of controlling global warming and climate change.

While the Montreal Protocol resulted in global action to eliminate the use of some ozone-depleting substances, concerns still remain because their substitutes (while less destructive of ozone) have a much longer life in the atmosphere and some contribute to global warming. Less global progress has been made in curbing GHG emissions and in regulating economic developments contributing to global warming than in controlling atmospheric ozone depletion. This is partly because the necessary changes in the nature of human activity and lifestyles needed to control global warming are very far reaching. The problem is further compounded by the biophysical and economic uncertainties involved in the evaluation of the problem. Various predictions, however, indicate the future economic cost of not regulating global warming will be high and that a net economic benefit can be obtained by restricting the anthropogenic forces that contribute to global warming.

Global agreement on policies to limit global warming face difficulties because of rivalry between nations in pursuing their own self-interest and because of international income distribution issues. These problems are intensified because different nations are at different stages of their economic development. Furthermore, access to and use of energy resources have implications for the global political and military power of individual nations. Whether or not the Paris Agreement (the successor to the Kyoto global agreement on policies to regulate global warming) can overcome these obstacles remains to be seen. In 2020, the signs were not promising.

Although global warming is currently a major international concern, the economic importance of local and regional air pollution should not be lost sight of. Additional economic policies are needed to address these environmental effects. Addressing such issues is complicated by political factors. Furthermore, the environmental regional spillovers from air pollution can have international (transboundary) consequences. Those nations which release pollutants having negative environmental impacts on other countries have no economic motivation to take these spillovers into account in regulating their economic activities. However, a bargained solution to the problem is possible — nations adversely affected by the spillovers may pay those countries generating these spillovers to moderate them. Nevertheless, an ideal social outcome is not assured.

13.10. Keywords

Acid precipitation; climate change due to global warming; footloose industries and the regulation of GHG emissions; fossil fuels; global per capita consumption forgone as a result of GHG emissions; global warming; GHGs; incidence of regulations on GHG emissions; infant industries; Intergovernmental Panel on Climate Change (IPCC); international (regional) air pollution; Kyoto Protocol; local air pollution; Montreal Protocol; ozone layer depletion; Paris Agreement on Climate Change; private versus public supply of electricity; regional air pollution; social costs of GHG emissions; solar energy; sources of energy supplies; taxes on GHG emissions; tradable permits for GHG emissions; transboundary or transfrontier air pollution; United Nations Framework Convention on Climate Change (UNFCCC).

13.11. Questions for Review and Discussion

1. The increased use of fossil fuels following the Industrial Revolution did much to raise standards of living but this has been achieved at considerable environmental cost, some aspects of which have only emerged in recent times. Explain and discuss.
2. What are the main natural resources used for supplying electricity? Why has the proportion of electricity supplied by fossil fuels declined in recent years?
3. Which sectors of the global economy are the main users of electricity? Why is the demand for electricity sensitive to the aggregate level of economic activity? Do you expect the consumption of electricity to increase substantially in the future? Why?
4. Electricity production is a major source of energy supply in the modern world. Outline major issues that need to be considered by governments in managing this supply.
5. Outline and discuss reasons why some governments have subsidized (or might decide to subsidize) emerging sectors of the electricity industry which produce electricity resulting in low levels of GHG emissions. What types of economic instruments might be used for this purpose?
6. Why should environmental externalities that occur throughout the whole chain of electricity production be taken into account when considering the desirable development and use

of energy sources? Give examples of cases where failure to do this can result in inappropriate dependence on particular energy resources.

7. Making polluters pay for their adverse environmental externalities has been widely advocated as a policy for limiting GHG emissions. However, given the perceived current climate emergency, it may be desirable for governments to support the development of energy sources which have a low GHG footprint. Discuss. In doing so, take account of infant industry arguments.
8. Why is it sometimes difficult to achieve global action by nations to improve global air quality? Illustrate your answer by models derived from game theory.
9. Why has depletion of the ozone layer occurred? What adverse consequences does destruction of this layer have? Why was it relatively easy to get a global agreement on stopping the use of CFCs; a group of ozone-depleting agents? Do concerns continue about depletion of the ozone layer?
10. What do most scientists believe is the basic cause of global warming? What effects is global warming predicted to have on climate change and on sea levels?
11. What types of economic methods have been used to estimate the economic impacts (costs) of global warming and the net benefits of controlling it? What are their main limitations?
12. Why are the predicted economic consequences of global warming subject to so much controversy? In your answer, take into account both biophysical and economic issues.
13. Nicholas Stern in his review of climate change claimed that it might result in a 20% reduction in per capita global consumption compared to what it would otherwise have been if global warming was restricted. What economic components does Stern include in his estimate? Would you include the same components in a similar way? Explain why.
14. What international agreements have been reached to limit global warming and how effective have they been in doing this? Why is it difficult to get international cooperation to limit GHG

emissions? Why are developing countries reluctant to refrain from deforestation even though forests act as a sink for carbon dioxide?

15. Economic considerations will be important in determining appropriate policies both to mitigate global warming and to adjust to it. What types of considerations are relevant?
16. Why is it desirable to announce economic policies for reductions in GHG emissions well in advance of their implementation, phase these regulations in gradually, and to not permit widespread exceptions to their application?
17. If the policies of different countries result in different prices being paid for allowing GHG emissions, this can affect the international location of industries. There will be an incentive for major emitters of GHGs to shift from countries where policies result in a high price or cost for these emissions to those with low or no costs for these emissions. Explain. Why do international differences in charges for GHG emissions reduce the effectiveness of policies to lower these emissions?
18. Potential new techniques for carbon storage have been touted as the answer to reducing levels of CO_2 in the atmosphere. Does this prospect justify not charging for GHG emissions? Explain your answer.
19. Taxes on GHG emissions or alternatively, tradable permits for GHG emissions can be used to limit these emissions. How do such methods operate? Compare and contrast the economics of these measures for limiting GHG emissions. Use a diagram to illustrate your answer.
20. It has been suggested that the taxes on GHG emissions or the price of tradable permits for these emissions should be uniform throughout the world. What is the basis for this view? Would you want to qualify this assertion and why?
21. More than one type of gas contributes to global warming, although CO_2 is a major influence. Different GHGs have different lengths of life in the atmosphere and vary in their global warming effects. Explain. How does this complicate the formulation and execution of economic policies to control GHG emissions?

22. Although emitters of GHGs may be required to pay for their emission of GHGs, ultimately, it may be the buyers who pay this charge or most of it. Explain.
23. Why are some governments concerned about the income distributional consequences of imposing charges on GHG emissions? Discuss alternative policies for offsetting these effects.
24. Although global warming is an important issue, the economic consequences of local and regional air pollution should not be ignored. What types of environmental spillovers may occur at the local and regional levels? What types of (political) factors may result in local and regional air pollution problems not being addressed?
25. International (transfrontier) regional air pollution involves environmental externalities. Why is it likely to be difficult to achieve the efficient regulation of such emissions? Illustrate your answer with reference to acid precipitation. You may also find it useful to use diagrams to elucidate the issues involved.

Readings and References

Anon (2020a). *Economics of Global Warming*, Wikipedia. http://wikipedia.org/wiki/Economics_of_global_warming [Accessed 7 July 2020].

Anon (2020b). Paris Agreement, *Wikipedia* [Online] Wikipedia. https://en.wikipedia.org/wiki/Paris_Agreement [Accessed 6 April, 2020].

Garnaut, R. (2019). *Superpower: Australia's Low-Carbon Opportunity*, La Trobe University Press and Black Inc., Carlton, Victoria.

Hall, J.V., D. Hall and R.B. Howarth (Eds.) (2001). *Long-term Economics of Climate Change: Beyond a Doubling of Greenhouse Gas Concentrations*, Elsevier Science, Amsterdam. [pp. 1–64, 315–336].

Hong, Z., K. Bao and C.A. Tisdell (1991). Cadmium exposure in Daye County: Environmental assessment and management, health and economic effects, *Environmental Management and Health*, 2, 20–25.

Hunt, C. (2009). *Carbon Sinks and Climate Change: Forests in the Fight Against Global Warming*, Edward Elgar, Cheltenham, UK and Northampton, MA, USA [Chapters 1 and 2].

International Energy Agency (2005). *Data and Statistics — Electricity/Heat in World in 2005*, https://www.iea.org/data-and-statistics/data-tables?country=WORLD&energy=Electricity&year=2005 [Accessed 9 March 2020].

International Energy Agency (2017a). *Data and Statistics — Electricity/Heat/World,* https://www.iea.org/data-and-statistics/data-tables?country=WORLD&energy=Electricity&year=2017 [Accessed 27 April 2020].

International Energy Agency (2017b). World Energy Outlook 2017 — Executive Summary, [Online] International Energy Agency. https://webstore.iea.org/download/summary/196?fileName=English-WEO-2017-ES.pdf [Accessed 27 April 2020].

International Energy Agency (2019). Electricity Information Overview, [Online] IEA, Paris. https://iea.blob.core.windows.net/assets/722cdfb8-a938-43d6-ad99-1fbf3e53bf8e/Electricity_Information_2019_Overview.pdf [Accessed 27 April 2020].

IPCC (2007a). Working Group I Report: Climate Change 2007: Summary for Policy Makers. Intergovernmental Panel for Climate Change (IPCC), Geneva, Switzerland. Available from: https://www.ipcc.ch/report/ar4/wg1/ [Accessed 8 July 2020].

IPCC (2007b). Climate Change 2007: Synthesis Report, [Online] IPCC, Geneva. http://www.ipcc.ch/publications_and_data/publications_ipcc_fourth_assessment_report_synthesis_report.htm [Accessed 8 July 2020].

IPCC (2011). IPCC Special Report on Renewable Energy Sources and Climate Change Mitigation. Cambridge University Press, Cambridge, UK and New York USA. Prepared by Working Group III of the Intergovernmental Panel on Climate Change (O. Edenhover, R. Pichs-Madruga, Y. Sokona, K. Seyboth, P. Matschoss, S. Kadner, T. Zwickel, P. Eickemeier, G. Hansen S. Schlőmer, C. von Stechow (eds.)). Available from: https://www.ipcc.ch/report/renewable-energy-sources-and-climate-change-mitigation/ [Accessed 8 July 2020].

IPCC (2014). Climate Change 2014 Synthesis Report. Contribution of Working Groups I, II and III to the Fifth Assessment Report of the Intergovernmental Panel on Climate Change, AR5. Intergovernmental Panel on Climate Change (IPCC), Geneva, Switzerland. [Core Writing Team, R.K. Pachauri and L.A. Meyer (eds.)]. Available from: https://www.ipcc.ch/report/ar5/syr/ [Accessed 8 July 2020].

Kahn, J.R. (2005). *The Economic Approach to Environmental and Natural Resources,* 3rd edn. South-Western, Mason, Ohio, USA [Chapters 7–9].

List, F. (1841 [1856]). *Das Nationale System der politischen Oekonomie (The National System of Political Economy),* GA Matile [trans.], J.B. Lippencott and Co, Philadelphia, USA. [Translated 1856].

Marshall, A. (1890). *Principles of Economics,* 1st edn. Macmillan, London.

Marx, K. (1967). *Capital,* Dent, London. [Translated from the 4th German edition of *Das Kapital,* published in 1890].

Napoli, C. (2012). Understanding Kyoto's failure, *SAIS Review of International Affairs,* 32, 183–196. doi: http://doi.org/10.1353/sais.2012.0033.

Nordhaus, W.D. (1994). *Managing the Global Commons: The Economics of Change,* MIT Press, Cambridge, MA.

Nordhaus, W.D. (1998). *Economics and Policy Issues in Climate Change,* Resource for the Future, Washington, D.C., USA.

Perman, R., Y. Ma, M. Common, D. Maddison and J. McGilvray (2011). *Natural Resource and Environmental Economics,* 4th edn. Pearson, Harlow, Essex UK [Chapter 9].

Quiggin, J. (2008). Uncertainty and climate change policy, *Economic Analysis and Policy,* 38, 203–210. doi: https://doi.org/10.1016/S0313-5926(08)50017-8.

Rogelj, J., M. den Elzen, N. Höhne, T. Fransen, H. Fekete, H. Winkler, R. Schaeffer, F. Sha, K. Riahi and M. Meinshausen (2016). Paris Agreement climate proposals need a boost to keep warming well below 2°C, *Nature,* 534, 631–639. doi: 10.1038/nature18307.

Searchinger, T., R. Heimlich, R.A. Houghton, F. Dong, A. Elobeid, J. Fabissa, S. Tokgoz, D. Hayes and T.-H. Yu (2008). Use of U.S. croplands for biofuels increases greenhouse gases through emissions from land-use change, *Science,* 319, 1238–1240.

Stern, N. (2007a). *The Economics of Climate Change: The Stern Review,* Cambridge University Press, Cambridge UK.

Stern, N. (2007b). Stern Review: The Economics of Climate Change [Online]. https://webarchive.nationalarchives.gov.uk/+/http:/www.hm-treasury.gov.uk/media/4/3/executive_summary.pdf [Accessed 27 April 2020].

Swarna Nantha, H. and C.A. Tisdell (2009). The orangutan-oil palm conflict: Economic constraints and opportunities for conservation, *Biodiversity Conservation,* 18, 487–502. doi: 10.1007/s10531-008-9512-3.

Tietenberg, T. and L. Lewis (2018). *Environmental and Natural Resource Economics,* 11th edn. Routledge, New York and Abingdon, Oxon, UK [Chapters 7 and 17].

Tisdell, C.A. (1966). Some bounds upon Pareto optimality of group behavior, *Kyklos,* 19, 81–105.

Tisdell, C.A. (2008). Global warming and the future of Pacific Island countries, *International Journal of Social Economics,* 35, 889–903.

Tisdell, C.A. (2017). *Economics and Environmental Change: The Challenges We Face,* Edward Elgar Publishing, Cheltenham, UK, and Northampton, MA, USA. [Chapters 5 and 8].

Tisdell, C.A. (2019). Renewable energy use and the renewable energy sector's development: Public finance, environmental externalities and sustainability, *Green Finance,* 1, 156–173. doi: http://dx.doi.org/10.3934/GF.2019.2.156.

Tisdell, C.A. and K. Hartley (2008). *Microeconomic Policy: A New Perspective,* Edward Elgar, Cheltenham, UK and Northampton, MA, USA [Chapter 10].

Tol, R.S.J. (2008). The social cost of carbon: trends, outliers and catastrophes, *Economics: The Open-Access, Open-Assessment E-Journal,* 2. doi: http://dx.doi.org/10.5018/economics-ejournal.ja.2008-25.

Victor, D.G., K. Akimoto, K. Kaya, M. Yamaguchi, D. Cullenward and H. C. (2017). Prove Paris was more than paper promises, *Nature,* 548, 25–27. doi: 10.1038/548025a.

Wang, M., M. Wu and H. Huo (2007). Life-cycle energy and greenhouse gas emission impacts of different corn ethanol plant types, *Environmental Research Letters,* 2, 024001. doi: 10.1088/1748-9326/2/2/024001.

Chapter 14

Recycling and Solid Waste Management

14.1. Introduction

Economic production and consumption generate wastes and these tend to increase in volume with the level of economic activity. These wastes may be released into shared environments in the air, in water or as solids or semi-solids and may become pollutants that damage living organisms and natural ecosystems. Often the form in which they are released can be varied and the way in which they enter the environment may alter with the passage of time. A general overview of waste disposal and recycling can be found in Wikipedia (Anon, 2020).

Earlier chapters concentrated on air and water pollutants but in this chapter, the economics of managing solid wastes is the central issue. The disposal of solid wastes has increased in global importance with growing urbanization and the development of large cities. The safe disposal of solid wastes can be costly. This waste also requires the use of space which is particularly scarce in cities and it can add to air and water pollution.

Apart from the management of the disposal of solid waste, the other major issue examined in this chapter is the economics of recycling wastes and commodities. Because recycling of solids reduces the quantity of solid wastes to be dumped, recycling and solid waste management are interrelated. Secondly, recycling can have other advantages: it usually reduces the rate at which natural resources are depleted and often has positive environmental consequences. For example, the recycling of many metals reduces the extent of mining and normally requires less energy use than their production from virgin materials. Because much of the energy used to produce metals is obtained from the combustion of fossil fuels, there is a reduction in pollution resulting from the use of these fuels (see Chapter 13). For instance, much less energy is needed to recycle aluminum than to produce aluminum from bauxite.

Attention is initially given in this chapter to the potential economic benefits and drawbacks of recycling and its alternatives. Then economic failures that occur in recycling are considered and policies to rectify these are outlined. Subsequently, the economics of solid waste disposal becomes the focus of attention. It is shown how economic failures can result in the uneconomic management of solid wastes and policies to address such failures are examined.

14.2. Why should Wastes and Economic Products be Recycled? What Factors Influence the Extent of Recycling?

14.2.1. *Reasons for recycling*

Not all solid wastes and economic products can be recycled economically. However, for several reasons (outlined below) some solid wastes and used products are not recycled or reused even though it would be a social economic advantage for this to happen. Those who favor the recycling of used materials and products believe that (1) it may add to economic sustainability by reducing the demand to utilize non-renewable virgin resources; (2) it may reduce collateral environmental damage that would occur if new products are produced from virgin materials; (3) up to a point, it may be more profitable to recycle used materials than obtain these materials from virgin sources and it may reduce pollution from solid waste disposed of in land fill or otherwise. This does not, however, mean that it is always economic to recycle recyclable materials.

When the costs of collecting, sorting and physically transforming recyclable material are taken into account, it may be uneconomic to recycle some recyclable materials. Sometimes, the amount of energy (and costs) required to collect, sort and transform recyclable materials can exceed that required to obtain the same end-products from virgin materials. This can be so even when all social costs are taken into account. Nevertheless, as discussed below, less recycling of materials seems to occur than is desirable from a social economic point of view.

14.2.2. *A simple model of the private economics of recycling*

Unless the demand for use of a material (that can either be obtained from recycling or from virgin sources) is contracting, it will usually be impossible to supply all of the demanded material by recycling it. For one thing, each time a resource is used for economic consumption and production some dispersion or entropy of the resource occurs even if the product is a durable product. Therefore, the volume of a recyclable resource tends to decline each time it is used. Furthermore, the composition of some recycled materials tends to alter each time they are recycled and this limits the end uses to which they can be put. Physical (as well as economic) factors need to be taken into account when considering the recycling of materials.

Figure 14.1 provides a simple illustration of the economic relationship between the private demand for recycled materials and that for virgin materials. It assumes that recycled materials are perfect substitutes for virgin materials. The right-hand side of the diagram shows the private marginal cost of obtaining a particular material, X, from virgin sources and the left-hand side shows the private marginal cost of deriving the same material by recycling. In this particular case, the marginal cost relationships are shown, respectively, by lines OAB and OCD. If users of material X wish to maximize their profit, they should distribute their sourcing of supplies of X from the different sources so that the marginal cost of its availability is equal for both sources. This ensures that the cost of supply of X is minimized whatever quantity of material X is used. Thus, if the total demand for material is $\bar{X} = \bar{x}_v + \bar{x}_r$, the private cost of obtaining this supply is (as illustrated in Fig. 14.1)

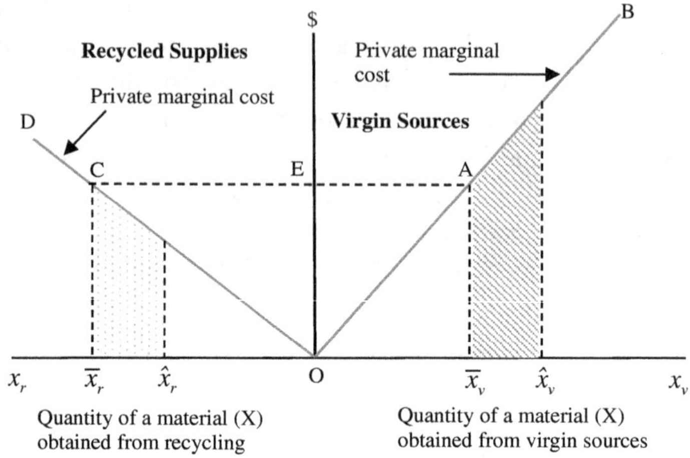

Fig. 14.1. This figure is used to show that the extent to which materials are recycled (e.g. metals, glass, plastics or paper) depends on the cost of recycling these materials compared to the cost of supplying them from virgin sources.

minimized by obtaining $\bar{x}_v$ of supplies from virgin sources and $\bar{x}_r$ by recycling. This ensures that the marginal cost of supply from each of the sources is equal. In this case, they are equal to OE. If a larger proportionate amount of $\bar{X}$ is obtained from either virgin sources or from recycling, this will add to the private cost of the material used.

This can be illustrated by reference to Fig. 14.1. For instance, suppose the sources of supply of $\bar{X}$ of material X are altered by increasing its supply from virgin sources by $\hat{x}_v - \bar{x}_v$ and decreasing its supply from recycled material by an equivalent amount of $\bar{x}_r - \hat{x}_r$. Consequently, the total cost of the supply of X from virgin sources rises by an amount equal to the area of the hatched quadrilateral and the total cost of its supply from recycling falls by an amount equal to the area of the dotted quadrilateral. Because the area of the hatched quadrilateral exceeds that of the dotted quadrilateral, the total cost of supplying $\bar{X}$ of material X rises. If the final marginal costs of supplying the material from the alternative sources are not equated, then the total private costs of supplying the material are higher than they need to be.

Note that other things equal, a decline in the marginal cost of supplying X from virgin sources (that is rotation of line OAB clock-wise) increases the proportion of the supply of X obtained from virgin sources and reduces the proportion obtained by recycling. Similarly, a reduction in the marginal cost of recycling, other things constant, would result in a greater proportionate supply of X being obtained by recycling. In the former case, the amount of solid wastes demanded for recycling falls, but rises in the latter case. Wastes need to be dumped or stored are likely to build up in the former case.

14.3. Adjusting the Simplified Recycling Model to Allow for Market Failures

The model considered in Fig. 14.1 does not allow for market failures. They are, however, likely to occur and cause social marginal costs to diverge from private marginal costs. For example, unfavorable externalities caused by mining and processing of materials obtained from virgin sources can cause the social marginal costs of supply from these sources to exceed their private marginal costs. The marginal unfavorable externalities from obtaining resources by recycling materials are often lower than those for obtaining the same materials from virgin sources, or the marginal externalities from recycling may even be positive. The latter can be considered to be the case if in the absence of recycling, solid wastes are dumped and subsequently generate unfavorable environmental externalities. The reduction in pollution avoided as a result of recycling materials and not dumping them as solid wastes can be regarded as a positive spillover from recycling.

Given the above pattern of environmental spillovers, private decisions about recycling result in a socially excessive proportion of materials being obtained from virgin sources and not enough being obtained as a result of recycling materials. This can be illustrated by modifying Fig. 14.1 as is done in Fig. 14.2.

Figure 14.2 has the same interpretation as Fig. 14.1 and as before, the private marginal cost of obtaining material X from virgin sources is as shown by line OAB and when obtained by recycling, it is as shown by line OCD. The social marginal cost of obtaining material X from virgin sources is shown by line OF and the difference between it and line OB represents the corresponding marginal unfavorable externality

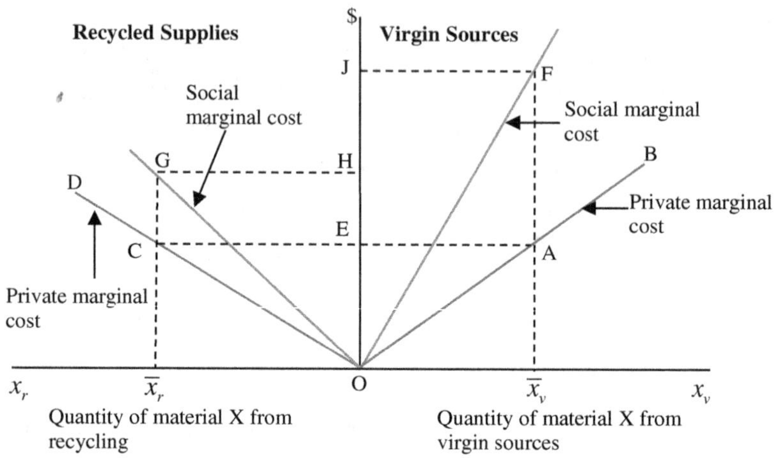

Fig. 14.2. An illustration of a case where the presence of environmental spillovers results in a socially excessive proportion of a material being obtained from virgin sources and an inadequate proportion being obtained by recycling.

costs. The social cost of supplying material X by recycling is shown by line OG. The difference between line OD and line OG represents the lower marginal externality costs from recycling. Now from a social point of view, whatever quantity of X is supplied ought to be supplied at minimum social cost. This requires that the social marginal cost of its supply from its alternative sources be equalized.

From Fig. 14.2, it is clear that decisions based on private marginal costs designed to minimize private costs will not minimize social costs. For example, if (as before) $\bar{X}$ of the material is being used, private decisions will result in $\bar{x}_v$ of it being supplied from virgin sources and $\bar{x}_r$ being obtained by recycling material. This will minimize private costs but not social costs. The social marginal cost of obtaining material X from virgin sources is equal to OJ whereas the social marginal cost of obtaining this material by recycling in only OH. Therefore, social marginal cost will be reduced if a larger share of $\bar{X}$ is obtained by recycling and a lower proportion is supplied from virgin sources compared to the allocations which would maximize private profit. Adjustment should take place until the social marginal cost of obtaining the material is the same for each of the sources.

In theory, the ideal social allocation could be achieved internalizing the economic costs associated with the spillovers. One possibility is to subsidize recycling and tax the use of virgin materials so as to allow for the spillovers present. This would, however, not necessarily be a socially ideal solution because it does not specifically target the particular spillovers involved (see Chapter 3). It is a Pigovian-type approach.

Note that if those disposing of solid wastes had to pay the full social costs of its disposal, they would be less inclined to acquire waste materials and would be more willing to supply wastes for recycling.

14.4. Some Additional Factors That Ought to Be Taken into Account in Modeling the Economics of Recycling

14.4.1. *Introductory observations*

The above models do not take into account the willingness of those who have recyclable wastes to supply these for recycling. Householders and others who have recyclable waste usually incur some costs in supplying this for recycling and may incur less cost by just dumping this waste, that is disposing of it as garbage or trash. Sometimes, suppliers of recyclable wastes have to sort these, arrange for recyclers to collect the waste or take it to some collection point. Arrangements for collection of wastes vary internationally. Nevertheless, one would expect suppliers of recyclable waste to take into account the cost of supplying it to recyclers and the relative cost of dumping it. While recyclers may pay for some types of recyclable material or wastes, sometimes there is no payment or they have to be paid to accept such wastes. It is, therefore, worthwhile considering the operation of markets for recyclable wastes and analyzing the decisions of individuals about whether to supply materials for recycling or reuse.

14.4.2. *Markets for recyclable wastes*

As discussed above, markets for obtaining materials from recycling or from virgin resources are interdependent. In order to provide more detailed analysis of the markets for recyclable wastes, let us assume that except in the market for the recyclable material under consideration, everything else remains constant.

Consider first a case in which suppliers of recyclable waste obtain a payment for it from recyclers. Let X represent the quantity of a material recycled and let the line DD indicate the demand of recyclers for this recyclable waste. Suppose that the line marked S_1S_1 is the marginal cost of supplying waste suitable for recycling to recyclers. Then in this market, equilibrium will correspond to point E_1 with recyclers paying P_2 for each unit of X supplied for recycling. The equilibrium supply of waste is X_1 per period. Should the demand curve for recyclable material shift upwards (for example, because the cost of obtaining material X from virgin sources rises) then, other things remaining equal, the price of recyclable wastes will tend to rise and a greater quantity of wastes can be expected to be recycled. The converse also applies. A shift downwards in the supply curve for recycled material (because, for example, of a reduction in costs of supplying it to recyclers) will tend to increase the amount of the material recycled. Note that the cost of dumping waste rather than recycling it influences its supply for recycling. For example, in Fig. 14.3, if FE_1 per unit is the cost of dumping recyclable

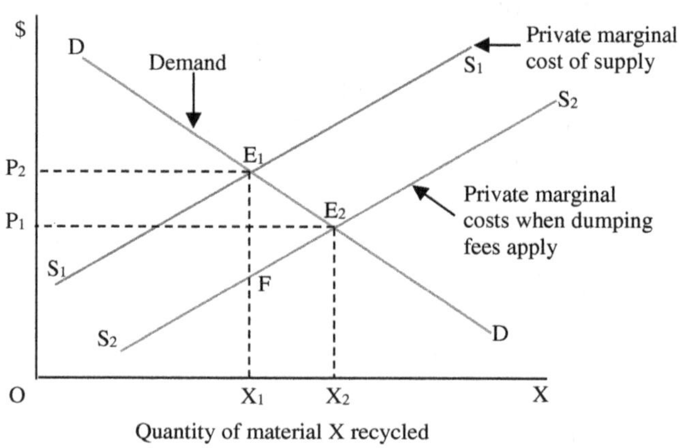

Fig. 14.3. Markets exist for some recyclable materials. In the case illustrated, the recyclable waste has a positive market price. The price for recyclable waste and the quantity recycled depends on the relative position of the relevant demand and supply curves.

wastes, this cost can be avoided by supplying the waste to recyclers. As a result, the supply curve for recyclable waste will be S_2S_2 rather than S_1S_1 and the market equilibrium for the waste will be established at E_2 rather than E_1. More waste is recycled, namely an amount X_2, but the price paid to suppliers falls to P_1. In general, the higher are the costs of dumping wastes, the greater is likely to be the volume of wastes recycled, other things remaining equal.

For many economic entities, wastes are nuisance goods — their presence is negative in value. Those with solid waste may have to pay to dump these and are inconvenienced by their presence if they cannot otherwise dispose of these wastes. Consequently, some materials may be supplied for recycling or for reuse even though the supplier has to pay for their removal or receives no payment for their supply. These possibilities are illustrated in Fig. 14.4 which once again relates to the market for recycling a type of material, X. The line DD indicates the demand for this material for recycling and the line S_3S_3 is its supply. This supply curve indicates that those with the waste would be prepared to pay to be rid of up to X_3 of it. Because the market equilibrium is established at E_3 in this case, the equilibrium price per unit of waste for recycling is zero, and X_3 of it is supplied for recycling.

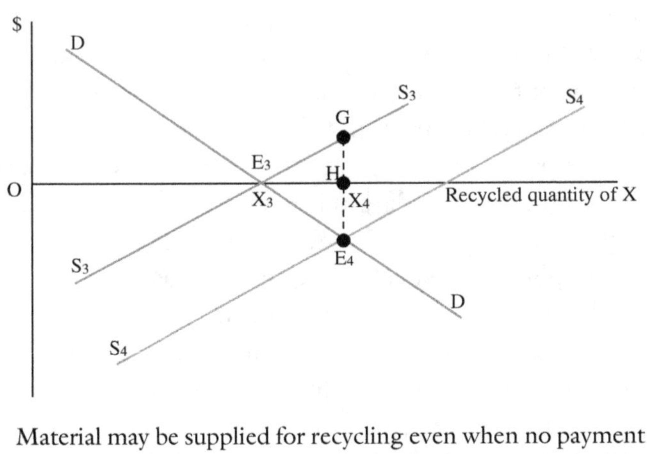

Fig. 14.4. Material may be supplied for recycling even when no payment is made for it by recyclers or in some cases, recyclers must be paid to remove it. The higher the costs of dumping recyclable wastes and the greater is their nuisance value, the more attractive is their recycling (other things held constant) to holders of recyclable wastes.

The higher is the cost of dumping recyclable waste, the greater is the incentive of the holders of such wastes to supply it to recyclers, other things remaining constant. For example, if in the case considered in Fig. 14.4, holders of wastes are charged an amount equal to E_4G for each unit of waste dumped, their supply curve for supplying the wastes to recyclers become S_4S_4 and a new market equilibrium for recyclable waste is established at E_4. Holders of waste now have to pay an amount equal to E_4H for each unit of recyclable waste recovered by recyclers. This, however, is lower than the dumping fee for such wastes. The recycling option costs suppliers of recyclable wastes the equivalent of HG less than if they dumped the waste.

14.4.3. *Decisions of individuals about supplying wastes for recycling*

Consider, in more detail, economic factors that influence decisions by individuals to supply items for recycling or reuse. Suppose that in each period of time an individual has a quantity of waste that can either be recycled or dumped. Let this quantity be $\bar{x}$. In Fig. 14.5, this flow of wastes is indicated by the vertical line HJ. Suppose that recyclers will pay OC per unit for this waste and assume that the individual's private marginal cost of supplying the waste is as shown by line OAB. Consequently, it is most profitable for the individual to supply x_1 of the waste per period for recycling and dump the rest, $\bar{x} - x_1$, if there is no marginal cost involved in dumping the waste. If, however, a charge of AG per unit is imposed on dumping the waste, the individual possessing waste will have an effective marginal cost curve for supplying waste for recycling equal to line GD. This will result in a greater quantity of waste being supplied for recycling (x_2 in this case) and a reduction in dumping of the waste to $\bar{x} - x_2$ per period.

Furthermore (as in the market-case illustrated in Fig. 14.4), individuals may supply waste for recycling even if they are not paid for its removal or have to pay for its removal. If the decision is made purely on financial grounds, then it will depend on whether it is less costly to supply the waste for recycling or alternatively, either to store it, dump it or otherwise dispose of it.

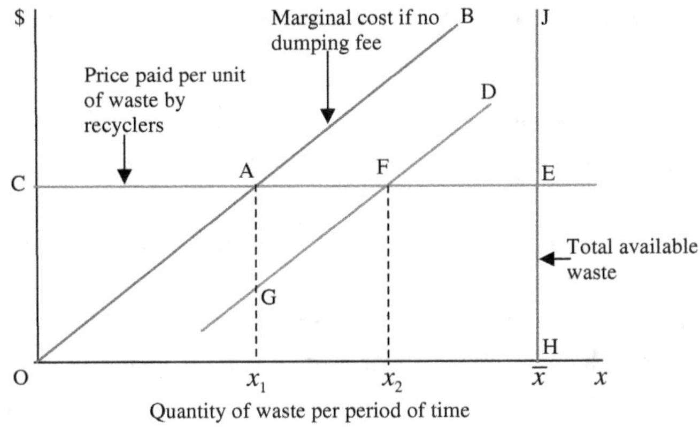

Fig. 14.5. An illustration of economic factors liable to influence decisions by individuals to recycle waste. From this figure, it can be observed that the higher is the cost of dumping waste, the more likely it is to be supplied for recycling, other things remaining unchanged. In the case shown, a dumping charge of AG per unit of recyclable waste increases the amount of waste that the individual supplies for recycling from x_1 to x_2 and reduces the quantity dumped.

Note that not all decisions about recycling of wastes and reuse of products are made purely on narrow economic grounds. Some individuals believe that it is morally more acceptable to recycle wastes than dump these because it is environmentally beneficial. Or again, some individuals believe that it is ethically desirable to donate used goods to charities for potential reuse by the poor and others. In such cases, they have a social preference for the recycling and reuse of commodities and may be prepared to make extra effort to ensure that their "waste" materials are recycled or reused. Both environmental and social welfare motives can have a strong influence on the extent of recycling and reuse of articles. In the case of charities, many volunteers contribute to the collection and distribution of goods for recycling and reuse and they may do so partly for ethical reasons. Social factors can significantly influence the recycling and reuse of articles as well as their accumulation and dumping. This accords with Etzioni's theory of human behavior (Etzioni, 1988). Etzioni (see Chapter 2) argues that human behavior reflects actions based on self-interest modified by moral or ethical feelings. The latter may be socially induced (Tisdell, 1997).

14.4.4. *Some additional factors that influence the extent of recycling*

The above models do not allow for some factors that influence the economics of recycling. For example, economies of scale and economies of scope may occur in recycling. The former implies that the per-unit cost of recycling materials falls with the quantity of material available for recycling. The latter implies that some economies in recycling could occur as the variety of materials available for recycling rises. In areas of high population density, such as large cities, these factors may increase the economic attractiveness of recycling. In addition, the per-unit costs of collecting recyclable materials are likely to be lower in such areas and the cost of dumping these materials in landfill, or otherwise disposing of them, is likely to be high.

Also bear in mind that institutional arrangements have significant influences on the dumping and recycling of materials. In most regions, public regulations govern where garbage (trash) may be disposed of and how. In most areas, laws restrict the rights of citizens to accumulate waste on their property. This may be done because it increases health hazards, because it is unsightly and such rubbish could give rise to various other negative externalities such as noxious smells and vermin. Such considerations result in most local governments arranging for the regular removal of garbage from properties. As a result, the management of the disposal of waste is influenced by political consideration. Let us consider this aspect.

14.5. The Management of the Disposal of Garbage (Trash) by Local Governments

14.5.1. *Marginal cost pricing of garbage disposal*

Ideally from a social economizing point of view, the pricing of garbage disposal should be such that the cost of disposing of it is covered and the marginal price for garbage disposal ought to reflect the social marginal cost of this disposal. The first part of this proposition is based on the view that those for whom services are provided should pay the costs

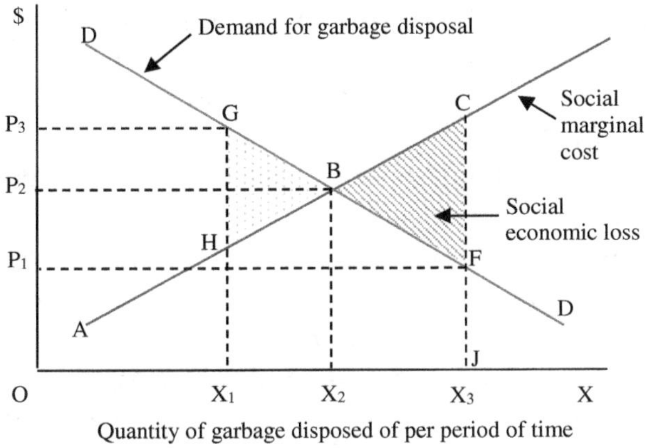

Fig. 14.6. The price for disposal of garbage should reflect the social marginal cost of disposing of it. The ideal economic policy in the case illustrated is for the price for garbage disposal to be P_2 per unit, because this equates the marginal value placed on garbage disposal with the social marginal cost of its disposal. If the price for garbage disposal is lower (say P_1) a deadweight social economic loss occurs which in the case illustrated is indicated by the hatched triangle. Social economic gain is also forgone if the price is set too high, say at P_3. In this case, the social economic gain that is unrealized is equal to the area of the dotted triangle.

of their supply. The second part of this proposition is based on the view that pricing should be such as to minimize collective economic scarcity. The latter proposition can be illustrated by the example given in Fig. 14.6. There line ABC represents the social marginal cost of disposing of garbage and the line DD represents the demand for disposal of garbage in a local government area. In this case, an efficient economic solution can be achieved by charging a price of P_2 per unit for each unit of garbage to be disposed of. At this price, X_2 units of garbage will be supplied for disposal and the extra value placed on the last unit of waste supplied for disposal will just equal the social marginal cost of its disposal. On the other hand, if the price for garbage disposal is P_1, X_3 units of garbage will be supplied per period, the social marginal cost of disposing of the last unit will equal to CJ and its value to those supplying the waste will only be equal to FJ. At the margin, the value of garbage disposal is less than its social marginal cost and therefore, this disposal is uneconomic. The total social economic loss resulting from this low price for garbage disposal is indicated by the area of the hatched triangle BFC. Furthermore, if the price for garbage disposal is very low, revenue obtained from the service may even fail to cover the actual cost directly incurred in disposing of the garbage. The local government will then have to subsidize garbage disposal from its general revenue.

It is also possible for local governments to charge a price for garbage disposal that is too high in the sense that a social economic gain would be made by charging a lower price. For example, in the case illustrated in Fig. 14.6, if P_3 is charged for each unit of garbage disposed of, this results in the value of the disposal of an extra unit of garbage exceeding the social marginal cost of disposal. As a result, social economic benefits equal to the area of the dotted triangle HBG are not realized.

The available evidence indicates that many local governments do not engage in marginal cost pricing of garbage disposal (Tietenberg and Lewis, 2018, pp. 191–193). A frequent practice is to charge a flat annual fee to cover the cost of garbage removal from household and its disposal. Usually, the amount of garbage accepted for removal by local governments is generous and therefore, there is little incentive for householders to economize on the amount of trash disposed of. However, systems vary widely. In Zurich, Switzerland for example, householders have to purchase paper bags of a fixed (relatively small) size for one-time only use for garbage disposal and consequently, the cost to the householder of garbage removal rises with the amount of garbage disposed of.

14.5.2. *Limitations of the above model*

Garbage disposal involves several complexities that are glossed over in the above model. Firstly, it is difficult to estimate exactly the social marginal cost of garbage disposal. The estimation requires account to be taken of the external economic consequences of garbage accumulation and its disposal as well as the direct cost of its disposal. Secondly, the above models assume that solid wastes are homogenous. They are not and the cost of their disposal varies. Ideally, therefore, the price of disposing of different types of garbage should vary. While some legal obligations may be put on providers of wastes to sort these according to type, transaction costs are involved in checking compliance. When these transaction costs are taken into account, it may be uneconomic to have differential prices for the disposal of some types of garbage which nevertheless, have differing disposal costs. Furthermore, transaction costs can be increased by having graduated prices for waste disposal that rise with the volume or weight of wastes. This limits the economic benefits of such a fee structure for the disposal of "regular" wastes.

Furthermore, households may have little control over their generated quantity of solid wastes. Consumers may, for instance, have only limited sovereignty in relation to the amount and type of packaging accompanying goods supplied by producers. This tends to make their demand for garbage disposal relatively inelastic. Consequently, variations in charges for garbage disposal would have little impact on the quantity of waste need to be disposed of. Therefore, the effectiveness of marginal cost pricing of garbage disposal is reduced. As argued below, it may be necessary to adopt policies which encourage producers to reduce the amount of garbage generated by their products.

14.5.3. *Institutional measures to increase the economic efficiency of garbage disposal, for example, contracting out*

Governments may undertake the tasks of collecting and disposing of garbage or they may contract these tasks to private industry. It is widely believed that private industry is likely to complete these tasks at lower cost than their provision by governments. This results in an economic gain. These tasks may be allocated by competitive tendering, thereby using market competition to secure the least cost of collection and disposal of garbage.

The potential economic benefit from this type of institutional approach can be illustrated in Fig. 14.7. In Fig. 14.7, the line marked DD represents the demand for garbage services. The line ABC represents the marginal cost of their supply by government and the line EFG the hypothetical marginal cost if provision of these services is

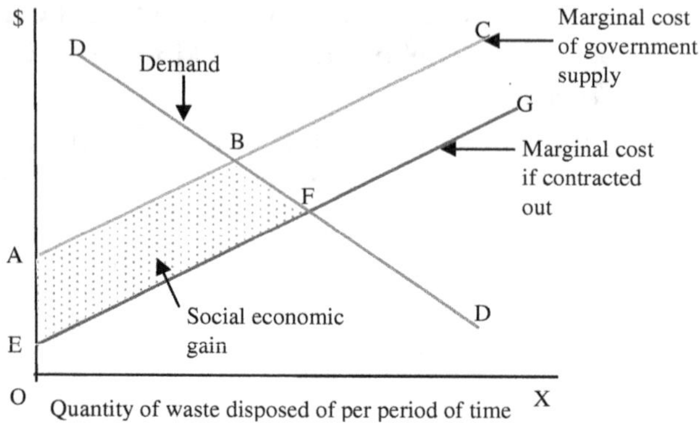

Fig. 14.7. In some cases, governments can reduce the cost of disposing of waste by contracting this activity out to private industry. In the hypothetical case illustrated above, a social economic gain equivalent to the dotted area can be achieved.

contracted out to private industry. Supposing no external costs and the adoption of marginal cost pricing, point B corresponds to the economic optimum if the government supplies the services and point F corresponds to the economic optimum if contracting out occurs. In this case, as a result of contracting out, social economic benefits are increased by the equivalent of the area of the dotted trapezium AEFB.

Furthermore, governments can also contract out rights to recycle waste materials gathered at garbage collection points. Even if the amount tendered for this recycling is less than the cost of collecting garbage, it can reduce the cost that would otherwise be incurred in disposing of the garbage. For similar reasons to those outlined in Section 14.4.2, it can even be economic for the local government to pay for the removal of recyclable rubbish.

The economics of rubbish disposal and recycling usually changes with the passage of time. For instance, technological progress may alter the economics of rubbish collection, disposal and recycling.

14.6. "Substitutes" for Recycling and Waste Creation

The above discussion has concentrated on recycling as an alternative to the dumping of solid wastes. However, recycling is not the only possible strategy to deal with the generation of wastes. The amount of wastes generated may be reduced by the following means:

1. Consuming less and being less wasteful of goods.
2. Reducing the amount of packaging of products.
3. Producing products that incorporate less material, but which perform the same functions as products that use more material.
4. Increasing the durability of products so they have a longer useful life.
5. Lowering the rate at which functioning products are discarded.
6. Encouraging the use of second-hand goods.
7. Employing reusable bags and containers rather than disposable ones, such as single use plastic bags.

While all of these strategies to reduce the flow of solid wastes, several have economic limitations.

Convincing the general public to consume less is not easy. Motives to acquire goods seem to be strong. In market economies both profits and employment are positively linked to the sale of products, so both employers and employees have a strong incentive to support measures to stimulate purchases, for example via advertising and promotions of products.

The extent to which the packaging of products can be reduced is limited. Some packaging is necessary to prevent damage of products in transport and storage. Sometimes "excessive" packaging of small products occurs because this makes it easier to detect those who may steal these items from shops. Nevertheless, much packaging of consumer products appears to be based on its anticipated positive psychological impact on consumers. As discussed in the next section, this may result in excessive packaging socially.

With technological progress, there has been a tendency to reduce the volume of materials used in many products and they function just as well or better than their predecessors. However, this does not necessarily translate into a reduction in the amount of solid wastes generated by economies because the number of items purchased often rises by a greater proportion than that by which the material content of each product is reduced.

Increased durability of products may also help to reduce the quantity of wastes generated by reducing the frequency with which durable items have to be replaced. On the other hand, if a less durable item contains less material or materials which are more likely to be recycled, the less durable product may be preferable from a resource use and waste-generation point of view to a more durable alternative product. For example, an item that lasts only one-tenth of the time of a more durable item may be preferable to the durable one if it incorporates less than one-tenth of the material used in the latter. Also, long-lived products delay the speed with which newer technologies are adopted, and these new technologies may reduce resource use.

Individuals often discard products before the end of their useful life, and do so for a variety of reasons. For example, a replacement product may involve lower operating cost and give superior performance. Sometimes replacement products lower resource use. On the other hand, social factors can play a major role in the replacement of durable products. Many individuals use their possession of particular types of durable goods as indicators of their wealth and social status or their aspirations in this regard. Social display of this type results in useful products being discarded quickly and their replacement with new products. Changing fashions and designs of products facilitate this process. They ensure the social display of "newness" of products. The types of social influences on consumption mentioned by Veblen (1934) are quite strong. Changing fashions and designs are partly fostered by producers, but in most societies, (some) consumers have a strong demand for being fashionable. As a result, an increased amount of solid waste is generated per period of time.

Improvements in the operation of markets for used goods can also reduce waste generation. Individuals may, however, be reluctant to buy used goods for reasons of social status. Furthermore, for some second-hand goods, there may be doubts about their quality and they may not be covered by product warranties. Problems of asymmetric information of the type mentioned by Varian (2006, Chapter 37) can lead to the collapse or partial collapse of markets for some second-hand products even though they are in demand. Sometimes, the repair of products extends their useful life but the cost of doing this has to be compared with the benefits of their replacement. Often repair of complex products proves to be uneconomic or repairs require the replacement of a whole module.

In some jurisdictions, it is believed that the reusable bags and containers can contribute significantly to reducing the costs of waste disposal. For example, shoppers may be required to bring their own bags or pay for plastic bags (or plastic bags may be banned) for environmental reasons. However, more durable bags involve more material and also have to be eventually disposed of. They are often made of synthetic material. Therefore, the comparative environmental costs of the alternative need careful analysis.

14.7. Policy Perspectives

14.7.1. *Some relevant observations*

As already observed, market failures may result in less recycling and more dumping of solid wastes than is optimal from a social economic point of view. In particular, adverse environmental spillovers or externalities may exist. They may not be internalized because governments fail to make those who cause these externalities pay for the spillover costs imposed on others. Furthermore, those who want to dispose of wastes may be charged less than the marginal cost of disposing of these wastes. Nevertheless, it was also observed that transaction costs limit the economic benefits available from marginal cost pricing. Also transaction costs (agency costs) may limit the economic scope for internalizing externalities.

Several possible ways of reducing the need for recycling materials and for reducing the amount of wastes for disposal were considered. It was found that many of these methods are less effective than appears to be the case at first sight. It was also suggested that consumers (buyers) may only have a limited amount of control over the type and amount of wastes they generate because producers may provide buyers with a restricted range of packed products. Furthermore, the ability or rationality of consumers in selecting products may be constrained. Let us consider this matter and then discuss the question of the extent to which producers rather than consumers should be responsible for wastes.

14.7.2. *Why might consumers have limited control over the type and amount of wastes generated by their purchases?*

Hotelling (1929) has argued that in competitive market situations, firms engage in minimum product differentiation (see also Tisdell and Hartley, 2008, Chapter 9). Most products are sold pre-packed in developed countries. Hotelling's principle may result in relative uniformity of packaging designed to attract buyers with median tastes or purchasing tendencies. This would result in more packaging and waste than demanded by buyers who prefer less packaging. Similarly, the design of some products often includes extra materials intended to improve the appearance of the product rather than its functioning because design is appealing to many buyers. If Hotelling's principle applies, producers will supply products with similar designs aimed at the median purchaser and incorporate a similar amount of extra material to complete these designs. Because suppliers are influenced by buyers with median tastes, this means that most buyers have limited consumer sovereignty.

If firms act according to Hotelling's rule, will they generate more waste on average than if maximum product differentiation occurred to satisfy consumers? If the preferences of buyers are such that the amount of wastes generated as a result of these preferences forms a symmetric relative frequency distribution (like that shown in Fig. 14.8), the mean and the median of the distribution will coincide. Therefore, the amount of waste generated will be the same whether individual tastes are fully catered for or only that of the median buyers. However, if the relative frequency distribution of tastes is skewed, this will not be so. For example, if the distribution has a negative skew (is skewed to the left), its median value exceeds its mean value. Therefore, in this case, the amount of waste generated rises. The opposite is the case if the relative frequency distribution has a positive skew.

However, a negatively skewed relative frequency distribution of the type mentioned above (combined with firm's following Hotelling's

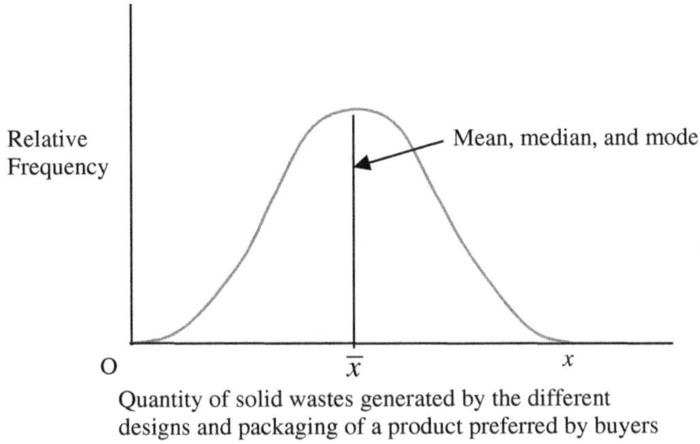

Fig. 14.8. In the case illustrated the relative frequency distribution of tastes is unimodel and symmetric, firms do not create extra wastes if they target median buyers rather than individual buyers in designing and packaging goods. This is not so if the relative frequency distribution has a negative skew.

principle of minimum product differentiation) is unlikely to be a major contributor to excessive waste generation. Excessive waste generation is more likely to be a result of the limited rationality of consumers in making their purchases. Visual cues are used to buy many products. If they look attractive as a result of superior packaging and design or the quantities offered for sale appear to be generous due to the packaging, this is likely to stimulate purchases. Some buying may be impulsive or involve an emotional element rather than an entirely rational one. At the time of purchase, many buyers may not consider (or may hardly consider) the costs of disposing of any wastes associated with their purchase. At the time of purchase of a commodity, all consequences of the purchase are unlikely to be assessed by the buyer. In retrospect, and after further consideration, many buyers may feel that they would have been better off if less packaging and designer-material had been included in the product they purchased. Sellers will, however, be interested mainly in how buyers react at the time of their purchases not in their considered evaluation in retrospect. These types of general differences have been noted by the social philosopher, John Elster (1985).

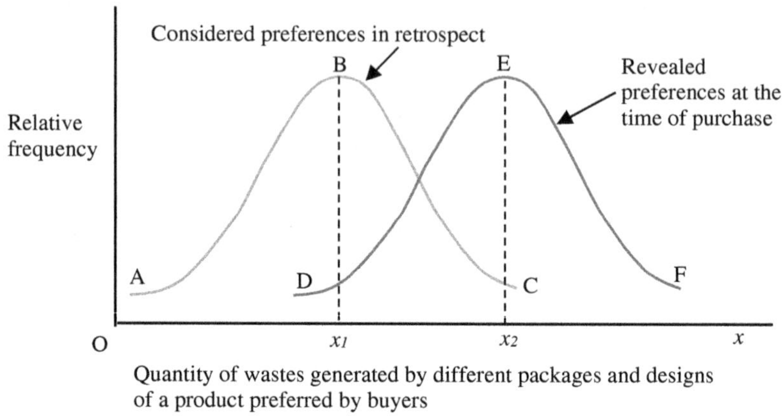

Fig. 14.9. The preferences expressed by consumers when buying may not be their considered preferences. When buying, consumers may be enticed to buy products that generate more waste than they want after later consideration.

As illustrated in Fig. 14.9, this type of psychological or behavioral phenomenon may result in a greater amount of waste being generated than is considered socially desirable in retrospect. On the basis of the considered views of buyers, the relative frequency distribution ABC might represent their distribution of tastes (Fig. 14.9). However, in the act of buying, buyers do not fully consider their situation and might act as if their tastes follow the relative frequency distribution DEF because they are positively influenced in their choices by the use of a greater amount of packing and designer-materials in products. Hence, the nature of buying activity results in a greater amount of waste being generated than is considered rational by buyers in retrospect.

Of course, some packaging is primarily functional. It helps to preserve and protect products. Packaging (not displayed to end buyers) for the bulk transport of products is mainly functional. It can be observed that many innovations have occurred that reduce the quantity of material used in this packaging while at the same time retaining attributes that help to protect the product in transport and storage. Savings in the quantity of packaging used to display materials to consumers does not appear to have occurred to the same extent.

14.7.3. *To what extent should the producers of products be made responsible for the wastes generated by their products rather than consumers or other buyers of these products?*

Given the restricted rationality of consumers when buying products and their limited sovereignty, it may be more effective to adopt regulations which require producers rather than buyers to reduce the amount of wastes generated by their products. Furthermore, producers may be prevented from or restricted in incorporating substances in their produces which are especially deleterious to the environment when they are disposed of. For one thing because there are usually fewer producers than consumers of a product and producers' activities are more concentrated geographically, the cost of monitoring compliance is likely to lower when policies focus on producers rather than consumers.

The following are some policies for reducing solid wastes and increasingly recycling that place obligations on producers and sellers:

1. Restrictions on type and amount of packaging provided by suppliers. For example, the provision of free single-use plastic shopping bags by supermarkets may be banned.
2. Producers of some durable products may be made responsible for the disposal of their products after the useful life of these is finished. This may provide producers with an incentive to design their products to reduce the cost of their disposal. This might be done by reducing the waste involved and increasing the recyclability of the components of the product. To ensure compliance, a refundable deposit might be lodged with the government by producers to cover the estimated cost of disposal of wastes associated with their products. This could be refunded to a producer if the producer carries out or arranges for the disposal of the product at the end of its useful life. Note that the economic incidence of the disposal cost would in such cases fall to some extent on buyers if sellers are forced to internalize these costs. The relative economic incidence of these costs on buyers and sellers will depend on the relative slopes of the demand and supply curves for the products involved.

3. In some cases, producers may be obliged by governments to accept their used products from buyers. To encourage buyers to return used products, a refundable deposit may be required from them at the time of purchase. This may provide an incentive for the recycling of some items, for example, glass and plastic bottles.
4. Producers may be required by governments to clearly identify the various types of materials in their products so as to facilitate their recycling. Otherwise, recyclers may have difficulty in identifying what components are recyclable.
5. Requirements may be placed on producers to design their products in ways that facilitate their recycling or economic incentives may be provided for using recyclable materials in products.

However, the economics of such policies needs to be assessed carefully. In some cases, policies of this type can reflect political popularism rather than rational scientific assessment.

14.7.4. *A note on the economic regulation of plastic wastes and anthropogenic marine litter*

Hundreds of millions of tonnes of plastics are produced each year and on average, the quantity of plastics manufactured has been rising by around 4% per year. Plastic wastes are the largest contributors to anthropogenic litter in marine environments, including in littoral areas. The nature of problems associated with marine litter is clear from a review of marine litter research by Ryan (2015), which is available as an open-access document.

Oceanic and coastal pollution from plastic waste (and other anthropogenic litter) results in considerable environmental costs and damages. The relevant literature is reviewed by Newman *et al.* (2015). Virtually all of this literature focuses on estimating the **costs** associated with different types of damages caused by anthropogenic marine litter. Costs considered include the cost of beach cleaning, extra costs incurred by the shipping and yachting industries, and by the fisheries. Mouat *et al.* (2010) estimated that the annual costs to the Scottish fishing industry (for example, removing litter from nets) amounted to about 5% of the fleet's total revenue. McIlgorm *et al.* (2011) found that marine debris in the Asia-Pacific cost marine industries 1 billion euros per year. Jang *et al.* (2014) and Leggett *et al.* (2014) measured the extent to which litter on beaches deters visits by tourists and recreationists and reduces their economic value. In many places (for instance in Australia) where beach recreation and tourism is important, local governments incur substantial costs as a result of regularly cleaning public beaches and disposing of the debris on them. Communities which depend heavily on beach tourism for their income can suffer tremendous declines in their income if their beaches become littered with rubbish, for instance plastic wastes (Jang *et al.*, 2014).

The review of the relevant economic literature by Newman *et al.* (2015), makes no mention of the adverse economic consequences of the impact of marine litter (including plastics) on marine life and on the sustainability of marine ecosystems. However, some marine animals (especially some species of sea turtles) suffer morbidity and mortality as a result of ingesting plastic waste. Populations of sea turtles have a total economic value consisting of both economic and intangible values such as existence value and economic non-consumptive use values, for instance for tourism, as well as consumptive use value in some communities, (Tisdell and Wilson, 2012, Chapters 9 and 10; Wilson and Tisdell, 2001). Reductions in populations of sea turtles are likely to diminish all of these values.

Newman *et al.* (2015) list and outline a range of public policies which could be adopted to reduce the amount of anthropogenic litter entering marine and coastal environments but they do not subject these policies to economic analysis. In particular, they do not consider the private benefits that may be forgone by such regulations, the cost of administering the different possible regulations, nor the likelihood that at least some of the regulations could result in some other products being substituted to some extent for plastics. These substitutes could also generate adverse environmental effects. Figure 14.10 can be used to help clarify some of the issues involved.

In this figure, X represents the amount of reduction in plastic entering the marine environment as a result of regulation. X_3 is assumed to be the amount of this plastic in the absence of regulation. The line

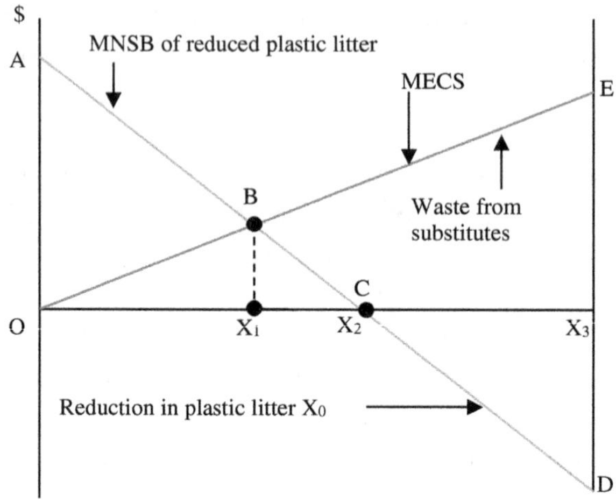

Fig. 14.10. An illustration of factors that should not be overlooked in determining the socially optimal regulation of plastic litter.

ABCD is in the assumed marginal net social benefit MNSB (marginal private benefit forgone less the reduction in marginal external environmental costs) as a result of regulations reducing the quantity of plastics entering marine areas. If only plastic waste is considered, the socially most economic level of reduction in this form of pollution is equal to X_2, the level at which MNSB = 0. However, since administering regulations involves a cost and the marginal administrative cost of regulation is likely to rise with the amount of attempted reduction of the pollutant, the socially optimal level of reduction in plastic litter as a result of regulation is liable to be less than X_1. For example, if the marginal cost of administering the regulations is MCA and positive, the MNSB–MCA is below the line ABD shown in Fig. 14.10. Consequently, this expression is zero for $X < X_2$ and therefore, less reduction in plastic litter is warranted.

As mentioned above, some regulations which reduce the amount of plastic litter can result in the increased use of substitutes. The production and disposal of these substitutes could also have negative environmental spillovers, even though their environmental costs might be smaller than for plastics. Ideally, these spillovers should be taken into account. They can reduce the extent to which it is socially optimal to limit the amount of plastic litter. For example, suppose in Fig. 14.10 that line OBE represents the marginal negative external costs attributable to the increased use of substitutes for plastics due to policies designed to reduce plastic litter. Then, the socially optimal level of reduction in plastic litter (given the modeling used) is equal to X_1. It corresponds to the level of reduction in plastic litter for which the MNSB of the reduction in plastic litter (considered on its own) equals the marginal externality costs arising from the increased use of substitutes (MECS) for plastics. Consequently, environmental effects from the increased use of substitutes for plastics should be considered in regulating the use and disposal of plastics.

This analysis shows that in evaluating the control of plastic litter, it is not only the environmental damages and costs from plastic litter which need to be taken into account. Social cost-benefit analysis requires also that account be taken of the costs of administering these policies. As well, any negative environmental externalities occasioned by the substitution of other products for plastics should be considered.

14.8. Concluding Comments

The economics of recycling and of solid waste management is complex. Reasons have been advanced in favor of the recycling of materials and factors that influence the extent of recycling of materials have been examined. These include the comparative costs of obtaining materials from virgin sources rather than by recycling material, the extent to which the private costs involved reflect social costs, and the relative costs involved in dumping material rather than recycling it.

The economics of managing solid waste disposal was also analyzed. Economic theory indicates that ideally the fee for disposing of garbage should be such that the social marginal cost of the last unit of garbage disposed of equals the extra value placed on its disposal by those who want to be rid of it. However, most garbage disposal is managed by local governments and failure to follow the above rule is widespread. Some writers have attributed this to political pressures by the electorate. However, considerable transaction costs can be involved in adopting marginal cost pricing. Because garbage can be very heterogeneous with different types of garbage varying in their marginal cost of disposal and in the environmental spillovers they generate, this adds to the transaction costs involved in following marginal cost pricing. Many local governments have tried to reduce the cost of garbage disposal by contracting out these services to private industry and the possible economic benefits of this were identified.

Recycling is not the only way to reduce the amount of solid wastes requiring disposal. A variety of other means for achieving this objective have been identified. It was claimed that social factors are responsible for "excessive" amounts of several types of wastes. Furthermore, some of these social factors are bound up with displays of social status and are so ingrained in society that it would be difficult or impossible to alter these by political means.

The limited ability of buyers to control the amount of wastes generated by their purchased products has been identified. Short-term psychological biases of consumers in purchasing products result in excessive packaging of products and waste generation. It, therefore, seems likely that effective control of many wastes and the encouragement of recycling depends on relevant policies being focused on producers and sellers rather than consumers and buyers. However, such policies do need rational economic evaluation — political popularism can result in policies that are costly from an economic point of view. One of the features of this discussion has been its identification of psychological factors and social forces as important influences on the amount of wastes generated by societies. This means that one must go beyond neoclassical economics to study the phenomena involved.

14.9. Keywords

Consumers' sovereignty and wastes; contracting out; environmental spillovers from product substitution; Hotelling's principle of minimum product differentiation; marginal cost pricing of garbage disposal; marine litter; markets for recyclable materials; plastic wastes; private marginal cost; recycled resources; recycling;

refundable deposits for recyclable products; social marginal costs; substitutes for recycling and waste creation; suppliers' responsibility for disposal of their products; transaction costs involved in waste disposal; virgin resources.

14.10. Questions for Review and Discussion

1. Why has it been contended that solid wastes ought to be recycled?
2. How are private incentives to recycle wastes related to the cost of obtaining materials from virgin sources? Illustrate your answer by means of a diagram.
3. Explain how failure to take adequate account of environmental spillovers can result in less recycling of materials and greater use of virgin sources than is socially optimal from an economic point of view. You may illustrate your answer by a diagram.
4. The operation of markets for recyclable wastes depends both on the demand of recyclers for such waste and the willingness of those who have such wastes to supply these to recyclers. Other things constant, those having wastes are likely to be more willing to supply these to recyclers, the higher are the fees for dumping these wastes. In such cases, those who have wastes may even be willing to pay for their removal. Explain.
5. In disposing of used items, many individuals are guided by social and ethical considerations rather than their narrow self-interest. Discuss.
6. Many economists believe that the fee for dumping the last unit of garbage should be such as to equate the social marginal cost of its disposal with the value placed on its disposal by the entity that wants to be rid of it. Why do they believe this? Illustrate the reasoning involved by means of a diagram.
7. Explain why the pricing rule stated in question 6 above is often not followed in practice.
8. Many local governments have attempted to reduce the costs of garbage disposal by contracting out the supply of these services to private industry. Why is such an approach expected to reduce the

cost of garbage disposal? How can its potential economic benefits be illustrated?

9. Recycling is just one means for reducing the amount of solid waste to be dumped as a result of economic activity? What other means exist for reducing wastes?
10. Why might several proposed means for reducing the generation of wastes not be as effective as they appear to be at first sight?
11. Explain how social factors may add to the amount of wastes generated by economic activity. Why is it likely to be difficult to alter behaviors of this type?
12. Discuss the view that consumers only have limited control over the amount and type of wastes generated by the products they purchase. In doing so, consider limits to the rationality of consumers when involved in the purchasing of products.
13. Discuss the desirability or otherwise of making producers or sellers rather than consumers or buyers responsible for the wastes generated by their products.
14. What types of regulations may be imposed on producers or sellers to reduce the amount of wastes generated by their products and to promote the recycling of materials contained in their products?
15. Why does neoclassical economics need to be supplemented by institutional economics and psychological considerations when studying the phenomena of waste generation and recycling?
16. Available economic estimates of the environmental cost of the presence of litter (e.g. plastics) in marine areas do not account for the total environmental cost of this litter. Discuss.
17. Sometimes policies which reduce the presence of one pollutant can result in the presence of other pollutants increasing. Explain. How can this affect the optimality of economic policies to limit the presence of a single pollutant? Illustrate your answer.

Readings and References

Anon (2020). *Waste management,* Wikipedia, https://en.wikipedia.org/wiki/Waste_management [Accessed 13 July 2020].

Elster, J. (1985). *The Multiple Self,* Cambridge University Press, Cambridge.

Etzioni, A. (1988). *The Moral Dimension: Towards a New Economics*, The Free Press, New York.

Hotelling, H. (1929). Stability in competition, *Economic Journal*, 39, 41–57.

Jang, Y.C., S. Hong, J. Lee, M.J. Lee and W.J. Shim (2014). Estimation of lost tourism revenue in Geoje Island from the 2011 marine debris pollution event in South Korea, *Marine Pollution Bulletin*, 81, 49–54. doi: https://doi.org/10.1016/j.marpolbul.2014.02.021.

Kahn, J.R. (2005). *The Economic Approach to Environmental and Natural Resources*, 3rd edn. South-Western, Mason, Ohio, USA [Chapter 10].

Leggett, C., N. Scherer, M. Curry and R. Bailey (2014). Assessing the economic benefits of reductions in marine debris: A pilot study of beach recreation in Orange County, California, Final Report, June 15, 2014. pp. 44. National Oceanic and Atmospheric Administration, Cambridge, USA. Available from: https://pdfs.semanticscholar.org/6dd0/dbb87b686df399be8f34640455d799703585.pdf?_ga=2.171257504.1880 867304.1589766459-2136311259.1589166722.

McIlgorm, A., H.F. Campbell and M.J. Rule (2011). The economic cost and control of marine debris damage in the Asia-Pacific region, *Ocean & Coastal Management*, 54, 643–651. doi: https://doi.org/10.1016/j.ocecoaman.2011.05.007.

Mouat, J., R.L. Lozano and H. Bateson (2010). Economic Impacts of Marine Litter. pp. 105. Kimo International, Available from: http://www.kimointernational.org/wp/wp-content/uploads/2017/09/KIMO_Economic -Impacts-of-Marine-Litter.pdf.

Newman, S., E. Watkins, A. Farmer, P.t. Brink and J.-P. Schweitzer (2015). The Economics of Marine Litter. In M. Bergmann, L. Gutow and M. Klages (Eds.), *Marine Anthropogenic Litter*, 367–394. Springer International Publishing, Cham.

Ryan, P.G. (2015). A Brief History of Marine Litter Research. In M. Bergmann, L. Gutow and M. Klages (Eds.), *Marine Anthropogenic Litter*, 1–25. Springer International Publishing, Cham.

Tietenberg, T. and L. Lewis (2018). *Environmental and Natural Resource Economics*, 11th edn. Routledge, New York and Abingdon, Oxon, UK [Chapter 8].

Tisdell, C.A. (1997). Local communities, conservation and sustainability: Institutional change, altered governance and Kant's social philosophy, *International Journal of Social Economics*, 24, 1361–1375. doi: 10.1108/03068299710193877.

Tisdell, C.A. and K. Hartley (2008). *Microeconomic Policy: A New Perspective*, Edward Elgar, Cheltenham, UK and Northampton, MA, USA.

Tisdell, C.A. and C. Wilson (2012). *Nature-based Tourism and Conservation: New Economic Insights and Case Studies*, Edward Elgar Publishing, Cheltenham, UK and Northampton, MA, USA.

Varian, H. (2006). *Intermediate Microeconomics: A Modern Approach*, 7th edn. Norton and Company, New York and London.

Veblen, T. (1934). *The Theory of the Leisure Class: An Economic Study in the Evolution of Institutions*, The Macmillan Company, New York.

Wilson, C. and C. Tisdell (2001). Sea turtles as a non-consumptive tourism resource especially in Australia, *Tourism Management*, 22, 279–288. doi: 10.1016/S0261-5177(00)00059-5.

Chapter 15

Health and Environmental Economics

15.1. Introduction

Given frequent statements that human beings value health, wealth and happiness, it comes as a surprise to find that little attention is given to environmental health in most textbooks dealing with environmental economics. One notable exception is Freeman (2003). This oversight is regrettable because studies demonstrate that environmental conditions have major consequences for health. For example, a study commissioned by the World Health Organization, WHO, (Prüss-Üstün *et al.*, 2016), found in 2012, that 23% of all deaths and 22% of the disease burden globally were attributable to environmental factors.

However, the distinction is imprecise between diseases which are primarily due to environmental factors and those which are not. For example, the WHO tally of environmentally related diseases excludes diseases spread by humans via the environment, for example, influenza. If these diseases were included the global health burden of environmentally dependent diseases would be much higher than are the WHO's estimates. In any case, it is clear that the state of the environment is a major influence on human health. Evidence of the importance of environmental pollution for human health can be found in Muller and Mendelsohn (2007). They found that about 94% of the gross annual economic damages from air pollution in the United States are accounted for by its adverse impact on human health and they point out that this is consistent with other findings in the economic literature (Muller and Mendelsohn, 2007, p. 8). In addition, environmental states influence the health of animals (such as livestock) and plants (such as food crops) used to sustain humans. Although some of the issues considered here (such as intervention to reduce the contagion of diseases and growing biological resistance to interventions to prevent or cure diseases) have applications to the health not only of human beings but also that of other living things, the emphasis here is on human health.

This chapter begins with discussion of the basic factors involved in the economic assessment of environmental health policies. This is followed by a consideration of economic failures in relation to environmental health, an examination of economic optimization models as applied to environmental health. Subsequently, the focus is on the economic consequences of chemical and physical environmental substances for health and then on the economic implications of biological spillovers for health. This is followed by some economic observations on pandemics giving particular attention to COVID-19.

15.2. Basic Considerations in the Economic Assessment of Environmental Health Policies

15.2.1. *The necessity of economic trade-offs*

A basic tenet of economics is that resources are scarce in relation to their valued uses and therefore, opportunity costs are incurred by allocating them to a particular use. Potential improvements in health (including environmental health) normally require the use of scarce resources and result in other valued opportunities for using these resources being foregone. This means that at the most general level, policies designed to alter resource use in order to improve health need to be assessed in an economy-wide context (see for example, Tisdell and Hartley, 2008, pp. 75–76).

Figure 15.1 provides a simplified illustration of the above proposition assuming that health improvements can be valued in monetary terms as can the commodities forgone to provide resources for

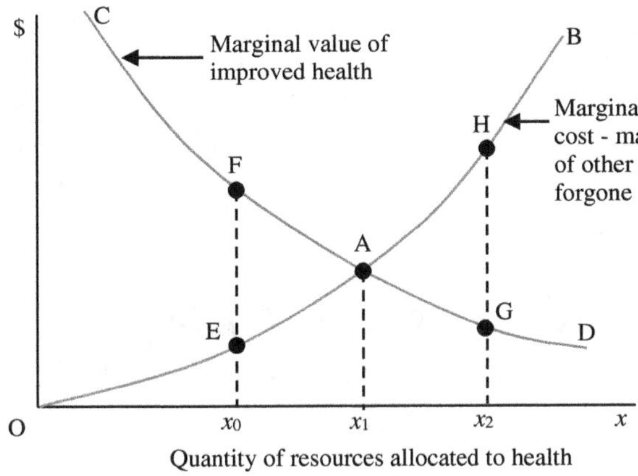

Fig. 15.1. When extra resources are allocated in order to improve health care, the opportunity cost of doing this needs to be taken into account. In the case illustrated, the socially optimal economic allocation occurs when x_1 of resources are used for improving health. At point A the extra value of improved health equals its marginal opportunity cost.

improving health. In this figure, curve OAB represents the marginal value placed on improved health produced by allocating increased resources (x) for this purpose and curve CAD indicates the marginal value of other commodities foregone in order to make more resources available for improving health.

In Fig. 15.1, the economically ideal allocation of resources for improving healthiness is x_1 because it ensures that marginal value of improved health equals the marginal value of all other commodities forgone. A smaller allocation of resources for improving health (for example, x_0) is suboptimal because the marginal value of better health exceeds its marginal opportunity costs. Similarly, an allocation of greater than x_1 (say x_2) is suboptimal because the marginal value of extra health benefits is less than the marginal opportunity cost of realizing these.

While, in principle, extra resource allocation for the purpose of improving health ought to be evaluated taking into account general economic interdependence, this may only occur to a limited extent in practice. Because of the cost of decision-making, there may be a tendency to compartmentalize the allocation of resources for different economic purposes (as suggested by some behavioral economists; see, for example, O'Curry, 1999) and politics may reinforce this compartmentalization in public financing. Thus, the allocation of aggregate resources for health purposes may not accord with the economic ideal which supposes perfect knowledge and zero decision-making costs.

15.2.2. *Factors that can be controlled in order to influence environmental health and their economic implications*

The processes by which environmental conditions can influence human health can be complex. In most cases, up to three different factors can be controlled in order to safeguard or improve the health of individuals subject to environmental health risks. These are:

(1) Reducing pollution emissions or changing their nature, or altering other initial environmental sources of health risks in a favorable manner. For example, the amount of an air-borne pollutant might be reduced or the population of mosquitoes carrying malaria could be reduced.
(2) Receptors of negative environmental health spillovers could engage in defensive action (averting behavior) to reduce their exposure to these spillovers. For example, householders could install air conditioning to remove particulate matter from the air and individuals can take various measures to avoid being bitten by mosquitoes, e.g. use repellent or mosquito nets.
(3) Medical treatment may be sought if an environmentally related illness occurs. For example, medication is available to relieve the symptoms of asthma triggered by air pollution. Cures are available for some diseases caused by environmental conditions.

These three types of interventions need to be taken into account simultaneously in considering optimal economic responses to environmental health risks. This is highlighted by Fig. 15.2.

Often the most economical response to an environmentally induced disease involves a **combination** of reducing the risk by lowering the

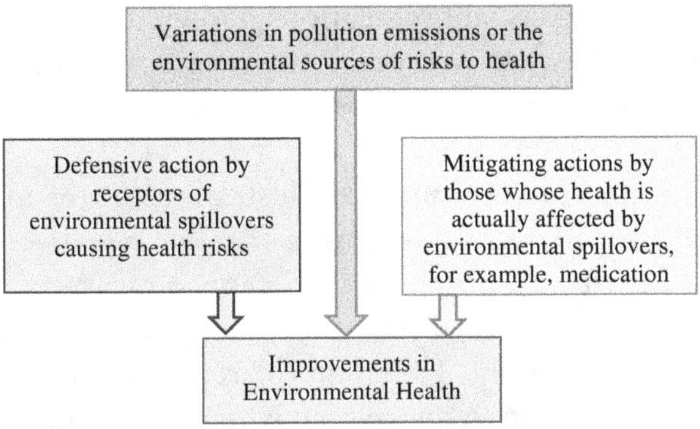

Fig. 15.2. Several different types of influences on environmental health need to be taken into account when considering economic strategies to improve environmental health.

degree of spillover from the environmental source (for example, reducing air pollution from power stations or lowering the population of pests that carry diseases, for example, reducing the presence of water bodies in which disease-bearing mosquitoes can breed), defensive measures, and where these measures fail, ensuring access to medical remedies. The optimal combination of these strategies can be expected to vary from case to case.

The question naturally arises of who should pay for these responses to environmental conditions. If polluters are the source of the environmental health problem and if the "polluter-pays principle" is adopted, then it follows that the cost burden of all these responses should fall on the polluters. This internalizes the polluters' externalities. Of course (as pointed out in Chapter 5), the polluter may pass on some of (and in the limit, all) of these costs to buyers but indirectly they are also responsible for the creation of the environmental problem. However, (as also pointed out in Chapter 5) transaction costs and other imperfections limit the scope for economically adopting such a policy.

15.3. Economic Failures and Environmental Health

15.3.1. *Environmental spillovers or externalities*

Economic agents can engage in activities which result in environmental spillovers that harm the health of others. Under free market conditions and in the absence of relevant regulations, individuals and organization have no economic incentive to take these spillovers into account in their decision-making and as discussed in Chapter 3, economic failure occurs.

Figure 15.3 provides a simplified illustration of this from an environmental health perspective **assuming** that the negative spillovers of an economic activity on human health can be measured in terms of money. This is the traditional assumption adopted in economic social cost-benefit analysis. In Fig. 15.3, line AC represents the marginal private net benefit from an economic activity (for example, emitting a pollutant or engaging in activities that increase the population of a vector that carries disease) and line AF indicates the social net benefit from that activity. It is lower than the line AC because of negative health spillovers. The difference between line AC and line AF measures the marginal external health costs of this activity. Indicating the intensity of the activity by x, individuals and organizations will maximize their private benefit by engaging in the activity at a level x_2; the level at which marginal private net benefit is zero. This is excessive from a social point of view because social net benefit is maximized when the level of the activity is restricted to x_1; the level at which social net benefit is zero.

Those whose health is adversely affected by activity x would be prepared to pay those engaging in this activity a minimum amount equivalent to the area of triangle DCB to reduce the intensity of activity from x_2 to x_1. They would then be better off by an amount equivalent to the area of triangle DFC. Therefore, a potential Pareto improvement is possible because those engaging in the activity causing environmental ill health would be well compensated for reducing the intensity of this activity. The area of triangle DFC is an indicator of the social economic loss occasioned by such an activity. However, this model does not resolve the ethical issue of who should compensate whom. In many cases, ethical considerations would suggest that it is polluters who should compensate victims rather than the other way around. Note that even if the intensity of the activity is reduced from x_2 to x_1, negative environmental health spillovers continue to exist. The total monetary costs of the negative spillovers are equivalent to the area of

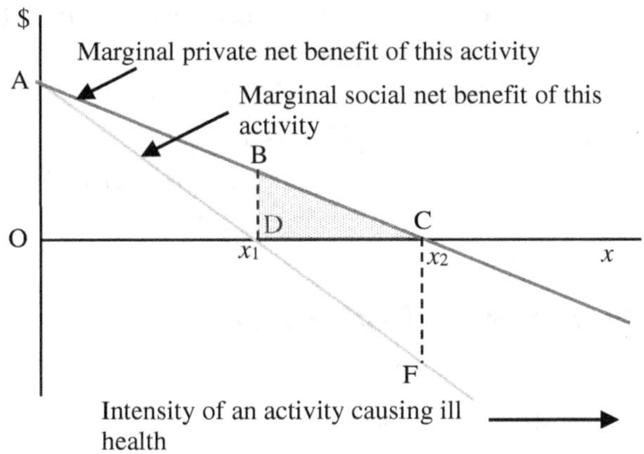

Fig. 15.3. A case in which negative health spillovers from human activity add to economic scarcity. In the absence of regulation, they result in a social economic loss. An economic measure of this loss is equivalent to the area of triangle DFC.

triangle ADB. Consequently, the moral question arises of whether entities that generate negative health spillovers should not only adjust these to achieve a Paretian optimum (in this case reduce the intensity of the activity from x_2 to x_1) but also be required to compensate fully for the ill health their activity generates. This would mean that spillover costs would be **fully** internalized, not just internalized at the margin.

15.3.2. *Public goods or bads and environmental health*

As specified in Chapter 3, public goods are such that no one can be excluded from the benefits of their supply and the consumption of their benefits is not rivalrous. In the case of public bads, no one can be excluded from their ill effects and if an individual suffers an ill effect, this does not prevent others from suffering the same effect.

Some actions which result in environmental improvement have beneficial health effects akin to public goods. Similarly, some forms of environmental deterioration that result in ill health can be classified as public bads. These may be of a local, regional or global nature. For example, measures that reduce the populations of disease-carrying mosquito species supply local or regional public goods. It is predicted that global warming will reduce human health. This can be regarded as a global public bad. Government intervention to alter the supply of such goods is usually needed to increase social economic welfare. In some locations, water resources for drinking are shared and pollution of these resources adversely affects all users. Public action is sometimes the most economical way to deal with the problem of contaminated shared water supplies used for drinking.

15.3.3. *Ignorance, behavioral variations and public health concerns*

Most models of health economics are based on neoclassical economics. As pointed out in Chapter 2, these models assume that individuals are well informed and choose rationally in order to promote their own self-interest to the maximum extent possible. Often these very strong assumptions are unlikely to be satisfied fully in practice. The extent to which they are satisfied can be expected to vary. This is one reason why governments can sometimes improve decisions about environmental health by increasing knowledge about environmental health relationships. Furthermore, bounded rationality and behavioral variations involving health are likely to be more important than allowed for in neoclassical economics.

15.4. Production Functions, the Cost-Effectiveness of Environmental Health Interventions and Maximization of Net Benefits

15.4.1. *A very simple environmental health production function*

The simplest production function used in economics involves a single variable input and a single output (see for example, Pindyck and Rubinfeld, 2005, Chapter 7). This can be adapted to provide a simplified way to consider policies intended to alter environmental health. One problem however, is how best to specify the quantity of health output. This is a greater problem than in the economic analysis of the production of goods because the economic output of particular

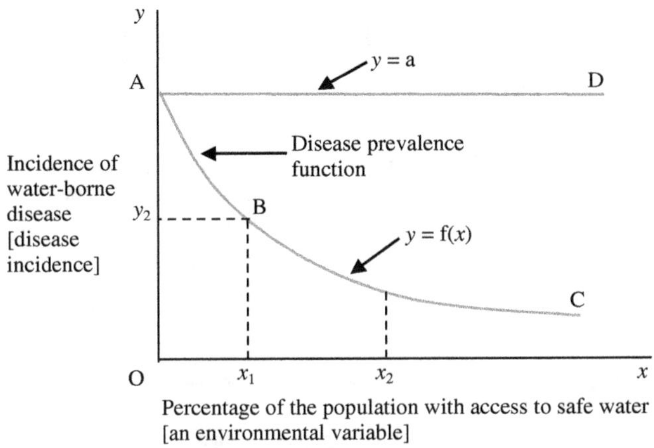

Fig. 15.4. The prevalence of a disease in relation to an environmental variable provides the basis for estimating the production function shown in Fig. 15.5.

types of goods is relatively homogenous whereas health outcomes can be highly heterogeneous. Nevertheless, some indicators of health outputs have been used, such as the incidence (prevalence) of occurrence of particular types of diseases per year or in some other period. Death rates from particular diseases could also be used as another indicator. The choice depends on the focus of concern.

Figure 15.4 provides an illustration of this approach. In this hypothetical case, x represents the percentage of a population with access to safe drinking water and y specifies the number of incidences of water-borne diseases per thousand of this population in a year. The curve ABC represents y (disease incidence) as function of x (safe-water access) and the difference between this curve and the horizontal line AD measures the reduction in the incidence of water-borne diseases as a function of access to clean water, other things held constant. Consequently, if the reduction in the incidence of water-borne diseases is taken to represent the output, the production formation in this case is like OEG in Fig. 15.5.

Simple relationships (such as those portrayed in Figs. 15.4 and 15.5) can provide useful information to planners. For example, if resources are available to increase safe-water coverage from x_1 to x_2, planners

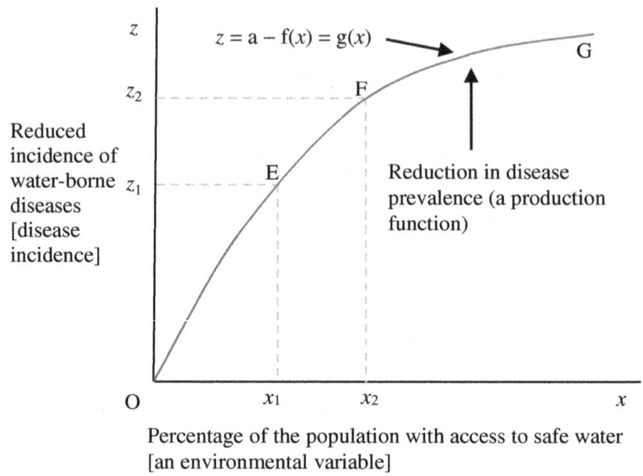

Fig. 15.5. A production function (derived from Fig. 15.4) indicating how the prevalence of a disease, or class of diseases, is related to an environmental variable.

may wish to know how effective this will be in reducing the prevalence of water-borne diseases — in this case, the incidence is reduced by $z_2 - z_1$. Alternatively, if the existing safe-water coverage is x_1 and if the incidence of water-borne diseases is z_1 and if health officials aim to reduce this incidence by $z_2 - z_1$, they may wish to know by how much they must increase the percentage of the targeted population having access to safe-water in order to achieve this goal. This is assuming that the extent of access to safe water is the only independent variable able to be controlled by health officials. In the case illustrated, safe-water coverage must be increased from x_1 to x_2 to achieve the desired goal. However, an important consideration will usually be the level of the costs involved in altering the environmental variable. A total cost function provides a general specification of this.

For the case discussed above, the total cost as a function of the reduced incidence of water-borne disease could take the form illustrated in Fig. 15.6. This relationship is specified by taking into account the cost of altering the environmental variable (safe-water coverage) and the production function (Fig. 15.5). The total cost of reducing the incidence of water-borne disease is shown in Fig. 15.6 to rise at the increasing rate. This is so, for example, if the marginal cost of increasing

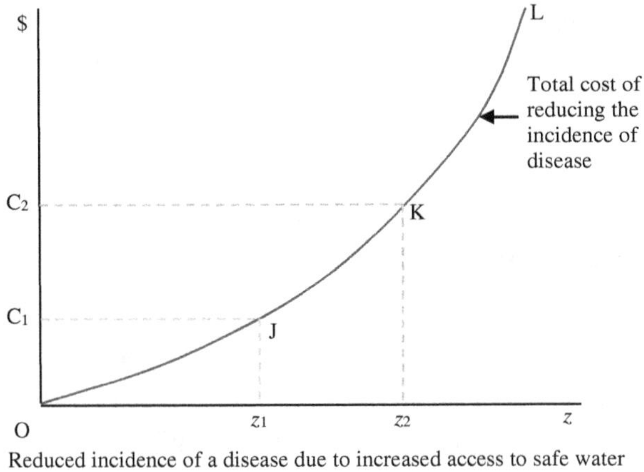

Fig. 15.6. A hypothetical total cost curve for reducing the incidence of a (water-borne) disease as a result of the alteration of an environmental variable: in this case, the extent of access to safe water.

safe-water coverage is constant or increasing **and** if the rate at which the incidence of the disease falls declines as safe-water coverage increased. The latter applies in the example shown in Fig. 15.5, because the production function OEG exhibits declining marginal productivity.

The type of cost function shown in Fig. 15.6 provides some useful information for policy-makers. It enables policy-makers to determine how much reduction in the incidence of water-borne diseases they can achieve by raising their expenditure on increased access to safe water by a particular amount, for example from C_1 to C_2, or conversely the costs they would need to incur to reduce the incidence of water-borne diseases by a designated amount, for instance from z_1 to z_2. This supposes that the only strategy available to policy makers is altering access to safe water.

If a benefit function can be defined in monetary terms for reducing the incidence of water-borne diseases, then net benefit can be maximized. Suppose that these benefits can be specified as $B(z)$. The **net** benefits, V, of reducing the incidence of water-borne diseases by providing greater access to safe water, other things held constant, is

$$V = B(z) - C(z) \tag{15.1}$$

Usually, the optimal value of z will be the value for which the marginal benefit from reducing the incidence of disease equals the marginal cost of doing this. The above is a simple form of cost-benefit analysis.

15.4.2. *Isoquants — health production functions involving multiple inputs*

Frequently more than one variable can be altered to improve environmental health. In such cases, environmental health actions depend on multiple inputs. Economic analysis can be applied to such cases. For simplicity, consider two variable environmental inputs, for example the degree of access of a population to sanitation and the extent of its access to safe water. In this case, the reduction in the prevalence of water-borne diseases in a locality can be expected to depend on both of these variables. Where z represents the reduction in the incidence of water-borne diseases, x_1 is the percentage of the population with access to safe water and x_2 represents the percentage of the population with access to sanitation, the relevant production function can be specified by

$$z = g(x_1, x_2) \tag{15.2}$$

This production function can be 'mapped' by a series of isoquants or equal-product contours. An isoquant shows the various combinations of inputs that result in the same level of output. For instance, the contour marked Q_1Q_1 in Fig. 15.7 is an isoquant showing the combinations of safe-water and sanitation access that result in a 5% reduced incidence of water-borne diseases in a community in a year. The shape of the isoquant indicates that some substitution between the environmental variables enables this degree of reduced incidence to be maintained. Nevertheless, substitutability is restricted as is indicated by the curvature of this isoquant. If perfect substitutability were possible, this isoquant would be a straight line and if there happened to be no substitutability, this isoquant would be right-angled. Wibowo and Tisdell (1993) found in their study in Indonesia of the impact of access to safe-water and of the availability of sanitation on the incidence of

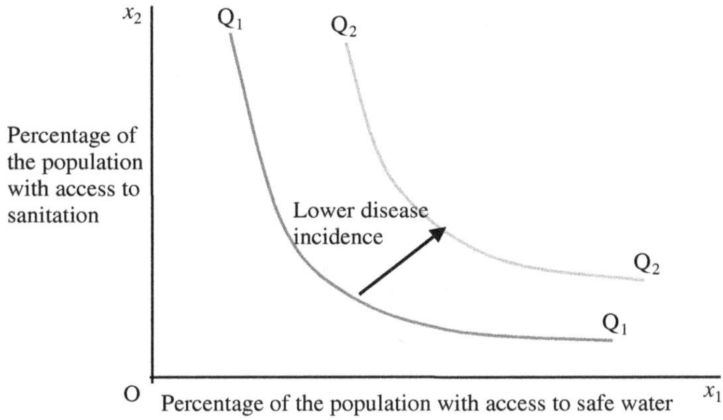

Fig. 15.7. Isoquants depicting combinations of environmental variables that result in constant reduced level of incidence of a disease. Higher isoquants correspond to a greater reduction in disease incidence and their shape indicates the degree of substitutability of the environmental variables in achieving the reduced incidence of disease.

water-borne diseases that the isoquants had a **similar** form to those in Fig. 15.7. Thus while some substitutability between the environmental variables was compatible with maintaining the same degree of environmental health, the extent of this substitutability was restricted. Note that higher isoquants in Fig. 15.7 correspond to greater levels of reduction in the incidence of disease. For example, the isoquant marked Q_2Q_2 in Fig. 15.7 might correspond to a reduction of 10% in the incidence of water-borne diseases.

15.4.3. *Isocosts*

In the multiple environmental input case, it is also important to consider the costs of achieving different health outcomes. Isocost curves can be used to advance this task. An isocost curve shows the combination of alternative quantities of inputs that can be obtained by undertaking a given level of expenditure. It is in fact a contour of the total cost curve. For example, in Fig. 15.8 the curve marked C_1C_1 is assumed to represent an isocost curve. It indicates the different percentages of safe water coverage and sanitation that can be achieved in a

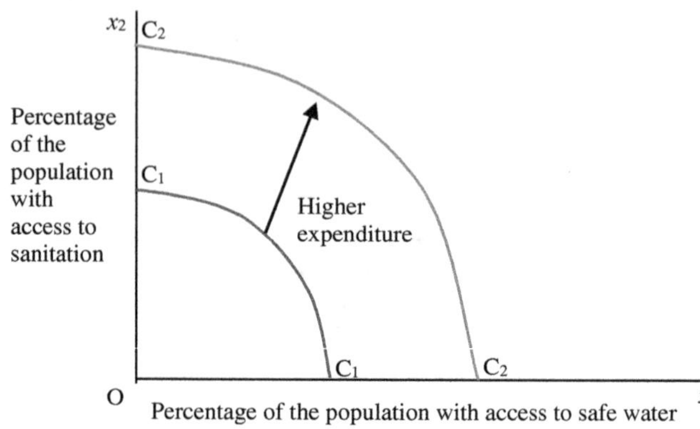

Fig. 15.8. Isocost curves showing the different levels of access to safe water and to sanitation a community can obtain by means of different levels of expenditure.

community by spending a given amount of money (say \$100 million) in a given period on their supply.

In the case shown, this isoquant is strictly concave. This implies that the marginal opportunity cost of increasing access to safe water rises as the provision of access to safe water rises. Conversely, as the level of access to sanitation increases, the marginal opportunity case of adding to sanitation in terms of reduced access to safe water rises. If the isocost line happened to be a straight line, the marginal opportunity costs would be constant.

Higher isocost curves correspond to a higher level of expenditure on improving environmental conditions. For example, if in the case illustrated, expenditure on access to sanitation and safe water were to be trebled, this might result in the isocost curve identified by C_2C_2. Greater access to both sanitation and water is now possible as a result of increased expenditure.

15.4.4. *Cost effectiveness*

Information about the output of environmental health in relation to environmental variables and the costs of achieving alternative environmental possibilities can be combined to assist decision-making about the economics of environmental health. For example, one can find the combinations of the quantities of the environmental variables that

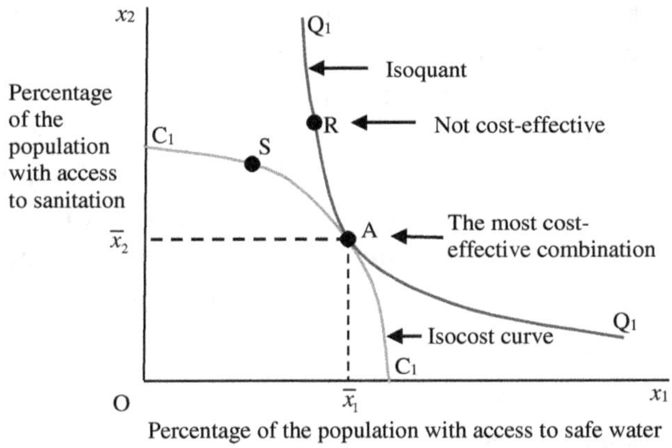

Fig. 15.9. The combination of the environmental variables at point A is the most cost-effective one if the aim is to obtain a reduction in the incidence of the disease corresponding to isoquant Q_1Q_1. It is also the most productive in reducing the disease incidence if expenditure is limited to that corresponding to the isocost curve C_1C_1.

minimize the cost of achieving a particular reduction in the incidence of a disease. Or conversely, the maximum reduction in the incidence of a disease can be found when a particular sum of money is to be spent on varying the environmental variables.

This is illustrated in Fig. 15.9. This figure reproduces isocost curve C_1C_1 from Fig. 15.8 and the isoquant Q_1Q_1 from Fig. 15.7 and these curves are tangential at point A. The combination of environmental inputs at point A, $(\bar{x}_1, \bar{x}_2)$, minimizes the cost of achieving the reduction in incidence of disease corresponding to Q_1Q_1. For example, while the same reduction in the incidence of the disease can be achieved by selecting the combination of environmental inputs corresponding to R, this combination would be on a higher cost curve and involves greater expenditure for the same result. It is not cost-effective. At point A, the slopes of the isoquant and the isocost curves are equal, and this is the cost-effective combination. Choosing any combination other than that at A on the isocost curve, C_1C_1 is inefficient because it is on an isoquant lower than Q_1Q_1. Consequently, the incidence of water-borne disease is not minimized for the expenditure undertaken, for example if the combination at point S is chosen.

To be more concrete, suppose that isoquant Q_1Q_1 indicates a 5% reduction in the incidence of water-borne disease and that isocost curve C_1C_1 corresponds to an expenditure of \$100 million. If this is so, the minimum cost of achieving a 5% reduction in the incidence of water-borne disease is \$100 million. Conversely, if \$100 million is available to provide safe water and sanitation, the combination of safe-water and sanitation coverage corresponding to point A maximizes the attainable reduction in the incidence of water-borne disease — a five per cent reduction in this case.

15.4.5. *Expansion paths, total costs and environmental health benefits*

This analysis can be extended by considering expansion paths. An expansion specifies the combination of inputs that minimize cost for each possible level of output. It is also the path that maximizes output for each possible level of cost outlay. It corresponds to the points of tangency of all the possible isocost and isoquant curves. In this context, output is the reduction in the incidence of a disease and the inputs are alterations in the relevant environmental variables.

Line OABD in Fig. 15.10 provides an example of an expansion path making use of the isoquant and isocost curves shown in Figs. 15.7 and 15.8. Point A corresponds to the tangency point identified in Fig. 15.9 and point B is a similar tangency point. All the points along the expansion path OABD are economically efficient in the allocation of resources required to achieve reductions in the incidence of the focal disease. The expansion path may but need not be linear.

The expansion path can be related to the total cost curves for reducing the incidence of a disease. Each point on the expansion path corresponds to a point on the total cost curve. For example, suppose that the isocost curve C_1C_1 corresponds to an outlay of \$100 million and that C_2C_2 corresponds to an outlay of \$300 million with Q_1Q_1 representing a reduction in the incidence of the focal disease by 5% and Q_2Q_2 that for a reduction of 10%. The points H and J on the total cost curve OHJ shown in Fig. 15.11 correspond to points A and B representatively in Fig. 15.10. In this case, the total cost of controlling

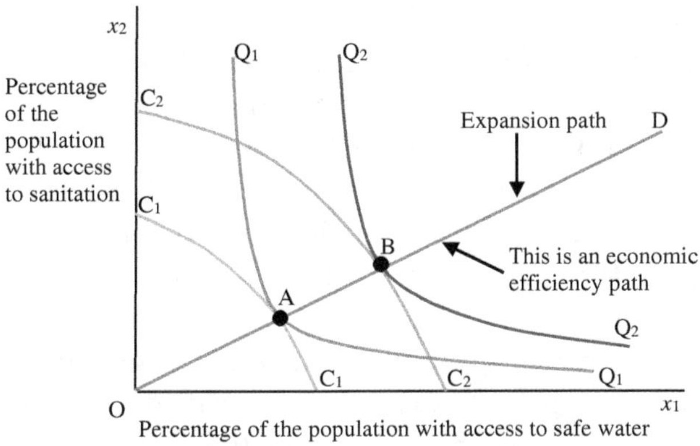

Fig. 15.10. A hypothetical expansion path (OABD) for a reduction in the incidence of water-borne diseases due to increased access to safe-water and sanitation. In the case illustrated, the most cost-efficient allocation of resources requires both access to safe water and sanitation to be provided. However, the relative access of the population to safe water should be greater than its access to sanitation when available resources are efficiently allocated.

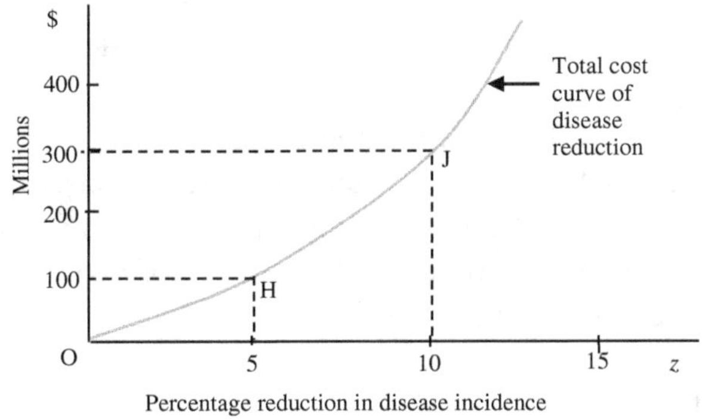

Fig. 15.11. The total cost curve for efficiently reducing the incidence of a disease by improving environmental conditions. This is based on economic expansion path analysis.

the incidence of a disease goes up at an increasing rate with a reduction in the incidence of the disease. Note also that the total cost curve is the lower boundary of potential costs because it is based on the assumption that resources are used efficiently in order to improve environmental health.

The cost curve in Fig. 15.11 is of the same type as that is shown in Fig. 15.6 but in specifying the cost function shown in Fig. 15.6 (see Eq. 15.1) substitutability of (environmental) inputs did not have to be taken into account. In both these cases, the total cost of reducing the incidence of an environmentally generated disease increase at an increasing rate as the incidence of the disease is reduced. In other words, marginal costs are positive. However, these total cost curves need not always take this form.

Once again, if benefits as a function of the degree of reduction in the incidence of the focal disease can be specified in monetary terms, then it is possible to determine the strategies that maximize net economic benefits. However, even if policy-makers merely set targets, the above models can be useful. For example, if policy-makers have a target to reduce the incidence of a focal disease by a particular amount, the minimum cost of achieving this can be determined and also the combination of environmental variables needed ensure cost efficiency can be found. Conversely, if a particular sum is budgeted for reducing the incidence of a focal disease by altering environmental variables, the maximum achievable reduction in incidence for this expenditure can be determined as well as the values of the environmental variables that ensure this result. A dual relationship exists.

The extent to which health benefits can be measured in monetary terms is nonetheless a contentious issue, but (as is clear from the above) such measurement is not required for aspects of economic decision-making about environmental health. For example, it is not needed for the cost-effective analysis of health decisions involving changes in the environment.

Wibowo and Tisdell (1993) provide empirical estimates of production functions of the above type for the incidence of water-borne diseases as a whole (and for diarrhea on its own) as a function of the access of households in Central Java to safe water and to sanitation. They also derived the isoquants for these functions and found that access to safe water was relatively more important than access to sanitation for reducing the incidence of these diseases.

15.5. Assignment of Monetary Benefits to the Valuation of the Avoidance of Ill-Health

15.5.1. *Monetary values facilitate social cost-benefit analysis*

The application of cost-benefit analysis depends on values being expressed in terms of money. This provides a common metric and facilitates mathematical optimization. At the same time, there is considerable controversy about whether all values can be expressed (or reliably expressed) in monetary terms and about how best to elicit or determine these values. This controversy is particularly pronounced when it comes to the valuation of health. In this chapter, it is only possible to introduce the subject of health valuation. Readers will find more detailed coverage of the subject in Brent (2003), Freeman (2003) and a useful overview is given in Dickie and List (2006). See also Watson *et al.* (2020).

In general, economic estimates of the value of avoiding ill-health focus on valuing longevity and on the value of avoiding morbidity. Many diseases and injuries to persons reduce their expected length of life or result in morbidity or sickness of varying intensities and duration. Placing acceptable monetary values on avoiding reductions in length of life and morbidity is very challenging but in reality, decisions are made that at least implicitly place values on these aspects of existence. This is unavoidable because available resources are scarce. Economists try to make these valuations explicit and wherever possible, assign monetary values to them.

Both revealed preference and stated preference methods have been used for this purpose (see Chapter 6, Hanley and Spash, 1993; Watson *et al.*, 2020). Revealed preference methods rely on observing decisions that individuals have made about health risks and inferring from these the monetary values they place on a variation in these risks. For example, wages may be higher in occupations involving greater health risks and this can be taken as an indicator of the willingness of those employed in such occupations to accept such risks in return for a higher monetary payment. Or, to give another example, difference in residential land prices in areas subject to air pollution (having adverse consequences for human health) may be compared with those prices in areas where less pollution occurs to infer the implicit economic value placed on improved environmental health in the focal area. Stated preference methods involve the direct questioning of individuals to elicit their preferences. Such methods include contingent valuation and choice modeling (see Chapter 6).

The value of a statistical life (VSL) is frequently used to estimate the economic mortality costs attributable to some environmental conditions, such as air pollution (Giannadaki *et al.*, 2018). This is based on the willingness to pay of a sample of the relevant population to avoid an increase in (or secure a reduction in) the risk of death (within a specified period of time) due to an environmental hazard. It is *average* willingness to pay per person in the sample. Its relevance depends on how representative the sample is of the focal population, and as a stated preference approach, it is subject to the same limitations as those involved in using this method.

Willingness to pay is dependent on the level of income and wealth of individuals. Therefore, VSL tends to be higher the higher is the level of income and wealth of individuals in the focal group. Consequently, those belonging to poorer groups are assigned a lower VSL than those belonging to well-off groups. This, for example, results in the statistical lives of those living in lower income countries being assigned a lower economic value than those in higher income countries. This disparity can be very large. For example, Giannadaki *et al.* (2018, Table A3) arrived at VSL estimates for 2010 for a large number of nations. They estimated that the value of a statistical life in the USA is more than 4 times that of a life in China and more than 6 times that of a life in India. Even wider differences in the statistical value of lives between countries are implied by their estimates. One can, therefore, see why the use of VSL can be controversial. It needs to be used with care, and its use should be qualified.

Another common method for valuing health is to consider variations in human capital that occur as a result of altered health conditions (Brent, 2003). For example, a reduction in the expected length of life of individuals will reduce their expected (discounted) life-time earnings. An increase in morbidity due to environmental conditions is likely to reduce the productivity of those affected and reduce their incomes. In addition, those with illness are likely to have medical and other expenses that they would have avoided in the absence of morbidity. All of these factors reduce the value of human capital and this reduction is sometimes taken as an indicator of economic loss occasioned by a rise in ill-health. Nevertheless, this approach has also been severely criticized, particularly as an economic measure of changes in the value of longevity (Mishan and Quah, 2007, Appendix 12).

15.5.2. *The economic value of expected longevity*

The valuation of human life in monetary terms is an extremely controversial subject. However, every day individuals risk their lives to survive and to obtain income. Hence, economists usually focus on how much individuals must gain financially in order to accept an increase in the likelihood of their longevity being reduced.

Alternatively, economists measure how much individuals are willing to pay in order to reduce the probability of their life being cut short. For most individuals, it is likely that they will need to be compensated monetarily at an increasing rate for the increased risk of dying in a specified period of time, for example a year, as a result of exposure to an environmental hazard. Furthermore, the willingness of most individuals to pay to avoid greater risk of death can be expected to accelerate as this risk rises but not indefinitely because the individual's available assets limit his/her possible payment. For example, curve ABC in Fig. 15.12 provides a hypothetical example of an individual's willingness to accept compensation for enduring an increased probability of death within one year. Curve ADE represents the same individual's willingness to pay to avoid increased risk of death in one year. Behavioral economists have found that normally willingness to pay is less than willingness to accept compensation (see for example, Kahneman *et al.*, 1991; Knetsch, 1989, 1990). In the example shown, the individual is willing to accept an increase in the probability of death from P_1 to P_2 if paid y_2 but will only pay y_1 to avoid this increase. Furthermore, the

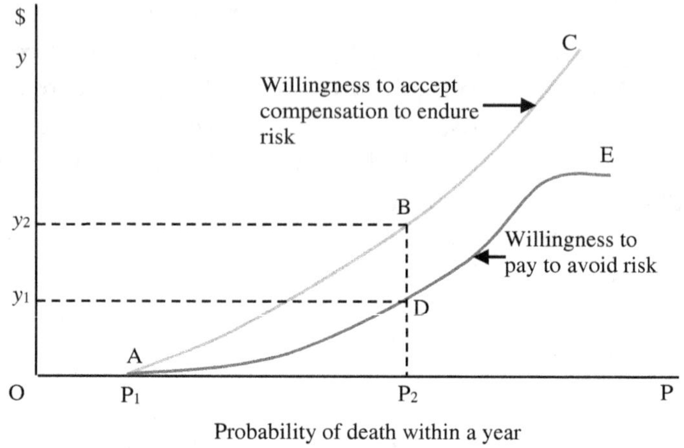

Fig. 15.12. Hypothetical curves showing the willingness of an individual to endure greater risk of death in return for compensation for this risk-taking (curve ABC) and the willingness of the same individual to pay (curve ADE) to avoid this increased risk. This risk could be created by an environmental hazard.

limited amount of assets and income of individuals will restrict their ability to pay to avoid an increase in environmental risk.

A dilemma arises in several cases about whether benefit-cost analysis should be based on willingness of potential victims of an environmental hazard to pay to avoid it or on their willingness to accept payment to endure it. If the latter approach is adopted, it will be more favorable to the potential victims, given a lower level of net social benefit and consequently, be more likely to result in the rejection of a project that creates an environmental hazard than if willingness to pay is adopted as the basis of social cost-benefit analysis.

A further issue is that those affected by an environmental hazard are often uncertain about the probable danger it poses to their life. Consequently, their subjective probabilities of adverse consequences from an environmental hazard can vary considerably as can their willingness to pay to avoid it or to accept compensation to bear the risk. Other things equal, increased uncertainty about the probability of death from an environmental hazard increases its perceived cost to potential victims. This follows because the curves shown in Fig. 15.12 increase at an increasing rate as the risk of death rises except for very high risks of mortality in the case of relationship ADE. In the case of function ABC and for probabilities confined to the convex portion of relationship ADE, greater dispersion of the probability of death about a given mean value tends to raise the average value of the dependent variable (see mathematical theorem 90, Hardy *et al.*, 1934, p. 74). Greater dispersion of the subjective probabilities of death is an indicator of heightened uncertainty about this event.

As mentioned above, a different approach to measuring the economic loss occasioned by death is that based on the loss of human capital. This approach regards an individual as a form of capital with a value equal to the discounted value of the stream of an individual's anticipated life-time earnings. However, this method has been severely criticized by some economists such as Freeman (2003) and Mishan and Quah (2007, Appendix 12). If earnings are only counted while an individual remains in the workforce, then those who are retired will have zero future life-time earnings as will most of the handicapped and housewives who decide not to work outside the home. Furthermore, the work of volunteer workers (including carers) may count for naught. Nevertheless, their continued life is not worthless. A consequence of the application of this approach is to favor the location of risky environmental projects in areas where the potential future earnings of the population is low. These are likely to be the areas where the poor reside. Application of this criterion would therefore, tend to reinforce political forces that could favor the location of risky environmental projects in areas inhabited primarily by the poor and the disadvantaged.

15.5.3. *The economic value of avoiding morbidity*

Revealed and stated preference methods can be used in principle to estimate the economic value of avoiding ill health generated by environmental conditions (Dickie and List, 2006). Often, however, estimates of this kind may not be available or the reliability of the available estimates may be questionable. Dickie and List (2006, p. 341) suggest that in these circumstances, health costs avoided (such as medical costs and lost income) can provide a useful lower bound to the economic benefits to be obtained by improving environmental health.

Alternatively, heath costs imposed as a result of a deterioration in the environment give a lower bound to the health costs imposed by this deterioration. Typically the type of costs taken into account are wages or other income lost by the individual as a result of sickness, and the costs of extra care and medication occasioned by the morbidity of the individual. If family members also incur extra costs in caring for a sick family member, this may also he taken into account. This approach was, for example, adopted by Hong *et al.* (1991) in assessing the net benefits of controlling cadmium pollution in a Chinese county. It has also been applied by Roy (2008).

Nevertheless, the question of whether this method really provides a lower bound to the costs of environmental ill-health can be debated. For example, if work involves disutility for an individual, income lost as a result of ill health could overstate the individuals economic loss.

Once again, it is evident that some economic approaches to evaluating the environmental health consequences of altered environmental conditions tend to disadvantage the poor. They will be unable (and less willing) to pay as much as the rich to avoid environmental risk and it is likely that they will be willing to accept a lower level of compensation to endure the same level of environmental risk. Similarly, if the averted cost method of valuation is adopted, the estimated costs of ill-health for the poor in the same environmental circumstances as the rich will be smaller than that for those better off because the income forgone by the poor as a result of ill health is lower than for the rich. Consequently, all these economic methods favor the location of projects that pose a risk to environmental health in locations where the poor are concentrated rather than in places where the rich reside. This is assuming the same health response to doses of pollutants (or other environmental hazards) by both those who are poor and those that are not poor. Because income and future earnings fall after individuals reach an advanced age, application of these methods also disadvantage the aged.

15.5.4. *Quality-adjusted-life years*

Those involved in health care and medicine rarely use the above economic approaches as a basis for evaluating environmental health policy (Dickie and List, 2006, p. 340). Many prefer to use the quality-adjusted-life years (QALYs) method, for example. This method is based on an index of the expected years of life of individuals taking into account their quality of life in each year based solely on their healthiness. The quality of an individual's life in any year is assigned a weight in the range zero to one. One corresponds to perfect health, zero corresponds to death and intermediate values indicate the relative state of health of individuals. Thus the quality of life-years index of a person expected to live for n years, where ρ_t represents their quality of life in year t is:

$$\text{QALYs} = \sum_{t=1}^{n} \rho_t \tag{15.3}$$

Clearly, the value of this approach depends on how well the ρ_t value can be predicted as well as on the accuracy of the individuals' estimated length of life.

One objective sometimes pursued using this measure is to try to maximize the aggregate quality-of-life years of a focal population for a given expenditure. This is a cost-efficiency approach similar to that discussed in Section 15.4.4. Now, however, the isoquants represent equal aggregate levels of quality-of-life years. For example, in Fig. 15.9, the isocost value C_1C_1 might represent the bundles of environmental possibilities available given the budget constraint and the isoquant Q_1Q_1 might represent the isoquant with the highest attainable quality of life-years. Point A corresponds to the environmental possibilities that maximize the total quality-of-life years for the community involved given the expenditure corresponding to C_1C_1.

One criticism sometimes made of this approach is that it displays an ageism bias because it tends to favor younger community members relative to older ones. A major problem for this method is the accuracy with which the quality of the life of a person can be determined in the range $0 < \rho \leq 1$ and whether or not the scales used for different individuals are comparable. Furthermore, it is not clear ethically that QUALYs should be the sole criterion for determining the access of individuals to health care. For example, would it be ethical to deny those who have saved for health care no greater access to it than those who had not? The moral basis of the quality-of-life-years criterion appears to be too restrictive. In addition, it does account fully for the fact that quality of life is not solely dependent on an individual's state of health.

15.5.5. *Further evaluation considerations*

A further consideration which needs to be allowed for in the analysis of health objectives is the value to others of the health of an individual. For example, a person's continuing life may be highly valued by others because the individual's dependents may rely significantly on his/her continuing to live and being healthy. For example, children are very dependent on the health and presence of their parents for their well-being. In many cases, health evaluation requires consideration not only of the individual's valuation of his/her health but also the valuations of an individual's health by others whose well-being depends on the health of the individual. This poses a difficulty for all the health evaluation methods outlined above, not just the QUALYs criterion.

An additional problem is that the major economic methods for valuing health assume that individuals are well informed and rational. This hypothesis needs to be subjected to greater scrutiny. Most economic models of health valuation suppose, for instance, that individuals are aware of the objective risks of morbidity and mortality in different occupations and locations, that these risks are applicable to them personally, and that they take these factors into account in their job choice and have job mobility. It seems that in practice, individuals' subjective probabilities of adverse events can frequently differ from more objective estimates of these (see for example, Celsi *et al.*, 1993) and job and locational mobility is more constrained than is typically assumed in most economic revealed preference models of health valuation. This is not to say that economic models can provide no guidance for health valuation but in all their applications, their assumptions and limitations need to be kept in mind.

15.6. Chemical and Physical Substances in the Environment and the Economic Consequences of their Health Impacts — Empirical Applications

15.6.1. *The purpose of this section*

Air and water-borne chemical and physical substances can be a significant source of ill health and can cause premature death. In this section, some selected empirical studies are reviewed that have assessed the economics of reducing these pollutants in the environment. Additional studies are reviewed in Voorhees *et al.* (2001) The focus is on studies that have taken into account the economic consequences of these substances for morbidity and mortality.

15.6.2. *Air quality in Los Angeles and Southern California*

In 1989, a plan was approved to reduce air pollution in Los Angeles Krupnick and Portney (1991) completed a benefit-cost analysis of it by taking into account its impacts on environmental health and came to the conclusion that the plan was uneconomic.

They estimated that the annual cost of the plan would be $13 billion and that its annual health benefits would amount to $3 billion per year. The health benefits comprised $2 billion for reduced mortality and $1 billion for lowered morbidity — benefits obtained mainly as a result of the reduction in respiratory health problems. They argued that because the $3 billion annual benefit falls far short of the annual cost ($13 billion) of the plan, it is patently uneconomic. They maintained that a higher economic return would be obtained by spending the $13 billion on other health-related programs, for example, campaigns to reduce the extent of the smoking of tobacco.

Several aspects of this study are worth noting. First, the economic health benefits were evaluated on the basis of secondary information about the willingness of individuals to accept an increased risk of mortality or morbidity **in a paid job**. Therefore, revealed preference was the fundamental basis used for evaluating the economic values of the environmental health effects of air pollution. For example, it was assumed that individuals would value each 0.001 reduction in the risk of annual mortality at $1000. However, the secondary empirical studies on which the authors draw displayed a range of $800 to $8,000 per year for this value (Krupnick and Portney, 1991, p. 437). Thus, the appropriate value was quite uncertain. Nevertheless, Krupnick and Portney decided to take a value towards the lower end of the range arguing that a greater proportion of elderly people lived in the Los Angeles area and that the economic value of their life would on average be lower than those still in the workforce. However, no empirical evidence is provided in support of this proposition. It can be observed that if estimates for the value of reduced mortality and morbidity towards the top of the range indicated by the secondary studies, that would considerably increase the benefits of the plan for Los Angeles. For example, at the very top of the range, benefits could be eight times those estimated by Krupnick and Portney (1991) that is $24 billion. In that case, the economic benefit of the plan to reduce air pollution in Los Angeles would far outweigh its costs, namely $13 billion.

This study demonstrates that data limitations can be a major constraint on the process of obtaining reliable estimates of the increased economic value of environmental health. At the same time, this study demonstrates how methods of valuation of environmental health can be applied and that complex issues can often be resolved by assessing limited alternatives. The problem considered by these authors was whether or not the Los Angeles plan was economic taking into account its predicted environmental health impacts. Thus, their focus was on a dichotomous choice problem rather than one assessing many alternative possibilities.

Jane Hall *et al.* (1992) also completed a study that assessed the likely net economic benefits from improved health as a result of cleaner air in southern California, and came to a conclusion different to that of Krupnick and Portney (1991). On the basis of their plausible estimates, they found that the net social economic benefit of meeting U.S. national ambient air quality standards in the South Coast Air Basin of California would most likely be positive. Their work underlines the sensitivity of the results of the analysis to allowances made for uncertain variables (for example, willingness to pay to avoid an increase in the risk of death) and to the range of health consequences assessed (for example, Hall *et al.* (1992) consider the health impacts of lower concentrations of air pollutants than do Krupnick and Portney).

15.6.3. *The economic costs of air pollution in the USA*

Muller and Mendelsohn (2007) undertook a detailed empirical study of the damages caused by air pollution in the USA and assigned economic costs to these. They found that the gross annual damage of air pollution in the US in 2002 most likely amounted to $74.3 billion per year. About 90.5% of these spillover costs were accounted for by adverse effects on human health with premature mortality being the major cost (see Muller and Mendelsohn, 2007, p. 6). Cost estimates for increased mortality were about three times those associated with greater morbidity. The greatest health costs were caused by the release of particulate matter (especially that of a small sizes and emissions of sulfur dioxide). Not surprisingly, environmental costs of air pollution were found to be much higher in urban areas than in rural ones. This is attributable mainly to higher population densities in urban areas than in rural ones.

As in the study by Krupnick and Portney (1991), Muller and Mendelsohn (2007) rely heavily on revealed preference hedonic wage models to obtain estimates for the willingness of individuals to accept increased risk of mortality and morbidity. When the full range of these findings are taken into account, they believe that the annual damages associated with air pollution in the US could range from $71 billion (0.7% of GDP) to $279 million (2.8% of GDP). Furthermore, their analysis suggests that the US Environmental Protection Agency over estimated the economic benefits to the US resulting from the introduction of the Clean Air Act.

15.6.4. *Pollution of water and air by the release of cadmium from a smelter in China*

Hong *et al.* (1991) completed a cost-benefit analysis of measures to reduce the release of cadmium from a smelting plant in Hubei Province,

China. It was planned to install a waste-water treatment plant and electrical dust removal apparatus at the smelter in order to substantially reduce emissions of both water-borne and air-borne cadmium. The expected cost of this equipment and increased variable costs associated with it were calculated. This extra cost was compared with the annual economic health benefits predicted for those living in Daye County as a result of reduced exposure to cadmium. Only morbidity benefits were taken into account.

The health benefits were estimated by taking into account the medical and nutrient costs avoided by the dwellers of the county and the wages no longer lost by those who avoided cadmium poisoning as well as those of their relatives who helped care for them. It was found that in just one year, the benefits for improved health due to the reduction in the incidence of cadmium poisoning in the county community exceeded the total cost of the control measures. The social benefit-cost ratio was found to be positive and was shown to be very high when benefits and costs over several years were taken into account.

15.6.5. *Water pollution in South Asia by arsenic*

Underground water in parts of India and Bangladesh has become contaminated with arsenic. This is partly due to geological factors but the problem has been exacerbated by lack of controls on the withdrawal of underground water supplies and inadequate treatment of this water for drinking purposes. The drinking of water contaminated with arsenic has adverse health affects and increases the risk of mortality (Singh, 2017). Bangladesh and India are the countries most exposed to this problem.

Roy (2008) undertook a case study in West Bengal to estimate the economic benefits of supplying those using arsenic-affected water with arsenic-free water. Roy also considered the economic benefits of reducing levels of arsenic concentration in drinking water. No account was taken of reduced mortality but cost savings due to improved health were taken into account as well as reduced averting expenditures, for example, extra costs avoided for traveling to collect safe water or adopting measures to reduce the arsenic content of available water.

Roy (2008, p. 5) comes to the conclusion that the health benefits of piping arsenic-free water to the arsenic-affected areas studied would substantially exceed its costs and that the payback period of the costs compared to the economic benefits would be short; just three years. While the general approach taken by Roy (2008) is useful, the fact that arsenic-related ill health is not distinguished from ill health due to other causes limits the validity of its findings. A later study by Singh (2017) has examined the cost-effectiveness of alternative arsenic mitigation technologies in Bihar, India. He found that the most cost-effective technologies in the different districts of Bihar varied with literacy rates in these districts.

15.6.6. *Additional observations on water quality and health*

There are many ways in which water can be polluted and its quality reduced. A useful general outline of the types of water pollution and their causes is given in Wikipedia, the free encyclopedia (Anon, 2020a). It has been claimed that water pollution is a leading worldwide cause of deaths and diseases (Anon, 2020a). When the full range of environmental health issues involving water quality are taken into account, considerable scope exists for applying economics to their assessment. It also becomes clear that the examples given in this section constitute a very small subset of potential applications of economics to the assessment of health effects associated with variation in water quality.

Of particular concern is the environmental release of heavy metals such as chromium, cadmium, lead and mercury which do not decompose and which can accumulate in humans and in fish and mollusks. If the latter are eaten by humans, this adds to the accumulation of these heavy metals in their body. Eating the affected organisms can result in human mortality and irreversible adverse health consequences. For example, the industrial disposal of mercury in Minamata Bay in Japan resulting in many victims suffering mercury poisoning with horrific consequences (Anon, 2020b). This case is of particular interest because it illustrates how political factors resulted in reluctance to address the problem and in long delays in victims of mercury poisoning obtaining compensation for the health effects of this poisoning; or the families of those who died as a result of this disease receiving 'sympathy' payments (Anon, 2020b).

15.7. Economic Considerations and Ecological and Biological Influences on Environmental Health

15.7.1. *Background*

Living organisms are the cause of much ill health and the likelihood that they will cause illness of human beings varies significantly with environmental conditions and the precautions that individuals take in interacting with organisms capable of transmitting diseases. The carriers (vectors) of infectious diseases may be humans (they are part of the environment) or other living things such as insects (species of mosquitoes in the case of malaria, Japanese encephalitis, dengue fever) or snails as in the case of schistosomiasis.

A large number of species can host organisms capable of causing ill health in humans. This is not to say that all organisms capable of causing human ill health rely on non-human hosts as part of their life-cycle. However, where they do, reducing populations of their hosts or alternatively, regulating human contact with their hosts are potential strategies for reducing illness (see Fig. 15.2).

Environmental conditions can also favor populations of pathogens and other organisms which are capable of causing ill health in humans and which survive independently of any particular hosts. For example, increased crowding of individuals in urban areas is favorable to the occurrence and evolution of particular infectious diseases such as influenza. Changing environments alter the prevalence of different diseases as do altered livelihoods. For example, as livelihoods change, humans are often less likely to come into contact with other species that may transmit diseases to them and so the composition of the prevalence of different diseases experienced by humans alters.

Environmental externalities are a major source of economic failures in controlling diseases that involve significant ecological interactions with humankind. These failures are the focus of this section. Subjects discussed include the economics of immunization and vaccination and the excessive use of antibiotics.

15.7.2. *Economic assessment of vaccination programs — existing analysis*

When individuals are vaccinated against a disease, they benefit by having increased resistance to the disease. Others are also likely to benefit because if infection fails to develop in a person vaccinated against an infectious disease, others are less likely to be exposed to infection and catch the disease. Economic modeling suggests that while individuals will take into account their private benefits from being vaccinated, they will not take account of the benefits that spillover to others. Thus is the absence of any public intervention, the private vaccination rate is likely to be lower than the socially optimal rate of vaccination. In these circumstances, there is an economic case for governments to subsidize vaccination against diseases.

Figure 15.13 illustrates the economic argument in favor of this, as for example, presented by Brent (2003, pp. 91–94) and Battacharya *et al.* (2014, Chapter 20). In this figure, line AC represents the marginal private benefit to individuals of being vaccinated against a disease as a function of the population vaccinated against it. It falls as the proportion of the population vaccinated against the diseases rises because the chance of any individual catching the disease declines. The difference between line AC and DC represents the marginal spillover benefits from vaccination. These decline as the percentage of the population vaccinated increases. The line DC shows the marginal social economic benefit of greater vaccination cover of the population. The line FG represents the marginal cost of vaccination. In these circumstances, if individuals pursue only their private economic interests, only x_1 of the population will seek vaccination whereas x_2 of the population ought to be vaccinated in order to maximize net social economic benefit. The net social gain in this case is equal to the area of the dotted triangle.

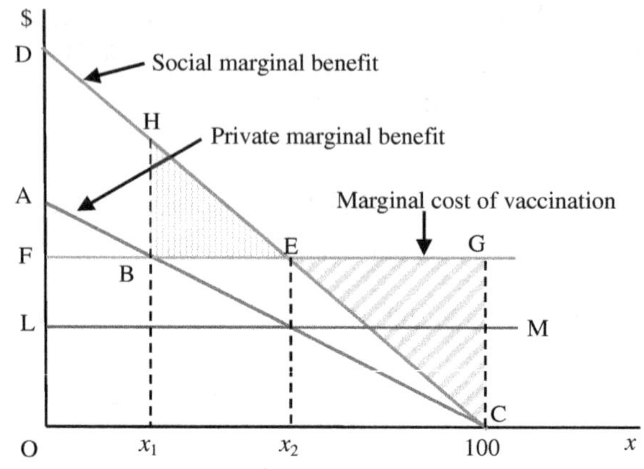

Fig. 15.13. Favorable spillovers from vaccination can result in an insufficient percentage of a population opting for vaccination when the spillover benefits from vaccination are taken into account. In the case illustrated, private decisions would result in only x_1% of the population deciding to vaccinate whereas x_2% would maximize social economic net benefits.

In order to rectify the market failure illustrated by Fig. 15.13, the government might subsidize vaccination against the disease. A subsidy of FL for each vaccination would lower private regional cost to OL per vaccination. Consequently, private benefits would be maximized when x_2 of the population obtained vaccination. The social deadweight economic loss in the absence of this intervention would be as represented by the area of the dotted triangle. Given this model, if the government made vaccination free, this would result in the whole population being vaccinated. However, this does not maximize social economic net benefit because beyond x_2 the marginal social benefit from extra vaccinations is less than the marginal cost of completing the vaccinations. If 100% vaccination coverage is achieved, the social economic deadweight loss is equivalent to the hatched triangle.

Brent (2003, pp. 101–103) reports the results of a U.S. study completed by Hannum (1997) which compares estimates of privately optimal ratios of vaccination against various diseases with socially optimum ratios and actual ratios. In the case of measles, the vaccination ratio in the period 1963–1967 (0.825) was well below the private optimum

(0.910) and below the social optimum (0.926) but by 1983, vaccination coverage was only slightly below (yet close to) the social optimum.

15.7.3. *A different possibility to that outlined above — a case in which eradication is an economic option*

The above model assumes that the marginal net social benefits from increasing the proportion of the population vaccinated against a disease decline as the coverage increases. However, for some diseases, once vaccination coverage becomes quite high, there could be an increasing probability that the disease will be eradicated, as happened with smallpox. Consequently, while the marginal expected social benefit from having an increased proportion of the population vaccinated may fall initially as coverage rises of high levels of coverage, it may begin to increase as in the case illustrated in Fig. 15.14.

In this figure, OF represents the marginal cost of vaccinating an individual against a disease. The curve DEHJK plus the segment LM represents the marginal expected social economic benefit from vaccination excluding the cost of vaccination. After the proportion of the population vaccinated reaches a level corresponding to point H, the expected marginal social benefit (excluding vaccination costs) from increased vaccination begins to rise as vaccination cover increases. This is because the likelihood of the disease being eliminated rises. In the illustration, it is assumed that if x_4 of the population is vaccinated that the disease is sure to disappear. Complete vaccination of a population may not be required to eliminate an organism carrying a disease. Vaccination coverage that exceeds x_4 is bound to be uneconomic in the case shown in Fig. 15.14.

In determining the socially optimal level of vaccination of a population against a disease, it is important to decide whether the standard type of model applies (as illustrated in Fig. 15.13) or a more complex model, such as the one illustrated by Fig. 15.14. Finding the socially optimal solution is likely to be more difficult in complex cases. An additional problem is that following the elimination of a disease in one population, it may be necessary to guard against its re-introduction

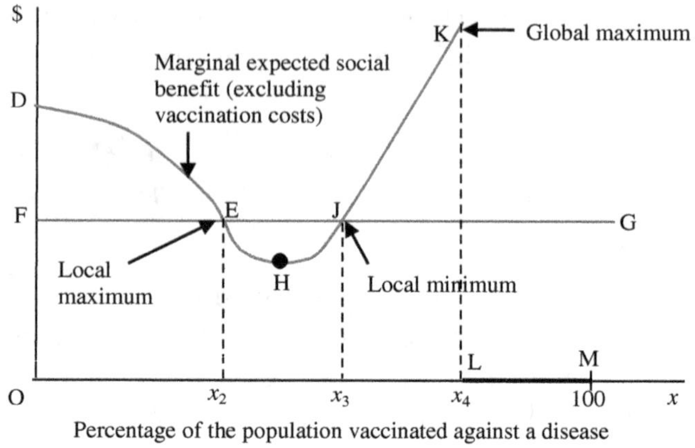

Fig. 15.14. A case in which the marginal expected social economic benefit from greater vaccination coverage does not fall continuously but after a point (in this example, J) rises. In this case, there is a separate local and global optimum for the social benefit from vaccination.

by contacts with other populations in which the disease continues to be present. Measures to prevent re-infection also involve economic decisions.

15.7.4. *Adverse health externalities — excessive use of antibiotics and measures to reduce contagion of diseases*

Not all practices intended to promote human health have favorable externalities. Some, such as the use of antibiotics to treat specific diseases, can result in adverse external effects. In the case of antibiotics, their effectiveness in killing targeted pathogens tends to decline with their increased use because these pathogens become more resistant (as a result of natural selection) to an antibiotic as its use grows (see for example, Tisdell, 1982; Battacharya *et al.*, 2014, Chapter 20). Eventually, the antibiotic becomes ineffective and future effective treatment of the targeted disease depends on the development of new antibiotics to which the targeted germs are not resistant (initially) or to the discovery of alternative methods of treatment. Some strains of tuberculosis

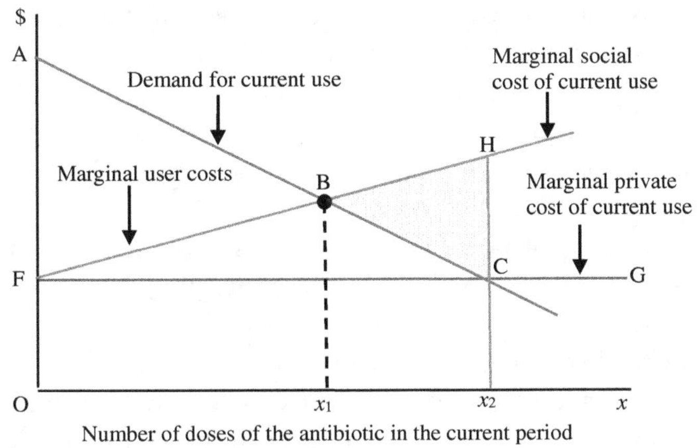

Fig. 15.15. Private decisions about the extent of the use of antibiotics are unlikely to take account of the user cost involved. In the case illustrated, marginal user costs are equal to the difference between line FG and FH. Private decisions result in x_2 of the antibiotic being used whereas x_1 is ideal from a social economic point of view.

are now resistant to available antibiotics and there is a need to find new alternatives.

The problem arises because users of antibiotics (and probably most doctors prescribing them) have no economic incentive to take into account the user costs of their consumption; that is their reduced effectiveness in the future as a result of their greater current use. Increasing biological resistance is of a similar nature to a public bad (see Chapter 3).

The problem can be illustrated by means of Fig. 15.15. In this figure, line ABC represents the current demand for the use of an antibiotic and OF is the current cost of each dose of the antibiotic so that the marginal cost curve is FG. The marginal user cost of current doses of the antibiotic is shown by the difference between line FG and line FH. Therefore, the marginal social cost of current uses of the antibiotic is as shown by line FH. Private decision-making will result in x_2 doses of the antibiotic being used in the current period whereas only x_1 doses are socially optimal.

In the case illustrated in Fig. 15.15, the use of the antibiotic in the range x_1 to x_2 results in the net marginal benefit from its current use being less than its reduced marginal benefit in the future; that is its marginal user costs. Private decisions will result in x_2 doses of the antibiotic being administered in the current period. This will result in an economic loss equivalent to the area of the dotted triangle. There may, therefore, be a case for governments to restrict the use of some antibiotics because of this consideration.

Other examples of negative externalities involving health include contagious diseases. Individuals with contagious diseases may be restricted in their interactions with other individuals. Such restrictions may be enforced by social rules or in extreme cases, by the state. The state may also place obligations on persons who have communicable diseases to take precautions not to pass them onto others. For example, persons with AIDS may have a legal obligation to inform potential partners of this.

15.8. New Pandemic Diseases Such as COVID-19

15.8.1. *New pandemic diseases and economic development*

Pandemic diseases are those that are present in the whole world or over a large geographical area, especially those for which the incidence is high. New highly infectious diseases which have become pandemics, such as COVID-19, can create serious health and economic problems because of the social transformations which have occurred as a result of economic development. As a consequence of economic development, the world's population has become increasingly urbanized and concentrated in large cities and as well, the level of the global human population has risen manifold. The density of human populations is greater than ever. In addition, the mobility of humans in all geographical dimensions has increased tremendously. These factors facilitate the outbreak of new infectious diseases and their spread. This is especially evident in the case of the corona viruses, such as different strains of influenza and more recently, COVID-19.

Developments in the nature of economic activity exacerbate the problem of controlling new infectious diseases transmitted as a result of human contact and presence. Increased economic specialization and greater division of labor accompanied by the expansion of markets and growing economic globalization increase the risk that individuals will come into contact with sources that result in infection by highly contagious diseases such as influenza and COVID-19. The adverse economic consequences of new forms or types of these diseases can be severe given the high degree of interdependence in economic activity in modern economies. For example, the absence of workers from work due to such infections, or the risks of these infections, can disrupt production at the workplace level as well as supply chains, and in addition, can have negative effects on purchases of commodities. This is evident from COVID-19 outbreak which resulted in a major worldwide economic depression.

15.8.2. *Economics and policies for controlling pandemics, especially COVID-19*

Contagious diseases capable of becoming pandemics can take varied forms and therefore, appropriate policies for controlling them often differ. Determining appropriate economic policies to respond to the outbreak and human-to-human spread of COVID-19 has proven to be extremely challenging because major measures to stem the level of infections and death rates from the disease involve a high economic cost in terms of the levels of income and economic production forgone. These measures have included the isolation of individuals, restrictions on gatherings and on travel. They were seen as necessary to flatten the upward trend in the curve of infections and reduce the increase in deaths and to enable hospitals to increase their capacity to provide for patients requiring hospitalization.

It is not possible here to consider all economic aspects of responding to the novel virus, COVID-19, but some economic issues raised by the objective of flattening the infection curve can be discussed. Figure 15.15 is helpful for conceptualizing one of the economic problems. There, curve JKEH represents the capacity of the hospital system to admit and care for patients requiring hospitalization for COVID-19. It might be of a logistic form because the initial expansion of this

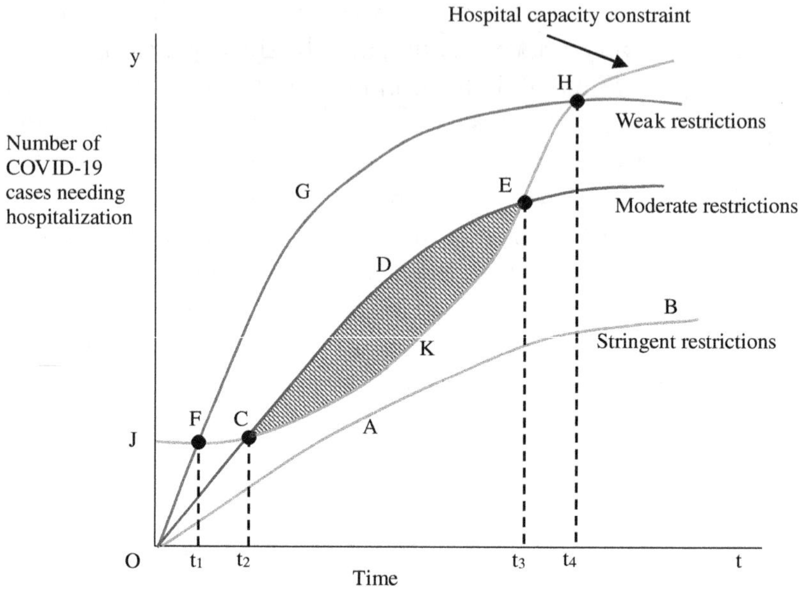

Fig. 15.16. An illustration of a choice problem involving COVID-19 patients needing hospitalization.

capacity takes time and once physical capacity ramps up, increasing scarcity of qualified staff to operate hospitals can become a major constraint. Three different hypothetical functions display the number of persons requiring hospitalization due to COVID-19 infections. Each corresponds to different levels of social restrictions imposed by the government to limit the spread of COVID-19. Curves OAB, ODE and OGH correspond respectively to substantial moderate and weak social restrictions to limit the spread of this disease.

It can be seen in Fig. 15.16 that as a result of the most severe restrictions, the hospital system would be able to accommodate all COVID-19 patients requiring hospitalization. Indeed, in this case hospital over capacity occurs. In the other two cases, hospital capacity is exceeded for a period of time and to a greater extent, the weaker are the social restrictions and precautions designed to reduce the transmission of the disease. For example, in the case of moderate restrictions, hospital capacity is exceeded between t_2 and t_3 and the number of

COVID-19 patients in need of hospitalization but unable to be admitted is equal to the difference between the segment CDE of the curve of COVID-19 patients requiring hospitalization and the segment CKE of the capacity of the hospital system to accommodate these patients. If weak restrictions and precautions are taken to limit the occurrence of COVID-19, then the period for which hospital capacity is exceeded increases to $t_4 - t_1$. Then the number of needy cases unable to be hospitalized rises from an amount indicated by the eye-shaped hatched area bounded by CKED in Fig. 15.16 to that enclosed by FKHG. This raises the question of how should COVID-19 sufferers be prioritized for admission if the capacity of hospitals to accommodate them is exceeded?

One possibility is to give priority to admitting those COVID-19 sufferers to hospital who have the largest increase in the expected value of their lives if they recover from COVID-19 as a result of being hospitalized. This can be formally analyzed as follows: Let

V_i = the expected value of the life of the *i*th sufferer from COVID-19 if this patient does not die;

PH_i = the probability of the *i*th COVID-19 sufferer recovering from the virus if admitted to hospital; and

PNH_i = the probability of the *i*th COVID-19 sufferer's recovery if not admitted to hospital.

Then the expected increase in the value of admitting the *i*th COVID-19 sufferer to hospital is

$$\Delta E[V]_I = (PH_i - PNH_i)V_i \tag{15.4}$$

A challenging moral and valuation issue is how to determine V_i. Also in many circumstances, the change in the probability of survival as a result of hospitalization can be uncertain.

Several different possibilities exist for determining V_i. One possibility is to estimate the quality of life years (QALYS) that a COVID-19 sufferer is likely to have left if the sufferer recovers from the disease. On this basis, other things being equal, the fewer are the number of years a sufferer is predicted to survive for after recovery from the virus, the lower would be the sufferer's V_i-value. This approach gives a reduced priority for hospital admissions to the elderly and to those with chronic conditions which are likely to reduce their life span. In addition, many belonging to these groups have a poor quality of life. Furthermore, they may have a smaller increase in the probability of recovery if admitted to hospital. This approach discriminates against the elderly and those with chronic health conditions. Chronic health problems are more prevalent in many ethnic minority communities and so it would also discriminate against these groups.

Another approach is to make hospital admissions of those infected by COVID-19 dependent on their willingness and ability to pay or partially dependent on this. This discriminates against the poor, and other socially disadvantaged groups. In addition, consideration may be given to the extent to which patients with other health conditions requiring hospital treatment should be prioritized for admission to hospital. In principle, the type of formula set out in Eq. 15.4 could also be applied to this group. Decisions also need to be made about the economics of expanding hospital capacity and the period for which this extra capacity is likely to be needed.

Furthermore, global pandemics substantially reduce global economic production and increase unemployment. In the case of COVID-19, government measures to stem the spread of this disease and the mortality and morbidity from it reduced worldwide employment and economic activity tremendously. Given that unemployment rises and aggregate economic activity falls when social restrictions to reduce the occurrence of COVID-19 are more stringent, governments have been faced with a difficult trade-off problem; namely how much to accept a reduction in employment and economic activity as a result of allowing more liberal opportunities for social interaction. This type of choice involves an opportunity cost and a trade-off problem and conceptually can be subjected to economic analysis. However, solving such a problem is difficult because of the uncertainty about many of the dimensions of a new pandemic, the problem of devising a social welfare function that is widely or universally acceptable and from a purely economic point of view, and the inability to measure (in a universally acceptable way) significant costs and benefits of measures which could be taken to control pandemics. This limits the scope for applying social cost-analysis to the problem. Despite this, exploring the potential trade-offs and opportunity costs involved in such measures remains important as a basis for rational decision-making. This aspect is given further consideration in Tisdell (2020).

It should be noted that collective responses to new pandemics, such as COVID-19, are significantly influenced by prevailing political systems and by the diverse objectives of rulers. In the case of COVID-19, this (along with the uncertainty about the epidemiology of the virus and its impacts on public health and economic activity) resulted in noticeable disparities in the methods adopted by different governments to manage the occurrence of COVID-19 infections and in the stringency of their precautionary social restrictions.

15.9. Concluding Observations

Environmental conditions have a major impact on human health and require a number of difficult and complex economic choices to be made. Economists have developed a variety of techniques for assisting with these decisions. These techniques have helped to highlight important economic trade-offs that are necessary in pursuing environmental health policy. This chapter has outlined several of these techniques and a variety of trade-off issues that arise in environmental health policy. Furthermore, a non-economic method that relies on QUALYs was also outlined and assessed. Despite its non-economic origin, this method can be linked (as was shown) to economic considerations involving cost-effectiveness.

Placing monetary values on the avoidance of ill-health is especially challenging. Several economic methods for doing this were outlined and discussed critically. Examples of application of these methods to environmental ill health arising from chemical and physical substances transported by air and water were outlined. The focus then shifted to considering the economics of controlling ecological and biological influences on environmental health. Both positive externalities (such as those arising from vaccinations) and negative externalities (such as those associated with excessive use of antibiotics and the spread of contagious diseases) were analyzed. Subsequently attention was given to economic issues involved in controlling the incidence of COVID-19.

Mendelsohn (2002) makes out a strong case for applying environmental economics to the development of policies to protect health (see also Arrow *et al.*, 1996). While it is clear from the coverage in this chapter that economics can help clarify many issues involving environmental health policy, it also has its limits. For example, individuals may be less well informed and rational than is assumed in many economic models. Furthermore, the lack of availability of reliable data after results in empirical estimates of net social benefits from environmental interventions being highly disparate, as was observed in Section 15.6. But sometimes, even if data is not completely reliable, it is sufficiently reliable to make an optimal social choice confidently. Complete certainty is not required for all rational choices (Tisdell, 1996, Chapter 3).

15.10. Keywords

Behavioral variations; cost-benefit analysis and health; cost effectiveness; cost efficiency; COVID-19; defensive health strategies; economic value of avoided morbidity; economic value of longevity; environmental health; environmental health externalities; environmental health spillovers; expansion paths and health; health production functions; health trade-offs; human capital; isocosts and health; isoquants for health; mitigating health strategies; pandemics; public goods and health; public bads and health; quality-adjusted-life years (QALYs); revealed preference; social economic benefits of vaccinations; stated preference; user costs of antibiotic doses; value of a statistical life (VSL).

15.11. Questions for Review and Discussion

1. How important in your view are environmental factors as influences on human health?
2. Improvements in health care usually involve the allocation of increased resources for this purpose. Explain the economic implications of this.

3. In many cases, three different factors can be altered to improve environmental health. Regulation of pollution emissions is just one possibility. Explain.
4. Economic failures are the source of many environmental health problems. What types of economic failures can be important influences on environmental health and why do they result in a social economic loss?
5. Using a single output and single input production function show how environmental health outcomes can be related to variations in an environmental condition. What are the limitations of this simplified approach?
6. How can the cost of environmental health be related to the simple type of production function mentioned in question 5 above? How could this sort of function be used in conjunction with a benefit function to maximize the net economic benefit of improving environmental health? What policy relevance could this production function approach have?
7. Often more than one environmental variable can be altered to improve environmental health. What types of economic issues arise in such cases? How can analysis using production functions help to resolve these economic issues?
8. Show how economic analysis can be used to determine a cost-efficient strategy for improving environmental health when more than one environmental condition can be varied. Use isoquants and isocosts to illustrate your answer.
9. The environmental strategy that minimizes the cost of achieving a particular level of environmental health is also the strategy that maximizes the level of environmental health for this level of cost (level of expenditure). Duality exists. Explain.
10. Explain the concept of an expansion path for improving environmental health. Relate an expansion path to the total cost of achieving a reduction in the incidence of an environmental disease.
11. Monetary values play an important part in facilitating cost-benefit analysis. What types of general methods have economists used to assign monetary values to improvements in human health? How useful and reliable are these assignments likely to be?

12. Human life is precious but does not have an infinite economic value. What evidence is there that this is so? What economic methods do economists employ to place economic values on probable variations in longevity? What are the limitations of these approaches?
13. Outline and discuss critically economic methods for placing monetary values on reduced morbidity.
14. Explain the method of QALYs as a procedure for determining optimal environmental health policy. What are the advantages and disadvantages of this approach?
15. Several empirical economic studies of the health impacts of chemical and physical substances in the environment are outlined in Section 15.6. Outline the limitations of at least two of these studies and explain the source of their limitations.
16. In what ways are ecological and biological environmental conditions likely to have important consequences for human health? Give examples.
17. Some health interventions have positive externalities. An example is vaccination against disease. When this favorable externality is taken into account, the proportion of the population vaccinated against disease is likely to be less than the social optimal proportion. Explain. Why is the traditional economic model for explaining this failure not applicable to all cases? Are government subsidies for vaccination justifiable on economic grounds? Should vaccination be free?
18. Why is there likely to be excessive use of antibiotics from an economic point of view? Illustrate your answer by a diagram?
19. The faster the rate at which new antibiotics are expected to be developed to replace existing ones, the less important the problem highlighted in question 18 above. Why?
20. Those with contagious diseases create a negative externality by mixing with individuals that are not infected. To what extent is it justifiable to restrict the movement of persons that have a contagious disease?

21. Economic development has made it easier for some types of new infections and diseases to develop and become pandemics. Why is this so?
22. The inadequacy of the hospital system to admit COVID-19 patients has raised significant issues about how human life should be valued and about how stringent precautionary measures should be to reduce the occurrence of this disease. What type of issues have been raised? How might those infected with a virus such as COVID-19 be prioritized for admission to hospital if hospital capacity is exceeded? What types of moral issues are involved?
23. Determining how stringent social restrictions should be to reduce the incidence of COVID-19 proved to be quite controversial. Why? Why have there been differences in the nature of restrictions imposed by different states?

Readings and References

Anon (2020a). *Water Pollution,* Wikipedia, https://en.wikipedia.org/wiki/Water_pollution [Accessed 20 July 2020].

Anon (2020b). *Minimata Disease*, Wikipedia, https://en.wikipedia.org/wiki/Minamata_disease [Accessed 22 July 2020].

Arrow, K.J., M.L. Cropper, G.C. Eads, R.W. Hahn, L.B. Lave, R.G. Noll, P.R. Portney, M. Russell, R. Schmalensee, V.K. Smith and R.N. Stavins (1996). Is there a role for benefit-cost analysis in environmental health and safety regulation? *Science,* 272, 221. doi: 10.1126/science.272.5259.221.

Battacharya, J., T. Hyde and P. Tu (2014). *Health Economics,* Palgrave Macmillan, Basingstoke, UK and New York [Chapter 20].

Brent, R.J. (2003). *Cost-Benefit Alaysis and Health Care Evaluations,* Edward Elgar, Cheltenham UK and Northampton, MA, USA [Chapter 1].

Celsi, R.L., R.L. Rose and T.W. Leigh (1993). An exploration of high-risk leisure consumption through skydiving, *Journal of Consumer Research,* 20, 1–23. doi: 10.1086/209330. Reprinted in C. Tisdell (2006) *The Economics of Leisure* Vol. II, pp. 182–204. Edward Elgar, Cheltenham, UK and Northampton, MA, USA.

Dickie, M. and J. List (2006). Economic valuation of health for environmental policy: Comparing alternative approaches. Introduction and overview, *Environmental & Resource Economics,* 34, 339–346. doi: 10.1007/s10640-006-9008-0.

Freeman, A.M. (2003). *The Measurement of Environmental and Resources Values: Theory and Methods,* 2nd edn. Resources for the Future, Washington, DC.

Giannadaki, D., E. Giannakis, A. Pozzer and J. Lelieveld (2018). Estimating health and economic benefits of reductions in air pollution from agriculture, *Science of The Total Environment,* 622–623, 1304–1316. doi: https://doi.org/10.1016/j.scitotenv.2017.12.064.

Hall, J.V., A.M. Winer, M.T. Kleinman, F.W. Lurmann, V. Brajer and S.D. Colome (1992). Valuing the health benefits of clean air, *Science,* 255, 812. doi: 10.1126/science.1536006.

Hanley, N. and C.L. Spash (1993). *Cost-Benefit Analysis and the Environment,* Edwar Elgar, Aldershot, UK and Brookfield, Vermont, USA [Chapter 6].

Hannum, R.J. (1997). *Using an Expected Utility Model to Analyze the Social Costs and Benefits of Childhood Immunizations.* PhD Thesis, New York, Department of Economics, Fordham University.

Hardy, G.H., J.E. Littlewood and G. Polya (1934). *Inequalities,* Cambridge University Press, Cambridge, UK.

Hong, Z., K. Bao and C.A. Tisdell (1991). Cadmium exposure in Daye County: Environmental assessment and management, health and economic effects, *Environmental Management and Health,* 2, 20–25.

Kahneman, D., J.L. Knetsch and R.H. Thaler (1991). The endowment effect, loss aversion and status quo bias, *Journal of Economic Perspectives,* 5, 193–206. doi: 10.1257/jep.5.1.193.

Knetsch, J.L. (1989). The endowment effect and evidence of nonreversible indifference curves, *The American Economic Review,* 79, 1277–1284. doi: https://www.jstor.org/stable/1831454.

Knetsch, J.L. (1990). Environmental policy implications of disparities between willingness to pay and compensation demanded measures of values, *Journal of Environmental Economics and Management,* 18, 227–237. doi: https://doi.org/10.1016/0095-0696(90)90003-H.

Krupnick, A.J. and P.R. Portney (1991). Controlling urban air pollution: A benefit-cost assessment, *Science,* 252, 522–528. doi: https://www.jstor.org/stable/2875476.

Landefeld, J.S. and E.P. Seskin (1982). The economic value of life: Linking theory to practice, *American Journal of Public Health,* 72, 555–566. doi: 10.2105/AJPH.72.6.555.

Mendelsohn, R. (2002). Environmental economics and human health, *Environmental Health Perspectives,* 110, A118–A119. doi: 10.1289/ehp.110-a118.

Mishan, E.J. and E. Quah (2007). *Cost-Benefit Analysis,* 5th edn. Routledge, London and New York.

Muller, N.Z. and R. Mendelsohn (2007). Measuring the damages of air pollution in the United States, *Journal of Environmental Economics and Management,* 54, 1–14. doi: https://doi.org/10.1016/j.jeem.2006.12.002.

O'Curry, S. (1999). Budgeting and mental accounting. In P.E. Earl and S. Kemp (Eds.), *The Elgar Companion to Consumer Research,* 63–65. Edward Elgar, Cheltenham, UK and Northampton, MA, USA.

Pindyck, R.S. and D.L. Rubinfeld (2005). *Microeconomics,* Pearson Education, Upper Saddle River, New Jersey, USA.

Prüss-Üstün, A., J. Wolf, C.F. Corvalán, R. Bos and M.P. Neira (2016). *Preventing Disease Through Healthy Environments: A Global Assessment of the Burden of Disease from Environmental Risks,* World Health Organization, Geneva.

Roy, J. (2008). Economic benefits of arsenic removal from ground water — A case study from West Bengal, India, *Science of The Total Environment,* 397, 1–12. doi: https://doi.org/10.1016/j.scitotenv.2008.02.007.

Singh, S.K. (2017). An analysis of the cost-effectiveness of arsenic mitigation technologies: Implications for public policy, *International Journal of Sustainable Built Environment,* 6, 522–535. doi: https://doi.org/10.1016/j.ijsbe.2017.10.004.

Tisdell, C.A. (1982). Exploitation of techniques that decline in effectiveness with use *Public Finance-Finances Publiques,* 37, 428–437.

Tisdell, C.A. (1996). *Bounded Rationality and Economic Evolution: A Contribution to Decision Making, Economics and Management,* Edward Elgar, Cheltenham, UK and Brookfield, VT, USA.

Tisdell, C.A. (2020). Economic, social and policy issues raised by the COVID-19 pandemic, *Economic Analysis and Policy,* 68, 17–28. doi: https://doi.org/10.1016/j.eap.2020.08.002.

Tisdell, C.A. and K. Hartley (2008). *Microeconomic Policy: A New Perspective,* Edward Elgar, Cheltenham, UK and Northampton, MA, USA.

Voorhees, S.S., R. Sakai, S. Araki, H. Sato and A. Otsu (2001). Cost-benefit analysis methods for assessing air pollution control programs in urban environments — A review, *Environmental Health and Preventive Medicine,* 6, 63–73. doi: 10.1007/BF02897948.

Watson, V., S. Luchini, D. Regier and R. Schultz (2020). Monetary analysis of health outcomes. In C. Guerriero (Ed.) *Cost-benefit Analysis of*

Environmental Health Interventions, 73–93. Academic Press, London UK and Cambridge, MA, USA.

Wibowo, D. and C. Tisdell (1993). Health, safe water and sanitation — a cross-sectional health production function for Central Java, Indonesia, *Bulletin of the World Health Organization*, 71, 237–245.

Index

D

E

H

M

S

U

V

Y

Z

www.ingramcontent.com/pod-product-compliance
Lightning Source LLC
LaVergne TN
LVHW021055220926
848484LV00021B/924